Language and Gender: A Reader

This book is dedicated to

Ulysse and Harriet Coates
Harry Coates Dhiman

and

Ilia and Maya Thelwell-Pichler

Language and Gender:
A Reader

Second Edition

Edited by

Jennifer Coates

and

Pia Pichler

WILEY-BLACKWELL

A John Wiley & Sons, Ltd., Publication

Library of Congress Cataloging-in-Publication Data

Language and gender : a reader / edited by Jennifer Coates and Pia Pichler. – 2nd ed.
   p. cm.
  Includes bibliographical references and index.
  ISBN 978-1-4051-9144-9 (hardcover : alk. paper) – ISBN 978-1-4051-9127-2 (pbk. : alk. paper)
 1. Language and languages–Sex differences. I. Coates, Jennifer. II. Pichler, Pia.
  P120.S48L338 2010
  306.44–dc22

                             2010035178

A catalogue record for this book is available from the British Library.

Set in 10/12.5pt Galliard by SPi Publisher Services, Pondicherry, India
Printed in Malaysia by Ho Printing (M) Sdn Bhd

1 2011

Contents

Editors' Note

Some papers in this Reader appear in their original form: Barrett; Cameron (Parts IV and X); DeFrancisco; Eckert and McConnell-Ginet; Ehrlich; Hall; Holmes (Part X); Holmes and Schnurr; Leap; Maltz and Borker; Nichols; Shaw; Tannen; Troemel-Ploetz; Waseleski; Weatherall; West and Zimmerman; Yang.

The other papers in the Reader have been edited and abridged, in consultation with the author(s): Abe; Bradley; Bucholtz; Cheshire; Coates (Part IV); Davies; Del Teso Craviotto; Eisikovits; Goodwin; Holmes (Part II); Kiesling; O'Barr, and Atkins; Ostermann; Reynolds; Schegloff; Swann (Part III); Trudgill; West (Part VII); Wetzel.

Four papers have been revised especially for the Reader by their authors: Herring, Johnson and DiBenedetto; Pichler; Coates ("Pushing at the Boundaries"); Swann (Part IX). The paper by Penelope Eckert was written specifically for the Reader.

We would like to thank all these writers for their generosity in allowing us to reproduce their work in this Reader.

JETC
PP

Transcription Conventions 1

As used in the papers by Bucholtz, DeFrancisco, Goodwin, Hall, Holmes and Schnurr, Kiesling, Ostermann, Schegloff, Swann, West, West and Zimmerman and based on those devised by Gail Jefferson (see, for example, Harvey Sacks, Emanuel A. Schegloff, and Gail Jefferson, "A simplest systematics for the organisation of turn-taking in conversation," *Language* 50 (1974), 696–735, and E. Ochs, E. A. Schegloff, and S. Thompson (eds), *Interaction and Grammar*. Cambridge: Cambridge University Press, 1996).

A: I had [them] B: [Did] you	Brackets around portions of utterances indicate that the portions bracketed overlap one another
//them	Double slashes provide an alternative method of marking overlap
A: 'swhat I said =	Equals signs indicate "latching": there is no interval
B: = But you didn't	between the end of a prior turn and the start of a next piece of talk
THIRteen	Capital letters mark speech that is much louder than surrounding talk
°thirteen	A degree sign marks speech that is much quieter than surrounding talk
thirteen	Italics indicate some form of emphasis
<u>thirteen</u>	Underlining indicates emphatic stress.
^thirteen	Circumflex represents sharp upward pitch shift
?, !.	Punctuation symbols are used to mark intonation, not grammar
↑	Upturned arrow indicates pitch accent in the syllable that follows
↓	Downturned arrow indicates lowered pitch in the syllable that follows
(0.5)	Numbers in parentheses mark silences in seconds and tenths of a second

(.)	Parentheses around a period/full stop indicate a micro pause
(#)	Parentheses around the symbol # indicate a pause of one second or less that wasn't possible to determine precisely
+	Pause of up to one second
we:::ll	Colons indicate that the sound just before the colon has been lengthened
but-	A hyphen marks an abrupt cut-off point in the production of talk
((chanting)) [laughs]	Double parentheses or square brackets enclose transcriber's comments or descriptions
(only)	Material in single parentheses indicates that the transcriber was uncertain of the exact word(s) heard
(x)	Parentheses enclosing an "x" indicate a hitch or stutter on the part of the speaker
(xxxx)	Parentheses enclosing several "x"s indicate untranscribable material
.hh	A series of "h"s preceded by a dot marks indicates an inbreath
hhh	A series of "h"s with no dot marks indicates an outbreath
h	Exhalation (e.g. laugh or sigh), single token marks one pulse
eh-heh-heh engh-hengh he, ha	These symbols mark laughter syllables (inhaled when preceded by a dot)
10-19-70-15 *or* (T15:50–60)	The citation preceding an example locates the transcript where the original data can be found

Additional Symbols
(as used in the bilingual transcripts in the paper by Ostermann)

thirteen	Bold indicates part of transcript marked for analysis
<u>thirteen</u>	Underlining indicates that talk overlaps with the activity of typing
italics	English gloss
(info)	Linguistic information that might have been lost in translation, e.g. grammatical gender (masc.) and (fem.) or number marking (pl.) and (sing.)
((*begins to cry*))	Factual information about the exchange or translation clarification
{}	Curly brackets enclose stretches of uncertain transcription
@	Laughter

Transcription Conventions 2

As used in the papers by Cameron, Coates, Davies, Pichler, and based on the system used in Jennifer Coates, *Women Talk* (Oxford: Blackwell, 1996).

1. A broken line marks the beginning of a stave and indicates that the words enclosed by the lines are to be read simultaneously (like a musical score):

```
-----------------------------------------------
A:  newspapers and stuff/
B:                     yes/
-----------------------------------------
```

2. Brackets around portions of utterances indicate the start of overlap:

```
-------------------------------------------
A:  papers and |stuff/
B:             |yes/good/
-------------------------------------------
```

3. Equals signs indicate "latching": there is no discernible gap between the two chunks of talk:

```
-----------------------------------------------------
A:  they're meant to be=
B:                      =adults/
-----------------------------------------------------
```

4. A slash (/) indicates the end of a tone group or chunk of talk:

```
she pushes him to the limit/
```

5. A question mark indicates the end of a chunk of talk which is being analysed as a question:

```
pregnant?
```

6. A hyphen indicates an incomplete word or utterance:

```
he's got this twi- twitch/
I was- I was stopped by a train/
```

7. Short pauses (less than 0.5 seconds) are marked as follows:

   `he sort of . sat and read`

8. Longer pauses are marked (1); (2) (timed in seconds)

9. Double round parentheses indicate that there is doubt about the accuracy of the transcription:

   `((I mean))`

10. Double round parentheses enclosing several "x"s indicate untranscribable material:

    `((xxxx))`

11. Angle brackets give clarificatory information, relating either to that point in talk or to immediately preceding underlined material:

    `nobody ever says that` <u>`do they`</u> `<LAUGHING>`
    `I can't help it <WHINEY>`

12. Capital letters are used for words/syllables uttered with emphasis:

    `MEXICO`

13. Bold is used for words spoken more loudly:

    `yeah but why would he?`

14. Emphatic stress on italicised item:

    `Mexico`

15. The symbol % encloses words or phrases that are spoken very quietly:

    `%bloody hell%`

16. The symbols >..< indicate faster speed of utterance delivery:

    `>did I tell you something<`

17. This symbol indicates that the speaker takes a sharp intake of breath:

    `.hhh`

18. The symbol [...] indicates that material has been omitted

Sources

The editors and publisher gratefully acknowledge the permission granted to reproduce the copyright material in this book:

Part I   Gender Differences in Pronunciation and Grammar

1   John Bradley (1988) "Yanyuwa: 'Men speak one way, women speak another'," *Aboriginal Linguistics* 1, 126–34. © John Bradley 1988. Reprinted with kind permission of the author.
2   Peter Trudgill (1983) "Sex and Covert Prestige," pp. 169–77 in P. Trudgill, *On Dialect*. Oxford: Blackwell. Reprinted with permission of Wiley-Blackwell.
3   Jenny Cheshire (1982) "Linguistic Variation and Social Function," pp. 153–64 in S. Romaine (ed.), *Sociolinguistic Variation in Speech Communities*. London: Arnold. Reprinted with permission of Edward Arnold Publishers.
4   Edina Eisikovits (1988) "Girl-talk/Boy-talk: Sex Differences in Adolescent Speech," pp. 35–54 in P. Collins and D. Blair (eds) *Australian English*. University of Queensland Press. Reprinted with permission of University of Queensland Press.
5   Patricia Nichols (1982) "Black Women in the Rural South: Conservative and Innovative," pp. 45–54 in B. L. Dubois and I. Crouch (eds) *American Minority Women in Sociolinguistic Perspective* (= vol. 17 of *International Journal of the Sociology of Language*). Mouton: The Hague (1978) pp. 45–54. Reprinted with permission of De Gruyter.
6   Penelope Eckert (1998) "Gender and Sociolinguistic Variation." Written especially for the first edition of this Reader.

Part II   Gender and Conversational Practice

7   Janet Holmes (1995) "Complimenting – A Positive Politeness Strategy," pp. 115–53 in J. Holmes, *Women, Men and Politeness*. London: Longman. Reprinted with permission of Pearson Education UK.
8   Marjorie Goodwin (1988) "Cooperation and Competition Across Girls' Play Activities," pp. 55–94 in A. Dundas Todd and S. Fisher (eds) *Gender and Discourse: The Power of Talk*. Norwood, NJ: Ablex. Reprinted with permission of ABC-Clio LLC.

Language and Gender: A Reader, 2nd edition, edited by Jennifer Coates and Pia Pichler
© 2011 Blackwell Publishing Ltd

Part III   Gender, Power, and Dominance in Mixed Talk

Part IV   Same-Sex Talk

Part V Women's Talk in the Public Domain

Part VI Language, Gender, and Sexuality

Part VII Theoretical Debates (1): Gender or Power?

Part VIII   Theoretical Debates (2): Difference or Dominance?

Part IX   Theoretical Debates (3): When is Gender Relevant?

Part X   New Directions in Language and Gender Research

Every effort has been made to trace copyright holders and to obtain their permission for the use of copyright material. The publisher apologizes for any errors or omissions in the above list and would be grateful if notified of any corrections that should be incorporated in future reprints or editions of this book.

Introduction

This second edition of the Reader has come about for a variety of reasons. The most obvious of these is that a huge number of fascinating books and articles on the topic of language and gender has been published since 1997 (the date of the first edition). While many users of the first edition responded to the publisher's survey – or communicated with us personally – to say they wanted the Reader to stay as it was, on balance we felt it was important that this new work was represented in a new edition of the Reader. We wanted to demonstrate the widening range of language and gender research, both in terms of geographically and socially diverse Communities of Practice. and in terms of changing theoretical and methodological approaches.

As well as allowing us to add new papers to existing sections, this second edition has also allowed us to make space for new areas of interest. It contains a new section on "Language, Gender, and Sexuality," a rapidly growing sub-area of language and gender research (Part VI). It also expands the later part of the first edition devoted to theoretical debates with a new section asking the question "When is Gender Relevant?" (Part IX).

For the editors, constructing a second edition has been a challenge because of the constant tension between wanting to preserve what is best about the first edition and wanting to bring the Reader up to date, to be representative of contemporary research in language and gender. We drew up an enormous long-list of papers which, in an ideal world, we would have liked to include, but inevitably we have only been able to include a minority of these. In the section introductions we have tried to refer to other relevant work on particular topics, and each section (as in the first edition) ends with a list of recommended further reading.

The papers which made it to the final cut have been selected for various reasons. First, they cover the spectrum of language and gender research over the last 30-odd years, with the earliest paper coming from 1977 and the most recent from 2009. This coverage will allow you to develop some understanding of the way the field has developed during this time. Secondly, papers have been chosen to represent a variety of sub-topics within the field, organized into 10 sections. Thirdly, the papers have been chosen to represent a variety of theoretical and methodological approaches. Fourthly, they have been selected to illustrate gender-related variation in a range of languages and cultures, including Brazil, China, and Japan (though research in English-speaking communities still predominates).

This book has several aims, not all of which are compatible. One aim is to introduce you to some of the best work in the field. Another is to give an idea of the breadth of the area, and to illustrate particular topics from as wide a range of material as possible. Some of the papers included are classics, or deserve to become so: they discuss innovative research and present their findings in ways that have had a profound influence on the language and gender field and on sociolinguistics generally. All the papers included in the Reader provide important insights into the complex interrelationship of language and gender.

Collections of papers such as this Reader exist to provide key material in a particular area, to accompany study in that area, or to be read for their own sake. With the growing use of introductory texts which summarize extant research there is a danger that students do not have first-hand contact with original work. It is very probable that you will use this Reader alongside a general introduction to the subject (such as Eckert and McConnell-Ginet 2003 or Coates 2004). To get a true feel for the subject, it is important not to rely solely on such texts, which are essentially second-hand accounts, but to go back to the original research. That is what a Reader is for.

Language and Gender

Early work on language and gender was inspired by the feminist movement of the 1970s and 1980s. Researchers aligned themselves with the Women's Liberation movement, and this led, unsurprisingly, to a new focus on women and women's language, and a move away from the androcentrism of early sociolinguistics. Seminal publications, such as Robin Lakoff's *Language and Woman's Place* (1975), Dale Spender's *Man Made Language* (1980), and Deborah Cameron's *Feminism and Linguistic Theory* (1985) were all explicitly feminist. This early work on the interplay of language and gender took it for granted that one of the goals of such research was to expose the links between language use and gender asymmetries. Researchers worked within a framework that aimed to expose gender discrimination and the ways in which language was coerced into the service of the patriarchy.

In more recent times, the feminist underpinnings of language and gender research have weakened, to the extent that some scholars have challenged their relevance. For example, Sara Mills (2003: 40) argued that "patriarchy" was a concept that had outlived its usefulness. Such "post-feminist" sentiments seemed to reflect a more apolitical phase in language and gender research. However, this does not mean that there was no important research going on. For example, during the 1990s there was growing interest in men and masculinity resulting in the first book to focus on language and masculinity (Johnson and Meinhof 1997). The concept of 'gender' was also put under intense scrutiny. The traditional binaries (male/female, masculine/feminine, gay/straight) were deconstructed, and queer linguistics was born (see Part VI). Research on the language of multiple masculinities, and of gay men, lesbians, drag queens, and transgendered individuals has enormously enriched our understanding of gender and the complexity of linguistic realizations of gender and sexuality. But at the same time many researchers felt intimidated by the new "political correctness" which made claims about "the way women speak" or "men's talk" liable to the accusation of "essentialism."

In the twenty-first century there has been a reappraisal of the roots of language and gender research, and some researchers have begun to argue explicitly for a revival of feminist awareness in language and gender research (see Baxter 2003; McElhinny 2003; Swann 2003; Holmes 2007 – this volume Part X). While it is not true to say that there is now consensus, there is a sense that a more pragmatic approach needs to prevail. Some are arguing for "strategic essentialism," a term coined by the postcolonial theorist Gayatri Chakravorty Spivak (1987), to refer to the careful and temporary use of essentialism when the main goal is to expose discrimination against subaltern (subordinate) groups. In such contexts, it may be strategically necessary to refer to categories such as "women" and "men."

Another interesting development captured in the second edition of the Reader is the changing understanding of the concept "gender" within sociolinguistics. In the early years (the 1970s), research into the interaction of language and gender relied on a predominantly essentialist paradigm which categorized speakers primarily according to biological sex, and used mainly quantitative methods. Next, in the late 1970s and the 1980s, came a period which recognized the cultural construction of categories such as gender; during this period, more qualitative, ethnographic approaches predominated. In recent research a more dynamic social constructionist approach has emerged which makes possible the combination of quantitative and qualitative approaches and which views gender as performative and as constantly "in formation" (Butler 1990).

The Reader in many ways retraces this historical route, in terms of both subject-matter and approach. It starts with work focusing on pronunciation and grammar and drawing on a quantitative paradigm (Part I). It then moves on to work focusing on conversational strategies and drawing on a more ethnographic paradigm (Part II). The concentration of early research on mixed talk inevitably led to an interest in conversational dominance, that is, in the ways male speakers employ particular strategies in conversation to dominate talk. Papers exploring conversational dominance are represented in Part III. The Reader then moves on to single-sex talk (Part IV), looking at both all-female and all-male interaction, and drawing on difference and social constructionist models. Interest in all-female talk has led researchers to examine the speech patterns of women beyond the private domain as they take up careers in the public sphere, to establish whether or not women have had to adapt to traditional – androcentric – speaking practices (Part V). Part VI is devoted to papers exploring gender and sexuality, and draws on Queer Theory and on theories of performativity. The papers in these opening six sections raise many questions, and three of the major debates in the field form the basis for Parts VII, VIII, and IX. Part VII focuses on the question: "Is the salient variable gender or power?", while Part VIII assesses the value of the two main theoretical frameworks adopted by researchers in the 1970s and 1980s, the difference (or two cultures) model and the dominance model. Part IX asks the Conversation Analysis-inspired question: 'When is gender relevant?'. The final section (Part X) is devoted to three papers which focus on theory and methodology in language and gender research and which signpost the direction in which language and gender research is moving in the twenty-first century, raising important questions about the future of language and gender research.

Notes on How to Use the Reader

The ten sections of the Reader are ordered to give some feel for the historical unfolding of the subject, and for the development of different theoretical frameworks to make sense of research findings. So you will find that some of the older papers are to be found in the early sections. The final section is designed to act as a springboard into the present, to give you a feel for the way contemporary researchers are thinking about language and gender now. Each section begins with a brief introduction, which discusses the topic or theme of the section and then summarizes the papers included in it.

You can choose to follow the Reader step by step, section by section: this would give you a clear idea of the way the field has developed, and would organize your reading into a number of coherent topics. But there are many other possibilities. You could equally well start with the last section (Part X), to get a feel for what's going on in language and gender *now*. Or you could construct your own topics or themes by picking out papers from different sections to form new groupings. For example, the Reader does not contain a separate section on children's talk, but you could pick out the papers by Cheshire (Part I), Eisikovits (Part I), Goodwin (Part II), Swann (Part III), Bucholtz (Part IV), and Pichler (Part IV), all of which deal with the construction of gender in the talk of children and adolescents. Or you could choose to focus on non-English-speaking cultures, picking out papers such as those on an Australian Aboriginal community (Bradley, Part I), on two Black communities in South Carolina (Nichols, Part I), on a Chinese community (Yang, Part III), on two contrasting Brazilian communities of practice (Ostermann, Part V); and on various Japanese communities of practice (Reynolds, Part V; Abe, Part VI; Wetzel, Part VII).

A question at the heart of sociolinguistic work is that relating to the relationship between language and identity. This is again a theme that can be followed throughout the Reader, both in terms of the ways in which women and men perform gender through differentiated language practices in specific groups and situational contexts, but also in terms of the complex intersection of gender with age, class, ethnicity, sexuality, and other non-linguistic variables.

Conclusion

As we have argued above, there are many ways to use this book. However you choose to map out your journey through the vast territory of language and gender research, the papers included here should provide you with more than enough material to enrich your understanding of the ways in which language and gender can intersect, and of the ways in which women and men in the early twenty-first century construct themselves *as* women or men.

References

Baxter, Judith (2003) *Positioning Gender in Discourse: A Feminist Methodology.* London: Palgrave.

Butler, Judith (1990) *Gender Trouble: Feminism and the Subversion of Identity.* New York: Routledge.

Cameron, Deborah (1985) *Feminism and Linguistic Theory.* London: Macmillan.

Coates, Jennifer (2004) *Women, Men and Language* (3rd edn). London: Longman.

Eckert, Penelope and McConnell-Ginet, Sally (2003) *Language and Gender.* Cambridge: Cambridge University Press.

Holmes, Janet (2007) "Social constructionism, postmodernism and feminist sociolinguistics," *Gender and Language* 1(1), 51–66.

Johnson, Sally and Meinhof, Ulrike Hanna (eds) (1997) *Language and Masculinity.* Oxford: Blackwell.

Lakoff, Robin (1975) *Language and Woman's Place.* New York: Harper & Row.

McElhinny, Bonnie (2003) "Theorising gender in sociolinguistics and linguistic anthropology," pp. 21–42 in Janet Holmes and Miriam Meyerhoff (eds) *The Handbook of Language and Gender.* Oxford: Blackwell.

Mills, Sara (2003) *Gender and Politeness.* Cambridge: Cambridge University Press.

Spender, Dale (1980) *Man Made Language.* London: Routledge.

Spivak, Gayatri Chakravorti (1987) *In Other Worlds: Essays in Cultural Politics.* New York: Routledge.

Swann, Joan (2003) "Schooled language: language and gender in educational settings," pp. 624–44 in Janet Holmes and Miriam Meyerhoff (eds) *The Handbook of Language and Gender.* Oxford: Blackwell.

Part I
Gender Differences in Pronunciation and Grammar

This section includes a range of papers which look at the way women's and men's speech varies in terms of pronunciation and grammar. As long ago as the seventeenth century, differences in the language used by women and men were remarked upon in anthropological writings. Missionaries and explorers came across societies where they claimed to find distinct languages for male and female speakers. In fact, their accounts exaggerated the reality: what we find in some languages are phonological, morphological, syntactic, or lexical contrasts where the speaker's gender determines which form is chosen. The first paper in this section, John Bradley's "Yanyuwa: 'Men speak one way, women speak another,'" describes an Australian Aboriginal language in which the choice of particular case-marking suffixes depends on the gender of the speaker.

Gender-exclusive differences of this kind mean that speakers who use a form inappropriate to their gender will be strongly reprimanded, as Bradley's paper makes clear: he quotes a Yanyuwa male who reminisces as follows: "I spoke like a woman and [my mother] yelled at me, 'Hey! you are a man, you have no foreskin, why do you talk like a woman? …' I was shamed." Such linguistic differences clearly function to keep gender roles distinct. However, most of the linguistic variation associated with gender found today involves *gender-preferential* rather than gender-exclusive differences. This means that, rather than there being linguistic forms associated exclusively with one gender, there is instead a tendency for women or for men to use a certain form more frequently. The difference between gender-exclusive and gender-preferential usage seems to correlate with differences between non-industrialized societies, such as the Yanyuwa, and industrialized societies, such as Britain and the USA. Non-industrialized societies tend to have clearly demarcated gender roles, whereas in modern industrialized societies gender roles are much less rigidly structured.

Modern industrialized societies are the setting for the other five papers in this section, which report on sociolinguistic research carried out in Britain, the USA, and Australia into gender-preferential differences in usage. They all use a quantitative approach: that is, results showing phonological or grammatical differences are presented in terms of either raw numbers or percentages, and statistical tests are used to demonstrate the significance of these findings. This approach is common throughout the sciences and social sciences, and it has proved a valuable tool for sociolinguists exploring gender-preferential differences (as it can demonstrate gender difference despite the fact that women and men are using the same linguistic forms). This approach was developed by William Labov in his pioneering book, *Sociolinguistic Patterns* (1972), and it has provided sociolinguists with a model for work on linguistic variation; the model is often referred to as the Variationist Paradigm.

The papers by Peter Trudgill and Penelope Eckert both deal with phonetic and phono-logical variation: that is, they both focus on gender differences in pronunciation. Trudgill's paper, "Sex and Covert Prestige," draws on his research into phonetic and phonological variation in the English town of Norwich. Trudgill shows how variation is correlated not only with the social class of speakers (with middle-class speakers using forms closer to Received Pronunciation than working-class speakers) but also with speaker's gender. Male speakers, in Trudgill's sample, were more likely than female speakers to use non-standard forms. Trudgill, following Labov, accounts for this pattern by appealing to the notion of "covert prestige." "Covert" prestige is hypothesized to inhere in vernacular variants, just as "overt" prestige inheres in standard variants. By carrying out self-evaluation tests (which asked speakers to say which pronunciation of particular words was closest to their own), Trudgill was able to show that men tended to claim that they used non-standard forms when recordings of their speech showed this was not the case, while women tended to over-report, that is, to claim that they used more standard forms than they actually did. These results suggest that covert prestige is a powerful force in the speech community of Norwich and that masculinity is strongly linked with non-standard forms.

The next two papers focus on the everyday interaction of adolescents, but they examine grammatical, not phonological, variation. Jenny Cheshire's paper, "Linguistic Variation and Social Function," is based on her research into the grammatical usage of young people in Reading, England, research which revealed significant gender differences. Cheshire col-lected her data through participant observation rather than through sociolinguistic interviews. Participant observation involves the researcher in long-term research: as the term suggests, the researcher becomes, as far as possible, a participant in the social group under scrutiny. The advantage of this research method is that large amounts of spontaneous speech can be collected over time, as participants become familiar with the researcher and lose self-consciousness about the presence of a tape-recorder. Cheshire spent nine months hanging around the adventure playgrounds where groups of young people collected after school or during school hours when they played truant. Her results revealed that non-standard grammatical forms were used less often by the girls than by the boys (apart from non-standard *do*), a finding which has been widely replicated in variationist studies.

What is particularly interesting about Cheshire's work is her use of social network the-ory. This was first applied to sociolinguistic research by James and Lesley Milroy in their work on linguistic variation in Belfast, Northern Ireland (see Milroy and Milroy 1978; Milroy 1980). At the heart of social network theory is its claim that members of a speech community are connected to each other in social networks, and that dense and multiplex networks reinforce vernacular norms. (Dense networks are those where everyone knows everyone else; multiplex networks are those where connections between people are of many different kinds – they may, for example, know each other as friends and as work-mates and as neighbors.) In other words, social networks operate as norm-enforcement mechanisms. In the case of language, this means that a closely knit group will have the capacity to enforce linguistic norms. Cheshire's research demonstrates that young people in Reading belong to social groups that are organized in terms of gender – the boys hang about with boys, the girls with other girls – and that membership of these close-knit single-sex groups results in different patterns of linguistic usage for boys and girls.

This was also the chief finding of Edina Eisikovits' research. Eisikovits' paper, "Girl-talk/ Boy-talk," arose from her study of the grammatical patterns typical of adolescents aged 13 and 16 living in working-class areas of Sydney, Australia. The adolescents were interviewed in self-selected pairs, to encourage informality. Eisikovits' findings for her 16-year-old informants correspond to the expected pattern, with female speech closer to the standard, and male speakers consistently using a higher proportion of non-standard forms. But, interestingly, this pattern was *not* apparent in the speech of the younger adolescent speakers she interviewed. In fact, the 13-year-old girls used a higher proportion of non-standard past-tense verb forms than any other group. It seems that many of the non-standard features of Sydney vernacular speech have prestige for young adolescents of both sexes. But, as they get older, girls learn to modify their speech in the direction of the standard, while boys seem to consolidate their perception of non-standard forms as having positive value. By the age of 16, young speakers have adjusted their speech to be more congruent with adult usage.

The next paper in this section, Patricia Nichols' "Black Women in the Rural South," is again about grammatical variation, but this time the research focuses on adult speakers. Nichols carried out fieldwork in two Black communities in South Carolina, USA, one on the mainland and one on a nearby island, in order to investigate the shift from an English creole known as Gullah to a more standard variety of English. Nichols found that the women in her sample did not behave uniformly. Older mainland women were the heaviest users of Gullah variants, but young and middle-aged island women, by contrast, were the most advanced in the shift to Standard English. Nichols explains this finding in terms of local job opportunities. Men of all ages in the area work in the construction industry, while older women work in domestic and agricultural jobs. These speakers have little incentive to speak Standard English. The younger island women, on the other hand, have different work opportunities in white-collar and service jobs. These jobs require Standard English and bring the younger women into contact with Standard English speakers. The younger Black women therefore have both the incentive and the opportunity to acquire the standard variety. (For more recent work on the talk of Black women in the rural South, see Childs and Mallinson 2004; Mallinson and Childs 2007.)

The last paper in this section is Penelope Eckert's "Gender and Sociolinguistic Variation." Eckert's data was obtained through participant observation: her subjects were students at Belten High, a high school in the suburbs of Detroit. The students she focuses on belong to two dominant groups in the school: "jocks" and "burnouts." "Jocks" are students who participate enthusiastically in school culture and aim to go on to college; "burnouts" are students who reject the idea of the school as central to their lives, and who are more interested in activities outside school. To put it simply, the jocks constitute a middle-class culture, the burnouts a working-class culture. Eckert studied phonological variation in the speech of these students: her analysis reveals the complex correlation between pronunciation, gender, and social category (jock or burnout). There is not a simple male–female divide in her findings; rather, jock girls are the most conservative group, while burnout girls are the most advanced speakers in terms of new vernacular forms. In other words, the girls' usage is more polarized than the boys'. Eckert argues that girls have to work harder at being good jocks or good burnouts, because, as females, they are marginalized in the linguistic "marketplace." We have placed this paper at the end of the section because it shows very clearly how variationist studies have developed. Eckert is concerned to demonstrate that there is no neat one-to one correlation between language use and gender. She also draws on a theoretical framework (Bourdieu and Boltanski's notion of a symbolic market) which illustrates the increasing influence of European social theory on sociolinguistics.

The six papers in this section deal not just with differences in linguistic usage between male and female speakers, but also with explanations for these differences. Explanations draw on a range of concepts: covert prestige – that is, the positive value assigned to vernacular forms by working-class and male speakers although this might be denied in interview (Trudgill; Eisikovits); social networks – that is, the power of social groups to enforce group norms (Cheshire); economic factors – that is, the pressures exerted by the job market which bring some speakers, but not others, into contact with more standard speech forms (Nichols); the linguistic market – that is, the idea that female speakers have to use more standard (or more vernacular) speech because they are marginalized in the linguistic marketplace (Eckert). All these explanations seek to clarify our understanding of *why* male and female speakers use language differently. Some additionally try to clarify why many studies find a pattern of female speakers using linguistic forms closer to the standard. But this pattern is not invariant; moreover, it is certainly not the case that male speakers invariably use more vernacular forms more frequently than women. Eckert's research shows the converse, as does Beth Thomas' work on language use in a small Welsh community (Thomas 1989).

The papers in this section reveal that there can be many different patterns of linguistic usage. Speakers' usage may vary in relation to age or social class or a whole host of other variables as well as gender. Whereas larger-scale quantitative studies like Trudgill's still aim to describe statistically significant differences between "women" and "men," several papers in this section already foreshadow our current understanding of gender as fluid and multiple, rather than treating "women" or "men" as monolithic categories. At any point in time, there will be a range of femininities and masculinities extant in a culture. This idea will be explored further in later sections of the Reader. (For a critique of early sociolinguistic explanations, see Cameron and Coates 1989; Cheshire and Gardner-Chloros 1998; Romaine 2003.)

References

Cameron, Deborah and Coates, Jennifer (1989) "Some problems in the sociolinguistic explanation of sex differences," pp. 13–32 in Jennifer Coates and Deborah Cameron (eds) *Women in their Speech Communities*. London: Longman.

Cheshire, Jenny and Gardner-Chloros, Penelope (1998) "Code-switching and the sociolinguistic gender pattern" in Beverly Hill and Sachiko Ide (eds) "Women's languages in various parts of the world," *International Journal of the Sociology of Language*, Special Issue.

Childs, Becky and Mallinson, Christine (2004) "African American English in Appalachia: dialect accommodation and substrate influence," *English Worldwide* 25, 25–50.

Labov, William (1972) *Sociolinguistic Patterns*. Philadelphia: University of Pennsylvania Press.

Mallinson, Christine and Childs, Becky (2007) "Communities of practice in sociolinguistic description: analysing language and identity practices among black women in Appalachia," *Gender and Language* 1(2), 173–206.

Milroy, James and Milroy, Lesley (1978) "Belfast: change and variation in an urban vernacular," in Peter Trudgill (ed.) *Sociolinguistic Patterns in British English*. London: Arnold.

Milroy, Lesley (1980) *Language and Social Networks*. Oxford: Blackwell.

Romaine, Suzanne (2003) "Variation in language and gender," pp. 98–118 in Janet Holmes and Miriam Meyerhoff (eds) *The Handbook of Language and Gender*. Oxford: Blackwell.

Thomas, Beth (1989) "Differences of sex and sects: linguistic variation and social networks in a Welsh mining village," pp. 51–60 in Jennifer Coates and Deborah Cameron (eds) *Women in their Speech Communities*. London: Longman.

Recommended Further Reading

Cheshire, Jenny (1982) *Variation in an English Dialect.* Cambridge: Cambridge University Press.

Cheshire, Jenny (2002) "Sex and gender in variationist research," pp. 423–43 in J. K. Chambers, Peter Trudgill, and Natalie Schilling-Estes (eds) *The Handbook of Language Variation and Change.* Oxford: Blackwell.

Coates, Jennifer and Cameron, Deborah (eds) (1989) *Women in their Speech Communities.* London: Longman.

Eckert, Penelope (2000) *Linguistic Variation as Social Practice: The Linguistic Construction of Identity in Belten High.* Oxford: Blackwell.

Eckert, Penelope and McConnell-Ginet, Sally (2003) "Working the market: use of varieties," ch. 8 in Penelope Eckert and Sally McConnell-Ginet, *Language and Gender.* Cambridge: Cambridge University Press.

Mallinson, Christine and Childs, Becky (2007) "Communities of practice in sociolinguistic description: analysing language and identity practices among black women in Appalachia," *Gender and Language* 1(2), 173–206.

Meyerhoff, Miriam (1996) "Dealing with gender identity as a sociolinguistic variable," pp. 202–27 in Victoria L. Bergvall, Janet M. Bing, and Alice F. Freed (eds) *Rethinking Language and Gender Research: Theory and Practice.* Harlow: Longman.

Milroy, Lesley (1980) *Language and Social Networks.* Oxford: Blackwell.

Romaine, Suzanne (2003) "Variation in language and gender," pp. 98–118 in Janet Holmes and Miriam Meyerhoff (eds) *The Handbook of Language and Gender.* Oxford: Blackwell.

1

Yanyuwa: "Men speak one way, women speak another"

John Bradley

Source: *Aboriginal Linguistics* 1, 126–34 (1988). © John Bradley 1988. Reprinted with kind permission of the author.

This paper describes briefly the apparently unique system within the Yanyuwa language of having separate dialects for male and female speakers. I will highlight some of the social and ethnographic features of language as it is used in day-to-day speech and in such specific examples as song and ritual. The system is pervasive and distinctly marks the way in which men and women must speak. As a result the roles of men and women in Yanyuwa society are not only contrasted by their social roles, such as ritual life, hunting and nurturing, such as can be found in other Aboriginal communities, but also explicitly by the use of different dialects by male and female speakers. The sex of the hearer has no relevance to the way the language is spoken: men speak their dialect to women and women speak their dialect to men.

The Yanyuwa people today are centred around the township of Borroloola some 970 kilometres south-east of Darwin. Traditionally the Yanyuwa people occupied the Sir Edward Pellew Group of Islands and the lower reaches of the McArthur River delta system and the Wearyan River. Today Yanyuwa speakers number approximately 90 to 150, ranging in age from the late twenties upwards. The younger generation have grown up speaking English with some influence from Kriol, though many have obtained a passive knowledge of Yanyuwa. The reasons for the decline in the language are many, varied and complex and have been described by Jean Kirton (1987). She has been working with the Yanyuwa since 1963 and has been in a position to document the language in considerable detail (see bibliography).

There have been a number of languages recorded throughout the world that have some sex differences. Edward Sapir (1923: 263–85) documented the now extinct Indian Yahi language, a dialect of the Yanna group in Northern California. Sapir noted dialect differences relating to sex and found that in Yana the male form was longer than the female form and included a final syllable as the root; dialectal differences occurred more in complete words than in suffixed elements. There was also a further non-structural distinction in pronunciation whereby men when talking to men spoken fully and deliberately and when speaking with a woman preferred a 'clipped' style of speaking. Three examples of the Yana speech are given below.

	male	female
'grizzly bear'	*t'en'na*	*t'et*
'see me'	*diwai-dja*	*diwa-tch*
'Yana'	*Yana*	*Yah*

Sapir concludes that there are or have been few if any languages in the world in which the split in a dialect has been so pervasive or so thorough: The sex-based dialect differences in Yanyuwa are at least as far-reaching. The following text illustrates the extent of divergence between the two dialects (see Kirton 1988 for a full discussion of the grammatical differences). Note that the same word stems are used in both dialects, but it is the class-marking prefixes on the noun classes, verbs and pronouns which are affected. (NB Yanyuwa has seven classes of common nouns: male (M); female (F); masculine (MSC); feminine (FEM); food (non-meat) (FD); arboreal (ARB); and abstract (ABS); and four cases: nominative (NOM); dative (DAT); ergative-allative (ERG/ALL) marking transitive subject and 'to' a person or location; and ablative (AB).)

Women's Dialect
Nya-ja nya-wukuthu nya-rduwarra   niya-wini nya-Wungkurli   kiwa-wingka
This-M M-short   M-initiated man his-name M-personal name he-go
wayka-liya   ji-wamarra-lu niwa-yirdi na-ridiridi   ji-walya-wu
down-wards MSC-sea-ALL he-bring   ARB-harpoon MSC-dugong/turtle-DAT

Men's Dialect
Jinangu φ-wukuthu φ-rduwarra   na-wini   φ-Wungkurli   ka-wingka wayka-liya
This   short   initiated man his-name personal name he-go   down-wards
ki-wamarra-lu na-yirdi na-ridiridi   ki-walya-wu
MSC-sea-ALL he-bring ARB-harpoon MSC-dugong/turtle-DAT

'The short initiated man whose name is Wungkurli, went down to the sea, taking a harpoon with him for dugong or sea turtle.'

The reason behind this dialect distinction is today unknown and the reason why a male and female dialect arose can only be left to the realms of speculation. The Yanyuwa themselves give no definitive answer as to why there are two dialects, and there is no mythological account for the distinction. In their mythology the female Creator Beings speak the women's dialect and the male Creator Beings speak the men's dialect. The Yanyuwa give no special terms for the two dialects and refer to them simply as *liyi-wulu-wu* 'for the men' and *liyi-nhanawaya-wu* 'for the women'. The most common statement given by the Yanyuwa people in relation to their language is as follows:

'Men speak one way, women speak another, that's just the way it is!' (Annie Karrakayn, 1986)

When I first asked why men and women had different dialects, people deferred to the knowledge of the elders who also readily admitted they did not really know, and thought that the question was a little peculiar. As one of the older Yanyuwa men put it:

'I am ignorant why there are languages for the men and women, maybe the Dreamings made it that way. I don't know, the old people spoke that way and we follow them. What about him, that "whitefella boss man" (scientist), he might know you should go and ask him.' (Old Tim Rakuwurlma, 1985)

Other people who profess a belief in Christianity believe that their language was given to them by God because that is the way He wanted the Yanyuwa people to speak. Only a few individuals offered opinions which were different from that of the general community.

'I don't really know, but I was thinking that men and women have to respect each other, so we talk different ways and so we show respect for each other, just like ceremony; you know men have their ceremony and their language well same way women have their own ceremony and their own language.' (Mussolini Harvey, 1986)

Two women, on hearing of Mussolini Harvey's comment, said they would do more thinking on the question and eventually came up with the following statement.

'Look at you, you're different you don't have *na-wunhan* [breasts] and you are a man, well same way you can't have woman's parts [vagina] so you see we're different, different body, different job, different language, that's why I can't talk like a man and you can't talk like us ladies.' (Amy Friday with Bella Charlie, 1986)

It is obvious then that some Yanyuwa people see the system of two dialects as a natural off-shoot of differing sex roles within their community, in terms of such matters as ritual divisions of labour and other more daily activities such as child nurturing, hunting, social and group dynamics.

Unfortunately the younger generation of Yanyuwa people no longer speak Yanyuwa, so it is very difficult to discuss the way in which the Yanyuwa language was acquired by children. However, conversations with the older Yanyuwa people have enabled at least a partial, albeit fragmentary, reconstruction. It appears that in very early childhood children spoke a form of neutral Yanyuwa, that is, the dialectal markers were removed from words, so that 'at or with the fire' became *buyuka-la* rather than the correct *ji-buyuka-la* for women and *ki-buyuka-la* for men. As the children grew up they were reared in a predominantly female atmosphere surrounded by grandmothers, mothers and aunts, so that the language for the children of both sexes was predominantly the women's dialect.

In early adolescence boys were, and still are, initiated through a series of rituals which culminated in circumcision, after which they were considered men and from which time onwards they were expected to speak the men's dialect. However, it was no smooth transition. For at least 10 years the boys had been speaking a predominantly female form of Yanyuwa and only passively hearing the men's dialect. As a consequence, for a short while after initiation they spoke a form of Yanyuwa which was a mixture of both men's and women's dialects. This was a situation which the older Yanyuwa apparently did not tolerate and the young men were disciplined for speaking incorrectly. A middle aged man gave the following account of such a situation.

'I was only a newly initiated man, and I asked my mother where Douglas [male cousin] was. I spoke like a woman and she yelled at me, "Hey! you are a man, you have no foreskin, why do you talk like a woman? Speak like a man, you are not a small child!" I was shamed, it was not easy to get the men's words right straight away.' (D.M. 1986)

Another man remembers asking to go dugong hunting with his uncle using the female dialect.

'When I spoke like a woman my father said to me, "Where are your breasts and woman's parts [vagina]?" I was really shamed. I was very careful for a while after that to speak the men's words.' (J.T. 1986)

To the Yanyuwa the two dialects are socially very important and after maturity it is considered only proper to speak the dialect of the sex to which one belongs.

Today most young people are more familiar with the female form of the language because of their frequent association with female company, for example at meal times and shopping trips to the store. Consequently when on the odd occasion a young Yanyuwa male uses Yanyuwa he often speaks the women's dialect, for which he is then disciplined. The following example is typical of such a situation.

SON:	Mum, did you buy *ni-warnnyi* [meat]?
MOTHER:	Hey! Are you a man or woman? Man got to talk *na-warnnyi* not *ni-warrnyi* that's women's talk, you got to talk properly, you not little kid you know.
SON:	Hey look you complain because young people don't talk language and when we do you got to laugh at us, man may as well not even bother.
MOTHER:	Well, you just got to learn to talk proper way just like we did. (A.I. and D.I. 1985)

It would appear that the system of having separate dialects for men and women invokes strong feelings about speaking correctly, which in itself creates a system where slovenliness of speech is not acceptable social behaviour. If individuals wish to speak Yanyuwa then they are expected to speak the dialect which is associated with their sex – there is no other alternative.

The groups neighbouring the Yanyuwa, such as the Mara, Garawa and Kurdanji, all say that Yanyuwa is 'too rough to learn', that is, the sex-differentiated dialects are somewhat obstructive to the understanding and learning of the language for a person of non-Yanyuwa descent. Only a few Garawa and Mara speakers today speak Yanyuwa with an easy fluency, while the Yanyuwa declare that Garawa and Mara are easy languages and the fact that many Yanyuwa people today have Mara and Garawa as second and third language is proof of this for the Yanyuwa.

There are occasions when the Yanyuwa men and women do speak each other's dialects, such as when they are relating a story where people of the opposite sex to the speaker have spoken, in which case the quotation will normally be in the dialect which relates to the sex of the person who has spoken. However, there are times especially in rapid general conversation where the distinctions are not highlighted and one must rely on other contextual clues to find out the sex of the speakers involved.

On rare occasions, men and women utilize the dialectal differences in Yanyuwa to draw attention to themselves. Once an elderly man in charge of certain public funeral rituals was not pleased with the way the performances were developing. He began orating his displeasure. At first people paid little attention until a woman pointed out that he was using the female dialect. When this was realized people listened to what was being said. I have witnessed such an occurrence once in eight years of fieldwork, though people present at the time said it had occasionally happened in the past. It is more common for both sexes to be somewhat hesitant to speak the dialect of the other sex unless it is for a specific reason, such as working for anthropologists or linguistic researchers, and on some occasions male Yanyuwa speakers have difficulty constructing the female form of the language and often defer to their wives or ask what they have stated to be checked with a female speaker; the women's dialect is the more complex of the two.

Both men and women will use the dialect of the opposite sex quite freely in joking situations, more specifically in situations relating to male and female relationships and sexual encounters. These situations are somewhat ribald and risqué and full of humour to the Yanyuwa. Amongst the men such occurrences take place after certain ceremonial performances, for example where a male dancer impersonates a woman, after which he will tease his brothers-in-law as if they are his prospective wives. An example is given below.

Female Dialect spoken by Male Speaker
Nya-ngatha nya-Nyilba   nya-yabi yinda   nya-marringaya nda-wuna
M-for me   M-pers.name   M-good you:sg   M-beautiful   your:sg-buttocks
'My Nyilba, you are too good, you have beautiful buttocks.'
(T.F. 1986)

Another unusual occurrence is the use of the female dialect form within the song cycles used by the Yanyuwa men during ceremonial performance. Many of the male mythological species are marked with the female dialect marker *nya-*. In everyday spoken Yanyuwa the men do not use the names of these creatures with this prefix. Examples are *nya-Yilayi*, Spotted Nightjar, *nya-Walungkanarra*, Rainbow Serpent, and *nya-Wurrunkardi*, the personal name of the Dingo Dreaming.

Within the song cycles, there are also female dialectal markers on common nouns and a number of verb stems from the female dialect. Two examples are given below:

Song Verse

Manankurra   'At Manankurra
kiya-alarri   He (a Shark Dreaming) stood.'

Manankurra
place name

kiya-alarri
he: stand

The prefix *kiya-* in the second line of the above verse is a women's dialect prefix, while in the men's dialect it is *ka-*.

Song Verse

Warriyangalayani   'The Hammerhead Shark
ni-mambul ni-ngurru   makes spray with its nose.'

Warriyangalayani
Hammerhead shark

ni-mambul ni-ngurru
its:spray   its:nose

The prefix *ni-* in the second line is the female masculine form. In the male dialect it would be *na-*.

When the men were questioned as to why the female dialect forms were found in song cycles, especially when some song cycles deal with male figures, they could give no answer and did not appear to be particularly disturbed. They classed such occurrences as 'That's just the Dreaming, they're different'. It is tempting to hypothesize that the female dialect may be the more archaic of the two, but without sufficient evidence such a hypothesis remains very tentative. The occurrences of feminine dialect forms in the song cycles are too irregular to form any definite conclusions.

A hypothesis put forward by Dixon (1968) suggests that in some Aboriginal languages there is evidence of an underlying logic in apparent exceptions. He puts forward rules which apply to transfer of class membership in Australian languages. He believes irregular occurrences are in fact a purposeful class transference which classifies according to mythological characteristics rather than observable ones or which mark some important property, quite often danger. Dixon's hypothesis may be relevant to the unusual prefixing which occurs in Yanyuwa song cycles.

There are other examples of unusual language usage which fit more into the mundane social life of the Yanyuwa. Two such examples are where root words are given irregular male and female prefixes:

nya-bardibardi
M-old woman

This word is used by women to refer to older men who associate with women, especially widows, and who constantly demand food or money from them.

rra-malbu
FEM-old man

This word is used by men to refer to older women who are said to associate with men too much, especially in relation to aspects of Yanyuwa life in which they should only be minimally involved. Both of the above terms are not regularly used and are meant to be somewhat insulting in their intent.

The Yanyuwa language also has complex avoidance and kinship terms, both of which are affected by the men's and women's dialects. This has been described by Kirton (1982, 1988).

In any given culture there will be differences in the way men and women speak, for example, in terms of address and the use of expletives, but it would appear that in Yanyuwa the speech differences of male and female speakers are so extensive that the two forms of speech have become dialects of the one language.

In Yanyuwa society the system of two dialects is all pervasive; in day to day usage the two dialects are an intrinsic part of the language. The Yanyuwa continually stressed when asked why there were separate dialects: 'It's just the way it is, no other reason.' In fact many of the Yanyuwa thought, and probably still think, the question a trifle stupid. None of the neighbouring languages share this feature, and in fact some of these people, such as the Garawa, Mara and Kurdanji, see Yanyuwa as a language too difficult to learn because of the separate dialects. Even though the Yanyuwa take for granted their system of male and female dialects they still place much importance on speaking correctly.

The reasons as to why two distinct dialects for female and male speakers have developed are lost in time. This feature has however served to make Yanyuwa a language unique within Aboriginal Australia, if not the world.

References

Dixon, R. M. W. 1968. Noun classes. *Lingua* 21, 104–24.
Grimes, B. J. ed. 1984. *Index to Tenth Edition of Ethnologue: Languages of the World*. Texas: Wycliffe Bible Translators.

Heath, J. 1981. *Basic Material in Mara Grammar, Texts and Dictionary.* PL.

Kirton, J. F. 1970. Twelve pronominal sets in Yanyuwa. *PL* series C, 13, 825–44.

Kirton, J. F. 1971. Complexities of Yanyuwa nouns. *PL* series A, 27, 15–70.

Kirton, J. F. 1987. Yanyuwa – a dying language. *Work Papers of SIL-AAB* Series B, 13, 1–19.

Kirton, J. F. 1988. Men's and women's dialects. *Aboriginal Linguistics* 1.

Kirton, J. F. and B. Charlie. 1978. Seven articulatory positions in Yanyuwa consonants. *PL* Series A, 51, 179–98.

Kirton, J. F. and N. Timothy. 1977. Yanyuwa concepts relating to 'skin'. *Oceania* 47, 320–2.

Kirton, J. F. and N. Timothy. 1978. Yanyuwa verbs. *PL* Series A, 51, 1–52.

Kirton, J. F. and N. Timothy. 1982. Some thoughts on Yanyuwa language and culture. *Work Papers of SIL-AAB* Series B, 8.

Kramer, C. 1975. Sex related differences in address systems. *Anthropological Linguistics* 17, 198–210.

Kroskrity, P. V. 1983. On male and female speech in the Pueblo South West. *IJAL* 49, 88–91.

Sapir, E. 1923. Text analyses of three Yana dialects. *America Archaeology and Ethnology* 20, 263–85.

Taylor, D. 1954. Diachronic note on the Carib contribution to Island Carib. *IJAL* 20, 28–33.

2

Sex and Covert Prestige

Peter Trudgill

Source: Peter Trudgill, *On Dialect*. Oxford: Blackwell (1988), pp. 169–77. Reprinted with permission of Wiley-Blackwell.

In this paper we present some data which illustrate quite clearly the phenomenon of sex differentiation in language in one variety of British English. We then examine an explanation for this differentiation. [...]

The results from which the following figures are taken are based on an urban dialect survey of the city of Norwich carried out in the summer of 1968 with a random sample, 60 in number, of the population of the city, and reported in detail in Trudgill (1974). This sociolinguistic research was concerned mainly with correlating phonetic and phonological variables with social class, age, and stylistic context. Some work was also done, however, in studying the relationships that obtain between linguistic phenomena and sex.

In order to relate the phonological material to the social class of informants and the other parameters, a number of phonetic and phonological variables were developed, and index scores calculated for individuals and groups in the manner of Labov (1966a) [...]. The first of these variables that I wish to discuss is the variable (ng). This is the pronunciation of the suffix -*ing* in *walking*, *laughing*, etc., and is a well-known variable in many types of English. In the case of Norwich English there are two possible pronunciations of this variable: [ɪŋ], which also occurs in the prestige accent, RP, and [ən ~ n̩]. The former is labelled (ng)-1 and the latter (ng)-2.

Index scores were developed for this variable by initially awarding 1 for each instance of (ng)-1 and 2 for each instance of (ng)-2. These scores were then summed and divided by the total number of instances, to give the mean score. Indices were finally calculated by subtracting 1 from the mean score and multiplying the result by 100. In this case, this gives an index score of 000 for consistent use of RP (ng)-1, and 100 for consistent use of (ng)-2, and the scores are equivalent to the simple percentage of non-RP forms used. (For variables with more than two variants this simple relationship, of course, does not apply.) Indices were calculated in the first instance for individual informants in each contextual style and subsequently for each group of informants. The four contextual styles:

Language and Gender: A Reader, Second Edition. Edited by Jennifer Coates and Pia Pichler.
© 2011 Blackwell Publishing Ltd except for editorial material and organization. © 2011 Jennifer Coates and Pia Pichler. Published 2011 by Blackwell Publishing Ltd.

word list style: WLS
reading passage style: RPS
formal speech: FS
casual speech: CS

are equivalent to the styles discussed by Labov (1966a) and were elicited in a similar manner. Indices for other variables were calculated in the same way.

Table 1 shows the average (ng) index scores for informants in the five social class groups obtained in the survey, in the four contextual styles. The social class divisions are based on an index that was developed using income, education, dwelling type, location of dwelling, occupation, and occupation of father as parameters. The five classes have been labelled:

middle middle class: MMC
lower middle class: LMC
upper working class: UWC
middle working class: MWC
lower working class: LWC

The table shows very clearly that (ng) is a linguistic variable in Norwich English. Scores range from a high of 100 percent non-RP forms by the LWC in CS to a low of 0 percent by the MMC in RPS and by the MMC and LMC in WLS. The pattern of differentiation is also structured in a very clear manner. For each of the social classes, scores rise consistently from WLS to CS; and for each style scores rise consistently from MMC to LWC.

Table 1 (ng) Index scores by class and style

		Style			
Class	*WLS*	*RPS*	*FS*	*CS*	*N*
MMC	000	000	003	028	6
LMC	000	010	015	042	8
UWC	005	015	074	087	16
MWC	023	044	088	095	22
LWC	029	066	098	100	8

In his study of this same variable in American English, Fischer (1958) found that males used a higher percentage of non-standard [n] forms than females. Since we have shown that (ng) is a variable in Norwich English, we could expect, if sex differentiation of the type we have been discussing also occurs here, that the same sort of pattern would emerge. Table 2 shows that this is in fact very largely the case. In 17 cases out of 20, *male* scores are greater than or equal to corresponding *female* scores. We can therefore state that a high (ng) index is typical not only of WC speakers in Norwich but also of *male* speakers. This pattern, moreover, is repeated for the vast majority of the other nineteen variables studied in Norwich.

[…] In this paper we seek an explanation for this phenomenon in terms of the fact that WC speech, like other aspects of WC culture, appears, at least in some western societies, to have connotations of masculinity (see Labov, 1966a: 495), probably because it is associated with the roughness and toughness supposedly characteristic of

Table 2   (ng) Index scores by class, style and sex

Class	Sex	WLS	RPS	FS	CS
MMC	M	000	000	004	031
	F	000	000	000	000
LMC	M	000	020	027	017
	F	000	000	003	067
UWC	M	000	018	081	095
	F	011	013	068	077
MWC	M	024	043	091	097
	F	020	046	081	088
LWC	M	060	100	100	100
	F	017	054	097	100

WC life which are, stereotypically and to a certain extent, often considered to be desirable masculine attributes. They are not, on the other hand, widely considered to be desirable feminine characteristics. On the contrary, features such as 'refinement' and 'sophistication' are much preferred in some western societies.

As it stands, this argument is largely speculative. What it requires is some concrete evidence. This need for evidence was discussed by Labov (1966b: 108) who wrote that in New York

> the socio-economic structure confers prestige on the middle-class pattern associated with the more formal styles. [But] one can't avoid the implication that in New York City we must have an equal and opposing prestige for informal, working-class speech – a covert prestige enforcing this speech pattern. We must assume that people in New York City want to talk as they do, yet this fact is not at all obvious in any overt response that you can draw from interview subjects.

It is suspected, in other words, that there are hidden values associated with non-standard speech, and that, as far as our present argument is concerned, they are particularly important in explaining the sex differentiation of linguistic variables. Labov, however, has not been able to uncover them or prove that they exist. We can guess that these values are there, but they are values which are not usually overtly expressed. They are not values which speakers readily admit to having, and for that reason they are difficult to study. Happily, the urban dialect survey carried out in Norwich provided some evidence which argues very strongly in favour of our hypothesis, and which managed, as it were, to remove the outer layer of overtly expressed values and penetrate to the hidden values beneath. That is, we now have some objective data which actually demonstrates that for male speakers, WC non-standard speech is in a very real sense highly valued and prestigious.

Labov has produced evidence to show that almost all speakers in New York City share a common set of linguistic norms, whatever their actual linguistic performance, and that they hear and report themselves as using these prestigious linguistic forms, rather than the forms they actually do use. This 'dishonesty' in reporting what they say is of course not deliberate, but it does suggest that informants, at least so far as their conscious awareness is concerned, are dissatisfied with the way they speak, and would prefer to be able to use more standard forms. This was in fact confirmed by comments New York City informants actually made about their own speech.

Overt comments made by the Norwich informants on their own speech were also of this type. Comments such as 'I talk horrible' were typical. It also began to appear, however, that, as suggested above, there were other, deeper motivations for their actual linguistic behaviour than these overtly expressed notions of their own 'bad speech'. For example, many informants who initially stated that they did not speak properly, and would like to do so, admitted, if pressed, that they perhaps would not *really* like to, and that they would almost certainly be considered foolish, arrogant or disloyal by their friends and family if they did. This is our first piece of evidence.

Far more important, however, is the evidence that was obtained by means of the Self-Evaluation Test, in which half of the Norwich informants took part. This is particularly the case when the results of this test are compared to those obtained by a similar test conducted by Labov in New York. In the Norwich Self-Evaluation Test, 12 lexical items were read aloud, to informants, with two or more different pronunciations. For example the word *tune* was read with two different pronunciations: (1) [tjuːn] (roughly, 'tyoon'); (2) [tuːn] (roughly, 'toon'). Informants were then asked to indicate, by marking a number on a chart, which of these pronunciations most closely resembled the way in which they normally said this word.

The corresponding Self-Evaluation Test in New York for the variable (r) – presence or absence of post-vocalic /r/ (a prestige feature) – produced the following results. Informants who in FS used over 30 percent /r/ were, very generously, considered to be (post-vocalic) /r/-users. Seventy percent of those who, in this sense, were /r/-users reported that they normally used /r/. But 62 percent of those who were *not* /r/-users *also* reported that they normally used /r/. As Labov says (1966a: 455): 'In the conscious report of their own usage … New York respondents are very inaccurate'. The accuracy, moreover, is overwhelmingly in the direction of reporting themselves as using a form which is *more* statusful than the one they actually use. Labov (1966a: 455) claims that 'no conscious deceit plays a part in this process' and that 'most of the respondents seemed to perceive their own speech in terms of the norms at which they were aiming rather than the sound actually produced'.

The full results of this test are shown in table 3. It shows that 62 percent of non-/r/-users 'over-reported' themselves as using /r/, and 21 percent of /r/-users 'under-reported', although in view of Labov's 30 percent dividing line, the latter were very probably simply being accurate.

Table 3 Self-evaluating of (r) – New York

	Percentage reported		
Used	/r/	ϕ	
/ɹ/	79	21	= 100
ϕ	62	38	= 100

In the Norwich test, the criteria used were much more rigorous. In comparing the results obtained in the Self-Evaluation Test to forms actually used in Norwich, *casual speech* was used rather than *formal speech*, since CS more closely approximates everyday speech – to how informants normally pronounce words, which is what they were asked to report on.

Table 4 Self-evaluation of (yu)

Used	(yu) Percentage reported		
	1	2	
1	60	40	= 100
2	16	84	= 100

Moreover, informants were allowed *no* latitude in their self-evaluation. It was considered that the form informants used in everyday speech was the variant indicated by the appropriate CS index for that individual informant. For example, an (ng) index of between 050 and 100 was taken as indicating an (ng)-2 user rather than (ng)-1 user. In other words, the dividing line is 50 percent rather than Labov's more lenient 30 percent. If, therefore, the characteristics of the Norwich sample were identical to those of the New York sample, we would expect a significantly *higher* degree of *over-reporting* from the Norwich informants.

The results, in fact, show the exact reverse of this, as can be seen from table 4. This table gives the results of the Self-Evaluation Test for the variable (yu), which is the pronunciation of the vowel in items such as *tune, music, queue, huge.* In Norwich English items such as these have two possible pronunciations: (yu)-1 has [j] as in RP-like [kjuː ~ kjʉː]; (yu)-2 omits [j] as in [kʉː ~ kɜʉ], *queue.*

Table 4 provides a very striking contrast to the New York results shown in table 3 in that only 16 percent of (yu)-2 users, as compared to the equivalent figure of 62 percent in New York, over-reported themselves as using the more statusful RP-like variant (yu)-1 when they did not in fact do so. Even more significant, however, is the fact that as many as 40 percent of (yu)-1 users actually *under*-reported – and the under-reporting is in this case quite genuine.

A further breakdown of the scores given in table 4 is also very revealing. Of the 16 percent (yu)-2 users who over-reported, *all* were women. Of the (yu)-1 users who under-reported, half were men and half women. Here we see, for the first time, the emergence of the hidden values that underlie the sex differentiation described earlier in this paper. If we take the sample as a whole, we have the percentages of speakers under- and over-reporting shown in table 5. Male informants, it will be noted, are strikingly more accurate in their self-assessment than are female informants.

Table 5 Percentage of informants over- and under-reporting (yu)

	Total	Male	Female
Over-r	13	0	29
Under-r	7	6	7
Accurate	80	94	64

The hidden values, however, emerge much more clearly from a study of the other variables tested in this way, (er), (ō) and (ā), illustrated in tables 6, 7, and 8, respectively. The variable (er) is the vowel in *ear, here, idea*, which in Norwich English ranges from [ɪə] to [ɛː]; (ō) is the vowel in *road, nose, moan* (but not in *rowed, knows, mown*, which are distinct) and ranges from [ɵu] through [u:] to [ʊ]; and (ā) is the vowel in the lexical set of *gate, face, name*, which ranges from [eɪ] to [æi].

Table 6 Percentage of informants over- and under-reporting (er)

	Total	Male	Female
Over-r	43	22	68
Under-r	33	50	14
Accurate	23	28	18

Table 7 Percentage of informants over- and under-reporting (ō)

	Total	Male	Female
Over-r	18	12	25
Under-r	36	54	18
Accurate	45	34	57

Table 8 Percentage of informants over- and under-reporting (ā)

	Total	Male	Female
Over-r	32	22	43
Under-r	15	28	0
Accurate	53	50	57

For each of these variables, it will be seen, there are more male speakers who claim to use a *less* prestigious variant than they actually do than there are who over-report, and for one of the variables (ō), the difference is very striking: 54 percent to 12 percent. In two of the cases, moreover, there are more male speakers who under-report than there are who are accurate.

Although there are some notable differences between the four variables illustrated here,[1] it is clear that Norwich informants are much more prone to under-report than New York informants, and that – this is central to our argument – *male* informants in Norwich are much more likely to *under*-report, *female* informants to *over*-report.

This, then, is the objective evidence which demonstrates that male speakers, at least in Norwich, are at a subconscious or perhaps simply private level very favourably disposed towards non-standard speech forms. This is so much the case that as many as 54 percent of them, in one case, claim to use these forms or hear themselves as using them *even when they do not do so*. If it is true that informants 'perceive their own speech in terms of the norms at which they are aiming rather than the sound actually produced' then the norm at which a large number of Norwich males are aiming is *non-standard WC speech*. This favourable attitude is never overtly expressed, but the responses to these tests show that statements about 'bad speech' are for public consumption only. Privately and subconsciously, a large number of male speakers are more concerned with acquiring prestige of the covert sort and with signalling group solidarity than with obtaining social status, as this is more usually defined. [...] By means of these figures, therefore, we have been able to demonstrate both that it is possible to obtain evidence of the 'covert prestige' associated with non-standard varieties, and that, for Norwich men, working-class speech is statusful and prestigious.

[...]

Note

1   These differences may be due to a skewing effect resulting from the necessity of using only a small number of individual lexical items to stand for each variable in the tests. (Informants' reports of their pronunciation of *tune*, for example, do not *necessarily* mean that they would pronounce or report *Tuesday* or *tube* in the same way.)

References

Fischer, J. L. (1958) 'Social influences on the choice of a linguistic variant'. *Word* 14, 47–56.

Labov, W. (1966a) *The Social Stratification of English in New York City*. Washington, DC: Center for Applied Linguistics.

Labov, W. (1966b) 'Hypercorrection by the lower middle class as a factor in linguistic change', in W. Bright (ed.) *Sociolinguistics*. The Hague: Mouton.

Trudgill, P. (1974) *The Social Differentiation of English in Norwich*. London: Cambridge University Press.

3

Linguistic Variation and Social Function

Jenny Cheshire

Source: S. Romaine (ed.), *Sociolinguistic Variation in Speech Communities*. London: Arnold (1982), pp. 153–64. Reprinted with permission of Edward Arnold (Publishers) Ltd.

The fact that linguistic variation is correlated with a wide range of sociological characteristics of speakers has been extensively documented over the last 15 years by the many studies that have been inspired by the work of William Labov. It is well established, for example, that the frequency with which speakers use non-standard linguistic features is correlated with their socioeconomic class. More recently, studies involving speakers from a single socioeconomic class have been able to reveal some of the more subtle aspects of sociolinguistic variation. It has been found, for example, that the frequency of use of non-standard phonological features in Belfast English is correlated with the type of social network in which speakers are involved (see Milroy and Margrain 1980). This paper will show that the frequency with which adolescent speakers use many non-standard morphological and syntactic features of the variety of English spoken in the town of Reading, in Berkshire, is correlated with the extent to which they adhere to the norms of the vernacular culture. It will also show that linguistic variables often fulfil different social and semantic functions for the speakers who use them.

The paper will consider nine non-standard features of Reading English:

1 the present tense suffix with non 3rd person singular subjects
   e.g. we *goes* shopping on Saturdays
2 *has* with non 3rd person singular subjects
   e.g. we *has* a little fire, keeps us warm
3 *was* with plural subjects (and singular *you*)
   e.g. you *was* outside
4 multiple negation
   e.g. I'm *not* going *nowhere*
5 negative past tense *never*, used for standard English *didn't*
   e.g. I *never* done it, it was him
6 *what* used for standard English *who, whom, which*, and *that*
   e.g. there's a knob *what* you turn
   are you the boy *what*'s just come?
7 auxiliary *do* with 3rd person singular subjects
   e.g. how much *do* he want for it?

8   past tense *come*
     e.g. I *come* down here yesterday
9   *ain't*, used for negative present tense forms of *be* and *have*, with all subjects
     e.g. I *ain't* going
     I *ain't* got any

Many, though not all, of these features function as markers of vernacular loyalty for adolescent speakers in Reading, though some are more sensitive markers than others. *Ain't*, in particular, is able overtly to symbolize some of the important values of the vernacular culture. Furthermore, some features are markers of loyalty to the vernacular culture for adolescent boys but not for adolescent girls, and vice-versa.

The Data

The analysis is based on the spontaneous, natural speech of three groups of adolescents, recorded by the method of long-term participant-observation in adventure playgrounds in Reading. The aim was to record speech that was as close as possible to the vernacular, or most informal style, of the speakers. Thirteen boys and twelve girls were recorded over a period of about eight months.

Some of the speakers were subsequently recorded at school, by their teacher, with two or three of their friends. The fieldwork procedures are discussed in detail in Cheshire 1982.

The Vernacular Culture Index

Labov (1966) maintains that the use of non-standard features is controlled by the norms of the vernacular subculture, whilst the use of standard English features is controlled by the overt norms of the mainstream culture in society. Any analysis of variation in the occurrence of non-standard features needs to take this into account, for it means that an adequate sample of non-standard forms is more likely to be found where speakers conform more closely to vernacular norms than to the overt norms of the dominant mainstream culture. The speakers who were chosen for the present study were children who often met at the adventure playgrounds when they should have been at school, and the boys, in particular, were members of a very well-defined subculture. In many respects this culture resembled a delinquent subculture (as defined, for example, by Andry 1960; Cohen 1965; Downes 1966; Willmott 1966 and many other writers). Many of the boys' activities, for example, centred around what Miller (1958) calls the 'cultural foci' of *trouble, excitement, toughness, fate, autonomy* and *smartness* (in the American English sense of 'outsmarting').

Since the vernacular culture was in this case very clearly defined, it was possible to isolate a small number of indicators that could be used to construct a 'vernacular culture index', in the same way that socioeconomic indices are constructed. It seemed reasonable to assume that those aspects of the peer-group culture that were sources of prestige for group members and that were frequent topics of conversation were of central importance within the culture. Six factors that met these requirements were selected. Four of these reflect the norms of trouble and excitement; three directly, and one more indirectly. *Skill at fighting, the carrying of a weapon* and *participation in minor criminal activities*, such as shoplifting, arson, and vandalism, are clearly connected with trouble and excitement.

Though interrelated, they were treated as separate indicators because not all boys took part in all the activities to the same extent. The job that the boys hoped to have when they left school was also included as a separate indicator, for the same reason. Again, acceptable jobs reflect the norms of trouble and excitement, though perhaps more indirectly here, and the job that the boys hoped to have when they left school (or, in a few cases, that they already had) was an important contributing factor to the opinion that they formed of themselves and of other group members. Some jobs that were acceptable were slaughterer, lorry driver, motor mechanic, and soldier; jobs that were unacceptable were mostly white-collar jobs. A fifth indicator was 'style': the extent to which dress and hairstyle were important to speakers. Many writers stress the importance of style as a symbolic value within adolescent subcultures (see, for example, Cohen 1972; Clarke 1973), and for many of the boys in the group it was a frequent topic of conversation.

Finally, a measure of 'swearing' was included in the index, since this appeared to be an extremely important symbol of vernacular identity for both boys and girls. Swearing is, of course, a linguistic feature, but this does not affect its use as an indicator here, since it involves only a few lexical items which could not be marked for any of the non-standard features of Reading English. [...]

The boys were then given a score for each of the indicators, and were divided into four groups on the basis of their total score. Group 1 consists of those boys who can be considered to adhere most closely to the norms of the vernacular culture, whilst group 4 consists of boys who do not adhere closely to vernacular norms. Groups 2 and 3 are intermediate in their adherence, with group 2 adhering more closely than group 3.

Linguistic Markers of Adherence to the Vernacular Culture

Table 1 shows the frequency of occurrence of the nine non-standard features in the speech of the four groups of boys.

The features are arranged into three classes, which reflect the extent to which they mark adherence to the vernacular culture. Class A contains four features whose frequency is very finely linked to the vernacular culture index of the speakers. The most sensitive indicator is the non-standard present tense suffix, which occurs very frequently in the speech of those boys who are most firmly immersed in the vernacular culture (group 1), progressively less frequently in the speech of groups 2 and 3, and rather infrequently in the speech of boys who are only loosely involved in the culture (group 4). This feature, then, functions as a powerful marker of vernacular loyalty.

The features in Class B (non-standard *never* and non-standard *what*) also function as markers of vernacular loyalty, but they are less sensitive markers than the features in Class A. Significant variation occurs only between speakers in Group 1 and speakers in Group 4, in other words, between the boys who adhere most closely to the vernacular culture, and the boys who adhere least closely. This type of sociolinguistic variation is not unusual: Policansky (1980) reports similar behaviour with subject–verb concord in Belfast English, where significant variation is found only between speakers at the extreme ends of the social network scale (cf. also Jahangiri and Hudson, 1982).

The fact that there is some correlation between the vernacular culture index and the frequency of use of Group B features can be clearly seen if the speakers in Groups 2 and 3 are amalgamated into a single group. Table 2 shows that non-standard *never* and non-standard *what* now show regular patterns of variation. These features, then, do function

Table 1   Adherence to vernacular culture and frequency of occurrence of non-standard forms

		Group 1	*Group 2*	*Group 3*	*Group 4*
Class A	non-standard -*s*	77.36	54.03	36.57	21.21
	non-standard *has*	66.67	50.00	41.65	(33.33)
	non-standard *was*	90.32	89.74	83.33	75.00
	negative concord	100.00	85.71	83.33	71.43
Class B	non-standard *never*	64.71	41.67	45.45	37.50
	non-standard *what*	92.31	7.69	33.33	0.00
Class C	non-standard aux. *do*	58.33	37.50	83.33	—
	non-standard *come*	100.00	100.00	100.00	(100.00)
	ain't=aux *have*	78.26	64.52	80.00	(100.00)
	ain't=aux *be*	58.82	72.22	80.00	(100.00)
	ain't=copula	100.00	76.19	56.52	75.00

NB. Bracketed figures indicate that the number of occurrences of the variable is low, and that the indices may not, therefore, be reliable. Following Labov (1970) less than 5 occurrences was considered to be too low for reliability.

Table 2   Frequency indices of group 1, groups 2 and 3, and group 4

	Group 1	*Groups 2 & 3*	*Group 4*
non-standard *never*	64.71	43.00	37.50
non-standard *what*	92.31	18.00	0.00

as markers of vernacular loyalty. But they are less sensitive markers than the features in Class A, showing regular patterning only with rather broad groupings of speakers.

Features in Class C, on the other hand, do not show any correlation with the speakers' vernacular culture index. For the most part, figures are completely irregular. All these features, however, are involved in other, more complex, kinds of sociolinguistic variation, and this could explain why they do not function as straightforward markers of vernacular loyalty. There is convincing evidence, for example, that non-standard auxiliary *do* is undergoing a linguistic change away from an earlier dialect form towards the standard English form (see Cheshire 1978. See also Aitchison 1981 for some interesting ideas concerning the mechanism of the change). Some forms of *ain't* appear to function as a direct marker of a vernacular norm, as we will see. We will also see that the use of non-standard *come* bears an interesting relation to the sex of speakers: it functions as a marker of vernacular loyalty for adolescent girls, but for boys it is an invariant feature, occurring 100 percent of the time in their speech, irrespective of the extent to which they adhere to the vernacular culture.

Stylistic Variation

We will now consider what happens to the frequency of occurrence of these linguistic features when the boys are at school. The Labovian view of style shifting is that formality–informality can be considered as a linear continuum, reflecting the amount of attention that speakers give to their speech. As formality increases, the frequency of occurrence of some non-standard linguistic features decreases (see Labov 1972, chapter 3). This approach has been questioned by a number of scholars. L. Milroy (1980) and Romaine (1980), for example, found that reading, where attention is directly focused on speech, does not consistently result in the use of fewer non-standard features. And Wolfson (1976) points out that in some situations speakers will monitor their speech carefully to ensure that they use *more* non-standard features, in order to produce an appropriately informal speech style.

The present study also found difficulties in applying the Labovian approach to the analysis of style, for the ability of some linguistic features to signal vernacular loyalty affects the frequency with which they occur in different speech styles.

The recordings made at school were clearly made in a more formal setting than the recordings made in the adventure playgrounds. The speakers were in school, where the overt norms of mainstream society are maintained (see, for example, Moss 1973), the teacher was present, the speaker knew that he was being recorded, and there had been no 'warm-up' session with the tape-recorder before the recording was made. On the other hand, the speaker did have two (at least) of his friends present. This was in an attempt to stop him 'drying up', as he may have done in a straightforward interview situation, and although the intention was to make the situation somewhat more relaxed, it nevertheless clearly represents a more formal setting than the adventure playground.

Unfortunately only eight of the thirteen boys could be recorded at school. Four boys had recently left school, and the fifth was so unpopular with the teacher that she could not be persuaded to spend extra time with him.

Table 3 shows the frequency of occurrence of the non-standard linguistic features in the vernacular style and in the school style of these eight speakers. We can see that those features that are sensitive markers of vernacular loyalty (Class A) all occur less often in the boys' school style than in their vernacular style, though the difference in frequency is very small in the case of non-standard *was*.

Non-standard *never*, in Class B, also occurs less often in the school recordings. Non-standard *what*, however, does not decrease in frequency; instead, it increases slightly in occurrence. The remaining features in the table do not decrease in frequency in the school style, either. Non-standard *come* remains invariant, and *ain't* increases in frequency by quite a large amount. (There were no occurrences of third person singular forms of auxiliary *do* in the school recordings.)

So far, of course, this is quite in accordance with the Labovian view of the stylistic continuum. Labov classifies linguistic variables into 'indicators' and 'markers', which

Table 3 Stylistic variation in the frequency of occurrence of non-standard forms

		Vernacular style	*School style*
Class A	non-standard *-s*	57.03	31.49
	non-standard *has*	46.43	35.71
	non-standard *was*	91.67	88.57
	negative concord	90.70	66.67
Class B	non-standard *never*	49.21	15.38
	non-standard *what*	50.00	54.55
Class C	non-standard *do*	—	—
	non-standard *come*	100.00	100.00
	ain't=aux. *have*	93.02	100.00
	ain't=copula	74.47	77.78

differ in that indicators show regular variation only with sociological characteristics of speakers, whereas markers also show regular correlation with style. We could, therefore, class the linguistic variables in Class A, together with non-standard *never*, as markers in Reading English, and class the other variables as indicators. But this would be oversimplistic. As we will see, there are some more complex factors involved in stylistic variation, which only become apparent if we compare the linguistic behaviour of individual speakers, rather than of groups of speakers.

Table 3 expressed the frequency of occurrence of the non-standard features in terms of group indices; in other words, the speech of the eight boys analysed together, as a whole. There are many practical advantages to the analysis of the speech of groups of speakers, particularly where morphological and syntactic variables are concerned. One advantage is that variables may not occur frequently enough in the language of an individual speaker for a detailed analysis to be made, whereas the language of a group of speakers will usually provide an adequate number of occurrences of crucial forms (cf. also the discussion in J. Milroy 1982).

The school recordings consisted of only about half an hour of speech for each boy. This did not provide enough data for an analysis in terms of individual speakers, and in most cases it did not even provide enough data for a group analysis. There was one exception, however. Present tense verb forms occur very frequently in speech, so that even within a half hour recording there were enough forms for an analysis of their use by individual speakers to be made. This enables us to investigate some of the more subtle aspects of sociolinguistic variation, that would be overlooked in a group analysis.

Table 4 shows the frequency of occurrence of non-standard present tense verb forms in the speech of each of the eight boys, in their vernacular style and in their school style. Noddy, Ricky and Perry are Group 1 speakers, with a high vernacular culture index; Kitty, Jed and Gammy are Group 2 speakers, and Barney and Colin are in Group 3.

Table 4 Frequency of occurrence of non-standard present tense verb forms

	Vernacular style	*School style*
Noddy	81.00	77.78
Ricky	70.83	34.62
Perry	71.43	54.55
Jed	45.00	0.00
Kitty	45.71	33.33
Gammy	57.14	31.75
Barney	31.58	54.17
Colin	38.46	0.00

There are considerable differences in the use of the non-standard forms by the different speakers. Noddy's use of the non-standard form, for example, decreases by only 3.22 percent in his school style, whereas the other Group 1 speakers (Ricky and Perry) show a much greater decrease. Jed (a Group 2 speaker) does not use the non-standard form at all in his school style, although the other Group 2 speakers (Kitty and Gammy) continue to use non-standard forms, albeit with a reduced frequency. Colin, like Jed, does not use the non-standard form in school style; Barney's use of the form, on the other hand, actually increases, by quite a large amount.

Present tense verb forms are sensitive markers of vernacular loyalty, as we have seen; and a group analysis of their occurrence in different speech styles showed that they were also sensitive to style. We saw that the feature could be classed as a marker, in the Labovian sense. Individual analyses, however, reveal that two speakers do not show the decrease in frequency that we would expect to find in their school style: Noddy, as we have seen, shows only a slight decrease, unlike the other boys in his group, and Barney's frequency actually increases. Their linguistic behaviour does not seem to be related to the vernacular culture index, for Noddy is a Group 1 speaker, showing strong allegiance to the peer-group culture, whilst Barney is a Group 3 speaker. One factor that could explain Noddy's behaviour is age: Noddy was only 11, whilst the other boys were aged between 13 and 16. Noddy may, therefore, have simply not yet acquired the ability to style shift. Labov (1965) suggested that children do not acquire this ability until the age of about 14, and there is some empirical evidence to support this (see Macaulay 1977). Other recent studies, however, have found evidence of stylistic sensitivity at a rather younger age (see Reid 1978; Romaine 1975), so that we cannot conclude with any certainty that this is a relevant factor here. In any case, Barney's behaviour cannot be explained this way, for he was 15, and old enough to show some signs of stylistic sensitivity. We need to explore further, then, to discover an explanation for this irregular behaviour.

Barney was recorded with Noddy and Kitty, by their teacher. The teacher was asking them about their activities outside school, and the boys were talking about a disco that they were trying to organize. The teacher was making valiant efforts to understand the conversation, but was obviously unfamiliar with the kind of amplifying equipment and with the situation that the boys were telling him about. It is worth noting that Barney and Noddy hated school and made very derisory remarks about their teachers. Barney had only just returned to school after an absence of a whole term, and Noddy attended school only intermittently. Kitty, on the other hand, attended school more regularly – his father was very strict, and he did not dare to play truant as often as his friends did.

These factors suggest an explanation for the boys' linguistic behaviour. A great deal of insight into linguistic behaviour has been gained from recent research by social psychologists, working within the framework of speech accommodation theory. It has been shown that speakers who are favourably disposed towards each other and who are 'working towards a common goal' adjust their speech so that they each speak more like the other, whereas speakers who are not working towards a common goal may diverge in their linguistic behaviour. One way in which speech convergence is marked is the frequency of occurrence of certain linguistic variables (see Thakerar, Giles and Cheshire 1982).

An explanation along these lines gives some insight into the behaviour of Noddy, Kitty and Barney in the school situation. Kitty knows the teacher, attends school fairly regularly, and we can imagine that he accepts the constraints of the situation. As a result his speech converges towards the teacher's, and he uses fewer non-standard linguistic forms than he does normally. Noddy, on the other hand, hates school and dislikes the teacher; as a result he asserts his allegiance to the peer-group culture rather than to the school, by refusing to acknowledge the situational constraints. The frequency with which he uses the non-standard form, therefore, does not change (or changes only slightly). Barney, who has only recently returned to school, asserts his total independence and hostility to the school by using more non-standard forms than he does usually. This is a very clear example of speech divergence. As we saw earlier, Barney is not closely involved in the vernacular culture, and this is reflected in his speech by a relatively low use of non-standard present tense forms. When he wants to assert his independence from the school culture, however, he is able to exploit the resources of the language system, by choosing to use a higher proportion of non-standard forms than he does usually.

Can an explanation in these terms account for the linguistic behaviour of the other boys in this study? For at least three of the boys, it seems that it can.

Ricky, Perry and Gammy were recorded together, by a teacher that they knew and liked. He had taken them on camping and fishing weekend expeditions, with some of their classmates. The conversation was initially about one of these weekends, and then moved on to racing cars and motorbikes, subjects that interested both the teacher and the boys. Speech accommodation theory would predict that in this situation the linguistic behaviour of the boys would converge towards that of their teacher (and, of course, vice-versa). This is precisely what happens – all three boys use a lower proportion of non-standard present tense forms here than they do in their vernacular speech style. The fact that they continue to use *some* non-standard forms, however, means that they are still able to show their allegiance to the vernacular subculture.

Jed and Colin behave rather differently from the other boys, for in their school recordings they do not use any non-standard forms at all. This is surprising, particularly in the case of Jed, who is a Group 2 speaker, like Kitty and Gammy. There are, however, some striking similarities between the linguistic behaviour of these two boys, and the situations in which the school recordings were made. They were recorded at different times, with a different speaker, but both recordings were made in a classroom situation, with about 20 pupils and the teacher. Both Jed and Colin participated a great deal in the discussions, partly because the teacher had purposely chosen topics on which they had strong views (football hooliganism, in Jed's case, and truancy, in Colin's case), and partly because they were encouraged to take part by the teacher. It is possible, though, that the situation was so drastically different from the situation in the adventure playground that the overall formality overrode the option of displaying linguistically their allegiance to the vernacular culture. Or perhaps the fact that no other members of the peer-group were present meant that the boys were more susceptible to the pressures of the norms of the school culture.

It seems, then, that a simple analysis in terms of the formality or informality of the situation cannot fully explain stylistic variation here. A better explanation can, perhaps, be achieved if we think in terms of situational constraints on exploiting the resources of the linguistic system. The non-standard present tense suffix is a powerful indicator of vernacular loyalty, and in some cases this function overrides other situational constraints on linguistic behaviour (as in the speech of Noddy and Barney, for example). In other cases (as with Jed and Colin), the situational constraints exclude the possibility of using the feature in this way.

The Linguistic Behaviour of Adolescent Girls

Many surveys of non-standard English have found that female speakers use non-standard speech forms less frequently than male speakers do. Table 5 shows that an analysis of the use of non-standard forms by girls and by boys confirms this pattern of behaviour.

Only non-standard auxiliary *do* is used more often by girls than by boys. As we have seen, this feature is involved in an on-going linguistic change, and has several irregular characteristics. The other non-standard features are all used less often by girls than they are by boys. In some cases the difference in frequency is very small (non-standard present tense verb forms, for example), but for most features the difference in frequency is more

Table 5 Linguistic variation and sex differences

	Frequency indices for non-standard features in boys' speech	Frequency indices for non-standard features in girls' speech
non-standard -*s*	53.16	52.04
non-standard *has*	54.76	51.61
non-standard *was*	88.15	73.58
negative concord	88.33	51.85
non-standard *never*	46.84	40.00
non-standard *what*	36.36	14.58
non-standard *do*	57.69	78.95
non-standard *come*	100.00	75.33
ain't=aux *have*	92.00	64.58
ain't=aux *be*	74.19	42.11
ain't=copula	85.83	61.18

striking. This kind of analysis, however, again conceals the ways in which linguistic features function as symbols of vernacular identity.

It was not possible to construct a vernacular culture index for the girls, as it was for the boys. The girls did not form structured peer-groups in the way that the boys did and, partly as a result of this, the norms of their vernacular subculture were less well-defined. It was possible, however, to divide the girls loosely into two groups, for three of the girls were clearly different from the others. They did not swear, steal, or set fire to the playground. They attended school regularly, and their parents did not approve of the adventure playground, because the children that their daughters met there were 'common' and 'rough'.

Table 6 shows the frequency of use of the nine non-standard features in the speech of these three girls, and also in the speech of the other girls in the group. This division of speakers is, of course, not ideal, since we are comparing the speech of a group of only three speakers with the speech of a group of nine speakers, but it can, nevertheless, give us an idea of the different ways in which linguistic features can function as markers of vernacular loyalty.

It can be seen from the table that some linguistic features appear to mark adherence to the vernacular culture, in that they are used less often by the 'good' girls than by the others. Other features, however, do not behave in this way. And if we compare table 6 with table 1, which showed those features that mark vernacular loyalty in the boys' speech, some interesting differences emerge.

Features 1–4, for example (non-standard -*s*, non-standard *has*, non-standard *was* and negative concord), all function as sensitive markers of vernacular loyalty for boys. Three of these features function in the same way for girls, as table 6 shows. Non-standard *has*, however, is used with approximately the same frequency by both 'good' girls and the other girls. This feature does not, therefore, function as a marker of vernacular loyalty for girls.

Non-standard *never* and non-standard *what* functioned only loosely as markers of vernacular loyalty for the boys. For girls, they do not appear to fulfil any symbolic function at all: the 'good' girls use them, in fact, more often than the other girls.

On the other hand, non-standard *come* and *ain't* appear to function as markers of vernacular identity for girls, although they do not for boys. Non-standard *come* is an invariant feature of the dialect for boys, occurring 100 percent of the time in the speech

Table 6 Use of non-standard features by 'good' girls and by other girls

	Frequency index: 'good' girls	Frequency index: other girls
non-standard -*s*	25.84	57.27
non-standard *has*	36.36	35.85
non-standard *was*	63.64	80.95
negative concord	12.50	58.70
non-standard *never*	45.45	41.07
non-standard *what*	33.33	5.56
non-standard *come*	30.77	90.63
ain't=copula	14.29	67.12

(There are no data for non-standard auxiliary *do*, nor for *ain't* as auxiliary *be* or as auxiliary *have*.)

of all speakers, in both speech styles (including those speakers who adhere only loosely to the norms of the vernacular culture). 'Good' girls, however, use non-standard *come* relatively infrequently (30.77 percent of the time), whilst the other girls use it much more often (90.63 percent of the time). Similarly, *ain't* is used much less often by the 'good' girls than it is by the other girls.

We can conclude, then, that male and female speakers in Reading exploit the resources of the linguistic system in different ways. Some linguistic features are markers of vernacular loyalty for both sexes (non-standard present tense verb forms, non-standard *was*, and negative concord). Some features function in this way for boys only (non-standard *never* and non-standard *what*). And others fulfil this function only for girls (non-standard *come* and *ain't*).

[…]

Conclusion

This paper has focused on the social function of linguistic variation in the speech of adolescent peer-groups. We have seen that non-standard linguistic features function in a number of different ways. Some are very sensitive markers of vernacular loyalty, showing a regular correlation in frequency with the extent to which speakers adhere to the vernacular culture. Others are less sensitive markers of vernacular loyalty. Finally, we have seen that the social function of non-standard features can vary with the sex of the speaker, and that this social function can sometimes override the constraints imposed on speakers by the formality of the situation. […]

References

Aitchison, J. (1981) *Language Change: Progress or Decay?* London: Fontana.

Andry, R. G. (1960) *Delinquency and Parental Pathology.* London: Methuen.

Cheshire, J. (1978) 'Present tense verbs in Reading English', in P. Trudgill (ed.) *Sociolinguistic Patterns in British English*, pp. 52–68. London: Edward Arnold.

Cheshire, J. (1982) *Variation in an English Dialect: A Sociolinguistic Study.* London: Cambridge University Press.

Clarke, J. (1973) *The Skinheads and the Study of Youth Culture.* Occasional paper. Birmingham: Centre for Contemporary Cultural Studies.

Cohen, A. K. (1965) *Delinquent Boys.* New York: The Free Press.

Cohen, P. (1972) *Subcultural Conflict and Working-Class Community. Working Papers in Cultural Studies, 2.* Birmingham: Centre for Contemporary Cultural Studies.

Downes, D. (1966) *The Delinquent Solution.* London: Routledge & Kegan Paul.

Jahangiri, N. and Hudson, R. (1982) 'Patterns of variation in Tehrani Persian', in S. Romaine (ed.) *Sociolinguistic Variation in Speech Communities.* London: Edward Arnold.

Labov, W. (1965) 'Stages in the acquisition of Standard English', in R. Shuy (ed.) *Social Dialects and Language Learning. Proceedings of the Bloomington, Indiana, Conference 1964.* Champaign, IL: National Council of Teachers of English.

Labov, W. (1966) *The Social Stratification of English in New York City.* Washington, DC: Center for Applied Linguistics.

Labov, W. (1970) 'The study of language in its social context'. *Studium Generale*, 23, 30–87.

Labov, W. (1972) *Sociolinguistic Patterns.* Philadelphia: Pennsylvania University Press.

Macaulay, R. K. S. (1977) *Language, Social Class and Education: A Glasgow Study.* Edinburgh: Edinburgh University Press.

Miller, W. B. (1958) 'Lower-class culture as a generating milieu of gang delinquency'. *Journal of Social Issues*, 14, 3, 5–19.

Milroy, J. (1982) 'Probing under the tip of the iceberg: phonological "normalization" and the shape of speech communities', in S. Romaine (ed.) *Sociolinguistic Variation in Speech Communities.* London: Edward Arnold.

Milroy, L. (1980) *Language and Social Networks.* Oxford: Blackwell.

Milroy, L. and Margrain, S. (1980) 'Vernacular language loyalty and social network'. *Language in Society*, 9, 43–70.

Moss, M. H. (1973) *Deprivation and Disadvantage?* Open University Course Book E 262:8. Milton Keynes: The Open University Press.

Policansky, L. (1980) 'Verb Concord Variation in Belfast Vernacular.' Paper delivered to the Sociolinguistic Symposium, Walsall.

Reid, E. (1978) 'Social and stylistic variation in the speech of children: some evidence from Edinburgh', in P. Trudgill (ed.) *Sociolinguistic Patterns in British English*, pp. 158–73. London: Edward Arnold.

Romaine, S. (1975) 'Linguistic Variability in the Speech of some Edinburgh School-Children.' University of Edinburgh, M. Litt thesis.

Romaine, S. (1980) 'Stylistic variation and evaluative reactions to speech: problems in the investigation of linguistic attitudes in Scotland'. *Language and Speech*, 23, 3, 213–32.

Thakerar, J. N., Giles, H. and Cheshire, J. (1982) 'Psychological and linguistic parameters of speech accommodation theory', in C. Fraser and K. R. Scherer (eds) *Advances in the Social Psychology of Language.* Cambridge: Cambridge University Press.

Willmott, P. (1966) *Adolescent Boys of East London.* London: Routledge & Kegan Paul.

Wolfson, N. (1976) 'Speech events and natural speech: some implications for sociolinguistic methodology'. *Language in Society*, 5, 2, 189–211.

4

Girl-talk/Boy-talk: Sex Differences in Adolescent Speech

Edina Eisikovits

Source: P. Collins and D. Blair (eds), *Australian English*. University of Queensland Press (1988), pp. 35–54. Reprinted with permission of University of Queensland Press.

[…]

Given the rigid sex divisions in Australian society (see Encel, McKenzie, and Tebbutt 1974) and especially the strong working class ethic of "Ockerism", the role of sex differences as a factor in determining linguistic behaviour in Australian English would seem to be an important area for investigation. Indeed, Mitchell and Delbridge's work on phonology (1965, 38) suggests that sex is a strong determinant of variation in Australian English:

> The distribution of boys in the vowel spectrum is significantly different from that of girls … These figures strongly suggest that the sex differences must be an important, perhaps an overriding influence in the distribution of the varieties of Australian speech.

Moreover, Shopen (1978, 44) in his study of the variable *-ING* in Canberra points out that "the most important distinction emerges as that between men and women in their roles both as speakers and listeners …". Horvath (1985) similarly identifies sex as a major variable in Australian English.

This chapter will look at sex differences from a developmental perspective, focusing on grammatical variation in a sample of adolescent speakers. Most past studies have tended to treat age and sex as separate categories, so we have little information about whether adolescent females behave like adults and if not when such behaviour is learnt.

On the other hand, we do know that adolescence is the period in which the use of non-standard forms is at its peak and that this usage tends to decline with increased age (Wolfram and Fasold 1974, 90ff). It is also the period during which social perceptions affecting linguistic behaviour are developed. The identification of when – if at all – these perceptions and hence changes in linguistic behaviour become evident is one of the goals of this chapter.

Methodology

The data for this study consist of more than fifty hours of tape-recorded conversation. The sample of informants was made up of twenty males and twenty females, equally divided into two age groups, a younger group in year 8 of secondary school, average age thirteen years eleven months and an older group in year 10, average age sixteen years one month. All were Australian-born of Australian-born parents and were long-term residents of inner-Sydney working class suburbs such as Glebe, Petersham, and Annandale. Their parents had occupations relatively low in social status; for example, cleaner, canteen assistant, truck driver. The informants were interviewed in pairs with the view of obtaining as broad a picture of their natural language as is possible within the limitations of a tape-recorded situation. In addition, those of the younger group in year 8 still at school two years later were interviewed a second time in year 10, thereby providing a small developmental group against which changes over apparent time could be compared.

In all, twelve grammatical variables were examined in the larger study of Inner-Sydney English (ISE) from which these data were drawn (Eisikovits 1981), but for the purposes of this chapter, three highly stigmatised variables have been isolated for consideration. It should be noted, however, that the patterns evident with respect to these three variables were similarly evident with respect to other grammatical variables examined in the larger study.

The three variables to be considered in detail here are:

1 non-standard past tense forms such as *seen* and *done*, as in:
   He woke up and seen something.
2 multiple negation; for example,
   They don't say nothing.
3 invariable *don't*; for example,
   Mum don't have to do nothing.

The occurrence of these forms is quantified using the paradigmatic Labovian model, that is:

$$\% \text{ frequency} = \frac{\text{number of occurrences of non-standard form}}{\text{total number of potential occurrences}}$$

Results

Non-standard past tense forms

Table 1 shows the frequencies of occurrence of non-standard past tense forms for each of the age/sex groupings in this study.

From this table it can be seen that males and females differ considerably in their use of these forms. Among the female speakers there is a significant decline in use with age ($\chi^2 = 14.79$; $p < .001$). This pattern may be observed even more dramatically in the case of individual verbs, especially past tense *done* and *come*. With *done*, the almost categorical use of this form among the younger girls (94.4 percent) may be contrasted with the

Table 1 Non-standard past tense forms for age/sex

Younger girls	Older girls
(N = 10)	(N = 10)
Occurrences: 134/313	Occurrences: 86/307
% : 42.8	% : 28.0
χ^2 = 14.79	
p < .001	
Younger boys	Older boys
(N = 10)	(N = 10)
Occurrences: 138/481	Occurrences: 137/411
% : 28.9	% : 33.3
χ^2 = 2.04	
p > .001	

Table 2 Occurrence of non-standard past tense forms of five verbs among male speakers

	Younger boys	*Older boys*
seen	58.9 (33/156)	67.9 (36/13)
done	65.5 (19/29)	61.3 (19/31)
come	55.8 (58/104)	75.9 (66/87)
give	4.8 (1/21)	14.3 (4/28)
run	23.1 (6/26)	0 (0/16)

significantly lower frequency of usage – 45.2 percent – among the older females. Similarly, past tense *come* decreases from 93.3 percent among the younger girls to 52.9 percent among the older girls.

Among the males, no such decline is apparent. Not only is a comparison of overall group results not significant (χ^2 = 2.04; p > .001), but also when the pattern of usage of the five most frequently occurring individual verbs is examined among the two male groups, only one – *run* – declines significantly. The remaining four occur in both groups with either a very similar or an increased frequency (see table 2). Indeed, for one verb, past tense *come*, there is a significant increase in the use of the non-standard form with increased age (χ^2 = 8.36; p < .01).

The same pattern may be observed in individual cases in the speech of the five male informants interviewed twice, once in year 8 and then again two years later in year 10. In almost all cases, these informants evidence either a very similar or an increased frequency in the use of non-standard past tense forms with increased age (see table 3). Informant 6B provides a dramatic example of this. Whereas in year 8 none of his past tense forms of *see, do* have the *seen/done* form, in year 10 there are eleven occurrences of *seen/done* compared with only five *saw/did*.

Multiple negation

A similar pattern of variation occurs with the use of multiple negation (see table 4). Again among the female speakers there is a significant decline in use of this form with age (χ^2 =

Table 3 Frequencies of occurrence of non-standard past tense forms among male developmental group

Informant:	1B Year 8	1B Year 10	2B Year 8	2B Year 10	4B Year 8	4B Year 10	5B Year 8	5B Year 10	6B Year 8	6B Year 10
seen	90	100	100	0	0	25	0	100	0	33.3
done	100	100	100	100	33.3	50	0	0	0	76.9
come	27.3	46.7	100	100	88.2	90.5	20	0	0	50
give	0	0	0	0	0	0	0	0	0	0
run	33.3	0	50	0 (0/1)	0	25	0	0	0	0

Table 4 Multiple negation within the clause for age/sex

Younger girls	Older girls
(N = 10)	(N = 10)
Occurrences: 56/115	Occurrences: 42/192
% : 48.7	% : 21.7
χ^2 = 24.72	
p < .001	
Younger boys	Older boys
(N = 10)	(N = 10)
Occurrences: 54/107	Occurrences: 56/127
% : 50.5	% : 44.1
χ^2 = 0.94	
p > .001	

24.72; p < .001). This pattern can be observed in individual cases in the speech of two girls, 1A and 6A, who were interviewed twice, once in year 8 and again two years later in year 10. Both of these speakers evidence a sharp decline in their use of multiple negation. Speaker 1A drops from a frequency of 30.8 percent in year 8 to 12.5 percent in year 10 while 6A declines even more dramatically from 87.9 percent in year 8 to 42.9 percent two years later in year 10. This is especially interesting for 6A in that in the earlier year 8 interview she evidences the highest frequency of use of this form (87.9 percent) of all speakers in the sample.

Among the male speakers, no such decline is apparent. Not only is a comparison of overall group results again not significant (χ^2 = 0.94; p > .001) but also, when the results of the five male speakers in the developmental group are examined, only one declines. The remaining four use either a very similar or an increased frequency of this variable (see table 5). This is especially interesting for the two speakers, 5B and 6B, who appear to have acquired this feature from year 8 to year 10. Note that it was 6B who also acquired the *seen/done* past tense forms in this period.

Invariable don't

This movement towards an increase in the use of non-standard forms among the male group is markedly apparent when we consider the use of invariable *don't* (see table 6).

Table 5 Multiple negation within the clause among male developmental group

Speaker	% frequency year 8	% frequency year 10
1B	62.5	52.9
2B	68.4	75
4B	40.9	52.4
5B	—	12.5
6B	—	7.1

Table 6   Don't/Doesn't for age/sex

Younger girls	Older girls
(N = 10)	(N = 10)
Occurrences: 3/63	Occurrences: 5/77
% : 4.8	% : 6.5
Younger boys	Older boys
(N = 10)	(N = 10)
Occurrences: 13/78	Occurrences: 31/60
% : 16.7	% : 51.7
χ^2 = 19.23	
p < .001	

The trends here are consistent with those evident with respect to other variables examined so far but they are not altogether parallel. With both of the other variables, it is the females who decline significantly in their use of the non-standard form with age whereas here it is the male group which significantly increases its usage with age (χ^2 = 19.23; p < .001). Among the girls on the other hand the use of *don't* is never favoured. The low frequency evident among the girls remains relatively constant with age, suggesting that this variable is heavily sex-marked.

Discussion

The existence of such different patterns of usage of non-standard forms among the two sex groups poses an obvious problem: why should an increase in age bring about such different patterns of usage among male and female speakers? Why is it only the girls who decline in their use of such forms as they grow older whereas, if anything, the boys increase their usage of such forms? If such forms are seen simply as developmental features we would expect a consistent decline with age among both groups. Clearly, at least two separate but intersecting factors are involved here: one developmental and the other relating to sex differences. Studies of sex variation in phonology in the past (Labov 1966; Shuy, Wolfram, and Riley 1966; Trudgill 1972 [revised version reprinted in Part I of this volume]) have tended to suggest that women regularly use more socially prestigious speech than men. Such sensitivity among female speakers is particularly evident in lower middle class and upper working class speech (compare Wolfram 1969).

In addition, women have been shown to evidence greater stylistic variation than men. Studies by Wolfram (1969), Labov (1972a), and Trudgill (1972), have shown that lower middle class women – especially younger females in the process of social mobility – are likely to evidence particular sensitivity to prestige norms in more formal speech situations.

Such sensitivity to social and stylistic variation is acquired by the child in various stages. Labov (1964, 81) presents a tentative model of language acquisition which incorporates the child's growing awareness of and control over variation in language. He specifies six levels of development; (i) the basic grammar, (ii) the vernacular, (iii) social perception, (iv) stylistic variation, (v) the consistent standard and finally, (vi) the acquisition of the full range. These stages are not entirely separate entities but are markers along a continuum of change. From Labov's model we would expect the informants in this study to be at stages (iii) and (iv); that is, initially at the stage of perceiving the social significance of speech and then gradually learning to modify their own speech in line with these perceptions. Such a view would account for the particularly high frequency of non-standard forms among the younger female group as well as for the decrease with age apparent in the use of such forms by the female informants. However, if this model is used to account for the use of non-standard forms here, we would expect a consistent decline with age among both the male and female groups. Hence, we are still left with the problem of accounting for the usage of the male speakers who, unlike their female counterparts, do not appear to modify their speech in the direction of the prestige standard.

One possible explanation for this is that the two groups do not share the same prestige standard; that is, forms perceived positively by one group are not similarly viewed by the other. Smith (1985, 83), citing research evidence from Labov (1966) and Trudgill (1972), suggests that such a difference in prestige norms may be widespread:

> Given the fact that men and women typically occupy quite different social niches, and are often clearly differentiated even in those they share, it would not be surprising to find that the sexes are habituated to different sets of context-dependent speech norms, and that their speech, and their impression of others' speech, reflect these differences.

Certainly, the attitudes and perceptions evidenced by the two sex groups in this study show some striking differences. Although both boys and girls were interviewed at similar points in their lives – the two older groups were at the conclusion of their high school education so that they were all looking outwards to the broader community – their orientations and "world views" differ significantly.

Among the older girls there is a serious and conservative acceptance of the responsibilities of adulthood. All are concerned with fitting in with society and its expectations rather than, as two years earlier, with the conflicts with it. No longer are they rebellious in their attitudes towards family, school, and society in general. All see themselves as having "grown up" – a process which for the girls means "settling down". This change is aptly summed up by 1E: "I think I've settled down a lot. It's better not being in trouble anyway."

A similar response comes from 1C, replying to the interviewer's question; "Do you feel a lot older than you did say two years ago?"

> That was funny you said that because, see I keep a diary an I was reading over what I'd written before and just from the beginning of the year you can see that what you've written, how stupid you must've been then to do that sort of thing, you know, 'cause whatever you've said or done or something you wrote, I've written it down, you know, the fights I've had with Mum an that. Then, like when you read it through you think, "Yeah, that was

ridiculous. Mum was right all the time," or summat like that, you know. Yeah, you notice how you do change an that. You realise your mistakes.

That this new conservatism is extended to attitudes to language may be seen in 1E's changed view of swearing. Asked what her fights with her boyfriend are about, she replies:

> Oh, petty things. Like, oh, sometimes he swears at me and I don't like swearing anymore. An he'll swear at me so we have a fight about that.

Even more telling are her later comments:

1E: We went – I've seen "One Flew Over the Cuckoo's Nest" – can't even say "cuckoo" properly. That was a good show. The only thing is they swear a lot in it.
INT: And that really bothers you?
1E: Mm. Sometimes, like, sometimes I'll be in the mood for it an other times I'll think, you know, "I don't wanna say that." Cause when you listen t'other people it sounds terrible, you know …
INT: You don't think about that when you're 13 or 14 doing it yourself.
1E: No, you don't. When you get older, you think, "Oh Jesus, what did I ever say that for?"

Among the boys, however, a rather different perception emerges. They, too, see themselves as having grown up, but for them this does not necessarily mean settling down or conforming to family or societal expectations of "good" behaviour. Instead, it is more usually seen as a movement towards self-assertion, "toughness" and an unwillingness to be dictated to. Again, some typical comments to illustrate this change:

9D: They said juniors are definitely not allowed to drink. We still drink though. They can't stop us really.
1D: I was pulled up by the police about 20 yards from me front door. They said, "Where do ya live?" That made me feel real good. I said, "Right there." You know you can give 'em cheek, bit a cheek back an they can't say nothing.
INT: Your Mum and Dad didn't try to push you into anything? [a job]
5F: No. If they did, I'd push 'em back.

Many spoke about on-going conflict with the police, the school, teachers, and to a lesser extent, parents, relating these stories with defiance and bravado. Incidents in which they were able to outwit authority were recounted with pride as evidence of toughness and skill. Never was there any admission of earlier errors as foolishness as there was among the older girls. Indeed, where family conflicts had diminished, this was because of reduced parental controls on the boys' actions rather than any recognition on their parts, as with the girls, of the validity of their parents' viewpoints. Consider, for example, the following dialogue:

INT: What sort of things do you have rows with your Mum and Dad about?
2D: Oh, we useta have rows. That was before I was 16. Useta have rows about comin home too late, early in the mornin an that. But now, it's just when I get in trouble off the police or something, you know. I just get in trouble for that … I don't stick around when they go off their heads.
INT: What happens if you come home really smashed?
2D: I do every week. But Dad doesn't mind.

INT: They don't nag you about stuff like that?

2D: Oh, me Mother used to. She still does a bit cause, you know, you're supposed to be a certain age to drink in a pub an if you're in there, you know, you get fined or sumpin, you know. But you can get away with it easy.

INT: What about homework?

1D: If I wanna do it, I do it. If I don't Mum don't care.

2D: They make me sisters an that do their homework.

This extract would suggest that not only are the older boys less conformist than their female counterparts but also that this independence is given tacit support by their parents and the community at large. Unlike the girls, they are encouraged to be independent and tough. Clearly, different behavioural norms as well as different social perceptions exist for the two sexes. Given these differences, it is hardly surprising that the two groups differ in their attitudes to and use of language. We have already seen the growing conservatism of the girls in their attitude to swearing. The boys on the other hand tend to move in a contrary direction:

INT: Did you used to get beltings when you were a kid?

6D: Oh, swore once when I was about five an I was belted off me mother. Tried to wash me mouth out with soap.

5D: Yeah, that's what they always say.

INT: You were in trouble for the same thing?

5D: Yeah, for swearing.

INT: What did they do to you?

5D: Oh, they just took me inside an smacked me. That's all.

INT: What about now?

5D: If I swear in front of me mother now she don't say nothing.

Such different social and linguistic perceptions may provide an explanation for the two groups' differing usage of non-standard forms here. That is, while the girls are increasingly ready to accept external social norms – a conformity mirrored in their readiness to modify their speech in line with external prestige norms – the boys are not so accepting. Indeed, they are learning to assert themselves, to express their opposition to authority and the middle class establishment – an opposition similarly mirrored in the maintenance/increase in their use of non-standard forms.

This increased use of non-standard forms among the males would suggest that for this group these forms carry their own prestige as a marker of masculinity and toughness, so that as the boys grow older and identify more strongly with their own class and sex their use of these forms is favoured.

That such prestige value is attached to non-standard forms by the males in this study may be seen from the direction of their self-corrections. Unlike the older females who self-correct towards standard forms, for example:

Our Deputy-Principal was really nice and he sort of let my group, the kids I hang – hung around with, get away with almost anything.

An me and Kerry – or should I say, Kerry and I – are the only ones who've done the project.

the older males self-correct in the opposite direction, favouring the non-standard over the standard form. For example:

I didn't know what I did – what I done.

He's my family doctor. I've known im ever since I was a kid. An 'e gave – give it to me an 'e said, "As long as it's helping you, I'll give it to you" you know.

That such consciousness of external prestige norms is only just developing among the older girls is evidenced in the contrary direction among the younger girls who self-correct in line with the males, for example:

It don't work out anyway – it don't work out noways.

[…]

Conclusions

What all this would suggest is that for the girls the norms which they become increasingly aware of are in line with those of external social usage. […] The boys, however, […] appear to use non-standard forms to affirm their own masculinity and toughness and their working class anti-establishment values.

Some anecdotal evidence of the boys' orientation may be drawn from the practice of individual speakers. Speaker 7D, for example, uses the non-standard forms, double negatives and invariable *don't*, in speech in which he is seeking in some way to affirm his own strength as a male in situations dominated by women or women's values. For example, in describing his part in housekeeping (he is the eldest of five children in a single parent family):

So I make sure the housework's done so Mum won't have to do nothing … All I have to do is put em clothes in the machine and turn the dial round and it goes for 40 minutes, then I just hang it up, so Mum don't have to do nothing.

Later, discussing his part in a fight with a girl:

She started hitting me again and again and I didn't do nothing then cause she was one of me friends.

Similarly with 1D, use of the double negative seems to be associated with the expression of anti-establishment values. Describing a confrontation with the police in which he outwits authority, he says:

That made me feel good … you know, you can give 'em cheek, bit a cheek back 'n they can't say nothing.

Again in a narrative recounting how he manages to drink in pubs though underage, he says:

Oh, it's pretty easy to get away with. Go down town, pubs down there. They don't say nothing to ya.

For 5D, the expression of his toughness and growing independence from his family, especially his mother, is couched in the use of non-standard forms. Having just described how in his childhood he was severely disciplined for swearing, he concludes:

If I swear in front of me mother now she don't say nothing.

Similarly for 6D, his attempt to assert himself in describing his relationship with his older sister is suggested in his comment:

Me sister don't boss me around.

That his assertiveness is still tempered by some dependence is evident as he continues:

Me brother, I don't worry about him much, but me Father is real strict. Doesn't like bad manners or talking at the table …

For other male speakers, the "them and us" attitude to society – school and teachers, employers and migrants – is suggested in their use of non-standard forms. Speaker 10D, for example, expresses his criticism of an authoritarian schoolmaster as follows:

He's always patrolling round, seeing what you're doing. Like he don't trust us …

Later, describing an unpopular migrant group, he concludes:

Everybody don't like 'em.

Similarly, 1D, discussing the attitude of the peer group to work, comments:

Half of 'em don't wanna work anyway. There's one kid, Roger, he don't wanna work so he told 'em down the Dole office he wanted to be an elephant trainer.

What we have then is very strong evidence for age and sex differences in this variety of Australian adolescent speech – differences which reflect different social and linguistic norms held by the two sex groups. The extent to which these norms are held by Australian adolescents in general and not just residents of the inner-city area of Sydney is a question well worthy of future investigation.

References

Adelman, C. 1976. The language of teenage groups. In *They Don't Speak our Language*, ed. S. Rogers, pp. 80–105. London: Edward Arnold.

Bourhis, R., and H. Giles. 1977. The language of intergroup distinctiveness. In *Language, Ethnicity and Intergroup Relations*, ed. H. Giles, pp. 119–35. European Monographs in Social Psychology, 13. London: Academic Press.

Cheshire, J. 1982. *Variation in an English Dialect*. Cambridge: Cambridge University Press.

Delbridge, A. 1977. The only known exception is Australia: A study in dialect variation (mimeograph).

Eisikovits, E. 1981. *Inner-Sydney English: An Investigation of Grammatical Variation in Adolescent Speech*. Unpublished Ph.D. thesis, University of Sydney.

Eisikovits, E., and J. Dixon. 1982. Learning to tell stories. *Developments in English Teaching* 1(1): 25–30.

Encel, S., N. McKenzie, and M. Tebbutt. 1974. *Women and Society: An Australian Study*. Melbourne: Cheshire.

Ervin-Tripp, S. 1964. Interaction of topic, listener and speaker. In *The Ethnography of Communication*, ed. S. Gumperz and D. Hymes, pp. 86–102. *American Anthropologist* 66(6), Part 2.

Fasold, R. 1972. *Tense Marking in Black English: A Linguistic and Social Analysis*. Urban Language Series, 8. Arlington, Virginia: Center for Applied Linguistics.

Feagin, C. 1979. *Variation and Change in Alabama English: A Sociolinguistic Study of the White Community*. Washington, DC: Georgetown University Press.

Giles, H. 1973. Accent mobility: A model and some data. *Anthropological Linguistics* 15: 87–105.

Giles, H. 1977. Social psychology and applied linguistics. *ITL: Review of Applied Linguistics* 33: 27–42.

Horvath, B. 1985. *Variation in Australian English: The Sociolects of Sydney*. Cambridge Studies in Linguistics, 45. Cambridge: Cambridge University Press.

Labov, W. 1964. Stages in the acquisition of Standard English. In *Social Dialects and Language Learning*, ed. R. Shuy. Champaign, Illinois: National Council of Teachers of English.

Labov, W. 1966. *The Social Stratification of English in New York City*. Washington, DC: Center for Applied Linguistics.

Labov, W. 1970. The study of language in its social context. *Studium Generale* 23(1): 30–87.

Labov, W. 1972a. *Language in the Inner-City: Studies in the Black English Vernacular*. Philadelphia: University of Pennsylvania Press.

Labov, W. 1972b. Some principles of linguistic methodology. *Language in Society* 1: 97–120.

Milroy, L. 1980. *Language and Social Networks*. Oxford: Blackwell.

Mitchell, A., and A. Delbridge. 1965. *The Speech of Australian Adolescents: A Survey*. Sydney: Angus & Robertson.

Romaine, S. 1984. *The Language of Children and Adolescents: The Acquisition of Communicative Competence*. Language in Society, 7. Oxford: Blackwell.

Romaine, S., and E. Reid. 1976. Glottal sloppiness? A sociolinguistic view of urban speech in Scotland. *Teaching English* 9(3): 12–16.

Sankoff, G., and H. Cedergren. 1971. Some results of a sociolinguistic study of Montreal French. In *Linguistic Diversity in Canadian Society*, ed. R. Darnell. Edmonton and Champaign: Linguistic Research Inc.

Shopen, T. 1978. Research on the variable (ING) in Canberra, Australia. *Talanya* 5: 42–52.

Shopen, T., W. Wolfram, and W. Riley 1976. Linguistic correlates of social stratification in Detroit speech. Final Report. Co-operative Research Project 6–1347. Washington, DC: US Office of Education, Department of Health, Education and Welfare.

Shuy, R., W. Wolfram, and W. Riley, 1966. *A Study of Social Dialects in Detroit*. Final report. Project 7–1347. Washington, DC: US Office of Education, Department of Health, Education and Welfare.

Smith, P. 1979. Sex markers in speech. In *Social Markers in Speech*, ed. K. R. Scherer and H. Giles, pp. 107–46. Cambridge: Cambridge University Press.

Smith, P. 1985. *Language, the Sexes and Society*. Language in Society, 8. Oxford: Blackwell.

Trudgill, P. 1972. Sex, covert prestige and linguistic change in the urban British English of Norwich. *Language in Society* 1: 179–95. Reprinted in B. Thorne and N. Henley, eds. 1975. *Language and Sex: Difference and Dominance*. Rowley, Mass: Newbury House.

Trudgill, P., ed. 1978. *Sociolinguistic Patterns in British English*. London: Edward Arnold.

Wolfram, W. 1969. *A Sociolinguistic Description of Detroit Negro Speech*. Urban Language Series, 5. Washington, DC: Center for Applied Linguistics.

Wolfram, W., and D. Christian. 1976. *Appalachian English*. Arlington, Virginia: Center for Applied Linguistics.

Wolfram, W., and R. Fasold. 1974. *The Study of Social Dialects in American English*. New Jersey: Prentice-Hall.

5

Black Women in the Rural South: Conservative and Innovative

Patricia C. Nichols

Source: B. L. Dubois and I. Crouch (eds), *American Minority Women in Sociolinguistic Perspective* (= vol. 17 of *International Journal of the Sociology of Language*). Mouton: The Hague (1978) pp. 45–54. Reprinted with permission of De Gruyter.

Recent sociolinguistic studies have discovered sex as an important variable in language use. Prior to the 1950s little attention was given to the speaker's sex when describing linguistic systems, except in a few European studies and some descriptions of more exotic languages. This paper will examine briefly the orientation of several sociolinguistic studies which have looked at sex-related language differences, and will present data from a more recent study of a black population in rural South Carolina. I will suggest both culture-specific and crosscultural reasons for the linguistic differences which have been found for men and women.

One of the first studies to recognize the importance of studying differences in speech behavior between members of a small group who engaged in frequent face-to-face inter-action was Fischer's 1958 comparison of boys' and girls' use of *ing/in* participle endings. This study of playmates in a semi-rural New England village revealed that girls consist-ently used more of the standard-prestige -*ing* ending than boys. Labov later found similar patterns for men and women in the much larger and more diverse population of New York City. His 1966 dissertation found, however, that women's linguistic behavior differed from that of men's in two general ways: in careful speech women used fewer stigmatized forms, but in shifting between casual and careful styles, women showed sharper shifts from stigmatized forms to prestige forms than did men. Lower middle-class women showed the most extreme style shifts. Studies in Detroit confirmed women's greater use of prestige forms. Shuy, Wolfram and Riley (1968) found women using the prestigious -*ing* ending more than twice as often as men among the general urban population of Detroit, while Wolfram (1969) found that, for the black speakers of that city, females within each social class used forms closer to standard norms than did males. A study of the black working-class population of Washington, DC, however, did not find females to use more standard forms than males; Fasold (1972) reported either no difference or slightly more use of standard forms by males. Other studies of whites in urban centers have found women to use more prestigious forms than men. In North Carolina, Levine and Crockett's study (1967) of a Piedmont community found equal use of the postvocalic *r*, a prestige form for that region, for both men and women in reading sentences. In a more formal

Language and Gender: A Reader, Second Edition. Edited by Jennifer Coates and Pia Pichler.
© 2011 Blackwell Publishing Ltd except for editorial material and organization. © 2011 Jennifer Coates and Pia Pichler. Published 2011 by Blackwell Publishing Ltd.

word-list style, women used the feature more frequently than men. Sankoff and Cedergren (1971) found women in Montreal using the standard Canadian French liquid *l* more frequently than men generally, although younger professional women used it less than older women within their class. In Norwich, England, Trudgill (1972, revised version reprinted in this volume, p. 21; 1974) found women to use the standard-prestige *-ing* ending more frequently than men.

Besides these studies of sex differences in use of prestige features which show women to exhibit more conservative linguistic behavior than men generally, studies of sound changes have been made which indicate that women exhibit innovative behavior and are far ahead of men in this portion of the language. Labov, Yaeger and Steiner (1972) have found women more advanced than men for several sound changes in a variety of U.S. communities. How are we to explain these two tendencies of women speakers, both the use of standard-prestige features and the spread of new sounds?

Several explanations have been advanced. Labov and Trudgill have suggested that women are 'linguistically insecure'. Trudgill elaborates on this point by observing that women achieve status in western societies more on the basis of how they look than on what they do. Use of prestigious language might be seen as one of women's limited means of achieving and signaling status, particularly in more formal situations. More recently, Labov (1972: 304) has postulated that the wide expressive range exhibited by women may be understood in terms of linguistic behavior considered more appropriate for one sex than for the other. Shuy (1970: 856) expresses general despair at arriving at some satisfactory explanation, with the comment, 'Women continue to be one of the mysteries of the universe.'

In addition to the general problem of failing to find convincing explanations for the seemingly paradoxical behavior of women speakers, most of these previous sociolinguistic studies exhibit three serious methodological problems. The most serious is that of methods used to assign women to particular social classes. In examining methods currently used for social stratification, some sociologists recently have maintained that no present method permits accurate classification of women in modern societies (Watson and Barth 1964; Acker 1973). Typically, occupation is the measure most heavily used as a major index of social class, and the family is arbitrarily taken to be the primary social unit. Most of the sociolinguistic studies discussed here have followed this practice, using the occupation of head of household as a major index of an entire family's social class. Problems are raised by the presence of unmarried women and widows. Some of the studies assign widows the occupation of their dead husbands. Single women are variously assigned their own occupations (typically low-status), their father's occupations, or are systematically eliminated from the study because of the problems they pose for classification (see Levine and Crockett 1967). Obvious problems are raised when trying to compare the speech of women in one study with that of women in another, particularly for single women. In addition, there is actually little or no evidence to support the general assumption that married women belong to the same social class as their husbands (Acker 1973). The social stratification procedures used raise questions about the validity of comparing men's and women's speech both within classes and from study to study. No sociolinguistic research has overtly dealt with these issues.

Related to the problem of social stratification is the seriousness with which sex is treated as a variable. Most studies have not taken care to match speakers for age and sex, as well as for social class. Those studies with a disproportion of one sex in some age groups, such as Fasold's (1972), have reported difficulties in drawing valid conclusions about sex differences in language use. While Labov has been in the forefront of recognizing the importance of sex differences as a factor in linguistic change, his New York study included far more women than men overall; his lowest class contained more than twice as many women as men, while his highest class contained almost twice as many men as women. His more recent studies have concentrated on speech used in male social groups. Trudgill uses an equal number of male and female speakers, but does not give figures on their distribution by social class. The studies of Fischer (1958) and of Sankoff and Cedergren (1971) are exceptions to the general failure to match speakers for both sex and age, within larger social groups.

A final methodological problem has been the general lack of discussion about community norms for language use. Labov has been an exception on this point, taking care to establish from his data the norms for a social group. Little discussion has been devoted to the problem of comparing linguistic behavior from group to group for the two sexes. Use of a given feature may represent conservative linguistic behavior within one social group and innovative behavior within another. To take only one obvious example, use of the *-ing* ending may mean preservation of an older form for a white middle class group, but introduction of a new form for a black working class group. The question of differences in community norms needs much fuller examination in order for sex differences in language use to be characterized accurately.

For the rural black population which I studied in coastal South Carolina for a five-month period in 1974–5, the use of standard-prestige features was innovative behavior. The language variety spoken by blacks in Georgetown County has been variously called 'Gullah', 'Geechee', or 'Sea Island Creole'. It has developed historically from a pidgin based on both English and West African languages, spoken by the earliest African immigrants to this region. The language now used by blacks in this region constitutes a post-creole continuum (see DeCamp 1971) which encompasses creole, non-standard, and standard varieties of English. The three syntactic variables chosen for study and their Gullah realizations were:

(1)　the *for-to* complementizer
　　　'I come *for* get my coat.'
(2)　the static-locative preposition *at*
　　　'Can we stay *to* the table?'
(3)　the third person singular pronoun *it*
　　　'Well, *ee* was a fun to me.'
　　　'Over there, they call *um* over the island.'

Based on previous studies of Gullah (Turner 1949; Cunningham 1970), the use of standard forms for these variables would be innovative for most black speakers in the isolated rural area I chose for study. Use of creole variants would be maintenance of archaic forms. More detailed linguistic analysis of these variables is provided elsewhere (Nichols 1976).

In order to become familiar with the natural age and social groups within the community I had initially selected, I obtained an unpaid job in the elementary school. Influenced by the concept of 'action anthropology', as discussed by Piddington (1960) and others, I sought to act in some functional capacity within the community under study. After several months of observing the language used by school children and participating in varied community activities, I recognized three subgroups within the black population, which constituted approximately half of the total county population. The all-black community of a river island accessible only by boat remained the primary focus of my study, but I recognized that two distinct mainland groups existed within the total black population. One of these groups was composed of the educated elite of the black community and included teachers, preachers, political figures, businessmen, and school board members; most of these families had owned land for several generations. The second mainland group had far less education (often none for older members), held laboring jobs, and usually had not owned land for more than one generation. The island community fell somewhere in between the two mainland groups, having kinspeople in both, with educational and economic levels about those of the lowest group but with no professional jobs among island residents. I subsequently included older members from the lower mainland group in my study, along with adults in three age groups from the island community.

The population of the river island was approximately two hundred, composed of several large families who owned land there and contributed to the support of a community church which was the center of much of the social life of the island. Residents engaged in frequent face-to-face interaction in church activities, meetings and parties in the abandoned schoolhouse, daily boat rides to mainland jobs and to mainland schools, and constant walks from the boat landing to homes at the interior of the island. The standard of living has been steadily rising since the forties, when subsistence rice farming was abandoned with the availability of motorized transportation. Daily commuting to mainland jobs is now the practice, with most families having at least two working members. Some jobs, particularly for women, are seasonal in nature, however. Electricity became available in the last decade, and a telephone cable was installed three years ago, bringing closer ties with the mainland. The level of education has risen since the county provided bus and boat transportation to county secondary schools about two decades ago.

Recordings of language used in the island community and one mainland group were made after I had become fairly well known and had observed daily life in both groups for several months. I taught a volunteer composition class on the island one night a week, which gave me the opportunity to be in that community regularly in a functional capacity and brought me into contact with younger adults of high school age and slightly older. I determined that the ages fell into natural groups of older adults who no longer worked outside the home and remained on the island most of the time; middle-age adults, with growing families, who commuted off the island daily; and young adults, not yet married, who engaged in social or school activities with each other. From each of these three groups I chose two men and two women to record in unstructured conversations of less than thirty minutes each. I was a participant in all of the conversations, together with other family members who happened to be present. All recordings were made with the knowledge of the participants, in their own homes. Subject matter with older residents was primarily history and customs; with middle-age, history and child-rearing practices; with younger adults, future plans and comparison of their childhood and their siblings'. No formal questionnaire was used, but efforts were made to learn the approximate age of the speaker and the amount of traveling he or she had done. For the mainland group, recordings were made of two men and two women in the older group only. Table 1 shows the frequency with which each variable was used by each speaker, according to sex and age, for the three island groups and the one mainland group. For each variable, the number of times non-standard variants were used is compared with the total possible times they could have been used; the figure in parentheses is the percentage of non-standard variants used.

Comparison of the figures for the oldest adults in both mainland and island communities indicates that women from the mainland group show more conservative linguistic

Table 1 Non-standard variants used for *for-to, at,* and *it*

	Speakers	for-to		at		it	
		Non-standard variants used for:					
		NS/tot	%NS	NS/tot	%NS	NS/tot	%NS
65–90 yrs mainland	f. SS	8/12	(.66)	7/7	(1.00)	6/10	(.60)
	f. SG	17/26	(.65)	17/20	(.85)	32/37	(.85)
	m. BD	1/5	(.20)	7/10	(.70)	12/20	(.60)
	m. MW	0/3	(.00)	2/4	(.50)	5/6	(.83)
65–90 yrs island	f. MC	3/7	(.43)	3/6	(.50)	4/30	(.13)
	f. MN	0/8	(.00)	3/5	(.60)	0/16	(.00)
	m. JW	3/28	(.11)	7/10	(.70)	21/77	(.27)
	m. JH	2/30	(.06)	9/11	(.82)	13/31	(.41)
30–50 yrs island	f. TW	0/7	(.00)	0/1	(.00)	0/5	(.00)
	f. GF	0/7	(.00)	1/3	(.33)	0/32	(.00)
	m. GW	0/24	(.00)	4/7	(.57)	13/75	(.17)
	m. JT	0/11	(.00)	6/7	(.86)	2/5	(.40)
15–25 yrs island	f. CW	0/3	(.00)	2/2	(1.00)	0/5	(.00)
	f. JTTT	0/36	(.00)	0/13	(.00)	0/57	(.00)
	m. JW	2/11	(.18)	3/4	(.75)	2/5	(.40)
	m. JTT	2/11	(.18)	0/1	(.00)	5/47	(.11)

behavior than mainland men, while those from the island are more innovative than the men. Mainland women use more archaic forms for the two variables *for-to* and *at*, while the two sexes are about the same for the other variable. Island women use fewer archaic forms than island men for variables *at* and *it*. One island woman, MC, uses more archaic forms for the variable *for-to* than either island man, but fewer nevertheless than both mainland women. MC is perhaps a transitional figure for island women, since she was confined to the island for most of her young life and engaged in work off the island only later in her life, when motor boats became more widely used. MN, the other island woman in the oldest age group, lived off the island for a portion of her young married life. In addition, both her mother and an aunt had some college education, although she herself had not. The two island men had worked and lived off the island for brief portions of their young adulthood, before and after marriage, with JW spending a five-year period away on a shipyard job during World War II. JH was the only island adult I encountered who had had no schooling. For the mainland group, both educational levels and mobility were lower. Only the man, BD, had attended school in this group; he had also lived outside the area for a time and had held better jobs than the other three mainland adults. The two older women in this group had done domestic work all their lives, and both were now caring for 'grands' for assorted relatives who either worked in the area or lived out of state. SS was the daughter of a former slave and had worked for one family, on the same plantation, all her life. The other older man, MW, had moved into the area as a young man and had worked on the same plantation for fifty years of his life; he had relatives on the river island.

In other age groups, island women were also more linguistically innovative than island men. For the middle-age group, women used more standard forms for *at* and *it*, while neither sex used archaic variants for the *for-to* complementizer – perhaps the most stigmatized of the three variables. In the youngest age group, males used non-standard forms for *for-to* and *it*, while females used none. Use of *at* was about the same for both sexes in this group. (*At* is probably the least stigmatized of the variables, since at least one member of both sexes in every age group uses some non-standard variant of it.) JTT and JTTT, a brother and sister who have jobs entailing conversation with diverse people, use no non-standard variants for *at*, while CW and JW, another brother and sister still in high school, both use some. In three different age groups for the island community, then, linguistic variation on selected syntactic forms suggests that women are moving toward standard-prestige forms faster than island men.

Both culture-specific and crosscultural explanations can be suggested for these differences in language use for the two sexes. For the particular communities in which these people live, the two sexes have very real differences in occupational opportunities. All island women work outside the home at some time during their lives, as do most black women in the area. Two of the top five occupations open to black women in the state are white-collar and require use of the standard language variety, while all of the top occupations open to black men are blue-collar and require few language-related tasks. Since the median salary for black women in the state for 1970 census figures is less than half that for black men, there is incentive for women to train for the available higher paying jobs. With good clerical skills or with a college education, a woman can make almost as much as some blue-collar construction workers; hence, many families invest in higher education for their daughters rather than for their sons, since the job choices for women have been basically domestic work or teaching. Island men sometimes attend trade school, but never college; most middle-age men work at good-paying jobs in the construction industry. In the mainland group studied, the low level of education characteristic of this group limits women to domestic or other low-paying jobs involving physical labor. Men in this group work at both unskilled labor within the community or at factory jobs in town, which entail some interaction with a more diverse population than that encountered by women in their group. Thus, for both groups studied, differences in occupational choices available to the sexes are associated with differences in linguistic experiences, though in different directions for each community. The standard language used by island women reflects their attraction to occupations requiring language-related tasks, as well as their membership in an economically mobile community. Mainland women, who have had no similar opportunities for change, maintain more archaic forms than the relatively more mobile men in their group.

On a crosscultural level, recent anthropological analyses have pointed out that men and women universally occupy different positions within their cultural and social groups, in terms of public authority and central cultural values of the group (Rosaldo 1974; Ortner 1974). Rosaldo has observed that women are considered anomalous figures by many societies. For both social groups studied here, women occupy lower relative positions than men in terms of earning power, occupational choices, and geographic mobility. Men hold more authority within their families, churches, and local government, while women are in charge of the domestic sphere and assume less public authority than men of their age. While women in one group hold higher status jobs than men, and lower status jobs than men in the other group, linguistic patterns are similar in that the sexes speak differently in both cases. Linguists have long understood that the interaction of language and social life has important consequences for linguistic behavior (Ferguson 1959; Hymes

1967, 1973). Hymes observes that inequality among speakers arises because some speakers participate in social situations not available to other speakers. If women are universally limited in their exercise of public authority, as Rosaldo suggests, we must expect certain linguistic consequences to follow from the different life experiences of the two sexes. Men and women will speak differently from each other in every social group.

A more adequate sociology of women will enable us to understand the linguistic behavior of women as a reflection of their peripheral status within their communities. The present study suggests that women lag behind men in the adoption of new forms within traditional, relatively stable societies. In more mobile groups, like that of the island community here, we might expect women to be in advance of men. Perhaps in transitional groups, women will exhibit both conservative and innovative behavior. Whatever the particular pattern, language used by women must be dealt with in terms of the social roles available to women rather than dismissed as one of the great mysteries of the universe.

References

Acker, Joan (1973), 'Women and social stratification: A case of intellectual sexism', *American Journal of Sociology* 78: 936–45.

Cunningham, Irma (1970), 'A syntactic analysis of Sea Island Creole ("Gullah")'. Unpublished University of Michigan dissertation.

DeCamp, David (1971), 'Toward a generative analysis of a post-creole speech continuum', in D. Hymes (ed.), *Pidginization and Creolization of Languages*. Cambridge, Cambridge University Press.

Fasold, Ralph (1972), *Tense Marking in Black English: A Linguistic and Social Analysis.* Washington, DC, Center for Applied Linguistics.

Ferguson, Charles A. (1959), 'Diglossia', *Word* 15: 325–40.

Fischer, John L. (1958), 'Social influence in the choice of a linguistic variant', *Word* 14: 47–56.

Hymes, Dell (1967), 'Models of the interaction of language and social setting', *Journal of Social Issues* 23: 8–28.

Hymes, Dell (1973), 'On the origins and foundations of inequality among speakers', *Daedalus* 102: 59–86.

Labov, William (1966), *The Social Stratification of English in New York City*. Washington, DC, Center for Applied Linguistics.

Labov, William (1972), *Sociolinguistic Patterns*. Philadelphia, University of Pennsylvania Press.

Labov, William, Yaeger, Malcah, and Steiner, Richard (1972), *A Quantitative Study of Sound Change in Progress*. Philadelphia, US Regional Survey.

Levine, Lewis, and Crockett, Harry J., Jr. (1967), 'Speech variation in a Piedmont community: Postvocalic r', in S. Lieberson (ed.), *Explorations in Sociolinguistics*. Bloomington, Indiana University.

Nichols, Patricia C. (1976), 'Linguistic change in Gullah: Sex, age, and mobility'. Unpublished Stanford University dissertation.

Ortner, Sherry (1974), 'Is female to male as nature is to culture?', in M. Rosaldo and L. Lamphere (eds.), *Women, Culture and Society*. Palo Alto, Stanford University Press.

Piddington, Ralph (1960), 'Action anthropology', *Journal of the Polynesian Society* 69: 199–213. In J. Clifton (ed.), *Applied Anthropology: Readings in the Use of the Science of Man*. Boston, Houghton Mifflin Co. (1970).

Rosaldo, Michelle Zimbalist (1974), 'Women, culture, and society: A theoretical overview', in M. Rosaldo and L. Lamphere (eds), *Women, Culture and Society*. Palo Alto, Stanford University Press.

Sankoff, Gillian, and Cedergren, Henrietta (1971), 'Some results of a sociolinguistic study of Montreal French', in R. Darnell (ed.), *Linguistic Diversity in Canadian Society*. Edmonton, Linguistic Research, Inc., 61–87.

Shuy, Roger (1970), 'Sociolinguistic research at the Center for Applied Linguistics: The correlation of language and sex', *International Days of Sociolinguistics*. Rome, Instituto Luigi Sturzo, 849–57.

Shuy, Roger, Wolfram, Walt, and Riley, William K. (1968), *Field Techniques in an Urban Language Study*. Washington, DC, Center for Applied Linguistics.

Trudgill, Peter (1972), 'Sex, covert prestige and linguistic change in the urban British English of Norwich', *Language in Society* 1: 179–95.

Trudgill, Peter (1974), *The Social Differentiation of English in Norwich*. Cambridge, Cambridge University Press.

Turner, Lorenzo (1949), *Africanisms in the Gullah Dialect*. Chicago, University of Chicago Press.

US Bureau of the Census (1973), 'Subject reports: Negro population'. *1970 Census of Population*.

Watson, Walter, and Barth, Ernest (1964), 'Questionable assumptions in the theory of social stratification', *Pacific Sociological Review* 7: 10–16.

Wolfram, Walt (1969), *A Sociolinguistic Description of Detroit Negro Speech*. Washington, DC, Center for Applied Linguistics.

6

Gender and Sociolinguistic Variation

Penelope Eckert

This paper was written especially for the first edition of this Reader.

Sociolinguistic Variation

We generally think of language as a means of communicating referential meaning – for telling each other what we think, what we want, what we see. The linguistic system is also constructed in such a way as to create resources for the expression of social meaning – nuances of emotion, attitude, social identity – without actually stating it in so many words. One of the subtlest of these resources is what is referred to as *sociolinguistic variation*, particularly phonological variation, or what is commonly referred to as "accent." Phonological variation, or nuances of pronunciation, can signal important information about aspects of speakers' social identity – about such things as class, age, ethnicity and gender. This chapter will explore the manifestations of gender in phonological variation, and the interactions between gender and some other aspects of identity.

I begin with a very brief description of phonological variation, taking as an example a well-known instance from American English. In the midwest, as in many parts of the United States, the vowel in *bad, ham* and *rag* can be pronounced as [æ] – the way it is pronounced in RP, or by careful newscasters in the US. It can also be pronounced as a high front vowel [e] or as a diphthong [eə] or even [iə], sounding much like the vowel in *beer*. This variability does not change the identity of the word – it has no effect on its referential meaning. A [hiəm] is every bit as much a smoked (or salted) pig's thigh as a [hæm], but the difference in pronunciation carries social meaning. The nature of this social meaning, particularly with respect to gender, is the subject of this chapter.

The most common approach to variation is to view variables as constituting a continuum between "standard" and "vernacular" language. [hæm] is what we call the "standard" pronunciation in American English, whereas [hiəm] is called "non-standard" or "vernacular." Standard pronunciations are part of the standard language – the variety of language that is associated with education, central government, and other institutions of national or global power. In opposition to the standard is what is commonly called the vernacular, the language of locally based communities – most people's everyday language. The vernacular has local and regional features – features that are muted in the standard. The closer a person's speech is to the standard the more difficult it is to tell

Language and Gender: A Reader, Second Edition. Edited by Jennifer Coates and Pia Pichler.

where he or she is from; the closer to the vernacular, the stronger and more identifiable their regional or local accent. The difference between standard and vernacular is not abrupt, but a matter of degree. The phonetic continuum between [æ] and [iʲ], for example, offers a range of possible pronunciations that lie somewhere in between the most standard and the most vernacular pronunciation. All speakers use a range of these pronunciations, varying in their use depending on who they're talking to, the topic, the degree of formality, etc. At the same time, the range of variants that a given speaker uses in this way reflects where she or he falls in the social matrix.

While the standard variety is associated with the people, settings and institutions of social and economic power, the non-standard variety is associated with locally based communities. The heart of these communities is in the working class and the lower middle class – in social networks based in local neighborhoods and workplaces (see Milroy 1980 for a thorough discussion of the relation between social class, social networks, and the use of the vernacular). The local vernacular has all the flavor of the community, and it both constructs and evokes solidarity among the community's members.

Since there is a relation between such broad social categorizations as socioeconomic class and the extent to which one's life is based in local networks, sociolinguistic variation is associated simultaneously with broad social categories like class, and with nuances of local meaning within communities. For example, in a study of Martha's Vineyard, an island off the coast of Massachusetts, William Labov (1972) found a relation between the use of vernacular features and local identity. Speakers who identified with the local traditional fishing culture used more of the vernacular features than people who identified with the emerging mainland-oriented tourist economy. Thus, the vernacular can be associated not simply with place, but with quite local issues.

Quantitative studies of correlations between linguistic variables and the social characteristics of speakers have shown a set of patterns that recur from community to community in the industrialized world. The best-known set of findings in this correlational enterprise has been class stratification. Predictably, as one moves up the socioeconomic hierarchy, people produce an increasing percentage of standard pronunciations (see, e.g., Labov 1966; Macaulay 1977; Trudgill 1974). But while the study of variation has traditionally focused on socioeconomic class, it has emerged that gender is at least as powerful a force in patterns of sociolinguistic variation. The traditional focus on class, however, has led many researchers to treat gender as secondary, and as independent of other social variables. This is not only a result of a particular academic practice, but of popular thought about gender. It is traditional to think of gender as oppositional – indeed, the expression "the opposite sex" is the only colloquial way to refer to the other sex. Gender is commonly thought of, therefore, as independent of other aspects of identity as well, so that being male or female is commonly thought to have the same effect on people's behavior, identities, etc. regardless of age, ethnicity, social class etc. But (as emphasized by Eckert and McConnell-Ginet [reprinted in Part X of this volume]) gender practices differ considerably from culture to culture, from place to place, from group to group, living at the intersection of all the other aspects of social identity. Nonetheless, it has become commonplace to speak of "men's speech" and "women's speech" – even of "men's language" and "women's language." Because gender is viewed as independent of other aspects of identity, it has been common practice to generalize on the basis of observations in a restricted population, and it has also been common practice to interpret gross statistical gender differences as reflecting a pure gender effect. The use of statistics in an area as understudied as gender can lead researchers down a garden path of naive assumption, encouraging them to attribute things to gender that may well be more closely related to other aspects of identity. One particular difficulty with a heavy-handed use of statistics is that explanations frequently lie in the exceptions, which are just the cases that statistical studies tend to ignore.

Is Women's Speech More Conservative?

One of the most popular generalizations about male and female speech is the common claim that women's speech is more conservative than men's. And connected to this popular generalization is a series of popular explanations for it: e.g. women are status-conscious or polite, men are rough and down-to-earth. Since the generalization that women's speech is more conservative than men's is not entirely accurate, it is important to examine the ways in which it is true and false, and to consider the nature of possible explanations for the patterns that do emerge.

The patterns in phonological variation are quite heterogeneous. However, there is one fairly general observation that can be made (Labov 1991). Certain sociolinguistic variables have been around for generations: the so-called "stable" variables such as the variation between *walking* and *walkin'*, or between *this* and *dis*, *that* and *dat*. Women tend to be more standard overall in their use of these variables than men. Other variables are a reflection of the progress of linguistic change (the raising of (ae) discussed above is one such variable). Men are frequently more conservative than women in their use of these variables. As we move away from phonological variation to the use of grammatical variables, such as negative concord (e.g. *I didn't do anything* vs. *I didn't do nothing*), women's usage is considerably more standard, or conservative, than men's. It is significant that these grammatical variables are quite clearly consciously recognized and stigmatized, and far more so than the phonological variables. These differences suggest that conservatism is not an all-or-nothing phenomenon. A variety of explanations have been proposed for women's more conservative usages.

One important factor in people's use of variation is their relation to linguistic "markets." The notion of a symbolic market, developed by Pierre Bourdieu and Luc Boltanski (1975) and extended to the study of variation by David Sankoff and Suzanne Laberge (1978), builds on the importance of symbolic capital for success in functioning in different parts of society. One will have little chance of succeeding in the diplomatic corps if one does not possess a range of knowledge that marks one as the "right kind" of person: the right table manners, the right style of dress, the right ways of entertaining guests, the right language. While the work of Bourdieu focuses on the symbolic capital of elites, this is equally true if one is to be accepted in a peasant village or in an urban ghetto (Woolard 1985) – what is "right" depends on the market in which one is engaged.

From the start, women and men overall stand in very different relations to linguistic markets. Peter Trudgill's account (1972 [revised version reprinted in Part I of this volume]) of gender differences in the pronunciation of English in Norwich found women overall to be more conservative in their use of almost all variables. He speculated that this was because of women's exclusion from the workplace. According to Trudgill, because women's position in society is generally subordinate to men's, and because women have fewer opportunities to secure their positions through occupational success or other abilities, they find it necessary to use symbolic means to enhance their position.

While overall exclusion from the workplace may throw women onto symbolic means of establishing a place in the world, the workplace itself also has a variety of ways of constraining women to use more standard language. While standard language is crucial to performing many white-collar jobs, it is more generally crucial to the kinds of jobs that Sankoff et al. (1989) refer to as "technicians of language" – writers, academics, secretaries, receptionists. The earliest white-collar employment of women as teachers puts women's work squarely in the standard language market. But outside of education as well, many women's jobs require standard language by virtue of the function of these jobs as "front end" workers. Secretaries, receptionists, flight attendants and hostesses all make their living by representing an organization to its clients. In some important sense, they are part of the organization's symbolic capital. Thus for women, the need for standard language is not restricted to prestigious or higher paid occupations.

And what of women in the more prestigious occupations? To the extent that men dominate institutions, and particularly elite institutions, one might think of them as more engaged in the standard language market. However, one might also consider that to the same extent, men have greater legitimacy in these institutions, while women moving into them are generally seen as interlopers, and are at greater pains to prove that they belong. One means for proving worthiness is meticulous attention to symbolic capital – hence the millions made in self-help books to help professional women "dress for success." The more meticulous use of standard language, by the same token – "talking for success" – could make women's speech more conservative than their male peers'.

Margaret Deuchar (1989) argues that women's place in society more generally makes them more vulnerable to criticism, and that the more meticulous use of standard language could be seen as a way of being "beyond reproach." This has particular meaning in the light of Walt Wolfram's findings in his study (1969) of variation in the Detroit African American community. Wolfram found women at all socioeconomic levels to be more conservative in the use of features of African American Vernacular English (AAVE) than men. This gender pattern is overwhelmingly consistent, and more consistent than has been found in any other speech community. It is worth considering that among women in our society, African American women are the most subject to denigration, and that their very systematic use of standard language may well be a response to their greater social vulnerability. This argument is related to Penelope Brown's analysis (1980) of women's politeness in a Mayan community, in which she argues that women employ forms of politeness towards men as a strategy to avoid physical abuse.

In the above cases, we are focusing on women's place with respect to the standard language market. But women are vernacular speakers as well. Nonetheless, description of the social meaning of the vernacular has commonly focused on the relation between the vernacular and masculinity. Peter Trudgill (1972) has argued that men's use of the vernacular is associated with the general value among men of the toughness or physical prowess associated with working-class masculinity. But working-class culture and the local marketplace has to do with much more than toughness and masculinity. Perhaps more important is the role of know-how in locally based networks. The vernacular is commonly associated with blue-collar professions – not only people who work on the factory floor, but people who keep the infrastructure operating: mechanics, electricians, plumbers, construction workers. These are people whose skills are essential to the well-being of our day-to-day physical environment. The vernacular is associated, then, with a range of capabilities for functioning in the physical world – capabilities that include, but extend well beyond, physical power. And many of these capabilities are shared by men and women. It is notable, though, that the occupations traditionally available to, and associated with, women in the local market – such as cleaning, sewing, cooking and childcare – are as essential and often as skilled as men's work in the equivalent market, but not equally valued. Thus in the vernacular market, as in the standard language market, women's pursuits are marginalized, hence marginalizing women's claims to social centrality. If marginalization in the standard language market leads women to use more standard language, one might expect marginalization in the local market to lead women to use more vernacular.

This relatively abstract discussion of gender and the linguistic market makes it clear that we cannot understand the relation between variation and gender unless we explore quite concrete situations. To this purpose, the following discussion will examine some patterns of variation in a well-defined adolescent population, with the purpose of seeing the linguistic relation between gender and other aspects of social identity.

Belten High

Belten High is a comprehensive public high school in the suburbs of Detroit, serving 2,000 predominantly white students from families ranging from working-class through upper middle-class. In most social science studies, children are assigned their parents' (usually their fathers') socioeconomic status. But adolescents are not just their parents' children – they are moving into their adult identities. The transition from parents' class to one's own commonly begins in school, and is articulated through one's forms of participation in the school. In Belten High, as in many high schools across the US, two class-based social categories dominate discourses of adolescent identity. Some students, primarily college-bound, participate enthusiastically in school, particularly in the extracurricular sphere; others, primarily bound for the blue-collar workplace, reject the school's pretensions to be a total institution, and base their lives and activities outside of school in the neighborhood and in the broader local urban–suburban area. These categories commonly have names, and in Belten High, as in high schools throughout the Detroit suburbs in the 1980s, the members of the school-oriented category were referred to (and referred to themselves) as *jocks* while the locally oriented category were referred to (and referred to themselves) as *burnouts*. The jocks constitute a middle-class culture, oriented to the global market that the school and its college- and career-bound emphasis represents. Spending most of their time in school, and engaged in the institutional enterprise, the jocks are very much in the standard language marketplace. The burnouts constitute a working-class culture, engaging in the school's downplayed vocational curriculum but minimizing their time in school in favor of independent engagement in the local and urban scene.

The jocks and the burnouts, together accounting for just less than half the students in the school, constitute mutually opposed and relatively hostile categories. This opposition is constructed through a broad range of symbolic means, from territory to clothing, hairdo, substance use, musical tastes and friendship patterns (for a full account of these categories, see Eckert 1989). And while many people are neither jocks nor burnouts, the importance of these two categories is underscored by the fact that almost all students in the school who are neither jocks nor burnouts are referred to (and refer to themselves) as *in-betweens*, and describe themselves in relation to those two categories.

Each of these categories is composed of several social network clusters, and roughly equal numbers of boys and girls. The categories began in late elementary school as two separate, and somewhat rival, heterosexual crowds, surfacing in junior high school as full-blown opposed social categories. The jocks and the burnouts constitute communities of practice, based in very different (and class-based) responses to the school institution. They are distinguished not simply by their attitudes towards school, but by a range of differences in social practice, some of them quite profound. The jocks and the burnouts are continually engaged in a mutual process of meaning-making, as individuals engage among themselves in making sense of who they are, why they're together, and what their place is in the world.

Eckert and McConnell-Ginet (1995) discuss at some length the complexities of the interactions among gender and social category in Belten High. The resources and constraints for girls' and boys' actions and construction of identities are radically different. Just as women are marginalized in the adult marketplace, so are girls in the adolescent marketplace. Most specifically, boys' actions and roles are defining of the jock and burnout categories, just as men's actions and occupations are defining of the adult professional and blue-collar worlds. While a boy can build a highly valued jock identity through athletics, a girl cannot (or could not in the early 1980s, when this work was done). And while a boy can build a highly valued burnout image by rumbling in the streets of Detroit, with dirt biking or working on his car, a girl cannot. Jock girls can gain status only through participation in the school social sphere – student government, cheerleading, organizing dances – all of which are seen as secondary, or even auxiliary, to boys' varsity athletics. Legitimized activities are harder for burnout girls to find, since there are relatively few interesting non-school activities open to girls. Rather, burnout girls gain status through their social skill, their networks, and their reputation for daring and fun. Furthermore, while a boy can gain importance and popularity without good looks, a girl cannot; and while a boy can experiment with quasi-legal behavior and maintain (perhaps even enhance) his status as a jock, a girl who does risks not only her status as a jock but her closest friendships. There is little latitude for jock and burnout girls to stray into each other's territories – a jock girl who behaves in the least like a burnout will be labelled a "slut," while a burnout girl who behaves in the least like a jock will be labelled a "snob." The relation between female jocks and burnouts, then, is truly a relation of opposition and avoidance. On the other hand, the relation between male jocks and burnouts is more one of competition around physical prowess. While the jocks establish their physical prowess through school sports, the burnouts establish theirs sometimes through independent sports, but more saliently through fighting ability and urban know-how. Jock and burnout boys, therefore, represent something of a mutual threat, since each is recognized for a different and important aspect of masculine physical capability.

Sociolinguistic Variation in Belten High

Virtually all of the students of Belten High speak a local version of white Anglo American English. To illustrate the range of gender dynamics in variation, I will focus on three vowels that show flux in this dialect: (ae) as in *bad*, (uh) as in *cut*, and (ay) as in *fight*.[1] As described above, the variable (ae) ranges from a conservative pronunciation [æ] to a raised variant [e], so that *bad* sounds more like *bade*. (uh) ranges from its conservative pronunciation [ʌ] to a backed pronunciation [ɔ], making *cut* sound more like *caught*. Finally, the diphthong (ay) monophthongizes to [a:] so that, for example, *right* sounds like a drawn-out pronunciation of *rot*. All speakers in Belten High produce a range of variants for each of these three variables. What differs from speaker to speaker, or from group to group, is the frequency with which they produce the different variants. In the following discussion, I will refer to raised (ae), backed (uh) and monophthongized (ay) as advanced (vernacular) variants.

Just as jocks and burnouts differ in their relation to the urban area, so do the linguistic variables. Belten High sits in the midst of the urban sprawl that surrounds Detroit, a vast social landscape, and as discussed above, an important part of social practice in the urban–suburban continuum involves orientation towards the city of Detroit. An important aspect

Table 1 Correlations of three phonological variables with gender and social category as independent variables

Variable	Girls	Boys	Burnouts	Jocks	Input	Significance
(ae)	0.573	0.438	—	—	0.371	0.000
(ay)	0.426	0.555	—	—	0.072	0.006
(uh)	—	—	0.571	0.437	0.494	0.000

of the social meaning of variables, therefore, is to be found in the distribution of uses of variants in the urban–suburban area. The backing of (uh) and the monophthongization of (ay) are considerably more advanced as one moves closer to Detroit, while the raising of (ae) is more advanced as one moves away from Detroit (Eckert 1999). Thus while (ay) and (uh) can be associated with urban white speech, (ae) is more closely related to the suburbs. For this reason, I refer to (ay) and (uh) as urban variables, and (ae) as a suburban variable.

As shown in table 1, these three variables show different statistical patterns across the population of jocks and burnouts in Belten High. The figures in this table represent the results of a variable rule analysis,[2] indicating the relative rates of use of advanced variants by categories of speakers.[3] Table 1 treats gender and social category as independent variables, following a common statistical approach to gender and variation. This mode of analysis assumes that gender and social category membership have completely independent effects on language use – that gender and social category are separable. Each of these three variables shows a quite different pattern of correlation with gender and social category. In the case of (ae) and (ay), only gender correlates significantly with the use of advanced variants, with opposite effects: girls lead in the raising of (ae) and boys lead in the monophthongization of (ay). In the case of (uh), only social category shows a significant correlation, with burnouts leading jocks in the use of advanced variants. On the basis of table 1, one might be tempted to say that (ae) is a "female marker", (ay) is a "male marker", and (uh) is a "burnout marker." If we assume that social category and gender are inseparable, though, we might do well to examine the behavior of male and female jocks and burnouts separately, as shown in table 2. The figures shown in table 2, and displayed graphically in figure 1, paint a very different picture of the use of these variables. There is a clear and quite complex interaction between gender, social category, and local orientation. While the gender differentiation of (ae) and (ay) is overwhelming and clearly greater than the social category differentiation, it is also clear that these variables are not simply gender markers. Particularly, there is an apparent relation between gender, social category, and urban–suburban orientation. Not only do boys lead in the use of the urban variable (ay), but burnouts lead jocks in its use among the girls (the jock–burnout difference among the boys is not statistically significant). And not only do girls lead in the use of the suburban variable (ae), but jocks lead burnouts in its use among the boys. This makes a complex association among masculinity, burnout affiliation and urban-ness on the one hand, and femininity, jock affiliation and suburban-ness on the other. In the case of (uh) backing, gender gives way to a more straightforward relation between urban orientation and burnout affiliation.

Another, more general way of considering these data is in terms of the overall accent. The burnout girls lead the jock girls in the use of all three variables, and indeed they lead the entire population in the use of (ae) and (uh). This means that their local accent is the strongest of all the four categories of speakers. Following the burnout girls in the localness of their overall accent are the burnout boys. However, the burnout boys' extremely low values for the suburban variant (ae) leave them with a specifically urban

Table 2 Correlations of three phonological variables with gender and social category as inter-acting variables

	Girls		Boys			
Variable	*Burnouts*	*Jocks*	*Burnouts*	*Jocks*	*Input*	*Significance*
(ae)	0.611	0.535	0.386	0.466	0.371	0.000
(ay)	0.483	0.336	0.579	0.545	0.070	0.008
(uh)	0.619	0.418	0.532	0.450	0.494	0.000

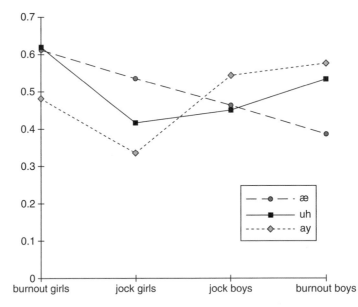

Figure 1 Patterning of three phonological variables with gender and social category

accent. The jocks, male and female, emerge as relatively conservative, but with the boys making greater use of the urban variables (uh) and (ay) and the girls making greater use of the suburban variable (ae). The jock boys' accent is more suburban than the burnout boys', and less than the jock girls'. The question of who is more conservative in this population, then, does not have a simple answer. But perhaps what is most striking is that the girls describe the overall envelope of variation in this community. The burnout girls are the most advanced speakers in the community overall, and the jock girls are the most conservative – if only marginally more conservative than the jock boys. This is consonant with the observations from earlier studies made above. The constraints on girls to conform to an exaggerated social category type are clearly related to their diminished possibilities for claiming membership or category status. In Eckert (1990), I argued that to the extent that men control material capital, women are constrained to accumulate symbolic capital. Thus while men develop a sense of themselves and find a place in the world on the basis of their actions and abilities, women have to focus on the production of selves – to develop authority through a continual proof of worthiness. Thus the jock and the burnout girls are continually working on their jockhood and their burnouthood, refining and elaborating their mutual differences, focusing on being good jocks or burnouts, just as later in life they will no doubt be focusing on being good mothers, wives, friends – focusing on how they are, while their male peers will be focusing on what they do.

Conclusions

One important lesson from these correlations is that across-the-board differences taken alone can seriously misrepresent the social meanings of variables. We clearly cannot talk about gender independently of other aspects of social identity, as no variable correlates simply with gender or social category. The major generalization in Belten High seems to be that girls are putting these phonological resources to greater use than the boys, as the greater social polarization between jock and burnout girls emerges in a greater linguistic polarization as well. This view of gender and variation can lead to a generalization, but not a generalization that would yield a consistent male–female difference across the board that would allow statements such as "women are linguistically more conservative than men." Rather, the generalization is likely to have more to do with women's greater use of symbolic resources to establish membership and status. And since the communities of practice in which women are seeking status vary widely, the particular linguistic nature of these symbolic resources will vary widely as well.

Notes

1   For a more thorough discussion of these and other variables in the same community, see Eckert (1999).
2   The variable rule program, in this case Goldvarb, a multiple regression package for the analysis of linguistic variation, is described in Rousseau and Sankoff (1978). The numbers shown in the tables and figure are probabilities of the occurrence of vernacular variants, within the context of an overall probability of occurrence in the population as a whole. These numbers should be regarded as indications of relations among the speaker groups represented, rather than as absolute values of occurrence.
3   These figures are based on 50 occurrences of each variable per speaker, extracted from free-flowing tape-recorded speech. For details of the methods used in data collection and analysis in this study, see Eckert (1999).

References

Bourdieu, Pierre and Boltanski, Luc (1975) 'Le fétichisme de la langue'. *Actes de la recherche en sciences sociales*, 4, 2–32.

Brown, Penelope (1980) 'How and why are women more polite: some evidence from a Mayan community', in S. McConnell-Ginet, R. A. Borker and N. Furman (eds) *Women and Language in Literature and Society*, pp. 111–36. New York: Praeger.

Deuchar, Margaret (1989) 'A pragmatic account of women's use of standard speech', in J. Coates and D. Cameron (eds) *Women in Their Speech Communities*, pp. 27–32. London and New York: Longman.

Eckert, Penelope (1989) *Jocks and Burnouts: Social Categories and Identity in the High School*. New York: Teachers College Press.

Eckert, Penelope (1990) 'Cooperative competition in adolescent girl talk'. *Discourse Processes*, 13, 92–122.

Eckert, Penelope (1999) *Variation and Social Practice: The Linguistic Construction of Social Meaning in Belten High.* Oxford: Blackwell.

Eckert, Penelope and McConnell-Ginet, Sally (1995) 'Constructing meaning, constructing selves: snapshots of language, gender and class from Belten High', in K. Hall and M. Bucholtz (eds) *Gender Articulated: Language and the Socially Constructed Self,* pp. 469–508. New York: Routledge.

Labov, William (1966) *The Social Stratification of English in New York City.* Washington, DC: Center for Applied Linguistics.

Labov, William (1972) 'The social motivation of a sound change', in W. Labov (ed.) *Sociolinguistic Patterns,* pp. 1–42. Philadelphia: University of Pennsylvania Press.

Labov, William (1991) 'The intersection of sex and social class in the course of linguistic change'. *Language Variation and Change,* 2, 2, 205–51.

Macaulay, Ronald K. S. (1977) *Language, Social Class and Education: A Glasgow Study.* Edinburgh: University of Edinburgh Press.

Milroy, Lesley (1980) *Language and Social Networks.* Oxford: Blackwell.

Rousseau, Pascale and Sankoff, David (1978) 'Advances in variable rule methodology', in D. Sankoff (ed.) *Linguistic Variation: Models and Methods,* pp. 57–70. New York: Academic Press.

Sankoff, D., Cedergren, H., Kemp, W., Thibault, P. and Vincent, D. (1989) 'Montreal French: language, class, and ideology', in W. Fasold and D. Schiffrin (eds) *Language Change and Variation,* pp. 107–18. Amsterdam: John Benjamins.

Sankoff, David and Laberge, Suzanne (1978) 'The linguistic market and the statistical explanation of variability', in D. Sankoff (ed.) *Linguistic Variation: Models and Methods,* pp. 239–50. New York: Academic Press.

Trudgill, Peter (1972) 'Sex, covert prestige and linguistic change in the urban British English of Norwich'. *Language in Society,* 1, 179–95.

Trudgill, Peter (1974) *The Social Differentiation of English in Norwich.* Cambridge: Cambridge University Press.

Wolfram, Walt (1969) *A Sociolinguistic Description of Detroit Negro Speech.* Washington, DC: Center for Applied Linguistics.

Woolard, K. (1985) 'Language variation and cultural hegemony'. *American Ethnologist,* 12, 738–48.

Part II
Gender and Conversational Practice

This section is devoted to research which finds that women and men characteristically draw on different strategies in conversational interaction. Such research moves away from the traditional linguistic preoccupation with phonetics/phonology and syntax/morphology to an investigation of linguistic strategies such as paying compliments, hedging, apologizing, or swearing. More recently, researchers have turned their attention to the use of *like* as a quotative and as a hedge by young speakers (see, for example, Tagliamonte and D'Arcy 2004), and also to the growing use of rising intonation patterns at the end of utterances, now common among young people all over the English-speaking world (see, for example, Britain 1998). Our knowledge of how to pay a compliment or how to replace *say* with *be like* is part of our communicative competence (Hymes 1972). Research like this suggests that women and men develop differentiated communicative competence: in other words, women's and men's behavior in conversation suggests that they have a different understanding of how a compliment is done, or of the gendered meaning of using *like* frequently in speech. Such differences led some researchers in the 1980s to talk of different female and male "styles" in conversation (a key work presenting such an argument is that by Maltz and Borker, included in Part VIII of this Reader).

The four papers in this section represent only a small fraction of the work carried out in recent years by researchers interested in gender differences in conversational style (for an overview, see Coates 2004). The first paper in this section focuses on compliments. Janet Holmes' paper, "Complimenting – A Positive Politeness Strategy," draws on the model of politeness developed by Brown and Levinson (1987). According to this model, politeness consists in respecting the face needs of others, that is, in showing consideration for other people's feelings. People have two kinds of face needs that have to be attended to in interaction: the need not to be imposed on (known as *negative face*); and the need to be liked and admired (known as *positive face*). Holmes argues that compliments are prime examples of speech acts which pay attention to the positive face needs of others. Her analysis of compliment usage in New Zealand reveals that female speakers both give and receive significantly more compliments than male speakers. This confirms research carried out in the USA and elsewhere (for example, Wolfson 1983; Herbert

1998). Holmes argues that it may be the case that women perceive compliments as positive politeness strategies while men are more ambivalent about the meaning of compliments and sometimes interpret them as face-threatening acts. Holmes suggests that the differential usage of women and men can be linked to women's subordinate social status.

The second paper is Marjorie Goodwin's "Cooperation and Competition Across Girls' Play Activities." Goodwin focuses on a single type of speech sequence, the directive, in a range of different situations (a directive is a speech act that tries to get someone to do something). This paper draws on her long-term research into the talk of Black children playing on a Philadelphia street. Goodwin looked at the way the children organized their play activities, in particular at the way they got each other to do things. She observed that, when they were engaged in a specific task activity (making slingshots), the boys preferred to use aggravated directives such as direct commands, while the girls, by contrast, preferred more mitigated forms such as *let's*. Goodwin argues that the linguistic forms used reflect (and in turn reproduce) the social organization of the group. The boys' group was hierarchically organized, with leaders using very strong directive forms to establish control, while the girls' group was non-hierarchical, with all girls participating in decision-making on an equal basis. But Goodwin is concerned to show that this is far from the whole picture: the second half of her paper examines directive usage when the girls play house. When the girls act out family relationships such as parent–child or older sibling–younger sibling, they use directives and directive-responses which accomplish asymmetry. In other words, Goodwin demonstrates that the girls have a repertoire which includes both cooperative and competitive ways of talking.

The third paper in this section, "Expressions of Gender," examines gendered discourse styles in the classroom. Julia Davies worked in three different secondary schools, focusing on small discussion groups involving 14-year-old pupils dealing with specific tasks, such as answering questions about a poem, or carrying out a role play of teachers dealing with bullying. These groups could be single-sex or mixed-sex (teachers made sure that pupils had experience of both, though pupils preferred working in same-sex groups). In this paper, Davies focuses on all-boy and all-girl discussion groups. She describes the girls' ways of talking as being characterized by "polyphony" (borrowing the metaphor from Coates 1996) and the boys' ways by "cacophony." Girls' discourse styles in the discussion groups involved both personal narrative and highly collaborative, jointly constructed text. Talk was highly cohesive, with lexical and grammatical repetition and the use of similar pitch levels and intonation patterns. By contrast, the boys' talk was full of interruptions, joking asides, and insults, and was frequently off-topic. The chief goal of boys in classroom discussion was to demonstrate that they were "real boys." Classroom goals of cooperation and focus on the task in hand were seen as non-macho or "gay," which made it very difficult for boys who wanted to engage with academic work. This is an important study, in that it not only demonstrates significant differences in discourse style between male and female speakers but also draws attention to the conflict between the discourse of learning and expressions of heterosexual masculinity.

The fourth paper in the section moves us from the spoken language of the streets and the classroom to contemporary electronic messages. Carol Waseleski's "Gender and the Use of Exclamation Points in Computer-Mediated Communication," examines the messages posted on two electronic discussion groups with a joint membership of over 3,500 users. She focused on the use of exclamation points (exclamation marks in British English) in these messages to test two claims: that females use exclamation points more than males, and that exclamation points are markers of "excitability." (The latter claim clearly draws on the sexist myth that women tend to be over-emotional in their language use.) She analyzed 200 examples of messages containing an exclamation point, using a 16-category coding frame. When she broke down her findings by gender, she found that 73 percent of all exclamations were made by females. Moreover, content analysis revealed that exclamation points are rarely markers of excitability; they more frequently function as markers of friendly interaction. This function is gendered, with 70 percent of all friendly exclamations made by female participants. These results were statistically significant.

All these papers show the role language plays in our construction of ourselves as *gendered beings*. It has been understood for a long time that language and identity are crucially intertwined (see, for example, Edwards 1985; Goffman 1959; Gumperz 1982; Joseph 2004; Preece 2009). More recently, with the insights afforded by post-structuralism, researchers in language and gender have begun to explore the way that language practices *accomplish* gender. Despite the differences in age and geography between the professional women interacting online in the US (studied by Waseleski) and the 14-year-old schoolgirls in the north of England (studied by Davies), both these groups accomplished gender in part by performing friendliness. For both groups, the performance of friendliness was closely linked to the performance of femininity. All of us make language choices all the time which index our identity, or rather identities, since none of us is monolithic (see Ochs 1992 for further discussion of the idea of gender and indexicality). It is through paying compliments, giving directives, swearing, being friendly, or being polite in particular ways in particular communities of practice that we constitute ourselves as women or men in these communities.

References

Britain, David (1998) "Linguistic change in intonation: the use of high-rising terminals in New Zealand English," pp. 213–39 in Peter Trudgill and Jenny Cheshire (eds) *The Sociolinguistics Reader*, vol. 1: *Multilingualism and Variation*. London: Arnold.

Brown, Penelope and Levinson, Stephen (1987) *Politeness*. Cambridge: Cambridge University Press.

Coates, Jennifer (1996) *Women Talk: Conversation Between Women Friends*. Oxford: Blackwell.

Coates, Jennifer (2004) "Gender differences in communicative competence," pp. 106–40 in *Women, Men and Language* (3rd edn). London: Longman.

Edwards, John (1985) *Language, Society and Identity*. Oxford: Blackwell.

Goffman, Erving (1959) *The Presentation of Self in Everyday Life*. New York: Anchor Books.

Gumperz, John (ed.) (1982) *Language and Social Identity*. Cambridge: Cambridge University Press.

Herbert, Robert K. (1998) "Sex-based differences in compliment behaviour," pp. 53–75 in Jenny Cheshire and Peter Trudgill (eds) *The Sociolinguistics Reader*, vol. 2: *Gender and Discourse*. London: Arnold.

Hymes, Dell (1972) "On communicative competence," pp. 269–93 in J. B. Pride and J. Holmes (eds) *Sociolinguistics*. Harmondsworth: Penguin Books.

Joseph, John E. (2004) *Language and Identity*. London: Palgrave.

Maltz, Daniel and Borker, Ruth (1982) "A cultural approach to male–female miscommunication," in J. Gumperz (ed.) *Language and Identity*. Cambridge: Cambridge University Press; reproduced in Part VIII of this Reader.

Ochs, Elinor (1992) "Indexing gender," pp. 335–58 in A. Duranti and C. Goodwin (eds) *Rethinking Context: Language as an Interactive Phenomenon*. Cambridge: Cambridge University Press.

Preece, Sian (2009) *Posh Talk: Language and Identity in Higher Education*. London: Palgrave.

Tagliamonte, Sali and D'Arcy, Alex (2004) "*He's like, she's like*: the quotative system in Canadian youth," *Journal of Sociolinguistics* 8(4), 493–514.
Wolfson, Nessa (1983) "An empirically based analysis of complimenting in American English," pp. 82–95 in Nessa Wolfson and Elliot Judd (eds) *Sociolinguistics and Language Acquisition*. Rowley, MA: Newbury House.

Recommended Further Reading

Goodwin, Marjorie Harness (1990) *He-Said-She-Said: Talk as Social Organisation among Black Children*. Bloomington: Indiana University Press.
Hall, Kira, and Bucholtz, Mary (eds) (1995) *Gender Articulated: Language and the Socially Constructed Self*. London: Routledge.
Holmes, Janet (1995) *Women, Men and Politeness*. London: Longman.
Holmes, Janet (ed.) (2000) *Gendered Speech in Social Context*. Wellington, NZ: Victoria University Press.
Pichler, Pia and Eppler, Eva (eds) (2009) *Gender and Spoken Interaction*. London: Palgrave.
Tagliamonte, Sali and D'Arcy, Alex (2004) "*He's like, she's like*: the quotative system in Canadian youth," *Journal of Sociolinguistics* 8(4), 493–514.

7

Complimenting – A Positive Politeness Strategy

Janet Holmes

Source: Janet Holmes, *Women, Men and Politeness*. London: Longman (1995), pp. 115–53. Reprinted with permission of Pearson Education UK.

[…]

Do women and men differ in the way they use particular speech acts to express politeness? How would one measure any differences? Should the relative frequency with which women and men use compliments, greetings, or expressions of gratitude be considered, for instance? The form of a directive (e.g. *Shut up!* versus *Let's have a bit of hush now*) is very obviously relevant in assessing how polite it is in any particular situation (Leech 1983; Brown and Levinson 1987). What can we deduce about female and male patterns of politeness by examining who uses particular speech acts to whom? In this paper I will focus on compliments to show how analysing particular speech acts can provide interesting suggestions about gender differences in politeness behaviour.

Paying Compliments

Example 1

Two colleagues meeting in Pat's office to discuss a report.

CHRIS: Hi Pat. Sorry I'm late. The boss wanted to set up a time for a meeting just as I was leaving.

PAT: That's OK Chris. You're looking good. Is that a new suit?

CHRIS: Mm. It's nice isn't it. I got it in Auckland last month. Have you had a break since I last saw you?

PAT: No, work work work I'm afraid. Never mind. Have you got a copy of the report with you?

Positive politeness can be expressed in many ways but paying a compliment is one of the most obvious. A favourable comment on the addressee's appearance, as illustrated in example 1, is a very common way of paying a compliment as we shall see. Compliments are prime examples of speech acts which notice and attend to the hearer's 'interests, wants, needs, goods', the first positive politeness strategy identified and discussed by Brown and Levinson (1987: 102).

What is a compliment?

But what is a compliment? There are a number of positively polite speech acts in the exchange between Pat and Chris – greetings, friendly address terms, expressions of concern and compliments. I would want to count *you're looking good* and *is that a new suit* as examples of compliments. The first is a direct compliment, while the fact that the second counts as a compliment is inferable from the discourse context and the fact that things which are new are generally highly valued in western society (see Manes 1983). When collecting and analysing examples of a particular speech act, it is important to have a clear definition in order to decide what counts and what does not. This is how I have defined a compliment:

> A compliment is a speech act which explicitly or implicitly attributes credit to someone other than the speaker, usually the person addressed, for some 'good' (possession, characteristic, skill, etc.) which is positively valued by the speaker and the hearer. (Holmes 1986: 485)

As the utterance *is that a new suit* illustrates, a compliment may be indirect, requiring some inferencing based on a knowledge of the cultural values of the community. There are other ways in which a compliment may be indirect too. Compliments usually focus on something directly attributable to the person addressed (e.g. an article of clothing), but examples 2 and 3 demonstrate that this is not always the case.

Examples 2 and 3
(2) *Rhonda is visiting an old schoolfriend, Carol, and comments on one of Carol's children.*
RHONDA: What a polite child!
CAROL: Thank you. We do our best.

(3) *Ray is the conductor of the choir.*
MATT: The choir was wonderful. You must be really pleased.
RAY: Yes, they were good weren't they.

The complimenters' utterances in these examples may look superficially like rather general positive evaluations, but their function as compliments which indirectly attribute credit to the addressee for good parenting in (2), and good conducting in (3), is unambiguous in context.

Why give a compliment?

Compliments are usually intended to make others feel good (see Wierzbicka 1987: 201). The primary function of a compliment is most obviously affective and social, rather than referential or informative. They are generally described as positively affective speech acts serving to increase or consolidate the solidarity between the speaker and addressee (see Wolfson 1981, 1983; Holmes 1986; Herbert 1989; Lewandowska-Tomaszczyk 1989). Compliments are social lubricants which 'create or maintain rapport' (Wolfson 1983: 86), as illustrated in all the examples above, as well as in example 4.

Example 4
Two women, good friends, meeting in the lift at their workplace.
SAL: Hi how are you? You're looking just terrific.
MEG: Thanks. I'm pretty good. How are things with you? That's a snazzy scarf you're
       wearing.

Compliments are clearly positive politeness devices which express goodwill and solidarity between the speaker and the addressee. But they may serve other functions too. Do compliments have any element of referential meaning, for instance? While the primary function of compliments is most obviously affective, they also convey some information in the form of the particular 'good' the speaker selects for comment. They provide a positive critical evaluation of a selected aspect of the addressee's behaviour or appearance, or whatever, which in some contexts may carry some communicative weight. Johnson and Roen (1992), for instance, argue that the compliments they analysed in written peer reviews simultaneously conveyed both affective (or interpersonal) meaning and referential (or ideational) meaning in that a particular aspect of the review was chosen for positive attention. It is possible that some compliments are intended and perceived as conveying a stronger referential message than others. Very clearly, the relationship between the complimenter and recipient is crucial in accurately interpreting the potential functions of a compliment.

In some contexts, compliments may function as praise and encouragement. In an analysis of over a thousand American compliments, Herbert (1990: 221) suggests some compliments serve as expressions of praise and admiration rather than offers of solidarity. This seems likely to reflect the relationship between the participants. Praise is often directed downwards from superordinate to subordinate. So the teacher's compliment about a student's work in example 5 would generally be regarded as praise.

Example 5
TEACHER: This is excellent Jeannie. You've really done a nice job.

Tannen seems to be referring to this function of compliments when she identifies compliments as potentially patronising.

> Giving praise … is … inherently asymmetrical. It … frames the speaker as one-up, in a position to judge someone else's performance. (Tannen 1990: 69)

It is possible, then, that in some relationships compliments will be unwelcome because they are experienced as ways in which the speaker is asserting superiority. Compliments directed upwards from subordinate to superordinates, on the other hand, are often labelled 'flattery'. In analysing differences in the way women and men use and interpret compliments, it will clearly be important to consider compliments between status unequals, exploring the possible alternative interpretations which they may be given.

Compliments may have a darker side then. For some recipients, in some contexts, an apparent compliment may be experienced negatively, or as face-threatening. They may be patronising or offensively flattering. They may also, of course, be sarcastic. When the content of a compliment is perceived as too distant from reality, it will be heard as a sarcastic or ironic put-down. I was in no doubt of the sarcastic intent of my brother's comment 'You play so well' as I was plonking away at the piano, hitting far more wrong than right notes. Focusing on a different perspective, Brown and Levinson suggest (1987: 66) that a compliment can be regarded as a face-threatening act to the extent that it implies the complimenter envies the addressee in some way, or would like something belonging to the addressee. This is perhaps clearest in cultures where an expression of admiration for an object imposes an obligation on the addressee to offer it to the complimenter, as in example 6.

Example 6
Pakeha woman to Samoan friend whom she is visiting.
SUE: What an unusual necklace. It's beautiful.
ETI: Please take it.

In this particular instance, Sue was very embarrassed at being offered as a gift the object she had admired. But Eti's response was perfectly predictable by anyone familiar with Samoan cultural norms with respect to complimenting behaviour. In other cultures and social groups too, compliments may be considered somewhat face-threatening in that they imply at least an element of envy and desire to have what the addressee possesses, whether an object or a desirable trait or skill (see Brown and Levinson 1987: 247). And in 'debt-sensitive cultures' (1987: 247), the recipient of a compliment may be regarded as incurring a heavy debt. In such cultures, then, the function of a compliment cannot be regarded as simply and unarguably positively polite.

Even if intended as an expression of solidarity, a compliment might be experienced as face-threatening if it is interpreted as assuming unwarranted intimacy. Lewandowska-Tomaszczyk (1989: 75) comments that in her Polish and British compliment data, compliments between people who did not know each other well caused embarrassment. Compliments presuppose a certain familiarity with the addressee, she suggests. This is likely to be true of certain types of compliments in many cultures. Compliments on very personal topics, for instance, are appropriate only from intimates, as in example 7.

Example 7
Young woman to her mother who is in hospital after a bad car accident.
Oh mum you've got your false teeth – they look great

The mother had been waiting for some time to be fitted with false teeth to replace those knocked out or broken in the car accident. There are not many situations in which such a compliment could be paid without causing embarrassment.

At the darkest end of the spectrum are utterances which have been called 'stranger compliments' or 'street remarks' (Kissling and Kramarae 1991; Kissling 1991).

Example 8
Man on building site to young woman passing by.
Wow what legs. What are you doing with them tonight sweetie?

These serve a very different interpersonal function from compliments between friends and acquaintances. Though some women interpret them positively as expressions of appreciation, others regard them as examples of verbal harassment. It seems likely that both the speaker's intentions and the hearer's interpretations of these speech acts are extremely variable, and require detailed analysis in context. Though I have mentioned them here for completeness, the discussion below is not based on data which included 'stranger compliments'.

Different analysts have thus identified a number of different functions of compliments in different contexts:

1 to express solidarity;
2 to express positive evaluation, admiration, appreciation or praise;
3 to express envy or desire for hearer's possessions;
4 as verbal harassment.

These functions are not necessarily mutually exclusive, but the relationship between the participants is crucial in interpreting the primary function of a particular compliment: analysis in context is essential. Distributional data can also be suggestive, however, as we shall see in the next section which describes the way compliments are used between New Zealand women and men, and discusses what this suggests about their function as politeness devices.

Who Pays Most Compliments?

Shall I compare thee to a summer's day?

The following analysis of the distribution of compliments between New Zealand women and men is based on a corpus of 484 naturally occurring compliments and compliment responses. The data was collected using an ethnographic approach (Holmes 1986), a method which derives from anthropology, and which has been advocated by Hymes over many years (1962, 1972, 1974), and very successfully adopted by researchers such as Nessa Wolfson (e.g. 1983, 1988). This approach combines some of the advantages of qualitative research with the generalisability gained from quantitative analysis. Compliments and their responses are noted down, together with relevant features of the participants, their relationship, and the context in which the compliment occurred. Using a number of people as data collectors, it was possible to gather a large number of compliments from a wide variety of contexts. Most, however, were produced by adult Pakeha New Zealanders, and it is therefore the compliment norms of this group which are being described.

The New Zealand compliments collected in this way revealed a very clear pattern. Women gave and received significantly more compliments than men did, as figure 1 illustrates. Women gave 68 percent of all the compliments recorded and received 74 percent of them. By contrast, compliments between males were relatively rare (only 9 percent), and, even taking account of females' compliments to males, men received overall considerably fewer compliments than women (only 26 percent). On this evidence, complimenting appears to be a speech behaviour occurring much more frequently in interactions involving women than men.[1]

Other researchers report similar patterns. Compliments are used more frequently by women than by men, and women are complimented more often than men in two different American studies (Wolfson 1983; Herbert 1990), and in research on compliments between Polish speakers (Lewandowska-Tomaszczyk 1989). This same pattern also turned up in a rather different context – that of written peer reviews (Johnson and Roen 1992). In this more information-orientated context which involved writing rather than speech, one would not have predicted gender contrasts. But even in writing women tended to use more compliments (or 'positive evaluative terms' to quote Johnson and Roen's precise measure) than men, though the differences were not quite statistically significant (Johnson and Roen 1992: 38).

These differences in the distribution of compliments between women and men have led to the suggestion that women and men may perceive the function of compliments differently. Women may regard compliments as primarily positively affective speech acts, for instance, expressing solidarity and positive politeness, while men may give greater weight to their referential meaning, as evaluative judgements, or to the potentially negative face-threatening features discussed above.

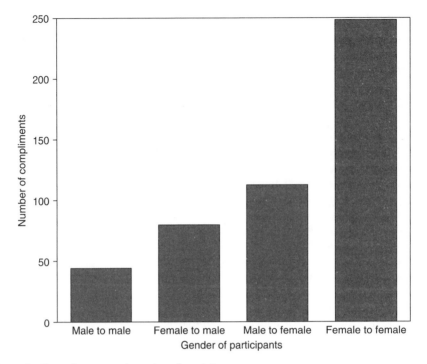

Figure 1   Compliments and gender of participants

Herbert (1990), for instance, draws a parallel between the lower frequency of compliments given by South Africans compared to Americans, and the lower frequency of compliments between men compared to women. Where compliments are frequent, he suggests, they are more likely to be functioning as solidarity tokens; where they are less frequent they are more likely to be referentially orientated or what he calls 'genuine expressions of admiration' (1990: 221). In support of this, he points to the fact that in his data the responses elicited by the rarer male–male compliments were more likely to be acceptances, reflecting the recipients' recognition of their evaluative function.

Example 9
Mick and Brent are neighbours. They meet at Brent's gate as he arrives home.
MICK: New car?
BRENT: Yeah.
MICK: Looks as if it will move.
BRENT: Yeah it goes well I must say.

Female compliments, however, were more likely to elicit alternative responses, such as shifting or reducing the force of the compliment.

Example 10
Friends arriving at youth club.
HELEN: What a neat outfit!
GERRY: It's actually quite old.

Responses which shift or reduce the compliment's force reflect the function of such compliments as tokens of solidarity, he suggests, since they indicate the recipient's desire to restore the social balance between speakers. There were no such gender differences in compliment responses in the New Zealand corpus, so this explanation cannot account for the less frequent use of compliments by New Zealand men.

It is possible, however, that men may more readily perceive compliments as face-threatening acts than women do. They may feel embarrassed or obligated by these unsolicited tokens of solidarity. The male threshold for what counts as an appropriate relationship to warrant mutual complimenting may differ from the female. Wolfson's 'bulge' theory (Wolfson 1988) suggested that certain linguistic behaviours, such as compliments, occurred more frequently between friends than between strangers or intimates. The bulge represented the higher frequency of such polite speech acts to friends and acquaintances. But the 'bulge' or the range of relationships within which compliments are acceptable politeness tokens may be much narrower for men than women. Female and male norms may differ. While one cannot be sure of the reasons for the imbalance in the distribution of compliments in women's and men's speech, it is widely agreed that women appear to use compliments mainly as a means of expressing rapport, while they do not appear to function so unambiguously for men.

This interpretation would be consistent with research which suggested that women's linguistic behaviour can often be broadly characterised as facilitative, affiliative, and cooperative, rather than competitive or control-orientated. In much of the research comparing patterns of male and female interaction, women's contributions have been described as 'other-orientated'. If women regard compliments as a means of expressing rapport and solidarity, the finding that they give more compliments than men is consistent with this orientation. Conversely, if men regard compliments as face-threatening or controlling devices, at least in some contexts, this could account for the male patterns observed.

In studies of compliments elsewhere, women also received more compliments than men (Wolfson 1984; Holmes 1988; Herbert 1990; Johnson and Roen 1992). Compliments between women are most frequent in all the studies, but it is noteworthy that men compliment women more often than they compliment other men. One explanation for this might be that women's positive attitude to compliments is recognised by both women and men in these speech communities. Perhaps people pay more compliments to women because they know women value them.

Alternatively, one might focus on why people do not compliment men as often as they do women. It appears to be much more acceptable and socially appropriate to compliment a woman than a man. One possible explanation based on an analysis of the power relations in society points to women's subordinate social position. Because compliments express social approval one might expect more of them to be addressed 'downwards' as socialising devices, or directed to the socially insecure to build their confidence. Nessa Wolfson (1984: 243) takes this view:

> women because of their role in the social order, are seen as appropriate recipients of all manner of social judgements in the form of compliments ... the way a woman is spoken to is, no matter what her status, a subtle and powerful way of perpetuating her subordinate role in society.

In other words, she suggests, compliments addressed to women have the same function as praise given to children, that is they serve as encouragement to continue with the approved behaviour. They could be regarded as patronising socialisation devices. Interestingly, even in classrooms it seems that females receive more praise or positive evaluations than males (e.g. de Bie 1987). It is possible that one of the reasons people do not compliment males so often as females is an awareness of men's ambivalence about compliments and of the possibility that men may regard some compliments as face-threatening acts, as embarrassing and discomfiting, or experience them as patronising strategies which put the speaker 'one-up'. If this is the case, then it is not surprising that the fewest compliments occur between men.

The way compliments are distributed suggests, then, that women and men may use and interpret them differently. While women appear to use them as positive politeness devices, and generally perceive them as ways of establishing and maintaining relationships, men may view them much more ambiguously as potentially face-threatening acts, or as having a more referential evaluative message which can serve a socialising function. In the next section an examination of the syntactic patterns of compliments will throw a little further light on these speculations.

How Do Women and Men Pay Compliments?

Examples 11–15
(11) You're looking nice today.

(12) What great kids!

(13) That's a beautiful skirt.

(14) I really love those curtains.

(15) Good goal.

Compliments are remarkably formulaic speech acts. Most draw on a very small number of lexical items and a very narrow range of syntactic patterns. Five or six adjectives, such as *good*, *nice*, *great*, *beautiful*, and *pretty* occurred in about two-thirds of the New Zealand compliments analysed. Wolfson noted the same pattern in her American corpus of nearly 700 compliments (1984: 236). And syntactic patterns prove similarly unoriginal. One of just four different syntactic patterns occurred in 78 percent of all the compliments in the New Zealand corpus (Holmes 1986). Similarly, three alternative syntactic patterns accounted for 85 percent of the compliments in the American corpus (Manes and Wolfson 1981). Compliments may be polite but they are rarely creative speech acts.

Nor are there many gender differences in this aspect of politeness behaviour. Most of the syntactic patterns and lexical items occurring in compliments seem to be fairly equally used by women and men, as table 1 demonstrates.

There are, however, two patterns which differ between women and men in an interesting way in the New Zealand corpus. Women used the rhetorical pattern *What (a) (ADJ) NP!* (e.g. *What lovely children!*) significantly more often than men. Men, by contrast, used the minimal pattern *(INT) ADJ (NP)* (e.g. *Great shoes*) significantly more often than women. The former is a syntactically marked formula, involving exclamatory word order and intonation; the latter, by contrast, reduces the syntactic pattern to its minimum elements. In other words, a rhetorical pattern such as *What a splendid hat!* can be regarded as emphatic and as increasing the force of the speech act. (D'Amico-Reisner (1983: 111–12) makes the same point about rhetorical questions as expressions of disapproval.) Using a rhetorical pattern for a compliment stresses its addressee- or interaction-orientated characteristics.

But the minimal pattern represented by *nice bike*, which was used more by men, tends to reduce the force of the compliment; it could be regarded as attenuating or hedging the compliment's impact. Interestingly, too, there were no examples of the more rhetorical

Table 1 Syntactic patterns of compliments and speaker gender

Syntactic formula*		Female %	Male %
1 NP BE (LOOKING) (INT) ADJ e.g. *That coat is really great*		42.1	40.0
2 I (INT) LIKE NP e.g. I *simply love that skirt*		17.8	13.1
3 PRO BE (a) (INT) ADJ NP e.g. *That's a very nice coat*		11.4	15.6
4 What (a) (ADJ) NP! e.g. *What lovely children!*		7.8	1.3
5 (INT) ADJ NP e.g. *Really cool ear-rings*		5.1	11.8
6 Isn't NP ADJ! e.g. *Isn't this food wonderful!*		1.5	0.6
	Subtotals	85.7	82.4
7 All other syntactic formulae		14.3	17.6
	Totals	100.0	100.0

* Following Manes and Wolfson (1981) copula BE represents any copula verb; LIKE represents any verb of liking: e.g. *love, enjoy, admire*; ADJ represents any semantically positive adjective; and INT represents any boosting intensifier: e.g. *really, very.*

pattern (*what lovely children!*) in the male–male interactions observed. So there seems good reason to associate this pattern with female complimenting behaviour.

Examples 16–18

(16) I love those socks. Where did you get them?

(17) I like those glasses.

(18) *Referring to a paper written by the addressee.*
I really liked the ending. It was very convincing.

Studies of compliments by other researchers provide support for this suggestion that women's compliments tend to be expressed with linguistically stronger forms than men's. Having analysed over one thousand American compliments, Herbert (1990: 206) reported that only women used the stronger form *I love X* (compared to *I like X*), and they used it most often to other women. In written peer reviews, Johnson and Roen (1992) noted that women used significantly more intensifiers (such as *really, very, particularly*) than men did, and, as in Herbert's data, they intensified their compliments most when writing to other women.

These observations provide further support for the point that it is important in analysing hedging and boosting behaviour to examine the particular types of speech acts which are being boosted, and, in particular, to note whether the speech act is intended and perceived as affectively positive or negative. It is possible to strengthen or alternatively to reduce the force of a positively affective speech act such as a compliment in a variety of ways. By their selections among a narrow range of syntactic formulae and lexical items, men more often choose to attenuate the force of their compliments, while women tend to increase their compliments' force. This supports the suggestion that women expect addressees to interpret compliments as expressions of solidarity rather than as face-threatening speech acts. By contrast, men's tendency to attenuate compliments supports the proposal that men perhaps perceive compliments as less unambiguously positive in effect. In other words, the differences which have been noted in the distribution of syntactic and lexical patterns between women and men is consistent with the view that women tend to regard compliments as primarily positively affective acts while men may feel more ambivalent about using them.

Examples 19 and 20
(19) You're looking stunning.

(20) I especially liked the way you used lots of examples.

In general, it is also true that women use more personalised compliment forms than men, while men prefer impersonal forms. There is some evidence for this in the New Zealand data, as table 1 illustrates, but it is even more apparent in Herbert's (1990) American corpus, and Johnson and Roen's (1992) written peer reviews. Well over half (60 percent) of the compliments offered by men in Herbert's corpus were impersonal forms, for example, compared to only a fifth of those used by women. By contrast women used many more forms with a personal focus (Herbert includes both *you* and *I* as personalised forms). Almost 83 percent of female–female interactions used personalised forms compared to only 32 percent of male–male compliments (Herbert 1990: 205). The peer reviews analysed by Johnson and Roen revealed a similar pattern. The women used more personal involvement strategies, especially to other women (1992: 44).

This evidence echoes the patterns noted in research on verbal interaction, which suggested that women tend to prefer personalised and expressive forms as opposed to impersonalised forms (see Kalcik 1975; Swacker 1979; Aries 1982), and supports a view of women's style as more interpersonal, affective and interaction-orientated compared to the impersonal, instrumental and content-orientated style more typical of male interaction (e.g. Piliavin and Martin 1978; Baird and Bradley 1979; Preisler 1986; Aries 1976, 1987; Schick Case 1988; Tannen 1990). So, where the linguistic features of women's compliments differ from men's, the differences tend to support the proposition that women regard compliments as other-orientated positive politeness strategies which they assume will be welcome to addressees, whereas for men, and especially between men, their function may not be so clear-cut.

What Do Women and Men Compliment Each Other About?

Examples 21–24
(21) *Appearance compliment.*
      I like your outfit Beth. I think I could wear that.

(22) *Ability/performance compliment.*
      Wow you played well today Davy.

(23) *Possessions compliment.*
      Is that your flash red sports car?

(24) *Personality/friendliness.*
      I'm very lucky to have such a good friend.

Women and men tend to give compliments about different things. To be heard as a compliment an utterance must refer to something which is positively valued by the participants and attributed to the addressee. This would seem to permit an infinite range of possible topics for compliments, but in fact the vast majority of compliments refer to just a

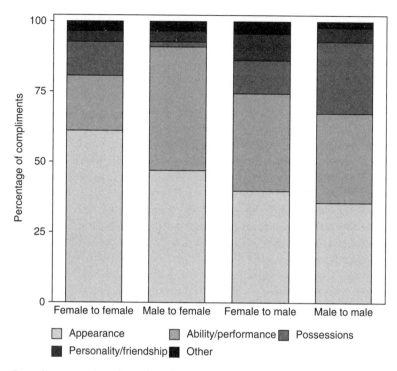

Figure 2   Compliment topic and gender of participants

few broad topics: appearance, ability or performance, possessions, and some aspect of personality or friendliness (Manes 1983; Holmes 1986). In fact, compliments on some aspect of the addressee's appearance or ability accounted for 81 percent of the New Zealand data.

Within these general patterns, there is a clearly observable tendency for women to be complimented on their appearance more often than men. Over half (57 percent) of all the compliments women received in the New Zealand data related to aspects of their appearance. And women give compliments on appearance more than men do, so that 61 percent of all the compliments between women related to appearance compared to only 36 percent of the compliments between males, as figure 2 demonstrates. Men, by contrast, appear to prefer to compliment other men, but not women, on possessions.

Provided it is not sarcastic, a compliment on someone's appearance such as *you're looking wonderful* is difficult to interpret as anything other than a positively polite utterance. An appearance compliment is clearly an expression of solidarity, a positively affective speech act. The predominance of this type of compliment in women's interactions is consistent with the view that women use compliments primarily for their positively polite function. Compliments on possessions, on the other hand, are much more vulnerable to interpretation as face-threatening acts since, as illustrated in example 6 above, there is the possibility that the complimenter will be heard as expressing desire for or envy of the object referred to. To this extent, men's greater use of these compliments reinforces the suggestion that they are more likely to perceive and experience compliments as potential face-threatening acts. In other words, if possession-orientated compliments are experienced as more face-threatening than others – which seems feasible since they focus on things which are in theory transferable from complimenter to recipient – then men certainly use more potentially face-threatening compliments than women.

Compliments on appearance seem to cause some men embarrassment.

Example 25
Middle-aged male to elderly male at a concert.
MALE 1:   I haven't seen you since the Festival.
MALE 2:   We haven't been here much since the Festival.
MALE 1:   You've got a new tie in the meantime.
MALE 2:   It's a very old one actually.
MALE 1:   It's quite splendid anyway.
MALE 2:   (*Looks extremely embarrassed.*) No no. What have you been up
           to anyway?

The recipient's response to the first somewhat indirect compliment is a disclaimer, while his response to the second overt compliment is acute embarrassment followed by a rejection. Wolfson comments (1983: 93) that appearance compliments are remarkably rare between American males. It seems that in America compliments on appearance may be experienced by males as very big face-threatening acts. And while New Zealand men do give and receive compliments on their appearance, there are a number of examples where compliments on their appearance clearly caused surprise.

Example 26
Two colleagues meet at coffee machine at work.
BILL: You're looking very smart today.
TOM: (*Looking very embarrassed.*) I'm meeting Mary and her mother for lunch.

Appearance compliments are clearly not the common currency of politeness between men that they are between women.
A number of men have commented that at least one of the reasons for the scarcity of appearance compliments between men is fear of the possible imputation of homosexuality.

> To compliment another man on his hair, his clothes, or his body is an *extremely* face threat-
> ening thing to do, both for speaker and hearer. It has to be very carefully done in order not
> to send the wrong signals. (Britain, personal communication)

In support of this David Britain provided the following example.

Example 27
Male flatmate, Alex, to Dave, referring to the latter's new haircut.
Jesus Christ tell me who did that and I'll go and beat him up for you!
Laughter. Then
No it's OK.
Finally, a week later.
That's a good haircut.

In this case, it took a week for Alex to get round to saying he liked Dave's haircut, that is to pay a clearly identifiable compliment on his appearance to another male.
Figure 2 also shows that nearly half (44 percent of all) the compliments given by males to females were compliments on abilities, skills or performance. Women do not

compliment men or other women so often on this topic. This raises the question of whether a compliment can act as a power play. As mentioned above, praise is often directed downwards. A compliment could be experienced as patronising if the recipient felt it was given as encouragement rather than as a token of solidarity. Compliments on skills and abilities are particularly vulnerable to being interpreted in this way.

Example 28
Husband to wife about her painting of a wall.
You've made a pretty good job of that.

One has the feeling that the husband is a little surprised his wife has done so well and is patting her on the head approvingly. The tendency for men to compliment women on their skills and abilities may reflect women's subordinate social status in the society as a whole, as well as, perhaps, a male tendency to perceive compliments as means of conveying referential or evaluative, as well as affective, messages. The next section will illustrate that the way compliments are used to those of different status provides further support for such an interpretation.

Can a Compliment Be a Power Play?

People pay most compliments to their equals. As Wolfson puts it, 'the overwhelming majority of all compliments are given to people of the same age and status as the speaker' (1983: 91). New Zealanders' compliments followed this pattern (see also Knapp et al. 1984; Herbert 1990). Almost 80 percent of the corpus consisted of compliments between status equals. Compliments typically occur in informal interactions between friends.

The distribution of the small proportion of compliments that occurred between people of different status is interesting, however, because it throws further light on the question of the functions of compliments for women and men.

If it is true, as Wolfson suggests, that the fact that women receive more compliments than men reflects their subordinate status in the society as a whole, then one would also expect more compliments to subordinates than to superiors, regardless of gender. Wolfson's American data evidently confirmed this expectation. She comments that 'the great majority of compliments which occur in interaction between status unequals are given by the person in the higher position' (1983: 91).

Example 29
Manager to her secretary.
You are such a treasure Carol. What would I do without you!

Another American study, which was based on self-report data rather than observation, reports the same pattern (Knapp et al. 1984). Most compliments occurred between status equals, but when there was a status imbalance, higher status participants complimented more often than lower status ones. In other words, people seem generally less willing to compliment someone of higher rather than lower status. Neither of these studies examined the interaction of gender and status, however.

In the New Zealand data, as mentioned, the great majority of compliments occurred between status equals. There were no significant differences in the numbers addressed to those of higher rather than lower status. But, interestingly, it was found that higher status females were twice as likely to receive compliments as higher status men.

Example 30
Secretary to boss.
That's a lovely dress.

If high status generally reduces the likelihood that one will receive compliments, then this data indicates it reduces it less with women than with men. This is true whether the complimenter is male or female, as can be seen in figure 3. In fact, despite the general pattern that women pay more compliments than men, males are even more likely to compliment women of higher status than women are.

Example 31
Male caretaker to woman executive as she leaves work.
You're a hard working woman Mrs Thomas. I hope they pay you well.

This is further support for the view that it is more acceptable to compliment high status women than high status men.

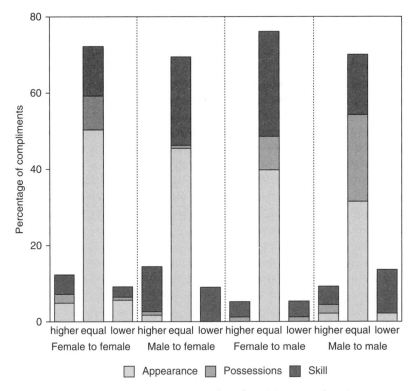

Figure 3   Compliments by relative status and gender of participants and topic

Perhaps higher status women are perceived as more receptive to compliments (especially from men) than their male counterparts, because in the society as a whole women are generally regarded as socially subordinate, and less powerful and influential than men. This may legitimate behaviour that might otherwise be considered presumptuous. Tannen's (1990: 69) suggestion that giving praise 'frames the speaker as one-up' is again relevant here. Higher status males may be perceived as high risk addressees by both genders. But female gender apparently overrides high status in determining how risky a compliment is perceived as being. Alternatively, perhaps women are seen as more approachable because they value solidarity more highly than status, and tend to reduce rather than emphasise status differences (Troemel-Ploetz 1992).

This interpretation of the patterns is consistent with the suggestion that men are more likely to experience a compliment as a face-threatening act whereas women are more likely to perceive compliments as positively affective speech acts, regardless of relative status. If true, this would be likely to encourage complimenters to address compliments upwards to women, and discourage compliments to higher status men where the risk of offence would be too great. Note the male's discouraging reaction in the following example.

Example 32
Young woman to Minister's personal secretary at a reception.
WOMAN: What an interesting job you have. You must be very bright.
MAN: I just do my job.

The young woman was lively and friendly. The tone of the man's reply made it clear he thought her presumptuous. Complimenting a higher status male is obviously a risky business. There is further support for this interpretation when we look at differences in the way women and men use compliments on appearance, in particular. As figures 2 and 3 illustrate, appearance was the most common topic of compliments in this corpus, as in others. Figure 3 shows that appearance was also by far the most frequent topic of compliments between equals (30–50 percent of all compliments). But status differences reduced the likelihood of appearance compliments quite dramatically, especially in cross-sex relationships. Fewer than 2 percent of the compliments analysed were appearance compliments between cross-sex pairs of different status – a clear indication of the link between appearance compliments and solidarity-based relationships.

On the other hand, appearance compliments are the most obvious examples of compliments which are likely to be interpreted or experienced differently by women and men, as discussed above, and illustrated in the following example.

Example 33
Office receptionist to high-status male whom she knew only slightly.
RECEPTIONIST: That's a nice suit.
MALE: Mr Avery's expecting me I think.

The man ignores the compliment completely. The receptionist was almost certainly being positively polite and intended her compliment as a solidarity signal. But an appearance compliment is vulnerable to being interpreted as presumptuous when addressed by a subordinate to a superior of either gender. If men also tend to regard compliments as potential face-threatening acts and find compliments on their appearance particularly discomfiting, the negative effect will be even greater.

The patterns revealed by the distribution of compliments in this corpus suggest, then, that women and men may use and interpret compliments differently. While women seem to use compliments to establish, maintain and strengthen relationships, they are much less clearly positive politeness devices for men, where they need to be used with care – especially to other men – since they can be face-threatening. The fact that men pay more compliments to women than they do to men may indicate that men are aware of the value of compliments in women's eyes – a solidarity-based explanation. Alternatively, this pattern may reflect the fact that men perceive compliments as appropriate encourage-ment or evaluative feedback to subordinates. In other words, male compliments to women may reflect the different social power positions of women and men.

[…]

Conclusion

In concluding this paper it is worth emphasising the range of functions any utterance may perform. The detailed analysis of compliments illustrated well that the 'same' utter-ance may simultaneously convey a range of meanings. The 'same' utterance may also be used and interpreted differently by different social groups, including women and men. Just as a gift expresses solidarity and appreciation in some cultures, but is a form of one-upping a rival in others (Tannen 1990: 295–6), so at least some compliments may be accepted as tokens of solidarity by women but experienced as an embarrassment by men. The same is likely to be true of other potential positive politeness devices. They are likely to be used and interpreted very differently in different contexts and cultures.

On the basis of a number of different aspects of the distribution of compliments in the New Zealand corpus, I have suggested that women tend to perceive and use compli-ments as positively affective speech acts and expressions of solidarity, whereas the responses of men may be more ambivalent. It seems possible that in some situations, at least, and with some types of compliment in particular, men may be more likely to inter-pret compliments as face-threatening acts. The pattern I have suggested provides an intriguing mirror-image of Kuiper's (1991) analysis of the way insults which would cer-tainly be experienced as face-threatening acts by women, appear to perform a solidarity-maintaining function for at least some men. Kuiper describes the verbal interaction of members of a rugby team in the locker room before a match. The team members insult and abuse each other, using terms of address such as 'wanker', 'fuck-face' and the more overtly sexist 'fucking old woman', and 'girl's blouse'. For this group 'sexual humiliation is used as a means of creating group solidarity through the loss of face the individuals who belong to the group suffer' (1991: 200). (See also Labov 1972 on ritual insults among Black gang members and Dundes et al. 1972 on Turkish boys' verbal duelling.) Insults function for these men as expressions of solidarity, whereas the data in this chap-ter has suggested women prefer compliments for this function.

It also seems possible that the way men use compliments to women, in particular, may reflect the subordinate status of women in the society generally. Like endearments, com-pliments gain their force from the context of the relationship in which they are used. When used non-reciprocally by superiors to subordinates, these may underline patterns of societal power which place women in a clearly subordinate position to men. When used between equals and friends, on the other hand, and especially female equals and friends, a compliment could be considered a quintessential example of a positive polite-ness strategy.

Note

1 As noted in Holmes (1988), the predominance of females among the data collectors was a potential source of bias. The figures nevertheless suggest that even with equal numbers of female and male data collectors, compliments between females will be more frequent than compliments between males, though the imbalance would not be so dramatic.

References

Aries, E. J. (1976) 'Interaction patterns and themes of male, female and mixed groups'. *Small Group Behaviour*, 7, 1, 7–18.

Aries, E. J. (1982) 'Verbal and non-verbal behaviour in single-sex and mixed-sex groups: are traditional sex roles changing?' *Psychological Reports*, 51, 127–34.

Aries, E. J. (1987) 'Gender and communication', pp. 149–76 in P. Shaver and C. Hendrick (eds) *Sex and Gender*. Newbury Park, CA: Sage.

Baird, J. E. and Bradley, P. H. (1979) 'Styles of management and communication: a comparative study of men and women'. *Communication Monographs*, 46, 101–11.

Brown, P. and Levinson, S. (1987) *Politeness: Some Universals in Language Use*. Cambridge: Cambridge University Press.

D'Amico-Reisner, L. (1983) 'An analysis of the surface structure of disapproval exchanges', pp. 103–15 in N. Wolfson and E. Judd (eds) *Sociolinguistics and Language Acquisition*. Rowley, MA: Newbury House.

De Bie, M. L. W. (1987) 'Classroom interaction: survival of the fittest', pp. 76–88 in D. Brouwer and D. de Haan (eds) *Women's Language, Socialisation and Self-Image*. Dordrecht: Foris.

Dundes, A., Leach, J. W. and Özkök, B. (1972) 'The strategy of Turkish boys' verbal dueling rhymes', pp. 130–60 in J. J. Gumperz and D. Hymes (eds) *Directions in Sociolinguistics*. New York: Holt, Rinehart & Winston.

Herbert, R. K. (1989) 'The ethnography of English compliments and compliment responses: a contrastive sketch', pp. 3–35 in W. Olesky (ed.) *Contrastive Pragmatics*. Amsterdam: John Benjamins.

Herbert, R. K. (1990) 'Sex-based differences in compliment behaviour'. *Language in Society*, 19, 201–24.

Holmes, J. (1986) 'Compliments and compliment responses in New Zealand English'. *Anthropological Linguistics*, 28, 4, 485–508.

Holmes, J. (1988) 'Paying compliments: a sex-preferred positive politeness strategy'. *Journal of Pragmatics*, 12, 3, 445–65.

Hymes, D. (1962) 'The ethnography of speaking', pp. 15–53 in T. Gladwin and W. Sturtevant (eds) *Anthropology and Human Behaviour*. Washington, DC: Anthropological Society of Washington.

Hymes, D. (1972) 'On communicative competence', pp. 269–93 in J. B. Pride and J. Holmes (eds) *Sociolinguistics*. Harmondsworth: Penguin.

Hymes, D. (1974) 'Ways of speaking', pp. 433–51 in R. Bauman and J. Sherzer (eds) *Explorations in the Ethnography of Speaking*. Cambridge: Cambridge University Press.

Johnson, D. M. and Roen, D. H. (1992) 'Complimenting and involvement in peer reviews: gender variation'. *Language in Society*, 21, 1, 27–57.

Kalcik, S. (1975) ' "… like Ann's gynaecologist or the time I was almost raped" – personal narratives in women's rap groups'. *Journal of American Folklore*, 88, 3–11.

Kissling, E. A. (1991) 'Street harassment: the language of sexual terrorism'. *Discourse and Society*, 2, 4, 451–60.

Kissling, E. A. and Kramarae, C. (1991) ' "Stranger compliments": the interpretation of street remarks'. *Women's Studies in Communication*, Spring, 77–95.

Knapp, M. L., Hopper, R. and Bell, R. (1984) 'Compliments: a descriptive taxonomy'. *Journal of Communications*, 34, 4, 12–31.

Kuiper, K. (1991) 'Sporting formulae in New Zealand English: two models of male solidarity', pp. 200–9 in J. Cheshire (ed.) *English Around the World: Sociolinguistic Perspectives*. Cambridge: Cambridge University Press.

Labov, W. (1972) 'Rules for ritual insults', pp. 265–314 in T. Kochman (ed.) *Rappin' and Stylin' Out*. Chicago: University of Illinois Press.

Leech, G. N. (1983) *Principles of Pragmatics*. London: Longman.

Lewandowska-Tomaszczyk, B. (1989) 'Praising and complimenting', pp. 73–100 in W. Olesky (ed.) *Contrastive Pragmatics*. Amsterdam: John Benjamins.

Manes, J. (1983) 'Compliments: a mirror of cultural values', pp. 96–102 in N. Wolfson and E. Judd (eds) *Sociolinguistics and Language Acquisition*. Rowley, MA: Newbury House.

Manes, J. and Wolfson, N. (1981) 'The compliment formula', pp. 115–32 in F. Coulmas (ed.) *Conversational Routine*. The Hague: Mouton.

Piliavin, J. A. and Martin, R. R. (1978) 'The effects of the sex composition of groups on style of social interaction'. *Sex Roles*, 4, 281–96.

Preisler, B. (1986) *Linguistic Sex Roles in Conversation*. Berlin: Mouton de Gruyter.

Schick Case, S. (1988) 'Cultural differences, not deficiencies: an analysis of managerial women's language', pp. 41–63 in S. Rose and L. Larwood (eds) *Women's Careers: Pathways and Pitfalls*. New York: Praeger.

Swacker, M. (1979) 'Women's verbal behaviour at learned and professional conferences', pp. 155–60 in B. Dubois and I. Crouch (eds) *The Sociology of the Languages of American Women*. San Antonio, TX: Trinity University.

Tannen, D. (1990) *You Just Don't Understand: Women and Men in Conversation*. New York: William Morrow.

Troemel-Ploetz, S. (1992) 'The construction of conversational equality by women', pp. 581–9 in K. Hall, M. Bucholtz and B. Moonwomon (eds) *Locating Power. Proceedings of the Second Berkeley Women and Language Conference* (4 and 5 April 1992), vol 2. Berkeley, CA: Berkeley Women and Language Group, University of California.

Wierzbicka, A. (1987) *English Speech Acts Verbs: A Semantic Dictionary*. New York: Academic Press.

Wolfson, N. (1981) 'Compliments in cross-cultural perspective'. *TESOL Quarterly*, 15, 2, 117–24.

Wolfson, N. (1983) 'An empirically based analysis of complimenting in American English', pp. 82–95 in N. Wolfson and E. Judd (eds) *Sociolinguistics and Language Acquisition*. Rowley, MA: Newbury House.

Wolfson, N. (1984) ' "Pretty is as pretty does": a speech act view of sex roles'. *Applied Linguistics*, 5, 3, 236–44.

Wolfson, N. (1988) 'The bulge: a theory of speech behaviour and social distance', pp. 21–38 in J. Fine (ed.) *Second Language Discourse: A Textbook of Current Research*. Norwood, NJ: Ablex.

8

Cooperation and Competition Across Girls' Play Activities

Marjorie Harness Goodwin

Source: A. Dundas Todd and S. Fisher (eds), *Gender and Discourse: The Power of Talk*. Norwood, NJ: Ablex (1988), pp. 55–94. Reprinted with permission of ABC-Clio LLC.

In an attempt to characterize women as speaking "in a different voice," recent research on female interaction patterns has tended to examine those features of female communication which are clearly different from those of males to the exclusion of those which females and males share in common. For example, cooperative aspects of female language usage have been examined (e.g., Brown, 1980; Maltz and Borker, 1982 [reprinted in Part VIII of this volume]), while ways in which disagreement may be expressed have been largely ignored. Investigations of girls' play have also neglected to analyze the full range of female interactional competencies. According to Piaget (1965: p. 77), Lever (1976: p. 482), and Gilligan (1982: pp. 9–20) the lack of complex rule structure and forms of direct competitiveness in girls' games (as for example are found in marbles (Piaget, 1965) or team sports (Lever, 1976)) limits their opportunities for practicing negotiational skills. [...]

Detailed ethnographic study of girls in play situations (Goodwin, 1985; Hughes, 1995) presents a different view of girls' competencies. In my studies of urban black girls I found that, with respect to boys, while some of girls' activities are conducted with what appears to be minimal disagreement or competition (Goodwin, 1980b), others provide for extensive negotiation (Goodwin, 1980a; Goodwin, 1985; Goodwin and Goodwin, 1987). The forms of social organization which girls select to carry out their play vary across different types of play activities. In order to investigate such variation, this paper focuses on a single type of speech sequence, yet the primary one through which children achieve organization in domains of play: sequences of "directives" or speech actions that try to get another to do something (Austin, 1962), and their responses. Directives will be examined within two play contexts – activities in which children are accomplishing a task and pretend play – as well as within cross-sex and caretaking situations. In this way it will be possible to examine how girls' directives and social organization take different forms across various activities.

For comparative purposes I will first summarize findings regarding how boys conduct themselves in a specific task activity, making slingshots and organizing a slingshot fight.[1] The types of hierarchical differences they establish between participants while performing a task permeate all aspects of their peer activities (comparing one another, arguing, storytelling, etc.). Next I will analyze how girls interact as they undertake a comparable task activity – making rings from the rims of glass bottles. In contrast to the boys, when girls organize tasks they select a more egalitarian form of social structure, avoiding the creation of distinctions between participants. Such a form of organization is consistent with the way in which they normally conduct their daily interactions with one another. When the full repertoire of female interaction patterns is investigated it can be seen that girls exhibit ways of formulating and sequencing their talk which display both cooperative and competitive forms. For example, in the activities of repairing utterances or disagreeing with one another girls use argumentative speech forms shared by the boys (Goodwin, 1983; Goodwin and Goodwin, 1987). Girls do not, however, customarily use bald commands, insults and threats – actions which are commonplace among the boys. Such actions are reserved for situations in which girls sanction the behavior of one of their members. Nonetheless the forms of accounts girls use in directive sequences express concerns that are distinctive from those used by the boys. Across different domains, girls exhibit a range of ways of executing decisions about courses of action and evolve distinctive forms of social organization.

Fieldwork and Background for the Study

The present study is based on fieldwork among a group of children in a black working class neighborhood of West Philadelphia whom I encountered during a walk around my neighborhood. I observed them for a year and a half as they played on the street, focussing on how the children used language within interaction to organize their everyday activities. The children (whom I will call the Maple Street group) ranged in age from four through 14 and spent much of the time in four same age/sex groups (older and younger girls and older and younger boys). Here I will be concerned principally with children in the older age group, from 10 to 13. As they played on the street after school, on weekends and during the summer months I audiotaped their conversation. In gathering data I did not focus on particular types of events that I had previously decided were theoretically important (for example stories or rhymes) but instead tried to observe and record as much of what the children did as possible, no matter how mundane it might seem. Moreover I tried to avoid influencing what the children were doing. The methods I used to gather data about the children were thus quite different from those characteristically used in psychological and sociological studies of children's behavior; in such studies efforts are typically made to systematically collect particular types of information deemed to be theoretically important in a carefully controlled fashion. Rather than being based on a laboratory model, the methodology I used was ethnographic, and designed to capture as accurately as possible the structure of events in the children's world as they unfolded in the ordinary settings where they habitually occurred. Therefore I did not have to rely on what subjects or interviewees might tell a researcher and could observe the conduct of children in a range of situations.

Alternative Forms of Directives

The ways in which speakers format their directives and sequence turns to them provide for a range of possible types of social arrangements between participants. Some directive/response sequences display an orientation towards a differentiation between participants, and result in asymmetrical forms of relationships. Others, by way of contrast, display an orientation towards seeking to minimize distinctions between participants and result in more egalitarian or symmetrical arrangements of social relationships. Within different clusters there may also be a division of labor with respect to the delivery of certain types of moves. This has consequences for the type of social organization a group evolves.

Directives have been discussed as forms of "social control acts" ("moves in which there is a clear intention to influence the activities of the partner" (Ervin-Tripp, 1982: p. 29)) and "persuasive talk" (Cook-Gumperz, 1981). One way in which directives may be formatted is in a very straightforward or "aggravated" (Labov and Fanshel, 1977: pp. 84–6) way, as imperatives (i.e., "Do X!"). Alternatively, directives may take more softened or "mitigated" (Labov and Fanshel 1977: pp. 84–6) forms, as requests ("Could you please do X?").
[...]

The Organization of a Task Among Boys

Making slingshots from wire coat hangers is a pastime which could be organized in a variety of different ways. The slingshot is an individual instrument, and, in theory, play with it could be construed as an individual activity in which all participants fend for themselves, the only preparation being that each have a slingshot and an adequate supply of "slings." Among the boys of Maple Street, however, the activity of making and using slingshots became organized into a competition between two separate "sides" or teams (not unlike those in football or basketball) with a hierarchical organization of participants on each team.[2] The slingshot fight itself was preceded by an extended preparation period during which, not only were weapons and slings made, but the organization of the group was also negotiated. All of the elements in this process, such as the allocation of necessary tools, the spatial organization of participants, where the preparation would occur, who would provide materials, who had rights to resources, when the activity was to move from stage to stage, what battle strategy would consist of, etc., became the focus for status negotiations between participants.

The formatting of leaders' directives and accounts in a boys' task activity

One key resource that was used in negotiation among the boys about their relative status was alternative formats for asking or ordering someone else to do something. A typical way that one party attempted to display or establish his position with respect to another party was by making directives in the form of explicit commands to that party rather than as hints, suggestions, or indirect requests. In organizing the slingshot session the team leaders, Michael and Huey, constructed their directives using the imperative form ("Do X!"). In the terminology developed by Labov and Fanshel (1977: pp. 84–6) they thus choose relatively "aggravated" or explicit directive forms. The following data are transcribed according to the system developed by Jefferson and described in Sacks, Schegloff, and Jefferson (1974: pp. 731–3). [A simplified version of this transcription system appears in Transcription Conventions 1 (p. x).]

(1) MICHAEL: *All* right. Gimme some rubber bands.
      CHOPPER: ((*Giving rubber bands to Michael*)) Oh.

(2) HUEY: Go downstairs. I don't care *what* you say you aren't – you ain't no good so
                 go down*stairs.*
     BRUCE: ((*Moves down the steps*))

(3)   ((*Regarding coat hanger wire*))
     MICHAEL: Give it to me man. Where's yours at. Throw that piece of shit out.
     CHOPPER: ((*Gives Michael his cut-off piece of hanger*))

The turn containing the imperative arguing for the speaker's relative control vis-à-vis the
recipient may be accompanied by various types of "semantic aggravators" (Becker, 1982:
p. 8) i.e., threats, phrases demanding immediate action, etc., which display the speaker's
view of the recipient's subordinate status. As is shown in examples 2 and 3, negative
descriptions of the other (e.g., "you ain't no good") or of his objects (e.g., referring to one
of Chopper's slings as "shit") may accompany the imperative to further denigrate the
recipient's character. In response to these sequences, recipients comply with the requests.
Of course other types of next responses, such as counters, are possible next moves, as in
lines 2, 4, and 7 of the following:

(4)   ((*Michael asks for pliers*))
     1 MICHAEL: Gimme the thing.
     2 POOCHIE:→   Wait a minute. I gotta chop it.
     3 MICHAEL: Come on.
     4 POOCHIE:→   I gotta chop it.
     5 MICHAEL: Come on Poochie. You gonna be with
     6   them? Give it to me. I'll show you.
     7 POOCHIE:→   I already had it before you.
     8 MICHAEL: So? I brought them out here. They
     9   mine. So I use em when I feel like it.

In this sequence Michael responds to counters with actions which argue for his ultimate
control of the situation. For example in line 5 through his question "You gonna be with
them?" Michael counters Poochie by threatening to make Poochie be on another team. In
lines 8–9 Michael refutes the relevance of Poochie's counter by arguing that he has ultimate jurisdiction concerning the allocation of resources. In other instances when players
counter Michael or Huey's imperatives, the leaders display their authority by reminding
subordinates that they can also make them leave their property (i.e., "Get off my steps."
or "I'll tell you to get out of *here* if I *want* you to.").

The imperative forms of the leaders' actions differ from the ways in which other players formulate actions to Michael and Huey. Requests for information such as "Can I
have some hangers?" or "Can me and Robert play if Robert be on Huey's team?" are
used in actions to team leaders. In contrast to the actions which Michael and Huey use
towards their teammates, requests for information display deference towards the
addressee and permit options in the way in which the recipient should respond. When
answering such mitigated types of directives, those assuming leadership positions do not
comply with the proposed actions, as in examples 1–3, but instead provide arbitrary definitions of the situation (example 5), return imperatives (example 6), and flat refusals
(example 7):

(5) BRUCE: Can me and Robert play if Robert be on Huey's team?
     MICHAEL: IT'S ALREADY TOO *MANY* OF US.

(6)   ((*Tokay takes a hanger*))
    TOKAY: Can I have some hangers?
    MICHAEL: Put that thing *back*!

(7) ROBBY: Michael could I be on your side?
    MICHAEL: *Heck* no!

A form of asymmetry is established through the alternative ways in which directives and their responses are formatted. While Michael delivers aggravated actions getting compliance in return, his teammates issue mitigated directives receiving counters as next moves.

Michael's actions are not only direct and aggravated but also arbitrary. To see the import of this it is important to note that not all direct imperatives constitute degrading actions to a recipient. Thus in many cases the situation of the moment itself warrants the use of directive formats that in other circumstances would be seen as aggravated. For example in the midst of a game of jump rope girls yell "Watch out!" as a car comes, or "Go ahead Nettie!" to urge a player to take her turn. Similarly, imperatives may be appropriate in work settings where differences in rank call for the subordination of one party to the other (Ervin-Tripp, 1976: p. 29). However, the directives Michael issues display no obvious reason why certain tasks need to be performed "right now" except for his own whims. The use of "need statements" (Ervin-Tripp, 1976: p. 29), "desire statements" (Ervin-Tripp, 1982: p. 30) or "explicit statements" (Ervin-Tripp, 1982: p. 35) has been argued (Garvey, 1975: pp. 52, 60; Ervin-Tripp, 1976: p. 29) to constitute among the most aggravated ways of formulating a directive. For example:

(8) MICHAEL: PL:IERS. I WANT THE PLIERS! Man y'all gonna have to get y'all *own*
                   wire cutters if *this* the way y'all gonna be.
    NATE: Okay. Okay.

(9)
→ MICHAEL: Everybody. Now I don't need all y'all down here in this little space. Get
                  back *up* there. Get *up* there. Now! Get back up there please.

In brief, through the way in which Michael constructs his directives he proposes his superior status with respect to others, and others' inferior positioning vis-à-vis him. He uses actions which imply that he independently can define for others how the task should proceed and how their actions can be interpreted. In response others assuming an inferior position with respect to him often provide compliance through either a nonvocal carrying out of the requested action (as occurred in examples 1–3) and/or signals of vocal agreement (as in examples 1 and 8).

Instructing others

There is one aspect of Michael's performance as team leader – instructing his subordinates – in which the use of aggravated social control acts appears less arbitrary. The job of teaching teammates how to make slings makes use of a participation framework common to other teaching situations. Instructing implies an asymmetrical relationship of participants, with the teacher providing actions such as getting the attention of the subordinates, giving them information, and criticizing them (Cazden, et al., 1979: p. 210). Assertions, such as "See this how we gonna do ours." in example 10 below may stand for speech acts with directive force. Frequently, as in the next two

examples, an account for why the stated course of action should be pursued is provided: either that the leader's way is a superior way of executing the task, as in example
10, or simply that the leader has a particular plan for how the activity should take
place (example 12):

(10)   MICHAEL: See this how we gonna do ours. It's a lot better and faster. Bend that side
              and then we bend this side too.

(11)   MICHAEL: Look I wanna show you how to do it so when you get the things you
              gonna know how to do it.

(12)   MICHAEL: I know what we gonna do. Poochie, a- after I cut these up all y'all- all y'all
              gonna cut these things off and Poochie gonna bend them and I cut em.
              And I just chop em. And then y'all pick em up. And they be ours.

Michael, as leader of his group, not only prescribes the working procedures and division
of labor for sling making; in addition he dictates team strategy:

(13)   1   MICHAEL: Now. Re*mem*ber what I sai:d. And
       2   don't try to shoot till
       3   TOKAY: Like- like they in sight?
       4   MICHAEL: That's ri̇ght.
       5   TOKAY: What if they ain't.
       6   MICHAEL: But if they- if they hidin in some
       7   bushes, don't you shoot. = You let them
       8   waste theirs. Count for the man how
       9   many he waste. Then after he waste as
       10   many as you got you let him shoot his.
       11   But then you let him waste some more.

As is clearly illustrated by this example, Michael's role as leader of the peer group is ratified through the types of actions, such as Tokay's requests for information (lines 3 and
5), which are initiated towards him. Because Michael is felt to be in control of knowledge regarding the craft, his opinion and assistance is summoned repetitively:

(14)   ((*Michael illustrates bending and cutting coat hangers*))
       MICHAEL: You bend it over like that and when- when you finish I'll show you how
              to just do these.
→   TOKAY: After it break, stomp down?
       MICHAEL: Just clap em.

(15)   MICHAEL: After I cut these up
→   POOCHIE: Who turn is it.
       CHOPPER: Mine. Mine. *Uh* uh. Ain't it my turn Michael,
       MICHAEL: ((*nods yes*))
       CHOPPER: See?

[...]
    As proprietors of the house where play occurs both Michael and Huey can exert con-
siderable leverage in getting boys to do what they want them to do, in that they can
threaten them with having to leave the premises:
[...]

(16)   ((*Michael moves into Poochie's space*))
       POOCHIE: Get outa here.
→   MICHAEL: Hell it's my house.
       POOCHIE: You always gettin in the way. You talkin about we can't even come up there.
       HUEY: That's *right*. It's mine *too*.
       POOCHIE: So.
→   MICHAEL: I'll tell you to get out of *here* if I *want* you to.
       HUEY: Yep.

Thus, despite the fact that participants other than those acting as team leaders may initiate instruction sequences or counter the instructions from them, there is an asymmetry with respect to whose instructions are treated as binding. Considerable power resides in the party who sponsors a task activity at his home, and this may account for the differential success with which his proposals are eventually heeded.

Summary of observations on how boys construct task activities

Within the boys' group a pattern of asymmetry in the formatting and usage of directives and their responses develops in the interaction between players, creating the positions of leaders and followers. Michael and Huey, who assume the position of leaders for this activity, issue bald imperatives to others and characteristically get compliance. These commands concern every aspect of the slingshot making, including access to resources, site for play, procedure for manufacturing "slings," future battle strategy, etc. Many of their imperatives contain insult terms or implicit comparisons which place the recipient in a degraded position with respect to the speaker; accounts that accompany Michael and Huey's directives propose that the activity should be performed because of their personal definition of the situation or needs of the moment, rather than any requirements of the current activity. Michael assumes the position of instructor vis-à-vis the others, and the other boys ratify this claim. A division of labor develops with respect to the distribution of various types of actions. Boys other than Michael and Huey do not initiate new phases of the activity through giving bald imperatives; instead they use more mitigated forms, requests for information. Michael's position in the group is displayed and validated in a number of different ways: through issuing direct commands while receiving indirect requests and through contradicting proposals and requests of others, while expecting and getting compliance to his own.

The Organization of Girls' Task Activity

In this section I will analyze how girls go about organizing a task activity which is comparable to that of the boys, making rings from glass bottle rims. In making the rings, girls carefully scrape bottle rims over metal manhole covers or other rough surfaces so that the rims break evenly, leaving as few jagged edges as possible. The jobs faced by girls in making their objects do not substantially differ from those faced by boys; they involve procuring and allocating resources and establishing techniques for the objects' manufacture. Thus, in making rings the girls must decide where they will get the bottles necessary to make the rings, how many bottles are needed, who should break the bottles, how precisely the rims of bottles should be broken over metal manhole covers, how used bottles should be disposed of, and how the rings should be decorated.

The formatting of directives and accounts
in girls' task activity

With the exception of the domain of pretend play, hierarchical forms of organization are uncommon in girls' play. In accomplishing a task activity girls participate jointly in decision-making with minimal negotiation of status. This process is both reflected in and achieved through the selection of syntactic formats for the production of directives as well as forms of accounts which are quite different from those selected by the boys. The following provide examples of the types of directives typically found among the girls:

(17)   ((*Girls are searching for bottles from which to make rings*))
TERRI: Well let's go- let's go around the corner- Let's let's go around the corner where whatchacallem.

(18)   ((*Girls are looking for bottles*))
TERRI: Let's go. There may be some more on Sixty Ninth Street.
SHARON: Come on. Let's turn back y'all so we can safe keep em. Come on. Let's go get some.

(19)   ((*Girls are looking for bottles*))
SHARON: Let's go around Subs and Suds.
PAM: Let's ask her "Do you have any bottles."

Whereas boys' directives typically constitute commands that an action should be undertaken at the time the imperative is issued, girls' directives are constructed as suggestions for action in the future. Syntactically the forms utilized by the boys generally differentiate speaker and hearer. One party is either ordering another to do something, or alternatively, requesting action from some other party. By way of contrast the verb used by the girls, "*let's*" (generally used only by the boys when shifting a major phase of the activity underway),[3] includes both speaker and hearer as potential agents of the action to be performed,[4] thus mitigating the appearance of control. *Let's* signals a proposal rather than either a command or a request and as such shows neither special deference towards the other party (as a request does) nor claims about special rights of control over the other (as a command does). Thus, through the way in which they format their directives, the girls make visible an undifferentiated, "egalitarian" relationship between speaker and addressee(s), that differs quite markedly from the asymmetrical, hierarchical relationship displayed in boys' directives.

The structure of directives used to organize making rings is not different from the types of actions which are used to direct other girls' activities which involve a joint task, as can be seen in the examples below in which participants undertake playing jacks (example 20), jumping rope to a particular rhyme called "one two three footsies" (example 21) and hunting for turtles (example 22).

(20)   DARLENE: Let's play some more jacks.

(21)   PAM: Let's play "one two three footsies." First!

(22)   ((*Searching for turtles*))
PAM: Let's look around. See what we can find.

In alternation to the use of "*let's*" the auxiliary verb "*gonna*" with a plural subject and the modal verbs "*can*" or "*could*" can also be used to format an action as a mitigated directive form (Blum-Kulka and Olshtain, 1984: p. 203), proposing a suggestion or a joint plan as in the following which occur in the midst of making glass rings:

(23) SHARON: We gonna paint em and stuff.

(24) PAM: We could go around lookin for more bottles.

(25) ((*Discussing keeping the ring making secret from boys*))
TERRI: We can ʎimp back so nobody know where we ɡettin them from.

In some cases the overt tentativeness of the modal is further intensified through the use of terms such as *maybe*:

(26) TERRI: Maybe we can slice *them* like that.

Directives which include verbs such as *gotta* (which place more demands on recipient than modal verbs) may also contain an account providing explicit reasons for why an action should be undertaken. Characteristically, such accounts consider the benefits which would accrue to all members of the group:

(27) SHARON: Pam you know what we could do, (0.5) We gotta *clean* em first, We gotta *clean* em.
PAM: Huh,
SHARON: We gotta *clean* em first, / / You know,
PAM: I know.
→ [[Cuz they got germs.
SHARON: Wash em and stuff cuz just in case they
→ got germs on em.
[[And then you clean em,
PAM: I got some paints.
(3.5)
SHARON: Clean em, and then we *clean* em and we gotta be careful with em before we get the glass cutters. You know we gotta
→ be careful with em cuz it cuts easy.

In circumstances of urgency, e.g., when the safety of a group member is at stake,[5] imperatives constitute the appropriate and even expected form (Brown and Levinson, 1978: pp. 100–1). Characteristically, when imperatives are used by girls they are accompanied by accounts which take into consideration the situation of the addressee, such as her safety:

(28) ((*Regarding Pam's finger cut while making glass rings*))
SHARON: Pam don't you lick your own blood.
→ That way it gonna go right back there through your body.

(29) ((*Terri and Sharon attempt to put mercurochrome on Pam's cut finger*))
TERRI: Take it out now Pam.
PAM: No I'm not.
TERRI: Get- it ain't gonna hurt you girl. You got-
→ and you want to get your hand infected and they take- they take the hand taken off?

Thus despite the relative infrequency of imperatives used in organizing girls' task activities, there are nevertheless circumstances which occur when imperatives constitute the most appropriate form of directive. The type of account which girls offer to support their imperatives during task activities contrast markedly with the accounts accompanying boys' commands. Rather than arguing that an action should be performed because of one party's personal desires, girls' imperatives deal with the requirements of the current activity.

Instructing others

When girls use imperatives during instruction they may qualify their talk in ways which are sensitive to both the form of their social organization and other aspects of context. In the next example girls actively negotiate who has the right to address others with imperatives while demonstrating how to break the glass rim of the bottles; it is not assumed that any one party has exclusive rights to instruct another. When Pam takes over the job of teaching in lines 11–18 she uses a range of paralinguistic cues to frame her talk (Goffman, 1974), or contextualize it in a particular way (Gumperz, 1982). Thus she speaks with singsong intonation, caricaturing a teacher (lines 14–18) and colors her talk with laughter.

(30)	1	PAM:	Get that one. Here! Yeah give it to
	2		her.
	3		(2.0)
	4	SHARON:	This won't know the difference.
	5	PAM:	Get outa the street.
	6		(0.8)
	7		See you gotta do it real hard.
	8	SHARON:	Gimme this. I wanna do it. You're
	9		cracked. I wanna show you how to do
	10		it. I know how to do it *Pam*!
	11	PAM:	*I* know. I ju- So you won't have to
	12		break it. Like y'know. Do it like ((*as she demonstrates scraping it against a metal manhole cover at the correct angle for getting a smooth bottle rim*))
	13	SHARON:	Yeah.
	14	PAM:	⌈[((*singsong instructing voice*)) But when
	15		│ you get at the end you do it hard so
	16		│ the thing would break off right, eh heh
	17		│ heh! ((*laughing at style of teaching*))
	18		⌊ Harder!
	19	SHARON:	Do it *har*der.
	20	PAM:	Eh heh heh! / / Oh:.

The negotiation which takes place here has features of what developmental psychologists Stone and Selman (1982: pp. 169–79) describe as a considerably advanced form of "social negotiation strategy." They note that in the "collaboration" stage of negotiation children make use of various paralinguistic expressions to "communicate multiple, often ironic, meanings" (Stone and Selman, 1982: p. 175), employing "a contrast between the form they use and the form generally used in peer interaction." Here, while instructing others, Pam gives them orders in lines 1–2, 5, and 7; Sharon in lines 8–10 counters that she wants to do it herself and does not need any instruction from Pam. Such active objection to letting another issue orders is congruent with the ways that the girls in other contexts actively monitor each other for actions that could be seen as claiming that one girl is setting herself above the others. When Pam takes up the instructor role again in lines 14–18 she modifies the intonation of her voice; by adopting a singsong lilt she mocks the way she is delivering her instructions to the group. Through this caricaturing of the talk of an instructor Pam distances (Goffman, 1961: pp. 120–32) herself from the teaching role she is currently enacting, thereby making herself a more equal partner in the play.

This sequence of instructing thus differs from comparable ones among the boys (examples 10–13). Michael took his instructor role quite seriously, with little deviation from a strict interpretation of his notion of himself as someone superior to the others present. Interaction from other parties supported the image of Michael as more knowledgeable than others (see example 13) and portrayed their current social relationships as asymmetrical. By way of contrast, Sharon's objections to Pam's teaching challenge the position of superordination Pam has adopted. Pam begins modifying her role as instructor when Sharon objects, and eventually even laughs at her own speaking style. The negotiation in this sequence thus resembles the symmetrical features of roles observable in other phases of task activities, with girls extending to one another equivalent types of actions and avoiding the appearance of hierarchy.

Achieving symmetry in interaction within girls' directive sequences

It was noted earlier that asymmetry among the boys was displayed not only in the formatting of particular directives, but also in the differential usage of both directives and responses to them. In the boys' group generally only the party acting as leader issued the directives prescribing actions for others, and he responded to others' directives with refutations. In the girls' group, however, proposals for certain courses of action can be made by many different participants, and the girls generally agree to the suggestions of others. For example:

(31) SHARON: You can get people to *cut* this though.
PAM: Yep.

(32) TERRI: Hey y'all. Let's use these first and then come back and get the rest cuz it's too *many* of em.
SHARON: That *right*.
TERRI: We can *limp* back so nobody know where we *gettin* them from.
(0.8)
SHARON: That's right.
TERRI: And w- and wash our hands. And wash your hands when you get *finish* now.
SHARON: If the boys try to follow us we don't know. Okay?
TERRI: Yep.

Thus in terms of both how directives are constructed, and the way in which others respond to them, the girls' system of directive use displays similarity and equality rather than differentiation among group members.

[...]

Although girls do not characteristically respond to directives in ways which show one party superior to another, they do counter one another's proposals for action. Argumentation is as common an activity in the girls' group as it is among boys or in mixed-sex groups (Goodwin and Goodwin, 1987). The following is an example of a directive/counter sequence in the midst of a task activity:

(33)   ((*On reaching a city creek while turtle hunting*))
1   PAM: Y'all gonna walk in it?
2   NETTIE: *Walk* in it, You know where that
3   water come from? The toilet.
4   PAM: So, I'm a walk in it in my dirty feet.
5   I'm a walk in it and I don't care if it
6   do come.=You would / / easy wash your
7   feet.
8   NETTIE: ((*to ethnographer*)) Gonna walk us
9   across? Yeah I'll show y'all where you
10   can come.

In this example negotiations occur with regard to directives. The directive initially posed by Pam in line 1 ("Y'all gonna walk in it?") is countered by Nettie (line 2). Pam then opposes Nettie's counter to her (line 4). Subsequently, in the midst of Pam's turn (line 6) Nettie interrupts to reinstate Pam's initial request and issue a second directive regarding where to step in the creek. Upon completion of this fragment, each of the major parties to the conversation has both given a directive and countered the other's action. The form of the argumentation, however, has not attempted to affirm the relative superiority of one party with respect to the other. The directives in lines 1 and 8 are requests for information and in line 6 the directive is framed as a proposal using a modal verb. Moreover the counters do not flatly refuse prior actions; instead they provide first (lines 2–3) an argument against the appropriateness of the suggested action and second (line 4) an argument against the consequentiality of the suggested action. The directive/ counter sequences promote a symmetrical rather than an asymmetrical social situation in that counters to proposals are themselves considered counterable, and a proposal initiated by one party may be reinstated subsequently by another.

Summary of findings about differences in the organization of task activities among girls and boys

Though boys and girls make use of a common system of directives for the coordination of behavior in task activities, they construct these actions in quite different ways. By selecting alternative directive forms and responses and by creating differing divisions of labor with respect to who can issue particular forms, they build different forms of social organization. Boys' directives are formatted as imperatives from superordinate to subordinate, or requests, generally upward in rank. The usage of alternative asymmetrical forms for the directive, such as the request and the command, is differentially distributed among members of the boys' group; however, among the girls all have access to similar types of actions. Girls characteristically phrase their directives as proposals for future activity and frequently mitigate even these proposals with a term such as *maybe*. They tend to leave the time at which the action being proposed should be performed somewhat open, while a boy in a position of leadership states that he wants an action completed *right now*.

Syntactically the directives of the boys differentiate speaker from hearer. Among the girls, however, the party issuing the directive is usually included as one of the agents in the action to be performed. From the point of view of cognitive psychologists who study "social perspective taking" ("an individual's capacity to coordinate psychological perspectives of self and other" (Stone and Selman, 1982: p. 164)) and "social negotiation strategies" (Stone and Selman, 1982) it can be argued that girls' directives *display* taking into consideration the other's point of view to a far greater extent than boys' directives do.[6] Thus the details of how participants select to build a turn either requesting another to do something or responding to talk make relevant two contrasting modes of interaction; hierarchical or more egalitarian social organization may be proposed through the syntactic structures which are chosen. Though within task activities a symmetrical form of social organization is established by the girls in their same-sex group, in other circumstances, girls can select more aggravated forms and construct quite different forms of social organization.

Directive Use in Playing House

Girls on Maple Street distinguish between various types of directives and degrees of mitigation, as is apparent from the ways in which they talk about alternative polite and impolite forms:

(34)   ((*Concerning a 4-year-old girl, Delin*))
  NETTIE: Delin wanted to come in the house. I said "You say 'exc*use* me.' = Not '*mo:*ve.' "

(35)   ((*Pam describing how she confronted another girl*))
  PAM: I s'd *I* said "You c'd *roll* your eyes all you *want* to. Cuz I'm *t*ellin you. (0.5) *T*ellin- I'm not *ask*in you." And I ain't say no plea:se *ei*ther.

A major circumstance in which girls make use of aggravated directives is when taking care of younger children and enacting such roles in their favorite pastime, playing house. For example when girls give directives to younger children in their charge, they frequently use aggravated forms or imperatives which resemble those their mothers use in disciplining them.[7] Directives may be accompanied by accounts which can explicitly describe a benefit (such as safety) for the recipient of the imperative as in example 37:

(36) SHARON: Stay out of the street now man. Come on punk. Hurry up Glen.

(37)   ((*Sharon cautions Delin to stand away from girls making glass rings*))
  SHARON: Delin you get back cuz I don't want nothin fallin in your eyes or in your face. Get back. Get back.

(38)   ((*Delin puts down the hood of her jacket on a windy day*))
  TERRI: *Don't* put that down. Put that back *up*! It's sup*posed* to be that way.

Such types of actions constitute the models for communication which takes place when older children play house with younger children.

Here a specific episode of playing house will be investigated. In order to provide a point of reference for observations made about interaction occurring within this session of pretend play, a diagram of dramatized kinship relationships will be provided. Deniece and Sharon, who enact "sisters" who are "mothers," establish two separate households at the onset of this session.[8] As this diagram shows, Aisha (age 10) is a childless sister of Deniece (10) and Sharon (12). At the onset of play Pam (12), Brenda (8), and Terri (age 12, who frequently acts as parental child[9] taking care of younger sibling Brenda) are the children of Deniece. However during the session Terri negotiates a position as sister of Deniece, Sharon and Aisha. Priscilla (7) and Shahida (5) are Sharon's children.

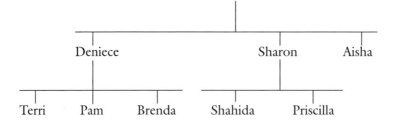

The structure of directives and accounts in house

When playing house girls enacting the role of mother address their "children" with directives that are very similar in structure to those that mothers or caretakers use. Such patterning is consistent with other research on role playing among children's groups (Andersen, 1978: p. 89; Corsaro, 1985: p. 82; Ervin-Tripp, 1982: p. 36; Garvey, 1974, 1977; Mitchell-Kernan and Kernan, 1977: pp. 201–7; Sachs, 1987) which has demonstrated that directives constitute the principal means through which children realize positions of dominance and submission between characters such as those in the mother/child relationship. "Mothers" typically deliver imperatives to their "children":

(39) DENIECE: Hurry up and go to bed!

(40) SHARON: BRING THOSE CARDS BACK, BRING THAT BOOK IN THE HOUSE AND C:OME HOME! Don't *climb* over that way. You climb over the *right* way.

(41) SHARON: PRISCILLA, BRENDA, SHAHIDA, GET IN THE CAR! Get in the car. Shahida and Brenda, and all y'all get in the car.=Where Priscilla at. GET IN THE CAR. YOU GOIN OVER *MY* HOUSE. GO ON OVER AND GET- UH- WHERE'S PRISCILLA AT.

In addition to the job of enacting the roles of characters relative to one another, a principal task for participants is determining what scene is being enacted and making visible that scene. Directives not only constitute the principal ways in which roles in house are dramatized; they also provide the means through which the stage is set and the plot line is developed, as scene-changing guides are embedded in them and reference is made to nonpresent objects and spaces as well as future undertakings.

Accounts which accompany mothers' directives (such as "IT'S TIME TO GO IN.=YOU GOTTA GO TO *SCHOOL* TOMORROW!") supply warrants for the imperatives, culturally appropriate reasons for why activities should be done in specific ways. They thus provide the primary ways that participants playing house develop domestic roles and introduce new information into the ongoing action. Consequently the accounts within "house" may be more elaborated than those that occur in actual interaction between caretakers and their charges:

(42)   DENIECE: Well if you don't want to go to sleep, don't go. But don't disturb your
sisters. Just because *you* don't wanna go. (2.8) Maybe *they* wanna go to
sleep. You don't know:: that. (3.6) That goes for *all* a you. Whether you
not my- children or not. You *too*. (2.2) *Don't* let this happen again.

In providing accounts girls playing mother talk about measures that must be heeded for
the safety and well-being of members of a group. Thus they express concerns which are
similar to those in accounts during girls' task activities.

The positions of those in control in house (as with the boys' slingshot episode) are
maintained not simply through the issuing of directives which maintain a particular format. They are also manifested through the *receipt* of various forms of action from others.
The actions enacted by smaller children are largely requests for permission, actions which
imply an asymmetry of role relationships:[10]

(43)   BRENDA: Mommy can um Aisha play with our baby brother?

(44)   SHAHIDA: Can I hold your book?

(45)   BRENDA: Mommy may *we* go out and play,

When speaking outside an enacted role concerning details of the drama, requests for
information are also used to address girls who manage the activity:

(46)   Pam: How old am *I*,

With respect to the roles of mother and children there is thus a form of asymmetry built
into the structure of behavior which closely models that in caretaker/child interaction as
well as that in leader/follower interaction among the boys during task activities.

Although Maple Street girls playing the roles of subordinates in "house" display deference through their requests for information they do not always display deference through
their *responses* to imperatives, as has been reported for other groups (i.e., Corsaro, 1985:
p. 83). Excuses rather than agreements are often provided – for example in line 4 of
example 47; a counter accusation occurs in line 7.

(47)   1   BRENDA: Maanaa. I want some *pea*nuts.
2   TERRI: Well you ain't *g*ettin none.
3   DENIECE: Hurry up and go to bed!
4   BRENDA: → ((*whining*)) I was *j*ust eating a *pea*nut.
5   DENIECE: GO TO *BED*! YOU SUPPOSED- YOU SUPPOSED
6   TO GET YOURS IN THE MORNINGTIME.
7   BRENDA: → ((*whining*)) Well *Y*ou eating them all
8   *u*:p.
9   DENIECE: Do you want me to tell her to go- uhm
10   make you go to bed?

[…]

In example 47 mother Deniece persists over several turns in her strategies to attempt to
get her child Brenda to comply with directives. Mothers' imperatives are repetitively answered
by children's counters as children negotiate their roles with respect to their caretakers.
[…]

By framing directives as requests for information, girls playing younger children display their subordination vis-à-vis girls playing mother. However, girls playing children do not assume passive roles in "house." Instead considerable negotiation occurs among girls playing subordinate roles, in both their responses to girls playing roles of mother and among themselves.

Asymmetry in roles in playing house

Symmetrical types of exchanges take place within house in interactions in which siblings exchange equivalent argumentative forms and "mothers" exchange stories about their "children." By comparison with task activities, however, there is a minimum of egalitarianism in decision making. In so far as those acting as children play subordinate roles there is asymmetry built into the activity itself. In addition girls who play the role of mother act in the capacity of stage manager. As overseers of the unfolding drama, both Deniece and Sharon monitor the actions of participants, commenting on them in utterances such as "Hey Brenda you supposed to be sleep." or "Priscilla you can't hear them." For example, in the following Deniece and Sharon, as commenters on Brenda's actions, describe for her appropriate behavior as a child (line 1) and warn her of her precarious tenure in the play through a negative categorization of her behavior ("not even *play*ing right") (lines 4–5), commands (lines 6 and 8) and an account "THAT'S WHY NOBODY WANT YOU FOR A CHILD." (lines 6–7):

(48)　1　DENIECE:　HEY BRENDA YOU OUGHTTA / / be sleep!
　　　　2　TERRI:　I can't even get her in the bed.
　　　　3　DENIECE:　I know.
　　　　4　DENIECE:　SHE'S NOT / / EVEN PLAYIN RIGHT. SHE
　　　　5　　　　　　NOT EVEN *PLAY*IN RIGHT.
　　　　6　SHARON:　BRENDA PLAY RIGHT. THAT'S WHY NOBODY
　　　　7　　　　　　WANT YOU FOR A CHILD.
　　　　8　DENIECE:　GET IN THERE AND GO TO SLEEP!

Girls in the position of "mother" can thus dictate for others dimensions of play *outside* the frame of play as well as within it. They not only can control who has rights to play what roles but also who can be members of the group. In example 48, important with respect to issues of social organization is the fact that while Deniece's actions towards Brenda are produced as complaints using third-person references, Sharon (line 6) delivers an imperative directly to Brenda. As the party who takes control of duties of principal stage manager, Sharon assumes the right to issue commands to players, even those not her own children.

Asymmetry is extended to other aspects of the activity as well. For example, while one might expect a certain equality among two girls who play mother, only one of them characteristically makes decisions for the group. In the present case Sharon assumes the right to change frame through "pretend" directives and in general it is she who plays the role of stage manager:

(49)　SHARON:　Hey y'all. = Pretend it's a- like- it's about twelve o'clock. = okay?
　　　　DENIECE:　It's twelve o'clock in the afternoon so y'all should settle down.
　　　　SHARON:　Don't be too late.
　　　　TERRI:　I'll fix their lunch!

(50) SHARON: Come on. = Pretend it's two o'clock in the morning.
      DENIECE: OH: I'm goin to *be*d.

(51) SHARON: Pretend it's gettin night time. =
      TERRI: *Good* night child*ren*!

Responses to pretend directives are not randomly distributed among participants. While many girls are present, generally the person responding to a request to pretend is another girl situated in an equivalent role. In these examples Deniece, a household head, and Terri, an older child performing caretaking responsibilities, are the ones who reply to Sharon's overt proposals for shifts in activity. Their talk elaborates the relevance of the directives for current and future activities. While not all initiations of frame shifts are begun by girls in the "mother" role, those who pass final judgment on proffered frame switches do overwhelmingly occupy that position. Thus asymmetrical role relationships are played out during "house."

Positions of subordination and superordination between Deniece and Sharon are further evident in forms of interactions between them. Deniece repetitively displays deference to Sharon. In the following, for example, Deniece relays a request made by someone in her household to Sharon rather than responding to it herself:

(52) TERRI: Okay. Pretend it's just about seven o'clock in the morning.
      DENIECE:→ What time is it Sharon, (1.8) What time is it Sharon.
                  (0.6) *Sh*aron what time is it.
      SHARON: Seven o *clock*.
      DENIECE: In the morning.

Meanwhile Sharon asserts her position as above that of Deniece in a variety of ways, for example by issuing imperatives to her:

(53) SHARON: Where Deniece go. You better get your children in the *house*.

(54) SHARON: Hey- you should beat your children cuz- You let her do her hair when she supposed to be in bed.

Repetitively Sharon's definition of the situation is asserted above Deniece's. In the following, after Sharon states that she has to fix dinner (lines 1–2), Deniece (line 3) offers an alternative plan of action using a modal verb: "*They* could eat dinner with *us*,". This suggestion is flatly opposed in a next turn by Sharon (lines 4–5), and subsequently the group follows up on Sharon's plan.

(55) 1 SHARON: Don't sit over here or stand over here
      2   cuz I gotta fix dinner.
      3 DENIECE: *They* could eat dinner with *us*,
      4 SHARON: No *uh* uh I'm fixin- I brought all this
      5   food out here and they gonna eat over here.

Not only do girls establish hierarchical arrangements among members of their groups. In addition they form coalitions against particular girls. Among the Maple Street girls, as occurs among other girls' groups (i.e., Eder and Hallinan, 1978; Lever, 1976; Thorne and Luria, 1986), negotiating who is to be included within the most valued roles is an important feature of social organization. Within task activities girls were positioned in equivalent identities. Greater social differentiation is possible while playing house as the division into families and households provides for the playing of alternative roles. The position of sibling to the party playing principal decision maker is the most coveted position. In the particular session of playing house being examined, Sharon's best friend Aisha had no difficulty acquiring the identity of sibling sister. However considerable negotiation took place regarding Terri's identity in a similar slot. In the following the girls conspire to exclude Terri from the position of sister to Sharon:

(56)	1	TERRI:	I'm not your daughter.=all right? Um,
	2		I'm- I'm her *sister*.
	3	DENIECE:	N:OO! / / You-
	4	SHARON:	YOU CAN'T BE STAYIN WITH ME!
	5	TERRI:	I know.=I'm staying with *her*! But I
			can-
	7	DENIECE:	[[YOU- Uh *uh*! You- you *my* daughter.
	8	TERRI:	Mm *mm*.
	9	DENIECE:	Uh *huh*, / / Until *P*am get back.
	10	TERRI:	*P*am *your* daughter.
	11	DENIECE:	I know.=I-
	12	SHARON:	[[WELL HOW CAN YOU BE HER *SI*STER,
	13	DENIECE:	UH *HUH* BECAUSE *WE S*:/ /ISTERS, HOW CAN
	14		YOU BE *HER* SISTER.
	15	SHARON:	NOW HOW CAN YOU BE *MY* SISTER,
	16	DENIECE:	How can you be my / / sister.
	17	AISHA:	That's r- that's right.
	18		(0.8)
	19	AISHA:	We all three *sis*ters.
	20	SHARON:	I *know*.
	21	AISHA:	Well how come you don't wanna be
	22		her daughter.
	23	BRENDA:	[[THERE SHARON, AISHA / / AND
	24	TERRI:	I'm another sister.
	25	BRENDA:	There Sharon and Aisha is her-
	26	SHARON:	[[N:O.
	27	BRENDA:	Is your- and / / she-
	28	SHARON:	WELL *YOU* STAY HERE WITH *HER*.

The dispute about Terri's position in playing house begins in lines 1–2, where Terri proposes that she enact the role of Deniece's sister rather than her daughter. This proposal is first objected to by Deniece (line 3) with "N:OO!" and then by Sharon (line 4): "YOU CAN'T BE STAYIN WITH ME!" Deniece counters Terri again in line 7, arguing that Terri is her "daughter," rather than sister. The dispute becomes more intense when Sharon (lines 12, 15, 20), Deniece (lines 9, 13–14, 16), and Aisha (lines 17, 19) argue that they are the only ones who can be sisters in playing house. The argument nears closure when Terri (line 24) states "I'm another sister." Subsequently Sharon (line 28) concedes that she can be a sister under the condition that she live with Deniece. In this way Sharon terminates the dispute while distancing herself from Terri. Thus in the midst of dramatic play, as in other of their interactions (Goodwin, 1982), girls take considerable care to delineate their friendship alliances. Though an issue which is highly charged is debated, the girls continue playing together for nearly an hour after this dispute.

Conclusion

Various researchers (Lever, 1976; Gilligan, 1982: p. 242) have proposed that the structure of games itself influences the form of social organization that children evolve. As the argument goes, because girls do not participate in complex games (team sports having a large number of players, high degrees of interdependence of players, role differentiation, rule specificity, and competitiveness), with respect to males females are considered less able to develop the negotiational skills which prepare one for "successful performance in a wide range of work settings in large, formal organizations" (Lever, 1974: pp. 240–1).

As can be seen from the data on playing house within a fairly unstructured form of play (that is, a form of play with relatively few explicit rules), an incipient hierarchy emerges. As within any focused gathering or activity requiring the close coordination of participants in differentiated roles, decisions regarding how the play is to proceed must be made from moment to moment; this allows for the emergence of the role of manager of the activity. Though both girls playing mother as well as the girl who is "parental child" may give directives to children in the play frame, one girl in particular controls the staging of the activity. She makes frequent use of imperatives in her talk, and in general uses explicit speech forms to oversee aspects of the activity. Concurrently those in positions subordinate to principal character (as both characters in the drama and actors in the dramatic play) display their positions of subordination vis-à-vis those in a position of authority, thereby constructing a complementarity of roles. Within dramatic play girls further create a differentiation of participants through the ways in which they criticize certain girls or exclude them from valued positions. Alliances of girls against particular individuals are played out in a fashion which resembles alliance formation in a gossip event called "he-said-she-said" (Goodwin, 1980a). Supportive evidence for girls' competence in developing elaborated forms of social organization while playing games comes from Hughes' (1983, 1995) studies of white middle class girls; within a nonteam game such as "foursquare," girls evolve quite sophisticated forms of social organization which entail contests between incipient teams.

The form of social organization which evolves in the midst of pretend play differs from that which characterizes girls' task activities. Girls, in contrast to boys, interpret task activities as needing relatively little control. In coordinating the actions of participants, events are treated as involving parallel rather than tightly interdigitated events, which are typical of a game such as jump rope or house. Girls make use of actions which include the speaker as well as others within the scope of the action and suggest rather than demand courses of next action. In addition, making decisions regarding what happens next is rotated among group members. When imperatives are used in this frame they are in some way modified from the bald forms which occur among the boys, either through accounts which specify safety of the individual involved, or benefits for the entire group. During the giving of instructions, imperatives are further modified through the shading of laughter and mimicry which surrounds them.

Thus girls exhibit a range of different types of social organization in the organization of their activities. Many studies of gender differences tend, as Thorne (1986: p. 168) argues, to promote the notion of "separate worlds" of males and females – "to abstract gender from social context, to assume males and females are qualitatively and permanently different." Here I have attempted to show that some features of girls' activities resemble the ways in which boys hierarchically structure their play. However, while girls in a stage manager position direct play in ways similar to the ways that boys in a leadership position make decisions for the group, the accounts they provide to support their imperatives speak to female rather than male concerns.

The findings reported here would thus seem to counter many of the prevalent notions about girls' social organization. Typically girls are seen as avoiding direct competition and spending little time on "negotiational involvements" (Lever, 1976; Sutton-Smith, 1979; Gilligan, 1982); such a view supports the view of females as powerless speakers. As I have argued here, within the "house" frame, girls devote considerable attention to negotiating features of their play, making use of language which expresses disagreement in an aggravated fashion. Moreover, such negotiation takes place without the disruption of the ongoing activity or a breach in social relationships, as is frequently argued to occur among girls (Lever, 1976: p. 482; Gilligan, 1982: pp. 9–10). The form of differentiated social organization within a comparatively large cluster that girls evolve within playing house defies the often cited typifications of girls as interacting within small groups or friendship pairs (Waldrop and Halverson, 1975; Eder and Hallinan, 1978; Maltz and Borker, 1982). The fact that girls' social organization varies substantially across different domains makes it imperative that studies of girls' play or interaction be grounded in detailed analysis of specific contexts of use.

Notes

An earlier version of this paper was presented at the American Folklore Society 1986 Annual Meeting and at the Indiana University Sociolinguistics Seminar. I am indebted to Charles Goodwin, Barrie Thorne and Linda Hughes for helpful and insightful comments on an earlier version of this analysis.

1 For more detailed analysis of how the boys organized their slingshot fight see Goodwin (1980b) and Goodwin & Goodwin (1990).
2 The organization of boys' activities into "teams" has been extensively commented upon by a number of researchers, most notably Lever (1974, 1976). Among the Maple Street boys, even the making of go carts evolved into play divided into two highly competitive "pit crews," each with its own professional secrets regarding the manufacture of the carts.
3 Among the boys, "let's" is used when a boy proposes to move to a new stage of an activity in utterances such as "Let's play some football Poochie. Two against two." or "Mi*chael*! Let's get a game." "Let's" was used two times during the boys' slingshot making session reported on here. Michael requested (a) that boys move around to the back of the house to make slings ("Let's go around back and make some slings") and (b) that boys move from a stairwell to a cement backyard area ("All right. It's too crowded in here. Let's go somewhere.").
4 According to Blum-Kulka and Olshtain (1984: p. 203), such a "point of view" provides a more mitigated form of directive.
5 Grant (1984: p. 108) in her study of peer interaction in a desegregated school found that "black girls were above the mean in care-giving in four classrooms."
6 This is not meant to imply that boys are *in fact* less able to deal with the perspective of the other than girls are.
7 Studies comparing child-rearing practices of black parents with those of Euro-American (Bartz and Levin, 1978; Baumrind, 1972) and Chicano parents (Bartz and Levin, 1978) report "a pattern of increased strictness, high control, and high support (nurturance) among African-American parents" (McLoyd, Ray, and Etter-Lewis, 1985: p. 40). The white middle class

mothers studied by Bellinger and Gleason (1982) deliver directives which appear far more mitigated than those I found in black mother–child interaction.

8   The importance of female sibling ties among black families has been discussed by Aschenbrenner (1975), Ladner (1971), McAdoo (1983), and Stack (1974). McLoyd, Ray, and Etter-Lewis (1985: p. 41) and Pitcher and Schultz (1983) report that among pre-school children there is little development of the father/husband role during pretend play.

9   Commenting upon the role of parental child within black families, McLoyd, Ray, and Etter-Lewis (1985: p. 40) state "Older children often assume caretaking responsibilities for younger children (Aschenbrenner, 1975; Lewis, 1975; Young, 1970) and, as a consequence, may acquire advanced role-taking skills."

10 Corsaro (1985: p. 83) also found that requests for permission were most frequently used by children playing younger children to "mothers" and constituted a way of displaying subordination. McLoyd, Ray, and Etter-Lewis (1985: p. 37) found that "children" used more direct forms with each other than with their "mothers." Gordon and Ervin-Tripp (1984: p. 308) argue that "true permission requests imply that the addressee has control over the speaker and that the speaker's wishes are subject to the hearer's approval."

References

Andersen, E. S. (1978). Learning to speak with style: A study of the sociolinguistic skills of children. Unpublished Ph.D. dissertation, Department of Linguistics, Stanford University.

Aschenbrenner, J. (1975). *Lifelines: Black Families in Chicago*. New York: Holt, Rinehart & Winston.

Austin, J. L. (1962). *How to Do Things with Words*. Oxford: Oxford University Press.

Bartz, K. W., and Levin, E. S. (1978). Childrearing by black parents: A description and comparison to anglo and chicano parents. *Journal of Marriage and the Family*, 40, 709–19.

Baumrind, D. (1972). An exploratory study of socialization effects on black children: Some black–white comparisons. *Child Development*, 43, 261–7.

Becker, J. (1982). Children's strategic use of requests to mark and manipulate social status. In S. Kuczaj II (Ed.), *Language Development*, vol. 2: *Language, Thought and Culture* (pp. 1–35). Hillsdale, NJ: Lawrence Erlbaum Associates.

Becker, J. A. (1984). Implications of ethology for the study of pragmatic development. In S. Kuczaj II (Ed.), *Discourse Development: Progress in Cognitive Development Research* (pp. 1–17). New York: Springer-Verlag.

Bellinger, D. C., and Gleason, J. B. (1982). Sex differences in parental directives to young children. *Sex Roles*, 8, 1123–39.

Blum-Kulka, S., and Olshtain, E. (1984). Requests and apologies: A cross-cultural study of speech act realization patterns (CCSARP). *Applied Linguistics*, 5, 196–213.

Brown, P. (1980). How and why are women more polite? Some evidence from a Mayan community. In S. McConnell-Ginet, R. Borker, and N. Furman (Eds.), *Women and Language in Literature and Society* (pp. 111–49). New York: Praeger.

Brown, P., and Levinson, S. C. (1978). Universals of language usage: Politeness phenomena. In E. N. Goody (Ed.), *Questions and Politeness. Strategies in Social Interaction* (pp. 56–289). Cambridge: Cambridge University Press.

Cazden, C., Cox, M., Dickerson, D., Steinberg, Z., and Stone, C. (1979). "You all gonna hafta listen": Peer teaching in a primary classroom. In W. Collins (Ed.), *Minnesota Symposia on Child Psychology* (Vol. 12, pp. 183–231). Hillsdale, NJ: Lawrence Erlbaum Associates.

Chance, M. R. A., and Jolly, C. J. (1970). *Social Groups of Monkeys, Apes and Men*. London: Jonathan Cape.

Cook-Gumperz, J. (1981). Persuasive talk – the social organization of children's talk. In J. L. Green and C. Wallat (Eds.), *Ethnography and Language in Educational Settings* (pp. 25–50). Norwood, NJ: Ablex.

Cook-Gumperz, J., and Corsaro, W. (1979). Social-ecological constraints on children's communicative strategies. *Sociology*, 11, 411–34.

Corsaro, W. A. (1985). *Friendship and Peer Culture in the Early Years*. Norwood, NJ: Ablex.

Eder, D., and Hallinan, M. T. (1978). Sex differences in children's friendships. *American Sociological Review*, 43, 237–50.

Ervin-Tripp, S. (1976). "Is Sybil there?": The structure of some American English directives. *Language in Society*, 5, 25–67.

Ervin-Tripp, S. (1982). Structures of control. In L. C. Wilkinson (Ed.), *Communicating in the Classroom* (pp. 27–47). New York: Academic Press.

Garvey, C. (1974). Some properties of social play. *Merrill-Palmer Quarterly*, 20, 163–80.

Garvey, C. (1975). Requests and responses in children's speech. *Journal of Child Language*, 2, 41–63.

Garvey, C. (1977). *Play*. Cambridge, MA: Harvard University Press.

Gilligan, C. (1982). *In a Different Voice: Psychological Theory and Women's Development*. Cambridge, MA: Harvard University Press.

Goffman, E. (1961). *Encounters: Two Studies in the Sociology of Interaction*. Indianapolis: Bobbs-Merrill.

Goffman, E. (1974). *Frame Analysis: An Essay on the Organization of Experience*. New York: Harper & Row.

Goodwin, M. H. (1980a). 'He-Said-She-Said': Formal cultural procedures for the construction of a gossip dispute activity. *American Ethnologist*, 7, 674–95.

Goodwin, M. H. (1980b). Directive/response speech sequences in girls' and boys' task activities. In S. McConnell-Ginet, R. Borker, and N. Furman (Eds.), *Women and Language in Literature and Society* (pp. 157–73). New York: Praeger.

Goodwin, M. H. (1982). "Instigating": Storytelling as social process. *American Ethnologist*, 9, 799–819.

Goodwin, M. H. (1983). Aggravated correction and disagreement in children's conversations. *Journal of Pragmatics*, 7, 657–77.

Goodwin, M. H. (1985). The serious side of jump rope: Conversational practices and social organization in the frame of play. *Journal of American Folklore*, 98, 315–30.

Goodwin, M. H., and Goodwin, C. (1987). Children's arguing. In S. Philips, S. Steele, and C. Tanz (Eds.), *Language, Gender, and Sex in Comparative Perspective* (pp. 200–48). Cambridge: Cambridge University Press.

Goodwin, C., and Goodwin, M. H. (1990). Interstitial argument. In A. Grimshaw (Ed.), *Conflict Talk* (pp. 85–117). Cambridge: Cambridge University Press.

Gordon, D., and Ervin-Tripp, S. (1984). The structure of children's requests. In R. L. Schiefelbusch and J. Pickar (Eds.), *The Acquisition of Communicative Competence* (pp. 295–321). Baltimore: University Park Press.

Grant, L. (1984). Black females' "place" in desegregated classrooms. *Sociology of Education*, 57, 98–111.

Gumperz, J. J. (1982). *Discourse Strategies*. New York: Cambridge University Press.

Hughes, L. A. (1983). Beyond the rules of the game: Girls' gaming at a Friends' school. Unpublished Ph.D. dissertation, University of Pennsylvania, Graduate School of Education.

Hughes, L. A. (1995). Children's games and gaming. In B. Sutton-Smith, J. Mechling, and T. Johnson (Eds.), *A Handbook of Children's Folklore* (pp. 93–119). Washington, DC: Smithsonian Institution Press.

Labov, W., and Fanshel, D. (1977). *Therapeutic Discourse: Psychotherapy as Conversation*. New York: Academic Press.

Ladner, J. A. (1971). *Tomorrow's Tomorrow: The Black Woman*. New York: Anchor Books.

Lever, J. R. (1974). Games children play: Sex differences and the development of role skills. Unpublished Ph.D. dissertation, Department of Sociology, Yale University.

Lever, J. (1976). Sex differences in the games children play. *Social Problems*, 23, 478–87.

Lewis, D. (1975). The black family: Socialization and sex roles. *Phylon*, 36, 221–37.

Maltz, D. N., and Borker, R. A. (1982). A cultural approach to male–female miscommunication. In J. Gumperz (Ed.), *Language and Social Identity* (pp. 196–216). Cambridge: Cambridge University Press.

McAdoo, H. P. (1983). *Extended Family Support of Single Black Mothers.* Columbia, MD: Columbia Research Systems.

McLoyd, V. C., Ray, S. A., and Etter-Lewis, G. (1985). Being and becoming: The interface of language and family role knowledge in the pretend play of young African American girls. In L. Galda and A. D. Pellegrini (Eds.), *Play, Language, and Stories: The Development of Children's Literate Behavior* (pp. 29–43). Norwood. NJ: Ablex.

Mitchell-Kernan, C., and Kernan, K. T. (1977). Pragmatics of directive choice among children. In S. Ervin-Tripp and C. Mitchell-Kernan (Eds.), *Child Discourse* (pp. 189–208). New York: Academic Press.

Piaget, J. (1965). *The Moral Judgment of the Child* (1932). New York: Free Press.

Pitcher, E., and Schultz, L. (1983). *Boys and Girls at Play: The Development of Sex Roles.* New York: Praeger.

Sachs, J. (1987). Preschool boys' and girls' language use in pretend play. In S. Philips, S. Steele, and C. Tanz (Eds.), *Language, Gender and Sex in Comparative Perspective.* Cambridge: Cambridge University Press.

Sacks, H., Schegloff, E. A., and Jefferson, G. (1974). A simplest systematics for the organization of turn-taking for conversation. *Language,* 50, 696–735.

Stack, C. (1974). *All Our Kin: Strategies for Survival in a Black Community.* New York: Harper & Row.

Stone, C. R., and Selman, R. L. (1982). A structural approach to research on the development of interpersonal behavior among grade school children. In K. H. Rubin and H. S. Ross (Eds.), *Peer Relationships and Social Skills in Childhood* (pp. 163–83). New York: Springer-Verlag.

Sutton-Smith, B. (1979). *Play and Learning.* New York: Gardner Press.

Thorne, B. (1986). Girls and boys together – but mostly apart: Gender arrangements in elementary school. In W. W. Hartup and Z. Rubin (Eds.), *Relationships and Development* (pp. 167–84). Hillsdale, NJ: Erlbaum.

Thorne, B., and Luria, Z. (1986). Sexuality and gender in children's daily worlds. *Social Problems,* 33, 176–90.

Vaughn, B. E., and Waters, E. (1980). Social organization among preschool peers. In D. R. Omark, F. F. Strayer, and D. G. Freedman (Eds.), *Dominance Relations: An Ethological View of Human Conflict and Social Interaction* (pp. 359–79). New York: Garland STPM Press.

Waldrop, M. F., and Halverson, C. F. (1975). Intensive and extensive peer behavior: Longitudinal and cross-sectional analyses. *Child Development,* 46, 19–26.

Wood, B., and Gardner, R. (1980). How children "get their way": Directives in communication. *Communication Education,* 29, 264–72.

Young, V. H. (1970). Family and childhood in a southern Negro community. *American Anthropologist,* 72, 269–88.

9

Expressions of Gender: An Analysis of Pupils' Gendered Discourse Styles in Small Group Classroom Discussions

Julia Davies

Source: *Discourse & Society* 14(2) (2003), pp. 115–32. Reprinted with permission of SAGE.

Introduction

This article presents aspects of data taken from a project (Davies, 1999) enquiring into the relationship among talk, gender and learning. The work contributes to debates about the apparent under-achievement of boys (Clark and Millard, 1998; Department for Education and Employment [DfEE], 1997; Office for Standards in Education [OFSTED], 1998; Woodhead, 1996) and resurrects unresolved issues raised in the 1980s about girls' position in schools (Arnot and Weiner, 1987; Mahony, 1985). Moreover, this investigation adds to the increasing body of research into language and gender (Cameron, 1985; Coates, 1996; Lakoff, 1975). The relationship between talk and learning has been well demonstrated (Barnes et al., 1969; Department of Education and Science [DES], 1975; Vygotsky, 1962) thus rendering research into spoken language and achievement pertinent. Moreover, pupils are commonly required, in UK schools at least, to work in discussion groups in order to share ideas, investigate problems, debate issues and so on. Thus, this research has broad cross-curricular ramifications.

Gender and Education in the 1980s

During the 1980s sociological education research demonstrated how girls' schooldays often saw them placed at a disadvantage relative to boys (Mahony, 1985; Spender and Sarah, 1980; Swann, 1992). For example, the work identified the disproportionate amount of teacher attention enjoyed by boys in comparison with girls (Spender and Sarah, 1980; Swann and Graddol, 1988) and highlighted boys' domination of classroom discourse (Spender and Sarah, 1980).

Mahony (1985: 70) also reported on male monopoly of linguistic and geographical space, arguing

> The construction of male identity and in particular the social construction of male sexuality is crucial in the maintenance of male power and it is this which we have witnessed in the mixed sex classroom.

Yet she noted also, how non-macho boys fall victim to male power – a theme I have found significant in my own research.

The National Curriculum for England and Wales (DES, 1989) was introduced in the 1980s, comprising statutory orders and non-statutory teaching guidance. The guidance warned, 'There are considerable differences between the sexes in typical speech styles, which carry implications for assessment' (DES, 1989: 11.14). The comments reflected the deterministic nature of popular gender and linguistics research of the decade (Spender, 1980), seeing girls as needy, quiet and passive (DES, 1989: 11.14).

Gender and Education in the 1990s

In contrast, more recent publications urge attention to boys' needs (Basic Skills Agency, 1997; Frater, 1997; Millard and Walsh, 2001; Qualifications and Curriculum Authority [QCA], 1998).

With the focus of the academic lens now turned towards boys, the casual observer could be forgiven for being reminded of Monty Python sketches of competing suffering. The scenario has been characterized as a 'pro-girl versus pro-boy shoot out' (Connell, 1996: 207).

Debate, in the UK at least, has been high profile (DfEE, 1998a, 1998b, 1998c). 'The phenomenon of boys underachievement' seems to have dominated educational discussion in the 1990s (Younger et al., 1999: 327) and seems set to continue with urges and polemic from a government intently focusing on statistics concerning measurable achievement (Mahony, 1998). Figures showing girls' accelerating dominance over boys in examination results have been used to identify the demise of boys' progress (DfEE, 1997).

Intended to render transparent the achievements (or otherwise) of pupils, the examination results presented in gendered sets offer a simplistic view obfuscating a more complex picture. The statistics provide a partial perspective ignoring ethnicity and class for example (OFSTED, 1998) and certainly do not reflect the full picture of either gender's social position in schools. Surely neither gender has drastically changed its behaviour as implied by the alternating descriptions across the decades. Different types of data have been presented to mourn the circumstances of first one, then the other, gender. As OFSTED (1998: 26) remarked.

> Gender differences … for educational performance is not self-evident. There is little research that directly links classroom interaction with academic outcomes. In view of the current interest in the effectiveness of different teaching methods and different forms of classroom organisation, this could be a fruitful area for future research.

Research needs to continue if we are to address the processes which maintain inequity and this project is intended to contribute to such a body of work, synthesizing arguments about socialization, language and educational achievement.

Data Collection and Analysis

During the late 1990s I taped 14-year-old pupils involved in several speaking and listening activities during their English lessons. Six classes (182 pupils) from three different comprehensive schools in the north of England were involved. The pupils were organized in both single and mixed sex settings so that a comparison could be made of the way group gender composition, as well as tasks, affected pupils' discussion work. The recordings were made during 'ordinary' lessons using unobtrusive equipment; the usual classroom teacher was present throughout. Whilst some of the transcriptions might suggest to many readers that the pupils were 'out of control', the classrooms all retained an orderly, unexceptional atmosphere. The extracts below were taken mainly from discussions of Tennyson's *Lady of Shalott*; a few further examples show pupils in a task involving them exchanging memories about earlier schooldays, whilst another was a role-play of teachers tackling a bullying problem.

A combination of mixed and single sex groups tackled each task. To achieve this arrangement, each pupil selected a partner, while the class teacher organized pairs to create four-person groups. Thus, pupils could work 'securely' with friends, whilst also meeting the challenge of articulating ideas to lesser known others. Owing to pupils' tendency to work in single sex groups (Davies, 1999), intervention was required to organize mixed sex groupings to allow comparative analysis. For the purposes of this article, examples are taken solely from single sex groups. Transcript conventions are explained in the Appendix.

Using Discourse Analysis techniques, the research considers whether discussions fulfilled the tasks set and whether there was variation according to gender. Dangers in such analysis include the temptation to over-generalize, to designate a linguistic feature as 'typical' of one gender and make brash conclusions regarding their signification. Although patterns were sought, the use of an intransigent framework was avoided. The precedent of progress has been made by other linguists (Coates, 1996; Eckert and McConnell Ginet, 1995; Eggins and Slade, 1997; Goodwin, 1998) and their findings and methods informed this work. Moreover the research is contextualized within current sociological debate (Connell, 1996), with awareness that the extent to which individuals lead gendered lives is varied. It has been demonstrated that there is an element of choice as to how far individuals perform gender in particular circumstances (Coates, 1996; Eckert and McConnell Ginet, 1995; Goodwin, 1998). Certainly, many of my subjects demonstrated variety in their performances, changing according to linguistic context (field, mode and tenor).

The data I gathered were complex: specifically the gendered variety of linguistic patterns, how tasks and group composition affected behaviour. Here, however, space permits representation of only a sample. In this article I focus on showing how:

- Girls demonstrate and cement their social loyalties via discussion work, challenging neither their membership of 'female culture' nor the work process, referred to as *polyphony* (Coates, 1996);
- Boys' demonstrations of their social loyalties severely challenges the work process and inhibits learning (referred to as *cacophony*);
- Boys' use of sexist language and stereotypes is rarely challenged by other boys – potentially harming themselves as well as girls;
- Boys tend to invoke the use of emblems from popular culture in order to avoid self-revelation.

In the discussions of the data below, lengthier examples of girls' discussions are given because of the way in which the points itemized earlier emerged more clearly in longer extracts for girls than in the more concise way the boys' language illustrated the contrasting features. Excerpts selected for this article concentrate on exemplifying ways in which pupils communicated gendered allegiances through their discussions.

Being Friends: The Girls' Discussions

The girls in my sample consistently produced friendly talk, comfortably fulfilling both social and educational work. The co-operative style required to achieve the tasks was easily accommodated by the girls and ran along congruent lines with their manner of forming friendships. Coates (1996) has already described the way in which talk forms the basis of women's friendships; building on her findings and analysis techniques, I have observed how well 'friendship talk' suits the learning process (Vygotsky, 1962). The unanimity of purpose characteristic of the girls' discussions supported the development of a group identity in which similarities among individuals were emphasized whilst, conversely, differences were relegated. The process by which this was achieved was performed implicitly through engagement styles. Coates (1996) uses the musical term 'polyphony' to describe the way in which discourse structure demonstrates, even enacts, harmonious relationships.

The all-girls groups did not express their gender in explicit ways nor did they articulate particular requirements, for indeed, such membership was never questioned. The stated goals of the work, to collaborate and negotiate through tentative exchanges of opinion, ideas and memories, represented no obstacle to the development of personal friendship goals. Gender allegiances were expressed in subtle ways; they were not foregrounded. The girls worked in a supportive climate in which they could experiment with words and struggle with ideas together. Their discussions showed that learning is facilitated in an environment in which participants share a sense of purpose and social goals could be achieved through academic agenda.

In many tasks, girls devoted time to storytelling. As Maybin (1997: 48) says, this technique allows a:

> revisiting … (of) issues in different stories and exchanges from different perspectives. Thus the recursive and iterative process of collaborative meaning-making between children is carried on at three inter-related levels: through the dialogues they reconstruct within stories, through the conversational exchanges from which the stories emerge and through the 'long conversations' across space and time.

In my observations, girls comfortably narrated anecdotes, confidently using a range of strategies to enliven them. The tales seemed familiar and well-rehearsed with pupils re-framing themes to suit different tasks.

Personal stories allow speakers to construct versions of themselves to entertain, and display linguistic expertise. Tellers not only shape versions of experiences past, they hold centre stage in constructing versions of themselves (Eggins and Slade, 1997; Hardy, 1975). […]

It is not just through the telling of stories that interlocutors collaboratively create texts. There are other ways of linking exchanges, offering mutual support, and expressing personal allegiance. In many of the discussion groups the pupils were able to share meanings and develop ideas using cohesive strategies which expressed a concerted effort, built on each others' contributions and afforded opportunities to learn together in a united way.

For example, in discussions of a Tennyson ballad (*The Lady of Shalott*) pupils were not required to offer a personal account of themselves. They needed to concentrate on the text, extracting information from it, deconstructing some of the meanings and to formulate opinions, nevertheless they did refer to personal details, albeit in a relevant way. It was again particularly the girls' groups which produced highly cohesive texts in which great attention was given to the poetry while relationships were simultaneously managed through the work.

Female discussants often even used similar intonation patterns and voice pitch to each other. Initial transcription of the texts was often tricky because pupils often spoke as if one voice. The high level of grammatical concord in the discourse allowed pupils to jointly construct a text which passed seamlessly from speaker to speaker. Thus, the value of individual contributions seemed less emphasized than the enterprise of jointly deconstructing the poetry and seeking consensus.

In this next example, for instance, the girls accumulated layer upon layer of adjectival and adverbial phrases to produce a verbal representation of the scene depicted in the ballad:[1]

11	CATH:	Well it's got lots of long fields/it's like countryside/
12	JULIE:	Peaceful place/
13	LISA:	Ermm (.)/
14	JULIE:	It's got lots of flowers and (.)/
15	KATIE:	Crops/
16	JULIE: LISA:	It's got (.) barley (.) and thyme (.)=/ Lots of fields and rivers/
17	EMMA:	Big countryside/
18	LISA:	It's got a river=/
19	JULIE:	It's got wildlife/
20	EMMA:	Very idealistic=/
21	JULIE:	Yes/
22	EMMA:	Like in a fairy tale/
23	LISA:	Picturesque/
24	JULIE:	The mood is like peaceful and silent and nice and relaxing/
25	EMMA:	Calm/

26	LISA:	Lazy. laid back/
27	JULIE:	Yes/
28	EMMA:	It seems (.) as if (.) <laughs> it's just got the (.) scenery (.)/
29	JULIE:	There's no like (.) towns springing up everywhere/
30	LISA:	It's just fields and sky <sing song voice>/
31	JULIE:	The same thing for every where (.) for ever and ever/
32	LISA:	The picture that is created is just like (.)/
33	EMMA:	Fields that go on for ever and meet the horizon so it just looks like it's meeting the sky?/
34	JULIE:	Yeah/
35	CATH:	It's a very peaceful picture/
36	JULIE:	Yeah (.)/

The discourse is poetic in its accumulation of descriptive lexicon, borrowing from the genre of idyllic romanticism. Pupils' vocabulary collocated with each other's across turns, responding in a sympathetic way to the tone of the poem as well as in keeping with each other's use of language. The pupils' syntax matched with each other's, such as in staves 11, 16, 18 and 19 there is repetition of 'It's got … + noun phrase'. In addition, the pupils' repetition of 'it's *just* + adverbial' on staves 28, 30 and 33 allowed them to jointly express the unobtrusive mood of the landscape. Moreover the minimal responses used at staves 21, 27, 34 and 36 emphasized a uniform approach. Lisa's use of a singsong intonation at stave 30 encapsulated the relaxed air of the whole group which seemed to be influenced by their total absorption with the poetry itself. Where there was overlap, there was no sense of competition to speak, more an enthusiasm to add to the chorus of an increasing catalogue of epithets in what became a verbal collage.

The pupils working in such collaborative groups attempted to elaborate fully on their answers to questions, seeking to satisfy all aspects of a problem and allowing input from everyone in each question. Responding to the question 'What is the Lady of Shalott weaving?' for example, these girls developed their answer fully in the following way:

220	LIZ:	Well er/what is The Lady of Shalott weaving?/
221	KIT:	Er a cloak?/
222	JO:	She's weaving a magic web/
223	SAL:	She's weaving her feelings into a fabric-/

224	KIT:	By night and day a magic	web with colours gay=/
	LIZ:		She's weaving a magic web/

225   JO: Yeah with lots of colours/

226   LIZ: What clues are there that The Lady of Shalott is tired of being isolated in the tower?/

227   SAL: We've done that one/

228   KIT: Yeah/

229   LIZ: Right/

230   JO: So she's weaving a magic web with colours gay/

231   LIZ: And it's like weaving her feelings into it/

232   KIT: It's her way of expressing her feelings/

233   LIZ: Yeah it's a way of expressing something/

234   SAL: There isn't a way of expressing in words/her way is through colour/

Beginning with an initial literal interpretation, Sal viewed the web as a metaphor and suggests that the Lady of Shalott 'is weaving her feelings into a fabric'. This idea was deconstructed by both Liz and Kit, so that Sal was able to conclude:

234   SAL: There isn't a way of expressing in words/her way is through colour/

This process of working on each other's words and phrases in jointly articulated responses to questions exemplifies the real jewels of active learning through talk. All participants freely played with ideas here, evaluating their own and other people's contributions in a secure context finally gaining a deeper understanding of the poetry. The pupils had helped each other to learn.

Proving Machismo: The Boys' Discussions

Many boys' perpetual attention to matters concerning membership of the 'male culture' required them to repeatedly define that culture and demonstrate their worthiness to belong. The discourse of work and the ways in which the boys expressed their gender allegiances were not compatible. Boys frequently had to choose whether to be accepted by their peer group and join in 'macho discourse' or to work hard and become ostracized and have their behaviour and language derided. Where these competing discourses of masculinity and academia collided, I refer to this as 'cacophony' emphasizing the converse way in which these discussions operate to polyphonous discourse (Coates, 1996).

Many groups, both male and female, began their discussions by addressing the tape recorder directly, perhaps introducing themselves by name, by identifying the gender of the group, or as here, by declaring a role for themselves:

---

177 BOB: Hello it's me again/I'm in control/

---

178 RICK: Yep/big gay/<laughs>

In every all-male group the term 'gay' was used frequently in a negative and gratuitous manner to defame other boys and to regulate group membership. Here, as typically, the use of the term did not denote homosexuality, but was used to disempower Bob. The designation 'gay' was never explicitly challenged; only through 'appropriate' behaviour could heterosexual conformity be proved. The term was also used to suggest homosexual tendencies:

---

61 SIM: You seen my bird?/

---

62 BOB: Morris has got a bi–ird/ <chanting/singing>(.)

---

63 SIM: And Bobby hasn't/

---

64 BOB: She's a right ugly get/(.)I haven't and I'm proud/

---

65 SIM: Yeah/because you are a gay bastard aren't you?/

In this example of off-task discussion, Sim referred to his girlfriend using proprietorial 'my' and denigrating language 'bird'. His question (stave 61) contained an assertion, reminding the group that he had a girlfriend. Bob answered the implicit assertion with a taunting intonation, thus undermining the status associated with coupling. Sim's retort that Bob had no girlfriend (so no associated kudos) was denigrated by Bob's answer to Sim's initial question in which he used slang to insult the girl and by implication, Sim. He reasserted his single status as superior 'I haven't and I'm proud'. Yet Sim concluded that not only was Bob 'gay', but also a 'bastard', playing the trump card in this particular game.

This was a venture of power fought on grounds where not only was it important to be sexually active, but also where girls were treated as mere ancillaries to the reputation being sought. Sim's status depended not only upon his possession of a girlfriend, but also upon her attractiveness. The signification of such associations is made clear here, that sexual credibility is based partly upon the marketability of the girl. The above exchanges show how boys use talk to socially engineer, to police each others' behaviour and to establish a pecking order of masculinity. It has all been off-task social work. Additionally pupils frequently empowered themselves at the expense of others, at times also alluding to great sexual appetite and an easy knowledge of acts which would repulse others (Davies, 1998). Their discourse placed them as perpetrators of sexual acts on passive subjects as seen in this next example:

154	Bob:	Right then(.)/We've got to think of lessons that we think we'd like/
155	Sim:	<laughs>
156	Ant:	Art and Design/
157	Bob:	SEX/
158	Rick:	Yeah
159	Bob:	Let's have sex sex sex sex sex/
160	Rick:	/practical sex
161	Bob:	<u>Practicals on sex education</u> <each word enunciated very clearly in R.P.>
162	Rick:	What if you just -/ what if you just stuck it in %her arsehole%?/
163	Bob:	<laughs>

The talk was saturated with references to sex, and through repeated references the boys impressed upon their peers their apparently irrepressible sexual urges. In this construction, girls were passive recipients of male sexual appetite at the mercy of the competence or otherwise of their impulses. The undercurrent of aggression was also manifest in behaviour towards each other in many of the discussions. In this way, the speakers used language which humiliated individual boys but all girls in general.

In announcing the gender of their group these boys emphasized that masculinity is an attribute to be earned rather than an assumed biological certainty. The precariousness of masculinity was emphasized through the declaration of the group's gender:

40	Jim:	Oh and by the way/this is an all boys group/OK?
41	Andy:	<laughs>/
42	Pierre:	It's a little bit late for that/
	Jim:	Most of us are boys<laughs>
43	Kirk:	We're close anyway <laughs>

Analysis of this group's work provides a number of examples in which Pierre was singled out as not possessing all the attributes required by 'real boys'. Life membership is not guaranteed; boys need continually to demonstrate that they deserve to be part of the male group. This same group demonstrated the positive value of maleness and the fragility of its attribution, for example at moments of conflict.

The earlier boys' examples arose from tasks requiring personal reflection on their schooldays. Such discussions saw boys persistently policing the talk, prohibiting 'female values' and embracing references to heterosexual prowess. Frequent diversions away from set tasks, with boys unable to combine gendered social goals with academic ones, were a strong characteristic of this task.

Concentration on literary work was sometimes more successful, but only if care was taken not to show too much absorption in the task. In the next extract, based on *The Lady of Shalott*, Pierre concentrated on answering the question about the colours mentioned in the ballad, spotting words and phrases as well as offering interpretative remarks. His enthusiasm was obvious, but the background of dissent led by Kirk clearly shows how resilient boys often need to be in order to work:

242	ANDY:	What are we on?/
243	PIERRE:	Part three/<high voice>
244	KIRK:	<u>Ooooh</u>/ <two tone high pitch in mockery of Pierre>
245	PIERRE: KIRK:	The sun dazzling through the leaves |like orange -/ |Pierre Pierre
246	PIERRE: KIRK:	|**and things it's gorgeous**/ |shut up/I'm not bothered/<high pitched mimicry>
247	PIERRE:	And the yellow gold/
248	KIRK:	You're just stupid you/
249	PIERRE:	And a GOLDEN GALAXY/erm/
250	KIRK:	Shut up Pierre/
255	ANDY:	Listen to him/Listen to him/oh God/
256	KIRK:	**He'll shut up now cos he's gonna smell it**/
257	ANDY:	**Oh God!**/
258	KIRK: PIERRE:	Oh |God |**Like crystals like with all colours coming out of it**/
259	KIRK:	See?/do you HAVE to speak like that and moving your hands about like a <u>queer?</u><laughs>/

Pierre commented relevantly on this poem using sophisticated vocabulary to deconstruct the ballad. He relished the poetry using such words as 'dazzling', 'gorgeous', 'yellow gold' and 'golden galaxy'. His utterances became increasingly loud, moving to an effective simile 'like crystals with all colours coming out of it'. Throughout this episode he was harangued repeatedly by Kirk, and eventually Andy, being called 'stupid', 'queer' and told to 'shut up' and later a 'turnip' and 'bum-bandit'.

Pierre's resilience was remarkable and his persistence in the face of extreme provocation instigated more assertive tactics from Kirk. Having not managed to interrupt Pierre's thought processes. Kirk spoke about him rather than to him, 'He'll shut up now cos he's gonna smell it'. On three occasions in this group Kirk referred to smells as a basis for distraction. The repulsed reaction from Andy was not echoed by Jim or Pierre who conformed to conventions of silence about such matters as bodily functions. Through acknowledging Kirk's remarks, Andy implicated himself in the strategy to prevent Pierre's continuance. Pushed to the limit, Pierre moved on to the next question, having approached this one unilaterally. It might be argued that Pierre dominated the discussion in a way that would have been unacceptable in the girls' groups. However, in this context if he had not done so it would be hard to envisage any work being achieved at all by this group.

Even in better-motivated boys' groups, members typically used 'distancing tactics' when tasks required personal reflection or anecdotal exchange. In order for the learning process to run smoothly alongside social development, amicable relationships were mediated through alternative versions of reality drawn through stereotyped concepts presented by the mass media, for example. Successful discussions arose from tasks which specifically *required* pupils to reflect on popular culture or to demonstrate familiarity with technology. Good relations were usually sustained through humour and if this could be achieved via inter-textual references, then so much the better. In the example below pupils were asked to role-play teachers tackling a bullying problem in their school. (Role-play has been argued to help boys 'save face' in expressing their own views; QCA, 1998.)

---

67   TOM: Right then./thirdly/

---

68   WES: Video cameras/

---

69   TOM: A list of ideas which you have/

---

70   JON: Err/Miss Jones is on camera/<laughs>

---

71   MAT: Suspect enters the room<laughs>

---

72   JON: I'm now showing suspect item two five A/<laughs>

---

73   MAT: D<laughs>

---

74   JON: Do you recognise this pen?

These boys subverted the teacher role-play and cleverly replaced it with their own ludic play. Pupils often sought opportunities to feed into the discourse an array of sketches which allowed them to display their familiarity with different genres and an ability to take on a range of voices. The above example evoked scenes from crime television with all four boys demonstrating they could enter into other spheres of life than that confined by domesticity and the institution of the school. Through appropriating this kind of language and using emblems from other networks, the boys were able to show through their familiarity with the language of the 'outside world' that they were part of it. The pupils seemed to stand 'at arms length' as it were, from each other and the topic, building relationships on shared understandings from without rather than within themselves. Other references included popular cartoon character impersonations, mention of satellite television sex channels, beer brands and football teams. These carefully chosen emblems were often used in competitive ways to accentuate familiarity with macho motifs; the wrong choices always attracted derision.

Conclusions

The way in which the girls in this study repeatedly told stories together emphasized their sense of being one group, not only in the way they shared the telling, but through the ways in which they sought to mirror each other's experiences through those stories. The girls created a sense of unity through their language creating texts in which individuals formed learning allegiances. The maintenance of amicable relationships seemed to be crucial to the process of learning support and the discussions tended to possess a highly positive aspect and to contain a high number of cohesive devices in the language.

Pressure to conform was not visible, for membership of their groups could be developed through the work as the styles used to manage friendship and work ran along congruent lines. Although the girls gained strength through their group solidarity, they nevertheless remained the often unconscious victims of boys' language. Although space does not allow me to present here moments of girls' conflict, or of their own sometimes sexist behaviour, it is worth noting nevertheless that they did occasionally accept the male construction of femininity in a manner which prevented them from developing their ideas freely.

The nature of the girls' harmonious scripts derived from the way in which pupils worked together on one theme, exploring possibilities by interweaving new ideas. Such discussions could be described as polyphonous (Coates, 1996: 133). However, where groups' discussions were less cohesive, a cacophonous, chaotic effect resulted. Here it was not possible to blend the work-related discourse with friendship or 'male bonding' discourses, because these did not run along congruent lines.

For the boys, difficulties presented by social constraints were at least as difficult to negotiate as the tasks themselves. The language the boys employed often restricted their freedom to experiment with words and ideas and they were highly reticent to challenge peer pressure. Where boys did experiment, they were sometimes able to enrich their work through intertextual references and humour, but this also had the potential to trivialize issues or to distract from the task. No pupils offered an alternative reading of 'gay', but boys usually adjusted their behaviour in order to avoid the term being directed at them. It was clear that the term represented a complex value system pervading the boys' attitudes to work, even when they were on task and interested.

It is often overlooked that many boys have problems conforming to a macho stereotype, often the butt of homophobic teasing and exclusion from the main group (Nayak and Kehily, 1996). As Connell (1996) has also witnessed, boys were often the victims of their own policing procedures. The vigilant monitoring of deviation from male heterosexual norms exerted great social pressure and this process made the work so much more difficult to negotiate for the boys than for the girls.

It is through verbally articulated displays of seeming homophobia, that the powerful boys in school often set the mood of an anti-school, anti-female culture. As my data demonstrate, boys frequently express both implicitly and explicitly, the view that conformity to educational expectations is feminine thus it is much less problematic for girls to conform to school expectations in this respect. Moreover, the ways in which boys are expected by their peers to behave is often counter to school expectations, requiring them to demonstrate very fine skills of dexterity in order to satisfy the conflicting pressures of their peers and the school. Girls' behaviour, however, gains approval not only from their peers, but also from the institution.

Some of the linguistic patterns I found in this data were very marked, with pressure from male peer groups enforcing social rules particularly strongly. Although girls in these examples remain the victims of the sexist language often employed by boys, the boys nevertheless win only a pyrrhic victory. In order to work towards equity in schools, commitment needs to be invested more broadly than just in the purely academic arena. Practitioners might question the validity of discussion work in the light of the above data; however, careful structuring of talk task, of group composition and pedagogical style can produce positive discussions in which all pupils can fulfil academic goals without the intrusion of negative social 'noise' (Davies, 1999; QCA, 1998). It remains important that teachers note the impact of gendered group dynamics and that both they and their pupils collaborate to improve the chances of all pupils.

Note

1 *Transcription conventions* can be found in Transcription Conventions 2, p. xii. The transcription layout is based upon that devised by Jennifer Coates (1996).

References

Arnot, M. and Weiner, G. (eds) (1987) *Gender and the Politics of Schooling*. Harmondsworth: Penguin.

Barnes, D., Britton, J. and Rosen, H. (eds) (1969) *Language the Learner and the School*. Harmondsworth: Penguin.

Basic Skills Agency (1997) *Our Quality Mark for Basic Skills in Secondary Schools*. London: Basic Skills Agency.

Cameron, D. (1985) *Feminism and Linguistic Theory*. London: Macmillan.

Clark, A. and Millard, E. (1998) *Gender in the Secondary Curriculum: Balancing the Books*. London: Routledge.

Coates, J. (1996) *Women Talk*. Oxford: Blackwell.

Connell, R.W. (1996) 'Teaching the Boys', *Teachers College Record* 98(2): 206–35.

Davies, J. (1998) 'Taking Risks or Playing Safe: Boys and Girls Talk in the Classroom', in A. Clark and E. Millard *Gender in the Secondary Curriculum*. London: Routledge.

Davies, J. (1999) 'Expressions of Gender', unpublished PhD thesis, University of Sheffield, UK.

Department of Education and Science (1975) *A Language for Life [The Bullock Report]*. London: HMSO.

Department of Education and Science (1989) *English for Ages 5–16 [The Cox Report]*. London: HMSO.

Department for Education and Employment (1997) *Excellence in Schools*. London: Stationery Office.

Department for Education and Employment (1998a) *Byers Outlines Co-ordinated Plan to Tackle Boys Underachievement – Byers DfEE Press Release 002/98*. London: DfEE.

Department for Education and Employment (1998b) *Secondary Education Report – Good Progress But Must Do Better – Byers Press Release: 296.98.* London: DfEE.

Department for Education and Employment (1998c) *Government Acts To Improve Boys' Performance – Morris DfEE Press Release 380/98.* London: DfEE.

Eckert, P. and McConnell-Ginet, S. (1995) 'Constructing Meaning, Constructing Selves: Snapshots of Language, Gender and Class from Belton High', in K. Hall and M. Bucholtz (eds) *Gender Articulated: Language and the Socially Constructed Self.* London: Routledge.

Eggins, S. and Slade, D. (1997) *Analysing Casual Conversation.* London: Cassell.

Frater, G. (1997) *Improving Boys' Literacy.* London: Basic Skills Agency.

Goodwin, M.H. (1998) 'Co-operation and Competition Across Girls' Play Activities', in J. Coates (ed.) *Language and Gender: A Reader.* Oxford: Blackwell.

Hardy, B. (1975) *Tellers and Listeners: The Narrative Imagination.* London: University of London/Athlone Press.

Lakov, R. (1975) *Language and Woman's Place.* New York: Harper & Row.

Mahony, P. (1985) *Schools for the Boys.* London: Hutchinson.

Mahony, P. (1998) 'Girls Will be Girls and Boys Will be First', in D. Epstein, J. Elwood, V. Hey and J. Maw (eds) *Failing Boys? Issues in Gender and Achievement.* Buckingham: Open University Press.

Maybin, J. (1997) 'Story Voices the Use of Reported Speech in 10–12 Year Olds "Spontaneous Narratives"', in L. Thompson (ed.) *Children Talking: The Development of Pragmatic Confidence.* Clevedon: Multilingual Matters.

Millard, E. and Walsh, J. (2001) *Improving Writing at Key Stage 2… Getting it Right for Girls and Boys.* Huddersfield: Kirklees Metropolitan Council Education Service.

Nayak, A. and Kehily, M.J. (1996) 'Playing it Straight: Masculinities Homophobias and Schooling', *Journal of Gender Studies* 5(2): 211–30.

Office for Standards in Education (Arnot, M., Gray, J., James, M. Rudduck, J. and Duveen, G.) (1998) *Recent Research on Gender and Educational Performance.* London: Stationery Office.

Qualifications and Curriculum Authority (1998) *Can Do Better.* London: QCA.

Spender, D. (1980) *Man Made Language.* London: Routledge & Kegan Paul.

Spender, D. and Sarah, E. (1980) *Learning to Lose: Sexism and Education.* London: The Women's Press.

Swann, J. (1992) *Girls, Boys and Language.* Oxford: Blackwell.

Swann, J. and Graddol, D. (1988) 'Gender Inequalities in Classroom Talk', *English in Education Oracy Edition* 22(1): 48–65.

Vygotsky, L.S. (1962) *Thought and Language.* London: MIT Press.

Woodhead, C. (1996, 8 March) 'Boys Who Learn to be Losers', *The Guardian.*

Younger, M., Warrington, M. and Williams, J. (1999) 'The Gender Gap and Classroom Interactions: Reality and Rhetoric?', *British Journal of Sociology* 20(3): 327–43.

10

Gender and the Use of Exclamation Points in Computer-Mediated Communication: An Analysis of Exclamations Posted to Two Electronic Discussion Lists

Carol Waseleski

Source: Journal of Computer-Mediated Communication 11(4) (2006), pp. 1012–24. Reprinted with permission.

Introduction

When elements of speech and writing are associated with female communication style, they tend to be described in negative terms (Mills, 1995). Tag questions, for example, are usually understood by grammarians to invite verification, confirmation, or consent, and by some linguists (e.g., Brown and Levinson, 1987), to function as politeness devices. When associated with female communication style, however, a tag question such as the last two words in "John is here, isn't he?" has been claimed (most famously by Lakoff, 1975) to indicate that the speaker lacks confidence in what she has said. Similarly, reference works on grammar and English usage describe the function of exclamation points as indicators of "emotive force" (Quirk, Greenbaum, Leech, Svartvik, 1985, p. 1633), or as a means to demonstrate that a "preceding word, phrase or sentence is an exclamation or strong assertion" (McArthur 1992, p. 394). When considered in relation to gender, however, exclamation points are often described as "markers of excitability," a phrase that implies instability and emotional randomness. Exclamation points are typically reported to be used by females significantly more than by males (Colley and Todd, 2002; Rubin and Greene, 1992; Scates, 1981; Winn and Rubin, 2001). However, the contexts in which the exclamation points appeared in these reports have generally not been examined for evidence of "excitability."

The present study begins by examining a body of research relating gender and the use of exclamation points. It shows how each piece of research built on its predecessors, further

Language and Gender: A Reader, Second Edition. Edited by Jennifer Coates and Pia Pichler.
© 2011 Blackwell Publishing Ltd except for editorial material and organization. © 2011 Jennifer Coates and Pia Pichler. Published 2011 by Blackwell Publishing Ltd.

developing the notion that exclamation points function as markers of excitability. Keeping in mind Mills' caution that linguistic elements should not simply be presumed to indicate factors such as deference, power, [or emotional state – CW], that "it is necessary to analyze the multiple possible uses of each element …" (1999, p. 27), the study then presents a 16-category coding frame as an alternative to the previous method of tallying up exclamation points and characterizing them exclusively as excitability markers. The results show that exclamation points function most often to indicate friendliness and to emphasize intended statements of fact, but only infrequently as markers of excitability.

"Markers of Excitability"

The notion that exclamation points function as markers of excitability can be traced in modern times to *The Way Women Write*, Mary Hiatt's (1977) study of women and men's writing styles. Extraordinarily ambitious for its time, Hiatt's content analysis of 100 literary works incorporated the use of computers to determine whether a feminine writing style actually existed and, if so, how it differed from masculine writing style. Hiatt proposed that certain types of punctuation could be used as a yardstick to analyze qualities in the prose of women and men; for example, she held that "the frequency of use of exclamation points is one indicator of what might be called 'emotionality' or 'excitability'…" (1977, p. 39), characteristics she believed were stereotypically associated with women. Hiatt did not formally define the term excitability, but operationalized "exclamatory style" as the use of four or more exclamation points in the 2,000-word writing samples that were randomly selected from each book. Samples were examined for the "presence (or absence) of certain elements [such as] numbers or words or other types of symbols" (1977, p. 19), and in the case of exclamation points, the elements were counted. Hiatt's computerized tallies indicated that the occurrence of exclamation points is greater in men's prose than in women's prose, i.e., that "women writers as a group do *not* exclaim more often than the men" (1977, p. 44).

Carol Scates' (1981) analysis of the gendered writing styles found in first year college students' compositions built on Hiatt's study, which she characterized as "the most comprehensive work on men's and women's writing styles to date" (Scates, 1981, p. 22). Scates analyzed many of the same stylistic elements that Hiatt had, among them exclamations. Content was analyzed to determine such elements as sentence type, syntax, use of figurative language, and approaches to topics, but some elements, such as exclamations, were simply counted. Scates' tallies indicated that females used exclamations substantially more than did males.

Building on Hiatt's (1977) and Scates' (1981) work, Rubin and Greene (1992) expected that sentence types such as exclamations would be among the "likely candidates" (1992, p. 15) to differentiate female and male prose in their study of college students' writing. Rubin and Greene analyzed the content of writing samples for rhetorical structure and tabulated the occurrence of stylistic features such as intensifiers, de-intensifiers, first person pronouns, perceptual verbs, and so on. Stylistic features were then combined into multivariate clusters including "markers of excitability" (exclamations and underlining). Although female and male styles were shown to be more similar to one another than different, Rubin and Greene reported that "where male and female styles did diverge, they differed in predicted directions. For example, women used far more exclamation points than men" (1992, p. 7). The term "Markers of Excitability" appears as a header in a results subsection. Although they didn't examine context for possible range of meaning of exclamations, Rubin and Greene proposed that, as an alternative to regarding exclamation points as signs of excitability, "a high frequency of exclamation points can be regarded as sort of an orthographic intensifier signaling 'I *really* mean this!'" (1992, p. 27). They also point out that this might convey the writer's lack of stature; that, in fact a confident person could "affirm their views by simply asserting them" (1992, p. 27).

Giving a new twist to the study of student compositions, Winn and Rubin (2001) investigated ways in which gender identity is enacted in the written language of personal ads. In separate writing tasks, college students composed self-descriptions for simulated personal ads and later composed responses to these ads. Winn and Rubin cite Hiatt's work as a source from which they derive gender-linked variables such as "markers of excitability (e.g., exclamation points)" (2001, p. 399) for their investigation. Like Rubin and Greene (1992), Winn and Rubin counted markers of excitability, but did not analyze the context in which they appeared for a possible range of meaning. Their results indicate that women use about "3 times more" (2001, p. 409) markers of excitability than do men.

In the area of computer-mediated communication, Colley and Todd's (2002) study of the gendered style and content of email examines many of the same stylistic markers for which Rubin and Greene (1992) had previously noted gender differences. Included among these was "excitability," as denoted by the use of exclamation marks and capitalization. Deriving the majority of their style categories from previous studies of email conducted by Rafaeli and Sudweeks (1993) and Savicki, Lingenfelter, and Kelley (1996), Colley and Todd asked college students to compose emails describing a recent holiday to (imaginary) friends interested in going to the same location. As did previous researchers, Colley and Todd coded text for the frequency of language features, but did not consider any characterization other than "excitability marker" for exclamation points. Like Winn and Rubin (2001), who "found that women used more nonessentials and excitability markers than men" (2002, p. 381), Colley and Todd's results indicate that women use exclamation points, especially multiple exclamation points, far more often than men do.

The Present Study

This study reports the results of a content analysis of 200 exclamations – words, phrases or sentences that end in exclamation points – in messages posted to two electronic discussion groups: dig_ref and JESSE. The entire message in which each exclamation appeared was recorded. As was the case with tag questions in previous research, it was expected that exclamations in these messages might have a "range of meaning … across contexts" (Cameron, McAlinden, and O'Leary 1989, p. 77); thus two raters reviewed the context in which the exclamations appeared and assigned each exclamation to one of 16 different content codes. The gender of the writer of each exclamation was also recorded, with gender being determined by the message writer's first name.

Setting

Electronic discussion lists where "people engage in socially meaningful activities online in a way that … leaves a textual trace" (Herring, 2004, p. 338) were chosen for this study, since their textual traces could be observed unobtrusively. Further, messages posted to electronic discussion lists reflect spontaneous discourse that is unmodified by others, and such messages have the additional advantage of being more or less permanently archived on the Internet and available for inspection by anyone (Sierpe, 2000).

The electronic discussion group dig_ref supports professionals who answer questions and provide expert information via the Internet, in settings that range from virtual library reference to online AskAnExpert services. At the time this study was conducted, dig_ref subscribership was 2,500. The electronic discussion group JESSE is not dedicated to a particular topic, but serves various professionals in library and information science (LIS) education. At the time this study was conducted, JESSE subscribership was 1,154.

The field of library and information science is predominantly female with distribution ranging from 62.7% female in academic and research libraries (Kyrillidou and Young, 2005) to 83.2% female for all types of libraries combined (US Bureau of Labor Statistics, 2006). Subscribership to LIS-related electronic discussion lists, then, might reasonably expected to be predominantly female; such is the case with dig_ref and JESSE (see Table 1). In addition, Herring (1996) has observed that electronic discussion lists serving female-predominant professions tend to exhibit features of female discourse style. Given the claim that use of exclamation points is a feature of female discourse style (Colley and Todd, 2002; Rubin and Greene, 1992; Scates, 1981; Winn and Rubin, 2001), dig_ref and JESSE seemed likely settings in which to locate exclamations.

While subscribership to dig_ref and JESSE is predominantly female, participation in both groups is predominantly male. Two samples were examined to determine female/male participation rates. The first sample consisted of the 607 messages from dig_ref and the 1,077 messages from JESSE that were used to retrieve the 200 exclamations used for this study. A larger "back-up" sample consisting of 1,400 messages from each list was also examined. (See Appendix for additional details regarding the two samples.) Participation was determined by the gender of the name of the poster of individual messages, and messages posted by each gender were counted. Participation rates by gender were very similar in the two samples. A comparison of subscribership and messages posted in dig_ref and JESSE is presented in Table 1.

Table 1 Participation in dig_ref and JESSE

	Subscribers identified as female	*Subscribers identified as male*	*Totals*	*Messages (from 2 samples) posted by identified females*	*Messages (from 2 samples) posted by identified males*	*Totals*
dig_ref	1,436 (72%)	558 (28%)	1994	1,138 (61%)	727 (39%)	1,865
JESSE	558 (64.5%)	307 (35.5%)	865	1,377 (63%)	794 (37%)	2,171
Combined totals	1,994 (70%)	865 (30%)	2859	2,515 (62%)	1,521 (38%)	4,036

Methods

Classification Scheme

ProjectH, an international analysis of computer-mediated communication conducted by Rafaeli and colleagues (1993, 1996), provided the basis for a classification scheme for collecting and evaluating data for the present study. Both the original ProjectH coding frame and an adapted coding frame used by Savicki, et al. (1996) in their study of 27 online electronic discussion groups consist of straightforward content codes that provided a range of objective alternatives to the more subjective descriptor "excitability marker." At the same time, when exclamations assigned to a given code (such as "Flame2") consistently expressed either positive or negative emotionality, the code could be acknowledged as indicating "excitability."

Examples of content codes include ACTION (meaning action or call for action by the individual posting the message, e.g., "Read e-books!"); APOLOGY (implied apology such as "I wish I hadn't said that!" also direct apology, i.e., "Sorry!"); COALITION (agreement with or support of those in the group or elsewhere), and FACT (facts whether correct or not; also, opinions stated as fact). Content codes such as "QUESTION" and "STATUS" (titles and words that identify the personal status of the message poster) were not relevant for this study and were not included. A complete list of the content codes adapted for this study, along with definitions and examples for each code, is provided in Table 2. Some of the examples in Table 2 are from Savicki et al. (1996), some from

Table 2 Codebook

Content code	Definition	Examples
Action	Action or call for action by the individual posting the message	I'm checking the search engine now! Read eBooks!
Apology	Implied or direct apology	I wish I hadn't said that! My apologies!
Challenge	Challenge, dares or bets	Prove it! Bet you won't find it!
Coalition	Agreement with / support of those in the group or elsewhere	You're right! Agnes makes a great point! I agree with those who say it shouldn't happen!
Fact	Intended statement of fact, whether or not the fact is correct; opinion stated as fact.	The world is flat! It turned my hair gray! They're freeloaders!
Firstperson 1	Self-disclosure, preferences using "I" or "my."	My hair is getting gray! I'd like to do reference at home in my robe!
Firstperson 2	Opinion using "I" or "my"	I like Blackboard! My side is better!
Friendly 1	Friendly greetings or closings	Hi! Hello everyone! Good luck! Bye!
Friendly 2	Friendliness, helpfulness, cordiality expressed within body of message	"Posts are archived at [URL] for your self-service convenience!"
Flame 1	Mild argument/annoyance	Not all answers take as long as 2 days!
Flame 2	Moderately aggressive/rude	I TOLD YOU- NOT IN THE LIBRARY!
Flame 3	Hostility, personal insult	You stupid jerk!
De-flame	Attempts to avoid tension, attempts to reverse flaming.	OK, calm down! Let's look at it another way!
Sarcasm	Sneering or cutting remarks	Big deal! Ooo, isn't that just too bad!
Thanks 1	Thanks used in closing or in opening	Thanks! Lisa
Thanks 2	Thanks expressed by sender in the body of the message.	Thanks for the information! I appreciate that!
Thanks 3	Effusive expressions of thanks.	It was wonderful of you to say that – thank you so very much!

dig_ref and JESSE, and some were created by the author. They were chosen to provide the clearest illustration of each category for an independent rater.

Procedures

The data collection method for this study consisted of using Internet Explorer's Edit > Find command to locate individual exclamation points, if any, in messages posted to dig_ref and JESSE. Beginning with the posting that was current at the time the study was conducted, messages were reviewed until a total of 100 exclamations were retrieved from each electronic discussion group. In the case of dig_ref, 607 messages were reviewed. In the case of JESSE, 1,077 messages were reviewed. Each exclamation and the entire message in which it appeared was stored in a database record that also included the first name and gender of the poster and a means of identifying and retrieving the message (e.g., a message number or a posting date) should that be required.

Exclamation points in trade names such as Yahoo! and Live! Chat were ignored. Moreover, parts or all of some messages had been copied and pasted from other sources, and those messages thus did not consist of original, spontaneously composed text. Such messages (e.g., calls for papers, announcements of trainings and conventions, job postings, requests to complete surveys, and promotional messages) were consequently ignored. Exclamations quoting other sources or other individuals ("Mary told them 'You should have thought of that sooner!'") were also ignored.

Inter-rater reliability

Two raters independently reviewed the content of each of the 200 exclamations retrieved from the sample of 607 messages from dig_ref and 1,077 messages from JESSE. Some messages contained more than one exclamation; each exclamation was treated as a separate unit of analysis. Each rater coded the 200 exclamations using the codebook shown in Table 2. Inter-rater agreement was established at 81% for the messages from dig_ref and at 85% for messages from JESSE.

In addition, each rater assigned a gender code "F" or "M" (a "U" was also available for "unknown," but was not needed) to the first name of each message poster. Gender ambiguous names were handled in different ways by the two coders. When the author encountered names of which she was uncertain, she consulted personal web sites, university web sites, and other web sources. She was able to confirm gender by viewing photos, by locating personal pronouns in "About our Staff" pages, and so on. The independent rater, however, was asked to assign gender codes based on conjecture. Interestingly, the independent rater's assignments were exactly the same as the author's. Thus, in assigning gender identity to the first names of the posters of the exclamations, 100% inter-rater reliability was established for both dig_ref and JESSE.

Findings

Table 3 indicates that most (i.e., 59) exclamations were statements of fact ("There's still time to register!" "Computers had an important impact in libraries before 1970!" "That makes us kindred souls!"). The codes "Thanks 1" and "Thanks 2" (thanks expressed either within the body of the message or as closing or greeting statements) both refer to

Table 3   Content codes for exclamations from dig_ref and JESSE

	DIG_REF			JESSE	
Code	Females	Males	Code	Females	Males
Action	8	2	Action	4	2
Apology	1	0	Apology	0	0
Challenge	1	0	Challenge	0	1
Coalition	5	1	Coalition	3	2
Fact	21	1	Fact	27	10
Firstperson 1	7	0	Firstperson 1	4	3
Firstperson 2	0	0	Firstperson 2	1	0
Friendly 1	6	2	Friendly 1	4	1
Friendly 2	3	3	Friendly 2	9	3
Flame 1	5	3	Flame 1	3	0
Flame 2	0	3	Flame 2	0	1
Flame 3	0	0	Flame 3	0	0
De-flame	1	1	De-flame	0	0
Sarcasm	6	2	Sarcasm	2	2
Thanks 1	9	5	Thanks 1	9	4
Thanks 2	2	0	Thanks 2	3	1
Thanks 3	2	0	Thanks 3	0	1
TOTALS	77	23	TOTALS	69	31

a friendly kind of thanking. Consequently, the exclamations in these categories were combined with the exclamations in the "Friendly 1" and "Friendly 2" categories (i.e., friendly greetings or closings such as "Hello, everyone!," "See you there!" or friendliness, helpfulness or cordiality expressed within the body of the message such as "I hope this helps!" and "Congratulations to Amanda!"). The adjusted results show that 62 (34%) of the exclamations were "friendly."

Because the content of exclamations from three other categories indicated "excitability," that is, the exclamations in these categories expressed positive or negative emotionality, the exclamations in these categories were also combined. The three categories were "Flame 2" (rude or moderately aggressive comments such as "Those damn programs are out of touch with reality!"); "Sarcasm" (sneering or cutting remarks such as "Surely anyone on JESSE could write better copy than that!"), and "Thanks 3" (effusive thanks such as "Thank you so much for your comments – they are very, very helpful and the list of resources is wonderful!"). The findings are summarized below.

Overall findings

Overall, 32% of the exclamations fell into the four "friendly" categories, i.e., Thanks1, Thanks2, Friendly1, and Friendly2. Another 29.5% of the exclamations fell into the Fact category, i.e., they were intended as statements of fact, whether or not the "fact" was correct. Only 9.5% of the exclamations fell into the three "emotional" ("excitable") categories, i.e., Flame 2, Sarcasm, and Thanks 3, effusive thanks. (There were no exclamations in the Flame 3 category.)

Gender-based findings

A breakdown of the results by gender indicates that 73% of all exclamations were made by females, and 27% by males. Similarly, 70% of all "friendly" statements (as defined above) were made by females, and 30% by males. Regarding statements of "fact," 81% were made by females, and 19% by males. Finally, females made 53% of all "emotional" statements (as defined above), compared to 47% by males.

Interpretation

While females posted 73% of the exclamations and males posted only 27%, participation rates in the two electronic discussion groups must also be factored into the analysis. Combined participation rates for both groups averaged 62% female and 38% male in both the original sample of 607 messages from dig_ref and 1,077 messages from JESSE and in the larger sample of 1,400 messages from each group. A Chi square analysis was conducted using exclamation rates (73% female and 27% male) as observed frequencies and participation rates (62% female and 38% male) as expected frequencies. Results (Chi-square = 5.136, df = 1, p = .0234) indicate that females did, indeed, use exclamations significantly more often than males did.

The results, however, do not show that exclamation points function solely – or even very often – as markers of excitability. Only 19 (9.5%) of the total of 200 exclamations examined indicated excitability, i.e., negative or positive emotionality. In contrast, exclamations functioned as markers of friendly interaction 32% of the time, and to emphasize intended statements of fact 29.5% of the time. Of the 19 "excitable" exclamations, 10 were made by females and nine were made by males. A Chi square analysis was performed using "excitable" exclamation rates (53% female and 47% male) as observed frequencies and participation rates (62% female and 38% male) as expected frequencies. The results (Chi square = 3.438, df = 1, p = .0637) suggest that a larger sample would be needed in order to better evaluate this relationship, but that the trend is in the direction of males using excitable exclamations more often than females use them.

A Chi square analysis was also attempted for use of "friendly" exclamations. Using the rates of 70.3% female and 29.7% male as observed frequencies and participation rates of 62% female and 38% male as expected frequencies, Chi square results (Chi square = 2.924, df = 1, p = .0872) again suggest that a larger sample would be needed in order to better evaluate this relationship, although the trend in this case favors female use of "friendly" exclamations. Finally, Chi square analysis (Chi square = 15.323, df = 1, p = .00009) using "intended fact" rates of 81% female and 19% male as observed frequencies and participation rates of 62% female and 38% male as expected frequencies clearly indicates that females use exclamation points to emphasize intended statements of fact significantly more often than do males.

Discussion

The results of this study do not support the notion that exclamation points function solely or even primarily as markers of excitability. However, the finding that females use exclamations significantly more than do males is consistent with the findings of Rubin and Greene (1992), Winn and Rubin (2001), and Colley and Todd (2002). Thanking, whether of the friendly or effusive type, was also a predominantly female behavior. These findings are consistent with Herring's (1994) observation that female online discourse style is characterized by "supportiveness," which includes "expressions of appreciation, thanking, and community building activities that make other participants feel accepted and welcome" (p. 4).

Moreover, the findings in this study relating to flaming were consistent with those of Herring (1994), who found "little or no flaming and cooperative, polite exchanges" (p. 2) in online discussion lists devoted to "feminized" professions such as librarianship. Only 11 exclamations in the Flame 1 category (mild argument/annoyance) were made, eight by females and four by males. Only four exclamations fell into the more emotional Flame 2 category, three of which were made by one male who had become angry over a single issue. In other results that are consistent with what Herring (1994) observed in female-predominant electronic discussion lists, there were only two "challenges," one from a female and one from a male ("Answer that one, why doncha!" and "I'd like to talk to those who think running DE is cheap!"). Only 12 of the exclamations were sarcastic, four made by males and eight by females.

These results echo the lack of flaming and other abusive behavior observed during Sierpe's (2000) monitoring of JESSE. Noting that questions posted to JESSE were not of a type that usually lead to heated debate, Sierpe wondered whether this "absence of passionate debate was the result of a different value system and one that permeates all LIS-related electronic discussions lists or is a particular feature of JESSE" (2000, p. 287). The present study's finding of mostly cooperative, polite exchanges and lack of heated debate, as well as the lack of extensive flaming and other abusive behavior, also suggests the presence of LIS-oriented (feminized) values.

Limitations and directions for future research

This study was limited to a sample of 200 exclamations that were posted to the library and information science electronic discussion groups dig_ref and JESSE, the latter being the subject of one of the few existing studies of gender and computer-mediated communication in library and information science (Sierpe, 2000). Although selection of LIS electronic discussion groups provided an opportunity to relate new findings to old in a field in which computer-mediated communication is becoming increasingly important, LIS-oriented values may have affected the results, limiting the possibility of generalization to other types of electronic discussion groups.

Future studies might address these limitations by comparing exclamations posted in electronic discussion lists associated with feminized professions to exclamations posted in lists associated with other, non-feminized professions. Comparisons might also be made in non-work online settings. More generally, a study of wider scope using larger samples could help to determine whether males use significantly more "excitable" exclamations than do females, or if females use significantly more "friendly" exclamations than do males. Further research should also address whether the use of exclamation points alters perceptions of, say, "friendliness" in email environments. For example, is "Thank you!" perceived as friendlier than "Thank you" in email?

Conclusions

The results of the present study bring to mind Coates' (1998) study of gossip (reproduced in Part IV of this Reader), in which she points out that women's uses of tag questions and other devices "had been interpreted as signs of weakness" (1998, p. 250). When considered in context, however, tag questions were found to "serve the function of asserting joint activity and of consolidating friendship" (Coates, 1998, p. 250). By considering the context in which exclamations were used, and by adopting a more nuanced methodology than has been adopted in the past, the present study has demonstrated that exclamation points do more than function as markers of excitability; they can also function as markers of friendliness.

This finding is important for two reasons. First, even though email is extensively used, it still lacks "universally agreed modes of behavior established by generations of use" (Crystal, 2001, p. 15) and precise means for conveying exactly the impressions the email sender wishes to convey. This study suggests that individuals of both genders can convey "friendliness" via the (non-excessive) use of exclamation points. Second, the results point to the need to re-consider the negative labels that have often been associated with female communication styles, and to investigate the multiple possible uses of linguistic elements for potential re-labeling and re-interpretation as they relate to email and other forms of computer- mediated communication.

Note

Thanks are due to Eileen Pearce who acted as a second independent rater for this study, to the owners of dig_ref for their cooperation, to Eino Sierpe for his advice, and to *JCMC*'s editor and reviewers for their invaluable recommendations.

References

Brown, P., and Levinson, S. (1987). *Politeness: Some Universals in Language Usage*. Cambridge: Cambridge University Press.

Cameron, D., McAlinden, F., and O'Leary, K. (1989). Lakoff in context: The social and linguistic functions of tag questions. In J. Coates & D. Cameron (Eds.), *Women in Their Speech Communities: New Perspectives on Language and Sex* (pp. 74–93). New York: Longman.

Coates, J. (1998). Gossip revisited. In J. Coates (Ed.) *Language and Gender*. (pp. 226–53). Oxford: Blackwell.

Colley, A., and Todd, Z. (2002). Gender-linked differences in the style and content of e-mails to friends. *Journal of Language and Social Psychology*, 21(4), 380–92.

Crystal, D. (2001). *Language and the Internet*. Cambridge: Cambridge University Press.

Herring, S. C. (1994). *Gender Differences in Computer-Mediated Communication: Bringing Familiar Baggage to the New Frontier*. Keynote address at the American Library Association Annual Convention, Miami, Florida. Retrieved July 25, 2006 from http://www.vcn.bc.ca/sig/comm-nets/herring.txt

Herring, S. C. (1996). Two variants of an electronic message schema. In S. C. Herring (Ed.), *Computer-Mediated Communication: Linguistic, Social and Cross-Cultural Perspectives* (pp. 81–108). Amsterdam: John Benjamins.

Herring, S. C. (2004). Computer-mediated discourse analysis: An approach to researching online behavior. In: S. A. Barab, R. Kling, and J. H. Gray (Eds.), *Designing for Virtual Communities in the Service of Learning* (pp. 338–76). New York: Cambridge University Press.

Hiatt, M. (1977). *The Way Women Write*. New York: Teachers College Press.

Kryllidou, M. and Young, M. (Eds) (2005). *ARL Annual Salary Survey 2004–2005*. Washington, DC: Association of Research Libraries.

Lakoff, R. (1975). *Language and Woman's Place*. New York: Harper & Row.

McArthur, T. (Ed.). (1992). *The Oxford Companion to the English Language*. Oxford: Oxford University Press.

Mills, S. (1995). *Feminist Stylistics*. London: Routledge.

Mills, S. (1999). Discourse competence; or how to theorize strong women speakers. In C. Hendricks and K. Oliver (Eds.), *Language and Liberation* (pp. 81–98). Albany, NY: SUNY Press.

Quirk, R., Greenbaum, S., Leech, G., and Svartvik, J. (1985). *A Comprehensive Grammar of the English Language*. London: Longman.

Rafaeli, S., and Sudweeks, F. (1997). Networked interactivity. *Journal of Computer-Mediated Communication*, 2(4). Retrieved July 25, 2006 http://jcmc.indiana.edu/vol2/issue4/rafaeli.sudweeks.html

Rafaeli, S., Sudweeks, F., Konstan, J., and Mabry, E. (1993). ProjectH overview: A collaborative quantitative study of computer-mediated communication. Retrieved February 2, 2006 http://www.it.murdoch.edu.au/~sudweeks/papers/techrep.html

Rubin, D., and Greene, K. (1992). Gender-typical style in written language. *Research in the Teaching of English*, 26(1), 7–40.

Savicki, V., Lingenfelter, D., and Kelley, M. (1996). Gender language style in group composition in Internet discussion groups. *Journal of Computer-Mediated Communication*, 2(3). Retrieved July 25, 2006 http://jcmc.indiana.edu/vol2/issue3/savicki.html

Scates, C. (1981). *A Sociolinguistic Study of Male/Female Language in Freshman Composition*. Unpublished doctoral dissertation. University of Southern Mississippi, Hattiesburg, Mississippi.

Sierpe, E. (2000). Gender and technological practice in electronic discussion lists: An examination of JESSE, the library information science education forum. *Library & Information Science Research*, 22(3), 273–90.

US Bureau of Labor Statistics. (2004). Table No. 604: Employed Civilians by Occupation, Sex, Race and Hispanic Origin: 2004. In US Census Bureau (Ed.). *Statistical Abstract of the United States*, 2006 (pp. 401–4). Washington, DC: US Census Bureau.

Winn, L., and Rubin, D. (2001). Enacting gender identity in written discourse: Responding to gender role bidding in personal ads. *Journal of Language and Social Psychology*, 20(4), 393–418.

Appendix

Appendix Subscribership of dig_ref and JESSE as of November, 2004

	dig_ref	*JESSE*
Subscribers with first names identified as "female" names	1436 (72%)	558 (64.5%)
Subscribers with first names identified as "male" names	558 (28%)	307 (35.5%)
Total "identified" female / male subscribers	1,994	865
Subscribers with first names that could not be identified as either "female" or "male"	318	203
Subscribers with first names used by both genders, e.g., Terry, Leslie, Jan, Lee, Chris, Pat.	133	48
Duplicates (individuals subscribed under more than one email address)	43	27
Institutional/corporate subscribers	12	11
Total subscribership as of November, 2004	2,500	1,154

Participation Rates in dig_ref and JESSE by Gender

	dig_ref Sample 1	*JESSE* Sample 1	*dig_ref* Sample 2	*JESSE* Sample 2	*Combined average*
Number of messages posted by subscribers with "female" first names	346 (60.38%)	598 (63.28%)	792 (61.3%)	779 (62%)	62% (rounded)
Number of messages posted by subscribers with "male" first names	227 (39.62%)	347 (36.72%)	500 (38.7%)	447 (38%)	38% (rounded)
Total number of messages with "gender-identified" names	573	945	1,292	1,226	
Number of messages posted by subscribers whose first names could not be identified as "female" or "male"	34	132	108	174	
Total number of messages reviewed	607	1,077	1,400	1,400	

Part III

Gender, Power, and Dominance in Mixed Talk

The last section focused on gender and conversational practice. In this section, we shall look at the way certain conversational strategies and discourses can be used to achieve dominance in talk. Research focusing on mixed talk in a variety of social contexts has revealed asymmetrical patterns, with men's greater usage of certain strategies being associated with male dominance in conversation. In the last 10 years there has been less research in this area – particularly on talk in the private sphere – as a result of the tension between the postmodern idea that "woman" cannot be treated as a uniform social category and the continuing awareness that "Gender relations are power relations" (Osmond and Thorne 1993: 593) and that "women are still systematically discriminated against" (Mills 2003: 240). Researchers are well aware of these tensions: DeFrancisco, for example, the author of the second paper included in this section, has addressed such concerns explicitly in a recent book (DeFrancisco and Palczewski 2007). Issues of power and dominance will be taken up again in Parts V, VII, and X. The first four papers in this section focus on conversational dominance, while the last paper brings us into the twenty-first century with its exploration of the impact sexist ideology can have on women's everyday lives.

Interruptions are perhaps the most unambiguous linguistic strategy which achieves dominance, since to interrupt someone is to deprive them – or at least to attempt to deprive them – of the right to speak. The classic paper on gender differences in interruptions is that of Zimmerman and West (1975). Zimmerman and West drew on the model of turn-taking established by Sacks, Schegloff, and Jefferson (1974) to refine the distinction between overlaps (brief, non-threatening instances of simultaneous speech) and interruptions (major incursions into another speaker's turn at talk). The first paper in this section is a later paper by the same writers, Candace West and Don Zimmerman. This paper – "Women's Place in Everyday Talk" – recapitulates their earlier research project and compares the patterns they found there with patterns found in parent–child interaction. Their earlier finding – that male speakers regularly interrupt female speakers in mixed pairs, even though interruptions are rare in male–male and female–female pairs – is compared with the finding that adults regularly interrupt children. West and Zimmerman claim that women in contemporary American society, like children, have

Language and Gender: A Reader, Second Edition. Edited by Jennifer Coates and Pia Pichler.
© 2011 Blackwell Publishing Ltd except for editorial material and organization. © 2011 Jennifer Coates and Pia Pichler. Published 2011 by Blackwell Publishing Ltd.

restricted rights to speak, and that interruptions are used both to exhibit and to accomplish socially sanctioned relations of dominance and submission. (More recent research, analyzing family interaction, supports West and Zimmerman's claims by showing how dinner-table talk reproduces a traditional gender-based division of labor, where "father knows best" – see, for example, Ochs and Taylor 1995; Kendall 2008.)

Interruptions are not the only linguistic strategy implicated in conversational dominance. The next paper in this section, Victoria DeFrancisco's "The Sounds of Silence: How Men Silence Women in Marital Relations," focuses on non-cooperation in interaction. DeFrancisco got seven married couples to record themselves at home for a week or more, using the method developed by Pamela Fishman (1980). She subsequently interviewed each of the participants on their own and asked them to comment on extracts from their recorded conversations. She found that, although the women talked more than the men, and introduced more topics, this was not associated with dominance. In fact, the women were less successful than the men in getting their topics accepted. The men used various non-cooperative strategies to control conversation: no-response, interruption, inadequate or delayed response, and silence. DeFrancisco concludes that men have the power to establish the norms of everyday conversation in the home, and that women have to adapt to these norms.

While DeFrancisco's research restricts itself to the domestic environment, the next two papers in this section look at patterns of dominance in language used in the public sphere. Joan Swann, in her paper "Talk Control," examines linguistic and paralinguistic behavior in the school classroom. She analyzes her data in terms of a range of variables: amount of talk, chipping in, teachers' gaze. Her paper problematizes various issues, in particular the notion that dominance can be achieved by male speakers without the complicity of women. She shows how, in the classroom situation, female teachers and girl pupils collude with boys to construct male dominance. Her insights into the construction of dominance and control suggest that change will be difficult to achieve.

The fourth paper in this section – Susan Herring, Deborah Johnson, and Tamra DiBenedetto's "Participation in Electronic Discourse in a 'Feminist' Field" – analyzes interactive behavior on the internet. It focuses primarily on amount of talk as a measure of dominance. Susan Herring had observed (Herring 1992) that participation on the e-mail discussion list known as Linguist (subscribed to by professional linguists worldwide) was highly asymmetrical, with male participants contributing 80 percent of the total discussion. Herring, Johnson, and Dibenedetto therefore undertook an investigation of a smaller, more woman-friendly list, to see if a less adversarial environment would facilitate more symmetrical patterns of participation. In fact, women still only contributed 30 percent of the discussion. But during the five weeks of discussion chosen for analysis, there were two days when women's contributions exceeded men's. The resulting disruption, with men claiming they were being "silenced" and threatening to "unsubscribe" from the network, suggests that there is an underlying cultural assumption that women and men do not have equal rights to speak.

The last paper in this section looks at the impact sexist ideology can have on women's everyday lives. Jie Yang's paper, "Zuiqian 'Deficient Mouth': Discourse, Gender and Domestic Violence in Urban China," examines the relationship between language, gender, and domestic violence. The author identifies a meta-pragmatic discourse on domestic violence around the term *zuiqian*, meaning "deficient mouth." This discourse includes a series of terms such as *zuisui* "broken mouth" (talking about trivial things in great detail) or *chang shetou* "long tongue" (being too inquisitive and nosey). This discourse in effect blames women's "deviant" speaking styles for the serious social problem of domestic violence. As feminist scholars have noted in many contexts, problems in male–female relations are frequently redefined as problems arising from failings in women themselves. In her ethnographic study of a community in Beijing, Yang talked to local women: their unsympathetic statements about abused women show how this sexist discourse has been internalized by members of the community. Moreover, women who are victims of domestic violence struggle to understand their situation and often blame themselves. As Yang says, "by attributing the root cause of domestic violence to women's 'deficient' mouths, the relation of gender domination is … simplified and disguised."

As these papers demonstrate, the use of language as a means of asserting dominance occurs world-wide, and the prevailing pattern is of men dominating women. This may be through interrupting, through holding the floor too long, or through withholding talk. Both DeFrancisco and Yang show that silence is used by husbands as a demonstration of power over wives. Male dominance can be achieved through non-violent means, as in the first four papers in the section, or through ideologies of female deficiency which excuse or condone male violence against women. The final paper reminds us of the power of discourses to construct a sexist reality. This is not specific to China: in the UK, a wife's "nagging" can be used as a defense against charges of violence (see the many cases collected by the group Justice for Women), while recent work in the educational sphere argues that language and violence are intrinsically linked in constructing and maintaining boys' dominance in school (see, for example, Kenway and Fitzclarence 1997; Francis 2000; Mills 2001; Skelton 2001). We shall return to issues of power and dominance in Part V, which looks at gender and interaction in public contexts, and in Part VII, which asks whether the linguistic features associated with women are related to power and powerlessness rather than gender. The role of ideology in constructing gender norms will be discussed further in the final section of the Reader (Part X).

References

DeFrancisco, Victoria Pruin and Palczewski, Catherine Helen (2007). *Communicating Gender Diversity: A Critical Approach*. Thousand Oaks, CA: Sage.

Fishman, Pamela (1980) "Conversational insecurity," pp. 127–32 in Howard Giles, Peter Robinson, and Philip Smith (eds) *Language: Social Psychological Perspectives*. Oxford: Pergamon Press.

Francis, Becky (2000) *Boys, Girls and Achievement: Addressing the Classroom Issues,* London: Routledge.

Herring, Susan (1992) "Gender and participation in computer-mediated linguistic discourse," Washington, DC: ERIC Clearinghouse on Languages and Linguistics. Document no. ED345552.

Kendall, Shari (2008) "The balancing act: framing gendered parental identities at dinnertime," *Language in Society* 31, 539–68.

Kenway J. and Fitzclarence, L. (1997) "Masculinity, violence and schooling: challenging 'poisonous pedagogies'," *Gender and Education* 9(1), 117–33.

Mills, M. (2001) *Challenging Violence in Schools*. Buckingham: Open University Press.

Mills, Sara (2003) *Gender and Politeness*. Cambridge: Cambridge University Press.

Ochs, Elinor and Taylor, Carolyn (1995) "The 'father knows best' dynamic in dinnertime narratives," pp. 97–120 in Kira Hall and Mary Bucholtz (eds) *Gender Articulated*. London: Routledge.

Osmond, Marie W. and Thorne, Barrie (1993) "Feminist theories: the social construction of gender in families and society," pp. 591–622 in Pauline Boss et al. (eds) *Sourcebook of Family Theories and Methods*. New York: Plenum.

Sacks, Harvey, Schegloff, Emanuel A., and Jefferson, Gail (1974) "A simplest systematics for the organisation of turn-taking in conversation," *Language* 50, 696–735.

Skelton, Christine (2001) *Schooling the Boys*. Buckingham: Open University Press.

Zimmerman, Don and West, Candace (1975) "Sex roles, interruptions and silences in conversation," pp. 105–29 in Barrie Thorne and Nancy Henley (eds) *Language and Sex: Difference and Dominance*. Rowley, MA: Newbury House.

Recommended Further Reading

Fishman, Pamela (1983) "Interaction: the work women do," pp. 89–102 in Barrie Thorne, Cheris Kramarae, and Nancy Henley (eds) *Language, Gender and Society*. Rowley, MA: Newbury House.

Hall, Kira and Bucholtz, Mary (eds) (1995) *Gender Articulated: Language and the Socially Constructed Self*. London: Routledge.

Itakura, Hiroko and Tsui, Amy (2004) "Gender and conversational dominance in Japanese conversation," *Language in Society* 33, 223–48.

Mills, M. (2001) *Challenging Violence in Schools*. Buckingham: Open University Press.

Osler, A. (2006) "Excluded girls: interpersonal, institutional and structural violence in schools," *Gender and Education* 18(6), 571–90.

Sattel, J. W. (1983) "Men, inexpressiveness and power," pp. 118–24 in Barrie Thorne, Cheris Kramarae, and Nancy Henley (eds) *Language, Gender and Society*. Rowley, MA: Newbury House.

Walsh, Clare (2001) *Gender and Discourse: Language and Power in Politics, the Church and Organisations*. London: Longman.

11

Women's Place in Everyday Talk: Reflections on Parent–Child Interaction

Candace West and Don H. Zimmerman

Source: Social Problems 24 (1983), pp. 521–9. Reprinted with permission of the University of California Press.

Introduction

It is sometimes said that children should be seen and not heard and that they should speak only when spoken to. To be sure, situations abound in which children are seen and most definitely heard without prior invitation to talk from adults. Nevertheless, these maxims do tell us that children have restricted rights to speak resulting in special problems in gaining adults' attention and engaging them in conversation. For example, Sacks (1966) has observed that children frequently use the form "D'ya know what?" when initiating talk with an adult. The answer to this particular question is ordinarily another question of the form "What?" and the adult so responding finds that he/she has given the child opportunity to begin an utterance to which a listener attends – at least for the moment.

Fishman (1975) observed that in fifty-two hours of tape-recorded conversation collected from three couples the women employed the "D'ya know what?" opening twice as frequently as men. Overall, the women asked almost three times as many questions as the men. The implication is, of course, that the greater reliance on such question forms by women stems from *their* limited rights as co-conversationalists with men.

The difficulties children encounter in verbal interaction with adults follow perhaps from their presumed lack of social competence. A child is a social actor whose opinion may not be taken seriously and whose verbal and non-verbal behavior is subject to open scrutiny, blunt correction, and inattention. It is thus potentially illuminating when parallels between the interaction of adults and children and men and women are observed.

Goffman (1976) characterizes the relation of middle-class parents to their children in face-to-face situations as one of benign control. The child is granted various privileges and the license to be a child, i.e., merely to play at or practice coping with the manifold demands of the social occasion. Goffman (1976: 72–3) notes that "there is an obvious price that the child must pay for being saved from seriousness," a price that includes

Language and Gender: A Reader, Second Edition. Edited by Jennifer Coates and Pia Pichler.
© 2011 Blackwell Publishing Ltd except for editorial material and organization. © 2011 Jennifer Coates and Pia Pichler. Published 2011 by Blackwell Publishing Ltd.

suffering parents' intervention in his/her activities, being discussed in the presence of others as if absent, and having his/her "time and territory ... seen as expendable" due to the higher priority assigned to adult needs. This sort of relation in face-to-face interaction can characterize other encounters between subordinate and superordinate parties:

> It turns out ... that in our society whenever a male has dealings with a female or a subordinate male (especially a younger one), some mitigation of potential distance and hostility is quite likely to be induced by application of the parent–child complex. Which implies that, ritually speaking, females are equivalent to subordinate males and both are equivalent to children. (Goffman, 1976: 73)

Perhaps this ritual equivalence of women and children includes as a common condition the risk that their turns at talk will be subject to interruption and hence control by a superordinate.

In this paper, we compare the results of our previous study of interruptions in same-sex and cross-sex conversations (Zimmerman and West, 1975) with similar data from parent–child verbal interaction and find striking similarities between the pattern of interruptions in male–female interchanges and those observed in the adult–child transactions. We use the occasion of this comparison to consider the function of interruptions in verbal exchanges, particularly in conversations between parties of unequal status. Since interruptions are a type of transition between speakers, our point of departure in this as well as the previous paper is the model of turn-taking in conversation advanced by Harvey Sacks, Emanuel Schegloff and Gail Jefferson (1974) which provides a systematic approach to speaker alternation in naturally occurring conversation.

The Turn-Taking Model

Sacks et al. (1974) suggest that speech exchange systems in general are arranged to ensure that (1) one party speaks at a time and (2) speaker change recurs. These features organize casual conversation, formal debate, and high ceremony. Conversation is distinguished from debate and ceremony by variable distribution of turns, turn length, and turn content.

A turn consists of not merely the temporal duration of an utterance but of the right and obligation to speak allocated to a particular speaker. Turns are constructed out of what Sacks et al. (1974) call "unit-types" which can consist of words, phrases, clauses, or sentences.[1] Unit-types are projective, that is they provide sufficient information prior to their completion to allow the hearer to anticipate an upcoming transition place.

Sacks et al. (1974) represent the mechanism for speaker transition as an ordered set of rules speakers use to achieve a normatively constrained order of conversational interaction. For each possible transition place, these rules provide, in order of priority: that (1) current speaker may select the next speaker, e.g., by using a term of address, and if not choosing to do so, that (2) a next speaker may self-select, and if not, that (3) the current speaker may continue. The exercise of any of these three options recycles the rule-set to the first option. The operation of the rule-set accounts for a number of regularly occurring features of observed conversations – including the alternation of speakers in a variable order with brief (if any) gaps or overlaps between turns, as well as variable length of turns. That is, the model provides for the systematic initiation, continuation and alternation of turns in everyday conversation.[2] Our concern here is with the phenomenon of simultaneous speech, i.e., the occurrence and distribution of overlap among categories of speakers.

Elsewhere (Zimmerman and West, 1975: 114) we have defined overlap as a brief stretch of simultaneous speech initiated by a "next" speaker just before the current speaker arrives at a possible transition place, often in a situation where the current speaker has elongated the final syllable of his/her utterance (cf. Sacks et al., 1974: 706–8; Jefferson and Schegloff, 1975: 3):[3]

(T14:213–214)　B2:　　Um so where's your shoror-sorORity
　　　　　　　　　　house. Is it on campus or off: :?
　　　　　　　B1:　　　　　　　　　　　　[No] it's
　　　　　　　　　off=all thuh sororities and fraternities
　　　　　　　　　are off campus.

The significance of overlap occurring in such an environment follows from the fact that speakers apparently "target" the starting of their stream of speech just at completion by the current speaker (Jefferson and Schegloff, 1975). When successfully managed, the next speaker "latches" his/her utterance to the utterance of the preceding speaker as in the following:

(Jefferson and Schegloff, 1975: 3)
　　　　　　EARL:　How's everything *look*.=
　　　　　　BUD:　=Oh looks pretty *goo*:d,

Jefferson and Schegloff (1975: 3) also observe that the addition of tag-questions or conjunctions to a possibly complete utterance furnishes another locus for overlap:

(Sacks et al., 1974: 703, n. 12)
　　　　　　BERT:　Uh *you* been down here before ⌈ havenche ⌉
　　　　　　FRED:　　　　　　　　　　　　　　⌊ Yeh. ⌋

(T14:59–60)　B1:　I don't like it at all ⌈ but- ⌉
　　　　　　　B2:　　　　　　　　　⌊ You d ⌋on't

An interruption, in contrast, involves a "deeper" intrusion into the internal structure of the speaker's utterance, i.e., prior to a possible transition place:

(T1:114–115) A1:　It really sur ⌈prised me becuz-⌉
　　　　　　　A2:　　　　　　⌊It's jus' so smo :g⌋gy ...

Thus, what we call "overlaps" (Sacks et al. use the term to refer to all instances of simultaneous speech) are events occurring in the immediate vicinity of a possible transition place and can be seen as generated by the ordinary workings of the turn-taking system (cf. Sacks et al., 1974: 706–8). Interruptions, however, do not appear to have a systemic basis in the turn-taking model as such, i.e., they are not products of the turn-constructional and turn-allocation procedures that make up the model. Moreover, there is nothing in the model to suggest that patterned asymmetries should occur between particular categories of speakers. Quite to the contrary, the model is posited to hold for all speakers and all conversations (cf. Sacks et al., 1974: 700) and represents a mechanism for the systematic allocation of turns across two or more speakers while minimizing gap and overlap.[4]

Viewed strictly in terms of the turn-taking model, then, the deep incursion into the turn-space of a current speaker constitutes a violation of turn-taking rules.[5] Interruptions accomplish a number of communicative acts, among them the exhibition of dominance and exercise of control in face-to-face interaction.

Findings

Our preliminary findings (Zimmerman and West, 1975) suggested marked asymmetries in overlaps, interruptions, and silences between, same-sex and cross-sex conversational pairs. These interactional episodes were (like the parent–child segments introduced below) selected from longer stretches of talk by excerpting all topically coherent segments exhibiting (a) two or more noticeable silences between speaker turns or (b) two or more instances of simultaneous speech, without regard for who overlapped whom. That is, they were selected precisely because of the presence of gaps and overlaps. Three fourths of the exchanges between eleven adult male–female, ten adult male–male, and ten adult female–female parties were recorded in coffee shops, drug stores, and other public places in a university community; the remainder in private dwellings (cf. Zimmerman and West, 1975: 111–12).

The same-sex transcripts displayed silences in nearly equal distributions between partners. And while overlaps occurred with greater frequency than interruptions, both were distributed symmetrically between male–male and female–female speakers. In all, there were seven interruptions in the same-sex conversations coming from three transcripts: in two of these there were three interruptions, and in one of them, a single interruption. These were divided as equally as possible between the two parties in each conversation: 2 vs. 1, 2 vs. 1, and 1 vs. 0. By comparison, cross-sex conversations displayed gross asymmetries. Interruptions were far more likely to occur than overlaps, and both types of simultaneity were much more frequently initiated by males than females. For example, forty-six out of forty-eight, or 96%, of the interruptions were by males to females.[6] Females, on the other hand, showed a greater tendency toward silence, particularly subsequent to interruption by males. These patterned asymmetries – most striking in the case of interruption – led us to conclude tentatively that these females' rights to complete a turn were apparently abridged by males with impunity, i.e., without complaint from females.[7]

Recall Goffman's (1976: 73) observation that children – in interaction with adults – are accorded treatment characteristically extended to "non-persons," i.e., their status as co-participants in conversation is contingent on adult forbearance, and their "time and territory may be seen as expendable." If we regard conversational turn-space as the "time and territory" of a speaker, then the tendency of males to interrupt females implies that women's turn at talk is – at least some of the time – expendable and that women can be treated conversationally as "non-persons." With these considerations in mind, we present our parent–child transcripts.

Five interactions between parents and children were recorded in a physician's office, either in the open waiting room, or in the examination room before the doctor–patient interaction began.[8] Each author inspected the transcripts of these exchanges to locate instances of simultaneous speech. In the five parent–child exchanges, we found seventeen instances of simultaneity, of which fourteen were interruptions. Of the fourteen, twelve, or 86%, were by the adult. The remaining two interruptions were by the same child to an adult (trying to get her attention).

Hence the striking asymmetry between males and females in the initiation of interruptions is reproduced in the transcripts of parent–child conversation. However, in contrast to the broader range of situations where the adult conversations were recorded, the parent–child segments are two-party conversations drawn from a single setting. But one might argue that interactions between children and their parents in other, more relaxed situations might have a markedly different character.[9] The pertinent point, in any event, is whether or not interruptions occur *when* the issue of who is to control the interaction is salient. Hence, the conversational exchanges recorded in the physician's office, while insufficient in themselves to establish the point, do suggest that interruptions are employed by the dominant party, the adult, to effect control in the exchange.[10] Let us consider some of the ways interruptions may function to achieve control and to display dominance in both parent–child and male–female conversations.

Discussion

Taking the similarities in the patterns of interruptions between adults and children and males and females to mean that females have an analogous status to children in certain conversational situations implies that the female has restricted rights to speak and may be ignored or interrupted at will. However, we suggest that the exercise of power by the male (or, for that matter, the parent) is systematic rather than capricious, and is thus subject to constraint. That is, wholesale trampling of speaker rights, even in the case of children, is not culturally approved, and those speakers who indiscriminately interrupt or otherwise misuse their conversational partner are subject to characterization as rude, domineering, or authoritarian. We believe interruptions are a tool used to fashion socially appropriate interactional *displays* which both exhibit and accomplish proper relationships between parties to the interaction.

Parent–child interaction

A common-sense observation about physicians' offices is: many (if not most) young children are apprehensive about what will happen to them there. Moreover, parents are likely to feel some anxiety about the behavior of their children in that setting: control over the child is necessary to insure cooperation in the medical examination, to suppress protest or other expressions of reluctance to participate, and to prevent uninvited handling of equipment in the examining room (cf. Goffman, 1976). We can thus expect interactions of the following sort:

```
CHILD:    But I don't wanna shot! ((sobs)) you said (x)
          said you said ⎡ I          ⎤
PARENT:              ⎣ Look ⎦ just be quiet and take that
          sock off or you'll get more than just a shot!
```

Or:

```
CHILD:    If I got one wi ⎡ th a   ⎤
PARENT:              ⎣ Leave ⎦ that alone Kurt
(1.8)
CHILD:    Huh?
PARENT:   Don't touch that roller
```

The rule-set described earlier is a system of rules governing the construction of speaker turns and the transitions between them. Observance of these rules results in the distribution of opportunities to speak among participants and hence, the allocation of a segment of time to the speaker. The time slot under control of a speaker is potentially (a) a time when the speaker may engage in activities other than speaking, e.g. handling some object, and (b) a time when the speaker's utterance itself may unfold as a definite *action*, e.g. as a complaint or insult. The turn-taking system assigns the current turn-holder the right to that interval, to reach at least a first possible transition place (Sacks et al., 1974: 706) and the listenership of those present and party to the talk ratifies that right. Given that many utterances project not only their ending but their sense as well (cf. Jefferson, 1973: 54–60), to listen (or to be witness to some unfolding behavior), is an *act* in its own right according at least provisional approval or acquiescence to the action heard (or witnessed), and acknowledging the right of the speaker to be speaking. What is said and *listened to* combine to permit inferences about the character and relationship of the speaker and hearer.

Thus, in the case of the parent–child interactions discussed above, adult forbearance of the child's protest or failure promptly to disrobe could be seen as tolerance of – if not acquiescence to – the child's "unruly" behavior. If the child is simultaneously engaged in taking a turn at talk *and* some problematic non-verbal behavior, or if *what* the child is using the turn to do (e.g., to protest) is problematic, then the parent's presumed obligation to correct or control the child's behavior may take precedence over the child's already uncertain right to complete a turn. Moreover, the parent's intrusion into the child's turn *exhibits* the adult's control over the situation and the child, displaying it to the parent, the child, and to any others witnessing the interaction. The parent's failure to act in problematic situations also shows a lack of control or the child's dominance. Insofar as the parent–child relationship is *essentially* asymmetrical by our cultural standards, those occurrences warranting adult intervention may warrant interruption of the child's turn at talk as well.

Woman's place

The similarity between parent–child and male–female conversational patterns in our data has been noted. The suggested parallel is clear: men interrupt women in situations where women's verbal or non-verbal behavior is somehow problematic, as in the following:

FEMALE: Both really (#) it just strikes me as too
           1984ish y'know to sow your seed or whatever
           (#) an' then have it develop miles away not
           caring i⌈f ⌉
MALE: ⌊Now: :⌋ it may be something uh quite
           different (#) you can't make judgments like
           that without all the facts being at your
           disposal

Or:

FEMALE: I guess I'll do a paper on the economy business
           he laid out last week if ⌈I can ⌉
MALE: ⌊You're⌋ kidding!
           That'd be a *terrible* topic.

And:

FEMALE: So uh you really can't bitch when you've got
all those on the same day (4.2) but I uh *asked*
my physics professor if I couldn't chan⌈ge that⌉
MALE: ⌊Don't⌋ touch that
(1.2)
FEMALE: What?
(#)
MALE: I've got everything jus' how I want it in that notebook (#) you'll screw it up
leafin' *through* it like that.[11]

Our reflections here touch on three matters. First, we take the view that the use of interruptions by males is a *display* of dominance or control to the female (and to any witnesses), just as the parent's interruption communicates an aspect of parental control to the child and to others present. Second, the use of interruptions is *in fact* a control device since the incursion (particularly if repeated) disorganizes the local construction of a topic, as in the following:

FEMALE: How's your paper coming?=
MALE: Alright I guess (#) I haven't done much in
the past two weeks
(1.8)
FEMALE: Yeah::: know how that⌈can⌉
MALE: ⌊Hey⌋ya' got an extra cigarette?
(#)
FEMALE: Oh uh sure ((hands him the pack))
like *my* ⌈pa⌉
              ⌊How⌋'bout a match?
MALE:
(1.2)
FEMALE: Ere ya go uh like *my* ⌈pa⌉
MALE: ⌊Thanks⌋
(1.8)
FEMALE: Sure (#) I was gonna tell you ⌈my⌉
MALE: ⌊Hey⌋I'd really like
ta' talk but I gotta run (#) see ya
(3.2)
FEMALE: Yeah

Third, and perhaps most important, the occurrence of asymmetrical interruption signals the presence of issues pertinent to the activation of dominating behavior by the male. That is, just as the physician's examining room is a setting likely to engender adult concerns for control of the child (and hence, interruption of the child's utterance, among other things) so too may various occasions, *and the talk within them* trigger male displays of dominance and female displays of submission. Thus, the presence of male-initiated simultaneity – particularly interruptions – provides a clue where to search in interactional materials to find the particulars accounting for the occurrence of situationally induced attempts at dominance, in part through the suspension or violation of the rule-set.[12] Those "situational inducements", viewed from within the matrix of our present culture, constitute the warrant for interruption of the female by the male.

Concluding Remarks

These are preliminary findings, based on suggestive but far from definitive results. We report them here to show their potential significance for the study of gender behavior. The notion that language and speech communicate the cultural significance of gender is reflected by the growing literature in this area (cf. Key, 1975; Lakoff, 1975; and Thorne and Henley, 1975). Earlier research has utilized verbal interaction as an index of power in familial interaction (Farina and Holzberg, 1968; Hadley and Jacob, 1973; and Mishler and Waxler, 1968).

However, the use of features of conversational interaction as measures of power, dominance and the like has produced inconclusive – and sometimes contradictory – findings (cf. Shaw and Sadler, 1969) in the absence of an explicit model of conversational interaction *per se*. The work of Sacks, Schegloff, and Jefferson (1974) provides a theoretical basis for analyzing the very organization of such social interaction. We have tried to sketch the outlines of an approach to the study of male–female interaction utilizing this model.

Notes

This is a revised version of a paper presented at the American Sociological Association Annual Meetings, August 25–30, 1975, San Francisco, California. We wish to acknowledge the many helpful comments and suggestions of Thomas P. Wilson and Michelle Patterson. We owe Gail Jefferson more than we could ever acknowledge.

1   The criteria for determining a unit-type are only partially syntactic. For example, the status of a word as a unit-type is a sequential and hence, social-organizational issue, as in saying "Yes" in answer to another's question.

2   The model is further characterized as *locally managed*, i.e., it operates to effect transitions between adjacent turns, the focus being upon the next turn and next transition. The turn-taking system is also said to be *party administered* and *interactionally managed*, i.e., under the control of speakers and employed on a turn-by-turn basis by conversationalists each exercising options contingent upon, and undertaken with the awareness of, the options available to the other.

3   The transcribing conventions used for our data are presented in Transcription Conventions 1, p. x.

4   The model is proposed as a context-free mechanism that is at the same time finely context-sensitive. "Context-free" here means that it operates independently of such features of actual conversations as topics, settings, number of parties, and social identities. Given this independence, the mechanism can accommodate the changing circumstances of talk posed by variation in topic, setting, number of speakers and their identities; that is, its context-sensitivity permits it to generate the particulars of unique conversations. The model is thus posited to pertain to "any speakers" and "any conversation" (cf. Sacks et al., 1974: 699–701, especially n. 10 p. 700 for a brief consideration of the issues raised by this claim). Such a proposal of course runs counter to the basic sociological notions of social and cultural variability. Can different ethnic groups, social classes, or even males and females within such categories be assumed to use the same mechanisms for effecting turn transition? Here we simply assume that white, middle-class university students – male and female alike – are oriented to turn-taking in the fashion Sacks et al. (1974) assert, thus permitting us to focus on the communicative and interactional implications of violations of turn-taking rules. The issue of the generalizability of the model across other social and cultural categories we leave to further inquiry.

5   The turn-by-turn organization of talk means that both the relevance and coherence of talk are locally managed by participants at any particular point in conversation (e.g. given a subsequent occurrence, what may have begun as topic X may be transformed into topic Y). Clearly, not all instances of simultaneous speech are disruptive. Jefferson (1973), for example, comments on the precision placement of a characteristic class of events which overlap a present speaker's utterance in such a way as to indicate both active listenership and independent knowledge of what the overlapped utterance is saying. Such displays occur *prior* to completion of a unit-type (i.e. by our schema, at points of interruption). Our point here is that beginning to speak prior to a possible transition place can be a communicative act with sequential consequences for conversation (cf. Jefferson and Schegloff, 1975).

6   Ten of the eleven cross-sex interactions exhibited interruptions, ranging from a low of two to a high of thirteen and averaging 4.2 per transcript. In every conversation, the male interrupted the female more frequently than vice versa.

7   The collection of conversations analyzed here and in Zimmerman and West (1975) does not constitute a probability sample of conversationalists or conversations. Hence, simple projections from findings based on this collection to conversationalists or conversations at large cannot be justified by the usual logic of statistical inference. Thus, the present research is intended to illustrate the utility of the Sacks et al. (1974) model as a means of locating significant problems in the area of language and interaction and as a point of departure for further study.

8   The children in these exchanges ranged from four to eight years of age. Parties to conversation include two mother–son pairs, two mother–daughter pairs, and one father–daughter pair.

9   For example, multi-party conversations in the home might be situations in which children have greater needs to compete for the attention of adults than in the case of two-party exchanges in public. Hence, these "competitive" situations would be more likely to produce instances of interruption of adults by children. We have seen some indications to this effect, in other transcripts of exchanges in this same setting (i.e. the physician's office). However for purposes of comparability with our adult conversations, we are interested only in two-party exchanges here.

10   We should note that more systematic study is called for to control for setting itself. Our current research utilizes variations on a standardized experimental setting in which dyads of equivalent ages and educational backgrounds – but differing sex compositions – interact.

11   This last excerpt is an exchange embedded in a longer sequence marked by pronounced "retarded minimal responses" i.e., silences prior to issuing a brief acknowledgement of prior speaker's utterance, e.g., "unhuh."

12   Clearly, to test a hypothesis that particular types of situations induce male displays of dominance and female displays of submission would require that we define such situations independently of the occurrence of interruption.

References

Farina, Amerigo, and Jules D. Holzberg (1968) "Interaction patterns of parents and hospitalized sons diagnosed as schizophrenic or non-schizophrenic." *Journal of Abnormal Psychology* 73: 114–18.

Fishman, Pamela (1975) "Interaction: The work women do." Paper presented at the American Sociological Association Annual Meetings, San Francisco, California, August 25–30, 1975.

Goffman, Erving (1976) "Gender advertisements." *Studies in the Anthropology of Visual Communication* 3: 65–154.

Hadley, Trevor and Theodore Jacob (1973) "Relationship among measures of family power." *Journal of Personality and Social Psychology* 27: 6–12.

Jefferson, Gail (1973) "A case of precision timing in ordinary conversation: Overlapped tag-positioned address terms in closing sequences." *Semiotica* IX: 47–96.

Jefferson, Gail and Emanuel Schegloff (1975) "Sketch: Some orderly aspects of overlap in natural conversation." Unpublished manuscript.

Key, Mary Ritchie (1975) *Male/Female Language*. Metuchen, NJ: Scarecrow Press.

Lakoff, Robin (1975) *Language and Woman's Place*. New York: Harper & Row.

Mishler, Elliot G. and Nancy E. Waxler (1968) *Interaction in Families: An Experimental Study of Family Process and Schizophrenia*. New York: Wiley.

Sacks, Harvey (1966) Unpublished Lectures, University of California, Los Angeles.

Sacks, Harvey, Emanuel Schegloff and Gail Jefferson (1974) "A simplest systematics for the organization of turn-taking for conversation." *Language* 50: 696–735.

Shaw, Marvin E. and Orin W. Sadler (1965) "Interaction patterns in heterosexual dyads varying in degree of intimacy." *The Journal of Social Psychology* 66: 345–51.

Thorne, Barrie and Nancy Henley (1975) *Language and Sex: Difference and Dominance*. Rowley, Massachusetts: Newbury House.

Zimmerman, Don H. and Candace West (1975) "Sex roles, interruptions and silences in conversation." Pp. 105–29 in Barrie Thorne and Nancy Henley (eds.), *Language and Sex: Difference and Dominance*. Rowley, Massachusetts: Newbury House.

12

The Sounds of Silence: How Men Silence Women in Marital Relations

Victoria Leto DeFrancisco

Source: *Discourse & Society* 2(4) (1991), pp. 413–24. Reprinted with permission of SAGE.

I want him to tell me what he's thinking, what he's feeling. … About a month ago I said, 'Hal talk to me, just don't sit there like a bump on a log. Talk to me …'. He'll, when we're arguing mostly, I'll say, 'just explain to me now, what are you saying, what is it?' And he won't. He takes it as an insult I guess that I don't understand what he's saying and he won't explain. … (A 21-year-old Hispanic woman describes communication with her husband.)

Part of the impetus for this research project was my personal dissatisfaction in conversing with some men; a dissatisfaction similar to that expressed above by a woman in the present study. This project was also influenced by the growing body of research on gender and conversation. Many earlier studies have seemed to accept gender differences as a given and have failed to consider social or relational contexts (see critiques by Rakow, 1986; Spitzack and Carter, 1989; Thorne et al., 1983). Instead, the research which seemed most insightful and challenging to me was that which attempted to link larger social hierarchies to the less assuming, day-to-day interactions between women and men (e.g. Davis, 1988; Fishman, 1983; Henley, 1977; Hite, 1987; Rubin, 1976, 1983; Sattel, 1983; Spender, 1980; West and Zimmerman, 1983). Nancy Henley (1977) called this the study of micropolitics, meaning that larger social inequalities can be observed in the microcosm of our personal relations where these inequalities are created, maintained and even justified.

An example of such research is Pamela Fishman's more naturalistic examination of ongoing interactions in white heterosexual couples' homes. She examined a number of conversational devices used to build conversation or to detour it and found that for the three couples studied, the women worked harder to initiate and maintain conversation than the men, but were less successful in their efforts. Her conclusion was that women do the 'shitwork' of conversation. This controversial thesis made an important connection between other domestic duties traditionally ascribed to women, and the work of conversational development and relational maintenance.

However, like much communication research on conversation, Fishman's work still omitted an important source of information: the individual speaker's views. I chose to extend Fishman's methods of studying conversational development in ongoing interactions by adding private interviews. The primary purpose of the interviews was to discover the individuals' communication preferences in reviewing specific interactions with their spouses.[1] When I combined these methods I found several intricate means by which these women have been silenced, not only by the non-responsive men in their lives, but also by the social science methods commonly employed in such communication research.

Participants and Methods Description

There were seven couples in the study. I accepted only those who worked outside the academy. Couples were paid US$20 for participation. The couples lived in two medium-sized midwestern cities. Their ages ranged from 21 to 63. They had lived together for between 2 and 35 years and this was the first marriage for all persons involved. Three of the couples had children living at home. All the participants described their marital relationships as being generally satisfying and stable, and their descriptions of relational and domestic duties suggested they follow fairly traditional gender-role behaviors (Fitzpatrick, 1988; Maltz and Borker, 1982 [reprinted in Part VIII of this volume]). One woman described herself as Hispanic, the others were Anglo-Americans.

I chose to study ongoing interactions where individual attempts to initiate conversation could be noted over time. To do so, a tape recorder with an omnidirectional microphone was set up in the central living area of each couple's home for a week to 10 days, which produced an average of 12 hours of recording. The participants were asked to run the recorder whenever both partners were present for an extended period of time and to go on about their regular household activities. They had the right to erase recordings or turn off the machine at any time, but only two brief comments were reportedly erased. The participants said they became comfortable with the taping and that the conversations were representative of their daily interactions, although I realize some degree of artificiality may be inevitable.

After the taping I conducted a private interview with each person. The individual listened to two or three different episodes, totaling approximately 30 minutes. The participant was asked to stop the recorder to note anything she or he liked or disliked about the episode. To help clarify this task I first asked the person to brainstorm some examples of what likes and dislikes might be, and I stressed that I was not looking for any one type of information. Interviews were conducted within one week of the tape recordings and lasted an average of 90 minutes.

The episodes participants reviewed, plus an additional 30 minutes of interaction per couple, were transcribed using an adaptation of Jefferson's system [see Transcription Conventions 1, p. x]. I worked with the transcripts, the actual recordings and participants' comments to compile relative frequencies on the following conversational components identified as problematic in previous gender research: talk time (Fitzpatrick and Dindia, 1986; Martin and Craig, 1983; Spender, 1980); question-asking (Fishman, 1978a, 1983); topic initiations (Fishman, 1978b; Tannen, 1984; West and Garcia, 1988); topic success/failure (Fishman, 1978a, 1978b, 1983); and turn-taking violations, including interruptions (Dindia, 1987; Kennedy and Camden, 1983; Roger, 1989) and turns at talk which seem minimal, delayed or complete failures to respond (labeled the no-response – Fishman, 1978a, 1983; West and Zimmerman, 1983).

Criteria for Identifying Conversational Components

I began with the assumption most gender and conversation research has been based upon Sacks et al.'s (1974) model of turn-taking. Underlying tenets of this model are that a turn at talk is seen as a right and an obligation to speak. Generally one person speaks at a time, and speaker turns recur. Conversational partners are said to be conscious of their speaker/listener roles, as turns at talk tend to occur with few or no silences between. Thus behavioral failures to follow these norms may be considered uncooperative, inattentive and turn-taking violations. I included in my analyses of turn-taking violations those which seemed delayed (1–3 seconds average); minimal (monosyllabic turns at talk, 'mhm', 'yeah', not to be confused with active-listening cues); complete failure to take one's turn at talk, the 'no-response' violation (Fishman, 1983, 1978a); and interruptive (the listener begins to speak at a point that is unlikely to be a completion point in the current speakers' utterance).[2]

While Sacks and his colleagues' (1974) model served as a guideline for identifying these violations, I soon realized, as others have noted (Murray, 1985), that the tenets of their model were not universal. Consequently, identifications were also based on information gleaned from the tapes and the interviewees' reactions (Murray, 1985). Topic changes were identified by criteria adapted from previous research (Fishman, 1978b; Tannen, 1984) and from contextual information. A number of indicators were used to distinguish successful and unsuccessful topics. These included responses which directly shut off an attempted topic; topics which received a higher frequency of interruptions, minimal, delayed or no-response violations from the other speaker; and indicators that the original speaker knew her or his topic was in trouble, such as increases in verbalized pauses (Fishman, 1978b: 14). Talk time was measured with a hand-held stopwatch and total word count.

Results

After learning first-hand how complex and interpretive the work of identifying conversational components is, the reader is cautioned against making any conclusive judgments based on the numbers reported below. While the risks of quantifying gender differences across individuals, couples, and contexts are apparent, I conducted these frequency counts in an effort to provide preliminary parallels with previous studies of gender and conversation. Thus the following should be viewed as suggestive and not exhaustive. Furthermore, the patterns of behaviour and other ethnographic information are what is important, not the individual results.

There are two general findings which lead to the conclusion that the men were relatively silent and that their behaviors silenced the women. First, the no-response was the most common turn-taking violation, particularly for the men. Second, results from the components of conversation combined with the ethnographic information strongly suggest that the women in this project worked harder to maintain interaction than the men, but were less successful in their attempts. Together these findings reveal the multiple ways in which these women have been silenced.

No-responses accounted for 45 percent of the total 540 violations; interruptions were the second most common violation, but only accounted for 24 percent. Among the total violations, the women were responsible for 36 percent and the men were responsible for 64 percent. The men were responsible for more turn-taking violations across all categories studied (no-response, 32 percent women, 68 percent men; interruption, 46 percent women, 54 percent men; delayed response, 30 percent women, 70 percent men; and minimal response, 40 percent women, 60 percent men).

The higher percentage of no-response violation was not expected given the previous focus in gender research on the interruption as a central dominance behavior (e.g. Dindia, 1987; Kennedy and Camden, 1983; Roger, 1989; West and Zimmerman, 1983). However, in general, these conversations were not interactive enough to necessitate interruption. The television ran the entire recording time in two couples' homes, and when simultaneous talk did occur, the participants did not always perceive it as a turn-taking violation. They heard it as a sign of their partner's enthusiasm toward the conversation. Among the fourteen participants, interruptions were rarely listed as a complaint about their partners. The problem, particularly for the women in this study, seemed to be more basic – getting a response at all.

The second point which led me to conclude that the men generally silenced the women is that, similar to Fishman's earlier work (1978a, 1978b, 1983), there were several indicators which suggested communication was more important for the women, that they worked harder at it than the men, and yet were less successful. The women talked more (139 minutes total, 63 percent; men spoke 83 minutes, 37 percent), yet seemed to have far less turn-taking violations (197, 36 percent to 343, 64 percent); and they raised more topics (236, 63 percent to 140, 37 percent), yet succeeded less often than the men in getting these developed into conversations (156, 66 percent succeeded compared to 106, 76 percent).

Certainly there may be other explanations for these results. First, talking more could have been a dominance behavior. However, when a person dominates by doing most of the talking, the person will also tend to interrupt more (Spender, 1980) and be more likely to have her or his topics succeed, neither of which occurred here. Second, merely raising a topic is not necessarily a positive effort toward conversation since some things may be better left unsaid. However, in the topic analysis, I found women and men were both as likely to raise all categories of topics except one – personal emotions or concerns. Since there were only five instances of this topic initiation on all the tapes (all raised unsuccessfully by the women), it seems reasonable to suggest that topic selection was generally not the problem. Furthermore, regardless of the topics' positive or negative nature, when one person seems to do most of the decision-making regarding which topics are successful and which are not, that decision-making may be a form of control and silencing.

The following is an example of the variety of strategies one man used to detour his partner's topic and her response efforts.

1 MARY: I went to Diana's ((food store)) today, for lunch, got a salad you know? (.)
2 BUD: Ahha.
3 MARY: = Ran into your mom.
4 BUD: = Ran into who? (1)
5 MARY: Your mom. (1) She didn't even know who 1 was. (2)
6 BUD: Ahhh. (1)
7 MARY: She was at the, she was at the meat case and, and I was looking at, you know I was gettin my salad, and I come around and she was at the meat case and then she took off, and then (2)
8 BUD: {Be right back ((goes outside)) Ouch, my elbow! (45) ((door bangs, he returns)) (7) Emm (2)
9 MARY: So I followed her all the way up through the store (1) and she was ((word))
10 BUD: {well, you have to remember my mom, my mom has tunnel vision, too, I mean she don see nothin but straight ahead.

*   *   *

11   MARY: I've got this all figured out. (3) I talked to Doyle today? (4) And, (4) you know explained to him the fact that you know, come April I'll probably have to (1) ahm (.)

12   BUD: {Excuse me, open the back door, I'm gonna give this to (the dogs). (8) ((He returns.))

13   MARY: I'll probably have to terminate my appointment.

During our interview Bud said he did not feel like talking at the time of the conversation and that he had 'heard it all before'. His lack of attentiveness was apparent: he went outside twice during her stories (lines 8, 12); he seemed to diffuse her punch-line for the first story (line 10); he seldom provided any apparent participative listening cues (lines 2, 6); and he seemed to exhibit no-response violations (e.g. lines 11, 12, 13). In the total 12.5-minute conversation, he had 18 turn-taking violations, she had 9. She raised 7 topics, 5 of which were successful; he raised 4, all successfully. Together these suggest she was working harder at the conversation, but with less success than Bud.

All the women expressed concern about getting their husband's attention and mentioned the extra efforts they made to try to do so. One woman, Sandy, said: 'He doesn't talk to me! If it were up to him, we wouldn't talk.' She described various attention-getting strategies: she quizzed him if she suspected he had not been listening; she used guilt and jealousy strategies, and she purposefully raised topics he enjoyed.

In contrast to the women's efforts to encourage talk, they noted in the taped interactions a variety of what they termed 'patronizing', 'put-down' and 'teachy' behaviors by their husbands. Paternalistic statements are said to limit another's behavior through what are presented as well-meant intentions (Davis, 1988: 23). In the taped interactions the men's patronizing comments seemed to detour the women's efforts to develop conversation. In a more blatant case, when Sharon asked Jerry's opinion about responding to a newspaper advertisement he warned, 'Be careful you don't get into somethin you can't get out of. Like don't give em your credit card number', to which she replied, 'I know. I'm not stupid.' In another case, Sue labeled her husband's behavior as 'teachy', because of the way he explained tennis or technical processes related to their joint careers in television production. On the tapes, her husband Robert slowed his speech and used more careful articulation, similar to the way adults sometimes try to teach children. Less blatant cases of condescending behaviors which silenced the women may be the several instances of husbands who cautioned their wives to quit worrying about a topic the wives had tried to discuss. 'Why worry about something until it happens?', Curt said.

A final type of patronizing behavior is what two women called 'faked listening', pretending to listen by offering only token acknowledgments. Sharon said when Jerry got bored with her topic he would change it by 'getting mushy', meaning he would make a romantic or sexual comment. She knew the next thing he said would have nothing to do with the topic she had raised. The effect of these various patronizing behaviors seemed to be to trivialize the women's concerns and make further discussion of a topic irrelevant.

There was also other evidence that talk was more important to the women than the men. I received eighteen responses to my solicitations for participants; women initiated the contact in all but one case. Of these, six chose not to participate (five were ineligible), because they said their husbands were not comfortable with the project. Of those who completed the project, four men (Curt, Hal, Ted and Warren) said they agreed to do so because their wives had been feeling lonely and they thought getting to talk with another woman (rather than increasing an awareness of their own communication inadequacies) might make their wives feel better.

I am not trying to suggest that the men in this study failed to value talk at all, or that the stereotypical 'silent male' is a universal phenomenon. However, the men consistently preferred 'not talking' and/or 'light conversation' in their continual vigilance for conflict avoidance. According to previous research, conflict-avoidance strategies are techniques people use to deal with unwelcome requests from others (Belk et al., 1988: 165). Both the women and men voiced desires to avoid conflict, but the strategies they preferred for doing so were different. The women chose to voice objections, seek compromises and talk out a problem. These are behaviors consistent with what previous researchers have labeled 'collaborative' conflict-avoidance strategies (Belk et al., 1988). The men chose what previous researchers have labeled 'unilateral conflict avoidance' (Belk et al., 1988), as exemplified by their desires to withdraw, for their wives to be less emotional, to have more efficient conflict resolutions, and to generally avoid sensitive topics of discussion.

The men's stated preference for conflict avoidance seemed consistent with their greater use of no-response violations because the conflict avoider is generally thought to be apathetic and disinterested (Fitzpatrick, 1988; Folger and Poole, 1984). It is plausible that a person who unilaterally avoids conflict may do so, as these men did: by avoiding sensitive topics; using more no-response violations as opposed to interruptions; talking less; and using patronizing behaviors to control conversation. The women's preferences for collaborative conflict avoidance seemed consistent with the greater amount of work they did to generate communication with their husbands.

The problem, then, is that these different preferences for how to avoid conflict may themselves come into conflict. And, while no one piece of evidence reported here would be highly meaningful alone, together the information demonstrates that when these needs did compete, the men seemed to be able to put forth less effort and still obtain their wishes more often than the women. As a result, the men seemed to have more control in defining the day-to-day reality of these couples' communication styles, and the women did more of the adapting.

Thus, through the variety of research methods employed, we can see connections between speaker preferences, components of conversation, and the consequences for relational and social control. Although this was a preliminary effort to understand how gender inequalities may be created and maintained on a daily basis, the methods do offer directions for future work. Analyses of isolated conversational components are not enough if we want to understand how relational and social realities are developed through interaction. Anita Pomerantz (1989) suggested that researchers need to bridge the gap between the more technical analyses of conversation and that which is socially relevant for the speakers. While such translational links are susceptible to misrepresentations (Jefferson, 1989), failure to make such attempts seems elitist and does little to inform people's lives. This concern is particularly important for feminists, since the violations of one's communication expectations and preferences in intimate relations may actually be covert dominance strategies. Research methods which fail to make such political links serve to further camouflage women's realities and maintain the silence.

Notes

A special thanks to Marsha Houston, Cheris Kramarae and Richard West for suggestions on earlier drafts of this paper.

1   The term communication preferences as used here refers to individuals' likes and dislikes in communication with their spouse, not the structure-based preferences Schegloff (1988) discussed.

2   In the transcripts, the symbol [is used at the beginning of an utterance to show overlap, that
    is, to show where a speaker began her/his turn within two or less syllables of the other speak-
    er's ending. The symbol { is used to show where a speaker interrupted the other's turn by
    beginning to speak when it was not a transition-relevance place (a point beyond the two-sylla-
    ble rule of thumb).

References

Belk, Sharyn S., Garcia-Falconi, Renan, Hernandez-Sanchez, Julita Elemi and Snell, William E.
    (1988) 'Avoidance Strategy Use in the Intimate Relationships of Women and Men from
    Mexico and the United States', *Psychology of Women Quarterly* 12: 165–74.

Davis, Kathryn (1988) 'Paternalism under the Microscope', in A. D. Todd and S. Fisher (eds)
    Gender and Discourse: The Power of Talk, pp. 19–54. Norwood, NJ: Ablex.

Dindia, Kathryn (1987) 'The Effects of Sex of Subject and Sex of Partner on Interruptions',
    Human Communication Research 13: 345–71.

Fishman, Pamela (1978a) 'Interaction: The Work Women Do', *Social Problems* 25: 397–406.

Fishman, Pamela (1978b) 'What Do Couples Talk about When They're Alone?', in D. Butturff and
    E. Epstein (eds) *Women's Language and Style*, pp. 11–12. Akron, OH: University of Akron.

Fishman, Pamela (1983) 'Interaction: The Work Women Do', in Barrie Thorne, Cheris Kramarae
    and Nancy Henley (eds) *Language, Gender and Society*, pp. 89–102. Rowley, MA: Newbury
    House.

Fitzpatrick, Mary Anne (1988) *Between Husbands and Wives: Communication in Marriage*.
    Newbury Park, CA: Sage.

Fitzpatrick, Mary Anne and Dindia, Kathryn (1986) 'Couples and Other Strangers: Talk Time in
    Spouse–Stranger Interaction', *Communication Research* 13: 625–52.

Folger, Joseph P. and Poole, M. Scott (1984) *Working through Conflict: A Communication
    Perspective*. Glenview, IL: Scott, Foresman & Co.

Henley, Nancy (1977) *Body Politics*. Englewood Cliffs, NJ: Prentice-Hall.

Hite, Shere (1987) *Women and Love: A Cultural Revolution in Progress*. New York: Alfred A.
    Knopf, Inc.

Jefferson, Gail (1989) 'Letter to the Editor', *Western Journal of Speech Communication* 53:
    427–9.

Kennedy, C. W. and Camden, C. L. (1983) 'A New Look at Interruptions', *Western Journal of
    Speech Communication* 47: 45–58.

Maltz, Daniel and Borker, Ruth (1982) 'A Cultural Approach to Male–Female Miscommunication',
    in John Gumperz (ed.) *Language and Social Identity*. pp. 196–216. Cambridge: Cambridge
    University Press.

Martin, J. N. and Craig, R. T. (1983) 'Selected Linguistic Sex Differences during Initial Social
    Interactions of Same-sex and Mixed-sex Student Dyads', *Western Journal of Speech
    Communication* 47: 16–28.

Murray, Stephen (1985) 'Toward a Model of Members' Methods for Recognizing Interruptions',
    Language in Society 14: 31–40.

Pomerantz, Anita M. (1989) 'Epilogue', *Western Journal of Speech Communication* 53: 242–6.

Rakow, Lana (1986) 'Rethinking Gender Research in Communication', *Journal of Communication*
    36: 11–26.

Roger, Derek (1989) 'Experimental Studies of Dyadic Turn-taking Behavior', in Derek Roger and
    Peter Bull (eds) *Conversation: An Interdisciplinary Perspective*, pp. 75–95. Clevedon:
    Multilingual Matters.

Rubin, Lillian (1976) *Worlds of Pain: Life in the Working-class Family*. New York: Basic Books.

Rubin, Lillian (1983) *Intimate Strangers*. New York: Harper & Row.

Sacks, Harvey, Schegloff, Emanuel, and Jefferson, Gail (1974) 'A Simplest Systematics for the
    Organization of Turn-taking for Conversation', *Language* 50: 696–735.

Sattel, J. W. (1983) 'Men, Inexpressiveness, and Power', in Barrie Thorne, Cheris Kramarae and Nancy Henley (eds) *Language, Gender and Society*, pp. 118–24. Rowley, MA: Newbury House.

Schegloff, E. A. (1988) 'On an Actual Virtual Servo-mechanism for Guessing Bad News: A Single Case Conjecture', *Social Problems* 35: 442–57.

Spender, Dale (1980) *Man Made Language*. London: Routledge & Kegan Paul.

Spitzack, Carole and Carter, Kathryn (1989) 'Research on Women's Communication: The Politics of Theory and Method', in Kathryn Carter and Carole Spitzack (eds) *Doing Research on Women's Communication: Perspectives on Theory and Method*, pp. 11–39. Norwood, NJ: Ablex.

Tannen, Deborah (1984) *Conversational Style: Analyzing Talk among Friends*. Norwood, NJ: Ablex Publishing.

Thorne, Barrie, Kramarae, Cheris and Henley, Nancy (1983) 'Language, Gender and Society: Opening a Second Decade of Research', in Barry Thorne, Cheris Kramarae and Nancy Henley (eds) *Language, Gender and Society*, pp. 7–24. Rowley, MA: Newbury House.

West, Candace and Garcia, Angela (1988) 'Conversational Shift Work: A Study of Topical Transitions between Women and Men', *Social Problems* 35: 551–75.

West, Candace and Zimmerman, Donald (1983) 'Small Insults: A Study of Interruptions in Cross-sex Conversations between Unacquainted Persons', in Barrie Thorne, Cheris Kramarae and Nancy Henley (eds) *Language, Gender and Society*, pp. 103–17. Rowley, MA: Newbury House.

13

Talk Control:
An Illustration from the Classroom
of Problems in Analysing
Male Dominance of Conversation

Joan Swann

Source: J. Coates and D. Cameron (eds), *Women in their Speech Communities*. London: Longman (1989), pp. 123–40. Reprinted with permission of Pearson Education UK.

Women and Men Talking

The stereotype of the over-talkative woman stands out in stark contrast to most research studies of interactions between women and men, which argue that, by and large, it is men who tend to dominate the talk.

[…]

However the notion of male 'dominance' itself is rather problematical. While many studies have shown that men's interests tend to be better served than women's in mixed-sex conversation (as, for instance, in Fishman's 1978 study, where topics initiated by men are more often followed up and pursued), it is likely that both women and men contribute to this state of affairs. In other words, the use of terms such as 'dominate' and 'control' should not suggest that men need linguistically to bludgeon women into submission. Where it is seen as normal that men talk more, etc. they may do so with the complicity of women. […]

Classroom Talk: An Illustration

Classroom talk is an interesting area of study partly because many educationists argue that talk itself is an important vehicle for learning:

> The way into ideas, the way of making ideas truly one's own, is to be able to think them through, and the best way to do this for most people is to talk them through. Thus talking is not merely a way of conveying existing ideas to others; it is also a way by which we explore ideas, clarify them, and make them our own. Talking things over allows the sorting of ideas, and gives rapid and extensive practice towards the handling of ideas. (Marland 1977: 129)

Language and Gender: A Reader, Second Edition. Edited by Jennifer Coates and Pia Pichler.

The classroom is also one place in which children learn social roles. An influential argument is that socially appropriate behaviour (including gender-appropriate behaviour) is learnt in part (though not by any means exclusively) through classroom talk.

Studies of classroom life have found many ways, linguistic and nonlinguistic, in which girls and boys are treated differently. For instance, pupils are often segregated by gender as an aid to classroom administration, or told to do things as boys or as girls as a form of motivation (girls may be told to leave first very quietly, boys to sing as nicely as the girls); pupils are often told that certain topics are 'boys'' topics or will 'mainly appeal to the girls'; topics are often chosen specifically with a view to maintaining boys' interests; boys insist on, and are given, greater attention by the teacher; in practical subjects such as science boys tend to hog the resources; boys are more disruptive; and boys, in various ways, dominate classroom talk. (See Byrne 1978; Deem 1978; and Delamont 1980, for a general discussion of these and other findings; Whyte 1986, for a report on science teaching; and Clarricoates 1983, for a discussion of classroom interaction.)

Talk may, therefore, be seen to play its part alongside much more general patterns of difference and discrimination. Studies that focus on characteristics of mixed-sex classroom talk produce results that are similar in many respects to general studies of talk between women and men. For instance, in an American study of over 100 classes Sadker and Sadker (1985) found that boys spoke on average three times as much as girls, that boys were eight times more likely than girls to call out answers, and that teachers accepted such answers from boys but reprimanded girls for calling out. French and French (1984) suggest that particular strategies may enable talkative boys to gain more than their fair share of classroom talk. In a study of (British) primary classrooms they found that simply making an unusual response to a teacher's question could gain a pupil extra speaking turns – and those who made such responses were more often boys.

Most studies of classroom talk focus on the role of the teacher as much as on different pupils. One characteristic of classroom talk (that distinguishes it from talk in many other contexts) is that this is often mediated (if not directly controlled) by the teacher. If boys are to dominate, therefore, they must do so with the teacher's assistance or at least tacit acceptance. The argument that teachers pay boys more attention and, in other ways, encourage them to talk more has led some people consciously to attempt to redress the balance. Such evidence as is available, however, suggests that old habits are hard to break. Spender (1982) claims that it is virtually impossible to divide one's attention equally between girls and boys. Whyte (1986) is less pessimistic. Observations of science lessons by researchers involved in the Manchester-based Girls Into Science and Technology project revealed that teachers were able to devote an equal amount of attention to girls and boys, and therefore to encourage more equal participation from pupils. This was only achieved with some effort, however. Whyte reports a head of science who, having managed to create an atmosphere in which girls and boys contributed more or less equally to discussion, remarked that he had felt as though he were devoting 90 percent of his attention to the girls (1986: 196).

While the fact of male dominance of classroom talk makes this similar to mixed-sex talk in other contexts, it's worth noting that not all of the same indicators of conversational dominance are present.

[...]

If boys are to attempt to dominate classroom talk (relative to girls), such dominance must fit with the context and with the behaviour of other participants – in this case chiefly the teacher, who is meant to be in control, overall, of what is going on.

I want to discuss some of these issues further in relation to an exploratory study of classroom talk that I carried out with a colleague, and which is described in greater detail elsewhere (see Swann and Graddol 1988).

An Exploratory Study of Classroom Talk

Given imbalances that had been found in earlier work between girls' and boys' participation in classroom talk the intention in this study was to examine in detail:

1 the mechanisms of turn allocation and turn exchange that support male dominance of classroom talk;
2 the roles played by different participants (girls, boys and the class teacher) in the achievement of such interactional dominance.

To do this, we made a close examination of video-recordings of two twenty-minute sequences of small-group teaching with primary school children. The sequences were recorded in two different schools: one, which I shall refer to as the 'pendulum' sequence, was recorded in the East Midlands; the other, the 'mining' sequence, was recorded in the north-east of England. In the 'pendulum' sequence there were six children (three girls and three boys) aged between 10 and 11 years, and a female teacher. The children were reporting back on experiments they had carried out with pendulums, and discussing their findings. The 'mining' sequence involved eight children (four girls and four boys) aged from 9 to 10 and a female teacher. These children were having a follow-up discussion after having seen a television programme on coal-mining (the school was situated in a mining area). In both cases the discussion was 'set up' to the extent that it was being recorded for research purposes. However, the work the children were engaged in was part of their normal classwork at the time.

Because the sequences were video-recorded we could observe teachers' and pupils' nonverbal behaviour as well as their talk (I shall return to this point below). We could also note any activities, etc. that accompanied the talk and that might contribute to the overall interpretation of what was going on. For instance, in the 'pendulum' sequence the seating arrangements were such that the teacher could more easily face the boys. In the 'mining' sequence the teacher was standing but turned more often towards the boys. In the 'pendulum' sequence a girl was helped by the teacher to adjust a slide on an overhead projector. Boys were not helped, but a boy was asked to focus the projector, and also to handle other equipment. In the 'mining' sequence the seating arrangements were such that the boys could more easily see a model pit that was used for part of the lesson. A boy was also asked to put on some miner's equipment. On any one occasion such factors may, of course, be coincidental, but it is interesting that they were similar to aspects of classroom organization recorded in the other general studies mentioned above (p. 162).

Having transcribed each video-recorded sequence we made various measures of the amount of talk contributed by each pupil. The number of turns and the number of words for each pupil are given in table 1.

On average, boys contributed more in each sequence, both in terms of the number of turns taken and the number of words uttered. There were, however, intra-group differences: there were quieter boys and more talkative girls – including one particularly talkative girl in the 'mining' sequence. Clearly we could not make any generalizations on the basis of word- and turn-counts from such small samples: as with the aspects of classroom activities and organization mentioned above our results at this point simply confirmed that the distribution of talk in our groups was similar to that recorded in work carried out in other classrooms and with larger samples of pupils (such as French and French 1984, and Sadker and Sadker 1985).

Table 1 Contribution to classroom talk from girl and boy pupils in 'pendulum' and 'mining' sequences

Pupils	Amount spoken		
	Total words spoken	*Total spoken turns*	*Average words per turn*
'Pendulum' sequence			
Sarah	79	17	4.6
Laura	20	5	4.0
Donna	37	5	7.4
Unidentified girls	18	9	2.0
Total girls	154	36	4.3
Matthew	133	23	5.8
Trevor	83	20	4.1
Peter	55	10	5.5
Unidentified boys	48	20	2.5
Total boys	319	73	4.4
'Mining' sequence			
Kate	127	9	14.1
Lorraine	13	7	1.8
Anne	23	8	2.9
Emma	8	4	2.0
Unidentified girls	—	—	—
Total girls	171	28	6.1
Mark	47	9	5.2
Ian	80	23	3.5
John	35	5	7.0
Darren	101	15	6.7
Unidentified boys	3	2	1.5
Total boys	266	54	4.9

When we came to examine more closely the interactional mechanisms by which boys obtained more turns than girls, we found differences between the two sequences. I shall describe briefly the findings from each sequence in turn.

The 'pendulum' sequence

This sequence was one in which pupils apparently had a great deal of freedom to contribute. However, there were differences between how girls and boys began an interchange with the teacher. When selecting pupils to speak by name the teacher chose girls rather more often than boys (11 occasions for girls and eight for boys). It was most common, however, for pupils simply to chip in to answer questions, without raising their hands or being selected by name. Boys were at a clear advantage here, chipping in or volunteering responses on 41 occasions, as opposed to girls' 13.

It seemed, then, as if boys were able to use the relatively unconstrained atmosphere to dominate the talk. However, certain aspects of the teacher's behaviour may also have favoured the boys. An example of this is the teacher's gaze behaviour, which we were able to analyse for part of the sequence. For the portion of the videotape in which the teacher was clearly in view and in which we could measure her gaze towards the pupils, we found that she looked towards the boys for 60 percent of the time and towards the girls for 40 percent of the time. The following brief extract provides an illustration of the distribution of the teacher's gaze and shows how this may encourage the boys to participate more. The extract comes about half way into the sequence, when pupils have finished reporting on their experiments and are engaged with the teacher in a more general discussion of their results.

Questions are numbered in sequence.[1]
. . . . = teacher's gaze towards the girls
- - - - - - = teacher's gaze towards the boys
(Where gaze is not marked this is because the teacher is looking elsewhere – for instance, at the overhead projector.)

TEACHER: If you have a pendulum (.) which we established last

week was a weight a mass (.) suspended from a string

or whatever (.) and watch I'm holding it with my hand

so it's at rest at the moment (.) what is it that makes

the pendulum swing in a downward direction for

instance till it gets to there? [1] | (.) just watch it
MATTHEW: | gravity

TEACHER: What is it Matthew? [2]

MATTHEW: Gravity

TEACHER: [Yes (.)] now we mentioned gravity when we were
BOY: [((xxx))]

TEACHER: actually doing the experiments but we didn't discuss it

too much (.) OK so it's gravity then that pulls it

down (.) what causes it to go up again at the other

side? [3]

BOY: [Force the force]
BOY: [The string Miss] it gets up speed going down.

TEACHER: It gets up speed going [down (.) does] anyone know the
BOY: [(force)(xxx)]

TEACHER:　word for it when you get up speed? [4] (.) as in a car
when you press the pedal? [5]

BOY:　[accelerate
BOY:　[momentum]

TEACHER:　You get momentum (.) [Matthew (.)] it accelerates
MATTHEW:　　　　　　　　　　　[(xxx)]

TEACHER:　going down doesn't it and it's the (.) energy the force
that it builds up that takes it up the other side (.)
watch (.) and see if it's the same (.) right (.) OK (.)
em (.) anything else you notice about that? [6] (.) so
it's gravity what about the moon? [7] (.) that's a bit
tricky isn't it? [8] (.) is [there grav]ity on the
BOYS:　　　　　　　　　　　　[(xxx)]

TEACHER:　moon? = [9]

BOYS:　　　　　= No no it would float

TEACHER:　There isn't gravity on the moon? [10] (.)

SEVERAL:　No

MATTHEW:　There is a certain amount

TEACHER:　A certain amount Matthew? = [11]

MATTHEW:　　　　　　　　　　　　= [(xxx)]

BOY:　　　　　　　　　　　　　　[Seven] times less

TEACHER:　You reckon it's seven? [12]

BOY:　Times less than on earth

TEACHER:　Yes (.) well it's a it's a difficult figure to arrive at but
it is between six and seven

The transcript shows, first of all, that the teacher is looking much more often towards the boys. The teacher is also more often looking towards the boys at critical points, when a question requires to be answered. (Of the 12 questions, eight are directed towards the boys and four towards the girls.)

Of the four girls' questions, two (numbers 4 and 6) occur after a last-minute switch of gaze from the boys to the girls. Another (number 8), although we coded it as a question to give it the benefit of the doubt, seems to function more as an aside, or a comment on the activity, than as an attempt to elicit information.

Although in the 'pendulum' sequence, then, the boys seemed able to contribute more to the discussion by simply 'chipping in', our analysis of the teacher's gaze behaviour during a portion of the interaction suggests she may be distributing her attention selectively between the pupils and thus favouring the boys. It is also worth noting from the transcript that boys' speech often overlaps the teacher's. General 'muttering' from the boys occurs at various points during the interaction and may have the function of attracting, or maintaining the teacher's attention.

The 'mining' sequence

The teacher in this sequence had a different teaching style. The interaction was lively but kept more directly under the teacher's control: pupils rarely called out an answer – normally they raised their hands and were selected to speak. The following interchange is an example of the commonest way pupils obtained a speaking turn. Gaze is marked as in the 'pendulum' transcript. The superscript shows the order of hand-raising.

Interchange between teacher and Kate:

		Notes
	- - - - - - - - - - - - - - - - - - - -	Teacher looking at boys but can see girls.
TEACHER:	How did they know that those (KJMEA)	As K's hand goes up, teacher turns to look
	- - - - - - - - -	at girls. By the time boys' hands are raised,
	men were alive? (.) yes	teacher has already begun to turn to girls.
	....	By the time E's hand rises, teacher's gaze
KATE:	Miss they were knocking	is already directed towards K.
	....	
TEACHER:	They were knocking	

(K = Kate; J = John; M = Mark; E = Emma; A = Anne)

Here the teacher looks towards the boys then switches to the girls. Kate is selected to answer, and hers was the first hand raised. The teacher seemed to have a strategy of occasionally selecting a quiet child whose hand was not raised and encouraging them to answer (Lorraine and Emma obtained all their speaking turns this way, and Anne half of hers). On the whole, though, when she was in a position to see it, the teacher responded to the first or most decisively raised hand (Kate, and the boys, obtained most of their speaking turns this way). The teacher was in fact extraordinarily sensitive to the first hand raised. Presumably she was responding intuitively to this (and no doubt to additional nonverbal cues) as hands were raised very rapidly and, in analysing the sequence, we had to play the video frame by frame to determine the order of hand-raising. Although the teacher appeared quite directive, therefore, this gave the pupils considerable scope: they could ensure they were selected to speak more often if they were confident enough to raise their hands first.

As with the 'pendulum' sequence there seemed to be an interaction here between the behaviour of different participants that guaranteed the boys (on average) more speaking turns:

First, more confident pupils (who tended more often to be boys) simply raised their hands first and more decisively, thereby attracting the teacher's attention.

Second, we were able to analyse the teacher's gaze behaviour for the whole of the 'mining' sequence. This analysis showed that, as with the 'pendulum' sequence, the teacher's gaze was more often directed towards the boys (for 65 percent of the time as opposed to 35 percent of the time towards the girls). This occurred during general exposition as well as during more interactive parts of the sequence. Furthermore, when the teacher began to formulate a question with her gaze towards the boys she tended to maintain this gaze direction (unless a girl's hand was raised before a boy's and attracted her attention). However, on those (fewer) occasions in which the teacher began a question with her gaze directed towards the girls she tended to switch towards the boys half-way through the question, or to switch back and forth between girls and boys. This overall pattern of gaze behaviour may give boys generally more positive feedback and encourage them to respond to questions when they came.

Third, all the girls (and not just Kate) did frequently raise their hands during this sequence. Even Emma, the quietest pupil, often had her hand in the air. As in the example given above, however, Emma normally raised her hand just after the teacher's gaze had been directed towards the pupil she intended to select to speak. Such girls' hand-raising strategies, then, contribute to their relatively poor level of participation just as much as many boys' strategies enable them to contribute more.

Male Dominance Reconsidered

Many points arising from a consideration of classroom talk, and from the exploratory analysis of teacher and small-group interaction that I have just described, can illuminate some of the issues raised at the beginning of this paper in relation to gender differences in conversation.

[...]

The exploratory study (in common with other studies of classroom talk) raises problems for the notion of female and male styles, first because differences between girls and boys are not categorical: boys may take more turns on average, but there are quiet boys (and more talkative girls). Second, while those who dominate classroom talk (in this case largely by talking more often) do tend to be boys, different interactional mechanisms are used in each context. In the relatively informal atmosphere of the 'pendulum' discussion, boys chip in much more often than girls. In the 'mining' sequence talk seems to be more overtly under the teacher's control and pupils (of either sex) rarely chip in: boys are selected to talk more often by the teacher, but this seems to be related to their ability to raise their hands more decisively and fractionally earlier than girls. It appears then that certain 'interactional resources' are available that might allow a speaker to have more say in a discussion, but that the resources available differ in different contexts. Rather than there being a particular set of 'controlling tactics', would-be dominant speakers would need to select features as appropriate to a context (taking account of the roles played by participants, the activities in which they are engaged, etc.).

It can be argued that a complete analysis of inequalities in talk would need to take account, not only of a range of linguistic factors, but also of nonverbal components of an interaction. It's worth pointing out here that many studies of talk have relied on audio-recordings and transcripts and so cannot take account of nonverbal features, nor (reliably) of any accompanying activities. Studies of gender and classroom life, or classroom interaction (carried out perhaps more often by sociologists or educationists than by linguists or conversation analysts) have often seen talk as playing a part *along with other factors* in establishing and maintaining inequalities between girls and boys. It might be useful now to have more detailed studies showing the interplay between these different factors. This would mean expanding the metaphorical box of 'interactional resources' to include nonverbal features that interact with talk and may fulfil similar functions. In the 'mining' sequence, for instance, hand-raising strategies were crucial in obtaining (or not obtaining) speaking rights. Gaze was an important interactional mechanism in both sequences (though we were not able to analyse its use by pupils). Other features such as posture and gesture no doubt played their part, though they did not form part of our analysis. Finally, other accompaniments to the talk such as seating arrangements and the positioning and use of equipment may have contributed to the overall achievement of 'male dominance', though more work is needed to see how, on any one occasion, such factors interact with talk. There is, of course, a methodological problem here, in that, while it would seem useful to have a more complete record of what is going on in any sequence of talk, two or three video cameras would be needed even to cope with a small group discussion (let alone a whole class). Any observation may affect what is going on but the introduction of so much hardware would probably be unacceptably intrusive. In our exploratory study we lost some (no doubt) valuable information in the interests of remaining rather less intrusive.

Finally, there are problems with the notion of male 'dominance' itself. The studies of classroom talk that I have discussed suggested that to speak of boys 'dominating' classroom talk, while a useful shorthand, may risk oversimplifying things. It seems more plausible to argue that there is an interaction between the behaviour of all participants: for instance, the greater attention paid by teachers towards boys may encourage boys' fuller participation, which in turn encourages greater attention from the teacher, and so on. It is likely that everyone is an accomplice in the tendency by boys to contribute more to classroom talk – girls too by, arguably, using the resources available in the interaction to contribute less.

The points made above have theoretical implications, and also practical implications for anyone wishing to analyse gender differences in talk. Studies of classroom talk are, however, also important in relation to (educational) policies on gender. For instance, if a whole variety of linguistic and nonlinguistic features can be used to achieve or support 'male dominance', how successful are local solutions (such as changes in teachers' classroom management strategies) likely to be?

Furthermore, if inequalities in talk between girls and boys are regarded as normal by all parties, they are likely to be resistant to change. If girls are encouraged to become more assertive, and to adopt conversational tactics more commonly associated with boys, will such behaviour be tolerated by others or regarded as deviant?

Note

This paper relies for part of its discussion on an analysis of classroom talk that I carried out with an Open University colleague, David Graddol.

The 'Pendulum' extract comes from data originally collected by Derek Edwards, Neil Mercer and Janet Maybin for their ESRC-funded project 'The Development of Joint Understanding in the Classroom' (ESRC No. C00232236). I am very grateful to Derek, Neil and Janet, and to the East Midlands school where the 'Pendulum' extract was recorded, for allowing access to these data. The 'Mining' extract comes from material collected at Escomb school, County Durham. Again, I am grateful to the staff and pupils for allowing one of their lessons to be video-recorded. (In both cases, I have changed the children's names to protect their identity, and the teachers are not referred to by name.)

1   Questions are marked with a ?. Utterances so marked were assessed by us to be functioning as questions, sometimes because of their syntactic form, but at other times for other reasons; we relied on cues such as intonation, but our interpretation relied on intuition. It is in fact difficult, on any occasion, to itemize the cues that are being attended to and that lead to an utterance being interpreted as a question.

References

Byrne, E. M. (1978) *Women and Education*. London: Tavistock Publications.

Clarricoates, K. (1983) 'Classroom interaction', in J. Whyld (ed.) *Sexism in the Secondary Curriculum*. New York: Harper & Row.

Deem, R. (1978) *Women and Schooling*. London: Routledge & Kegan Paul.

Delamont, S. (1980) *Sex Roles and the School*. London: Methuen.

Fishman, P. M. (1978) 'What do couples talk about when they're alone?', in D. Butturff and E. L. Epstein (eds) *Women's Language and Style*. Akron, OH: University of Akron, Department of English.

French, J. and French, P. (1984) 'Gender imbalance in the primary classroom: an interactional account'. *Educational Research*, 26, 2, 127–36.

Marland, M. (1977) *Language Across the Curriculum*. London: Heinemann.

Sadker, M. and Sadker, D. (1985) 'Sexism in the schoolroom of the 80s'. *Psychology Today*, March 1985, 54–7.

Spender, D. (1982) *Invisible Women: The Schooling Scandal*. London: Writers and Readers Publishing Cooperative Society.

Swann, J. and Graddol, D. (1988) 'Gender inequalities in classroom talk'. *English in Education*, 22, 1, 48–65.

Whyte, J. (1986) *Girls into Science and Technology: The Story of a Project*. London: Routledge & Kegan Paul.

14

Participation in Electronic Discourse in a "Feminist" Field

Susan C. Herring, Deborah A. Johnson and Tamra DiBenedetto

Source: Kira Hall et al. (eds), *Locating Power. Proceedings of the 2nd Berkeley Women and Language Conference*. Berkeley: BWLG (1992), pp. 250–62. Reprinted with permission of the authors.

Introduction

Studies of gender differences in amount of talk have shown that men consistently talk more than women in public settings. Talk in such settings – which include conferences, seminars, formal and informal meetings, and television discussions – draws attention to the speaker in ways that are potentially status-enhancing (Holmes 1992). Moreover, sheer amount of talk may garner speakers credit they do not deserve, as when subjects in a study conducted by Rieken attributed insightful solutions to those who had talked the most during the discussion, even when the solutions had in fact been proposed by other participants (reported in Wallwork 1978). In short, amount of talk is related to status, power, and influence in the public domain.

In recent decades, a new forum for public discourse has emerged: the Internet. The possibility of communicating via computer networks has led to the formation of multi-participant electronic discussion groups (known variously as lists, conferences or news-groups, depending on the technology involved), in which individuals scattered in diverse locations around the world can participate in discussions on topics of common interest by sending electronic mail (e-mail) messages to a common site, where they are posted for others to read and respond to. Participation is typically open to all interested parties, and some groups are exceedingly active, generating hundreds of messages per week.

Enthusiasts of the new electronic medium claim that it exercises a democratizing influence on communication. Citing studies conducted in educational settings, Kahn and Brookshire (1991: 245) conclude that individuals communicating via computer "tend to participate more equally in discussions, and discussion is likely to be more democratic in the absence of nonverbal status cues". Users also wax enthusiastic. As one male member of a discussion list recently wrote to another:

> One of the greatest strengths of e-mail is its ability to break down socio-economic, racial, and other traditional barriers to the sharing and production of knowledge. You, for example,

Language and Gender: A Reader, Second Edition. Edited by Jennifer Coates and Pia Pichler.

have no way of knowing if I am a janitor or a university president or an illegal alien – we can simply communicate on the basis of our ideas, not on any preconceived notions of what should be expected (or not expected) from one another.

The electronic medium is claimed to break down gender barriers as well. Graddol and Swann (1989: 175) observe that "the introduction of [computer conferencing] ... [leads] to a change in the traditional pattern of contributions from female and male participants". A number of characteristics of the medium mitigate the likelihood of gender asymmetries: sex non-specific electronic return addresses,[1] the absence of physical (including intonational) cues signaling relative dominance or submission, and the fact that interruption and overlap are effectively precluded – a participant may choose to delete messages, but each message selected appears on his or her screen in its entirety, in the order in which it was received.[2]

Despite this optimistic early prognosis, what little research has directly investigated the relationship between gender and participation in electronic discourse calls into question the claim that computers exercise an equalizing effect. In a study of the participation patterns of professional linguists on the Linguist electronic discussion list, Herring (1992) found that female linguists contributed significantly less overall than male linguists – 20% and 80%, respectively. Moreover, when surveyed, both men and women reported feeling put off by the bombastic and adversarial postings of a small minority of male contributors who effectively dominated the discussions. Herring concluded that women refrain from participating on Linguist due in part to their aversion to the adversarial tone of such discussions.

In the present study, we report on an investigation of participation on a smaller list serving an academic field – composition and rhetoric – in which feminism currently enjoys considerable influence.[3] This list, Megabyte University (hereafter MBU), is considered by its members to be especially "friendly" and "supportive" relative to other lists. We hypothesized that in a non-adversarial computer-mediated environment, women would be more likely to participate equally in discussions, as predicted by the claims cited above. However, this hypothesis was not supported: while the overall tone of the list was indeed less adversarial, women still contributed only 30% of the messages as compared to 70% contributed by men. Even more revealing patterns emerge when participation is considered on a day-by-day and topic-by-topic basis. In discussion of a feminist topic, the contributions of women at one point exceeded those of the men for two consecutive days. The subsequent disruptions that took place, including male accusations of being "silenced" in the discussion and threats from several men to unsubscribe from the list, provide support for the view that women and men do not have equal rights to speak in public; by contributing more, even temporarily, and on a feminist (and female-introduced) topic, women in the group violated the unspoken convention that control of public discourse belongs rightfully to men.

The "Men's Literature" Discussion

Our investigation focuses on a particularly lively discussion that took place on MBU between November 7 and December 16, 1991. It began as a request by one of the subscribers for reading suggestions for a university course he planned to offer on "men's literature". The "men's literature" question soon revealed itself to be controversial, with participants becoming polarized along gender lines regarding the legitimacy of offering such a course.[4] Some women feared that the course might be used to perpetrate male hegemony, e.g., by co-opting resources that might otherwise be used for women's literature courses. The men, in turn, argued that women on the list were trying to deny them the right to talk about how gender shapes their identity. In addition to being concerned with gender issues, the "men's literature" discussion contains meta-commentary on gender and "silencing" in the discussion itself.

Participation by Gender

The first and most obvious indication of gender-based inequality comes from the figures for participation in the "men's literature" discussion as a whole. These figures are summarized in table 1.

Table 1   Participation in the "men's literature" discussion

	Female	Male
Number of contributors	18 (30.5%)	41 (69.5%)
Number of contributions	87 (36%)	155 (64%)
Average words per contribution	162	211.5
Total words contributed	14,114 (30%)	32,774 (70%)

As table 1 shows, men contributed significantly more than women to the discussion overall. 69.5% of the participants were men, who in turn were responsible for contributing 70% of the total words and 64% of the total messages.[5] Moreover, the average message length for men was 211.5 words, as compared with 162 words for women. Rather than demonstrating a new, democratic form of discourse, these figures support "the traditional pattern of contributions from male and female participants" alluded to by Graddol and Swann, whereby men dominate (i.e., in face-to-face conversation) by taking longer and more frequent turns.

A rather more complex picture emerges if we consider a day-by-day breakdown of the number of messages contributed by participants of each sex to the "men's literature" discussion, as shown in figure 1.[6]

Figure 1 shows that males (M) contributed more than females (F) nearly every day on which the discussion took place. However, the number of contributions by both sexes rose dramatically in the period between November 21 and November 27, and during a two-day span (November 22–23), the contributions of women exceeded those of the men. Immediately thereafter, participation in the discussion soared to a peak of intensity (November 24–27), dropping off and stabilizing after Thanksgiving, which was celebrated on November 28 that year.

What accounts for this variability in participation? Explanations begin to suggest themselves when we take into account what MBU-ers were talking about at any given time. The vertical lines in figure 1 indicate transitional points at which new topics of discussion were taken up by the group. Five such topics arose in the course of the discussion as a whole:

Topic 1:   Men's literature course (M)
Topic 2:   Silencing of women in the discussion (F)

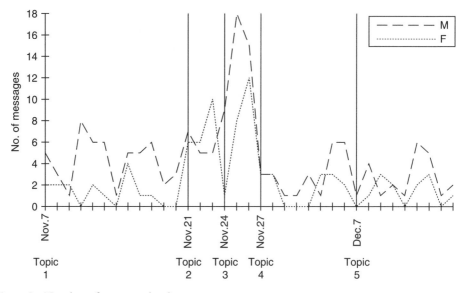

Figure 1 Number of messages by day

Topic 3: Threats of three members to unsubscribe, and reactions to this (M)
Topic 4: Male hegemony in English departments (F)
Topic 5: Statistics posted by one of the members (similar to those in table 1) show-
          ing male and female participation in the discussion to date (M)

Topics 1, 3, and 5 were introduced by males; Topics 2 and 4 were introduced by females. Participation by gender and topic is shown in figure 2.

As figure 2 shows, men contributed the greatest number of messages on Topics 1 and 3, both introduced by men, and the least on Topic 2, which was introduced by women. Women, on the other hand, contributed the most on Topic 2. Indeed, this is the only period in the discussion when the usual pattern of men posting more messages than women is reversed. We suggest that this reversal – the fact that women were participating more, and on a female-introduced topic – made men uncomfortable to the point of threatening to unsubscribe, and that it was ultimately responsible for male perceptions of having been "silenced" and of women having dominated the discussion.

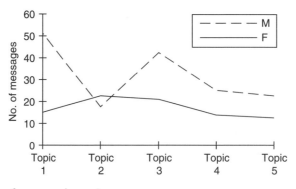

Figure 2 Number of messages by topic

It might seem strange that when men participated significantly more than women in the five-week discussion overall, two days in which women happened to contribute more would be perceived as a threat. Several factors may have contributed to producing this effect. First, the number of women's contributions took a leap on November 21 relative to what had come before, as can be seen from figure 1. Second, female participants continued to contribute actively the next day and the next, exceeding the contributions of men for two days straight, a situation without precedent in the discussion thus far. Finally, Spender (1979) found that male academics perceive women as dominating in public when they contribute as little as 30% of the talk. What would men then feel if women contributed more than half, as they did in this case?[7] It is likely that from the perspective of the men in the group, the women's increased participation was not only unexpected, it also appeared to be more than it actually was.

In support of this view, note that during Topic 2 men posted no fewer messages in absolute terms than they had previously. Yet on November 23, a male contributor (the one who posted the original request for texts on "men's literature") wrote and, addressing two of the more vocal women in the group by name, complained, "You may not feel very powerful outside this net or this discourse community, but here on the inside you've come very close to shutting all of us men up and down". The perception that men had been shut up (or down) is clearly contradicted by the fact of their participation – this man's message alone is 1,098 words, the longest in the entire discussion, and four other lengthy messages were contributed by men on the same day as well – yet it is consistent with Spender's observation that women need not truly dominate in order to be perceived as doing so.

What happened next is also revealing. The evening of November 23, and the morning of November 24, three men (none of whom had participated in the discussion thus far) posted public messages in which they announced their intention to unsubscribe from the list.[8] The reasons given were that the discussion, having begun as a well-intentioned request for help in selecting texts for a course, had degenerated into "insults", "vituperation", and "vilification". It was not, of course, that they had any problem with discussing gender issues; rather, what upset them was the "tone" of the debate.

However, if one examines the messages posted during the immediately preceding days, one finds little evidence of a vituperative tone. With one exception, the contributions of the women appear to be aimed primarily at furthering communication: they raise questions about the interaction at hand (specifically, the lack of male response to female concern about the proposed course), explain their own views, and encourage others to respond in kind.[9] The only message indisputably negative in tone was posted by the man who proposed the men's literature course in the first place. In it, he accuses women on the list of "posting without thinking [their contributions] through carefully first", of leveling "charges" [rather than questions] at the men, and in general, of "bashing", "guilt-tripping", and "bullying" men who didn't toe a strict feminist line. A man who overtly sided with the female participants also comes under attack: he is accused of betraying his brothers out of feminist-induced guilt.

If the only vituperation comes from the man whose cause they allegedly support, why then did the three men threaten to leave the list? The real reason did not escape the notice of participants on MBU at the time: it was a "boy"cott, a "power play" intended to silence those women who persisted in speaking uncomfortable truths about the gender/power dynamics on the list. It is no coincidence that threats of withdrawal occurred on and immediately following a day when the majority of messages were posted by women.

Ironically, however, the boycott had the reverse of its intended effect – it shamed the other men on the list into cooperating, at least temporarily, with the women's attempts to change the topic of discussion to one of feminist concern: the issue of male hegemony within the field of English. The period labelled "Topic 3" in figures 1 and 2 above was thus a turning point in the gender dynamics of the discussion, a turning point, as we demonstrate below, that is reflected on various levels of the discourse.

A Temporary Reversal of Control

Responses

The first evidence of a temporary reversal of influence in the discussion comes from a consideration of how – and how often – participants of each sex were responded to. Male participants received more responses than female participants overall: 89.2% of male post-ings in the "men's literature" discussion received explicit responses, as compared with only 70.6% of female postings. This disparity led one female participant to observe:

> I am fascinated that my thoughtful ... response on the "men's lit" thread was met with silence ... while an anonymous man ... with a silly little 3-liner gets fascinated and committed responses. ... When threads initiated by women die from lack of response that's silencing; when women do not respond on threads initiated by men for reasons to do with fear (and the fear may be fear of verbal or other reprisal, ridicule, whatever) ... – that's silencing.

Lack of response to postings questioning the proposed "men's literature" course prompted another frustrated woman to write, "Are you (in general) listening to what's being communicated?", and a third to conclude a message by "shouting" in capital letters: "IS THERE ANYBODY OUT THERE?"

Figure 3 charts the percentage of response (100% = 1 response per message posted) received by females and males according to topic.[10]

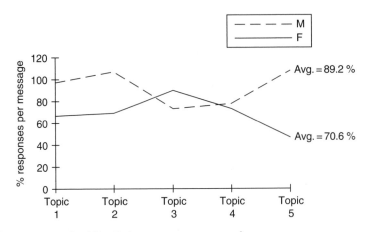

Figure 3   Responses received in relation to messages posted

As figure 3 shows, men were responded to more than women at all times during the discussion, except during Topic 3, the period immediately following the threats by several men to leave the list. The reversal of the usual pattern of response during Topic 3 appears

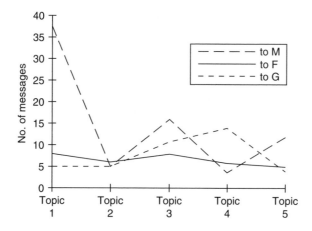

Figure 4 Responses to males, females, and group by topic (men only)

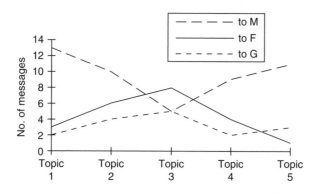

Figure 5 Responses to males, females, and group by topic (women only)

to be a reaction to the reversal in participation during Topic 2 (see figure 2 above), and reinforces the notion that amount of talk is power: by contributing more, women earned a higher rate of response to their messages.

Also of interest is the matter of who responds to whom. The most frequent direction of response is men to men (33.4%), followed by women to men (21.3%), men to women (15.8%), and finally women to women (11.2%). (The remaining responses (18.3%) were addressed to the group as a whole.) Both men and women thus respond more to men, an indication of the more powerful status of men in the group overall. The number of responses directed to participants of each sex is shown for men in figure 4, and for women in figure 5.

Men on MBU are consistent in responding most to men on topics introduced by men, as shown in figure 4. Their rate of response to postings by women is consistently low throughout. Note that in acknowledging the women's topic of hegemony – Topic 4 – men avoided responding directly to women (to do so would be to concede power) by addressing most of their postings to the group (G) as a whole.

Women show a different pattern. As figure 5 indicates, women respond most to men throughout, except during Topic 3, when the pattern of response is temporarily reversed.

It might appear from figure 5 that women responded most to other women about the threats of men to leave the list (Topic 3). In fact, however, many women at this point are virtually ignoring Topic 3 and pursuing the topic of hegemony (Topic 4) among themselves instead. This is further evidence that the control of the discourse has shifted; the women, after struggling throughout the earlier part of the discussion to make themselves heard, and having succeeded in gaining the floor on the topic of silencing (Topic 2), are finally empowered to talk about what they want, and they do so among themselves. The increases in both women's responses to women during the time period identified as Topic 3, and men's responses to the group during Topic 4, can be seen as reactions to women having gained control of the conversational floor.

Hedges

Yet another revealing piece of evidence comes from the use of hedges. Hedges – qualifiers such as *sort of, a little,* and *somewhat,* the modals *may* and *might,* and expressions such as *perhaps, conceivably,* and *it seems* – have been observed to occur more frequently in the speech of women especially in situations where women are relatively powerless (Lakoff 1975; O'Barr and Atkins 1980, reprinted in this volume, p. 377). In the "men's literature" discussion, women use more hedges than men overall.[11] However, while women's use of hedges *decreases* steadily throughout the discussion, men's use of hedges *increases* as the discussion builds in intensity, dropping off after the worst of the conflict has passed. This is charted in figure 6.

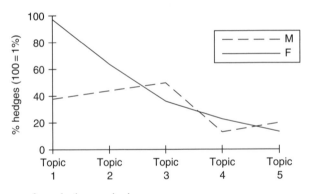

Figure 6   Percentage of words that are hedges

Men hedge most during the period identified as Topic 3, thus exhibiting features of powerless language at a time when women are relatively more empowered in the discourse. This results in another temporary reversal of the overall pattern.

Survey results

Finally, the hypothesis that power relations underwent a reversal in the discussion is supported by the results of a survey we created and disseminated on MBU two months after the "men's literature" discussion had ended. The survey included the following two questions:

(1)   In the course of the debate, two basic positions were expressed: a "pro" position, which essentially supported the offering of courses on men's literature, and a "con" position opposed

Table 2 Survey results for question (1): Who won the "men's literature" debate?

	Pro	*Con*	*Neither*	*Other*
Female	10.0%	30.0%	*40.0%*	20.0%
Male	11.1%	*50.0%*	33.3%	5.6%
Both	10.7%	42.9%	35.7%	10.7%

to or concerned by the offering of courses of this type. If you had to choose, which side would you say was ultimately more successful in persuading the group as a whole to its point of view?

(2)   How satisfied were you personally with the outcome of the debate?

Twenty-eight people responded to the survey (M = 18; F = 10) either privately or by posting their responses publicly to the list.[12] Their responses to question (1) are summarized in table 2. While the greatest percentage (40%) of women responded that neither side had been more persuasive, the majority of men (50%) indicated that the "con" (i.e., female) position had prevailed. These responses are especially revealing in that the original question could be interpreted as biased towards a "pro" response: the person who suggested the "men's literature" course did, in fact, go on to teach it, and survey respondents were aware of this fact. Why did more men than women say that the "women's side" had won the debate? Clearly, they perceived the women to have been more powerful than the women perceived themselves to have been, or than the external circumstances warranted.

Not coincidentally, male survey respondents also indicated a lower level of satisfaction than females with the outcome of the debate (question 2). On a scale where 2 = very satisfied, 0 = indifferent, and –2 = very dissatisfied, the men's responses averaged –.06 (indifferent to somewhat dissatisfied), while the women's averaged .6 (somewhat satisfied). Additional comments made by survey respondents on the tone of the debate provide further evidence of differing levels of satisfaction. Female respondents tended to comment that they found the discussion 'interesting", "provocative", "gratifying", and "impressive", although several also expressed weariness at having to fight the "same old battles". The comments of the male respondents, in contrast, range from "initially shocked", to a "no-win" discussion, "whining", "yelling and screaming", and (from the man who posted the original "men's literature" request) "a bad-tempered festival of condemnation and defense". Such comments are consistent with Spender's (1980) observation that women who express feminist views, no matter how rationally and calmly, tend to be perceived as hostile and emotional by men.

Ironically, these attitude differences emerge despite the fact that subscribers to MBU – male and female alike – overwhelmingly consider themselves to be feminists. In response to a question on the survey asking: "Do you consider yourself to be a feminist, and if so, how strongly?", 100% of respondents of both sexes indicated that they were either strong feminists or supporters of feminist principles.

Conclusions

We have presented data to show that despite considerable external evidence to the contrary (amount of participation, rate of response, real-world outcome of the debate), men perceived women as having dominated the "men's literature" discussion. This perceptual reversal of dominance can be traced to a two-day period during which women contributed more messages than men. Immediately following this period, men threatened to leave the list, began hedging more, and ultimately abandoned a male-introduced topic to talk about a female-introduced topic instead (although without responding directly to the women involved). Moreover, when surveyed later, men were more inclined to state that the women's side of the argument had "won", and to express dissatisfaction with the discussion overall.

The feminist overtones of the women's contributions, along with the fact that they were critical of a topic introduced and supported by men, no doubt contributed to the discomfort experienced by the men in the group. Yet the implied accusations that the women were "vituperative" and "unreasonable" are not supported by our analysis, nor indeed is such a characterization consistent with the women's supposedly greater rhetorical effectiveness in persuading others to their point of view, as male survey respondents claimed. In fact, we suggest that women on the list were neither vituperative, nor especially persuasive – what won them the floor was their persistence in participating, and male (over)reactions to that persistence.

These findings have implications for participation in electronic discourse more generally. It is significant that after their brief period of more-or-less equal participation, women on MBU retreated back to a lower level of participation, such that their contributions to the discussion overall did not exceed 30%. Moreover, in discussions on MBU in the four months following the "men's literature" discussion, women's contributions averaged slightly less than 20%, even on topics of broad general interest.[13] The 20% figure is also consistent with earlier findings (Herring 1992) for women's participation on the Linguist list. If it is true that women, including successful, well-educated, academic women, are accorded less than equal speaking rights in mixed-sex public discourse on the Internet, then it appears that the amount they are expected to speak, all other factors being equal, is between 20–30%.

The 20–30% figure is supported by evidence from a variety of other public discourse types, both spoken and written. In an academic seminar, Spender (1979) found that 30% was the upper limit before men felt that women were contributing more than their share. In publishing, women writers average only 20% of those published; despite the fact that more women than men buy books, male publishers consider that to publish more women authors would be "risky" (Spender 1989). Finally, in two recent surveys of American television commercials, students in sociolinguistics courses taught by the first author of this article found that although women are frequently depicted, they have significant speaking roles in only 28% of the commercials aired. This last observation is particularly interesting, given the normalized appeal of commercial television: it suggests that society at large recognizes as normal a less than equal amount of talk by women. In a society where such an expectation is conventionalized and even exploited for commercial ends, it is small wonder that the electronic medium does not – cannot – by itself make for equal communication between the sexes.

Nevertheless, increased feminist awareness may help. The fact that MBU women spoke up, persisted in speaking up even when ignored, and appealed successfully to other women in the group for support can be attributed to widespread feminist consciousness within the field of composition/rhetoric. Further, the political reality of feminism in the field constrained the males in the group (according to self-report) to hedge their objections and ultimately to concede the floor – at least temporarily – to the women. Of course, these results did not come about without effort (as one woman later put it, "a small war was necessary on MBU for a bit of consciousness raising"), and female participants' communicative efforts were met with resistance as soon as they appeared to be taking up more than their rightful "share" of the discussion.

Women may never gain the right to equal participation, however, unless we assume that the right is ours already, and act accordingly. Given the growing importance of computer-mediated communication in the current information age, electronic discussion groups might well be a good place to start.

Notes

This is a slightly revised version of an article by the same title published in 1992 in *Locating Power: Proceedings of the Second Berkeley Women and Language Conference* (Berkeley, CA: Berkeley Women and Language Group). An expanded analysis of male reactions to women's participation in the "men's literature" discussion can be found in Herring, Johnson and DiBenedetto (1995).

1 Gender non-specific return addresses (such as those containing sender's last name only, or a more or less random sequence of letters and numbers) were apparently used in the communication observed by Graddol and Swann, which took place at the Open University in the United Kingdom. In the lists reported on in this paper, however, the sex of participants is generally known, either because their first name is part of their return address, or because they sign their messages, or because their address is otherwise known within the community.

2 Messages on lists and computer conferences are typically posted to an intermediary machine, or listserver, before being distributed to subscribers. Some lists have a moderator who exercises a degree of editorial control over the content (and less commonly, the order) of messages; generally, however, messages are distributed on a strict "first come, first served" basis.

3 For example, at the 1992 College Composition and Communication Conference (CCCC) in Cincinnati, the number of sessions on "gender and feminist theory" ranked third out of 27 topics. The only two topics that had more sessions were devoted to practical teaching issues.

4 One man supported the feminist position throughout, and several others supported parts of it during the later portions of the discussion; overall, however, most men favored the idea of a men's literature course, and all participating women expressed concerns about such a course.

5 The subscription figures for MBU are 42% female and 58% male (out of a total of 178 subscribers), based on a count of names from which gender can reliably be determined. The majority of subscribers are teachers and graduate students in English departments at United States universities.

6 The intervals between dates in Topics 1, 4, and 5 are fewer than the number of calendar days, as we have included in figure 1 only those days on which messages related to "men's literature" were contributed.

7 At the height of the "reversal", on November 23, women contributed 66.6% of the day's messages. However, since the women's messages were shorter, men still contributed more words on that day.

8 One man did in fact unsubscribe; the other two were persuaded to remain on the list.

9 The one exception is a contribution in which the writer presents her feminist views dogmatically, rather than cooperatively; this message accuses one of the male participants of "intellectualizing".

10 *Responses* were counted as only those messages which explicitly acknowledge an earlier posting. Excluded were messages pertaining to the topic under discussion but addressed to the group as a whole, as well as first postings on a new topic.

11 Hedges constitute .48% of the words contributed by women, and .36% of the words contributed by men.

12 Of these, 18 (M = 13; F = 5) had participated in the original discussion.

13 For example, in a discussion of the usefulness of composition theory in teaching writing, contributions by women accounted for only 16.9% of the 142 message total.

References

Graddol, David and Joan Swann (1989) *Gender Voices*. Oxford: Basil Blackwell.

Herring, Susan (1992) Gender and participation in computer-mediated linguistic discourse. Washington, DC: ERIC Clearinghouse on Languages and Linguistics. Document no. ED345552.

Herring, Susan, Deborah Johnson, and Tamra DiBenedetto (1995) 'This discussion is going too far!' Male resistance to female participation on the Internet. In K. Hall and M. Bucholtz (eds.), *Gender Articulated: Language and the Socially Constructed Self*. New York: Routledge, 67–96.

Holmes, Janet (1992) Women's talk in public contexts. *Discourse and Society* 3.2; 131–50.

Kahn, Arnold and Robert Brookshire (1991) Using a computer bulletin board in a social psychology course. *Teaching of Psychology* 18.4; 245–9.

Lakoff, Robin (1975) *Language and Woman's Place*. New York: Harper & Row.

O'Barr, William & Bowman K. Atkins (1980) 'Women's language' or 'powerless language'? In Sally McConnell-Ginet, Ruth Borker & Nelly Furman (eds.), *Women and Language in Literature and Society*. New York: Praeger, 93–110.

Spender, Dale (1979) Language and sex differences. In *Osnabrücker Beiträge zur Sprachtheorie: Sprache und Geschlect II*; 38–59.

Spender, Dale (1980) *Man Made Language*. London: Pandora Press.

Spender, Dale (1989) *The Writing or the Sex (or Why You Don't Have to Read Women's Writing to Know it's No Good)*. The Athene Series. New York: Pergamon.

Wallwork, Jean (1978) *Language and People*. London: Heinemann Educational Books.

15

Zuiqian "Deficient Mouth": Discourse, Gender and Domestic Violence in Urban China

Jie Yang

Source: *Gender and Language* 1(1) (2007), pp. 107–18. Reprinted with permission of Equinox Publishing Ltd.

1 Introduction

Feminist scholarship has paid attention to particular social problems such as domestic violence and rape (cf. Jacobson, Gottman, Waltz, Rushe, Babcock and Holtzworth-Munroe 1994; Erhlich 1998; Johnson 2001; Sokoloff with Pratt 2005), but the problem of domestic violence has only gained cursory scholarly attention in language and gender studies (Trinch 2004). The absence of a strong research focus on language and male violence against women may be, on the one hand, because of the difficulty in collecting verbal data; on the other hand, it may be an unintended consequence of the shift in analytical categories in language and gender studies from face-to-face interactions between heterosexual couples (cf. Tannen 1990) to macro, institutional activities and practices (Gal 1991; McElhinny 2003). Indeed, a focus on face-to-face interactions that directly provoke male violence may trivialize the serious social problem of domestic violence as a private, family issue.[1] Therefore, instead of using gender as the primary explanatory model (Sokoloff and Dupont 2005:10), domestic violence can be examined from a broader social, political and economic perspective, because gender inequality is intertwined with other systems of power and oppression such as class, race and sexuality. This 'intersectionality' approach (Crenshaw 1994) to domestic violence also de-centers the predominant cultural approach to domestic violence in feminist writing, which often obscures the material conditions that intensify gender inequality and cause male violence against women.[2]

As Scott (1986) suggests, to understand social meaning, 'we need to deal with the individual subject as well as social organization and to articulate the nature of their interrelationships, for both are crucial to understanding how gender works, how change occurs' (1986:1067). This article, combining an analysis of the broader political economy with a micro discourse analysis, contextualizes the study of language and domestic violence in postsocialist China. In the course of China's current neoliberal restructuring, the number of cases of domestic violence has been reportedly increasing. In 1991, the rate of domestic violence (husbands beating wives) was 1.67 per cent (Wang 2003). However, according to a recent survey conducted by the All China Women's Federation, about 30 per cent of women suffered domestic violence in China (Wang 2003:151). This increase is, on the one hand, a result of women's declining social status and, on the other, by changes in the acceptability of reporting domestic violence. With the breakdown of the supposedly all-encompassing socialist work-unit system and the establishment of a modern enterprise system corresponding to the market economy, state enterprises have been reduced and downsized. This process has produced massive unemployment and women suffer unemployment to a greater degree than men. Sixty percent of the unemployed population is women. When full-time jobs are their major source of income, women's job loss, to a great extent, means poverty. Thus there is a tendency towards feminized poverty in cities. The feminized poverty and economic difficulties make women more vulnerable to domestic violence. On the other hand, reform-era social activism may also motivate more women to report their battery. Although domestic violence previously was construed as a private concern, it is now the subject of public discourse and public legislation in China. Since the public/private distinction often has ideological implications and can be used as tool to defend certain political or economic interests (Gal 2002; McElhinny 1997), the recent public attention to the 'private' issue of domestic violence in China may be part of neoliberal trends or technologies (see below).

This article examines a metapragmatic discourse on domestic violence – *zuiqian* 'deficient mouth' – which, by blaming women's mouths and 'deviant' speaking styles, individualizes the serious social problem of domestic violence and downplays the structural force that causes male violence. This discourse of *zuiqian* serves as an anatomic mode of power (anatomo-politics) for the state to discipline women and safeguard society. It also constitutes a repudiating site (that is, a site at which subjects are condemned and criticized in order for them to emerge) to construct a kind of subject identified with China's neoliberal interests. The data used in this article were collected during my doctoral research on China's neoliberal restructuring in a working-class community in Beijing between 2002 and 2003. In this community, massive gendered layoffs had devastated women's social status and increased the number of reported cases of domestic violence. The data include media discourse/public discourse on domestic violence and in-depth interviews with both battered women and cadres from grassroots trade unions and women's organizations in charge of domestic violence.

2   Zuiqian 'Deficient Mouth' – 'Condemned' Body and 'Deviant' Language

The current approach to domestic violence in China is predominantly through legislative measures, which often pay attention to women's physical injuries but overlook their mental and emotional suffering. Also, legislative measures cannot change the ideologies that blame women for their battery and legitimize male violence. These ideologies are epitomized in a metapragmatic discourse on domestic violence – *zuiqian* 'deficient mouth' – in the local community where I conducted my doctoral research in Beijing. *Zuiqian* 'deficient mouth' is an indiscriminate term delineating women's 'deviant' and 'deficient' talk. It includes a series of terms and propositions such as *zuisui* 'broken mouth' (talking about trivial things in great detail); *da zuiba* 'big mouth' (talking loudly and aggressively); *chang shetou* 'long tongue' (being too inquisitive and nosey); and *zui-jian* 'cheap mouth' (talking too much and out of context, etc.).[3] Any of these forms of talk, together with a wide variety of other women's practices such as earning too much money, being too social, nagging, and complaining about men's bad behaviors, can provoke men's anger and violence against women. For example, in this community, a young woman worker who could not bear her husband's infidelity and complained and argued with her husband was constantly beat up by her husband. Finally, she went to her work-unit to seek official assistance.[4] After the battered woman explained how and why she argued with her husband, the middle-aged female party secretary of the work-unit gave her some personal advice.

> …If I had such a rich husband, I just would seal my mouth and serve him well to win his heart back. Nowadays, it's hard to have a man who can make money and meanwhile be nice to you. Men work outside the whole day, and they need peace at home. You just tend every one of his needs. Don't argue with him. Don't complain….

Instead of condemning the abusive husband, the party secretary advised the woman to be quiet, docile and tolerant. This folk ideology on how to avoid male violence at home not only further victimizes women but also discredits and essentializes women's speaking styles. This inevitable link between women's speaking styles and male violence even constitutes an 'iconization process' (Irvine 2001) so that any woman that suffers domestic violence is iconically associated with a 'deficient' mouth to a greater or lesser degree. The correlation between women's speaking styles and their battery is not a causal relationship, but serves to legitimize the state's non-interference or tolerance of male violence.[5]

Zuiqian is not a neologism in this working-class community but has gained new discursive power after a sensational TV series on domestic violence in 2002 entitled *Buyao he moshengren jianghua* 'Don't talk to strangers' drew public attention to language's role in domestic violence. The TV series, while setting out to combat domestic violence, seemed to enrich men's linguistic repertoire and provide an overarching narrative structure for men to justify their violent practices. For example, in the community, men often used this sentence 'Don't talk to strangers' to show spousal jealousy and restrain their wives' contact with men. Language has thus become one of the main foci for the debate on domestic violence in China. In one of my interviews with a female official from a local women's organization in Beijing, the leader of an international anti-domestic violence collaboration, she described her understanding of the role of language in triggering domestic violence.

> Although men should be blamed for their violence, women should also improve their *suzhi* (roughly translated as 'quality'). For example, they should mind their language. Some women have really 'cheap mouths,' and they cannot control their mouths. They often *jihuo* 'stimulate fire' (e.g. trigger men's anger and violence). I mentioned this element in domestic violence to my Canadian counterparts. But they just ignored this element, saying that women could not leave the home, and therefore they had to vent their frustration at home, and this shows women's disadvantaged position in society. I think those Canadians just don't really understand Chinese situations.

This local official emphasized that women do need to improve their language as part of their overall *suzhi* 'quality' in order to avoid male violence. The discourse of *zuiqian*, by condemning women's mouths and their linguistic performances that presumably provoke male anger and violence, blames individual victims and obscures the root causes for domestic violence – the political and economic structure that intensifies gender inequality and disadvantages women. In China, women have paid the highest price for the neoliberal restructuring as it impacts women in a particularly negative way, by cutting back on funds for health, education, etc.

This discourse of *zuiqian* is both a diagnostic and a condemning discourse. Women's mouths are perceived as the source of aberrant violence against themselves. Male violence is the deserving punishment for those non-conforming female bodies. Thus, it is not only linguistic performances but the performing body part that is specified and condemned. This kind of condemnation is more permanent and hegemonic. When a talking mouth becomes a modality to regulate women, the politics of gender is then played out in biological terms. To put male dominance over women in biological forms may constitute a nascent means of governing gender in China.

3 The Anatomo-politics of the Female Body and the Repudiating Mode of Subjectivity Formation

The discourse of *zuiqian* is imbued with the kind of ideologies that discredit women's bodies and legitimize male violence. Ideology, according to Foucault (1978), is not only a theory of ideas, signs, and the individual genesis of sensations, but also a theory of the social composition of interests, which can be a doctrine of 'the regulated formation of the social body' (1978:134). The ideology of the social body can be in the form of concrete arrangements that make up the anatomic technology of power. In this study, to subjugate women by disciplining their mouths/bodies seems to be an example of Foucault's (1978) anatomo-politics of the human body. According to Foucault (1978), starting in the seventeenth century, the power over life evolved in two basic forms: one is anatomo-politics and the other biopolitics/biopower. Anatomo-politics refers to political strategies targeting man-as-body in an attempt to make individual human bodies more productive and docile. For instance, one's ability to enter in, and advance within, educational institutions depends on the assessment of an examination. Biopolitics, by contrast, refers to political strategies aimed collectively at man-as-species. Biopolitics is the attempt to regulate aggregate biological occurrences at the population level such as lowering the mortality rate, increasing life expectancy, stimulating birth rate, etc. (1978:139). The power over life in China to discipline individuals and regulate the population is often through the discourse of *suzhi*, which has undergone a re-organization in the realm of the biopolitical in which human life becomes a new frontier for capital accumulation (Anagnost 2004:189). Thus, an anatomo-politics refers to the seizure of power over the body in an individualizing mode (Foucault 1978:139). Rather than seeking to contain subjects by the threat of death that a sovereign exercises, an anatomo-politics seeks to optimize the usefulness and docility of the human body by disciplinary procedures. It includes mechanisms directed towards the performances of the body by individualizing it as man-as-body so that individual bodies can be kept under surveillance, used or punished. Such procedures include observation, judgment and examination. Anatomo-politics as a technique of power presents at every level of the social body and is utilized by diverse institutions for segregation and social hierarchization in order to guarantee relations of domination and effects of hegemony (1978:141). This anatomic mode of power employs procedures that measure, distribute, or order the human body according to social norms rather than the juridical system of the law (1978:144). In fact, the discourse of *zuiqian* is itself the embodiment of the local gender norms. Women who suffered domestic violence were inevitably perceived as having 'deficient mouths.' They were often considered as undeserving of protection from local institutions and less sympathy was then afforded them, because they violated normative definitions of the helpless victim and did not appear properly gendered. A workshop party secretary from the factory where I did my fieldwork told me about a woman who could not control her mouth and thus did not deserve protection.

> We live in the same unit of the same apartment building. Everyone heard her curse and scream mixed with her husband beating. I heard the husband yell, 'If you curse again, I'll beat you to death.' I could not help going to their door to knock, and they could not hear my knock, I shouted out, but her screams and curses were louder. I just stood outside, wondering why she was just so stupid, you just shut up, your husband would not feel that irritated and would stop beating you. She was not. So stubborn. How can I help?

Gendering is thus, among other things, the differentiating relationship by which speaking subjects come into being and are judged (Butler 1993:7). But to judge women as 'deserving' victims based on their speaking styles trivializes and even denies the victimization of battered women.[6] The discourse of *zuiqian* composed of condemning judgments is regulatory and exclusionary in nature. Through the discourse of *zuiqian*, grassroots institutions diagnostically identify and scrutinize the 'pathological' (battered) women and reformulate their subjectivities. Thus, the construction of the subject works through an act of foreclosure in discourse. The female trade union leader described one of the regularly battered women in the factory.

> You can see she's becoming fat and fat, *yi shen lan rou*, 'full of lazy flesh.' If her husband does not beat her, she doesn't work. You can see her always carrying her baby outside gossiping and chatting with men. She *yexin* 'has a wild heart.' She seldom stays at home, having no patience doing housework. Her apartment must be a mess. Her husband said if he does not beat her, she never wants to work. She just has a poor memory. So her husband has to remind her regularly by beating her up to make her work.

The above narrative entails a foreclosing discourse through which the 'lazy' woman was criticized, condemned and battered in order to become a 'normal' subject. According to Zizek (1989), any theory of the discursive constitution of the subject must take into account the domain of foreclosure, of what must be repudiated for the subject itself to emerge. To paraphrase Butler (1993), the forming of a subject requires identification with the norm, and this identification takes place through a repudiation which produces a domain of abjection, a repudiation without which the subject cannot emerge (1993:3). This foreclosing mode of subjectivity construction works through a series of regulatory and condemning discursive devices such as terms and discourses labeling women's linguistic practices as 'deficient' or 'deviant'.

The discourse of *zuiqian* is regulatory in nature, but to avoid male violence seems to rely on individual disciplines and constraints. It seems that women can do something on their own (by controlling their mouths) to avoid or combat male violence. Further, by attributing the root cause of male violence to women's 'deficient' mouths, the relation of (gender) domination is thus simplified and disguised. Indeed, in the model of anatomic

power, the state is no longer the sole agent of control but individuals themselves participate in their own self-monitoring, self-scrutiny, and self-discipline through mundane and
taken-for-granted regulatory mechanisms. This individualization in combating domestic
violence implicitly coincides with the 'technology of the self' employed in China's neoliberal restructuring. These technologies of the self operate in a process through which
individuals are made in charge of their own behaviour, competence, improvement, secu-
rity, and 'well-being' (Rose 1999). But the emphasis on individual responsibility in solving
the problem of domestic violence shouldn't make us overlook the political and economic
conditions which devastate women's social status and place them at risk of domestic violence, because lack of economic resources reduces women's ability to alter the environments in which they suffer male violence.

4   Conclusion

One of the important features of neoliberalism or neoliberal restructuring is the displace-
ment of the public into the individual and market. Thus, the private, the individual and
the body have increasingly been the bases for political legitimacy (Rofel 1999; Rose
1999). This study shows that both language and gender can be integrated either as disciplinary modes of power or repudiating sites for subjectivity construction into the process
of economic restructuring and the process of globalization. In this instance, the discourse
of *zuiqian* serves as an anatomic technology of power for the state to regulate the female
body and safeguard society. Ideologies of the deficient social body/mouth in the discourse of *zuiqian* systematize and rationalize relationships between linguistic phenomena
and social formations (e.g. domestic violence). To fragment women and subjugate their
body parts for scrutiny and regulation seems to be a more objective and hegemonic mode
of subjectivization. The politics of gender is played out on a biological basis, which appears
to be devoid of ideological biases. This resembles the surveillance techniques involving
the use of biometrics – physical attributes such as fingerprints, DNA patterns, retina, iris,
face, voice, etc. Which are used to collect, process, and store biometric samples onto a
database for scrutiny and control. To reduce women's subjectivities to 'body parts' seems
to set women up for self-management and self-regulation. For example, a woman who
suffered *jiating leng baoli* 'spiritual torture' from her husband, said to me:

> For a long time, he came back with only three sentences. 'Hungry'. 'Tired.' 'Go to sleep.' Only
> these words, nothing else. No fight, no argument. These words rendered all that I said mean-
> ingless. I really hope he told me what's wrong with me and what I should do to make him talk
> to me again. That's really a torture. For a long time, I searched my soul for what is wrong with
> me. I went to talk with my sister-in-law who was a workshop party secretary before she retired
> and I thought she might give me some advice. She warned me to be more cautious in my
> everyday behaviour as nowadays men always find excuses to divorce their wives and find
> younger women. She asked me to control my mouth – don't talk too much and control my
> legs – work hard at home. I do. I really do. I talk cautiously to him and serve him well. I'm
> really afraid of saying something wrong to annoy him further.

Thus (patriarchical) power does not need to be enforced but merely 'internalised'
through men's hegemonic silence shown in the above or other regulatory schemas
(e.g. the party secretary's warnings). Such mechanisms render the regulated as simultaneously the subject of and the one subjected to power. Also, this withering away of
subjectivity makes such anatomic power more effective and less obtrusive.

As shown in this study, the investigation of the social body can provide an angle on the study of subjectivity. The recent research focus towards theorizing gender as a way of defining access to resources or as a terrain for political or economic struggle in nation-building rather than as a personal trait or identity may downplay the significance of the multiple features and modes of subjectivity construction. This article thus explores one mode of subjectivity formation through the regulatory and repudiating discourse of *zuiqian*. The subject is constituted through the force of exclusion and abjection, which produces a constitutive outside to the subject, yet 'inside' the subject as its own founding repudiation (Butler 1993:3). The 'deviant,' 'deficient,' and 'lack' categories are thus essential to construct the hegemonic subject identified with the state interests. As Laclau (1990) suggests, 'the hegemonic relationship can be thought only through assuming the category of lack as a point of departure' (1990:96). The analysis of the discourse of *zuiqian* thus reminds us of the performativity of discourse, which, in this case, refers to its reiterative power to embody and cite gender norms and produce the phenomena that the discourse regulates and constrains (Butler 1993). Finally, this study demonstrates that domestic violence often indexes the general politics of gender and class. Therefore, in combating domestic violence, social, structural inequalities between genders as root causes of male violence should be identified, and structural solutions are required in order to redress aggravating, causal factors associated with domestic violence.

Notes

The data used for this article were collected during my field research in Beijing between 2002 and 2003. I am grateful for the financial support from the Department of Anthropology at the University of Toronto. This article benefits greatly from the detailed and insightful comments from Professor Hy Van Luong, the editors, and two anonymous reviewers. I especially thank Bonnie McElhinny for her constant encouragement, insights and guidance.

1   Perhaps 95 per cent of domestic violence victims in China are women, and practically all of the perpetrators are men. Many women who do kill their spouses kill out of self-defense after years of enduring violence (Wang 2003; Wang 2004). Given the feminine face of domestic violence, some scholars choose to use the term 'woman battery' (cf. Johnson 2001).

2   Feminist scholarship on domestic violence often points to the traditional culture and the preeminence of the patriarchal family as the primary historical and social roots of domestic violence against women. And domestic violence is perceived as a product of male-dominated culture (Sokoloff with Pratt 2005).

3   Lakoff's (1975) research suggests that women's language (essentialized as more polite, cooperative and gentle) is often perceived as 'deviant' and 'deficient,' which serves to affirm the sexist notion of women as culturally subordinate. However, being deficient and deviant in speech can be defined the other way around in this community where I conducted my fieldwork in Beijing – speaking impolitely, loudly, confrontationally, and aggressively. These 'deviant' speaking styles are often perceived as important factors that trigger male violence against women.

4   Although the supposedly all-encompassing socialist work-unit system in which people worked and lived together has been gradually collapsing in a market economy, workers still habitually returned to their work-units (factories) to seek official assistance or spiritual support.

5   Although Deborah Tannen finds that high-involvement speakers are often female – women produce more utterances, interrupt more aggressively, and feel that making their feelings obvious is more important than not hurting others – the philosopher Jean-Paul Sartre suggests that argument is sometimes the strength of groups who have had to live with violence

against them but are not able to counter it with violence, as is historically the case with the Jews. Sartre's argument may also be made about women (Kalmar 2000). However, contradictory cases are also found. Based on laboratory interviews and clinical research, Jacobson, Gottman, Waltz, Rushe, Babcock and Holtzworth-Munroe (1994) study the roles that male batterers and female victims play during violent altercations. When husbands show the same level of verbal aggression as their wives during verbal arguments, wife beating is likely to be present in the relationship. There is an absence of gender differences among domestic violent couples in rates of verbal aggression; these findings should not be construed as supporting the notion that battered women cause or are in some way provoking violence through their verbal aggression. These results simply illustrate that the battered women, despite their history of being beaten, had not been beaten into submission (cf. Cordova, Jacobson, Gottman, Rushe, and Cox, 1993). And women seem to have little recourse when it comes to stopping the fight once it starts. It is the men who are driving the system (Jacobson, Gottman, Waltz, Rushe, Babcock and Holtzworth-Munroe 1994:987).

6 Victimization can also be denied when domestic violence is defined as culturally 'normal' and when human suffering is neutralized or obscured. For example, in this community, a very popular metadiscourse on domestic violence is *da shi qin, ma shi ai*, 'Beating is intimacy, and cursing is love.' This metadiscourse, by lumping intimate interactions (including domestic violence) between couples into playful fights or love relationship, trivializes women's victimization and fixes domestic violence in the family domain. Metadiscourses of this sort are ideological barriers to the prevention of male violence.

References

Anagnost, Ann. 2004. The corporeal politics of quality (*suzhi*). *Public Culture* 16(2):189–208.

Butler, Judith. 1993. *Bodies that Matter: On the Discursive Limits of 'Sex.'* New York and London: Routledge.

Cordova, James V., Neil S. Jacobson, John M. Gottman, Regina Rushe and Gary Cox. 1993. Negative reciprocity and communication in couples with a violent husband. *Journal of Abnormal Psychology*. 102:559–64.

Crenshaw, Kimberle. 1994. Mapping the margins: Intersectionality, identity politics, and violence against women of color. In M. Fineman and R. Mykitiuk (eds). *The Public Nature of Private Violence*. New York: Routledge, pp. 93–118.

Ehrlich, Susan. 1998. The discursive reconstruction of sexual consent. *Discourse and Society* 9 (2):149–71.

Foucault, Michel. 1978. *The History of Sexuality*, vol. 1: *An Introduction*. New York: Pantheon Books, pp. 135–59.

Gal, Susan. 1991. Between speech and silence. In Micaela di Leonardo (ed.). *Gender at the Crossroads of Knowledge: Feminist Anthropology in the Postmodern Era*. Berkeley, CA: University of California Press, pp. 175–203.

Gal, Susan. 2002. A semiotics of the public/private distinction. *Differences: A Journal of Feminist Cultural Studies* 13(1):77–95.

Irvine, Judith T. 2001. Style as distinctiveness: The culture and ideology of linguistic differentiation. In Penelope Eckert and John R. Rickford (eds). *Style and Sociolinguistic Variation*. Cambridge: Cambridge University Press, pp. 21–43.

Jacobson, Neil S., John M. Gottman, Jennifer Waltz, Regina Rushe, Julia Babcock and Amy Holtzworth-Munroe. 1994. Affect, verbal content, and psychophysiology in the arguments of couples with a violent husband. *Journal of Consulting and Clinical Psychology* 62(5):982–8.

Johnson, Janet Elise. 2001. Privatizing pain: The problem of woman battery in Russia. *National Women's Studies Association (NWSA) Journal* 13(3):153–68.

Kalmar, Ivan. 2000. *Word, Sign, Culture: Notes on Linguistic and Semiotic Anthropology*. Toronto: Quirk Press.

Laclau, Ernesto. 1990. Psychoanalysis and Marxism. In Ernesto Laclau (ed.). *New Reflections on the Revolution of our Time*. London and New York: Verso, pp. 93–6.

Lakoff, Robin. 1975. *Language and Women's Place*. New York: Harper & Row.

McElhinny, Bonnie. 1997. Ideologies of public and private in sociolinguistics. In Ruth Wodak (ed.). *Gender and Discourse*. London and Thousand Oaks, CA: Sage, pp. 106–39.

McElhinny, Bonnie. 2003. Theorizing gender in sociolinguistics and linguistic anthropology. In Janet Holmes and Miriam Meyerhof (eds). *The Language and Gender Handbook*. Oxford: Basil Blackwell, pp. 21–42.

Rofel, Lisa. 1999. *Other Modernities: Gendered Yearnings in China after Socialism*. Berkeley, CA: University of California Press.

Rose, Nikolas. 1999. *Powers of Freedom: Reframing Political Thought*. Cambridge: Cambridge University Press.

Scott, Joan. 1986. Gender: A useful category of historical analysis. *American Historical Review* 91(5):1053–75.

Sokoloff, Natalie J. with Christina Pratt (eds). 2005. *Domestic Violence at the Margins: Readings on Race, Class, Gender and Culture*. New Brunswick, NJ: Rutgers University Press.

Sokoloff, Natalie J. and Ida Dupont. 2005. Domestic violence: Examining the intersections of race, class, and gender – an introduction. In Nalatie Sokoloff with Christina Pratt (eds). *Domestic Violence at the Margins: Readings on Race, Class, Gender and Culture*. New Brunswick, NJ: Rutgers University Press, pp. 1–14.

Tannen, Deborah. 1990. *You Just Don't Understand: Women and Men in Conversation*. New York: Morrow.

Trinch, Shonna L. 2004. *Latinas' Narratives of Domestic Abuse: Discrepant Versions of Violence*. Amsterdam and Philadelphia: John Benjamins Publishing Company.

Wang, Fengxian. 2003. Shou bao funu ruhe baituo jiating baoli (How women battery victims get out of domestic violence). In Wang Hongqi (ed.). *Zhongguo nuxing zai yanshuo* (Chinese women are speaking). Beijing: Zhongguo Shidai Jingji Chubanshe, pp. 148–75.

Wang, Xingjuan. 2004. Domestic violence in China. In Tao Jie, Zheng Bijun and Shirley L. Mow (eds). *Holding Up Half the Sky: Chinese Women Past, Present and Future*. City University of New York: The Feminist Press, pp. 179–92.

Žižek, Slavoj. 1989. *The Sublime Object of Ideology*. London and New York: Verso, pp. 153–200.

Part IV
Same-Sex Talk

By contrast with the previous section, which focused on interaction involving both women and men, this section deals with women's and men's talk in same-sex groups. The first three papers in the section focus on all-female talk, the last three on all-male talk. These papers mark the shift from a theoretical approach emphasizing difference (the two-cultures model) to a social constructionist approach, which treats gender as something which is accomplished through talk. Not only does more recent work view gender as fluid and malleable, but masculinity and femininity are no longer viewed as singular: analysts explore a range of femininities and masculinities.

The publication in 1973 of Robin Lakoff's classic paper "Language and Woman's Place" (reprinted in 1975 as a slim book) marked the beginning of a new, less androcentric, phase in sociolinguistic research. The topic of all-female talk, however, was not explicitly addressed until 1980 in Deborah Jones' paper, "Gossip: Notes on Women's Oral Culture." Since then, a great deal of research has been carried out on same-sex talk, though much of it has had a comparative focus. For example, Deborah Tannen (1990) compared the talk of same-sex pairs of friends at different ages; Jenny Cheshire (see paper in Part I) compared the language used by adolescent single-sex groups in adventure playgrounds in Reading, England; Marjorie Goodwin (see paper in Part II) compared the language used by pre-adolescent single-sex peer groups in a Philadelphia street; and Julia Davies (see paper in Part II) compared single-sex groups of girls and boys in classroom discussion. All these papers focus on children or adolescents, and all investigate both female and male speakers. It is still relatively rare to find research being carried out which has as its aim the description of women's conversational practices for their own sake (but see Mallinson and Childs 2007; Mendoza-Denton 2008; Pichler 2009a).

The first paper in this section, "Gossip Revisited," was written in response to Jones' innovative piece on all-female talk, with the aim of moving the debate on. Jennifer Coates aimed to provide detailed linguistic evidence in support of Jones' claims about women's oral culture. The paper presents a qualitative analysis of a 45-minute conversation between five women friends. Coates argues that women's friendly talk has as its chief goal the establishment and maintenance of good social relations. This has consequences

Language and Gender: A Reader, Second Edition. Edited by Jennifer Coates and Pia Pichler.
© 2011 Blackwell Publishing Ltd except for editorial material and organization. © 2011 Jennifer Coates and Pia Pichler. Published 2011 by Blackwell Publishing Ltd.

for the way talk is structured: friendly talk, or talk-as-play, is very different from talk-as-serious-business. In the paper the following features of all-female talk are selected for analysis: topic development; minimal responses; simultaneous speech; epistemic modality (or hedging); and tag questions. The paper ends with the claim that women's friendly talk is cooperative in the strong sense that speakers collaborate in the construction of talk, and that the voice of the group has priority over the voice of the individual. (This finding is corroborated by more recent research on all-female talk, for example, Davies in Part II, Eppler 2009, as well as Coates' later work – see in particular Coates 1996, 1997.)

The second paper in this section is Mary Bucholtz's "Why Be Normal?" This paper focuses on the talk of adolescent girls rather than that of adult women, and explores the linguistic practices associated with the social identity "nerd." Bucholtz argues that nerd identity is not necessarily something to be avoided but may be deliberately chosen as an alternative to mainstream gender identities. The girls she studies attend a high school in California and form a small cohesive friendship group with four central members and two peripheral members. These girls define themselves in opposition to "cool" groups or communities of practice such as Jocks and Burnouts (see Eckert in Part I of this volume; Eckert 1989). They are good students and value intelligence (in this way they fit the existing social order), but at the same time they reject conventional femininity (thus subverting the social order). They place a high value on individuality and deliberately flout the norms of the in-groups. Bucholtz shows how in their talk the girls display their intelligence in playful discussions of, for example, the kind of seed found on a bagel. When one of the girls, Carrie, introduces the slang term "bootsie," it is received negatively by the rest of the group since it is part of "cool" youth culture and therefore in direct conflict with their anti-cool identity practices. For these girls, nerd identity offers a crucial alternative to hegemonic femininity, which is antipathetic to female intellectual achievement. (For an account of a group of adolescent girls balancing displays of intelligence with coolness, see Pichler 2009b.)

The third paper in this section is Pia Pichler's "Hybrid or In Between Cultures: Traditions of Marriage in a Group of British Bangladeshi Girls." Several papers in the Reader highlight the fluid, constructed nature of gender, and Pichler takes the same constructionist approach to ethnic culture in order to capture the identity work of the five girls who are the subject of her paper. The girls come from a very different background from those in the previous paper; they are all British Bangladeshi and form a friendship group at their single-sex school in the East End of London. Pichler's aim in the paper is "to provide a space in language and gender research for the voices of adolescent Asian girls." She presents an analysis of an extract from the girls' talk about a wedding proposal, which demonstrates how they position themselves as "British" or "Londoni," but at the same time index their Bangladeshi identities by their overall alignment with a "modified discourse of arranged marriage." The topic of marriage is positioned as central to their adolescent femininities (in complete contrast to the preoccupations of the nerd group analyzed in the previous paper); but the girls also draw on and negotiate other, competing, discourses with various inflections of (ethnic) culture and gender, allowing them to accomplish hybrid British Bangladeshi femininities in their talk.

The section finishes with three papers focusing exclusively on male speakers. The best-known example of sociolinguistic research into all-male talk is probably Labov's (1972) study of the language of Black adolescent peer groups in Harlem, but the unmarked character of maleness is demonstrated by the title of Labov's book: *Language in the Inner City*. Presumably because of the semantic conflation of being-a-male and being-a-human-being, research focusing specifically on male speakers qua male speakers – particularly in informal settings – was rare until the 1990s, when the growth of Men's Studies, and a general sense that current forms of masculinity are in crisis (see, for example, Kimmel 2000; Clare 2001) brought masculinities into the spotlight. The first collection of papers focusing on language and masculinity was published in 1997 (Johnson and Meinhof 1997).

Deborah Cameron, in her paper "Performing Gender Identity," analyzes the conversation of a group of male students. Cameron shows how gender is performed through talk, drawing on Butler's (1990) notion of performativity. The group was recorded while they watched sport on television (one of their commonest shared activities), and one of the ways that these men perform gender in their talk is through their comments on the basketball game they are watching. Cameron suggests that "sportstalk" is a typically masculine conversational genre (see Johnson and Finlay 1997 for discussion of the way adult males use sportstalk as a form of gossip). Besides sport, these friends talk about women and about alcohol, topics stereotypically associated with all-male conversation. But they also gossip about non-present others: they discuss in great detail certain males of their acquaintance, accusing them of being gay. Overall, the talk is solidary: the five friends are bonded by their shared denigration of the supposedly gay outsiders. Cameron argues that, for men in a context such as this, demonstrating that they are not gay is as important as demonstrating that they are not women. In other words, they perform not just masculinity, but heterosexual masculinity. Interestingly, Cameron shows how the talk of these men involves several features normally associated with "cooperative" women's talk – hedges, overlapping speech, latching. But it also displays more competitive features – two speakers dominate the talk, and speakers vie for the floor. She argues that cooperation and competition as styles of talking cannot be simplistically attributed to one gender or the other. In fact, one of her aims in this paper is to deconstruct the opposition cooperative/ competitive.

While Cameron focuses on the talk of a small group of male friends, the next paper draws on a corpus of all-male conversation involving a wide range of male friendship groups, ranging in age from 18 to 55 and coming from both middle- and working-class backgrounds. In this paper, "Pushing at the Boundaries," Jennifer Coates examines friendly all-male interaction to explore the ways in which male speakers construct alternative masculinities through talk. The paper demonstrates that men can use friendly conversation as an arena in which the boundaries of conventional masculinities can be challenged and in which alternative masculinities can be explored. But the constraints of hegemonic masculinity are ever present and make it difficult for many men to express vulnerability or to explore more personal topics.

The final paper in the section is also concerned to demonstrate the pressures of dominant forms of masculinity. Scott Kiesling's "Playing the Straight Man" examines the all-male talk of an American fraternity. Fraternities are by definition all-male: as Kiesling says, "the 'greek' letter society system is arranged through an ideology of sexual difference." Kiesling has carried out a long-term ethnographic study of this fraternity. In this paper he explores the tensions that are ever present in a group where dominant discourses of masculinity are intrinsically heterosexual, while group activities are inevitably homosocial. Like the young men discussed in Cameron's paper, these students emphasize their heterosexuality; they boast about sexual conquests and use terms such as "bitch" to insult each other. The speech activities which are central to this group are based on the notion of sexual difference and heteronormativity. Kiesling concludes that displays of heterosexuality are used by the men as part of a same-sex status competition.

The extracts from the men's talk in Kiesling's paper illustrate an aspect of men's talk that is sometimes forgotten in discussion of language and masculinity. The evidence of a wide range of sociolinguistic and sociological research is that all-male talk can be misogynistic, homophobic, and full of swearing and obscenities (see, for example, Kuiper 1991; Kaminer and Dixon 1995; Gough and Edwards 1998; Coates 2003). Both Cameron and Kiesling help us to understand why this might be so by drawing attention to the pressures on men to constantly demonstrate that they are not gay. The paper by Coates shows that men do resist these pressures at times, in groups where they feel able to push back the boundaries of dominant masculinities. But generally the need to display heterosexuality leads to in-group competition of a kind not found in all-female talk.

References

Butler, Judith (1990) *Gender Trouble: Feminism and the Subversion of Identity*. London: Routledge.

Clare, Anthony (2001) *On Men: Masculinity in Crisis*. London: Arrow Books.

Coates, Jennifer (1996) *Women Talk: Conversation Between Women Friends*. Oxford: Blackwell.

Coates, Jennifer (1997) "The construction of a collaborative floor in women's friendly talk," pp. 55–89 in T. Givon (ed.) *Conversation: Cognitive, Communicative and Social Perspectives*. Philadelphia: John Benjamins,.

Coates, Jennifer (2003) *Men Talk: Stories in the Making of Masculinities*. Oxford: Blackwell.

Eckert, Penelope (1989) *Jocks and Burnouts: Social Categories and Identity in the High School*. New York: Teachers College Press.

Eppler, Eva (2009) "Four women, two codes and one (crowded) floor: the joint construction of a bilingual collaborative floor," pp. 211–34 in Pia Pichler and Eva Eppler (eds) *Gender and Spoken Interaction*. London: Palgrave.

Gough, B. and Edwards, G. (1998) "The beer talking: four lads, a carry out and the reproduction of masculinities," *The Sociological Review*, Aug., 409–35.

Johnson, Sally and Finlay, Frank (1997) "Do men gossip? An analysis of football talk on television," pp. 130–43 in Sally Johnson and Ulrike Hanna Meinhof (eds) *Language and Masculinity*. Oxford: Blackwell.

Johnson, Sally and Meinhof, Ulrike Hanna (Eds) (1997) *Language and Masculinity*. Oxford: Blackwell.

Jones, Deborah (1980) "Gossip: notes on women's oral culture," pp. 193–8 in Cheris Kramarae (ed.) *The Voices and Words of Women and Men*. Oxford: Pergamon Press.

Kaminer, Debra and Dixon, John (1995) "The reproduction of masculinity: a discourse analysis of men's drinking talk," *South African Journal of Psychology* 25(3), 168–74.

Kimmel, Michael S. (2000) *The Gendered Society*. Oxford: Oxford University Press.

Kuiper, K (1991) "Sporting formulae in New Zealand English: two models of male solidarity," pp. 200–9 in Jenny Cheshire (ed.) *English Around the World*. Cambridge: Cambridge University Press.

Labov, William (1972) *Language in the Inner City*. Oxford: Blackwell.

Lakoff, Robin (1975) *Language and Woman's Place*. New York: Harper & Row.

Mallinson, Christine and Childs, Becky (2007) "Communities of practice in sociolinguistic description: analysing language and identity practices among black women in Appalachia," *Gender and Language* 1(2), 173–206.

Mendoza-Denton, Norma (2008) *Home Girls: Language and Cultural Practices among Latina Youth Gangs*. Oxford: Wiley-Blackwell.

Pichler, Pia (2009a) *Young Femininities*. London: Palgrave.

Pichler, Pia (2009b) "'All I've gotta do is wank on about some bollocky poem': cool and socially aware positions in the talk of London private school girls," pp 87–114 in Pia Pichler and Eva Eppler (eds) *Gender and Spoken Interaction*. London: Palgrave Macmillan.

Tannen, Deborah (1990) "Gender differences in topical coherence: creating involvement in best friends' talk," *Discourse Processes* 13(1), 73–90.

Recommended Further Reading

Charteris-Black, Jonathan and Seale, Clive (2009) "Men and emotion talk: evidence from the experience of illness," *Gender and Language* 3(1), 81–113.

Coates, Jennifer (1996) *Women Talk: Conversation Between Women Friends*. Oxford: Blackwell.

Coates, Jennifer (1999) "Changing femininities: the talk of teenage girls," pp. 123–44 in Mary Bucholtz, A. C. Liang, and Laurel A. Sutton (eds) *Reinventing Identities*. Oxford University Press.

Coates, Jennifer (2003) *Men Talk: Stories in the Making of Masculinities*. Oxford: Blackwell.

Edley, Nigel and Wetherell, Margaret (1997) "Jockeying for position: the construction of masculine identities," *Discourse & Society* 8(2), 203–17.

Frosh, Stephen, Phoenix, Ann, and Pattman, Rob (2002) *Young Masculinities: Understanding Boys in Contemporary Society*. London: Palgrave..

Goodwin, Marjorie Harness (1990) *He-Said-She-Said: Talk as Social Organisation among Black Children*. Bloomington: Indiana University Press.

Johnson, Sally and Meinhof, Ulrike Hanna (eds) (1997) *Language and Masculinity*. Oxford: Blackwell.

Mendoza-Denton, Norma (2008) *Home Girls: Language and Cultural Practices among Latina Youth Gangs*. Oxford: Wiley-Blackwell.

Pichler, Pia (2009) *Young Femininities*. London: Palgrave.

Pichler, Pia and Eppler, Eva (eds) (2009) *Gender and Spoken Interaction*. London: Palgrave.

16

Gossip Revisited:
Language in All-Female Groups

Jennifer Coates

Source: Jennifer Coates and Deborah Cameron (eds), *Women in their Speech Communities*. London: Longman (1989), pp. 94–122. Reprinted with permission of Pearson Education UK.

Introduction

During the last ten years, interest in, and knowledge of, the relationship between language and gender has grown enormously. But attention has focussed on gender *differences*: sociolinguistic research has aimed to quantify differences in women's and men's usage of certain linguistic forms. The linguistic forms examined range from phonological or syntactic variables to interactive forms such as interruptions, directives and questions. Where the latter are concerned, a majority of researchers have drawn their data from mixed interaction (that is, interaction involving both male and female speakers); research has rarely focussed on women in single-sex groups. As a result, we know little about the characteristics of all-female discourse. Worse, we accept generalisations about 'the way women talk' which derive from women's behaviour in *mixed* groups, groups where the differential use of linguistic features such as interruptions, directives or questions is part of the social process which maintains gender divisions.

Deborah Jones's paper, 'Gossip: notes on women's oral culture' (1980), was a landmark. While Jones was not the first to focus on all-woman interaction (cf. Abrahams 1975; Kalcik 1975; Aries 1976; Jenkins and Kramer 1978), she was the first to locate her analysis firmly in the sociolinguistic field. Jones glosses 'female oral culture' as 'language use in women's natural groups' (using 'natural' to refer to groupings which in our *culture* are construed as 'natural'). Her paper offers a description of such language use in terms of the relations between setting, participants, topic, form and function, following Ervin-Tripp (1964). The strength of Jones's paper is that it puts women talking to women firmly centre-stage; its weakness stems from the lack of empirical data. Her common-sense description of the setting, participants and topics typical of all-woman talk provides a clear set of norms to be tested in further research. Her statement that 'Little is known about any distinctive formal features of women's language in all-female groups' is a challenge to linguists which this paper will take up.

Since the publication of Jones's paper, some linguists have developed the notion, originally used in inter-ethnic communication studies, that linguistic differences might be the result in part of subcultural differences rather than simply a reflection of dominant–

subordinate relationships. Work adopting this model has explored miscommunication between the sexes (e.g. Maltz and Borker 1982 [reprinted in Part VIII of this volume]; Tannen 1982, 1987). Such work makes the assumption, either implicitly or explicitly, that the conversational strategies which lead to miscommunication in mixed groups are acquired and developed in single-sex groups. But this assumption is unverified. The evidence presented in the few studies available (Kalcik 1975; Aries 1976; Goodwin 1980; Wodak 1981) is hardly conclusive (but does suggest that such conversational strategies may not be restricted to white middle-class women). We still know very little about the norms of spoken interaction in single-sex groups.

While they lack detail, the papers listed above all draw on a notion of **co-operativeness** to characterise all-female interaction. Early work on women's language had labelled it as 'tentative' or 'powerless'. More recently, and in reaction to this, there has been a move to value women's language more positively, using terms such as 'co-operative'. This is laudable; but in order to avoid the creation of new linguistic myths, it is important that such claims are substantiated by linguistic evidence.

In this paper, I want to analyse in detail part of a corpus of conversation between women friends. The corpus is small (135 minutes of running text), and the approach used is qualitative rather than quantitative.[1] I want firstly to see whether the evidence supports Jones's general claims, secondly to establish what formal features are typical of all-woman discourse, and thirdly to explore the notion of co-operativeness.

The Data

I recorded a group of women friends over a period of nine months during 1983–4. These women were an established group who met once a fortnight at each other's houses in the evening to talk. I had belonged to this group since 1975, when it began to meet, and I recorded my friends surreptitiously each time it was my turn to have the group to my house during the period in question. All participants were informed subsequently that recordings had been made, and they agreed to this material being used for research purposes.[2] I shall discuss this data in relation to Jones's five headings, dealing briefly with setting, participants and topic, and at greater length with formal features and functions.

Setting

Jones follows Ervin-Tripp (1964) in using the term **setting** to cover both time and place. She identifies the private domain as the **place** for women's talk, and names the home, the hairdresser's, the supermarket as typical locations. Her identification of the private sphere as the setting for women's subculture seems to me to deserve more emphasis than she gives it. The division between public and private as we now understand it was established at the beginning of the nineteenth century (see Hall (1985) for an account of the historical background). As the division became more highly demarcated, patterns of gender division also changed: 'men were firmly placed in the newly defined public world of business, commerce and politics; women were placed in the private world of home and family' (Hall 1985: 12). This split was to have significant sociolinguistic consequences.

Jones describes the setting of gossip in terms of **time** as brief and fragmented: 'Time to gossip is usually snatched from work time' (1980: 194). The claim that snatched episodes are an intrinsic feature of gossip seems debatable, and depends too heavily on seeing women as mothers with small children. Old women, for example, sit on park benches or in social clubs, chatting for extended periods; adolescent girls often congregate on neutral territory (not home or school) and have considerable spare time in which to talk, especially if they are playing truant from school (see Cheshire 1982). Even mothers with small children meet in settings where the quality of the talking cannot be defined as 'snatched' – outside the school gate at the end of the day; waiting in the clinic to weigh the baby; at the mother and toddler group. According to Milroy, in traditional working-class communities such as Belfast, 'speakers valued various kinds of conversational arts very highly. *Many hours were spent simply chatting*' (my italics) (Milroy 1980: 100). Of course, some interaction between women which we would want to label as typical women's talk is brief, but it seems that length of time is not a salient feature of gossip.

The setting for the conversations I recorded was the living room of my home in Birkenhead, Merseyside. People sat on sofas or on the floor around the gas fire, drinking wine. Sessions lasted three hours or more, starting at about 9.0 in the evening. Food was served about half way through the evening; this was usually bread and cheese, but sometimes something more elaborate such as home-made soup or pizza.

Participants

'Gossip is essentially talk between women in our common role *as* women' (Jones 1980: 195). Jones argues that gossip arises from women's perception of themselves as a group with a great deal of experience in common. The members of the women's group I recorded are white, middle class, aged in their late 30s and early 40s. The group was formed (in 1975) at a time when all members had children still at school, and some had babies (who attended in carry cots). The group's *raison d'être* shifted gradually over the years: it initially provided a support network for mothers with young children; it now encourages these same women in their struggle to establish a career in their middle age. Urwin (1985) has commented on the importance for young mothers of friendships with other women. The need for contact with other women at various stages of one's life, not just as young mothers, is certainly borne out by the Birkenhead group which has now existed for 12 years.

Topic

Jones claims that the topics discussed by women are crucially related to their roles as wives, girlfriends and mothers. This claim seems to me to be over-strong, and again to overemphasise the place of motherhood in women's lives. The conversations that I recorded cover a wide range of topics, from discussions of television programmes, to mothers' funerals and child abuse. However, as I have commented in an earlier paper (Coates 1987), it seems to be typical of all-women groups that they discuss people and feelings, while men are more likely to discuss things. This finding fits Jones's general claim that 'the wider theme of gossip is always personal experience' (1980: 195).

Functions

Unlike Jones, I shall discuss the functions of gossip before I discuss its formal features, since I want to argue that the linguistic forms which characterise women's interaction can be explained in terms of the functions they serve. Jones's section on functions is weak: she merely catalogues four different types of gossip. I want to use the term **function** in relation to the **goals** of all-woman interaction. All-woman conversation, like most informal interaction between equals, has as its chief goal the maintenance of good social relationships.

Grice's conversational maxims (Grice 1975) assume that referential meaning is all-important, and that speakers' only aim is to exchange information. The falsity of this assumption has been demonstrated by Lakoff (1973) and discussed by many other linguists subsequently (e.g. Brown 1977; Leech 1983; Tannen 1984). The distinction between public and private spheres, discussed above, leads to a distinction between public and private discourse. In public discourse, the exchange of information is an important goal. Male speakers in our culture are socialised into public discourse, while female speakers are socialised into private discourse (cf. Gilligan 1982; Smith 1985; Wells 1979). Until recently, the androcentric view that information-focussed discourse should be the object of linguistic analysis was not challenged. In private discourse, the exchange of information is not the chief goal. I hope to show in the central section of this paper that the formal features which are typical of women's language in all-female groups can be explained by direct reference to the functions of such interaction, that is the establishment and maintenance of social relationships, the reaffirming and strengthening of friendship.

Formal Features

I shall examine in detail four aspects of the interactional pattern found in the all-female conversation I recorded. I shall look at topic development, at minimal responses, at simultaneous speech, and finally at epistemic modality. I have chosen to concentrate on these aspects of women's talk because they have been picked out by other writers as markers of co-operative style.

Topic development

It has become a truism in accounts of women's discourse that women develop topics progressively in conversation (see Maltz and Borker 1982: 213). Yet, as far as I know, this claim has not been supported by empirical evidence. The claim is multifaceted: women are said to build on each other's contributions, preferring continuity to discontinuity, and topic shift is supposed to occur gradually (rather than abruptly, as in all-male conversation). Consequently, the discussion of a single topic can last for some time (up to half an hour according to Aries 1976: 13).

In order to examine the nature of topic development in all-female conversation, I shall analyse one episode in detail from one of my recordings. This passage is about mothers' funerals and lasts just under $4\frac{1}{2}$ minutes. There are five participants. The structure of the funeral extract is as follows:

1   A introduces topic;
2   B tells anecdote on same theme;
3   C tells another anecdote on same theme, leading into;
4   general discussion;
5   D summarises;
6   A has last word.

In musical terms, (1), (2) and (3) form the exposition, (4) is the development, (5) the recapitulation, and (6) the coda. The development section is by far the longest (2 minutes 47 seconds). This pattern of topic development is typical of the material I have transcribed (see Coates 1987, where I analyse the development of a different topic).

The telling of anecdotes is a common way of introducing a new topic in conversation; sometimes one anecdote is sufficient, sometimes more than one occurs. What characterises these introductory sections, and sets them off from the central development section, is that they are **monologues**: the telling of a story gives the speaker unusual rights to speak. Example 1 below is a transcript of A's introductory anecdote. [A key for the transcription notation used is given in Transcription Conventions 2, p. xii.]

Example 1

....

A: this bloke I met today who's doing . he- he's doing some postgraduate research at- at
    Stirling/ . anyway I asked him- he- he wanted to talk to me about a professional matter/
    and I . I said- . I was asking him his sort of background/ and he said that he'd done
    philosophy/ . so I was just interested with little snippets of philosophy that came my way
    you see/ and he said one of the things that he was interested in was taboo/ . the nature
    of taboo/ . and he said that- . a- and he gave this example that um . if you didn't go to
    your mother's funeral . because you'd got something else to do/ . it would be very

....

A: much frowned ⌈upon/ um   even though what you had to do could
B: ⎢   =mhm/
D: ⌊oh god =

....

A: easily be more important/ and after all she was dead= .   and
C: = mhm/

....

A: wouldn't know you weren't going kind of thing/

....

Note that A's fellow participants say nothing until the very end of her narrative. They accord her the right to establish a new topic – something she doesn't do until the end of her turn – and it is only when this point is reached that other participants volunteer supportive noises. No one attempts to make a substantive contribution until it is clear that A has finished her turn.

Once A has finished – and the group has accepted the new topic – B tells a personal anecdote which illustrates A's general theme of whether it is taboo to miss your mother's funeral. B's anecdote is reproduced below.

Example 2

....

   B: oh we – it's so odd you see because we had this
   ?: ((xxx))

....

2 A: = mhm =
   B: conversation at dinner tonight=   =because Steve

....

   B: MacFadden's mother died at the weekend+ and she

....

4 B: 1- . well she lived in Brisbane/ ((they were

```
B:  at Brisbane/))  ⌈so he's going over there/ Australia/
E:                  ⌊what – Australia?

6  B:  so he's going to the ⌈funeral/     it's obviously
   D:                       ⌊oh my god/

   B:  gonna cost him a f⌈ortune/ . and John said
   E:                    ⌊fortune/<WHISPERS> ((s'about

8  B:  –                        ((he was)) just astonished/
   E:  four hundred pounds/))

   B:  I said . well I wouldn't go Steve/ . and the- and the

10 B:  whol- as you say it was just taboo/ I mean as far
   C:                                            mhm/

   B:  as Steve was concerned I mean that was ⌈just
   C:    mhm/                                 |
   D:                                         ⌊you just

12 B:              no/ and I s- and my response I
   D:  can't say that/
   ?:              no/

   B:  must 'oh John' – but sorry ((xxx))/⌈it's so
   ?:                         ((xxx))     |
   C:                                     ⌊I didn't

14 B:  odd that you should-
   C:  go over for my father/ ....
```

While B's right to hold the floor is never challenged, the other participants are far more active than they were during A's narrative. They support her with well placed minimal responses (staves 2, 6, 10, 11, 12), they complete her utterances either at the same time as her ('fortune', stave 7) or by briefly taking over from her ('you just can't say that', staves 11–12), they ask for clarification ('what – Australia?', stave 5). None of these contributions constitutes an attempt to take the floor from B – they are signals of active listenership.

B's final comment is unfinished as C starts at a point which she interprets as the end of B's turn (though co-participants were clear what B intended to say, namely, that it was a coincidence that A should bring up this subject when she herself had been discussing it that evening in relation to her neighbour). Clearly, the members of the group now feel they have established what topic is under discussion. Thus, C is granted the normal monologue rights when she begins *her* personal anecdote, but as soon as she reaches her first punch line, other speakers intervene and the discussion section begins.

Discussion sections, where speakers evaluate the topic, are multiparty in nature. Often several speakers speak at once, and speaker turns tend to be brief. Example 3 below gives C's anecdote and the opening of the general discussion.

Example 3

```
   C:  ⌈I didn't go over for my father/ I asked my mother
   B:  ⌊it's so odd that you should-
...................................................................................
2  C:  if she wanted me/ I mean . I- I immediately said
...................................................................................
   C:  'Do you want me to come over?'/ – and she said
...................................................................................
4  C:  'Well no I can't really see the point/ he's dead
...................................................................................
   C:  isn't he?'/ <LAUGHS>     . and .            ⌈and she
   A:             mhm/                             |
   B:                        well that's right/    ⌊that's
...................................................................................
   C:  said no/ I mean          ((xxx))  ⌈no point in
6  B:  what John was saying/ . that they- |
   E:                                     ⌊you've got
...................................................................................
   C:  coming/                      so-
   A:                                   ⌈yeah/
   E:  terribly forward-looking parents you ⌊see/ it
...................................................................................
8  C:
   E:  depends on the attitude of- . mean is- is his
...................................................................................
   C:                                  ⌈I don't
   B:              %I don't know/%     |
   E:  father still alive?              ⌊because
...................................................................................
10 C:  think- I don't think they had a funeral either/
   E:  that would have a very big bearing on it/
...................................................................................
   C:
   D:  if they were religious I mean/ yes/ ⌈it would all
   E:                                      ⌊yeah/
...................................................................................
   C:  yeah I don't think they had a funeral/ .
12 D:  depend/                  ⌈if there were life
   E:           yeah/ . I mean  ⌊if there was- if there
...................................................................................
   C:  they had a memorial service/
   D:  after death/                 ⌈then they'd KNOW
   E:  was-                         ⌊if they- if-
...................................................................................
   C:
14 D:  that you hadn't come/
   E:                      that's right/ ((xx))
...................................................................................
```

Discussion sections are complex. At one level, individual speakers are dealing with their own feelings about the topic under discussion. In the funeral episode, C keeps returning to the theme of missing her father's funeral, expanding on the reasons for this, and hypothesising that she would go now. A says that she would be upset if her brothers and sister failed to come to her mother's funeral (and since her sister, like C's father, lives in the United States, A is implicitly challenging the assumption that the Atlantic is an insuperable barrier). E, whose parents live in Sheffield, asserts that she would definitely go to their funerals and that it is unthinkable that she wouldn't. These speakers are in effect asking for support from the group, even though their positions are to some extent mutually exclusive; they need to air their feelings in order to deal with them.

At another level, speakers are debating more general points: is it the purpose of funerals to comfort surviving relatives? or are they a public statement about one's feelings for one's dead mother? How important is distance in the decision about whether or not to attend a funeral? The general and personal are intertwined; crucially, speakers work together to sort out what they feel.

From an analytical point of view, the taken-for-granted view of conversation (originating in Sacks, Schegloff and Jefferson 1974) as interaction where one speaker speaks at a time is of little use when dealing with such material. As Example 3 illustrates, more than one speaker speaks at a time: C continues her account of not attending her father's funeral, while B ties this in with her anecdote and E adds a comment about C's parents, responding both to C ('you' in stave 6 refers to C) and to B ('is his father still alive?', staves 8 and 9, is addressed to B – 'his' refers to B's neighbour Steve). E's comment ('that would have a very big bearing on it' at stave 10) coincides with C providing further information to fit E's description of her parents as 'forward-looking'. The link between having or not having a funeral service and religious belief is picked up, slightly tongue-in-cheek, by D; E joins in with D, while C continues to refine her account.

The discussion section is long and there isn't space to give it in full nor to analyse it in detail here: specific aspects relating to minimal responses, simultaneous speech and epistemic modality will be picked up in the following three sections. Example 4 gives the end of the discussion, with D's summary and A's final comment.

Example 4

```
       ............................................................................................................
       C:  I probably I mean it would have also would have
       ............................................................................................................
   2   C:  been if- . I'd go now/ – Daniel was sort of
       ............................................................................................................
       A:                          ⌈mhmmhm/
       C:  . 18 months old⌊ and it would have been rather
       ............................................................................................................
       A:  ⌈yes/      ⌈yes/
   4   C:  ⌊difficult and ⌊this kind of thing=
       D:                              =that's right/
       ............................................................................................................
       C:                  um              I think I
       D:  I suppose there's two things/ there's-
       ............................................................................................................
   6   C:  would go now/ because probably because I would want
       ............................................................................................................
```

```
       C:  to go=      =cos it would be be very easy to go=
       D:                                            =yeah=
       E:        =mhm=

       A:  =yeah =
   8   C:         =it would have been- – I don't⌈know/ –
       D:                                      ⌊there's TWO

       C:                        ⌈anyway ((xx perfectly all-
       D:  things aren't there/⌊there's the- the other people

  10   C:  right xx))
       D:  like your mother or father who's left/ and- or- or

       D:  siblings/ and there's also how how you feel at that

       A:                                          mhm/
       B:                                                yeah/
  12   C:                                    mhm/
       D:  time about . the easiness of going/
       E:                               mhm/

       A:                 ⌈well to go to Australia seems a bit
       D:  I mean I would ⌊I-

  14   A:  over the top/
```

It seems that the group jointly senses that this topic has been satisfactorily dealt with: C receives lots of support in her final statement that she *would* go now since circumstances have changed. Note that D has to make two attempts to provide a summary, starting once before C has finished. C's last turn gets two *yeahs* in sequence (staves 7 and 8). D's summary, like A's initial anecdote, is notable for *lack* of interruption: only when she has completed it do the others respond, all four co-participants indicating, in a perfectly timed sequence of *mhm* and *yeah*, their acceptance of what D has said. A, who initiated the topic, then has the last word.

This brief account of the development of one topic in a conversation between women friends provides an example of the way that women develop topics progressively. These women work together to produce the funeral episode, both by recognising opening and closing moves (i.e. granting one speaker the right to initiate a topic through the telling of an anecdote, or to summarise at the end), and by jointly negotiating an understanding of the problem in question (is it taboo to miss your mother's funeral?). This latter part of joint production involves both the right to speak and the duty to listen and support. The five speakers deal with their own and each other's feelings and experiences, juggling speaker and listener roles with great skill. There is no sense in which it is possible to sum up the funeral topic by saying 'A talked about taboo and funerals' or 'C talked about not going to her father's funeral'. The funeral episode is jointly produced by all speakers.

Aries' claim that topics can last up to half an hour is not apparently borne out by this example (which lasts 4 minutes 29 seconds), but this may depend on the definition of 'topic'. Certainly, topic shift is normally gradual rather than abrupt as the following example demonstrates (Example 5 follows on from Example 4).

Example 5

....
```
A:    a bit over the top =
E:                         =yeah/ what- what did the- oh yeah
```
....
```
A:                                            ⎡((xxx he
D:                                            ⎣oh yeah
E:    what was your bloke saying about taboo?
```
....
```
A:    just xxx))
D:    what? I've just written my CHAPter on taboo so I'm
```
....
```
A:    well-              =I didn't get much more from
D:    terribly interested=
```
....
```
A:    him than that/ except um . he's looking at . er ba- battering/ and his sort of thesis is-
      and the way social services deal with these kind of problems/ . men that batter women/ .
      and men that . sexually abuse their children and um their . other children and he was
      just looking at . attitudes to that/ and he said that he's come across incredible taboo- .
      taboos/ um you- you know this just world hypothesis . business/
```
....

Note how E's question refers back to A's original anecdote (see Example 1), thus providing a very cohesive link.

In fact, this kind of gradual topic shift continues for many topics:

These five topics are smoothly linked and overall they last for 15 minutes 54 seconds. Perhaps Aries' figure more appropriately refers to coherent sequences of topics such as the above. At all events, my data suggest that women do build progressively on each other's contributions, that topics are developed jointly, and that shifts between topics are gradual rather than abrupt.[3]

Minimal responses

Research on the use of minimal responses is unanimous in showing that women use them more than men (Strodtbeck and Mann 1956; Hirschmann 1974; Zimmerman and West 1975; Fishman 1980). This research is, however, mainly concerned with **mixed** interaction; the finding that women use minimal responses more frequently, and with greater linguistic sensitivity, in such contexts is said to demonstrate yet again the fact that women do the 'interactional shitwork' (to use Fishman's 1977 term).

It shouldn't be automatically assumed that the use of these forms denotes power-lessness, however. The same form functions in different ways in different contexts (see Cameron, McAlinden and O'Leary, 1989). Certainly it is clear from my data that the use of minimal responses also characterises linguistic interaction between women who are friends and equals.

Minimal responses are used in two different ways in the women's conversations I recorded. In the interaction-focussed discussion sections, they are used to support the speaker and to indicate the listener's active attention. The opening of Example 4 (the end of the funeral discussion section) illustrates this. While C talks, first A (staves 3 and 4), then E (stave 7), then D and A one after the other (staves 7 and 8) add their minimal responses. These responses are well placed: they are mostly timed to come at the end of an informa-tion unit (e.g. a tone group or clause), yet so well anticipated is this point that the speaker's flow is not interrupted. (Both Zimmerman & West and Fishman have shown how the *delayed* minimal response is used by male speakers to indicate lack of interest and/or attention.) These minimal responses signal the listeners' active participation in the conversation; that is, they are another aspect of the way text is *jointly* produced.

In the narrative or more information-focussed sections of the conversation, minimal responses seem to have another meaning. They are used far less frequently, and when they occur they signal agreement among participants that a particular stage of conversa-tion has been reached. For example, when a speaker introduces a new topic, as in Example 1, it is only at the very end that other speakers indicate that they are attending. At this point it seems that D, B and C are indicating to A that they have taken the point of her anecdote, and that they accept it as a topic.

In Example 4, D's summary is followed by minimal responses from all the other participants (stave 12). Clearly the women feel the need to indicate their active agree-ment with D's summing-up. In both these examples, it is not just the presence of mini-mal responses at the end, but also their absence during the course of an anecdote or summary, which demonstrates the sensitivity of participants to the norms of interac-tion: speakers recognise different types of talk and use minimal responses appropriately.

So while it is true to say that the use of minimal responses characterises women's speech in both mixed and single-sex conversation, it would be wrong to claim that you have only to say *mhm* or *yeah* every few seconds to talk like a woman. On the contrary, women's use of minimal responses demonstrates their sensitivity to interactional proc-esses; they use them where they are appropriate. In mixed conversations, the use of minimal responses by women will only become 'weak' where women's skill as listeners is exploited by male speakers. In all-female groups, it seems that the use of these linguistic forms is further evidence of women's active participation in the joint production of text.

Simultaneous speech

The Sacks, Schegloff and Jefferson (1974) model of turn-taking in conversation views simultaneous speech by two or more co-conversationalists as an aberration. Their model assumes a norm of one speaker speaking at a time. The evidence of my data is that, on the contrary, for much of the time (typically in discussion sections) more than one speaker speaks at a time. The same phenomenon has been observed by Edelsky (1981) and Tannen (1984), both of whom analysed mixed conversation. Edelsky's analysis of five staff meetings reveals what she describes as two types of 'floor': F1, where one speaker dominates, and F2, where several speakers speak at once to jointly produce text. Tannen's analysis of a Thanksgiving dinner involving six speakers (two women, four men) describes two kinds of talk, one more information-focussed, the other more interaction-focussed: the latter involves more than one speaker speaking at the same time.

It is certainly not the case in the conversations I have recorded that where more than one speaker speaks this normally represents an attempt to infringe the current speaker's right to a turn. I have analysed all instances of simultaneous speech which occur during the funeral episode; only a minority can be described in this way (see table 1).

Table 1   Simultaneous speech in the funeral episode (4 mins 29 secs)

Type I.	Two speakers self-select at the same time, one stops	3
Type II.	Speaker B self-selects at TRP, A carries on, B stops	3
Type III.	Speaker B self-selects at TRP, A tails off	3
Type IV.	Speaker B completes A's utterance	5
Type V.	Speaker B asks question or comments while A is speaking	7
Type VI.	Speaker B comments, A stops speaking	2
Type VII.	Two speakers speak at the same time	7
		30

(TRP = Transition Relevance Place, i.e. the end of a 'unit type' such as a phrase or clause. See Sacks, Schegloff and Jefferson 1974.)

Type I, where more than one speaker starts at the same time, is trivial: where next speaker self-selects, such infelicities are inevitable. Types II and III are more serious: they are illustrated in Examples 6 and 7 below. In Example 6, E's interruption fails and B completes her own utterance: in Example 7, B stops talking and C claims the floor.

Example 6

....

B: I mean ⌈it's not as if I'm particularly religious/
E: ⌊but if-   yeah/ but if

....

E: you've got a fa- if there's a spouse then perhaps they would

....

E: want you to go/

....

Example 7

....

B: but sorry ((xxx))/ ⌈it's so odd that you should-
?:   ((xxx)) |
C: |I didn't go over for my father/

....

C: I asked my mother if she wanted me/....

....

Even with these two examples, the term 'interruption' seems inappropriate. In Example 6, speaker E is guilty of what Tannen calls the 'overlap-as-enthusiasm' strategy: she is not so much trying to stop B from talking as jumping in too soon because of her enthusiasm to participate. She realises her mistake and comes in again once B has finished. (Another example of this phenomenon can be seen in Example 5 where D's enthusiasm delays the start of A's turn.) In Example 7, C assumes that B has finished, and in fact B is one of those speakers, like D (see Example 4, stave 13) who typically tail off rather than finishing their turns crisply. It could be argued that B and D's personal style results from their expectation that others know what they mean (so they don't need to say it in full), and that they invite overlap by their habit of ending their turns with utterances which peter out, both syntactically and prosodically. An example of such tailing-off is given below:

Example 8

....
E: but if there's no spouse I mean <u>and there's very few</u>
....
B: mhm/
E: <u>relatives left it doesn't really seem much of a-</u> <LAUGHING>
....

In Example 8, E's contribution is not overlapped: this example therefore illustrates more starkly how such tailing-off turns are not 'unfinished', in the sense that E has made her contribution and her co-participants know what she means. (To get the full quality of this utterance, it is of course necessary to hear the tape.)

Type IV simultaneous speech is closely related to the above: if a speaker tails off, then it is open to other participants to complete the utterance. Speaker B's habit of not completing her turn often results in others (usually E) doing it for her:

Example 9

....
B: I just thought/ if the car breaks down on the way home
....
B: I mean I'll die of fear/ <LAUGHS> I'll never get out/
....
B: I'll just-
E: just sit here and die/
....

In this case there is no overlap, but often speakers' completion of each other's utterances results in simultaneous speech:

Example 10

....
B: I mean that was ⌈just-   =no/
D: ⌊you just can't say that=
....

Note that B acknowledges D's contribution and in fact continues speaking: D's overlap in no way constitutes an attempt to get the floor.

Such completion-overlaps can involve more than two speakers:

Example 11

....
A: i- it'll become a s- public statement about=
E: =the family/

....
A: er   ⌈((xx))   yeah/
D: yeah/ |and that YOU're close/
E: ((to do with))⌊you/

....

Again, as in Example 10, the current speaker (A) acknowledges the others' contributions before continuing.

Type V is a very common type of simultaneous speech: it involves one of the co-participants asking the speaker a question, or commenting on what the speaker is saying, during the speaker's turn. One could describe this phenomenon as a relation of the minimal response: the questions or comments function as a sign of active listenership, and do not threaten the current speaker's turn. Speakers in fact acknowledge such questions/comments while continuing to hold the floor. Examples 12 and 13 illustrate the question, where listeners seek clarification.

Example 12

....
B: well she lived in Brisbane/ ((they were at Brisbane/))

....
B: ⌈so he's going over there/ Australia/ so he's going
E: ⌊what – Australia?

....
B: to the funeral/

....

Example 13

....
A: and I imagine that my two far-flung sibs will
E:

....
A: actually make the journey/ ⌈I'm just- . I'm ((almost-))
E: ⌊what . to your parents?

....
A: ⌈yes/ I'm sure they will/ but it'll be because
E: ⌊to- to your mother's?

....
A: i- it'll become a s- public statement about=
E: =the family/

....

In Example 12, B tucks 'Australia' into her exposition to satisfy E, while A, in 13, interrupts herself to say 'yes' to E before continuing her statement about her sister and brother.

Comments occur more frequently than questions and normally don't threaten a speaker's turn:

Example 14

....

A: I'm absolutely sure they'll come/ but I mean in fact it

....

A: won't make any odds/ but I think I . would be .

....

A: ⌜. hur- hurt and angry if they hadn't/
E: ⌊it'll be nicer for you/

....

In this example, E's comment goes unacknowledged, but speakers often do respond to listener comments:

Example 15

....

A:
E: if there's a spouse then perhaps they WOULD want

....

A: yeah for their comfort/ for them=
E: you to go/   you know/ but if- but if   =that's

....

E: right/ comfort for them/ but if ...

....

Here E acknowledges A's comment before continuing.

Occasionally comments of this kind coincide with the current speaker stopping speaking (Type VI). In the following example, C finishes making her point during E's comment about her parents, and it is E who then takes the floor. C's *so* is ambiguous: it could be a bid for a longer turn (which fails), or it could be a tailing-off noise.

Example 16

....

C: and she said 'no'/ I mean ((xxx)) ⌜no point in
E: ⌊you've got

....

C: coming/   ⌜so-
E: terribly forward-looking parents ⌊you see/ it

....

C:
E: depends on the attitude...

....

This example is complicated by the fact that B is also talking at the same time (see Example 3, staves 5–9 for the full version). However such an example is categorised, what is important is that E's contribution here is constructive: she is embellishing C's turn, putting C's mother's behaviour in context.

The final type of simultaneous speech, Type VII, involves two or more speakers speaking at once; for this type it is not possible to say one speaker has the floor and the other is merely interjecting a comment. There are seven examples of this during the funeral episode (i.e. nearly a quarter of all examples of simultaneous speech). The obvious analogy is again a musical one: the speakers contribute simultaneously to the same theme, like several instruments playing contrapuntally (the notion of contrapuntal talk is also invoked in Reisman 1974). Examples 17 and 18 below illustrate this type:

Example 17

....

```
C:                                          ⌈I don't
B:                    %I don't know/%        |
E:   is his father still alive?              ⌊because
```

....

```
C:   think- I don't think they had a funeral either/
E:   that would have a very big bearing on it/
```

....

Example 18

....

```
A:   I mean I've o- I've op- for many year⌈s ((have wondered))
E:                                         ⌊cos that's what
```

....

```
A:   about my own mother's funeral/
E:   funerals are for/ it's for the relatives/
```

....

Without providing an audio-tape, it is hard to describe the quality of such passages: crucially, there is no sense of competition, or of vying for turns. Speakers do not become aggrieved when others join in. The feel of the conversation is that all the participants are familiar with each other and with the way the interaction is constructed. It is very much a joint effort, with individual speakers concerned to contribute to a jointly negotiated whole.

A final more extended example, containing four instances of simultaneous speech, will serve to give the flavour of the conversation as a whole.

Example 19

....

```
C:   I mean I think it really depends on the ATTitude of the
```

....

```
B:                      ⌈yeah/
C:   surVIvors who are  ⌊THERE/ . if- if they want the person
```

....

```
A:          I don't think it depends on that Cathy/
C:   to ⌈go/   . then the person should go/
E:     ⌊mhm/
```

....

```
A:   I think it depends on ⌈um-
E:                         ⌊oh I do/ if one of mine died/
```

....

```
E:   and . er I mean – my- . if it were- whichever one
```

....

```
E:   it were the other one would expect me to go/ –
```

....

```
D:                                      ⌈mhm/
E:   they'd be ABSolutely STAggered if I didn't/ – ⌊especially
```

....

```
C:                                                =no I mean if
D:                                    ⎡ Sheffield= <LAUGHS>
E:   as it's only. <LAUGHS> two hours a ⎣ way/
```

```
C:   my mother had wanted me to come/ if she'd said 'oh yes
```

```
A:        mhm/                                    yeah/
C:   please'/   ⎡ or 'of course' or- or something/        then
E:              ⎣ you would've gone/
```

```
A:                                                yeah/
C:   I would've- . of course I would've gone/
```

At the beginning of Example 19, A's conflicting point of view overlaps with C's talking (note that C completes her utterance) and E's support for C overlaps with A, who tails off. That an interpretation of this as conflict is false is shown by A's support (given in minimal responses) for C's restatement of her point of view at the end. The contrapuntal nature of such text is exemplified by D's contribution 'Sheffield', which glosses E's 'it's only two hours away', and by E's anticipation of C's words which leads her to butt in with 'you would've gone' before C herself says it.

As someone who was a participant in this discourse, there is no doubt in my mind that the term 'interruption' is hardly ever appropriate as a description of instances of simultaneous speech which occur in gossip. In public domains, where the norm is that one speaker speaks at a time, and where the goal of participants is to grab speakership, then interruption is a strategy for gaining the floor. In private conversation between equals, on the other hand, where the chief goal of interaction is the maintenance of good social relationships, then the participation of more than one speaker is iconic of joint activity: the goal is not to take the floor *from* another speaker, but to participate in conversation *with* other speakers. The examples of simultaneous speech given here illustrate the way in which women speakers work together to produce shared meanings.[4]

Epistemic modality

Epistemic modal forms are defined semantically as those linguistic forms which are used to indicate the speaker's confidence or lack of confidence in the truth of the proposition expressed in the utterance. If someone says *Perhaps she missed the train*, the use of the word *perhaps* indicates lack of confidence in the proposition 'she missed the train'. Lexical items such as *perhaps, I think, sort of, probably*, as well as certain prosodic and paralinguistic features, are used in English to express epistemic modality.

Such forms, however, are used by speakers not just to indicate their lack of commitment to the truth of propositions, but also to hedge assertions in order to protect both their own and addressees' face (for a full account of the role of epistemic modality in spoken discourse, see Coates 1987). It is my impression (based on an admittedly small corpus of data) that women in single-sex groups exploit these forms more than men. Table 2 gives the totals for the most commonly used forms in two parallel texts, each lasting about 40 minutes.[5]

Utterances such as those in Examples 20 and 21 below are typical of the discussion sections of the all-women conversations recorded (epistemic modal forms in italics).

Table 2 Sex differences in the use of epistemic modal forms

	Women	Men
I mean	77	20
well	65	45
just	57	48
I think	36	12
sort of	35	10

Example 20
[funeral discussion]
I mean I think it *really* depends on the ATTitude of the survivors who are THERE/

Example 21
[speaker describes old friend she'd recently bumped into]
she looks very *sort of* um – *kind of* matronly *really*/

It is my contention (see Coates 1987: 129) that women exploit the polypragmatic nature of epistemic modal forms. They use them to mitigate the force of an utterance in order to respect addressees' face needs. Thus, the italicised forms in Example 21 hedge the assertion *she looks matronly* not because the speaker doubts its truth but because she does not want to offend her addressees by assuming their agreement (describing a friend in unflattering terms is controversial). Such forms also protect the speaker's face: the speaker in Example 21 can retreat from the proposition expressed there if it turns out to be unacceptable. Where sensitive topics are discussed (as in Examples 20 and 21), epistemic modal forms are used frequently. This seems to provide an explanation for women's greater use of such forms (see table 2). The women's conversations I have analysed involve topics related to people and feelings (see, for example, the topic sequence given above, page 208); in the parallel all-male conversation I have analysed, the men talk about *things* – home beer-making, hi-fi systems, etc. Presumably such topics do not trigger the use of epistemic modal forms because they are not so face-threatening.

Women also use these forms to facilitate open discussion (and, as I've said, epistemic modal forms are mostly found in the discussion sections of conversation). An underlying rule of conversation between equals, where the exchange of information is not a priority, is 'Don't come into open disagreement with other participants' (see Leech 1983: 132). Examples 20 and 21 are contributions to discussion which state a point of view but allow for other points of view. More positively, epistemic modal forms can be used to invite others to speak, a function often fulfilled by the tag question.

As Perkins (1983: 111) says: 'since questions qualify the truth of a proposition by making it relative to the speaker's uncertainty, they may be regarded as expressing epistemic modality'. An analysis of the tag questions used in the conversations I have recorded shows that the vast majority are addressee-oriented rather than speaker-oriented (cf. Holmes, 1984; Cameron, McAlinden and O'Leary, 1989). In one of the conversations (about 40 minutes of taped material) there are 23 tag questions, yet of these only four are used to elicit information (i.e. only four are speaker-oriented), as in Example 22:

Example 22

you don't know what colour their bluè is dó you (Note the rising intonation contour on the tag.)

Addressee-oriented tags can be used either to soften the force of a negatively affective utterance, or to facilitate interaction. Of the 19 addressee-oriented tags in the conversation, only one functions as a softener; the rest are all facilitative. Facilitative tags are given this name precisely because they are used to facilitate the participation of others; they invite them into the discourse. The following examples illustrate this (tags are italicised):

Example 23

E: but I mean so much research is male-dominated/ I mean it just.

A: =mhm/
E: it's staggering *isn't it*=

Example 24

D: it was dreadful *wasn't it*=
E: =appalling Caroline/ absolutely

E: appalling/

What is surprising about the tag questions in my data is that, while I would argue that they are facilitative, they are mostly not found in contexts like Examples 23 and 24, that is, where the tag results in another speaker taking a turn. Instead, they occur in mid-utterance, and the speaker seems to expect no verbal response (or at most a minimal response). Examples 25 and 26 illustrate this type:

Example 25

B: I think the most difficult thing is is that when you love someone you you half the time you forget their faults (yes) *don't you* and still maybe love them but I mean ...

Example 26

A: and they had they had a very accurate picture of him
D:

A: *didn't they?* they roughly knew his age=
D: =at one point

A: =yeah=
D: they knew about his gap teeth too *didn't they*=

A:
D: =then they got rid of that/

A further example is given in Example 4 (page 206), where D's summary at the end of the funeral discussion begins *there's twò things àren't there*. Of the 18 facilitative tags, nine occur in mid-utterance, like these; another three come at the end of a speaker's turn but elicit no overt response – for example, during the funeral discussion, E comments on the theme of missing a funeral *it's just not gòing isn't it*. Most of the other facilitative tags appear as comments by active listeners (Type V simultaneous speech) as in Example 27:

Example 27

....

D: cos I'm fed up of travelling to conferences/ ⌈but I'm
B: ⌊oh it's so

....

D: giving a paper/
B: typical *ìsn't it?*

....

All these examples involve falling intonation, and all expect the answer *yes* (like *nonne* in Latin).

The women conversationalists seem to use these tags to check the taken-for-grantedness of what is being said. Paralinguistic cues, and sometimes minimal responses, signal to the speaker that what she is saying has the support of the group. [...]

I want to argue that these tags are not only addressee-oriented, in the normal sense of 'facilitative', but that they also function, sometimes simultaneously, to mark the speaker's monitoring of the progress of the conversation. This may involve the establishment and development of new topics. The following example is taken from the point in the conversation where the topic shifts from child abuse to wives' loyalty to husbands.

Example 28

....

A: =mhm/   ‖ [*end of*
B: =mhm/ . mhm/ ‖ *child abuse*
C: and your husband has become a monster=   ‖ *topic*]

....

C: mhm/
E: I mean it's like that woman that turned in- was it Pri- Prime?

....

E: [...] one of those . spy cases/ it was his wife/ *wasn't it?*

....

A: =yeah/
D: =oh yes/
E: who turned him in=

....

E's tag question here serves to get agreement from the group to pursue a new aspect of the topic; it functions as a *check* on the co-operative progress of the discourse.

Co-operativeness

In some senses, co-operativeness is a taken-for-granted feature of conversation: Grice, in his well known analysis of conversational norms (Grice 1975), used the term 'co-operative' to underscore the obvious but often overlooked fact that conversations can only occur because two or more participants tacitly agree to co-operate in talk. The notion of co-operativeness that has become established in the literature on women's language, however (see, for example, Kalcik 1975; Aries 1976; Goodwin 1980; Maltz and Borker 1982), is less general: co-operativeness in this sense refers to a particular *type* of conversation, conversation where speakers work together to produce shared meanings. Set against this notion of co-operativeness is the notion of competitiveness; competitiveness is used to describe the adversarial style of conversation where speakers vie for turns and where participants are more likely to contradict each other than to build on each other's contributions. (Whether competitiveness in this sense is typical of all-male discourse is a folklinguistic myth which has still to be tested.)

At the heart of co-operativeness is a view of speakers collaborating in the production of text: the group takes precedence over the individual. How far does my data support the idea that women's language is co-operative in this more specific sense? Do the formal features described in the previous section function as collaborative devices?

At one level, we have seen that topics develop slowly and accretively because participants build on each other's contributions and jointly arrive at a consensus. At a more delicate level, both minimal responses and epistemic modal forms function as enabling devices. Participants use minimal responses to signal their active listenership and support for the current speaker; they use them too to mark their recognition of the different stages of conversational development. Epistemic modal forms are used to respect the face needs of all participants, to negotiate sensitive topics, and to encourage the participation of others; the chief effect of using epistemic modal forms is that the speaker does not take a hard line. Where a group rather than an individual overview is the aim of discussion, then linguistic forms which mitigate the force of individual contributions are a valuable resource. Finally, simultaneous speech occurs in such discourse in various forms, and is rarely a sign of conversational malfunctioning. On the contrary, in much of the material I have collected, the norm of one-speaker-at-a-time clearly does not apply. Co-conversationalists ask questions or make comments which, like minimal responses, are signals of active listenership, but which more substantially help to produce joint text. Simultaneous speech also occurs when speakers complete each other's utterances: this seems to be a clear example of the primacy of text rather than speaker. Finally, simultaneous speech occurs most commonly because speakers prefer, in discussion, the affirmation of collaborative talk to the giving of the floor to one speaker. Participants in conversation can absorb more than one message at a time; simultaneous speech doesn't threaten comprehension. On the contrary, it allows for a more multilayered development of themes.

Topic development, minimal responses, epistemic modal forms and simultaneous speech are formal features of very different kinds. Yet where minimal responses and epistemic modal forms are used frequently and with sensitivity, where simultaneous speech is contrapuntal and doesn't mark conversational breakdown, and where topics develop slowly and progressively, all can be seen to function to promote co-operative talk. It seems that in conversations between women friends in an informal context, the notion of co-operativeness is not a myth.

Conclusions

In this chapter I have tried to refine Jones's description of gossip, in particular by analys-ing some of the formal features which characterise all-female discourse. A comprehen-sive account of the formal features typical of gossip remains to be carried out. But it is possible on the basis of the four features analysed here to conclude that women's talk *can* be described as co-operative. This, however, brings us up against the conflicting findings of those working on women's language in the context of *mixed* interaction. Women's use of minimal responses, tag questions, and hedging devices in general (epis-temic modal forms) has been interpreted as a sign of weakness, of women's subordinate position to men (see, for example, Lakoff 1975; Fishman 1977, 1980). Moreover, research on interruption and overlap in mixed and single-sex pairs has shown that men use interruptions to dominate conversation in mixed interaction, but that simultaneous speech of any kind is rare in single-sex conversation (Zimmerman and West 1975; West and Zimmerman 1983).

Firstly, it is clearly not the case that any one linguistic form has one single function irrespective of contextual factors; linguists are now aware that linguistic forms are potentially multifunctional (see Cameron, McAlinder and O'Leary, 1989, for a full discussion of this point). Secondly, as I argued above, the forms that characterise all-female discourse need to be understood in the framework of the goals they serve. Since it is the aim of such talk to create and maintain good social relationships, then forms which promote such ends will be preferred. I have tried to show that women's frequent use of minimal responses and epistemic modal forms, their way of develop-ing topics progressively, and their preference for all-together-now rather than one-at-a-time discussion, all serve the function of asserting joint activity and of consolidating friendship. Women's talk at one level deals with the experiences com-mon to women: individuals work to come to terms with that experience, and partici-pants in conversation actively support one another in that endeavour. At another level, the *way* women negotiate talk symbolises that mutual support and co-operation: conversationalists understand that they have rights as speakers and also duties as listeners; the joint working out of a group point of view takes precedence over indi-vidual assertions.

This discussion of underlying goals should help to explain the differences between language use in same-sex and mixed interaction. It is undoubtedly the case, all other things being equal, that when women interact with other women they interact with equals, while when they interact with men they are relating to members of the domi-nant group. This means that analysis of mixed interaction has to be conducted in a framework which acknowledges dominance and oppression as relevant categories. Giving a minimal response to an equal in conversation, for example, is very different from giving a minimal response to a superior. Where the main goal of relaxed informal conversation between equals is the maintenance of good (equal) social relationships, one of the goals of mixed interaction is inevitably the maintenance of gender divisions, of male–female inequality.

Furthermore, it is now agreed that sociocultural presuppositions are a key factor in explaining how speakers make sense of conversation (Gumperz 1982). Since it is arguable that women and men in our culture do not share these sociocultural presuppositions, then another difference between same-sex and mixed interaction will be that the latter will exhibit communication problems similar to those found in inter-ethnic conversation.

For both these reasons, it is very important that we do not conflate the 'women's language' said to be typical of mixed interaction with the 'women's language' which characterises all-female discourse. The two need to be analysed separately. However, growing awareness of the norms of all-female discourse may help us to reassess our interpretation of the linguistic forms used by women in mixed interaction.

Jones's original paper marked the beginning of an important shift in focus in work on language and gender differences. It drew attention not just to women's language *per se*, but to the *strengths* of such discourse. This positive approach has provided an important counterbalance to the more negative tone of researchers who see women's language as weak and tentative. Much remains to be done in the study of women and language: the majority of studies so far have concentrated on white educated women in the United States and Britain. We still know very little about variation in women's language relating to age or class or ethnic group. The notion of co-operativeness needs to be tested against all these parameters. Jones's argument is that, despite differences of age or class or ethnicity, women form a speech community. In so far as human interaction is constitutive of social reality, and in so far as interaction with other women plays an important role in our dealing with our experiences as women, then the study of interaction in all-woman groups is, as Jones says, 'a key to the female subculture'.

Notes

1   I describe, and give a justification of, this approach in greater detail in Coates (1987).
2   I would like to place on record my gratitude to my friends for their tolerance and support.
3   Abrupt shifts do occur, when the emphasis switches from interaction-focussed to more information-focussed episodes. Such shifts, however, form a minority of cases.
4   See Coates 1996 (ch. 6) and 1997 for further development of these ideas.
5   The two texts used were one of my own, and one from the Survey of English Usage (University College, London). The speakers in both were white, middle-class, well educated, aged in their 30s and early 40s. Both texts were recorded in the evening in the homes of linguists who had invited their friends over for a drink. Five women are involved in the first text; three men in the other. (My thanks to Professor Greenbaum for allowing me to use SEU material.)

References

Abrahams, R. (1975) 'Negotiating respect: patterns of presentation among black women', in C. R. Farrar (ed.) *Women in Folklore*. Austin: University of Texas Press.

Aries, E. (1976) 'Interaction patterns and themes of male, female and mixed groups'. *Small Group Behaviour*, 7, 1, 7–18.

Brown, G. (1977) *Listening to Spoken English*. London: Longman.

Cameron, D., McAlinden, F. and O'Leary, K. (1989) 'Lakoff in context: the social and linguistic functions of tag questions', in J. Coates and D. Cameron (eds) *Women in Their Speech Communities*. Harlow: Longman.

Cheshire, J. (1982) *Variation in an English Dialect*. Cambridge: Cambridge University Press.

Coates, J. (1987) 'Epistemic modality and spoken discourse'. *Transactions of the Philological Society*, 110–31.

Coates, J. (1996) *Women Talk: Conversation Between Women Friends*. Oxford: Blackwell.

Coates, J. (1997) 'The construction of a collaborative floor in women's friendly talk', in T. Givón (ed.) *Conversation: Cognitive, Communicative and Social Perspectives*. New York: John Benjamins.

Edelsky, C. (1981) 'Who's got the floor?' *Language in Society*, 10, 383–421.

Ervin-Tripp, S. (1964) 'An analysis of the interaction of language, topic and listener'. *American Anthropologist*, 66, 6 (part 2), 86–102.

Fishman, P. M. (1977) 'Interactional shitwork'. *Heresies*, 2, 99–101.

Fishman, P. M. (1980) 'Conversational insecurity', in H. Giles, W. P. Robinson and P. Smith (eds) *Language: Social Psychological Perspectives*. Oxford: Pergamon.

Gilligan, C. (1982) *In a Different Voice*. Cambridge, MA: Harvard University Press.

Goodwin, M. H. (1980) 'Directive–response speech sequences in girls' and boys' task activities', pp. 157–73 in S. McConnell-Ginet, R. Borker and N. Furman (eds) *Women and Language in Literature and Society*. New York: Praeger.

Grice, H. P. (1975) 'Logic and conversation', pp. 41–58 in P. Cole and J. L. Morgan (eds) *Syntax and Semantics*, vol. 3: *Speech Acts*. New York: Academic Press.

Gumperz, J. (1982) *Discourse Strategies*. Cambridge: Cambridge University Press.

Hall, C. (1985) 'Private persons versus public someones: class, gender and politics in England, 1780–1850', pp. 10–33 in C. Steedman, C. Urwin and V. Walkerdine (eds) *Language, Gender and Childhood*. London: Routledge & Kegan Paul.

Hirschmann, L. (1974) 'Analysis of supportive and assertive behaviour in conversations.' Paper presented to the Linguistic Society of America, July 1974 (see abstract in B. Thorne and N. Henley (eds) (1975) *Language and Sex: Difference and Dominance*. Rowley, MA: Newbury House).

Holmes, J. (1984) 'Hedging your bets and sitting on the fence: some evidence for hedges as support structures'. *Te Reo*, 27, 47–62.

Jenkins, L. and Kramer, C. (1978) 'Small group process: learning from women'. *Women's Studies International Quarterly*, 1, 67–84.

Jones, D. (1980) 'Gossip: notes on women's oral culture', pp. 193–8 in C. Kramarae (ed.) *The Voices and Words of Women and Men*. Oxford: Pergamon Press.

Kalcik, S. (1975) '"… like Ann's gynaecologist or the time I was almost raped": personal narratives in women's rap groups'. *Journal of American Folklore*, 88, 3–11.

Lakoff, R. (1973) 'The logic of politeness'. *Papers from the Ninth Regional Meeting of the Chicago Linguistics Society*, 292–305.

Lakoff, R. (1975) *Language and Women's Place*. New York: Harper & Row.

Leech, G. (1983) *Principles of Pragmatics*. London: Longman.

Maltz, D. N. and Borker, R. A. (1982) 'A cultural approach to male–female miscommunication', in J. Gumperz (ed.) *Language and Social Identity*. Cambridge: Cambridge University Press.

Milroy, L. (1980) *Language and Social Networks*. Oxford: Blackwell.

Perkins, M. (1983) *Modal Expressions in English*. London: Frances Pinter.

Reisman, K. (1974) 'Contrapuntal conversation in an Antiguan village', in R. Bauman and J. Sherzer (eds) *Explorations in the Ethnography of Speaking*. Cambridge: Cambridge University Press.

Sacks, H., Schegloff, E. and Jefferson, G. (1974) 'A simplest systematics for the organization of turn-taking for conversation'. *Language*, 50, 696–735.

Smith, P. (1985) *Language, the Sexes and Society*. Oxford: Blackwell.

Strodtbeck, F. and Mann, R. (1956) 'Sex role differentiation in jury deliberations'. *Sociometry*, 19, 3–11.

Tannen, D. (1982) 'Ethnic style in male–female conversation', in J. Gumperz (ed.) *Language and Social Identity*. Cambridge: Cambridge University Press.

Tannen, D. (1984) *Conversational Style: Analyzing Talk among Friends*. Norwood, NJ: Ablex.

Tannen, D. (1987) *That's Not What I Meant*. London: Dent.

Urwin, C. (1985) 'Constructing motherhood: the persuasion of normal development', in C. Steedman, C. Urwin and V. Walkerdine (eds) *Language, Gender and Childhood*. London: Routledge & Kegan Paul.

Wells, G. (1979) 'Variation in child language', in V. Lee (ed.) *Language Development*. London: Croom Helm.

West, C. and Zimmerman, D. (1983) 'Small insults: a study of interruptions in cross-sex conversations between unacquainted persons', in B. Thorne, C. Kramarae and N. Henley (eds) *Language, Gender and Society*. Rowley, MA: Newbury House.

Wodak, R. (1981) 'Women relate; men report: sex differences in language behaviour in a therapeutic group'. *Journal of Pragmatics*, 5, 261–85.

Zimmerman, D. and West, C. (1975) 'Sex roles, interruptions and silences in conversation', in B. Thorne and N. Henley (eds) *Language and Sex: Difference and Dominance*. Rowley, MA: Newbury House.

17

"Why Be Normal?":
Language and Identity Practices
in a Community of Nerd Girls

Mary Bucholtz

Source: *Language in Society* 28(2) (1999), pp. 203–24. Reprinted with permission of Cambridge University Press.

[…]

In this article, I build on the theory of the community of practice to develop its potential as an analytic tool for the sociolinguistics investigation of gendered identities. The framework is applied to a social identity, that of the nerd, which has remained out of bounds in traditional sociolinguistic research based on the speech community. This identity is analysed within the community of practice framework because only this concept permits us to draw on the linguistic and social information necessary to understand the production of nerd identity. I argue that nerd identity, contrary to popular perceptions, is not a stigma imposed by others, but a purposefully chosen alternative to mainstream gender identities which is achieved and maintained through language and other social practices.

[…]

Nerds, Gender, and the Community of Practice

The inadequacies of the speech community model for scholars of language and gender are overcome in the theory of the community of practice as articulated by Eckert and McConnell-Ginet 1992, 1995.[1] Rather than investing language with a special analytic status, the community of practice framework considers language as one of many social practices in which participants engage. By defining the community as a group of people oriented to the same practice, though not necessarily in the same way, the community of practice model treats difference and conflict, not uniformity and consensus, as the ordinary state of affairs. The inherent heterogeneity of the community of practice also brings marginal members to the forefront of analysis. One reason for this shift to the margins is that some peripheral members are recognized as novices, as in Lave and Wenger's original formulation (1991). More importantly,

Language and Gender: A Reader, Second Edition. Edited by Jennifer Coates and Pia Pichler.
© 2011 Blackwell Publishing Ltd except for editorial material and organization. © 2011 Jennifer Coates and Pia Pichler. Published 2011 by Blackwell Publishing Ltd.

however, the community of practice, unlike the speech community, may be constituted around any social or linguistic practice, no matter how marginal from the perspective of the traditional speech community. Likewise, by focusing on individuals as well as groups, the theory of the community of practice integrates structure with agency. And because identities are rooted in actions rather than categories, the community of practice model can capture the multiplicity of identities at work in specific speech situations more fully than is possible within the speech community framework. Such nuanced description is also facilitated by Eckert and McConnell-Ginet's intrinsically ethnographic approach to language and gender research. The remainder of this article draws on the above characteristics of the community of practice to demonstrate the theory's utility in the investigation of an understudied social identity as it emerges locally in a high-school setting.

Eckert 1989a offers an account of the social organization of a typical suburban US high school. She found that students' social worlds and identities were defined by two polar opposites: the Jocks (overachieving students who oriented to middle-class values) and the Burnouts (underachieving students who were bound for work, rather than college, at the end of their high-school careers). Yet the dichotomy that separated these students also united them in what can be understood as a single community of practice, since the ultimate goal of members of both groups was to be COOL. The difference lay in how each group defined coolness.

Not all high-school students, however, share the Jocks' and Burnouts' preoccupation with coolness. A third group, the nerds, defines itself largely in opposition to "cool" students – whether Jocks, Burnouts, or any other social identity. Nerds stand as the antithesis of all these groups, a situation that Eckert succinctly captures in her observation, "If a Jock is the opposite of a Burnout, a nerd is the opposite of both" (1989a:48). But despite the structural significance of the nerd in the organization of youth identities, few researchers have examined its implications, and those who have tried have fallen far short of the mark in their analyses. Thus the sociologist David Kinney, in a rare study of nerds (1993), argues that, in order to succeed socially, nerds must undergo a process of "recovery of identity" that involves broadening one's friendship network, participating in extracurricular activities, and heterosexual dating: In short, they must become Jocks. Another scholarly treatment (Tolone and Tieman 1990) investigates the drug use of nerds in an article subtitled "Are loners deviant?" – in other words, are nerds really Burnouts?

What both studies overlook is that being a nerd is not about being a failed Burnout or an inadequate Jock. It is about rejecting both Jockness and Burnoutness, and all the other forms of coolness that youth identities take. Although previous researchers maintain that nerd identity is invalid or deficient, in fact nerds, like Jocks and Burnouts, to a great extent consciously choose and display their identities through language and other social practices. And where other scholars tend to equate nerdiness with social death, I propose that nerds in US high schools are not socially isolated misfits, but competent members of a distinctive and oppositionally defined community of practice. Nerdiness is an especially valuable resource for girls in the gendered world of the US high school.

Elsewhere (Bucholtz 1998) I describe the social identity of the nerd and detail the phonological, syntactic, lexical, and discourse practices through which nerd identity is linguistically indexed. Here I propose a framework for the classification of such practices. These linguistic indices are of two kinds: NEGATIVE IDENTITY PRACTICES are those that individuals employ to distance themselves from a rejected identity, while POSITIVE IDENTITY PRACTICES are those in which individuals engage in order actively to construct a chosen identity. In other

Table 1 Linguistic identity practices of nerds at Bay City High School

Linguistic level	Negative identity practices	Positive identity practices
Phonology	Lesser fronting of (uw) and (ow)[a]	
Phonology	Resistance to colloquial phonological processes such as vowel reduction, consonant-cluster simplification, and contraction	Employment of superstandard and hypercorrect phonological forms (e.g. spelling pronunciations)
Syntax	Avoidance of nonstandard syntactic forms	Adherence to standard and superstandard syntactic forms
Lexicon	Avoidance of current slang	Employment of lexical items associated with the formal register (e.g. Greco-Latinate forms)
Discourse		Orientation to language form (e.g. punning, parody, word coinage)

[a] In Bucholtz 1998 I offer a fuller discussion of the phonological and syntactic patterns of nerds. The present article focuses primarily on lexicon and on discursive identity practices. The variables (uw) and (ow) are part of a vowel shift that is characteristic of California teenagers (Hinton et al. 1987, Luthin 1987). It is stereotypically associated with trendy and cool youth identities.

words, negative identity practices define what their users are *not*, and hence emphasize identity as an intergroup phenomenon; positive identity practices define what their users *are*, and thus emphasize the intergroup aspects of social identity. The linguistic identity practices of nerds in the present study are shown in Table 1.

The negative identity practices listed here work to disassociate nerds from non-nerds, and especially from cool teenagers. Each of these practices, which mark nerdy teenagers as avowedly uncool, constitutes a refusal to engage in the pursuit of coolness that consumes other students. Meanwhile, all the positive identity practices listed contribute to the speaker's construction of an intelligent self – a primary value of nerd identity. These linguistic practices also have non-linguistic counterparts in positive and negative identity practices of other kinds (see below).

But linguistic practices can often reveal important social information that is not available from the examination of other community practices alone. For example, Eckert and McConnell-Ginet 1995 apply the theory of the community of practice to Eckert's study of Jocks and Burnouts. Linguistic analysis revealed that the two groups were participating at different rates in the Northern Cities Vowel Shift, with the most innovative vowels being those used by the "Burned-Out Burnout girls", the most extreme adherents to this social identity. Eckert and McConnell-Ginet's finding runs counter to the sociolinguistic tenet that "in stable variables, women use fewer non-standard variants than men of the same social class and age under the same circumstances" (Chambers 1995:112).[2] The researchers argue that the vowels employed by the Burned-Out Burnout girls are resources through which they construct their identities as tough and streetwise; unlike the boys, who can display their toughness through physical confrontations, female Burnouts must index their identities semiotically, because fighting is viewed as inappropriate for girls. Thus Burnout girls and boys share an orientation toward toughness in their community of practice, but the practice of toughness is achieved in different ways by each gender. By viewing language as equivalent to other social practices like fighting, Eckert and McConnell-Ginet are able to explain the ethnographic meaning of the Burnout girls' vowel systems, and to show how, as symbolic capital (Bourdieu 1978), language can acquire the empowering authority of physical force itself.

Nerds, of course, attain empowerment in very different ways than either Burnouts or Jocks. One of the primary ways they differ from these other, more trend-conscious groups is through the high value they place on individuality. Compared to both Jocks and Burnouts – who must toe the subcultural line in dress, language, friendship choices, and other social practices – nerds are somewhat less constrained by peer-group sanctions.

For girls, nerd identity also offers an alternative to the pressures of hegemonic femininity – an ideological construct that is at best incompatible with, and at worst hostile to, female intellectual ability. Nerd girls' conscious opposition to this ideology is evident in every aspect of their lives, from language to hexis to other aspects of self-presentation. Where cool girls aim for either cuteness or sophistication in their personal style, nerd girls aim for silliness. Cool girls play soccer or basketball; nerd girls play badminton. Cool girls read fashion magazines; nerd girls read novels. Cool girls wear tight T-shirts, and either very tight or very baggy jeans; nerd girls wear shirts and jeans that are neither tight nor extremely baggy. Cool girls wear pastels or dark tones; nerd girls wear bright primary colors. But these practices are specific to individuals; they are engaged in by particular nerd girls, not all of them.

The community of practice model accommodates the individuality that is paramount in the nerd social identity, without overlooking the strong community ties that unify the nerd girls in this study. The community of practice also allows us to look at nerd girls in the same way that Eckert and McConnell-Ginet 1995 view the Burnout girls: as speakers AND social actors, as individuals AND members of communities, and as both resisting and responding to cultural ideologies of gender.

Identity Practices in a Local Nerd Community

To illustrate the value of the community of practice framework, I will focus on a single social group that displays the nerd social identity. Nerds at the high school in my study constitute a single community insofar as they engage in shared practices, but this identity is divided into particular social groups whose members associate primarily with one another, and these groups form their own communities of practice. In communities of practice, unlike speech communities, the boundaries are determined not externally by linguists, but internally through ethnographically specific social meanings of language use. As suggested above, ethnographic methods therefore become crucial to the investigation of communities of practice.

The ethnographic fieldwork from which the data are taken was carried out during the 1994–95 academic year at a California high school that I call Bay City High. The social group of nerd girls that is the focus of this discussion is a small, cohesive friendship group that comprises four central members – Fred, Bob, Kate, and Loden – and two peripheral members, Carrie and Ada. (Ada does not appear in the data that follow.) All the girls are European American except Ada, who is Asian American. The same group also formed a club, which I will call the Random Reigns Supreme Club.[3]

Random Reigns Supreme is more properly described as an anti-club, which is in keeping with the counter-hegemonic orientation of nerd identity. It was created by members in order to celebrate their own preferences, from Sesame Street to cows to Mr. Salty the pretzel man. Members emphasize the "randomness" of the club's structure. It is not organized around shared preferences; instead, any individual's preferences can be part of the club's de facto charter, and all six members are co-presidents. This structure contrasts with the corporate focus and hierarchical structure of most school clubs, which bring together people who are otherwise unconnected to perform a shared activity (Eckert 1989a). The Random Reigns Supreme Club centers around members' daily practices, not specialized activities. It has no goals, no ongoing projects, and no official meetings. Nevertheless, members proudly take their place among the corporate clubs in the pages of the school's yearbook. The girls' insistence on being photographed for the yearbook has a subversive quality: The photo publicly documents the existence of this otherwise little-recognized friendship group, and demands its institutional legitimacy on par with the French Club, the Backpacking Club, and other activity-based organizations. Like their yearbook photograph, the language used by the girls not only marks their nerd identity but also expresses their separation from outsiders. As shown by the following examples (taken from a single interaction), the details of interaction are important and contested resources in defining a shared oppositional nerd identity within the club's community of practice.

Positive identity practices

As indicated above, many positive identity practices in which nerds engage contribute to the display of intelligence. The community value placed on intelligence is reflected in non-linguistic identity practices oriented to the world of school, books, and knowledge. This orientation is amply illustrated in the following.[4] Carrie's question in line 1 creates the conditions for intellectual display. Although the humor of the question is acknowledged through laughter (line 2), it receives immediate, serious uptake from two participants, Bob and Fred (lines 4–5). Carrie's subsequent question (line 6), however, forces an admission of ignorance from Fred (line 7).

(1)	1	CARRIE:	Where where do those seeds come from?
	2		((points to her bagel))
	3	((laughter))	
	4	BOB:	[Poppies.]
	5	FRED:	[Sesame plants.]
	6	CARRIE:	{But what do they look like?} ((high pitch))
	7	FRED:	I have no idea. hh
	8	BOB:	Sesame:.
	9	CARRIE:	[Is anybody–h]
	10	FRED:	Ask me (.) [tomorrow.]
	11		I'll look it up for you. h
	12	CARRIE:	h Is anybody here knowledgeable about (.)
	13		the seeds on top of bagels?/
	14	FRED:	/Sesame.
	15	BOB:	They're sesame?
	16		They're not sunfl–?
	17		No,
	18		of course they're not sunflower.

19	LODEN:	Yeah,	
20		[What kind of seeds <u>are</u>–	]
21	CARRIE:	[Because sunflower are those whopping ones?]	
22	BOB:	[Yeah.	
23		Yeah.	
24		I know.	]
25	((laughter))		

Carrie's question in line 1 creates the conditions for intellectual display. Althoug the humor of the question is acknowledged through laughter (line2), it receives immediate, serious uptake from two participants, Bob and Fred (lines 4–5). Carrie's subsequent question (line 6), however, forces an admission of ignorance from Fred (line 7).

Because knowledge is symbolic capital within the nerd community of practice, Fred's admission results in some loss of face. She recovers from this (minor) social setback by invoking the authority of a reference book (*I'll look it up for you*, line 11). In this way Fred can safely assure her interlocutor that, although she does not yet know the answer, she soon will. She is also able to one-up Bob, who has misidentified the bagel seeds (line 4) and continues to show some skepticism about Fred's classification of them (*Sesame:*, line 8). Fred tracks this indirect challenge for five lines, through her own turn and Carrie's next question; rather than continuing to participate in the series of adjacency pairs that Carrie has initiated (lines 12–13), she responds to Bob (line 14). Fred thus succeeds in displaying both actual knowledge, about the type of seeds under discussion, and potential knowledge, about the appearance of sesame plants.

Claims to knowledge are, however, often disputed in this community of practice. After Bob provides an incorrect answer to Carrie and receives a correction from Fred, she continues to exhibit doubt about Fred's knowledge (line 15). She offers a second incorrect identification of the seeds in line 16, but this time she interrupts herself and self-corrects (lines 17–18), in an effort to prevent further other-correction. She does not succeed, however; and when Carrie explains why Bob is mistaken, the latter overlaps with her, offering three quick acknowledgments that are designed to cut off Carrie's turn (lines 22–4).

This passage shows several deviations from the preference organization of repair in conversation (Schegloff et al. 1977), according to which self-initiation and self-repair are preferred over initiation and repair by another. Bob twice initiates dispreferred repairs of Fred's turns (lines 8, 15), and she even begins to carry out the repair itself in line 16. When Bob initiates a repair of her own utterance through self-interruption in the same line, Carrie performs the repair despite Bob's efforts to prevent her from doing so (lines 21–4). The frequent apparent violations of repair organization suggest that, in this community of practice, self-repair is preferred only by the speaker; the listener's positive face (the desire to be viewed as intelligent) wars against and often overrides consideration of the speaker's negative face (the desire not to be viewed as unintelligent).

Bob's loss of face in example 1 leads her, in example 2, to initiate a new conversational direction:

(2)	26	BOB:	They come from trees.	
	27		They have big trees and they just	
	28		[ra:in down seeds]	
	29		[((laughter))]	
	30	CARRIE:	[<u>No they don't</u>.]	
	31		Uh uh.	

32   Why would little tiny seeds [come from–   ]
33   FRED: [{into baskets.}] ((smiling quality))
34   Ye:p,
35   [({I've been there.})] ((smiling quality))
36   CARRIE: [No:.   ]
37   LODEN: [No:.   ]
38   BOB: [[Little tiny <u>leaves</u> come from trees,   ]]
39   FRED: [[And the whole culture's built <u>around</u> it,]]
40   like in: some countries,
41   All they do is like the women come out and they have ba(h)skets on
42   th(h)eir h(h)eads and they st(h)and under a [tree,]

Bob jokingly provides an authoritative answer to Carrie's question (lines 26–8) and thereby skillfully shifts attention from her own lack of knowledge to Carrie's. Fred eagerly joins in with the parody of scientific discourse, amplifying on the theme while supplying invented anthropological details that invoke the didactic style of a typical high-school classroom or public television documentary (33–5, 39–42). Such teasing episodes are frequent in this friendship group. But more importantly, this exchange is a collaborative performance of nerd identity: The participants collude in sustaining the frame of an intellectual debate, even as laughter keys the talk as play. Nerd identities are here jointly constructed and displayed.

In example 3, Carrie – who up to this point has mostly provided opportunities for others to display their nerd identities, rather than participating herself (but see below) – shifts the topic, which she sustains for the rest of the interaction:

(3)   43   CARRIE: [My–]
      44   You sound like my crusty king,
      45   I'm writing this (.) poem because I have to like incorporate these
      46   words into a poem, and it's all about–
      47   ⟨interruption, lines omitted⟩
      48   FRED: So what about this king?

Carrie's discussion of a class assignment returns to a central value of nerdiness: school. The topic is sustained for 56 lines and 26 turns; and although it is interrupted immediately after Carrie introduces it (line 47), Fred prompts her to return to the subject several minutes later (line 48). Carrie's enthusiastic description of her poem – and the eager participation of others in this topic – is rare among students with cool social identities, but it is quite common among nerds, for whom academic pursuits are a central resource for identity practices.

At the same time, however, Carrie's selection of subject matter for her poem, with its mildly scatological – or at least "gross" theme (line 80) – is playfully subversive of school values and emphatically counter to traditional feminine topics, as example 4 illustrates:

(4)   49   CARRIE: He's like (.) has this (.) castle,
      50   (xxx: Is he xxx king?)
      51   CARRIE: No–
      52   Yeah,
      53   he is.
      54   LODEN: hh
      55   CARRIE: He has this–
      56   {He has this castle right?

57		except it's all crusty,}
58		((rustling of lunch bag, clanging of aluminum can))
59	(FRED:	Uh huh.)
60	CARRIE:	And so he lives on a boat [in the moat.]
61	BOB:	[A crusty–]
62	((Fred crushes her aluminum can))	
63	KATE:	Who:a!
64	((quiet laughter))	
65	BOB:	Is it really [crusty?]
66	CARRIE:	[He's–]
67		And so like the– like because– the people are trying to convince
68		him that like he should stay in the castle and he's all,
69		{"No, it's crusty!"} ((high pitch, tensed vocal cords))
70		[((laughter))]
71	CARRIE:	[{"I'm in the moat!"}] ((high pitch, quiet))
72		right,
73	BOB:	What's wrong with [crusty castles?]
74	CARRIE:	[And so–]
75		Well,
76		Would [you want to live]=
77	KATE:	[Crusty (castles).]
78	CARRIE:	=in a castle full of crust?
79		{[iəi]} ((noise of disgust and disapproval))
80	KATE:	[How gross.]
81	BOB:	[I mi:ght.]
82	CARRIE:	Huh?

Bob here enters into the unfeminine spirit of Carrie's narrative, even outdoing Carrie with her repeated insistence on her own immunity from "gross" subjects like crustiness (lines 73, 81). A competitive tone is also evident in the multiple challenges she issues to Carrie throughout the latter's narrative (lines 65, 73). As questions, these challenges echo Carrie's earlier questions (lines 1, 6, 12–13); but whereas Carrie's appeared to be genuine information-seeking questions, Bob's are not. Carrie's recognition of this fact is shown by her failure to respond at all to the first question, and by her answering the second question with an equally challenging question of her own (*Would you want to live in a castle full of crust?*, lines 76, 78). Bob's face-threatening response (*I mi:ght*, line 81) perpetuates the jocular-combative tone. In ex. 5, however, this combativeness becomes not a shared resource for joint identity construction, but a marker of social division. The positive identity practices that dominate in the earlier part of the interaction are replaced by negative identity practices, as community members experience a threat not only to their face but also to their identities.

Negative identity practices

Example 5 is a continuation of Bob's face-threatening questions to Carrie. This final series of questions is unified through a shared template (*like* + ADJ + *crust*); their syntactic similarity emphasizes that they are designed as a series, and it thus produces an effect of unremitting interrogation.

```
(5)   83   BOB:    What kind of crust?
      84           Like,
      85               bread crust?
      86   CARRIE:  Like
      87   BOB:     Like [eye crust?   ]
      88   CARRIE:       [crusty crust.]
      89            Like {boo:tsy} ((high pitch, tensed vocal cords))
      90            crust.
      91   ((laughter))
      92   BOB:     Oh.
      93            Well,
      94            Maybe if it's bootsy,
      95            I don't know.
      96   FRED:    {Boot[sy!          ]} ((falsetto, sing-song))
      97   KATE:         [((coughs))]
      98   ((laughter))
```

These questions display Bob's nerd identity through her use of puns on the word *crust* (lines 85, 87). Punning, as a discourse practice that orients to linguistic form, is characteristic of nerds' discourse style (see Table 1). Carrie's refusal (line 88) to participate in Bob's punning thus constitutes a negative identity practice – one which, moreover, indexes a rejection of nerd identity as it has been constructed through preceding interactional practices. The refusal is made more evident by her exploitation (lines 86, 88–90) of Bob's syntactic template. By conforming to the syntactic form of Bob's turn, while failing to conform to the discourse practice of punning, Carrie separates herself from Bob at a point when the latter is fully engaged in nerdy identity practices.

This analysis is confirmed by Carrie's choice of upgraded adjective in line 89. *Bootsy* is a slang term with a negative evaluative sense; it is not used by other members of the Random Reigns Supreme Club. The introduction of youth slang into a group that explicitly rejects such linguistic forms is part of a strongly negative identity practice, and the reactions of Carrie's interlocutors are correspondingly negative: Bob's response (lines 92–5) jokingly concedes the point, while underscoring that Carrie has violated the rules of nerdy argument by appealing to the authority of cool youth culture. Fred's mocking repetition of the term (line 96) demonstrates that the use of slang is itself worthy of comment. With Carrie's narrative entirely derailed – it never becomes clear how it is connected to the earlier discussion – she soon afterward moves away from the group.

The complex interaction presented above reveals Carrie's peripheral status in this community of practice. As a non-core member, she moves between friendship groups – in fact, the interaction occurred when Carrie approached the core group in the middle of lunch period. Carrie's social flexibility has made her a cultural and linguistic broker for the Random Reigns Supreme Club, whose members become aware of current youth slang in large part through contact with her. Hence many slang terms that circulate widely in the "cool" groups are labeled by club members as "Carrie words".

Yet Carrie also demonstrates her ability and willingness to participate in the group's positive identity practices. She does so most obviously by engaging in sound play in recounting her poem (*crusty king*, line 44; *a boat in the moat*, line 60). More significant, though, is the subtle shift in her speech practices at the beginning of the interaction. Thus Carrie's question *Is anybody here knowledgeable about (.) the seeds on top of bagels?* (lines 12–13) draws on the formal register through her choice of the word *knowledgeable*. Among nerds, this register projects a speaker's persona as smart and highly educated.

But the use of the formal register is strategic, not a mechanical result of membership in a particular social category. This point is supported by the fact that Carrie employs the nerd identity practice only after she asks two related questions in colloquial register (lines 1, 6). Her unwillingness to overlap her turn with Fred's (lines 9, 10) further suggests that the question is a performance of nerdiness, not just a manifestation of it; she does not produce her utterance until she is assured of an attentive audience. That is, Carrie is simultaneously displaying and commenting on nerd practice – showing her awareness of nerdy linguistic forms, and announcing her willingness to enter a nerdy interactional space by carefully gauging her utterance to match the group's practices. Thus Carrie's performance of nerdiness places her within the community of practice; but her use of slang, as the other members are quick to let her know, moves her outside it. Such adjustments at interactional boundaries may reflect adjustments at community boundaries.

Conclusion

Because all the participants in the above exchange are middle-class European American girls from the same California city, the traditional sociolinguistic perspective would classify them unproblematically as members of the same speech community. Such an analysis would overlook the details of greatest interest to language and gender researchers: the performances of identity, and the struggles over it, which are achieved through language. However, by viewing the interaction as the product of a community of practice, we can avoid this problem, as well as others associated with the speech community model.

The ethnographic method brings into view the social meanings with which participants invest their practices. These meanings emerge on the ground in local contexts; thus what it means to display academic knowledge, or to use slang, depends not on fixed identity categories but on where one is standing. Nor do participants necessarily agree on the meanings of their actions; nerdiness, like all identities, is a contested domain in which speakers struggle both over control of shared values, via positive identity practices (Who's better at being a nerd?), and over control of identity itself, via negative identity practices (Who counts as a nerd?). Such conflicts reveal the heterogeneity of membership in the community of practice – its constitution through the work of central and peripheral members alike. In this project, the interactional choices of specific individuals matter. Thus Carrie's identity is on display – and at risk – in a way that Loden's, for example, is not. These actions must be seen as choices, not as the outputs of interactional algorithms. While some practices reproduce the existing local social structure (as does Carrie's use of the formal register), others undermine it (e.g. her use of slang). Likewise, some nerdy practices (such as being good students) comply with the larger social order, while others (such as rejecting femininity) resist it. Linguistic practices, moreover, have no special status in this process. Instead, they work in conjunction with other social practices to produce meanings and identities. Bob's interactional work to distance herself from hegemonic femininity, for instance, is part of her overall participation in anti-feminine practices and her non-participation in feminine practices, as evidenced also by her physical self-presentation.

For sociolinguists, the community of practice represents an improvement over the speech community in that it addresses itself to both the social and the linguistic aspects of the discipline. As a well-grounded framework with currency in a number of fields, practice theory in general, in particular the community of practice, revitalizes social theory within sociolinguistics. What is more, it does so at a sufficiently general level to accommodate multiple dimensions of social analysis – including both structure and agency, both ideology and identity, both norms and interactions. The community of practice also provides an avenue for a more complete sociolinguistic investigation of identity. Although introduced for gender-based research, the community of practice has never been restricted to the analysis of a single element of identity. Indeed, it lends itself to the simultaneous investigation of multiple aspects of the self, from those at the macro level – like gender, ethnicity, and class – to micro-identities like Jocks, Burnouts, or nerds. The framework also allows for the study of interaction between levels of identity. The concepts of positive and negative identity practices, as proposed in this article, are intended as one way to develop the potential of the community of practice in this arena.

In addition to its benefits for social analysis, the community of practice offers an integrated approach to linguistic analysis. By understanding all socially meaningful language use as practices tied to various communities, the model enables researchers to provide more complete linguistic descriptions – along with social explanations – of particular social groups. Moreover, the community of practice provides a way to bring qualitative and quantitative research closer together. Because both kinds of linguistic data emerge from practice, both can be included in a single analysis. This richly contextualized approach to both language and society is one of the great strengths of the community of practice as a sociolinguistic framework.

The community of practice, having revolutionized the field of language and gender almost as soon as it was first proposed, enables researchers of socially situated language use to view language within the context of social practice. Perhaps the most valuable feature is that the community of practice admits a range of social and linguistic phenomena that are not analyzed in other theoretical models. Local identities, and the linguistic practices that produce them, become visible to sociolinguistic analysis as the purposeful choices of agentive individuals, operating within (and alongside and outside) the constraints of the social structure. To describe and explain such complexity must be the next step not only for language and gender scholars, but for all sociolinguists concerned with the linguistic construction of the social world.

Notes

My thanks to Janet Holmes, Chris Holcomb, Stephanie Stanbro, and members of the Ethnography/Theory Group at Texas A&M University for comments on and discussion of the ideas in this article.

1 A fuller discussion of the advantages of practice theory for language and gender research is provided by Bucholtz 1999.
2 Eckert 1989b calls this simple formulation into question; see also Labov 1990 for a response.
3 Though this is not its actual name, it preserves the flavor of the original. All other names are pseudonyms chosen by the speakers.
4 Transcription conventions are given on p. x.

References

Bourdieu, Pierre (1978). *Outline of a Theory of Practice*. Cambridge: Cambridge University Press.
Bucholtz, Mary (1998). Geek the girl: Language, femininity, and female nerds. In Natasha Warner et al. (eds.), *Gender and Belief Systems: Proceedings of the Fourth Berkeley Women and Language Conference*, 119–31. Berkeley: Berkeley Women and Language Group.

Bucholtz, Mary (1999). Bad examples: Transgression and progress in language and gender research. In Mary Bucholtz et al. (eds.), *Reinventing identities*. To appear, New York: Oxford University Press.

Chambers, J. K. (1995). *Sociolinguistic theory*. Oxford: Blackwell.

Eckert, Penelope (1989a). *Jocks and Burnouts: Social Categories and Identity in the High School*. New York: Teachers College Press.

Eckert, Penelope (1989b). The whole woman: Sex and gender differences in variation. *Language Variation and Change* 1:245–67.

Eckert, Penelope and McConnell-Ginet, Sally (1992). Think practically and look locally: Language and gender as community-based practice. *Annual Review of Anthropology* 21:461–90.

Eckert, Penelope and McConnell-Ginet, Sally (1995). Constructing meaning, constructing selves: Snapshots of language, gender, and class from Belten High. In Kira Hall & Mary Bucholtz (eds.), *Gender articulated: Language and the socially constructed self*, 459–507. London: Routledge.

Hinton, Leanne, et al. (1987). It's not just the Valley Girls: A study of California English. *Berkeley Linguistics Society* 13:117–28.

Kinney, David A. (1993). From nerds to normals: The recovery of identity among adolescents from middle school to high school. *Sociology of Education* 66:1.21–40.

Labov, William (1990). The intersection of sex and social class in the course of linguistic change. *Language Variation and Change* 2:205–54.

Lave, Jean and Wenger, Etienne (1991). *Situated Learning: Legitimate Peripheral Participation*. Cambridge: Cambridge University Press.

Luthin, Herbert W. (1987). The story of California (ow): The coming-of-age of English in California. In Keith M. Denning et al. (eds.), *Variation in Language: NWAV-XV at Stanford*, 312–24. Stanford, CA: Department of Linguistics, Stanford University.

Tolone, W. L., and C. R. Tieman (1990). Drugs, delinquency and nerds: Are loners deviant? *Journal of Drug Education* 20:2.153–62.

18

Hybrid or In Between Cultures: Traditions of Marriage in a Group of British Bangladeshi Girls

Pia Pichler

Source: Jose Santaemilia and Patricia Bon (eds), *Gender and Sexual Identities in Transition: Cross-cultural Perspectives*. Newcastle upon Tyne: Cambridge Scholars Publishing (2008), pp. 199–218. Reprinted with permission of Cambridge Scholars Publishing.

1   Introduction

This chapter presents a discourse analytic investigation of the negotiation of cultural practices and subject positions in a group of five adolescent British Bangladeshi girls. In their spontaneous talk the girls position marriage as central to their adolescent femininities. My analysis will focus on what I call a "modified discourse of arranged marriage", which, I argue, emerges locally as a hybrid during the complex interactive negotiations of a wide range of cultural discourses with ethnic and gendered inflections in the girls' talk about a wedding proposal. However, I shall also present an extract from a different source of data, loosely structured interviews between myself and one of the girls. In this extract my in-group informant Hennah appears to challenge my post-structuralist celebration of hybrid British Bangladeshi femininities with regard to the girls' positioning to traditions of marriage.
[…]
  Language and gender scholars have generated a substantial amount of research on adolescent girls and their friendship or peer groups, focusing both on structural and on discoursal features of young women's talk (Bucholtz 1999; Coates 1999; Eckert 1993; Eckert and McConnell-Ginet 1995; Eder 1993; Goodwin 1999; Mendoza-Denton 1999). Like the extensive body of cross-disciplinary research on young Asian women many of these linguistic studies take a constructionist approach to identity, and some of them also show an interest in exploring gender in non-white groups (Goodwin 1999; Mendoza-Denton 1999; Pichler 2006a). However, language and gender research has, to my knowledge, so far not turned its attention to the talk and the identity practices of British Asian girls. My own work therefore builds on non-linguistic research into young hybrid British Asian identities and the topic of arranged marriage.

Popular media representations of arranged marriage continue to perpetuate the stereotype of the suppressed Asian girl as a victim of culture clash (e.g. Cramb, writing in *The Daily Telegraph* 25/04/2002; Kelbie, writing in *The Independent* 30/08/2006). Early academic work such as Watson (1977) and the Community Relations Commission (1976) did not present an altogether different perspective, describing the situation of second generation Asian adolescents in Britain as being trapped "between two cultures". On the other hand, during the last two decades pathologising culture-clash theories have been challenged both by feminists presenting a structuralist argument focused on racism, gender, social class and education (Amos and Parmar 1981; Brah and Minhas 1985) and, more recently, by scholars taking a constructionist rather than a structuralist stance. The work of Ahmad (2003), Alexander (2000), Archer (2002a, 2002b), Brah (1996), Dwyer (2000) and Shain (2003) challenges earlier studies and conceptualisations of British Asian adolescents for their essentialist approach to culture and identity as fixed and static, with "Asian-ness" and "British-ness" as independent, a priori and, moreover, homogenous categories. Frequently this work from anthropology, cultural studies, sociology and education is framed as a 'celebration' of hybridity (Puwar 2003: 31–6), with a particular focus on second and third generation South Asian young women.

This recent, cross-disciplinary research adopts a (feminist) poststructuralist approach to culture, conceptualising it 'not [as] an essence but a *positioning*' (Hall 1990: 226), or, in other words, viewing culture not as a reified, homogenous entity (Bauman 1997: 211) but instead as a 'process' and as 'semiotic space with infinite class, caste, gender, ethnic or other inflections' (Brah 1996: 234, 246). The spontaneous conversational data that I collected from a group of Bangladeshi girls on the topic of marriage contain what I would interpret as rich evidence of the process of invoking, challenging and synthesising cultural practices and discourses with various 'inflections' and thus of the local negotiation of 'cultures of hybridity' (Hall 1992: 310). However, my second source of data, consisting of interviews, suggests that this performative notion of culture and the celebration of cultural hybridity are not always shared by the research participants themselves. My combination of data sources therefore encouraged me to adopt a critical and reflexive approach to the topic of (arranged) marriage, building both on academic theorization and my participants' lived experience of culture and hybridity, and even considering the possible limitations of my linguistic data.

After presenting some background information about my two data sources, the participants in my study and previous research on "arranged marriage", I shall first focus my analysis on the girls' spontaneous talk and then turn to the interviews with my in-group informant. The final section of this chapter will draw conclusions about the girls' positioning in relation to the topic of marriage on the basis of my analysis of these diverse and seemingly contradictory data.

2   Data and Participants

The girls in this group, who I shall refer to as Ardiana, Dilshana, Hennah, Varda and Rahima, all attended year 11 (15–16 years old) and formed a friendship group at their single-sex comprehensive school in the East End of London, which recruited students mainly from the surrounding working class areas. Three girls were born in Bangladesh but all of the girls had received between two and eight years of schooling in Britain.

The conversational extracts I present in this chapter derive from the self-recorded spontaneous talk of the girls during their lunch breaks at school. I supplemented these spontaneous conversational data with recordings and notes of several loosely structured interviews resulting from my in-depth, long-term collaboration with one of the girls who helped me to translate the Bengali/Sylheti utterances in the girls' talk. These "interviews" with Hennah not only provided me with valuable ethnographic information about the girls themselves, their families and communities but they also allowed one of the partici-pants to add her own interpretation of the conversational data to mine and encouraged me to reflect on my own stance and perspectives as a researcher.

3   Arranged Marriage: A Research Overview

Ahmad (2003: 44–5) is critical of what she feels to be an 'overemphasis' on arranged marriage in relation to South Asian women in academic work. My own study on young femininities was not led by any a priori interest in the topic of marriage, but instead the topic was positioned as significant by Ardiana and her friends themselves in their group talk. My exploration of these conversational data on marriage, however, benefits greatly from the wealth of previous, non-linguistic research on and with young British Asian women.

Most of this cross-disciplinary research suggests that "arranged marriage" continues to be prominent among second and third generation Asians in the UK, but that it is also undergoing significant changes. However, individual studies vary greatly in how they present this tradition. Although some of the large-scale studies such as Anwar (1998), Ghuman (1994, 2003), Modood et al. (1994) emphasise that there might not be any inter-familiar conflicts about the tradition, they tend to take a more critical, or, at least, non-celebratory stance to arranged marriage, arguing that there is 'reluctant obedience, especially among the young Muslims' (Modood et al. 1994: 79) to the tradition, or even describing it as 'most troublesome [custom]' (Ghuman 1994: 71). On the other hand, recent long-term or small-scale ethnographic and feminist studies by Basit (1997), Gavron (1997) Shain (2003) provide evidence for Brah's (1996: 77) conceptualisation of arranged marriage as a 'joint undertaking between parents and young people'.

4   Talking Traditions of Marriage: Young British Asian Femininities

4.1   Negotiating hybrid positions – the girls' spontaneous talk

My own conversational data from the group of British Bangladeshi girls appear to con-firm Brah's stance, but also show the heterogeneity of the practices and positions within the group, and the complex negotiations that are necessary for the girls to achieve a consensus (Eckert 1993) on the topic of marriage. Unlike the cross-disciplinary research on the topic of arranged marriage, my aim in this chapter is to focus on the process of these negotiations and identity formations by linking my analysis of discourse to an exploration of lexical and syntactic features, the sequential organisation of the interac-tion, including pauses, non-verbal signs such as laughter and paralinguistic features like a change of voice.

The following narrative and subsequent discussion of a wedding proposal from the girls' spontaneous talk is divided into three sections. The first section focuses on the girls' accommodation strategies to the discourse of arranged marriage, the second on the girls' resistance against this discourse, and the third section on the evolution of what I define as a modified discourse of arranged marriage.

(a) Discourse of arranged marriage: accommodation. The story of the wedding proposal reveals a discourse which positions parental choice of children's future spouses as the appropriate form of marriage arrangement (staves 1–9).

Extract 1.1: The Wedding Proposal[1]

(1)   A: .hh >did I tell you something< er [thingie] my brother
       D: [what]

(2)   A: came from Bangladesh innit like   (.) a wedding proposal
       D: \huh

(3)   A: (-) f [or me] for me (.) and I was so: shocked they wrote
       D: (-) [WHA::T]

(4)   A: a letter to my s- my mum and dad right saying that .hh

(5)   A: *{drawling}* "she's really ni::ce she s- talks politely"

(6)   A: and everything *{swallows}* and I was shocked my brother

(7)   A: (>was like<) my sister was like reading it to me yeah and

(8)   A: she goes "<they want me to be their bride>" and everything

(9)   A: and I was like saying (.)   ["EXCUSE ME-"]
       D: wh[o are they]   related to you

(10) A: =they just live next door to m[y h]ouse in
       D: (.) cousins=   [ah]

(11) A: Bangladesh (.) and they just want **me** (.) as their

(12) A: son's bride
       H: oh [my God]
       V: [(Ardiana)] did you see the photo (.)

(13) A: *{swallows}* I've seen the guy when I went to
       V: (that-) *{swallowing}*

(14) A: Bangladesh [(he is alright)] looking he's alright
       ?D: [is he nice]
       ?   (xxx)

(15) A: looking   [but he's::-] the same height as me EXCUSE ME
       H: *{- laughs -}*
       ?V: *{amused}*[(yeah:::)]

This extract shows the group's familiarity with and acceptance of a discourse of arranged marriage which allocates a significant (matchmaking) role to the two families of the couple-to-be. Although two of her friends express their surprise in stave 3: 'WHAT' and stave 12: 'oh my God', this surprise is directed at Ardiana's (cleverly introduced) news of having received a wedding proposal, rather than at the procedures adopted by the two families. Thus, despite Ardiana's repeated claims that 'she was (so) shocked' (staves 3, 6) her friends display less shock than curiosity about the wedding proposal. They have no difficulties in understanding the reference of the third person personal pronoun 'they' (staves 3, 8, 9, 10, 11), showing no sign of surprise that the authors of the letter turn out to be the parents of the suitor, rather than the young man himself (staves 9–12). Similarly, they do not question the fact that the proposal is not addressed to the bride-to-be but instead to Ardiana's parents (stave 4). Dilshana's assumption that the family of the suitor is in fact related to Ardiana (staves 9–10) signals her knowledge of the cultural practice of consanguineous marriage (Basit 1997; Dwyer 2000; Gavron 1997; Phillipson et al. 2003). Both Varda and Dilshana express their curiosity about the physical appearance of the young man, asking Ardiana whether she has seen a photo of him and whether the boy is good looking (staves 12 and 14). The enquiries and reactions of Ardiana's friends show that their aim is to find out the particulars of the wedding proposal, but it does not suggests that the girls question the practice of arranged marriage itself. It seems that the girls do not expect to choose their future spouse on their own; instead they align themselves with a discourse where the role of active matchmaking is assumed by the families of the young couple.

(b)   Discourse of arranged marriage: resistance?   However, the above extract also appears to suggest that there may be some resistance to the discourse of arranged marriage in the group. Ardiana's claims of being shocked in extract 1.1 also serve to introduce her critical position towards this wedding proposal. In stave 9 she raises her volume to protest: 'EXCUSE ME' but is prevented from voicing her objections by Dilshana's question. Significantly, Ardiana's resistance to the wedding proposal does not appear to go hand in hand with a critical position towards the role of her own family in the match-making. Whereas she creates a distance between herself and the groom's parents by subverting their voice when reporting details of the wedding proposal in stave 5, she does not change the quality of her voice when she reports what her sister said in stave 8. The change of voice quality is one possible strategy for a speaker to mark a detachment from the voice that she is reproducing (Bakhtin 1986; Coates 1999; Maybin 2003).

However, after being temporarily prevented from displaying her resistance fully by her friends' eager questions about the proposal and the suitor, Ardiana vehemently airs her opposition to the proposed marriage when she switches into a discourse which appears to value love-marriages:

Extract 1.2: The Wedding Proposal - continued:

(15)   A: [but he's::-] the same height as me EXCUSE ME I LOVE
       H:
       ?V: [(yeah:::)]<*amused*>

(16)   A: MY BOYFRIEND here right I don't wanna get married to

(17)   A: somebody else I don't /**know**
       H: (-)   [((inn]it))] (.)
       R: (-) innit ma[n]
       ?V: (-) {--- *laughs* ---}

(18)   A: [but then
       H: *<amused>* he may be gorgeous but then again he mig[ht have a

(19)   A: again (a] ha-)
       H: (a)]   personality like a (.) **ape** or some thing=

Ardiana here introduces a discourse of romantic love, which constitutes the popular norm in a large majority of western communities. Initially, it seems as if the other girls were following Ardiana's lead and accepted her switch into a discourse of romantic love (stave 17 'innit man'; 'innit'). Following Ardiana's criticism of marrying a young man she does not know, Hennah provides the reasons for their reservations in staves 18–19: if a girl does not know her future husband before getting married, she runs the risk of ending up with a husband who may be good looking, but could have a flawed personality. Hennah's joke and the girls' agreement with Ardiana appear to signal the group's unanimous alignment with the tradition of love marriage, and consequently their rejection of arranged marriages. However, on a sequential, micro-linguistic level, the presence of a hesitation in the form of a pause after Ardiana's utterance signals that the group's acceptance of Ardiana's switch into a discourse of romantic love is not entirely smooth (see Conversation Analytic work, e.g. Pomerantz 1984, Levinson 1983: 334 on the significance of pauses as markers of dispreferred seconds). Moreover, the remainder of the conversation does not provide any further evidence of the group's unanimous resistance to the tradition of arranged marriage and instead highlights a much more complex process of positioning within the group.

(*c*)   *Modified discourse of arranged marriage.* Ardiana's protest is expressed in her utterance 'EXCUSE ME I LOVE MY BOYFRIEND here right I don't wanna get married to somebody else I don't **know**'. Whereas the first part of the utterance clearly voices a western notion of romantic love, the second can be interpreted as positioning Ardiana in a modified discourse of arranged marriage, emphasising solely her resistance to getting married to somebody she does not know.

I argue that the other girls align themselves only with the latter part of Ardiana's proposition. The third extract of the conversation provides evidence for this claim, showing that the girls do not object to the tradition of arranged marriage per se, but instead resist a particular version of it.

Extract 1.3: The Wedding Proposal - continued:

(20)   A: =YEAH:: [that's] true (.)
       D: [yeah]   (.) yeah when they come to England

(21)   A: they just wanna get
       H: [(they just]xxx-)
       D: yeah they just lea[ve you man]

(22)   A: married to girls from London [because like they are
       V: [yeah because of the

(23)   A: Londoni] (.) **yeah** [they are from London they are
       V: passport] (.)   [they want their passport
       D: (ah[::)*<agreeing>*

(24)   A: British] they are British and they wanna come to this
       V: inn]it

(25)   A: country as well
       V: (-) <swallows> they want the passports

(26)   A: so what's wrong with you Rahima
       ?V: (the British) passport
       ?   <dental click>   <laughter>

What the girls *do* challenge in this extract is the tradition of being married to men
from Bangladesh. The interactive manner in which they formulate this challenge is
highly collaborative, mirroring and building on each others' contributions in a way
that Coates (1996, 1999) found to be characteristic of the friendship talk of white
adult middle-class women. Thus, the girls use many thematic repetitions ('Londoni-
British') and lexical repetitions ('passport'), supportive minimal agreements such as
'yeah' and 'joint constructions involving simultaneous speech' (Coates 1996: 121)
as in staves 22 to 24. One explanation for their objection to men from Bangladesh is
based on the girls' view that Bangladeshi men are only interested in British citizenship and that they leave their wives once they have established themselves in Britain.
All the girls reject their role in this alleged pursuit: in staves 22–24 Ardiana and
Varda collaboratively and simultaneously express their condemnation of the men's
motivation to get married to girls from Britain because of their British passport.
They receive support from Dilshana, who voices her agreement with their claim in
stave 23.

It is hard to imagine that the girls' concern about their role as potential gateway to
British citizenship has not been affected by a widespread popular anti-immigration
discourse in the UK (see also Ahmad 2003: 48–49). However, this anti-immigration
discourse appears to overlap with a trend among many young British Asians and a substantial number of their parents to object to marriages of British girls being arranged
with suitors from the Indian subcontinent (Anwar 1998: 112; see also Gardner and
Shukur 1994; Ghuman 1994; Shain 2003: 90; but for conflicting evidence see Gavron
1997: 124). On the other hand, connections with Britain are still valued highly by
Bangladeshi families, as the term 'Londoni', which tends to be applied to people,
houses and entire villages that have connections to Britain (Gardner and Shukur 1994:
147) shows. In stave 23 it is used by Ardiana to signal her understanding of the value
attributed by many Bangladeshis to a potential link with Britain and therefore with girls
like themselves.

Moreover, when Hennah says that a Bengali groom might have 'a personality like
an ape' (extract 1.2, stave 19), the connotation of the word 'ape' suggests that Hennah
expects the men's behaviour to be ill-mannered or even uncivilised. By referring to
Bangladeshi men in these derogatory terms Hennah's utterance also reveals an influence of a discourse of imperial Darwinism, which allows the girls to establish their own
superiority. At the same time the girls reveal their anxiety about feeling alienated from
their future husbands' (Sylheti village) background, which they appear to contrast
negatively with their own (urban British Bangladeshi) background. This discourse of
cultural incompatibility between British Asian girls and grooms from the Indian subcontinent due to cultural and educational differences appears to have established itself

recently in many parts of the British Bangladeshi and other British Asian "communities" (Anwar 1998: 112; Basit 1997: 81–4; Gardner and Shukur 1994: 156; Phillipson et al. 2003: 51; but see also Gavron 1997 for counter arguments). However, I would argue that by engaging in this (essentialist) discourse and by orienting to their own "Londoni" or "British" identities, the girls in this group in fact acknowledge their own hybrid identities, which they position in opposition to the identities of their Bangladeshi suitors.

4.2   Torn between cultures? The interview data

In the girls' spontaneous group talk about Ardiana's wedding proposal, popular 'culture clash' discourses therefore at best serve to explain the girls' rejection of grooms from Bangladesh, and not the girls' relationship with their parents or their position to (a modified version of) the tradition of arranged marriage. However, my interview data present a different perspective. I had originally planned these ethnographic-style interviews with my ingroup informant, Hennah, as a means to collect additional information about individual girls, their friendship group, families and wider community. However, in the course of these "interview sessions", which took place a year after the recordings, I was also able to give Hennah feedback on my progressing analysis of the girls' talk, as for example on my interest in the girls' bicultural or hybrid identities. At times Hennah aligned herself with my interpretation by arguing that the girls did have agency in choosing their future husbands or by acknowledging her own ability to, as she said, 'do both', that is, to align herself with what she perceived to be 'English' as well as 'Muslim' and/ or 'Bangladeshi' discourses and practices. However, she also spoke about hardship in relation to coping with different sets of norms (Pichler 2008; 2009). The following example will show an instance in which she goes very far in distancing herself from a celebration of 'hybrid identities'.

Extract 2: Torn Between Two Cultures

1)   P: the thing is I I do not you know from from like looking

2)   P: at **this**   I do not think that it's: like true: .hhh ah:
     H: =yeah

3)   P: how a lot of like sociologists have said *<slightly dramatic>*

4)   P: "oh you know like .hh erm: .hh it's so: difficult and

5)   P: people: and and (.) you know like (.) girls .hh they are

6)   P: completely torn between the two cultures"[2] **[I]**   think
     H: [hhhh]

7)   P: that you are doing really /**well (.) you know** with the
     H: *<laughs>*

8)   P: two (-) I mean [don't you /think]
     H: *<laughs>*   [no nono]   nonono hh you know this

9)   P: yeah
     H: yeah   this i- we're (-) there's so much teasing there

10) P: =yeah yeah
     H: yeah   that it makes it look like but it isn't (.)

11) H: honest to God <*almost staccato*> it is **not like** cause if you

12) P: yeah   =yeah
     H: look at Dilshana Ardiana yeah   look at the mess

13) P: yeah
     H: they're in (-)   and look at Rahima .hhh if it was erm:

14) H: (-) if it was OK they wouldn't be torn now (-) do

15) P: yeah
     H: you get me because .hhh   %her parents are really

16) H: angry% they **know** that she's going out with someone .hh

17) P: [yeah]
     H: but she won't tell them .hh [who it] yeah is or who erm

18) H: when he's gonna come for her ((like)) for good and stuff like

19) H: that and they aks her <*authoritarian*> "**tell** him to come to you

20) H: for good cause (-) I don't like what people are saying to me"

21) P: (-) yeah [yeah]   yeah
     H: (-)   [d'you] get me   and erm: <*laughing*> Ardiana she's

22) P: ye[ah]   yeah
     H: in aboard   [and] Shashima she's already **married** d'you get me

In this extract Hennah objects to my assessment of the girls 'doing well' (stave 7) and my challenge of the 'torn between cultures' discourse (stave 6). Hennah points out that (at the time of this interview more than ever) several of her friends in the group, including Dilshana, are in a 'mess' (stave 12): Ardiana abroad (in Bangladesh amongst speculations that she would be "married off") and another friend, Shashima, already having been married (after her parents' discovery that she was dating), see staves 21–2. Interestingly, Hennah also indirectly challenges my interpretation of the relevance of teasing for the group (which I had told her about previously), positioning it as a strategy to cover up difficulties (staves 9–10), rather than as a strategy to resolve difficulties and synthesise different cultural discourses and norms, as I had suggested on the basis of the girls' spontaneous talk (Pichler 2006a, 2006b). Thus, in the extract above Hennah argues that some of the girls in the group are in fact torn 'between two cultures' (Watson 1977), rather than stressing their bicultural or hybrid identities, clearly positioning the different norms on dating and marriage as incompatible and adopting a rather essential-ist definition of culture.

My analysis of the interview data elsewhere (Pichler 2008) takes into consideration that interviews, just like conversations, are co-constructed events, in which subjects take on a range of frequently conflicting discourses and subject positions. It is also essential to acknowledge that Hennah's stances and positioning may or may not be representative of the entire group. Nevertheless, I felt that this extract also required me to ask whether Hennah's alignment with this discourse of 'being trapped between two cultures' reveals an experience of a "reality" of the girls' heterosexual relationships out-side the context of conversational interaction, which is more difficult to manage than what the spontaneous talk of the girls suggests. In connection with this I felt it was necessary to ask whether a focus on conversational micro-phenomena can wrongly pri-oritise an emphasis on the participants' agency. Critiques of extreme constructionist approaches to language and identity share their concern about a focus on conversa-tional micro-phenomena which may draw a distorted picture of participant agency. Bonnie McElhinny (2003: 26–7) highlights the relevance of this question for language and gender research:

> It is worth considering why post-structuralist models of gender have been so readily embraced by sociolinguists and linguistic anthropologists working on gender. Our very sub-ject matter – language – may lend itself to an ability to focus on gender and the social con-struction of "sex". People's ability to adapt language readily and rapidly from situation to situation, addressee to addressee, may accord people an unusual degree of agency and flex-ibility in their construction of themselves in a way that other forms of cultural and actual capital can and do not […].

In the light of the above quote the girls' difficulties in balancing cultural norms in relation to marriage and dating, which Hennah claims in the interview, could partly be explained by the fact that in the cultural field (Bourdieu 1991) of the girls' wider com-munity, gender norms about heterosexual relationships are considerably less flexible than the diverse and shifting discursive positions which I have identified in their spontaneous conversations.

5 Conclusion

The spontaneous talk about the wedding proposal shows that the girls draw on and negotiate a wide range of discourses and cultural practices in their heterogeneous group. On one hand, the topic of marriage is clearly positioned as very central to the adolescent femininities of Ardiana and her friends, whereas marriage was simply not a topic pursued in the other two non-Asian groups of adolescent girls I was working with at the time (see Pichler 2009). On the other hand, one of the girls briefly adopts a discourse of romantic love and all girls insist on 'knowing their partners'. The girls also voice their opposition to marrying men from Bangladesh, by drawing on anti-immigration discourses as well as on discourses of cultural incompatibility and imperial Darwinism. However, in the modi-fied discourse of arranged marriage, which is negotiated by the girls in the group, the wish to get married to men the girls "know" does not constitute an expectation or even a wish to marry their boyfriends. Although several girls in the group actually date, choosing a boyfriend without the knowledge of their parents is positioned as slightly more acceptable (albeit not to all the girls) in the group's talk than choosing a husband without the knowledge and help of their families. Rather than aligning themselves fully with a discourse of love marriage, it seems that the group's consensus is to favour grooms they consider compatible with their "British" or "Londoni" Bangladeshi identities, without challenging the discourse of arranged marriage per se.

I would argue that, in the girls' spontaneous conversations about marriage, ethnic boundaries and cultural differences are frequently constructed interactively and locally (Brah 1996: 163); they mostly remain implicit, as for example when Ardiana objects to her marriage proposal on the grounds of loving her boyfriend. These ethnic and cultural boundaries are constantly de-constructed, re-negotiated and/or synthesised by the girls in their talk, allowing them to engage in 'identity formations which cut across and intersect [...] frontiers' (Hall 1992: 310), that is, in the construction of hybrid identities.

The significance of an essentialised and stereotypical notion of ethnic culture is also acknowledged explicitly on some occasions by the girls in the group talk, as when they position themselves as British and Londoni in opposition to Bangladeshi suitors, and much more frequently so by Hennah in our interviews (Pichler 2008). As Bauman (1997: 209) argues, dominant and essentialist notions of culture(s), equated with discrete and homogeneous ethnic groups, remain relevant aspects in a critical examination of culture as a process, as they 'form [...] part of the discursive competence of citizens from 'ethnic minorities' themselves, and continue [...] to function as one element in the negotiation of difference'. Whereas in some instances Hennah aligns herself with my own celebration of flexible, hybrid cultural practices and identities, in others she relies on much more essentialist discourses of culture and difference. However, these discourses, I believe, can reveal cultural experiences and norms which are much less easily synthesised than the linguistic practices that can be identified in the group's conversational data.

As I argued above, one way to resolve what appears to be a discrepancy between my emphasis on cultural hybridity and Hennah's alignment with a discourse of culture clash is to acknowledge our different foci, my own, initially mostly on linguistic micro-phenomena, and Hennah's, on non-linguistic experiences. Another solution is to refrain both from a re-alignment with the dominant popular discourse of 'being torn between cultures' and from an academic over-romanticisation of hybridity (Puwar 2003).

The comparison of my two sources of data suggests that the translation and negotiation between cultural practices and identities which Hall (1992: 310) deems essential for the formation of hybrid identities is not necessarily free of contradictions and conflict (see also Ballard 1994: 31). There is some evidence for this already in the girls' spontaneous talk about marriage, as the group needs to engage in complex negotiations of individual stances and cultural practices to achieve a consensus in the form of what I defined as a modified discourse of arranged marriage. These complex discursive negotiations that the girls carry out locally in their friendship talk possibly reflect some of the issues and difficulties which, as Hennah indicates in her interview, the girls face in relation to cultural norms and practices surrounding dating and marriage outside their friendship group. At the same time, however, I would argue that their spontaneous talk offers the girls a platform to negotiate different traditions of marriage, and therefore not only reflects but also potentially affects discourses and cultural practices of marriage well beyond their adolescent friendship group.

Notes

1 Transcription conventions are given in Transcription Conventions 2, p. xii. Speakers are marked as follows:
    A   Ardiana
    D   Dilshana
    H   Hennah
    R   Rahima
    V   Varda
    P   Pia
    ?   identity of speaker not clear
2 Apologies for this generalisation based on Watson's 1977 work.

References

Ahmad, F. 2003. "Still in 'In Progress?'– Methodological dilemmas, tensions and contradictions in theorizing South Asian Muslim Women." In *South Asian Women in the Diaspora*. Ed. N. Puwar and P. Raghuram. Oxford: Berg, 43–66.

Alexander, C. 2000. *The Asian Gang*. Oxford: Berg.

Amos, V. and P. Parmar. 1981. "Resistances and responses: the experience of black girls in Britain." In *Feminism for Girls: An Adventure Story*. Ed. A. McRobbie and T. McCabe London: Routledge & Kegan Paul, 129–52.

Anwar, M. 1998. *Between Cultures: Continuity and Change in the Lives of Young Asians*. London: Routledge.

Archer, L. 2002a. "Change, culture and tradition: British Muslim pupils talk about Muslim girls' post-16 'choices'." *Race, Ethnicity and Education* 5.4: 59–376.

Archer, L. 2002b. "It's easier that you're a girls and that you're Asian': interactions of 'race' and gender between researchers and participants." *Feminist Review* 72: 108–132.

Bakhtin, M. 1986. *Speech Genres and other Late Essays*. Ed. C. Emerson and M. Holquist. Trans. Vern W. McGee. Austin: University of Texas Press.

Ballard, R. 1994. "Introduction: the emergence of Desh Paradesh." In *Desh Paradesh: The South Asian Presence in Britain*. Ed. R. Ballard. London: C. Hurst & Co., 1–34.

Basit, T. 1997. *Eastern Values, Western Milieu: Identities and Aspirations of Adolescent British Muslim Girls*. Aldershot: Ashgate.

Bauman, G. 1997. "Dominant and demotic discourses of culture: their relevance to multi-ethnic alliances." In *Debating Cultural Hybridity: Multi-cultural Identities and the Politics of Anti-Racism*. Ed. P. Werbner and T. Moodod. London: Zed Books, 209–25.

Bourdieu, P. 1991. *Language and Symbolic Power*. Cambridge: Polity Press.

Brah, A. 1996. *Cartographies of Diaspora*. London: Routledge.

Brah, A. and R. Minhas. 1985. "Structural racism or cultural difference? Schooling for Asian girls." In *Just a Bunch of Girls: Feminist Approaches to Schooling*. Ed. G. Weiner. Milton Keynes: Open University Press, 14–25.

Bucholtz, M. 1999. "'Why be normal?': Language and identity practices in a community of nerd girls." *Language in Society* 28: 203–23.

Coates, J. 1996. *Women Talk. Conversation between Women Friends*. Oxford: Blackwell.

Coates, J. 1999. "Changing femininities: the talk of teenage girls." In *Reinventing Identities. The Gendered Self in Discourse*. Ed. M. Bucholtz, A.C. Liang and L. A. Sutton. Oxford: Oxford University Press, 123–44.

Community Relations Commission. 1976. *Between Two Cultures*. CRC.

Cramb, A. 2002. "It was my fault says mother of arranged marriage girl, 16." *The Daily Telegraph* (25/04/2002).

Dwyer, C. 2000. "Negotiating diasporic identities: young British South Asian Muslim women." *Women's Studies International Forum* 23.4: 468–75.

Eckert, P. 1993. "Cooperative competition in adolescent 'girl talk'." In *Gender and Conversational Interaction*. Ed. Deborah Tannen. Oxford: Oxford University Press, 32–61.

Eckert, P. and S. McConnell-Ginet. 1995. "Constructing meaning, constructing selves: snapshots of language, gender and class from Belten High." In *Gender Articulated: Language and the Socially Constructed Self*. Ed. K. Hall and M. Bucholtz. New York: Routledge, 49–508.

Eder, D. 1993. "'Go get ya a french!': Romantic and sexual teasing among adolescent girls". In *Gender and Conversational Interaction*. Ed. D. Tannen. Oxford: Oxford University Press, 17–31.

Gardner, K. and A. Shukur. 1994. "'I'm Bengali, I'm Asian, and I'm living here': The changing identity of British Bengalis." In *Desh Paradesh: The South Asian Presence in Britain*. Ed. R. Ballard. London: C. Hurst & Co, 142–64.

Gavron, C. 1997. *Migrants to Citizens: Changing Orientations among Bangladeshis of Tower Hamlets, London*. Unpublished PhD thesis, University of London.

Ghuman, P. A. Singh. 1994. *Coping with Two Cultures. British Asian and Indo-Canadian Adolescents*. Clevedon: Multilingual Matters.

Ghuman, P. A. Singh. 2003. *Double Loyalties. South Asian Adolescents in the West*. Cardiff: University of Wales Press.

Goodwin, M.H. 1999. "Constructing opposition within girls' games". In *Reinventing Identities: The Gendered Self in Discourse*. Ed. M. Bucholtz, A. C. Liang and L. A. Sutton. Oxford: Oxford University Press, 388–409.

Hall, S. 1990. "Cultural identity and diaspora." In *Identity: Culture, Community, Difference*. Ed. J. Rutherford London: Lawrence & Wishart, 222–237.

Hall, S. 1992. "The question of cultural identity." In *Modernity and its Future*. Ed. S. Hall, D. Held and T. McGrew. Cambridge: Polity Press, 273–316.

Kelbie, P. 2006. "Mother appeals for safe return of daughter, 12, feared abducted by father for forced marriage." *The Independent* (30/08/2006).

Levinson, S. 1983. *Pragmatics*. Cambridge: Cambridge University Press.

Maybin, J. 2003. "Voices, intertextuality and introduction to schooling." In *Language, Literacy and Education: A Reader*. Ed. S. Goodman, T. Lillis, J. Maybin and N. Mercer. Stoke on Trent: Trentham Books in association with The Open University, 159–70.

McElhinny, B. 2003. "Theorizing Gender in Sociolinguistics and Anthropology". In *The Handbook of Language and Gender*. Ed. J. Holmes and M. Meyerhoff. Oxford: Blackwell, 21–42.

Mendoza-Denton, N. 1999. "Turn-initial no. Collaborative opposition among Latina adolescents." In *Reinventing Identities. The Gendered Self in Discourse*. Ed. M. Bucholtz, A. C. Liang and L. A. Sutton. Oxford: Oxford University Press, 273–92.

Modood, T., S. Beishon and S. Virdee. 1994. *Changing Ethnic Identities*. London: Policy Studies Institute.

Phillipson, C., Nilufar A. and J. Latimer. 2003. *Women in Transition*. Bristol: The Policy Press in association with University of Bristol.

Pichler, P. 2006a. "Multifunctional teasing as a resource for identity construction in the talk of British Bangladeshi girls." *Journal of Sociolinguistics* 10.2: 226–50.

Pichler, P. 2006b. "'This sex thing is such a big issue now': Sex talk and identities in three groups of adolescent girls." In *Sexual Identities and Desires across Cultures*. Ed. S. Kyratzis and H. Sauntson. Houndmills, Basingstoke: Palgrave Macmillan, 68–95.

Pichler, P. 2008. "Gender, ethnicity and religion in spontaneous talk and ethnographic-style interviews: balancing perspectives of researcher and researched." In *Gender and Language Research Methodologies*. Ed. K. Harrington, L. Litosseliti, H. Sauntson and J. Sunderland. Basingstoke: Palgrave Macmillan, 56–72.

Pichler, P. 2009. *Talking Young Femininities*. Houndmills, Basingstoke: Palgrave Macmillan.

Pomerantz, A. 1984. "Agreeing and disagreeing with assessments: some features of preferred/ dispreferred turn shapes." In *Structures of Social Interaction*. Ed. J. Heritage and J. M. Atkinson. Cambridge: Maison des Sciences de l'Homme and Cambridge University Press, 57–101.

Puwar, N. 2003. "Melodramatic postures and constructions." In *South Asian Women in the Diaspora*. Ed. N. Puwar and P. Raghuram. Oxford: Berg, 43–66.

Shain, F. 2003. *The Schooling and Identity of Asian Girls*. Stoke on Trent: Trentham Books.

Watson, J. 1977. *Between Two Cultures: Migrants and Minorities in Britain*. Oxford: Basil Blackwell.

19

Performing Gender Identity: Young Men's Talk and the Construction of Heterosexual Masculinity

Deborah Cameron

Source: Sally Johnson and Ulrike Meinhof (eds), *Language and Masculinity*. Oxford: Blackwell (1997), pp. 47–64. Reprinted with permission of Wiley-Blackwell.

Introduction

In 1990, a 21-year-old student in a language and gender class I was teaching at a college in the southern USA tape-recorded a sequence of casual conversation among five men; himself and four friends. This young man, whom I will call 'Danny',[1] had decided to investigate whether the informal talk of male friends would bear out generalizations about 'men's talk' that are often encountered in discussions of gender differences in conversational style – for example that it is competitive, hierarchically organized, centres on 'impersonal' topics and the exchange of information, and foregrounds speech genres such as joking, trading insults and sports statistics.

Danny reported that the stereotype of all-male interaction was borne out by the data he recorded. He gave his paper the title 'Wine, women, and sports'. Yet although I could agree that the data did contain the stereotypical features he reported, the more I looked at it, the more I saw other things in it too. Danny's analysis was not inaccurate, his conclusions were not unwarranted, but his description of the data was (in both senses) *partial*: it was shaped by expectations that caused some things to leap out of the record as 'significant', while other things went unremarked.

I am interested in the possibility that Danny's selective reading of his data was not just the understandable error of an inexperienced analyst. Analysis is never done without preconceptions, we can never be absolutely non-selective in our observations, and where the object of observation and analysis has to do with gender it is extraordinarily difficult to subdue certain expectations.

One might speculate, for example, on why the vignettes of 'typical' masculine and feminine behaviour presented in popular books like Deborah Tannen's *You Just Don't Understand* (1990) are so often apprehended as immediately *recognizable*.[2] Is it because we have actually witnessed these scenarios occurring in real life, or is it because we can so

Language and Gender: A Reader, Second Edition. Edited by Jennifer Coates and Pia Pichler.
© 2011 Blackwell Publishing Ltd except for editorial material and organization. © 2011 Jennifer Coates and Pia Pichler. Published 2011 by Blackwell Publishing Ltd.

readily supply the cultural script that makes them meaningful and 'typical'? One argument for the latter possibility is that if you *reverse* the genders in Tannen's anecdotes, it is still possible to supply a script which makes sense of the alleged gender difference. For example, Tannen remarks on men's reluctance to ask for directions while driving, and attributes it to men's greater concern for status (asking for help suggests helplessness). But if, as an experiment, you tell people it is women rather than men who are more reluctant to ask for directions, they will have no difficulty coming up with a different and equally plausible explanation – for instance that the reluctance reflects a typically feminine desire to avoid imposing on others, or perhaps a well-founded fear of stopping to talk to strangers.[3]

What this suggests is that the behaviour of men and women, whatever its substance may happen to be in any specific instance, is invariably read through a more general discourse on gender difference itself. That discourse is subsequently invoked to *explain* the pattern of gender differentiation in people's behaviour; whereas it might be more enlightening to say the discourse *constructs* the differentiation, makes it visible *as* differentiation.[4]

I want to propose that conversationalists themselves often do the same thing I have just suggested analysts do. Analysts construct stories about other people's behaviour, with a view to making it exemplify certain patterns of gender difference; conversationalists construct stories about themselves and others, with a view to performing certain kinds of gender identity.

Identity and Performativity

In 1990, the philosopher Judith Butler published an influential book called *Gender Trouble: Feminism and the Subversion of Identity*. Butler's essay is a postmodernist reconceptualization of gender, and it makes use of a concept familiar to linguists and discourse analysts from speech-act theory: *performativity*. For Butler, gender is *performative* – in her suggestive phrase, 'constituting the identity it is purported to be'. Just as J. L. Austin (1961) maintained that illocutions like 'I promise' do not describe a pre-existing state of affairs but actually bring one into being, so Butler claims that 'feminine' and 'masculine' are not what we are, nor traits we *have*, but effects we produce by way of particular things we *do*: 'Gender is the repeated stylization of the body, a set of repeated acts within a rigid regulatory frame which congeal over time to produce the appearance of substance, of a "natural" kind of being' (p. 33).

This extends the traditional feminist account whereby gender is socially constructed rather than 'natural', famously expressed in Simone de Beauvoir's dictum that 'one is not born, but rather becomes a woman'. Butler is saying that 'becoming a woman' (or a man) is not something you accomplish once and for all at an early stage of life. Gender has constantly to be reaffirmed and publicly displayed by repeatedly performing particular acts in accordance with the cultural norms (themselves historically and socially constructed, and consequently variable) which define 'masculinity' and 'femininity'.

This 'performative' model sheds an interesting light on the phenomenon of gendered *speech*. Speech too is a 'repeated stylization of the body'; the 'masculine' and 'feminine' styles of talking identified by researchers might be thought of as the 'congealed' result of repeated acts by social actors who are striving to constitute themselves as 'proper' men and women. Whereas sociolinguistics traditionally assumes that people talk the way they do because of who they (already) are, the postmodernist approach suggests that people are who they are because of (among other things) the way they talk. This shifts the focus away from a simple cataloguing of differences between men and women to a subtler and more complex inquiry into how people use linguistic resources to produce gender differentiation. It also obliges us to attend to the 'rigid regulatory frame' within which people must make their choices – the norms that define what kinds of language are possible, intelligible and appropriate resources for performing masculinity or femininity.

A further advantage of this approach is that it acknowledges the instability and variability of gender identities, and therefore of the behaviour in which those identities are performed. While Judith Butler rightly insists that gender is regulated and policed by rather rigid social norms, she does not reduce men and women to automata, programmed by their early socialization to repeat forever the appropriate gendered behaviour, but treats them as conscious agents who may – albeit often at some social cost – engage in acts of transgression, subversion and resistance. As active producers rather than passive reproducers of gendered behaviour, men and women may use their awareness of the gendered meanings that attach to particular ways of speaking and acting to produce a variety of effects. This is important, because few, if any, analysts of data on men's and women's speech would maintain that the differences are as clear-cut and invariant as one might gather from such oft-cited dichotomies as 'competitive/cooperative' and 'report talk/ rapport talk'. People *do* perform gender differently in different contexts, and do sometimes behave in ways we would normally associate with the 'other' gender. The conversation to which we now turn is a notable case in point.

The Conversation: Wine, Women, Sports ... and Other Men

The five men who took part in the conversation, and to whom I will give the pseudonyms Al, Bryan, Carl, Danny and Ed, were demographically a homogeneous group: white, middle-class American suburbanites aged 21, who attended the same university and belonged to the same social network on campus. This particular conversation occurred in the context of one of their commonest shared leisure activities: watching sports at home on television.[5]

Throughout the period covered by the tape-recording there is a basketball game on screen, and participants regularly make reference to what is going on in the game. Sometimes these references are just brief interpolated comments, which do not disrupt the flow of ongoing talk on some other topic; sometimes they lead to extended discussion. At all times, however, it is a legitimate conversational move to comment on the basketball game. The student who collected the data drew attention to the status of sport as a resource for talk available to North American men of all classes and racial/ethnic groups, to strangers as well as friends, suggesting that 'sports talk' is a typically 'masculine' conversational genre in the US, something all culturally competent males know how to do.

But 'sports talk' is by no means the only kind of talk being done. The men also recount the events of their day – what classes they had and how these went; they discuss mundane details of their domestic arrangements, such as who is going to pick up groceries; there is a debate about the merits of a certain kind of wine; there are a couple of longer narratives, notably one about an incident when two men sharing a room each invited a girlfriend back without their roommate's knowledge – and discovered this at the most embarrassing moment possible. Danny's title 'Wine, women, and sports' is accurate insofar as all these subjects are discussed at some length.

When one examines the data, however, it becomes clear there is one very significant omission in Danny's title. Apart from basketball, the single most prominent theme in the recorded conversation, as measured by the amount of time devoted to it, is 'gossip': discussion of several persons not present but known to the participants, with a strong focus on critically examining these individuals' appearance, dress, social behaviour and sexual mores. Like the conversationalists themselves, the individuals under discussion are all men. Unlike the conversationalists, however, the individuals under discussion are identified as 'gay'.

The topic of 'gays' is raised by Ed, only a few seconds into the tape-recorded conversation (6):[6]

ED: Mugsy Bogues (.) my name is Lloyd Gompers I am a homosexual (.) you know what the (.) I saw the new Remnant I should have grabbed you know the title? Like the head thing?

'Mugsy Bogues' (the name of a basketball player) is an acknowledgement of the previous turn, which concerned the on-screen game. Ed's next comment appears off-topic, but he immediately supplies a rationale for it, explaining that he 'saw the new Remnant' – *The Remnant* being a deliberately provocative right-wing campus newspaper whose main story that week had been an attack on the 'Gay Ball', a dance sponsored by the college's Gay Society.

The next few turns are devoted to establishing a shared view of the Gay Ball and of homosexuality generally. Three of the men, Al, Bryan and Ed, are actively involved in this exchange. A typical sequence is the following (14–16):

AL: gays=
ED: =gays w[hy? that's what it should read [gays why?
BRYAN: [gays]   [I know]

What is being established as 'shared' here is a view of gays as alien (that is, the group defines itself as heterosexual and puzzled by homosexuality: 'gays, why?'), and also to some extent comical. Danny comments at one point, 'it's hilarious', and Ed caps the sequence discussing the Gay Ball (23–5) with the witticism:

ED: the question is who wears the boutonnière and who wears the corsage, flip for it? or do they both just wear flowers coz they're fruits

It is at this point that Danny introduces the theme that will dominate the conversation for some time: gossip about individual men who are said to be gay. Referring to the only other man in his language and gender class, Danny begins (27):

DANNY: My boy Ronnie was uh speaking up on the male perspective today (.) way too much

The section following this contribution is structured around a series of references to other 'gay' individuals known to the participants as classmates. Bryan mentions 'the most effeminate guy I've ever met' (29) and 'that really gay guy in our Age of Revolution class' (34). Ed remarks that 'you have never seen more homos than we have in our class. Homos, dykes, homos, dykes, everybody is a homo or a dyke' (64). He then focuses on a 'fat, queer, goofy guy … [who's] as gay as night' [*sic*] (78–80), and on a 'blond hair, snide little queer weird shit' (98), who is further described as a 'butt pirate'. Some of these references, but not all, initiate an extended discussion of the individual concerned. The content of these discussions will bear closer examination.

'The antithesis of man'

One of the things I initially found most puzzling about the whole 'gays' sequence was that the group's criteria for categorizing people as gay appeared to have little to do with those people's known or suspected sexual preferences or practices. The terms 'butt pirate' and 'butt cutter' were used, but surprisingly seldom; it was unclear to me that the individuals referred to really were homosexual, and in the one case where I actually knew the subject of discussion, I seriously doubted it.

Most puzzling is an exchange between Bryan and Ed about the class where 'everybody is a homo or a dyke', in which they complain that 'four homos' are continually 'hitting on' (making sexual overtures to) one of the women, described as 'the ugliest-ass bitch in the history of the world' (82–9). One might have thought that a defining feature of a 'homo' would be his lack of interest in 'hitting on' women. Yet no one seems aware of any problem or contradiction in this exchange.

I think this is because the deviance indicated for this group by the term 'gay' is not so much *sexual* deviance as *gender* deviance. Being 'gay' means failing to measure up to the group's standards of masculinity or femininity. This is why it makes sense to call someone '*really* gay': unlike same- versus other-sex preference, conformity to gender norms can be a matter of degree. It is also why hitting on an 'ugly-ass bitch' can be classed as 'homosexual' behaviour – proper masculinity requires that the object of public sexual interest be not just female, but minimally attractive.

Applied by the group to men, 'gay' refers in particular to insufficiently masculine appearance, clothing and speech. To illustrate this I will reproduce a longer sequence of conversation about the 'really gay guy in our Age of Revolution class', which ends with Ed declaring: 'he's the antithesis of man'.

....

BRYAN: uh you know that really gay guy in our Age of Revolution class who sits in front
         of us? he wore shorts again, by the way, it's like 42 degrees out he wore shorts
         again [laughter] [Ed: That guy] it's like a speedo, he wears a speedo to class (.)
         he's got incredibly skinny legs [Ed: it's worse] you know=
ED: =you know
         like those shorts women volleyball players wear? it's like those (.) it's l[ike

....

BRYAN: [you know what's even more ridicu [lous? when
ED: [French cut spandex]

....

BRYAN: you wear those shorts and like a parka on …
(5 lines omitted)

....

BRYAN:	he's either got some condition that he's got to
	like have his legs exposed at all times or else he's
	got really good legs=
ED:	=he's probably he'[s like
CARL:	[he really likes

....

BRYAN:	=he
ED:	=he's like at home combing his leg hairs=
CARL:	his legs=

....

| BRYAN: | he doesn't have any leg hair though= [*yes* and oh |
| ED: | =he *real* [*ly* likes |

....

| ED: | his legs= |
| AL: | =very long very white and very skinny |

....

BRYAN:	those ridiculous Reeboks that are always (indeciph)
	and goofy white socks always striped= [tube socks
ED:	=that's [right

....

| ED: | he's the antithesis of man |

....

In order to demonstrate that certain individuals are 'the antithesis of man', the group engages in a kind of conversation that might well strike us as the antithesis of 'men's talk'. It is unlike the 'wine, women, and sports' stereotype of men's talk – indeed, rather closer to the stereotype of 'women's talk' – in various ways, some obvious, and some less so.

The obvious ways in which this sequence resembles conventional notions of 'women's talk' concern its purpose and subject-matter. This is talk about people, not things, and 'rapport talk' rather than 'report talk' – the main point is clearly not to exchange information. It is 'gossip', and serves one of the most common purposes of gossip, namely affirming the solidarity of an in-group by constructing absent others as an out-group, whose behaviour is minutely examined and found wanting.

The specific subjects on which the talk dwells are conventionally 'feminine' ones: clothing and bodily appearance. The men are caught up in a contradiction: their criticism of the 'gays' centres on their unmanly interest in displaying their bodies, and the inappropriate garments they choose for this purpose (bathing costumes worn to class, shorts worn in cold weather with parkas which render the effect ludicrous, clothing which resembles the outfits of 'women volleyball players'). The implication is that real men just pull on their jeans and leave it at that. But in order to pursue this line of criticism, the conversationalists themselves must show an acute awareness of such 'unmanly' concerns as styles and materials ('French cut spandex', 'tube socks'), what kind of clothes go together, and which men have 'good legs'. They are impelled, paradoxically, to talk about men's bodies as a way of demonstrating their own total lack of sexual interest in those bodies.

The less obvious ways in which this conversation departs from stereotypical notions of 'men's talk' concern its *formal* features. Analyses of men's and women's speech style are commonly organized around a series of global oppositions, e.g. men's talk is 'competitive', whereas women's is 'cooperative'; men talk to gain 'status', whereas women talk to forge 'intimacy' and 'connection'; men do 'report talk' and women 'rapport talk'. Analysts working with these oppositions typically identify certain formal or organizational features of talk as markers of 'competition' and 'cooperation' etc. The analyst then examines which kinds of features predominate in a set of conversational data, and how they are being used.

In the following discussion, I too will make use of the conventional oppositions as tools for describing data, but I will be trying to build up an argument that their use is problematic. The problem is not merely that the men in my data fail to fit their gender stereotype perfectly. More importantly, I think it is often the stereotype itself that underpins analytic judgements that a certain form is cooperative rather than competitive, or that people are seeking status rather than connection in their talk. As I observed about Deborah Tannen's vignettes, many instances of behaviour will support either interpretation, or both; we use the speaker's gender, and our beliefs about what sort of behaviour makes sense for members of that gender, to rule some interpretations in and others out.

Cooperation

Various scholars, notably Jennifer Coates (1989 [reprinted in Part IV of this volume]), have remarked on the 'cooperative' nature of informal talk among female friends, drawing attention to a number of linguistic features which are prominent in data on all-female groups. Some of these, like hedging and the use of epistemic modals, are signs of attention to others' face, aimed at minimizing conflict and securing agreement. Others, such as latching of turns, simultaneous speech where this is not interpreted by participants as a violation of turn-taking rights (cf. Edelsky, 1981), and the repetition or recycling of lexical items and phrases across turns, are signals that a conversation is a 'joint production': that participants are building on one another's contributions so that ideas are felt to be group property rather than the property of a single speaker.

On these criteria, the conversation here must be judged as highly cooperative. For example, in the extract reproduced above, a strikingly large number of turns (around half) begin with 'you know' and/or contain the marker 'like' ('you know like those shorts women volleyball players wear?'). The functions of these items (especially 'like') in younger Americans' English are complex and multiple,[7] and may include the cooperative, mitigating/face-protecting functions that Coates and Janet Holmes (1984) associate with hedging. Even where they are not clearly hedges, however, in this interaction they function in ways that relate to the building of group involvement and consensus. They often seem to mark information as 'given' within the group's discourse (that is, 'you know', 'like', 'X' presupposes that the addressee is indeed familiar with X); 'you know' has the kind of hearer-oriented affective function (taking others into account or inviting their agreement) which Holmes attributes to certain tag-questions; while 'like' in addition seems to function for these speakers as a marker of high involvement. It appears most frequently at moments when the interactants are, by other criteria such as intonation, pitch, loudness, speech rate, incidence of simultaneous speech, and of 'strong' or taboo language, noticeably excited, such as the following (82–9):

....

ED: he's I mean he's **like** a real artsy fartsy fag he's **like** (indeciph) he's so gay he's got this **like** really high voice and wire rim glasses and he sits next to the ugliest-ass bitch in the history of the world

....

ED: [and
BRYAN: [and they're all hitting on her too, **like** four

....

....

ED: [I know it's **like** four homos hitting on her
BRYAN: guys [hitting on her

....

It is also noticeable throughout the long extract reproduced earlier how much latching and simultaneous speech there is, as compared to other forms of turn transition involving either short or long pauses and gaps, or interruptions which silence the interruptee. Latching – turn transition without pause or overlap – is often taken as a mark of cooperation because in order to latch a turn so precisely onto the preceding turn, the speaker has to attend closely to others' contributions.

The last part of the reproduced extract, discussing the 'really gay' guy's legs, is an excellent example of jointly produced discourse, as the speakers cooperate to build a detailed picture of the legs and what is worn on them, a picture which overall could not be attributed to any single speaker. This sequence contains many instances of latching, repetition of one speaker's words by another speaker (Ed recycles Carl's whole turn, 'he really likes his legs', with added emphasis), and it also contains something that is relatively rare in the conversation as a whole, repeated tokens of hearer support like 'yes' and 'that's right'.[8]

There are, then, points of resemblance worth remarking on between these men's talk and similar talk among women as reported by previous studies. The question does arise, however, whether this male conversation has the other important hallmark of women's gossip, namely an egalitarian or non-hierarchical organization of the floor.

Competition

In purely quantitative terms, this conversation cannot be said to be egalitarian. The extracts reproduced so far are representative of the whole insofar as they show Ed and Bryan as the dominant speakers, while Al and Carl contribute fewer and shorter turns (Danny is variable; there are sequences where he contributes very little, but when he talks he often contributes turns as long as Ed's and Bryan's, and he also initiates topics). Evidence thus exists to support an argument that there is a hierarchy in this conversation, and there is competition, particularly between the two dominant speakers, Bryan and Ed (and to a lesser extent Ed and Danny). Let us pursue this by looking more closely at Ed's behaviour.

Ed introduces the topic of homosexuality, and initially attempts to keep 'ownership' of it. He cuts off Danny's first remark on the subject with a reference to *The Remnant*: 'what was the article? cause you know they bashed them they were like'. At this point Danny interrupts: it is clearly an interruption because in this context the preferred interpretation of 'like' is quotative (see note 7) – Ed is about to repeat what the gay-bashing article in *The Remnant* said. In addition to interrupting so that Ed falls silent, Danny contradicts Ed, saying 'they didn't actually (.) cut into them big'. A little later on during the discussion of the Gay Ball, Ed makes use of a common competitive strategy, the joke or witty remark which 'caps' other contributions (the 'flowers and fruits' joke at 23–5, quoted above). This, however, elicits no laughter, no matching jokes and indeed no take-up of any kind. It is followed by a pause and a change of direction if not of subject, as Danny begins the gossip that will dominate talk for several minutes.

This immediately elicits a matching contribution from Bryan. As he and Danny talk, Ed makes two unsuccessful attempts to regain the floor. One, where he utters the prefatory remark 'I'm gonna be very honest' (20), is simply ignored. His second strategy is to ask (about the person Bryan and Danny are discussing) 'what's this guy's last name?' (30). First Bryan asks him to repeat the question, then Danny replies 'I don't know what the hell it is' (32).

A similar pattern is seen in the long extract reproduced above, where Ed makes two attempts to interrupt Bryan's first turn ('That guy' and 'it's worse'), neither of which succeeds. He gets the floor eventually by using the 'you know, like' strategy. And from that point, Ed does orient more to the norms of joint production; he overlaps others to produce simultaneous speech but does not interrupt; he produces more latched turns, recyclings and support tokens.

So far I have been arguing that even if the speakers, or some of them, compete, they are basically engaged in a collaborative and solidary enterprise (reinforcing the bonds within the group by denigrating people outside it), an activity in which all speakers participate, even if some are more active than others. Therefore I have drawn attention to the presence of 'cooperative' features, and have argued that more extreme forms of hierarchical and competitive behaviour are not rewarded by the group. I could, indeed, have argued that by the end, Ed and Bryan are not so much 'competing' – after all, their contributions are not antagonistic to one another but tend to reinforce one another – as engaging in a version of the 'joint production of discourse'.

Yet the data might also support a different analysis in which Ed and Bryan are simply *using* the collaborative enterprise of putting down gay men as an occasion to engage in verbal duelling where points are scored – against fellow group members rather than against the absent gay men – by dominating the floor and coming up with more and more extravagant put-downs. In this alternative analysis, Ed does not so much modify his behaviour as 'lose' his duel with Bryan. 'Joint production' or 'verbal duelling' – how do we decide?

Deconstructing oppositions

One response to the problem of competing interpretations raised above might be that the opposition I have been working with – 'competitive' versus 'cooperative' behaviour – is inherently problematic, particularly if one is taken to exclude the other. Conversation can and usually does contain both cooperative and competitive elements: one could argue (along with Grice, 1975) that talk must by definition involve a certain minimum of cooperation, and also that there will usually be some degree of competition among speakers, if not for the floor itself then for the attention or the approval of others (see also Hewitt, 1997).

The global competitive/cooperative opposition also encourages the lumping together under one heading or the other of things that could in principle be distinguished. 'Cooperation' might refer to agreement on the aims of talk, respect for other speakers' rights or support for their contributions; but there is not always perfect co-occurrence among these aspects, and the presence of any one of them need not rule out a 'competitive' element. Participants in a conversation or other speech event may compete with each other and at the same time be pursuing a shared project or common agenda (as in ritual insult sessions); they may be in severe disagreement but punctiliously observant of one another's speaking rights (as in a formal debate, say); they may be overtly supportive, and at the same time covertly hoping to score points for their supportiveness.

This last point is strangely overlooked in some discussions of women's talk. Women who pay solicitous attention to one another's face are often said to be seeking connection or good social relations *rather than* status; yet one could surely argue that attending to others' face and attending to one's own are not mutually exclusive here.

The 'egalitarian' norms of female friendship groups are, like all norms, to some degree coercive: the rewards and punishments precisely concern one's status within the group (among women, however, this status is called 'popularity' rather than 'dominance'). A woman may gain status by displaying the correct degree of concern for others, and lose status by displaying too little concern for others and too much for herself. Arguably, it is gender-stereotyping that causes us to miss or minimize the status-seeking element in women friends' talk, and the connection-making dimension of men's.

How to do Gender with Language

I hope it will be clear by now that my intention in analysing male gossip is not to suggest that the young men involved have adopted a 'feminine' conversational style. On the contrary, the main theoretical point I want to make concerns the folly of making any such claim. To characterize the conversation I have been considering as 'feminine' on the basis that it bears a significant resemblance to conversations among women friends would be to miss the most important point about it, that it is not only *about* masculinity, it is a sustained performance *of* masculinity. What is important in gendering talk is the 'performative gender work' the talk is doing; its role in constituting people as gendered subjects.

To put matters in these terms is not to deny that there may be an empirically observable association between a certain genre or style of speech and speakers of a particular gender. In practice this is undeniable. But we do need to ask: in virtue of what does the association hold? Can we give an account that will not be vitiated by cases where it does *not* hold? For it seems to me that conversations like the one I have analysed leave, say, Deborah Tannen's contention that men do not do 'women's talk', because they simply *do not know how*, looking lame and unconvincing. If men rarely engage in a certain kind of talk, an explanation is called for; but if they do engage in it even very occasionally, an explanation in terms of pure ignorance will not do.

I suggest the following explanation. Men and women do not live on different planets, but are members of cultures in which a large amount of discourse about gender is constantly circulating. They do not only learn, and then mechanically reproduce, ways of speaking 'appropriate' to their own sex; they learn a much broader set of gendered meanings that attach in rather complex ways to different ways of speaking, and they produce their own behaviour in the light of those meanings.

This behaviour will vary. Even the individual who is most unambiguously committed to traditional notions of gender has a range of possible gender identities to draw on. Performing masculinity or femininity 'appropriately' cannot mean giving exactly the same performance regardless of the circumstances. It may involve different strategies in mixed and single-sex company, in private and in public settings, in the various social positions (parent, lover, professional, friend) that someone might regularly occupy in the course of everyday life.

Since gender is a relational term, and the minimal requirement for 'being a man' is 'not being a woman', we may find that in many circumstances, men are under pressure to constitute themselves as masculine linguistically by avoiding forms of talk whose primary association is with women/femininity. But this is not invariant, which begs the question: under what circumstances does the contrast with women lose its salience as a constraint on men's behaviour? When can men do so-called 'feminine' talk without threatening their constitution as men? Are there cases when it might actually be to their advantage to do this?

When and Why do Men Gossip?

Many researchers have reported that both sexes engage in gossip, since its social functions (like affirming group solidarity and serving as an unofficial conduit for information) are of universal relevance, but its cultural meaning (for us) is undeniably 'feminine'. Therefore we might expect to find most men avoiding it, or disguising it as something else, especially in mixed settings where they are concerned to mark their difference from women (see Johnson and Finlay, 1997). In the conversation discussed above, however, there are no women for the men to differentiate themselves from; whereas *there is* the perceived danger that so often accompanies Western male homosociality: homosexuality. Under these circumstances perhaps it becomes acceptable to transgress one gender norm ('men don't gossip, gossip is for girls') in order to affirm what in this context is a more important norm ('men in all-male groups must unambiguously display their heterosexual orientation').

In these speakers' understanding of gender, gay men, like women, provide a contrast group against whom masculinity can be defined. This principle of contrast seems to set limits on the permissibility of gossip for these young men. Although they discuss other men besides the 'gays' – professional basketball players – they could not be said to gossip about them. They talk about the players' skills and their records, not their appearance, personal lives or sexual activities. Since the men admire the basketball players, identifying *with* them rather than *against* them, such talk would border dangerously on what for them is obviously taboo: desire for other men.

Ironically, it seems likely that the despised gay men are the *only* men about whom these male friends can legitimately talk among themselves in such intimate terms without compromising the heterosexual masculinity they are so anxious to display – though in a different context, say with their girlfriends, they might be able to discuss the basketball players differently. The presence of a woman, especially a heterosexual partner, displaces the dread spectre of homosexuality, and makes other kinds of talk possible; though by the same token her presence might make certain kinds of talk that take place among men *im*possible. What counts as acceptable talk for men is a complex matter in which all kinds of contextual variables play a part.

In this context – a private conversation among male friends – it could be argued that to gossip, either about your sexual exploits with women or about the repulsiveness of gay men (these speakers do both), is not just one way, but the most appropriate way to display heterosexual masculinity. In another context (in public, or with a larger and less close-knit group of men), the same objective might well be pursued through explicitly agonistic strategies, such as yelling abuse at women or gays in the street, or exchanging sexist and homophobic jokes. *Both* strategies could be said to do performative gender work: in terms of what they do for the speakers involved, one is not more 'masculine' than the other, they simply belong to different settings in which heterosexual masculinity may (or must) be put on display.

Conclusion

I hope that my discussion of the conversation I have analysed makes the point that it is unhelpful for linguists to continue to use models of gendered speech which imply that masculinity and femininity are monolithic constructs, automatically giving rise to predictable (and utterly different) patterns of verbal interaction. At the same time, I hope it might make us think twice about the sort of analysis that implicitly seeks the meaning (and sometimes the *value*) of an interaction among men or women primarily in the style, rather than the substance, of what is said. For although, as I noted earlier in relation to Judith Butler's work, it is possible for men and women to performatively subvert or resist the prevailing codes of gender, there can surely be no convincing argument that this is what Danny and his friends are doing. Their conversation is animated by entirely traditional anxieties about being seen at all times as red-blooded heterosexual males: not women and not queers. Their skill as performers does not alter the fact that what they perform is the same old gendered script.

Notes

1 Because the student concerned is one of the speakers in the conversation I analyse, and the nature of the conversation makes it desirable to conceal participants' identities (indeed, this was one of the conditions on which the data were collected and subsequently passed on to me), I will not give his real name here, but I want to acknowledge his generosity in making his recording and transcript available to me, and to thank him for a number of insights I gained by discussing the data with him as well as by reading his paper. I am also grateful to the other young men who participated. All their names, and the names of other people they mention, have been changed, and all pseudonyms used are (I hope) entirely fictitious.

2 I base this assessment of reader response on my own research with readers of Tannen's book (see Cameron, 1995, ch. 5), on non-scholarly reviews of the book, and on reader studies of popular self-help generally (e.g. Lichterman, 1992; Simonds, 1992).

3 I am indebted to Penelope Eckert for describing this 'thought experiment', which she has used in her own teaching (though the specific details of the example are not an exact rendition of Eckert's observations).

4 The German linguist Karsta Frank (1992) has provocatively argued that so-called gender differences in speech-style arise *exclusively* in reception: women and men are heard differently, as opposed to speaking differently. I do not entirely accept Frank's very strong position on this point, but I do think she has drawn attention to a phenomenon of some importance.

5 I mention that this was 'at home' because in the United States it is also common for men, individually or in groups, to watch televised sports in public places such as bars and even laundromats; but this particular conversation would probably not have happened in a public setting with others present. It appears to be a recurrent feature of male friends' talk that the men are engaged in some other activity as well as talking. The Swedish researcher Kerstin Nordenstam, who has an impressive corpus comprising data from twelve different single-sex friendship groups, has found that the men are far less likely than the women to treat conversation as the exclusive or primary purpose of a social gathering. Many of the women's groups recorded for Nordenstam were 'sewing circles' – a traditional kind of informal social organization for women in Sweden – but they frequently did not sew, and defined their aim simply as 'having fun'; whereas the men's groups might meet under no particular rubric, but they still tended to organize their talk around an activity such as playing cards or games. (Thanks to Kerstin Nordenstam for this information.)

6 Numbers in parenthesis refer to the lines in the original transcript. Transcription conventions are given in Transcription Conventions 2, p. xii.

7 For example, *like* has a 'quotative' function among younger US speakers, as in 'and she's like [= she said], stop bugging me, and I'm like, what do you mean stop bugging you?'. This and other uses of the item have become popularly stereotyped as markers of membership in the so-called 'slacker' generation.

8 It is a rather consistent research finding that men use such minimal responses significantly less often than women, and in this respect the present data conform to expectations – there are very few minimal responses of any kind. I would argue, however, that active listenership, involvement

and support are not *absent* in the talk of this group; they are marked by other means such as high levels of latching/simultaneous speech, lexical recycling and the use of *like*.

References

Austin, J. L. (1961) *How to Do Things with Words*. Oxford: Clarendon Press.

Butler, Judith (1990) *Gender Trouble: Feminism and the Subversion of Identity*. New York: Routledge.

Cameron, Deborah (1995) *Verbal Hygiene*. London: Routledge.

Coates, Jennifer (1989) 'Gossip revisited', pp. 94–121 in J. Coates and D. Cameron (eds) *Women in Their Speech Communities*. London: Longman.

Edelsky, Carole (1981) 'Who's got the floor?' *Language in Society*, 10, 3, 383–422.

Frank, Karsta (1992) *Sprachgewalt*. Tubingen: Max Niemeyer Verlag.

Grice, H. P. (1975) 'Logic and conversation', pp. 41–58 in P. Cole and J. Morgan (eds) *Syntax and Semantics*, vol. 3: *Speech Acts*. New York: Academic Press.

Hewitt, Roger (1997) '"Box-out" and "taxing"', pp. 27–46 in Sally Johnson and Ulrike Hanna Meinhof (eds) *Language and Masculinity*. Oxford: Blackwell.

Holmes, Janet (1984) 'Hedging your bets and sitting on the fence: some evidence for hedges as support structures'. *Te Reo*, 27, 47–62.

Johnson, Sally and Finlay, Frank (1997) 'Do men gossip? An analysis of football talk on television', pp. 130–43 in Sally Johnson and Ulrike Hanna Meinhof (eds) *Language and Masculinity*. Oxford: Blackwell.

Lichterman, Paul (1992) 'Self-help reading as a thin culture'. *Media, Culture and Society*, 14, 421–47.

Simonds, Wendy (1992) *Women and Self-Help Culture: Reading between the Lines*. New Brunswick, NJ: Rutgers University Press.

Tannen, Deborah (1990) *You Just Don't Understand: Women and Men in Conversation*. New York: Ballantine Books.

20

Pushing at the Boundaries: The Expression of Alternative Masculinities

Jennifer Coates

Source: Janet Cotterill and Anne Ife (eds), *Language Across Boundaries*. London: BAAL/Continuum (2001), pp. 1–24. Reprinted with kind permission of Continuum International Publishing Group.

1 Introduction

This paper focuses on language and masculinity, on the constraints exerted by the discourses of hegemonic masculinity, and on the ways in which male speakers construct alternative and competing masculinities through talk. I shall begin by looking at an example. Example (1) is a story told by Rob during conversation with friends in the pub. It is one of a series of stories about the workplace – this one focuses on a colleague who had an alcohol problem.[1]

(1) **The Fight**
[*Context: 3 men in their 20s in a pub talk about an engineer at work who was an alcoholic*]
he came in this one time,
drunk,
and he started ordering me about.
With kind of personality I've got
5 I told him to piss off,
I wasn't taking any of it.
So I was making these um alarm bell boxes,
the alarm boxes,
you put this bell on and you wire these-
10 can't remember how to do it now anyway but-
wiring these up,
and he come out,
and he sss, sss, sss, <MIMICS NOISE>
what he did was he threw this knife at me,
15 this is honest truth,
threw a knife at me,

and then- and there was this cable,
you know um like on the workbenches where you connect the cables into these three
        points,
a bare wire,
20   he fucking chased me with it,
and I thought "Fuck this",
and he kept like having a go and teasing me,
and I just smashed him straight round the face with a bell box in front of the boss,
crack,
25   got away with it as well,
I said "Look", I said, "he's thrown knives at me",
it sounds like something out of a film but it's honest truth.
[...]
Honestly it was unbelievable.

'The fight' is a typical first person male narrative (see Coates 2000a). It is typical in that it contains the following features: the narrator presents himself as a lone protagonist who gets involved in conflict, conflict which involves physical violence; all the characters in the narrative are male; the setting is the workplace; the narrator goes into detail about technical things such as alarm boxes and cables; the language used includes taboo words (e.g. *piss off, fucking*) and sound effects (e.g. *sss, crack*); a key theme is that he 'got away with it' (line 24).

Rob's story focuses on action and, through his story, he presents himself as a winner, someone who will not be pushed around, someone who stands up for himself, and also as someone who gets away with things. His story foregrounds the workplace as a key arena for action, and the storyworld he creates is populated entirely by men: women do not exist in this world. The story, 'The fight', is a performance of masculinity; moreover, it is a performance of **hegemonic masculinity**. By this, I mean that Rob uses his account of his fight with the drunken engineer to align himself with dominant norms of masculinity, norms which are exemplified by the main characters in popular films such as *Rambo* and *The Terminator*.

2   Hegemonic Masculinity

The concept of hegemonic masculinity was developed by Robert Connell and his colleagues working in feminist sociology. According to Connell (1995), in order to carry off 'being a man' in everyday life, men have to engage with hegemonic masculinity. Hegemonic masculinity maintains, legitimates and naturalises the interests of powerful men while subordinating the interests of others, notably the interests of women and gay men. Kiesling (1998: 71) puts it like this: 'hegemonic masculinity [is an] ideology based on a hierarchy of dominant alignment roles, especially men over women, but also men over other men'.

But it is important to remember that the concept of hegemonic masculinity relies on the recognition of multiple masculinities. At any point in time there will be a range of masculinities extant in a culture. Moreover, masculinity cannot be understood on its own: the concept is essentially relational. In other words, masculinity is only meaningful when it is understood in relation to femininity and to the totality of gender relations (Connell 1995: 68; Kimmel 1987: 12; Roper and Tosh 1991: 2). This means that hegemonic masculinity is 'the masculinity that occupies the hegemonic position in a given pattern of gender relations' (Connell 1995: 76).

If we accept that hegemonic masculinity is not fixed but is always contestable, then the masculinity occupying the hegemonic position is always open to challenge from alternative masculinities. What I want to explore in this paper is the way that men express alternative masculinities through pushing at the boundaries of currently accepted hegemonic masculinity. I shall look in detail at some examples from my corpus to show the ways in which male speakers subvert dominant discourses of masculinity and construct, or attempt to construct, alternative masculinities.

3 My Data

I shall draw on a corpus of naturally occurring all-male conversation, focusing particularly on the narratives told by male speakers to each other in the course of friendly talk. The corpus consists of 30 conversations, which were audio-recorded with the agreement of the participants.[2] They involve a wide range of speakers in terms of both age and class, ranging from public schoolboys in the home counties to carpenters in Somerset and retired working class men in the Midlands. Altogether the thirty conversations contain a total of one hundred and eighty-five stories (though this statistic inevitably begs the question: What counts as a story?, a question I won't attempt to answer here – see Coates 2000b).

I have chosen to focus on conversational narrative since narrative has a crucial role to play in our construction of our identities, in our construction of the 'self' (Kerby 1991; Linde 1993). Just as we use narrative modes of thinking to make sense of what we call our 'life', so we present ourselves to others by means of narratives, shaping and selecting events to create particular versions of the self. And given that the self is gendered, then one of the most important things being accomplished in narrative is the construction and maintenance of gender.

Many stories in the conversations I've collected are like example (1) – in other words, they construct a masculinity where achievement and success are central ingredients. The corpus contains examples of adolescent speakers competing to tell ever more extreme stories about getting drunk; young men (in their 20s) telling stories which exaggerate feats of aggression and getting the better of authority figures; older men with a more working class background telling stories about run-ins with the police; and older men with a more middle-class background vying with each other to appear well-travelled or up-to-date in terms of technology and science, or as connoisseurs of good wine.

4 The Struggle to Express Vulnerability

But analysis of the whole range of conversations I've collected suggests that the picture is complex: many of the stories in these conversations reproduce the dominant values of masculinity – emotional restraint, ambition, achievement, and competitiveness, but these values inevitably jostle for position with other, competing, values. We are all involved, whether we like it or not, in the ceaseless struggle to define gender (Weedon 1987: 98), and it is not the case that the men whose conversations I have listened to adopt the dominant discourses of masculinity at all times and without protest. Some of the stories reveal men struggling to reconcile competing discourses of masculinity.

The next story – example (2a) – is a good example of this: in many respects this story performs conventional masculinity, but alternative discourses are voiced, and the discussion which follows the story shows the men struggling with these competing discourses. The story comes from a conversation involving four men, all carpenters, aged between 25 and 40, having a drink in a pub after work. Alan says he has been digging out 'the grange' over the weekend, and he goes on to tell the following story.

(2a) The Digger

```
 1   should of seen Jason on that digger though
 2   yeah he- he come down the ((park)) part
 3   where it's- the slope
 4   then he's knocking down the front wall
 5   and there was this big rock
 6   and he couldn't get it out
 7   so he put a bit more . power on the thing
 8   and . and the thing- the digger went <<SCOOPING NOISE>>
 9   it nearly had him out <LAUGHS>
10   he come out all white.
```

This story constructs a dominant version of masculinity, where masculinity is bound up with physical strength. It tells of a man knocking down a wall, and using a huge and powerful machine to achieve this. The point of the story, though, is that when Jason tries to employ more power to dig out the recalcitrant rock, he almost loses control of the machine. This brief story has three key themes, and these mutually reinforce a dominant and conventional John Wayne image of masculinity: there is the lone man battling with nature represented by the big rock; the story shows that men's work can be dangerous; and the story also testifies to the awesome power of machines.

The last line of the story, however, positions the audience slightly differently: Alan ends the story with the line *he come out all white*. 'To go white' is recognised as being a physical manifestation of fear, so Alan here portrays Jason not as a hero but as someone who nearly lost control of a powerful machine and who is frightened by the experience. Note that in lines 2–7 Jason is the subject of active verbs, but in lines 8 and 9, the climax of the story, the machine becomes the subject, with Jason becoming the object. This twist in the power relations between the man and the machine results in Jason *com[ing] out all white* in line 10.

In the next extract (2b), two of Alan's co-participants (Kevin and John) orient to the narrator's evaluation of the story, but the third (Chris) resists. The talk following Alan's story is transcribed in stave format to allow the interplay of voices to be clearly seen (transcription conventions are given on page xii).

(2b) The Digger

```
--------------------------------------------------------------------------------
 8  ALAN:    it nearly had him out/ <LAUGHS> he come out all white/
    CHRIS:                          <LAUGHS>
    KEVIN:                                    <LAUGHS>
    JOHN:
--------------------------------------------------------------------------------
 9  ALAN:
    CHRIS:   <LAUGHS>
    KEVIN:              I bet that could be dangerous |couldn't it/
    JOHN:                                            (((|hurt himself/))
--------------------------------------------------------------------------------
```

```
10  ALAN:
    CHRIS:
    KEVIN:  if it fell |on your head))                it's quite–
    JOHN:           |he-        you know/ -
```

```
11  ALAN:
    CHRIS:                        <LAUGHS>        | can I have some
    KEVIN:  |it's quite big/
    JOHN:   |he crapped himself/           he     |crapped himself/
```

```
12  ALAN:
    CHRIS:  pot noodles please Kevin <SILLY VOICE>
    KEVIN:                      <LAUGHS> |no/
    JOHN:                               |did he have to sit down
```

```
13  ALAN:               he- he- well . he was quite frightened
    CHRIS:
    KEVIN:
    JOHN:   and stuff? .
```

```
14  ALAN:   |actually/                               |well yeah/
    CHRIS:                        was it for you as well |mate?
    KEVIN:
    JOHN:   |I know/I must admit-
```

```
15  ALAN:                                ((well
    CHRIS:  did you go a bit white as well then did you?
    KEVIN:
    JOHN:
```

```
16  ALAN:   I still-))
    CHRIS:
    KEVIN:
    JOHN:          god/ he was thinking "god please don't
```

```
17  ALAN:
    CHRIS:         don't get any blood on it/ <SARCASTIC>
    KEVIN:                              is that the one
    JOHN:   wreck it"/
```

```
18  KEVIN:  with all the loa- lots of different things on it?
```

[*Discussion continues about different types and sizes of diggers*]

Kevin and John both orient to Alan's move to bring Jason's fear into focus in stave 8: Kevin comments on the danger of such machines, while John surmises that Jason could have got hurt, and that he *crapped himself*, another physical manifestation of fear. Kevin's comments are met by taunting from Chris – at least, that is how I interpret Chris's remark *can I have some pot noodles please Kevin*. Chris uses a silly voice to say this and since at face value the remark is totally irrelevant, we have to use conversational inferencing to interpret it. Superficially this utterance is a polite request for food: it is the sort of thing you might expect somebody relatively powerless – a child, for example – to say to someone more powerful – a mother or a dinner lady. By saying this, is Chris implying that Kevin's utterances *I bet that could be dangerous couldn't it if it fell on your head, it's quite – it's quite big* would be more appropriate in the mouth of a caregiver, that is, in the mouth of a woman? Certainly, Chris seems to be trying to humiliate Kevin, to position him as being cowardly, a wimp, of being un-masculine. Perhaps by producing an utterance as irrelevant as this, he is implying that Kevin's utterances are equally out of place. Chris clearly finds Kevin's view of Jason's near-accident threatening. However, Kevin does not seem to be intimidated: he laughs and says *No* to Chris, meaning 'No you can't have any pot noodles', which defuses the challenge by treating it humorously.

John continues to explore the theme of Jason and fear with his question to Alan: *did he have to sit down and stuff?* This leads to Alan, who was an eye witness, admitting: *he-he-well . he was quite frightened actually.* Note the hesitations and false starts in this response, as well as the presence of several hedges: Alan is clearly uncomfortable with his answer. Predictably, given his taunting of Kevin, Chris now has a go at Alan with the direct challenge *was it for you as well mate?*, that is, 'was it frightening?'. Alan replies, "*Well yeah*", with his *well* again signalling that this is a dispreferred response. Chris's subsequent question *did you go a bit white as well then did you?* ends with an aggressive tag. It is aggressive in that it demands an answer from Alan, and at the same time the repetition of *did you?* has overtones of motherese (*does he want his dindins, does he?*) which rudely suggests that Alan is behaving like a baby. Chris's question is highly face-threatening. His use of the phrase *go a bit white*, which picks up Alan's earlier utterance, mocks the euphemistic aspect of it and implies that to 'go white' is un-manly. This question challenges Alan to align himself with Jason and, by extension, with un-manliness. Alan begins a reluctant response: *well I still-* before he is rescued by John's intervention: *god/ he was thinking "god please don't wreck it".* John in effect answers for Alan with the claim that if Alan had gone white it was because he was worried about the machine. This utterance shifts the ground of the discussion by suggesting that the men's anxiety is to do with damaging the machine rather than with their own vulnerability. This interpretation of events is obviously more palatable to Chris, who here stands for hegemonic masculinity, but he still adds the sarcastic comment *don't get any blood on it* as if determined to wrong-foot Alan. But Kevin and John then steer the conversation into a discussion of exactly what kind of digger it was and how it compares to a fork-lift truck, an impersonal discussion involving lots of detail which re-establishes the solidarity of the group and their alignment with dominant norms of masculinity.

The tension and conflict in this short extract demonstrate how difficult it is for male speakers to discuss vulnerability, and how peer group pressure works to silence those who try to voice alternative masculinities. Alan, Kevin and John attempt to explore their feelings about the danger of large machines and their fear of losing control. In so doing, they push at conventional gender boundaries, but violations of gender boundaries will always be resisted, and will be met with sanctions ranging from ridicule, as here, to violence (Davidoff and Hall 1987: 29).

[…]

5   Self-Disclosure

Talk about vulnerability is particularly difficult because of men's avoidance of self-disclosure. However, there are men in the conversations I've collected who risk personal self-disclosure, who talk about times when they have been vulnerable and who therefore make themselves vulnerable to their friends. This happens only rarely (7% of the stories in the corpus discuss personal problems or involve self-disclosure of more than a trivial kind).

The avoidance of self-disclosure is all the more striking given that the majority of the stories in my corpus are first-person narratives, that is, the narrator and the chief protagonist are one-and the same person. First person narratives in all-female talk very often involve self-disclosure, because the narrative will tell of an event that occurred in the speaker's life, usually very recently, which had some kind of emotional impact (Coates 1996; Johnstone 1993; Langellier and Peterson 1992). Men's first-person narratives, by contrast, focus more on achievement and triumph, or on the more banal happenings of everyday life, and are not designed to reveal feelings or to lead into talk where feelings can be compared and discussed (Baumann 1986; Johnstone 1993; Labov 1972). The only stories I could really label as self-disclosing came in conversations involving older rather than younger men, well-educated middle-aged men who seem more comfortable with reflecting on themselves (though they still choose impersonal topics more often than personal ones).

The story in (3b) is an example of a story involving self disclosure. It comes from a conversation between four middle-aged middle-class men in the pub after work; they are having a general discussion about peaks and troughs in social history. Example (3a) gives a brief chunk of the preceding conversation to contextualise the story:

(3a) Progress or Decay

BRIAN: we keep having this idea that things are going to get better/ which was an earlier part of the conversation/

TONY: yes/

BRIAN: it's parallelled by this- I think what tends to happen/ you- you ((just)) have peaks and troughs/ you know the thing goes- there's a wave/ it does- it doesn't suddenly turn into an exponential growth pattern/

PETE: right/

BRIAN: you know it goes up and it comes down again/ |you know and I think-

PETE: but |do you think- do you think- but do you think that there's a- within the p- peaks and troughs/ do you think there's a- there's a upward or a downward trend?

At this point Brian gives an example from his own life (note how it is Pete's question that allows Brian this opportunity):

(3b) Suicidal [*words in italics are contributions from other speakers*]

→   well at the moment ((I mean)) this is partly personal

2   cos I mean I- my own life sort of has been (*ah*) up and down

3   and I've . you know sort of- . if you'd t- if you'd had this conversation with me about a term ago

4   I mean I was just about as down as you could get

5   because I'm er- really was quite seriously suicidal

6   and . it HAS come up again

7   you know my life HAS improved/ (*mhm/ mhm/*)

8   ((xx)) it hasn't actually got any better

9   but my attitude to it and psychologically I'm a lot straighter and clearer about what's going on

10   so it has picked up
11   and it was just literally a case of hanging on in there
12   I mean about . towards . about the middle of last term
13   I quite seriously- . I went out and I bought a big bottle of pills
14   they were codeine and aspirin mix
15   and a bottle of whisky
16   and I went and sat on Twickenham Green
17   and I was going to kill myself [*mhm*]
18   I was going to eat the pills and drink the whisky
19   er well <u>it was only a little bottle of whisky</u> <GREATER SPEED>
20   err sitting there y'know TOTALLY just about as depressed as you could possibly get
21   and then I just thought "you stupid sod"
22   so I threw away the pills
23   drank the whisky
24   and went home
25   [*everyone laughs*]
26   but you know that was the turning point
27   I started <u>coming up again</u> <LAUGHING QUALITY TO VOICE>
28   [Pete: *good*; Tony: *good*]

This rare example of a man talking about a difficult moment in his life is introduced with some tentativeness. First, he warns his fellow conversationalists that he is about to talk about something *partly personal* (the hedge *partly* here is semantically nonsense, but functions to soften the force of his utterance and protect his addressees' face). Secondly, he ties his story in very carefully to the theme of *peaks and troughs* which has been established in the preceding conversation: the phrase was used first by Brian himself, then repeated by Pete. Brian paraphrases this with *it goes up and it comes down again*, and he uses these words again in the second line of his story: *cos I mean I- my own life sort of has been up and down*. This careful tying in of his story to the more general conversational theme reveals his anxiety about telling the story, anxiety which is expressed in the many hedges which appear in lines 1–5 (3 tokens of *I mean*, 2 tokens of *sort of*, and 1 each of *you know* and *really*). This density of hedging is unusual in men's talk (but is typical of all-female conversation where sensitive topics are under discussion, see Coates 1996). After this he seems to settle down to tell his story, perhaps reassured that his fellow conversationalists have not raised any objections.

However, the reactions of the other men – laughing with Brian at line 25, then saying "Good" after Brian's coda – express both relief and embarrassment. This interpretation is borne out by a later conversation involving just Pete and Tony who arrive at the pub the following week ahead of their friends, and who mull over Brian's self-disclosing behaviour the previous week. Example (4) gives an extract from this conversation:

(4)   <u>Englishness</u>
TONY: I don't know Brian THAT well/ but every time I've met him/ he's been pretty .
          free with whatever happened to be on his mind at the time/
PETE: I don't know many people like that/ . you know who are able to sort of [*no*] just
          tap into . their- I don't know their situations their problems/ I know I take a long
          time to sort of er . warm to people I think=
TONY: =you . might wonder really how he . overcame the- the education that the rest of
          us obviously |succumbed to/ <LAUGHS>
PETE: |<LAUGHS> yeah/ %yeah%/ (1.0) I think I must be quite a
          typical Englishman in that sense/ being quite sort of er-

TONY: I k- I'm less English than I was/ <LAUGHS>

PETE: is that because you've been ab- abroad?

TONY: no/ |((xx))

PETE: er |how did you- how did you manage to- to become less English?

TONY: I think it's because I decided that- . that (1.0) I ((really)) didn't like this way of relating to people very much/ and that . life actually would be . improved by . people being more open with each other/ . not that I'm . brilliant at it/ <QUIET LAUGH>

PETE: makes you vulnerable though don't you think? . um don't- don't you feel vulnerable? . sometimes?

TONY: yeah but . I suppose that . that's a useful reminder really isn't it/ ((I mean)) . vulnerability is er- (1.0) all the- all the- the- the masks and so on are supposed to keep vulnerability at bay/ but . .hh they only do this at a very high cost/

PETE: yeah/ I suppose that's another kind of pain isn't it/

TONY: yeah/

PETE: you know putting up barriers/ distancing yourself/ and maybe- . maybe more damage is done that way than actually=

TONY: =it's not impossible/

This is an extraordinary stretch of talk. I have found nothing comparable anywhere else in the conversations in the corpus. Pete and Tony not only address a topic that demands reflexivity, something men normally avoid; they stick to the topic and explore the issues that arise from it in a way that is relatively common in women's friends' talk but is extremely rare in all-male talk. It is probably significant that there are only two speakers present: this conversation arises when two friends meet in the expectation that other friends will join them. When three or more males meet, it seems that peer group pressures make talk of this kind difficult, but where there are just two males, then a kind of intimacy is possible that is precluded otherwise.[3] For all speakers, self-disclosure seems, not surprisingly, to be more a feature of two-party talk than of multi-party talk; but this tendency is far more apparent in all-male than in all-female talk.

Pete and Tony make some fascinating observations on men's talk (though note that they gloss male inexpressivity as 'Englishness' and seem to overlook the gendered nature of the masks they are forced to wear). Tony argues for greater openness, which Pete responds to with a series of three questions: *makes you vulnerable though don't you think? don't- don't you feel vulnerable? sometimes?* Pete obviously feels vulnerable just talking like this, but wants to question Tony's assertion that it is better to be more open. Tony accepts that being open can make you vulnerable, but pursues his line of thinking by asserting that vulnerability is not necessarily bad but may be a useful reminder of our humanity. While feeling vulnerable can be uncomfortable, wearing masks all the time is a much worse option. Tony here voices an alternative discourse which challenges hegemonic masculinity and asserts the value of emotional honesty and openness.

6   Men and Masks

The metaphor of the mask which he voices is a powerful one, and seems to express the experience of many men. Andrew Tolson (1977: 10), for example, describes conventional male interaction as follows: 'we would fall into the conventional "matiness" of the pub, a mutual back-slapping, designed to repress as much as it expresses. It was impossible to talk to other men about personal feelings of weakness or jealousy. A masculine "mask of silence" concealed the emptiness of our emotional lives'. The phrase 'to mask up' is an expression coined by male prisoners to describe 'the conscious adoption each day of a defensive emotional wall that provides a barrier between the man's real feelings and the outward facade he presents to the inmate group' (Looser, personal communication, 1999). This 'mask' takes the form of an extreme kind of tough masculinity where the concealment of all traces of vulnerability is viewed as an essential part of men's self-presentation. Much earlier this century, a very different kind of male, a member of the privileged Bloomsbury group in England, Leonard Woolf, wrote about the mask he felt forced to adopt as follows: 'I suspect that the male carapace is usually grown to conceal cowardice. ... It was the fear of ridicule or disapproval that prompted one to invent that kind of second-hand version of oneself which might provide for one's original self the safety of a permanent alibi' (Woolf quoted in Segal 1990: 108). It is this 'kind of second-hand version' of self which Tony challenges in his bid for fuller, more honest interpersonal interaction.

7 Conclusion

In this paper I have tried to show that hegemonic discourses of masculinity are open to challenge from other competing discourses. In their talk with each other, men align themselves with dominant ideologies, but resistant discourses are also expressed. The examples I have looked at show men constructing themselves as achievement-oriented, competitive, and unemotional; but also exploring more feminine sides of themselves. [...] Most men in most conversations avoided self-disclosure, but a few men took the risk of engaging in a more self-reflexive discourse.

Does men's self-presentation change when conversation involves women as well as men? I have a corpus of eighteen mixed conversations involving speakers of all ages. In many of these, male speakers seem to see the presence of women as an excuse for an exaggerated performance of hegemonic masculinity, boasting of heroic achievements in fields as disparate as sport and wine buying. But in a sub-set of the mixed conversations, involving heterosexual couples, male speakers collaborate with female speakers to perform linguistic duets. These duets involve complex collaborative talk and are typically about less macho topics such as looking after kittens or being frightened by bats on holiday in Italy. In analysing these, I was initially persuaded that here at last male speakers were removing their masks. But after further analysis, I realised that in these duets it was the female partner who expressed the more emotional parts of the story. And crucially, I also realised that when a man constructs a duet with a female partner he is not pushing at the boundaries of masculinity: on the contrary, he is performing an extremely powerful version of hegemonic masculinity through displaying his heterosexuality to others present.

What I have tried to do in this paper is to explore masculinity as it is actually constructed by men. Discourses of masculinity evolve through a constant dynamic process of negotiation between speakers. The speakers whose talk has been examined in this paper can be seen to reproduce the dominant discourses of masculinity, yet at the same time speakers are not passive victims of such discourses, but can use friendly conversation as an arena in which the boundaries of conventional masculinities can be challenged and in which alternative masculinities can be explored. The importance of these alternative discourses cannot be under-estimated: as a male student said in one of my classes, heroism may have high status, but having to present yourself to others always as a hero is a burden. As Tony in example (4) put it, keeping vulnerability at bay has a very high cost.

Notes

This is a revised and abridged version of a paper originally given at the BAAL conference of autumn 2000. I would like to thank those who commented on the original paper and also those who gave me feedback on the original written version (especially Linda Thomas). I would also like to acknowledge the support of the following grant-giving bodies who made this research into men's narratives possible: the British Academy (small grant) and the Arts and Humanities Research Board (Research Leave). I would also like to thank the English Department of Roehampton University for giving me a semester's study leave.

1   Transcripts of narratives are presented in numbered lines, each line corresponding to one of the narrator's breath-groups or intonation units, typically a grammatical phrase or clause (Chafe 1980).
2   I am enormously grateful to all the men and boys who agreed to allow their conversations to be used in this project. (All names have been changed.) Some of the recordings were made initially by other researchers, including students taking my Conversational Narrative course at Roehampton University. I would like to put on record my gratitude to the following for giving me access to these recordings: Alex Bean, Keith Brown, Noni Geleit, Jacqueline Huett, Emma Ogden-Hooper, Janis Pringle, Andrew Rosta, Karl Stuart, Mark Wildsmith, John Wilson.
3   The difference between two and three participants in friendly conversation seems to be highly salient for male speakers. A male friend of mine told me that he has two good friends who he goes running with, and that when he runs with either of them on their own, conversation is personal and engaging, but when all three of them run together, conversation is impersonal and stilted.

References

Bauman, Richard (1986) *Story, Performance, and Event*. Cambridge: Cambridge University Press.

Chafe, Wallace (1980) 'The deployment of consciousness in the production of narrative', pp. 9–50 in W. Chafe (ed.) *The Pear Stories: Cognitive, Cultural and Linguistic Aspects of Narrative Production*. Norwood, NJ: Ablex.

Coates, Jennifer (1996) *Women Talk: Conversation Between Women Friends*. Oxford: Blackwell.

Coates, Jennifer (2000a) "So I thought 'Bollocks to it'": Men, stories and masculinities', pp. 11–38 in Janet Holmes (ed.) *Gendered Speech in Social Context*. Wellington, NZ: Victoria University Press.

Coates, Jennifer (2000b) 'What do we mean by "a story"?', *Roehampton Working Papers in Linguistics*, 2, 1–43.

Connell, R. W. (1995) *Masculinities*. Cambridge: Polity Press.

Davidoff, Leonova and Hall, Catherine (1987) *Family Fortunes: Men and Women of the English Middle Classes 1780–1850*. London: Hutchinson.

Johnstone, Barbara (1993) 'Community and contest: Midwestern men and women creating their worlds in conversational storytelling', pp. 62–80 in Deborah Tannen (ed.) *Gender and Conversational Interaction*. Oxford: Oxford University Press.

Kerby, Anthony (1991) *Narrative and the Self*. Bloomington: Indiana University Press.

Kiesling, Scott F. (1998) 'Men's identities and sociolinguistic variation: the case of fraternity men', *Journal of Sociolinguistics*, 2(1), 69–99.

Kimmell, Michael S. (1987) 'Rethinking "masculinity"', pp. 9–24 in M. S. Kimmell (ed.) *Changing Men: New Directions in Research on Men and Masculinity*. London: Sage.

Labov, William (1972) *Language in the Inner City*. Philadelphia: University of Pennsylvania Press.

Langellier, Kristin and Peterson, Eric (1992) 'Spinstorying: an analysis of women storytelling', pp. 157–80 in E. Fine and J. H. Speer (eds) *Performance, Culture and Identity*. London: Praeger.

Linde, Charlotte (1993) *Life Stories: The Creation of Coherence*. New York: Oxford University Press.

Roper, Michael and Tosh, John (1991) 'Introduction', pp. 1–19 in M. Roper and J. Tosh (eds) *Manful Assertions: Masculinities in Britain since 1800*. London: Routledge.

Segal, Lynn (1990) *Slow Motion: Changing Masculinities, Changing Men*. London: Virago.

Tolson, Andrew (1977) *The Limits of Masculinity*. Tavistock Publications.

Weedon, Christine (1987) *Feminist Practice and Poststructuralist Theory*. Oxford: Blackwell.

21

Playing the Straight Man: Displaying and Maintaining Male Heterosexuality in Discourse

Scott F. Kiesling

Source: Kathryn Campbell-Kibler, Robert Podevsa, Sarah J. Roberts, and Andrew Wong (eds), *Language and Sexuality: Contesting Meaning in Theory and Practice*. CSLI Publications (2002), pp. 2–10. Reprinted with permission of CSLI Publications.

[...]

In this paper I will be concerned with the discourse of heterosexuality: how a group of men define, police, and display heterosexual relationships within their same-sex group, and how these practices also help to create and display relationships among the men – relationships of homosocial desire and dominance.

The heterosexual identities I explore are not just displays of difference from women and gay men. They are also, more centrally, displays of power and dominance over women, gay men, and other straight men. A discourse of heterosexuality involves not only difference from women and gay men, but also the dominance of these groups. In fact, we will see that, through the use of address terms, men display *same-sex* dominance by metaphorically referring to other men as 'feminine', thus drawing on the cultural model of the heterosexual couple to index a homosocial inequality.

'Greek' Society and Compulsory Heterosexuality

The men's discursive indexing of their heterosexuality is embedded in a community of practice that is organized around heterosexuality and sexual difference. Thus, not only the practices within speech activities, but2also the organization, purposes, and rituals of speech events and activities in this community help to create a heterosexual and homosocial community.[1] This heterosexual organization begins with a separation of genders: The 'greek' letter society system is arranged through an ideology of sexual difference, such that fraternities are all-male, sororities all-female.

The system also polices heterosexuality through its organization and naming of social speech events and activities. The most obvious example of this is a 'mixer' speech event, at which one fraternity and one sorority hold a joint party, and 'mix' with one another. This terminology also reinforces an ideology of difference: Men and women are metaphorically different ingredients that must be mixed.

'Open' parties, while not being so overtly focused on heterosexual desire, nevertheless are similar in their focus on sex and alcohol. This focus is seen most in how the men evaluate parties, as Flyer does in the following excerpt. He is speaking during a meeting held to discuss fraternity problems. In this context, he compares his fraternity's parties to another's:

Excerpt 1[2]

```
 1  FLYER:  I-I-I went-
 2          I even went to a party the other night to investigate
 3          just to see who was gone
 4          not that I really wanted to go there
 5          I didn't have a great time
 6          I tried to get the fuck outta there but my ride dumped me.
 7          I went to- what the fuck-
 8          I went to see what happened.
 9          it was fuckin packed.
10          it was wall to wall chicks.
11          chicks hookin' up with guys everywhere
12          they're havin such a great time
13          they decided to fuck on the floor or whatever (??)
14  ??:     (who?)
15  FLYER:  this was Sig Ep OK.
16          and this- what this-
17          I- I thought *Jesus Christ.*
18          this was our parties.
19          good music,
20          they had a couple of trash cans of beer
21          and a couple bottles of liquor.
```

In this excerpt, Flyer is in fact implying that Gamma Chi Phi's parties have become too focused on drinking and homosocial activity, by suggesting another fraternity's party was better primarily because *it was wall to wall chicks* (*chicks* is the term the men most often use for women, especially young women to whom they are sexually attracted). Moreover, these women are *hookin' up* with the men, and are having such a great time, claims Flyer, that they *decided to fuck on the floor.* Thus it is because of this heterosexual activity that the party is rated highly – notice that Flyer goes out of his way to suggest that the drinks were not special (line 20: *they had a couple trash cans of beer*). This high evaluation of heterosexual activity creates a social context in which heterosexual sex is glorified as an end in itself, thus creating an ideology of heterosexual desire as an important social goal.

Some heterosexually organized speech activities constitute these larger speech events, and have been named by the men and women. Flyer's phrase *hook up* is an example. [...]

The men thus have a range of named heterosexual speech events, activities, and sexual relationships. Other social displays, such as the display of posters of nude or nearly-nude women in their apartments and dorm rooms, are similarly heterosexually-focused. In sum, the institutions of greek society, the speech events that make up this society, and the speech activities within those events are constructed principally around the display of sexual difference and heterosexual desire. They reflect the cultural models for men and women as different and unequal: men as dominant and hunting for sex, women as submissive and existing as sexual prey for the men.

The Heterosexuality of Homosociability in the Fraternity

Now let us turn to how the men talk in these interactions, and how this talk serves to create and reinforce the heterosexual model. The men use several different strategies to police and construct sexuality. However, most involve the taking or assigning of specific stances either to themselves or to others, including women and subordinated men. specifically, one revolves around the telling of stories, both performed in meetings and told in more private conversations. Another type is speech in which men take on roles of women and homosexual men – or have these roles forced upon them. A man is 'assigned' the role of a woman or gay man when he is in a subordinate position.

Cultural models of sex in interaction: Public valorization of 'man as hunter for sex'

Many of the stories the men tell present women and men in sexual relationships. These stories comprise a recognized, ratified genre in which men display sexual relationships. This 'genrification' of such narratives is an important component for policing/reinforcing hegemonic heterosexuality, because it means that one kind of sexual relationship is valorized in narrative performances.

This genre is a linguistic object, and its importance in the verbal repertoires of the men is a way of valorizing this kind of heterosexuality. There is status (and solidarity) to be gained from telling a story of this sort, or in being a character of one of these stories. In investigating how identities are created and how social values are transmitted, we need to look at the deployment of genres in the community, which includes the content of these genres. [...]

'Fuck stories' in gavel

Gavel is a story round at the end of Sunday meetings in which men often tell of their sexual exploits over the weekend. These are explicitly named by the men as 'fuck stories.' They can be particularly graphic, and portray women as sexual objects for the men, including for men who are voyeurs. The gavel stories were one of the highlights of the week for the men; they were performances for the entertainment of the members, usually told at the expense of the performer or one of the other members. (Fuck stories are not the only kind of narrative; another common type is the 'drunk story,' in which one member tells about the usually embarrassing actions of another member while very intoxicated; drunk stories and gavel stories are often the same.)

During most of my research I was not permitted to tape-record gavel. This fact shows how important this story round is for the social cohesion of the group – it is a form of ritual gossip which may never leave the group. They are a powerful way of creating a cultural model and placing value on it.

Conversational narrative and alternate sexual identities

While fuck stories are perhaps the most overt and obvious genre in which a certain heterosexual norm is reproduced, the men do not see this as the only kind of relationship with women, although it is the most 'public' representation their relationships with women. Let's have a look at one of the members who displays this public/private dichotomy. First, consider a portion of Hotdog's report to Mack of his trip to Atlanta, in which he creates a stance with respect to women similar to that in gavel stories. This excerpt is from the beginning of the narrative, on the day Hotdog arrived in Atlanta.

Excerpt 3

1	HOTDOG:	Then we went to a Ma:ll
2		and just like sat in the food court
3		and just looked at all the *beautiful* fuckin' hot ass *chicks*
4	MACK:	(are they) really dude.
5	HOTDOG:	Oh my *go:d*
6	MACK:	Where was it?
7	HOTDOG:	In Atlanta
8	MACK:	I know but what school?
9	HOTDOG:	Ahh Georgia Tech.
10	MACK:	I'm movin to Atlanta dude
11	ANDY:	We're movin there
12	HOTDOG:	We weren't like at the school
13		We were like
14		We were like in like the business district
15	MACK:	Oh
16	HOTDOG:	So it was just like all business ladies dressed up
17		and they're like (.) *in*credible.
18		then that night we registered
19		that's that *first* night is when we went to Lulu's,
20	MACK:	Let's move to Atlanta when we graduate [dude.
21	HOTDOG:	[I want to. I *de*finitely
		want to. Definitely.
22	ANDY:	I told you I wanna move down there.
23		I'm movin down there as soon as I graduate.

In this excerpt, Hotdog evaluates a shopping mall in Atlanta by describing the physical appearance of the women he sees there. We can see the impact of this evaluation and the importance of the appearance of women through the reaction of the men: Just this description of the women prompts them to talk about moving there when they graduate. This response constructs Hotdog's evaluation, then, as the highest compliment for the city.

Contrast this positioning with the one Hotdog presents in the interview situation, with only myself present. The following excerpt begins after I have asked Hotdog about his plans for the future, specifically marriage.

Excerpt 4

1	HOT:	I don't ever intend to be close to getting married any time soon.
2	SK:	You think you'll get married eventually?
3	HOT:	Yeah.(0.8)Probably (1.0) °let's see today's ninety three°
4		I probably could see myself getting married by like
5		nineteen ninety seven nineteen ninety eight.(1.4)
6		So about (.) four years.
7	SK:	Wow. Do you- I mean- do want to or is that just a matter of-
8	HOT:	No I-
9		it's not that I want to I have I have had a girlfriend sinc:e
10		°I guess we were°

11		I was in high school we've been datin' on and off.
12		Kinda got a little more serious *once* we went away believe
		it or not.
13		and uh (.) yknow if things stay the same way with her,
14		I could see us getting married like: ninety seven ninety eight
15		but if: we-
16		if things don't stay the same
17		I can't see u- me gettin married
18		until after the year two thousand (laughing).
19		|So.|
20	SK:	|Laugh| (1.7) So you guys are pretty close then.
21	Hot:	Yeah. We're very close.

Because Hotdog evaluates all the women he sees in the Atlanta mall as sexual objects, we would get an impression that his status on the heterosexual marketplace is unattached: For most of the men, the definition of having a 'girlfriend' is monogamy with that person. Thus, if Hotdog publicly shows a face of sexual veracity, it would be logical to think that he does not have a girlfriend. However, he *does* have a girlfriend, one with whom he is 'very close,' and one whom he is considering marrying in the near future. So Hotdog represents his sexuality quite differently in two different situations with different audiences and purposes: he performs two different kinds of identity in each of these situations.

In fact, it seems that he is a little unsure of exactly how to perform his identity with me in the interview. My status is not one he is familiar with: I am similar to a member, but not quite a member. At the beginning of this excerpt, Hotdog seems to want to present the same kind of identity as he did in the Atlanta recount. He denies quite strongly an interest in getting married: *I don't ever intend to be close to getting married any time soon.* But after I rephrase the question, he reveals that marriage may only be four years off. It takes several moves on my part before Hotdog tells me about his girlfriend, even though he later says 'we're very close' (line 19).

Hotdog's relationship with me has shifted over these turns, so has his identity. He begins with a stance similar to the one he takes publicly in the fraternity, and eventually admits to having a close, loving relationship with a woman. We thus see how the linguistic construction of sexuality for these men is based not just on the actual relationships they have with women but also on the relationships they are creating with other men. This allows the men to 'have' in fact more than one (hetero)sexual identity.

Metaphorical representations of other members as women

Morford (1987) and Hall and O'Donovan (1996) show that an address term indexes not simply such things as power and solidarity, but specific cultural models which are part of speakers' knowledge, and which interact with context to create local relationships between speakers. To the extent that speakers share these cultural models and scripts, the address terms are interactionally successful. Address terms in the fraternity work in this way as well, on several levels of linguistic and cultural awareness. All of the address terms I consider position a man as subordinate through the use of a female address term.

In the first case, the address term occurs within a culturally recognized phrase, thus indexing a certain heterosexual cultural model. It occurs while the men are playing monopoly, in which players pass through other players' property and pay rent. I will particularly focus on line 26, but I reproduce here some relevant context as well.

Excerpt 5

```
 9   ((Pete rolls, moves))
10   DAVE:   Nice, pay me. (2.3)
11   PETE:   I can't. Aren't you in jail or something?
12           Don't I not have to pay you this time?
13                   |Free pass.|
14   BOSS:   You  |got a    | free pass.
15           He's got one more.
16   DAVE:   No that's your last one.
17   PETE:   I have one more.
             I've got one left.
18   DAVE:   No that's it
19   PETE:   I have one left. I've only used two.
20   DAVE:   That's right And these over here. OK.
21   PETE:   The deal was for fi:ve.
22   DAVE:   God damn I needed that money too you son of a *bitch*.
23   ((Dave rolls))
24           The deal was for TWO.
25   (4.3)
26   PETE:   HI: HI: hi: honey I'm home.
27   BOSS:   I'm gonna blow by Dave right here.
28   ((Boss rolls))
```

The phrase 'Hi Hi honey I'm home' in line 26 does a large amount of contextually-dependent identity work for Pete. First, we need to understand the game situation: Pete has landed on a property owned by Dave, which would usually mean that Pete has to pay rent to Dave. However, because of an earlier deal in which Dave gave Pete a number of 'free passes,' Pete is allowed to 'stay' at Dave's property without paying rent. Pete draws on this metaphor and extends it. The metaphor taunts Dave and puts him down, in part by metaphorically vandalizing Dave's property, but also through the phrase 'Hi Hi honey I'm home.'

Without the correct background knowledge and cultural ideologies, the remark makes no sense, especially as a taunt. The phrase brings to mind the stereotype of a husband returning from work to a 'housewife' in a stereotypical American nuclear family, in which the woman is an unpaid houseworker. So it metaphorically positions Pete not only as one of the family staying for the night, but as 'the man of the house,' in a dominant position over his wife. This interpretation was confirmed through an informal poll of the members. Dave is then put in a metaphorically subordinate position as a housewife in a particular stereotype of a family. It thus makes sense as a taunt because Pete is not only staying for free but claiming that Dave is in a servant position to him. Without this background knowledge, the phrase makes little sense. Thus it reinforces an ideology as a woman/wife in that subordinate servant role for the man/husband, even as it is constructing a local dominance relationship between Pete and Dave.

This kind of dominance relationship was even clearer in the naming of one of the pledges.[3] During the pledge period, the members gave all the pledges a nickname which was often insulting to the pledge, or highlighted the subordinate position of the pledge. One pledge was given the name 'Hazel,' and was made to perform household cleaning duties for several of the members for a few weeks. Here again, the name of the subordinate male is female. But it also refers to a 1950's television show of the same name, about a character of the same name who is a domestic worker for a nuclear-family household. The men draw on the show and the larger cultural metaphor of women as domestic workers, to name a structurally subordinate position for 'Hazel.'

One of the most common examples of this kind of positioning is the use of *bitch* to insult another man. I collected several examples of this, and heard many more which I did not record or note down. In the next excerpt, Pete uses bitch in the prototypical way. It takes place during the chapter correspondent election. Like several other members (including Mack), Pete suggests three offices and the proper candidate for each. Mick reminds him not to argue for other offices and Pete then argues he can say whatever he wants when he has the floor.

Excerpt 6

1	MICK:	Pete
2	PENCIL:	You're a moron ((to Mitty, who just spoke))
3	PETE:	Kurt for chapter correspondent,
4		⌈Ritchie for sch-olarship,
5	?:	⌊no no:::::
6	PETE:	and Ernie for hi⌈storian.
7	?:	⌊Ritchie for chaplain.
8	PETE:	allright well Ritchie for historian,
9		and Ernie for scholarship.
10	MICK:	We're on one vote right now.
11	PETE:	Hey I get to say my piece I got the floor bitch.
12	MICK:	Darter.

Here we see Pete clearly in opposition to his addressee, here Mick. He finishes his statement by calling Mick 'bitch,' normally a term used to refer derogatorily to a woman (or a female dog, from where the insult derives). This insults Mick both through the 'conventional' manner of calling him a dog, and by drawing on a social ideology of female as subordinate.

We have evidence that 'bitch' is associated with this subordinate role through another derogatory term used by the men: 'bitch boy.' This term is loaded with dominant-subordinate meaning: first through 'bitch,' and second through the term 'boy', also used to refer to a servant. First let's look at how it is used in a meeting by Speed:

Excerpt 7

1	SPEED:	All right look.
2		first of all, you guys need to realize
3		we do not *ha:ve* to ne- necessarily make a:ll the new brothers,
4		put them in positions right away.
5		a *lot*-of the new brothers already have positions.
6		they can get elected next year *or* next semester.
7		there *are* some positions that are semesterly.
8		we don't have to make sure that every one of them has a position.
9		they need time to *learn* and grow-
10		it's better that ⌈they're- ⌉that they're=
11	?:	⌊(I need an assistant,)⌋
12	SPEED:	=SHUT THE F:UCK UP.
13		it's better that they're-
14		that they're almost like I was with Tex.
15		I was Tex's like little bitch boy, graduate affairs,
16		and I learned a lot more there,
17		than I would if I got stuck in some leadership role,
18		so *fuck* em,

Here Speed refers to the fact that he was Rex's assistant in the graduate affairs position, doing any tedious work Rex gave him. It is clearly a subordinate role, and therefore 'bitch' in its subordinate, servant meaning fits in. In addition, we have the story of the origin of the term from Mack:

Excerpt 8

1	MACK:	So bitch boy um
2		Chicken hawk and I don't know if you've ever met him KW um
3		one time was tellin a story
4		and I don't know if there were other people around
5		or if he's just told this story so many times
6		but um he apparently was at another school I think
7		maybe with his brother,
8		he was in a bar with his brother,
9		the details of it I'm not- I don't remember very well.
10		Anyway he was at this bar
11		and I think maybe he was talking to this- he was talking to a girl.
12		another guy some strange guy bigger than K though
13		um came over and started hassling him
14		either about the girl or he was standing in his place
15		you know the normal bar nonsense, and um
16		so K kinda left it be for a while and uh
17		he he I think he mentioned it to his brother
18		now they were there with a friend of his brother's
19		and apparently this friend of his brother's
20		they were at the bar
21		this friend of his brother's was quite a big man
22		very large you know
23		like six four you know like two hundred and fifty pounds or something
24		strong
25		big guy
26		and um so K went back over I think to talk to this girl
27		and uh apparently this same guy started giving him problems again
28		eh and this guy this big friend of Ks brother
29		comes up behind- behind this guy this guy that's bothering K,
30		and just puts his arm around him very gently
31		and kind of pulls him in close
32		and starts talking to him r:::really kind of
33		y- you know I don't even wanna I don't even wanna try and do the voice
34		that K does you're gonna have to ask K for it.
35		but t- he starts really talkin to him
36		like he's pimpin this guy or somethin' you know
37		and he goes you know what we gon do?
38		You gon be my bitch boy fa the rest of the night
39		and then he just went down the list of things that he's gonna make=
40		this guy do for him an
41		it wasn't- it was demeaning things like
42		you know you gonna get me drinks
43		your gonna come in and wipe my ass and
44		you know nothing nothing like
45		I'm gonna kick your ass or anything like that.
46		he spoke real calmly and real coolly and

47	you know You gon be my bitch boy tonight. you know
48	and so that's where it came from and
49	bitch boy you know it's pretty self explanatory
50	you know it's just a little boy
51	who's gonna do all the bitch work for me I dunno

The bitch boy relationship is clearly one of dominance. Not a dominance of actual physical violence, but one of potential violence symbolized by the things the dominant male makes the subordinate do. But it also has an essential sexual component as well, one that on the surface looks to be homosexual. Under the surface, though, the relationship is a metaphorical male dominant – female subordinate metaphor. Notice in line 31 that Mack says 'he starts talking to him like he's pimpin' this guy,' indicating he's treating him like a prostitute under his care. Here we see clearly Mack equate *bitch* with *woman*, and stating that the relationship is metaphorically a heterosexual one, not homosexual. So in using one of the most overt named dominance relationships in the fraternity group, the men use a term that not only has a lexical association with women (*bitch*), but also draws on the metaphor of a woman as a (sexual) servant to a (physically) powerful, dominant man. Thus, the meaning of bitch boy, which Mack claims is 'pretty self explanatory' in line 44, is only self explanatory if you have access to this cultural script of heterosexual relationships of this type. Moreover, the use of the term presupposes an understanding of this relationship and through its repetition reifies the existence of the dominance heterosexual model. The 'male' half of the term (*boy*) also helps to create the subordinate position of the addressee through age and race hierarchies. *Boy* is clearly an address term used with a younger and less powerful person; a male who has not yet made it to his full dominant position. It also indexes a racial cultural model in which powerful White men address Black men with the term, such as in Ervin-Tripp's (1969) example of an exchange between a Black physician and a White police officer. The fraternity men, then, when they use *bitch boy*, are creating a number of different identities and relationships. Most immediately for the discourse, they are creating a relationship between who is the bitch boy and who is his dominator. However, they are also crucially drawing on a shared ideology of gender relationships in which a woman is dominated by a man.

What about other address terms, especially those which are more clearly (heterosexual) male? Consider again the address terms in the monopoly game, where we saw Pete use 'Hi honey I'm home' to taunt Dave. Notice that Pete also uses the address term *dude*, particularly in line 5: 'Dave, dude, dude Dave,' in which he is clearly playing with language by using alliteration and chiasmus. Pete is here having fun with language given the resources of the game. But the relationship he has – and wants to construct -with Dave is quite different. In the *dude* situation, Pete is not clearly dominating Dave, but rather Dave has something Pete wants (the red property). So Pete is constructing a solidary and perhaps even a subordinate relationship with Dave. This is the way the two clear 'masculine' address terms are used in the fraternity (*dude* and *man*): as solidarity indexes to focus on cooperative actions, and even to diffuse tensions during confrontations. So the generic masculine address terms focus on equality and solidarity, whereas the female terms are terms of dominance and insult. Thus, not only are male and female separated, they are treated unequally. Moreover, through the term *bitch boy* (and similar creative terms such as 'Hazel') male and female are related metaphorically through an assumed heterosexual ideology.

The address terms I have considered thus do more than just position a man as a woman. They position a man as a woman *in a narrative* – a cultural script. This woman, moreover, is clearly in a subordinate position in the narrative: as a housewife, as a prostitute, as a domestic servant. Each use of the address term makes sense only if the interlocutors share access to the cultural script.

This has implications for the way we understand language to index social identity. The standard assumption is that a certain variant of a variable becomes associated with a recognized cultural group, and people who identify with that cultural group are statistically more likely to use the variant. This is the 'acts of identity' model of language and identity (LePage and Tabouret-Keller 1985). It requires a knowledge of groups and the way they act, and a direct, one-to-one indexing of linguistic form to group identity. What we see here is that heterosexual identities and ideologies are being created in a much more complex way: there is really no separated group of heterosexuals in the dominant culture. This group, like men a few decades ago, is considered the norm, and is indeed hardly a coherent group. But as we have seen here we can identify heterosexuality as part of these men's socially constructed identity. We must therefore have a model of language and identity that is itself much more complex than the acts of identity model, one that can take account of mocking and metaphorical positionings within a group that perpetuate its ideologies.

Such a model would recognize a multilayered social indexing of language, similar to Silverstein's (1996) orders of indexicality. The model would index at least four levels of social relationship: a local stance within an ongoing speech event, a position within an institution, a status in wider society, and, potentially at least, a place within a cultural model or script. And we have seen that there could be indexing within these levels as well, as local dominance relationships are indexed by a primary indexing of the cultural model.

Summary

We have seen how language is used by the men to reproduce a hegemonic heterosexuality which is embedded in the larger context of hegemonic masculinity. We saw that their society (Greek-letter society) is organized around an ideology of difference and how the speech activities which make up this society – both mixed and single sex – are based on the notion of sexual difference and heterosexuality. There is an elaborate cultural script around different kinds of heterosexuality, and these have led to the naming of these scripts and speech activities: throwing raps, scamming, a drunk story, the commitment thing. One of the most secret and sacred genres of the fraternity is centered around narratives of heterosexuality: fuck stories. In interaction, men metaphorically represent other men as women in order to claim dominance over that man (even in play), as we saw for the 'Hi honey I'm home' line, as well as 'bitch.' The metaphorical assignment of homosexuality worked in a similar way. These two metaphors find a complex but telling synthesis in the term 'bitch boy'. Importantly, in all of these examples the men were performing relationships for the men. We thus see that heterosexuality is embedded in the more important relationships of male dominance hierarchies and homosociability.

Similar practices of cathexis have been discussed by ethnographers of other European cultures. For example, Almeida (1996) describes a variant of the 'fuck story' genre told by the men he studied in a Portuguese village. He also describes a similar dichotomy of heterosexuality focusing on women as sexual partners and women as marriage partners. The fraternity men and the Portuguese men show how much time and effort go into displaying these kinds of heterosexuality: For both groups of men, these stories are central to their socializing, and are something exalted and enjoyed, not merely expected.

Most importantly, these speech strategies of heterosexuality are how men in both cultures create status among their peers. Heterosexuality is thus not just about sexual object choice, but it also has a social construction that is primarily used by social actors to compete within same sex groups. This pattern suggests that patterns of male domination are not simply about men dominating women. Rather, in both cultures, male domination in heterosexual displays is about men displaying power *over* other men (and women) *to* other men. The stories and other forms of heterosexual display therefore represent same-sex status competition in which heterosexual gender differentiation and dominance is not the goal, but one strategy with which to construct a hegemonic masculinity. This finding suggests that in order to understand language and gender patterns, we need to understand how language is used to create difference and status within gender groups.

Notes

1   I am using speech activities to denote actions smaller than a speech event but larger than a speech act. Speech activities can be made up of several speech acts; speech events are longer in duration and are made up of speech activities.
2   For transcription conventions see Transcription Conventions 1 (p. x).
3   A pledge is essentially a probationary member of the fraternity. Theoretically, it is a time when the new member learns the history and lore of the fraternity, and gets to know his fellow members better. In practice, it is also when most of the hazing occurs, as pledges are put through demeaning and sometimes dangerous rituals in order to attain full membership.

References

Almeida, Miguel Vale de. 1996. *The Hegemonic Male: Masculinity in a Portuguese Town*. Providence, RI: Berghahn Books.

Ervin-Tripp, Susan. 1969. Sociolinguistics. *Advances in Experimental Social Psychology*, ed. Leonard Berkowitz, Vol. 4, 93–107. Academic Press.

Hall, Kira and Veronica O'Donovan. 1996. Shifting Gender Positions among Hindi-speaking Hijras. *Rethinking language and Gender Research: Theory and Practice*, ed. Victoria Bergvall, Janet Bing, and Alice Freed, 228–66. London: Longman.

LePage, R. B. and Andree Tabouret-Keller. 1985. *Acts of Identity : Creole-based Approaches to Language and Ethnicity*. Cambridge, New York: Cambridge University Press.

Morford, Janet. 1987. Social Indexicality in French Pronominal Address. *Journal of Linguistic Anthropology* 7.3–37.

Silverstein, Michael. 1996. Indexical Order and the Dialectics of Sociolinguistic Life. *SALSA III: Proceedings of the Third Annual Symposium About Language and Society – Austin*, ed. Risako Ide, Rebeca Parker, and Yukako Sunaoshi, 266–95. Austin, Texas: Univeristy of Texas Department of Linguistics.

Part V
Women's Talk in the Public Domain

This section will focus on language use in the public domain. The public domain is a male-dominated domain, and the discourse patterns of male speakers are still the norm in public life. Now, in the twenty-first century, as a consequence of Equal Opportunities legislation, women are entering the public domain with growing expectations in terms of career progression. Yet "Women still struggle for acceptance within institutional settings such as government, politics, law, education, the church, the media and the business world" (Baxter 2006: xiv). Women are expected to adapt to androcentric norms, for example, to use the more adversarial, information-focused style characteristic of all-male talk, and typical of talk in the public domain. But women who successfully adapt to characteristically male linguistic norms run the risk of being perceived as aggressive and confrontational, as un-feminine, while those who choose to use a more affiliative, cooperative style risk being marginalized. Moreover, in the public sphere feminist discourses are often ignored or simply not heard.

In this section we will cover a range of workplaces – parliament, a police station, a feminist crisis intervention center, a law court, as well as professional and white-collar workplaces in Japan and New Zealand. (The educational sphere is represented in Swann's paper in Part III; doctor–patient interaction is the focus of West's paper in Part VII.) The first paper in this section, Katsue Akiba Reynolds' "Female Speakers of Japanese in Transition" explores the conflict in Japan between the contemporary ideology that women and men are equal, and the pressure on women to speak in a way that is *onna-rasiku*. *Onna-rasiku* language expresses an older female identity, one which is more in line with the Confucian doctrine of "men superior, women inferior." Reynolds shows that, in Japanese, some rules for gender-marking are categorical, and that, overall, women have a much more restricted stylistic range available to them than men have. This asymmetry is in conflict with the communicative requirements of contemporary life where women are taking on new roles in the public sphere and need to talk to men as equals. "In order to be accepted as a 'good' woman, a female speaker of Japanese must choose to talk non-assertively, indirectly, politely, deferentially: but in order to function as a supervisor, administrator, teacher, lawyer, doctor, etc. or as a colleague or associate, she must be able to talk with assurance." This sort of conflict exists

Language and Gender: A Reader, Second Edition. Edited by Jennifer Coates and Pia Pichler.
© 2011 Blackwell Publishing Ltd except for editorial material and organization. © 2011 Jennifer Coates and Pia Pichler. Published 2011 by Blackwell Publishing Ltd.

world-wide, but the Japanese situation is more extreme that most. Reynolds reports current perceptions of women in public life (many of whom deny that they have experienced any problems relating to language) and describes the linguistic strategies they are (often unconsciously) adopting to resolve the conflicting demands on them. These strategies seem to consist predominantly of "defeminizing" their language, that is, choosing variants towards the middle of an imaginary masculine–feminine spectrum, and avoiding variants associated with the feminine end of the spectrum.

The next paper examines the same tensions but in the context of the British House of Commons. Sylvia Shaw, in "Governed by the Rules? The Female Voice in Parliamentary Debates," looks at the experience of women members of parliament (MPs). Parliaments have been, until very recently, an arena reserved for the male voice. Women MPs have to learn the norms of this Community of Practice (or CoP) in particular the official rules for formal debate, as laid out in Erskine May. To be accepted as a core member of the CoP, a new member must demonstrate they have mastered these rules. An important way to "do" power in parliamentary debate is to hold the floor. Shaw analyzes floor apportionment and establishes that women MPs have trouble holding the floor, even when it is legally theirs, because male MPs frequently break the rules, making illegal comments (such as "Rubbish") without being censured by the Speaker (who moderates parliamentary behavior). In five debates, male participants made 90 percent of all individual illegal utterances, suggesting that this kind of rule-breaking is seen as normal by male MPs, while women MPs are disadvantaged because they are reluctant to break the rules. Moreover, women's non-participation in filibustering (speaking for so long – often on unrelated topics – that a debate runs out of time) marks them out as peripheral members of the CoP. Like the Japanese women discussed in Reynolds' paper, these British MPs find themselves subject to contradictory expectations: they are expected to be as able as the men, but simultaneously to demonstrate that women in parliament can "make a difference." They are in a no-win situation, either adhering to the rules of parliamentary debate (thus marking themselves out as peripheral members of the CoP) or flouting the rules like the men and becoming part of the "bear pit."

The tension between dominant norms of femininity and acting effectively in the workplace is taken up by Janet Holmes and Stephanie Schnurr, but with the interesting twist that they look more broadly at femininity and its performance by both women and men in the workplace. In their paper "'Doing Femininity' at Work," they draw on data collected as part of the Wellington Language in the Workplace project to explore the ways in which participants manage and interpret the notion of "femininity" in workplace discourse. They show how using good "relational practice," that is, subtle discursive work that attends to collegial relationships and ensures that things run smoothly, is an asset in the workplace. Such behavior is normatively feminine, and associated with collaborative linguistic strategies typically linked with women. But in some workplaces (labeled more feminine by participants), Holmes and Schnurr found examples of men as well as women using such strategies, which were treated as unmarked in these contexts. These tended to be organizations which dealt directly with clients or with people-oriented social issues or with education, and not IT companies or manufacturing organizations, which were assessed as more "masculine." Overall, Holmes and Schnurr demonstrate that there are multiple femininities in the workplace, some affiliative, but others more contestive. (These findings are supported by Baxter (2010), who found that, in male-dominated and gender-divided corporations, women leaders have to develop an extraordinary linguistic expertise just to survive, whereas in what she calls "gender-multiple" corporations, their linguistic expertise helps them to be highly regarded and effective leaders.)

In the next paper we see that working in an all-female space can make a huge difference to women's ability to act effectively. Ana Cristina Ostermann's "Communities of Practice at Work: Gender, Facework and the Power of *Habitus* at an All-Female Police Station and a Feminist Crisis Intervention Center in Brazil," compares two institutions that work with victims of domestic violence in Brazil. Both workplaces are all-female, but the interactional patterns found in them are very different. Those used at the feminist crisis intervention center were more cooperative and functioned to produce solidarity. By contrast, those used by the women police officers were less cooperative and more face-threatening, and turn-taking was less smooth. It seems that female police officers, working in a male-dominated system, use more distancing and controlling interactional strategies, in part because they fear that using interactional patterns seen as more typical of women will disadvantage them in the symbolic market of the police system. Ostermann shows that these two groups of women professionals belong to distinctive communities of practice, with distinctive ideologies, and their ways of interacting with victims of domestic violence differ accordingly.

A similar contrast emerges in the next paper, Susan Ehrlich's "Trial Discourse and Judicial Decision-Making: Constraining the Boundaries of Gendered Identities." Ehrlich looks at the language used in a Canadian courtroom, in a trial about sexual assault, and shows how "a feminist perspective, when manifest in a public context, can be distorted or rendered invisible by the androcentric discourses that often dominate in these contexts." Ehrlich argues that, while many researchers have focused on the agency and creativity of social actors in constructing gendered identities, it is important not to forget what Butler (1990) calls the "rigid regulatory framework" within which gendered identities are produced. Ehrlich analyzes question-and-answer sequences in transcripts of the courtroom discourse to show how lawyers' questions to a large extent determine what witnesses can say. The Crown Attorney (in support of the complainant) invokes a feminist sense-making framework, and shows how the woman complainant was worried about being alone with the defendant and how she went along with many of his suggestions because she was frightened that he might become violent. The complainant's strategies of resistance were not precursors to consensual sex, but the trial judge and the appeal court judge both fail to recognize the complainant's account as representing resistance – they only recognize resistance when it takes the form of persistent physical struggle. As Ehrlich comments, feminist discourse has difficulty making itself heard in public institutions like law courts.

These five papers do not give a unified message. As Holmes and Schnurr demonstrate, in workplaces which function as more "feminine" communities of practice, both women and men can adopt more collegial and collaborative strategies of interaction. But in many other workplaces women have to adapt to traditional – androcentric – working practices, and here the conflict between gender and status is highly problematic for them. Moreover, different ideologies shape very different contexts: where women work together in explicitly feminist professional groups (as in Ostermann's example), then much can be achieved, but as Ehrlich's analysis of courtroom discourse shows, hegemonic discourses of women's passivity in heterosexual contexts mean that feminist discourses go unheard.

References

Baxter, Judith (2006) "Introduction," pp. xiii–xviii in Judith Baxter (ed.) *Speaking Out: The Female Voice in Public Contexts*. London: Palgrave.

Baxter, Judith (2010) *The Language of Female Leadership.* London: Palgrave.
Butler, Judith (1990) *Gender Trouble: Feminism and the Subversion of Identity.* London: Routledge.

Recommended Further Reading

Baxter, Judith (ed.) (2006) *Speaking Out: The Female Voice in Public Contexts.* London: Palgrave.
Baxter, Judith (2010) *The Language of Female Leadership.* London: Palgrave.
Coates, Jennifer (1995) "Language, gender and career," in Sara Mills (ed.) *Language and Gender: Interdisciplinary Perspectives,* London: Longman.
Ehrlich, Susan (2001) *Representing Rape: Language and Sexual Consent.* London: Routledge.
Ford, Cecilia E. (2008) *Women Speaking Up: Getting and Using Turns in Workplace Meetings.* New York: Palgrave Macmillan.
Holmes, Janet (2006) *Gendered Talk at Work: Constructing Gender Identity through Workplace Discourse.* Oxford: Blackwell.
Holmes, Janet and Stubbe, Maria (2003) *Power and Politeness in the Workplace: A Sociolinguistic Analysis of Talk at Work.* London: Pearson.
Holmgreen, Lise-Lotte (2009) "Metaphorically speaking: construction of gender and career in the Danish financial sector," *Gender and Language* 3(1), 1–32.
McElhinnie, Bonnie (2005) "Gender and the stories Pittsburgh police officers tell about using physical force," pp. 219–30 in Caroline Brettell and Carolyn Sargent (eds) *Gender in Cross-Cultural Perspective,* London: Pearson Prentice Hall.
McRae, Susan (2009) "'It's a bloke's thing': gender, occupational roles and talk in the workplace," pp. 163–85 in Pia Pichler and Eva Eppler (eds) *Gender and Spoken Interaction.* London: Palgrave.
Mullany, Louise (2007) *Gendered Discourse in the Professional Workplace.* London: Palgrave.
Walsh, Clare (2001) *Gender and Discourse: Language and Power in Politics, the Church and Organisations.* London: Longman.
West, Candace (1984) *Routine Complications: Troubles with Talk between Doctors and Patients.* Bloomington: Indiana University Press.
West, Candace (1990) "'Not just doctor's orders': directive-response sequences in patients' visits to women and men physicians," *Discourse & Society* 1(1), 85–112.

22

Female Speakers of Japanese in Transition

Katsue Akiba Reynolds

Source: S. Ide and N. McGloin (eds), *Aspects of Japanese Women's Language*. Tokyo: Kurosio Publishers (1991), pp. 129–46.

Introduction

The Confucian doctrine of "men superior, women inferior" (*Dan-Son Jo-Hi*) an indispensable element in the hierarchical structure of Japanese society, began to give way when women were guaranteed equal status in the new Constitution soon after the end of World War II. At that time, women began to assert their existence in various public fields. However, the average person's image of women has not changed significantly, and the notion that women should behave *onna-rasiku* "as expected of women" is still predominant.
[…]

When one inspects the ways in which Japanese women talk at a variety of social levels, a complex interaction between social change and language change emerges, and changes in women's speech become visible. There is no doubt that social changes during the post-war era have had an incalculable impact on women's perceptions of reality, giving rise to "status conflict" (Pharr 1984) in various areas of social life. Language use is one such area: the female/male speech dichotomy stands in obvious contradiction to the new social order based on egalitarian ideology. As shown in Reynolds (1985), language use reflects Japanese society of the past, in which women were viewed as the inferior, weaker sex and were expected to talk accordingly. Women may perceive themselves as equals of men but women's language calls up the older image of women.
[…]

Historical Background

During the feudal era, which lasted up to 1868, Japan maintained its internal integrity under one of the most extreme forms of hierarchical society. The *samurai* "warrior" class held control and people were required to adhere strictly to behavioral norms. The slightest deviation from the norms could provoke the most severe punishment – decapitation. The introduction of the ideology of democracy into the Japanese political system at the time of the Meiji Restoration in 1868 led to the outlawing of such extreme feudal practices, but interactional expectations based on social ranking, an outgrowth of two hundred years of feudalistic practices, have persisted as a cultural characteristic. Even after the radical changes in social institutions after the war, the expectations remain at almost all levels of interaction among the Japanese. Thus, Nakane (1970) analyzes contemporary Japanese society as a hierarchical society governed by the "vertical" principle of human interaction. Because of intransigent adherence to this principle, many social scientists, including Nakane, maintain that the changes in political/social institutions have not reached down to the foundation of the culture. To many researchers Japan still appears to be a hierarchically organized, harmonious society with a high degree of internal integrity.

Recently, this view has been explicitly challenged by Krauss, Rohlen and Steinhoff (1984). They present examples of intergroup conflicts in Japan during the post-war period, and convincingly argue that the hierarchy/harmony model of Japanese society, which does not take such conflicts into consideration, is not adequate, being unable to account for the source, development, and outcome of various social phenomena. [...]

Japanese Female Speech

It was only two or three generations ago that women were all but prevented from entering the public arena: they occupied their respective positions within family structures as wives, mothers or mothers-in-law and had contact with the world outside the family only through male relations, or as substitutes. In Reynolds (1985), I attempted to show that most linguistic rules applying only if the speaker is female have the effect of reducing assertion, or expressing formality or politeness (hearer orientation), which indicates that the social foundation of female speech is a sex-segregated hierarchical society in which women are viewed as inferior.

[...]

I do not mean to imply by my analysis of Japanese female speech that the normative rules for female speakers are always strictly adhered to. On the contrary, this study takes note of the fact that many women deviate from the norm in many situations. But certain features of female speech can still be extensively observed among the majority of Japanese women, and some rules are even obligatory if the speaker is female. For example, as a woman I am not allowed to say to anybody, even to my younger sibling *Tot-te-kure* "Get (it) for me" using Informal-Benefactive-Imperative. I have to say instead *Tot-te*, applying the imperative deletion rule. I am not allowed to say *It-ta ka?* "Did you go?". I must suppress the interrogative marker *ka* and say *It-ta* (/), shifting the rising intonation to the tense marker. Some rules for gender-marking in Japanese are categorical, while in English rules are variable. However, this does not mean that the distinction between female speech and male speech is always clear-cut. Furthermore, there are several stylistic variants of female and male speech signifying different degrees of femininity or masculinity. Roughly speaking, the division between female and male speech is schematized as in the diagram below, V_1 being the most masculine – assertive/forceful variants – and Vn its opposite extreme.

That is, women are supposed to choose a style closer to the least assertive end, which men are supposed to avoid. Also, it seems that the risk of stepping into the overlapping area (Vk–m) is greater for females than for males. A woman using a style in this area may be considered impolite in more situations than a man talking in the same way. If we limit ourselves to informal speech (i.e., excluding from our consideration formal and written styles, which exhibit different patterns of distribution), the option for a style is much narrower in the case of a female speaker.

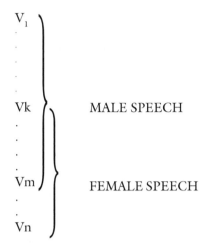

This asymmetric linguistic division may not have created serious problems in a sex-segregated society, where the wife, a woman in the only legitimate female category, occupied "the lowest rung on the entire social ladder, subordinated within the feudal hierarchy and within the family hierarchy as well" (Pharr 1984: 224). There was no need for women to talk assertively/forcefully/authoritatively since they were defined as subordinate to others. With the legal and economic changes after the war, however, the barriers between women and men were removed in most social and educational institutions: women are no longer confined to the home but are taking up various social/public roles which used to belong to men. Inevitably, mixed sex interactions have significantly increased, causing remarkable changes in the way people relate. Mixed sex interaction in which women and men can talk almost as equals is no longer taken as exceptional. There are many situations in which a woman talks as a superior to her male subordinates. It is mostly in such emerging patterns of interaction that speakers (especially, female speakers) face the conflict between traditional patterns and the need to meet the communicative requirements arising from their new roles. In order to be accepted as a "good" woman, a female speaker of Japanese must choose to talk nonassertively, indirectly, politely, deferentially: but in order to function as a supervisor, administrator, teacher, lawyer, doctor, etc. or as a colleague or associate, she must be able to talk with assurance. Given the constraint that a woman should talk *onna-rasiku* "as expected of women" regardless of her role, which is far more mandatory in Japanese than in English, the presence of an "objective condition for conflict" (Pharr 1984) is common.

Women and Status Conflict

In analyzing the "tea-pourers" rebellion (a rebellion in Kyoto, Japan, in the early 1960's by a group of female clerical workers in a city government office who were protesting against having to make and pour tea several times a day for the male members of their respective sections) as a sample case of status conflict, Pharr (1984) argues that conflict develops in five stages: (1) the objective basis for the conflict, (2) the subjective awareness of the conflict, (3) the initiation of conflict behavior, (4) the escalation/deescalation of conflict behavior and (5) the termination of conflict. Examination of female/male speech conflicts according to this model reveals a number of important facts.[1]

There are at least two types of mixed sex interactional situations where the objective conditions for conflict are inherent: a situation in which a female speaker is superior in social status to a male speaker and a situation in which both sexes are supposed to have equal status.

A woman in a superior position – a position defined as such by the male-established hierarchy – is expected to signify her authoritative power in her language, but female speech does not provide a means to this end. Formal speech may be interpreted as the speaker's means of keeping a distance from the addressee, or it may be taken as a manifestation of the speaker's genuine humility – a virtue – only if it comes from someone who has an option of a more overtly assertive/intimidating style, i.e., a male speaker. But formal speech is a sign of deference, an expected quality of the powerless, when it is used by a speaker who is constrained to using a nonassertive style, i.e. by a female speaker.

In mixed sex conversations where there is no vertical relationship among the participants, linguistic equality will be maintained only if both female and male members talk in formal speech, keeping a distance from each other. The odds are in favor of male speakers in any competition in informal speech.

Actions such as tea-pouring are intentional and the actors are well aware of what they are doing, so the fact that the duty is a burden imposed only on female workers is apparent to everybody. The question of what can be done to make the situation more fair can be discussed openly. But decisions as to what linguistic style to use must often, on the other hand, be made subconsciously by individuals. It is characteristic of linguistic conflict that subjects are seldom aware of it. Initially, interviews with women who are in social positions that require assertive talk – women who administer predominantly male groups or mixed sex groups with large percentages of male members, women critics, women in the media, women teachers and women politicians – suggest that they have never experienced any difficulties due to their language use. Yet later in the same interviews these women admit that their language does not have the same authoritative force as that of their male counterparts, that they must be aware of their language so they will not offend others, or be considered improper as women. However, there is evidence that women are attempting, subconsciously, to resolve the conflict, mostly by defeminizing their speech within limits, using variants in the Vk–m area in the diagram shown earlier. They even use some variants closer to V_1 than Vk when sentences are not explicitly directed towards the addressee: e.g., *Sooda naa* (/) instead of *Soo (desu) nee* (/), both of which are reflexive questions – questions directed towards the speaker him/herself; or the use of *sikasi*, the conjunction "however/but" commonly used in male speech/public discourse, instead of *desukere-do, kere-do, kedo, demo*, conjunctions with the same semantic function as *sikasi* but more commonly used in female speech/conversational discourse. I hear these expressions when women talk to me, a female stranger: this suggests that they are used more extensively in communication in work situations, especially when conflict is intense. One incident might be seen as an escalation of conflict behavior. A woman principal's thundering *Bakayaroo!* "Stupid!" silenced a group of faculty members. (*Yaroo* is a vulgarism referring to men: the word does not belong to the female vocabulary.) She said, "We must sometimes show who is the boss," when the incident, which must have been spread among the teachers and other principals in the community, was brought up by another woman principal. Variants at the V_1 level were employed by several angry women among about 200 observers of a Diet session discussing a bill to legislate equal employment opportunities for men and women (Notes, July 24, '84, no taperecording permitted).

A social conflict like the one concerning tea-pouring duties is externally observable and the existence of conflict is apparent. The conflict of male/female linguistic style under discussion, however, takes place mostly within individuals: subjects may not have full awareness of the existence of the objective conditions for conflict and may not consciously initiate conflict behavior. An individual who initiates conflict behavior under such conditions might easily yield to the pressure of society and be persuaded that it is she who is wrong, that it is her behavior that must be corrected. The role of society in this process is crucial, especially in Japan, where the desire for harmony is so deep-rooted in the culture that deviating from the cultural norm – destroying the harmony – is almost suicidal. The government proposal to put into law the principle of equal employment opportunity for men and women in response to the egalitarian ideology of the International Decade for Women was met with strong opposition by proponents of a "cultural ecology" theory.

Michiko Hasegawa, a female philosophy teacher, states, "The pattern of men's and women's roles is an important element of the system of each culture. It is analogous to religion or language, and if one attempts to change it recklessly, one might destroy the whole system of the culture" (Hasegawa 1984: 83). She argues that the Law, if it is ratified, would undermine the well-balanced system of Japanese traditions. To think of removing the male/female speech dichotomy is absurd to her, and to many others. It is understandable that individual female speakers' attempts to rebel against traditional female speech patterns do not escalate beyond a very limited domain. Conflicts either remain unresolved or end in failure.

Linguistic Dilemmas: The Example of Women Teachers

One group of women who are particularly vulnerable to the linguistic dilemma are female teachers in junior high schools,[2] as well as teachers teaching older age groups in elementary schools. They must handle boys and girls (the average class of a Japanese school has more than 40 students) who demand that the teacher be attentive and friendly to them while at the same time displaying a defensive and resistant attitude themselves. Displays of both solidarity and authority are necessary for a teacher to be successful in a Japanese junior high school: it is informal male speech that can satisfy these two requirements simultaneously. Let us look at an example of a male teacher's discourse in class.[3]

T:	… Please present a lot of your opinions or impressions. First, the boy. About the boy … You probably remember what you have written down yesterday. Well, what have you thought about the boy? *I want you to present it, OK? (Kore o dasi te-morai-tai na.)*
P (MALE):	…
T:	Yes, that's right. That's correct … What I wanted you to write about … among the subjects that you had strong feelings about, there are probably a lot besides it, aren't there? Well … to confirm those points with each other. *Well how about you A, first? (Ee, mazu saisyo ni A doo da.)*
P (MALE):	…
T:	Yes. *You felt thrilled at what the boy was doing, is it? (Syoonen ga yat-te-iru koto ni suriru o kanzi -ta, da na.)*

The italic parts are in an informal male speech style and those which are not marked are either formal or are in a written language style, which is very common in lecturing. Note that this male teacher teaching Tolstoy in Japanese translation to seventh graders regularly switches the code from formal to informal at the point where he attempts to elicit responses from students. Female informal speech, which has long been limited to private discourse among women, does not work in the same way as male informal speech in the public environment. For a woman teacher to be successful under the present circumstances, she has no choice but to use defeminized patterns to strengthen solidarity with her students without losing authority.

However, a teacher is evaluated not only by students but also by parents and the principal, who are critical if female teachers' behavior deviates from traditional standards. All the female principals that I interviewed criticized female teachers' language one way or another, although most of them admit that female teachers cannot be like "normal" women. One of the principals revealed that she had called in a young female teacher to admonish her about her language. The principal said that since that time the teacher in question seemed to be improving her language.

In the discussion on female speech held during a three-day seminar on women's studies at the National Women's Education Center (*Kokuritu Huzin Kyooiku Kaikan*)[4] a participant expressed concern about her daughter's language, which she thought was too rough for a girl, "perhaps, because of her (female) teacher's influence." Several younger participants who could still identify themselves with students rather than mothers responded that when they were students they always favored female teachers who talked a little bit like male teachers over those who talked too formally. It is the conflict inherent in being a female teacher that has been brought into focus by these two opposing views, the view of the mothers and the view of students as recalled by younger participants at the seminar.

The social expectation that women, regardless of their roles, should talk *onna-rasiku* is so strong that women teachers themselves often view defeminization negatively. A 26-year-old female teacher responds to a newspaper reporter. "I tend to speak rough language with an imperative tone in spite of my efforts not to, perhaps, because I am a teacher. I always think regretfully that this is not good for me" (the *Asahi*, July 18, 1984), and she adds that she, ambivalent about language use, won't be able to meet the demands of the career. It is interesting that the reporter (female or male?) admiringly describes the teacher as sitting *onna-rasiku* on the floor with her hands arranged in front of her folded knees in a poised manner. It seems to be only a matter of time before this teacher will terminate the conflict by returning to the traditional woman's place – home. Sensing society's disapproval of her language, this female teacher is punishing herself while the same society (represented by the reporter) lauds her for her femininity.

Female principals are in positions where they can control the female speech conflict to a certain extent. Unlike teachers, principals do not come into direct contact with students, and they can handle most interactions in formal language. Furthermore, even if they use rough language like [*Bakayaroo!*] they are relatively free from others' criticism since they are at the top rank within a school system. Difficulties that women principals experience are more subtle. First, a woman principal must demonstrate that she does not display linguistic traits which are believed to be typical of women: especially, she must avoid giving an impression in her talk that she is indecisive, indirect or picky. At the same time she cannot be as authoritative as a male counterpart would be. One of the women principals interviewed who seemed to be quite successful in establishing a good rapport with the teachers confided that she was careful not to be too informal with the teachers so that the male headmaster,[5] who is in between herself and the teachers, would not be crowded out (Recorded, July 18, 1983). A male headmaster talks to the principal deferentially according to the traditional principle of vertical relationships and at the same time he attempts to maintain his face as the superior *vis-à-vis* the teachers. Thus, the principal must allow enough distance between the teachers and herself to make room for the headmaster. She said, "I am formal and short with teachers in my office, but I try to make up for it by saying one or two words in a personal/casual manner to convey to them that I remember their cooperation and support when I see them around." Second, a woman principal has to deal with difficulties in her communication with male principals. A woman principal who talks to male principals too informally does not have a good reputation among male principals – the majority. Male principals' informal talk of course creates no difficulty. "We should not be carried away and address male principals with -*san* – a suffix very roughly corresponding to *Mr.* in English – just because male principals do so among themselves. We should address them with the title *Sensei* 'Master/Teacher' or *Kootyoo Sensei* 'Mr. Principal' or with family name and title (e.g., *Yamada Sensei* and *Yamada Kootyoo*) as we are expected."

It has been noted that the use of *boku* "I" (Male) by junior high school girls has recently become quite common in Tokyo. Girls who were interviewed in a TV program explain that they cannot compete with boys in classes, in games or in fights with *watasi* "I" (Female), reports Jugaku (1979). What we see here is a case of conflict behavior consciously initiated by a large group of female speakers who are fully aware of the disadvantage of female speech in school situations where they are expected to compete with boys for good grades and choose to ignore traditions openly. The use of *boku* and other expressions in the male speech domain by young female speakers has escalated to a larger area and to older groups of speakers.[6] However, since they know that *boku*-language is not acceptable in the society outside schools, they use *watasi*-language in talking to "members of the society."[7] In other words, as school girls they are bilinguals who have two distinct codes, *boku*-language and *watasi*-language. They select a code according to the situation.

In spite of the surface defiance of the trend, however, *boku*-language may not have as much subversive force as it appears. The avowedly rebellious behavior on the part of teenage girls rouses curiosity but never the anger that would be invoked if females with full membership in society stepped over the gender boundary in a less self-conscious and less forthright manner. This is because *boku*-language can be dismissed as a passing phase – it does in fact taper off by the time the students leave school – while defeminization/masculinization by adult female members is a serious threat to the established norms of society.

Conclusions

The female/male language dichotomy in Japanese is not a mere differentiation of the two sexes but it reflects the structure of a society where women were defined as the inferior sex. Jugaku (1979) points out that the structure of the Japanese language has a far greater effect on the way Japanese women live than one may expect. The examples of conflict processes that we have seen show that female speech plays a crucial role in keeping Japanese women in traditional roles. Attempts to remove the boundary between the male/female speech division inevitably end in failure, as a result of self-restraint on the part of female speakers who foresee social punishment. It appears that the way women are supposed to talk has changed little; the norm functions as a conservative force.

To predict from this, however, that female speech has not changed and will not change may be wrong. Even though individual processes of conflict may terminate in failure, "the effects of the conflict feed back into the objective conditions that potentially will give rise to further conflicts" (Pharr 1984: 219). One individual's conflict behavior can have an impact on a wide range of female speakers who come into contact with it, who may initiate conflict behaviors and influence in turn other women. As long as there are objective conditions for female language conflict, conflict behaviors will recur in various social segments and will spread with increasingly greater speed. Even if all conflict behaviors are suppressed, the ripple effect of conflict may eventually generate the energy necessary to undermine the traditional division of the language, into assertive styles for men and nonassertive/polite styles for women. It is certain, to say the least, that the female/male speech dichotomy will not remain as it is at present, just as the traditional role division based on sex has been fluctuating widely in various aspects of social life.

[...]

If equality between men and women enhances linguistic equality, and if linguistic equality entails equal access for all the speakers of a language to all the resources of the language, it is a logical conclusion that the female/male speech dichotomy must be removed. Although the observations that I have presented here may very well be proof that the change towards linguistic equality is already under way, there is no guarantee that the change will proceed without interruption or digression. It is in fact quite likely that the present form of dichotomy will simply shift to another – perhaps less obvious – form of dichotomy. Inoue (1984) concludes her essay on the image of women presented through the mass media saying that, in place of the traditional role division of domestic work for women and career work for men, a new system of dividing men's and women's roles may be developing: for example, a system in which administrative positions are assigned to men and secretarial positions to women, cooking to entertain the guests is men's work and cleaning up afterward women's.[8] If Inoue's analysis is correct, language may follow the same pattern of change: even if the obvious dichotomy between female and male speech disappears, the overall dominance of male speakers over female speakers may survive in a different form. I would like to suggest therefore that it is an important task for researchers of gender in relation to language to observe and analyze various phenomena related to the sex dichotomy, especially conflict phenomena, and to work against changes that create a new male/female language dichotomy rather than leading to linguistic equality.

Notes

1   Georganne Weller, Director of Center for Interpretation and Translation. University of Hawaii, has brought to my attention that the sociolinguistic studies using aspects/variants of conflict theory have increased during the past decade. E.g., Chapter IV, "The Conflict Paradigm," of Christina Bratt Paulson's *Bilingual Education: Theories and Issues* (Newbury House, 1980).

2   According to *Nihon Kyooiku Nenkan* (The Almanac of Japanese Education) 1985, the percentages of female teachers in Japanese schools are as follows (as of May 1, 1984): elementary schools, 56.0%; junior high schools, 33%; senior high schools, 18.1%. Female teachers in junior high schools are still a minority. Furthermore, the subjects that female teachers teach are often, though not always, limited: most of them teach home economics, gymnastics for girls, Japanese, or perhaps music.

3   The sample was taken from the transcribed material published in "*Rokuonki*" in *Gengo Seikatu* 172, 1966.

4   This seminar of women's studies is held for three days every summer with over 200 participants who include teachers at various levels, women working in government offices and in other professions, students and housewives, and is subsidized by the Ministry of Education. The discussion in question was held in the evening of the second day of the 1984 seminar.

5 There seems to be an unwritten rule that a female headmaster is never assigned to a school with a female principal.

6 Jugaku (1979) made a study of *boku* used by school girls in Osaka and discovered that *boku* is used quite often by high school girls in Osaka, too, although the use is accompanied by a joking playful tone. Several people have pointed out to me that *boku* is easier to use in woman-to-woman communication than in mixed sex communication. It seems that in the process of expansion of *boku* from high school girls to college girls the sociolinguistic significance of *boku*-language used by girls has undergone a slight change.

7 At the commencement ceremony, Japanese students are congratulated by guest speakers for "becoming members of society," that is, students are not regarded as members of society in Japan.

8 *The Asahi* (July 25, 1985) reports a tendency for male employees to be placed in the main office while female employees of the same company are placed in branch offices.

References

Hasegawa, M. (1984) "Danzyo koyoo byoodoo hoo wa bunka no seitaikei o hakai suru. [The law of equal employment opportunity will destroy the ecological system of the culture]." *Tyuuoo Kooron* 5, 78–87.

Inoue, T. (1984) "Masukomi to zyosei no gendai. [Today's women and mass media]". *Onna no Imeezi* [Image of Woman], ed. Zyoseigaku Kenkyuukai, 316–29. Tokyo: Keisoo-syoboo.

Jugaku, A. (1979) *Nihongo to Onna* [Japanese and Women]. Tokyo: Iwanami-syoten.

Krauss, E. S., T. P. Rohlen and P. G. Steinhoff, eds. (1984) *Conflict in Japan*. Honolulu:University of Hawaii Press.

Nakane, C. (1970) *Japanese Society*. Berkeley: University of California Press.

Pharr, S. J. (1984) "Status conflict: The rebellion of the tea pourers." *Conflict in Japan*, eds. E. S. Krauss, T. P. Rohlen and P. G. Steinhoff, 214–40. Honolulu: University of Hawaii Press.

Reynolds, Katsue Akiba (1984) "Evidence for masculinity constraint: Fillers in Japanese." Paper presented at the annual meeting of the Linguistic Society of America, Baltimore.

Reynolds, Katsue Akiba (1985) "Female speakers of Japanese." *Feminist Issues* 5, Fall, 13–46.

23

Governed by the Rules?
The Female Voice
in Parliamentary Debates

Sylvia Shaw

Source: Judith Baxter (ed.), *Speaking Out: The Female Voice in Public Contexts*. London: Palgrave (2006), pp. 81–102. Reprinted with permission of Palgrave Macmillan.

Introduction

Speaking out is the business of parliamentary debate. In possibly no profession other than politics does success depend so strongly upon an individual's ability to speak effectively in public and often adversarial contexts. Parliaments have been almost exclusively the realm of male politicians until the latter half of the twentieth century, and as they are governed by rules devised to constrain the debate discourse they provide a unique context within which to examine the relationship between language use, gender and power in public institutions. Here I investigate the female voice in the archetypal parliamentary context: the British House of Commons. This parliament is often characterised as an adversarial 'bear pit' where opposition parties face each other and fight out issues in a confrontational manner. I also consider some of these findings with a comparative analysis of data from a much newer political assembly, the Scottish Parliament.

Previous research into language, gender and political debates includes Edelsky and Adams' (1990) investigation into gender, language and floor apportionment in US televised debates. Walsh (2001) asks whether women uncritically accept pre-existing discursive practices in institutional contexts that have been previously dominated by men (such as parliaments and the Church of England), whether they seek to change them, or whether they shift between these two positions. Wodak (2003) investigates female role construction in the European Union (EU) parliament, and Harris (2001), Ayala (2001) and Christie (2003) have used the adversarial context of the British House of Commons to investigate and develop theories of linguistic politeness. In this paper, I aim to find out what makes women speakers powerful or powerless in parliamentary settings. In particular I relate the female voice to the rule-governed nature of parliamentary discourse and explore the ways in which these rules are negotiated differently by men and women within the House of Commons.

Most of the women Members of Parliament (MPs) I have interviewed speak of a 'terror' of speaking within the House of Commons debating chamber. Many male MPs probably share this sentiment, but they do not face the sexist barracking and negative media representations commonly directed at women MPs.[1] There are overt indications that women and men are not treated equally in this context: for example, male MPs in the debating chamber have made 'melon weighing' gestures (intended to represent a woman's breasts) while a woman MP makes a speech; the media characterise the 1997 intake of new Labour MPs as 'Blair's babes'; and women have been assigned to stereotypical 'women's' portfolios and topics. It has been claimed that 'institutions are organised to define, demonstrate and enforce the legitimacy and authority of linguistic strategies used by one gender – or men of one class or ethnic group – whilst denying the power of others' (Gal, 1991: 188). This means that women's language and behaviour are more likely than that of male colleagues to be affected by contradictory expectations and institutional constraints. As the House of Commons was an exclusively male forum until the latter stages of the twentieth century, it is likely that men from the dominant ethnic and class groups in Britain will be the most powerful participants, and that men and women are participating on unequal terms: 'organisations and structures institutionalise the predominance of particular masculinities, thereby empowering and or advantaging certain men over almost all women and men' (Lovenduski, 1996: 5). Here I adopt the idea that particular settings can be the domain of some groups and not others as expressed in Bourdieu's notion of linguistic habitus (1991) which he describes as a 'linguistic sense of place' that:

> governs the degree of constraint which a given field will bring to bear on the production of discourse, imposing silence or hyper-controlled language on some people while allowing others the liberties of a language that is securely established. (1991: 82)

Similarly, Freed's notion of 'gendered spaces' suggests that the setting and communicative tasks together become an index (Ochs, 1992) of a gendered style and that 'certain social activities and practices may themselves become symbolically gendered if they are regularly and consistently associated with women or men' (Freed, 1996: 67).

I found that to be constructed as powerful speakers in debates MPs must be conversant with both formal and informal rules in their 'communicative tasks'. Debates consist of not only formal written rules which relate to the 'ideal' or canonical form of debates but also sets of rules that have come to be accepted over time and form part of the 'actual' debate rules (Edelsky and Adams, 1990; Shaw, 2000). The ability of an MP to assimilate, use or 'play' with these rules relates to their power in the debating chamber, and are part of what constructs them as 'core' or 'peripheral' members of this Community of Practice (CoP) (Eckert and McConnell-Ginet, 1992). A CoP can be thought of as a group of people who come together to engage in a particular set of activities or 'practices'. Individuals belong to multiple, changing CoPs upon different terms of participation and the relationship of a 'core' member of this CoP to the rules is complex and variable. To signal their membership they must be faultless in their adherence to some rules (such as those governing the use of formal address terms) but yet have the ability to transgress other rules for their own advantage.

The Research Study

The methodology adopted for this research aims to be qualitative, highly contextualised and reflexive (Stacey, 1988; Furnow and Cook, 1991). A detailed ethnographic description (according to Hymes (1972, 1974) ethnography of speaking framework) was undertaken to contextualise the parliamentary discourse. An ethnographic approach is particularly useful in identifying interactional norms in relation to gender as it:

> highlights speaker competence, local understandings of cultural practice, and cross-cultural variation. It therefore contributes to the feminist project of calling attention to women's abilities and agency, whilst reminding scholars that gendered language use is not everywhere the same. (Bucholtz, 2003: 48)

This research aims to be 'anti-essentialist' in that it recognises the diversity of women's identities and linguistic practices. However, gender is seen as one of the factors that may affect an individual's membership of, and participation within, this CoP. I therefore view gender as both a flexible and a fixed category. The flexibility comes from the fact that gender is not viewed as a 'given' social category reflecting a pre-existing identity, but rather as constructing and maintaining an individual's identity in the ongoing process of talk. The fixity comes from the way in which men and women are constrained by 'institutional arrangements based on sex category' (West and Zimmerman, 1987: 146) typical of this type of institutional context. This means that women 'actively work out their subject positions and roles in the process of negotiating discursive constraints' (Smith, 1990: 86).

The linguistic analysis is based upon transcriptions taken from a 60-hour corpus of video data from different House of Commons speech events between 1997 and 2001. Additionally semi-structured interviews with MPs gave insights into my interpretations of the transcribed events. A range of discourse analytic approaches were used to investigate the different linguistic practices which were identified as possibly constituting speakers as powerful participants in debates. As mentioned above, power in debates is strongly related to an individual's ability to adhere to or transgress rules. Here I discuss examples from the data that relate specifically to the ways in which the female voice negotiates rules in debates and the ways in which this disadvantages women in comparison to their male colleagues.

Rule-Breaking in Debates

Introduction

Previous research into political debates suggests women do not transgress rules to gain advantage in debates as much as their male counterparts. Edelsky and Adams' (1990) research into U.S. televised debates showed that male candidates transgressed rules governing turn length and time restrictions more than their female opponents and thus gained an advantage by maximising their own televised talk time whilst minimising that of their opponents. Christie's (2003) work on language, gender and politeness in political debates found that women MPs in House of Commons debates conform to transactional discourse norms. Women MPs in Christie's data corpus were not repetitive and managed to be sufficiently brief, whereas male MPs were admonished by the Speaker (moderator) 30, times for breaching these rules. My own research on floor apportionment supports these claims (Shaw, 2000). I found that in five debates 38 illegal interventions were made by male MPs, and only 4 by female MPs. Here I focus on two key ways in which women MPs may 'lose out' by their relationship to the debate rules. First, through their greater difficulty with acquiring the rules of parliamentary debate and secondly through their tendency to conform to debate rules when their male counterparts break them for interactional advantage.

Gaining an advantage by adhering to the rules

In political debates rules exist to permit the 'equalization of turns' and to preserve the rights of a speaker so that only one person speaks at a time. The debate can be viewed as the 'most extreme transformation of conversation – most extreme in fully fixing the most important (and perhaps nearly all) of the parameters that conversation allows to vary' (Sacks, Schegloff and Jefferson, 1974: 731). In the House of Commons, the formal rules of debates are listed in *Erskine May's Treatise on the Law, Privileges, Proceedings and Usage of Parliament* and are enforced by interventions made by the moderator or 'Speaker' of the House of Commons. Rules must ensure interactional equality and also maintain 'order' within the chamber. The maintenance of 'order' is to avoid confrontation that could possibly lead to the breakdown of the debate through heated arguments within the chamber. The line drawn in front of both government and opposition benches shows the historical importance of these rules: MPs must stay behind the line to ensure that they are more than a sword's length apart and cannot engage in bloody dueling across the chamber. Today the emphasis of the rules is more on preventing verbal rather than physical dueling and the preservation of 'order' guarantees the orderly progression of the debate and preserves MPs' speaking rights.

MPs must be able to adhere to some formal debate rules such as those governing 'parliamentary language' in order to be powerful speakers in debates. The failure of an MP to acquire the rules governing these linguistic practices may construct a speaker as a junior or peripheral member of the CoP. The rules governing parliamentary language ensure that exchanges do not become too personal and confrontational and include the rule that all speeches should be addressed to the Speaker and not directly to a political opponent. In order to achieve this indirect mode, all turns should be initiated with the address term 'Madam/Mister Speaker' and MPs must only address or refer to other MPs in the third person according to the office they hold, and not by using the pronoun 'you'.[2] These linguistic constraints (together with restrictions on using taboo language and directly accusing another MP of being a liar) form the set of rules that make up what is known as 'parliamentary language'. As noted earlier, the ability of an MP to acquire these rules is part of what constructs them as a powerful or 'core' member of this CoP. The transcript below shows a newly elected woman Labour MP[3] failing to use the correct forms of address in her speech in the debate on the Stephen Lawrence Inquiry:[4]

Transcript one

Transcription Key: (.)=micropause of under a second; (1)=timed
pause in seconds
<u>underline</u>=emphasis on word or syllable
[ ]=utterances overlapping with the line above
JH=John Hayes (Conservative male MP)

FEMALE MP:	the problem the police f<u>a</u>ced (.) was the fact that	1
	they were institutionally <u>ra</u>cist (.) institutionally	2
	inc<u>ompe</u>tent <u>and</u> institutionally cor<u>ru</u>pt and I	3
	<u>wo</u>uld say that corr<u>u</u>ption is the twin brother	4
	of <u>racism</u> (.) and it affects us <u>all</u> and this <u>why</u>	5

	the debate is so imp<u>or</u>tant (.) and the L<u>aw</u>rence	6
	inquiry is so important for <u>white</u> people as	7
	well as <u>black</u> people	8
JH:	would the right Honourable Lady give way	9
FEMALE MP:	yes	10
JH:	I'm very <u>grate</u>ful to the Honourable Lady (.)	11
	the Honourable Lady is <u>tell</u>ing this House is	12
	she the police suffers from instit<u>ut</u>ionalised	13
	corr<u>up</u>tion (.) leaving aside that outr<u>a</u>geous	14
	claim (.) doesn't she r<u>e</u>alise that by <u>blam</u>ing an	15
	institution coll<u>ect</u>ively (.) by assuming there is	16
	some unconscious collective g<u>ui</u>lt (.) she is	17
	letting off the hook (.) those officers who are	18
	<u>cert</u>ainly guilty of these charges (.) because	19
	they are hiding be<u>hind</u> the very sort of	20
	collective allegations that she <u>makes</u>	21
FEMALE MP:	thank you (.) well if we can look at the issue	22
	you <u>raise</u> by per<u>haps</u> taking another –ism and	23
	another instit<u>ut</u>ion (.) just to see whether (.)	24
	the point you make is corr<u>ect</u> or not (.)	25
FEMALE MP:	oh I'm sorry	26
SPEAKER:	o o <u>ord</u>er the Honourable Lady must use the	27
	corr<u>ect</u> parliamentary language	28
FEMALE MP:	Mr Deputy Speaker I suffer from an ina<u>bili</u>ty	29
	to get that into my mind even after two years	30
	in this house (.) yes um the H<u>o</u>nourable	31
	G<u>en</u>tleman er opposite um will perhaps look	32
	at another example we can use another –ism I	33
	was <u>say</u>ing and a another instit<u>ut</u>ion lets take	34
	s<u>ex</u>ism (.) and lets take (.) er p<u>ar</u>liament lets	35
	take the House of C<u>omm</u>ons (.) lets look	36
	across the benches here (.) and in fact when	37
	the Home Secretary rose to his feet there was	38
	<u>o</u>ne w<u>o</u>man opposite and twenty-six m<u>e</u>n (.)	39
	on the opposition benches (.) now s<u>ure</u>ly you	40
	would not deny that that means we have an	41
	instit<u>ut</u>ion which is <u>bias</u>ed against women (.)	42
	would the Honourable Gentleman deny that	43
	I presume he would not (.) now <u>e</u>qually	44
	<u>e</u>qually(.) so y<u>ou</u> would say (.) well I sorry	45
	the H<u>o</u>nourable Gentleman	46
SPEAKER:	order the Honourable Lady must th<u>ink</u> carefully	47
	before she <u>choos</u>es her <u>words</u> (1)	48
FEMALE MP:	absolutely right er (.) Mr Deputy Speaker er	49
	the H<u>o</u>nourable G<u>en</u>tleman just said yes he	50
	w<u>ou</u>ld deny that there is a discrimination	51
	against women when eff<u>ec</u>tively there are no	52
	women well two women at this moment in	53
	time sitting on the benches opposite	54

(Speech Continues)

The MP uses the more informal address form 'you' four times in this extract (lines 23, 25, 40 and 45). The Speaker intervenes twice (lines 27 and 47) in order to tell the MP giving the speech to use correct 'parliamentary language'. This is a powerful speech, critical of both the police for being institutionally racist[5] and parliament itself for being institutionally sexist. One interpretation of the persistent use of this informal address form is that the MP is flouting the parliamentary rules. Her apologies for the rule-breaking (lines 26, 29–31 and 49) could be interpreted as sarcastic and her intention could be to show that the 'correct' formal address term is archaic and awkward. This resistance to the parliamentary rules would seem all the more appropriate here as the topic of her speech is highly critical of public institutions in general and the House of Commons in particular.

However, the MP makes it clear when interviewed that the rule-breaking was not intentional, and that she sees this rule-breaking as her own inability to master the interactional constraints of the debate floor. Furthermore, an error she made later in the same debate (when she presses an MP to 'give way' but then forgets her intervention) has a lasting effect upon her attitude towards speaking in debates:

Interview extract one

MP: I was pleased with my speech and I even thought oh maybe I've got the hang of this Commons thing and maybe that's why I was very insistent on him on this MP giving way because I felt that I was easily an equal with him in the chamber to have an argument about it [...] but I have never felt carefree about speaking in the chamber again because it's the fear thing if that kicks in you don't have the logic to fall back on it becomes a psychological thing the 'oh that's happened' it is very difficult to get round it and when I speak to other (women) MPs about it they all say yeah that's how I've always been in the chamber and I think maybe that I am. I didn't start off that way a lot of MPs start off that way.

INTERVIEWER: Which is a shame because your speech in that debate shows you are a good speaker.

MP: Oh well I can't any more I am not any more I find it makes you want to write things down more which is a bit of a killer for speaking because you know you don't speak freely.[6]

The consequences of breaking these rules are great as the MP has lost confidence in her speech-making abilities and has decided to speak with more caution in the future. The factors contributing to this reaction are undoubtedly complex and partly relate to the emotive nature of the topic of the debate itself as well as the specific role that this MP plays within the debate. However, this transgression of the rules may be particularly difficult for this MP because of the masculinised nature of the 'habitus' of this CoP. Not only are women more 'visible' than men in this forum (Puwar, 2004) but they may have to work harder than men to gain respect and be seen as equal colleagues. As Eckert and McConnell-Ginet point out in relation to their own findings:

> Such data suggest an extension of the generalization that women have to do much more than men simply to maintain their place in the standard language market [...] women may have to use linguistic extremes in order to solidify their place, wherever it might be. (1999: 195)

The 'linguistic extremes' for women MPs could be strict adherence to the debate rules. The pressure upon a woman MP to perform faultlessly when she rises to stand in the chamber may therefore be greater than upon her male counterparts.

Although women may have more pressure upon them to conform to the rules, there is no definite evidence to suggest that they break such rules regarding parliamentary language more than male MPs. However, it is surprising that there were no examples in the data corpus of newly elected male MPs failing to use the correct parliamentary language. The behaviour of the Speaker(s) and that of newly elected male MPs would have to be examined more closely in order to investigate this. Anecdotally there are reports that the Speakers of the House of Commons favour old members over new, have their favourite MPs, and choose to be pedantic about some rules but not about others. I found that in five debates the Speaker corrected the use of parliamentary language much more than s/he corrected MPs who spoke out of turn. It is also possible that the Speaker(s) call women MPs 'to order' more than men. An analysis of the behaviour of all newly elected MPs may also reveal a different explanation. One female MP I interviewed claims that '*men who are nervous are more likely just to stay out and not be there. There are lots of men never ever speak at all.*'[7] If this is the case male MPs may be avoiding making the kind of public error discussed above by non-participation within the chamber.

The House of Commons seems to be a particularly punishing forum in which to make mistakes of this kind. The Scottish Parliament is a CoP that shares many of the procedural characteristics of the House of Commons, but differs in some key respects. It is a relatively new parliament (opened in 1999) and has a higher proportion of women Members of the Scottish Parliament (MSPs).[8] Furthermore, women were founder members and it was designed with democratic and egalitarian notions of representation to the fore (Mitchell, 2000). Although most of the rules governing the interaction are the same as the House of Commons, one difference is that members can address each other by their first names. The transcript below shows Margo MacDonald asking the First Minister[9] a question in 'First Minister's Question Time'.

Transcript two[10]

MM=Margo MacDonald (SNP), PO=Presiding Officer, FM=First Minister (Henry MacLeish)

MM:	thank you Presiding Officer (1) if we could return to	1
	earth and leave Mars behind (.) I wonder if the First	2
	Minister recalls with me that following the winter crisis	3
	(.) in the NHS	4
PO:	[no I'm sorry] you haven't asked (.) order	5
MM:	oh I know (.) he knows what my first question was though	6
	I think	7
PO:	no no order you must read out your first question	8
MM:	oh (.) right we'll go through the form (laughs) to ask the	9
	First Minister	10
MSPs:	[laughter]	11
MM:	how he plans to (1) recruit the required number of nurses for	12
	hospitals to cope with seasonal admissions this winter (1)	13
FM:	er Margo (.) I'm really sorry that the procedures of the	14
	House force me to answer your first question and then we	15
	can get onto the real business after that (turn continues)	16

In this example Margo MacDonald starts her turn by making a joke (if we can return from Mars … on line 1). Then she starts to ask the First Minister a question but does not follow the correct procedures[11] (lines 2–4). The Presiding Officer (moderator) says she must read her question first (line 5) to which she replies that it is not necessary because the First Minister knows what her question is (line 6). The Presiding Officer insists she must read the question correctly (line 8) and she does so (lines 12–13). When the First Minister responds to the question he apologises to the MSP (using her first name only) for having to follow the procedures (lines 14–15).

This example provides a striking contrast with the transcript from the House of Commons. The woman MSP either forgets to ask the initial formal question or does not do so because she regards it as an unnecessary procedure. In either case she challenges the fundamental procedures of the chamber by contradicting the correction of the Presiding Officer. She is right in saying the First Minister knows her question already, he does. So in omitting to read out the initial question she is transgressing the accepted and official norms before agreeing to 'go through the form' which she clearly regards as unnecessary. This exchange also shows the lack of formality in the Scottish Parliament when compared with the House of Commons as first names are used, and the Presiding Officer even apologises for having to enforce the rules (line 14). The data from the House of Commons suggests that MPs are unlikely to challenge the Speakers' authority in this way (although some male MPs directly challenge debate rules when intervening or filibustering, discussed later). Furthermore the Speaker's style when intervening is much more authoritarian and direct than the intervention made by the Presiding Officer. The woman MP in the first transcript invokes negative consequences by transgressing the rules but there is no indication that this is case in the example from the Scottish Parliament. On the contrary it is the rules that appear misguided rather than the MSP's transgression of the rules.

This comparison[12] suggests that it is the particular culture of the House of Commons CoP and the way in which linguistic rules are enforced by the Speaker which makes the woman MP's transgressions so awkward. In contrast, the apparent lack of concern the woman MSP shows for Scottish Parliament rules suggests that she feels in a strong enough position to challenge the Presiding Officer when she transgresses the rules. In turn, the Presiding Officer is much less authoritarian than the Speaker in the House of Commons. Women MSPs were also found to illegally interrupt other MSPs, use adversarial language and to use humour to manipulate the 'key' of speech events, whereas these practices were extremely rare amongst women MPs in the House of Commons (Shaw, 2002). It is likely that the involvement of women in the Scottish Parliament from its origins, the higher proportion of women MSPs, and even possibly such factors as the design of the debating chamber may contribute to a more egalitarian culture than exists in the House of Commons.

Gaining an advantage by breaking the rules

Floor apportionment　The extent to which an MP is able to control the resource of the debate floor as evidenced by linguistic exchanges is one element that relates to the amount of power an MP has in debates. In an analysis of floor apportionment in debates (Shaw, 2000), it was found that there was nominal equality between male and female MPs with respect to 'legal' turns that follow the rules of debate. Women and men took equal amounts of legal debate turns and 'give way' interventions (in relation to their numbers in parliament). However, women MPs made far fewer illegal interventions than men MPs. Speaking or shouting from a sedentary position whilst another 'legal' speaker holds the floor is one of the most common transgressions in debates, and one that is often tolerated by the Speaker. Illegal interventions can be collective shouts of disapproval or approval (for instance cheering), individual short interventions (such as 'rubbish!') or substantive individual interventions that interfere with the 'legal' debate floor. The transcript below shows how the focus of the debate can be drawn away from a 'legal' speaker and the floor 'hijacked' by illegal intervenors.

A combination of legal and illegal interventions in this transcript result in the female speaker (who has all the legal rights to the floor) struggling to maintain her status as the main speaker. The transcript also shows the lack of interventions by the Speaker to stop these transgressions and enforce the rules. As male speakers made 90 per cent of all the individual illegal utterances in five debates this suggests that this type of rule-breaking has to some degree been accepted as a masculine 'norm' in debates. As illegal interventions account for a high proportion of all the interventions made in the House of Commons, and women do not participate in these type of interventions, men dominate the debate floor and women are disadvantaged by their reluctance to transgress these rules.

Transcript three[13]
Transcription Key: CMP=Current MP (with legal rights to the floor);
IMP=intervening MP; C=Conservative; L=Labour;
m=male; f=female

CMP f(C):	it is very significant that this has not taken	1
	place (.) there is an element in my view of	2
	deceit in the way in which this legislation	3
	(.) has been protect er presented in this	4
	house	5
IMP m(L):	would the right honourable lady give way	6
CMP f(C):	I will	7
IMP m(L):	(Give way) has the Hon. Lady been asleep	8
	for the last two years the European Court of	9
	Human Rights have ordered us to change	10
	our laws (.) we have to we have to change	11
	the law	12
IMP m(C):	rubbish (1)	13
IMP m(L):	(Give way contd.) the honourable gentleman	14
	from his lazing position says rubbish (.)	15
	unfortunately life is life (.) and life says we've	16
	got to change the law and we're doing it (.)	17
	it's not there is no hidden agenda there	18
IMP m(C):	of course there is	19
IMP m(L):	(Give Way contd) oh rubbish Winterton (.) you	20
	really are a silly man (1)	21
MPs:	[laughter]	22
CMP f(C):	gentlemen (.)	23
IMP m(C):	no more silly than you	24
CMP f(C):	I'm really I'm as aware as he is that there's been	25
	a debate on the issue from that perspective and	26
	that the honourable gentleman opposite has	27
	made his (.) contribution to some extent but	28
	that does not alter the fact that we are still here	29
	debating (.) what is going in this case to be	30
	domestic legislation (turn continues)	31

(Shaw, 2000: 411)

Filibustering

The practice of filibustering is probably the most extreme example of rule-breaking in the data corpus. Filibustering is the practice by which a group of MPs from one party attempts to speak for so long in a debate that there is no time left for the debate to be resolved, or for the following debate to be started. It is a tactic which 'plays with' and challenges the debating rules for political gain. It is also a process that manipulates the serious 'key' of debates into an ironic one: everyone in the chamber (including the Speaker) knows that an MP is breaking the rules by talking about irrelevancies and minor details, but they are unable to do anything about it. Filibustering is also a highly collaborative enterprise undertaken by a number of MPs from one party who help each other to prolong the speeches by intervening and suggesting further topics with which to prolong the debate. There are three examples of filibustering in the 60-hour data corpus and women MPs do not take part in any of them.

The ability to resist and challenge the Speaker's authority is perhaps the strongest expression of an MP's dominant behaviour in debates. Filibustering MPs regard them-selves as being powerful enough to disregard the Speaker's interventions. Furthermore, the irony mentioned earlier exploits the fact that everyone in the chamber is aware that the MP is breaking the rules, but nothing can be done to stop him. An example of this ironic tone is when the filibustering MP repeatedly emphasises the 'importance' of what everyone present knows is an utterly unimportant point. In one of these filibusters the video recording clearly shows an MP laughing and sniggering behind his papers when his filibustering colleague makes an obvious deviation from the topic of the amendment, and when he defies the Speaker's interventions. This covert humour is a highly collaborative enterprise in which the amusement is shared by the MPs taking part in the filibuster (and other members of their political party). The collaborative and gendered nature of filibus-tering seems (like humour (Shaw, 2002)) to help to establish and maintain the 'fraternal networks' (Walsh, 2001: 19) made manifest in 'bonds based on competitive mastery and subordination'. The fact that women either cannot or will not engage in this linguistic practice only serves to underline their position as peripheral members of this CoP.

Conclusion

These examples show that women MPs may be more conscious of adhering to debate rules than their male colleagues. One explanation for this could be that women MPs consciously choose to behave differently by rejecting the male, elitist, old-fashioned tra-ditions of the House of Commons. This would mean that women MPs are *choosing* not to break the rules in debates. Given the interactional advantage contingent upon rule-breaking this would seem ill-advised, but it could be that women MPs are actively seek-ing to alter the culture and norms of the debating chamber. Alternatively, the different behaviour of men and women MPs could be a result of the coercive forces within the CoP which mean that women are made to feel like 'interlopers' (Eckert, 1998) in the community, subject to negative sanctions like sexist barracking and negative stereotyp-ing. It is likely that both these explanations play a part in explaining men and women MPs' differential linguistic practices. In an analysis of the marginal position of women priests in the Church of England, Walsh (2001) finds that their position is partly the effect of their own belief in women's 'civilizing difference' and partly the effect of sexist reactions to them by male priests and by the media. As noted in the introduction Walsh finds that 'what *is* clear is that their language and behaviour is more likely than those of

male colleagues to be fractured by competing, and often contradictory norms and expectations' (2001: 201).

Women MPs in interviews expressed contradictory views. They identified practices
such as barracking and cheering as male activities in which they consciously did not
participate.[14] They also expressed the belief that women MPs behave differently from
men: *'we're doing things differently and we know we're doing things differently'*.[15]
However, some of the interviewees expressed contradictory attitudes in this respect.
Having identified 'male' practices and stated they did not engage in them, they also
claimed that they had to *'ape the men's behaviour because that's the only way you're
going to get anywhere'*.[16] The fact that women MPs do not have consistent reactions to
the avoidance of these 'male' linguistic practices suggests that women MPs' *choice* of
non-participation in these practices cannot fully explain the differences found.

Eckert (1998) suggests some explanations for the importance of women's adherence
to norms and rules. In her research on phonological variation in two CoPs of U.S. high
school adolescents ('Jocks' and 'Burnouts') she finds that: 'the constraints on girls to
conform to an exaggerated social category type are clearly related to their diminished
possibilities for claiming membership or category status' (1998: 73). This conformity
may be realised by other forms of linguistic behaviour, such as conforming to or transgressing linguistic rules, and related to different types of CoPs. Eckert argues that women
moving into prestigious occupations and especially elite institutions 'are generally seen as
interlopers and are at greater pains to prove that they belong' (1998: 67). With this
'interloper' status, women are more subject than men to negative judgements about
superficial aspects of their behaviour (such as dress or style of speech).[17] The way in
which women can 'prove their worthiness' is 'meticulous attention to symbolic capital'
(1998: 67). She notes that:

> While men develop a sense of themselves and find a place in the world on the basis of their
> actions and abilities, women have to focus on the production of selves – to develop authority
> through continual proof of worthiness. (1998: 73)

Women MPs' desire to adhere strictly to the rules and their desire to avoid rule-breaking
can therefore be viewed as one of the ways in which women MPs make sure they are
'beyond reproach' in a CoP which views them as 'outsiders'.

There is evidence to suggest that women MPs' lack of participation in male discursive
practices may be due to coercive forces leading them to have a marginal 'interloper' status within the CoP. Some women MPs recognise their status as that of 'interloper':

> My strategy was to try and be an insider. When quite clearly I was never going to be an
> insider in the House of Commons my strategy was to build up my strength outside.[18]

Women MPs are constructed as outsiders by sexist barracking, which is common, and
their exclusion from cross-party exchanges expressing solidarity. This may serve to
strengthen the 'fraternal networks' (Walsh, 2000: 301) against women MPs. Negative
sanctions outside the chamber are also pertinent, as the media characterisation of women
MPs as 'Stepford wives', 'clones' and 'Blair's babes' clearly have an effect on the women
themselves[19] and are taken up and used against women MPs through barracking within
the chamber. The imposition of these negative sanctions upon women MPs may mean
that they can only pay 'meticulous attention to symbolic capital' rather than attention to
their actions and abilities in order to prove their worthiness (Eckert, 1998: 67–73).

These coercive forces may therefore result in women MPs avoiding rule-breaking or norm-challenging practices in order to satisfy the requirements of their 'interloper' status by being 'beyond reproach' with respect to the formal CoP rules. Women MPs may also be constructed as outsiders because of the contradictory and impossible expectations upon them. For example, they are expected to be just like (or just as able as) male politicians, but they must also prove that it makes a difference when more women are elected (Dahlerup, 1988: 279). Additionally, the ideological salience of such ideas as a women's 'consensual' style of speech or the critical mass theory[20] can only fracture their behaviour further. In one study (Childs, 2000, 2004), women MPs claimed that they are 'less combative and aggressive, more collaborative and speak in a different language to men' (2004: 14). In my interviews with women MPs I found that they were often reluctant to characterise a women's style of speech but that women's language was nevertheless described as being 'less hectoring' but 'equally forceful'. One MP comments:

> One of the good things about women and debating is that we all listen to each other and we're all constructive, but actually when you have that sort of debate I didn't enjoy it.[21]

This sort of contradictory position is typical of the stance that women MPs have in relation to gendered 'styles' and their own participation in House of Commons speech events. Furthermore, women MPs who believe there are male and female styles put themselves in an uneasy position in relation to their own performances in debates – what place in the 'bear pit' for a consensual style? It has been noted that there has been a recent shift towards a perception of 'female verbal superiority' (Cameron, 2003: 458) where private rather than public communication skills are highly valued. However, it is difficult to see how the strong traditions of adversarial public speaking in the House of Commons can be undergoing a process of 'conversationalization' (Fairclough, 1992) of public discourse. As Holmes (1992: 144) points out, 'there is no obvious incentive for adult males to give up highly valued talking time in public contexts'.

Dahlerup (1988) and Walsh (2000; 2001) view institutional change as contingent upon the 'critical acts' undertaken by the female minority group.

> Even a small number of women can make an impact upon dominant discursive norms, if they pursue a 'critical difference' approach, whereas the voices of large numbers of women can be assimilated, if they choose to adopt a policy of accommodation to pre-existing norms and practices. (Walsh, 2000: 273)

The most significant factor in changing the position of the minority is the 'willingness and ability of the minority to mobilise the resources of the institution to improve the situation for themselves and the whole minority group' (Dahlerup, 1988: 296). Walsh (2001) finds that groups like the Northern Ireland Women's Coalition (NIWC) in the Northern Ireland assembly have helped to promote an alternative set of linguistic norms for political debates through an organised campaign focussed upon increasing the presence and treatment of women in the assembly. However, women MPs in the House of Commons expressed uncertainty at their ability to instigate political solidarity beyond the divisions created by party allegiances:

> I think it would be good if we could get women of all parties together but I don't think it will happen [...] the men would use it and say 'Oh look there's a group of women they must be weak to need that'. You just can't afford to draw attention to the fact that you're a woman.[22]

Given these constraints it is difficult to see how women MPs can undertake a critical difference approach and challenge their interloper status. Nevertheless, women MPs in the House of Commons may benefit from understanding how they are governed by the rules of this particular institutional language game, and what the real costs and rewards of their existing strategies might be.

Notes

1 Interviewees identified sexist barracking that was typically directed at women's physical appearance or intellectual capabilities. Similarly negative media characterisations often took up the idea that new women MPs could not think for themselves. For example, they were described as 'Stepford wives' (Interview data from Shaw, (2002)).

2 For example, when addressing an opposition MP the address term should be 'The Honourable Lady/Gentleman' and when addressing an MP in their own party, the address term should be 'My Honourable Friend'.

3 I have preserved the anonymity of this MP because although she granted me permission to use her interview data she did not know I would publish it with an analysis of her speech in this way.

4 This debate on 29th March 1999 discussed the finding that the metropolitan police was 'institutionally racist' in its failure to investigate the murder of a black teenager, Stephen Lawrence.

5 The full speech can be found in the Hansard Report for Monday 29th March 1999 at http://www.publications.parliament.uk.

6 Shaw (2002), Appendix 2, interview transcript E pages 347–8.

7 Shaw (2002), Appendix 2, interview transcript C pages 332–3.

8 At the time this data was collected, women occupied 37 per cent (48 MSPs) and men 63 per cent (81 MSPs) of the seats in the Scottish Parliament.

9 The 'First Minister' is the leader of the government party (in this case Labour), and is the equivalent of the Prime Minister in the House of Commons.

10 From First Minister's Question Time: (07/12/00).

11 In question times, the first question (which has been written and submitted in advance) must be read by the questioner. This is a formality as the questioner invariably wants to ask the Minister or First Minister the supplementary questions that follow (for which the Minister/First Minister has not had time to prepare).

12 A full comparison of the two parliaments was undertaken as part of the larger study (Shaw, 2002).

13 This extract is from the Sexual Offences Bill: Amendment one on the age of consent on 01/03/99. The female Conservative MP is Teresa Gorman, the male Labour MPs is Gerald Bermingham, and the interrupting male Conservative MP is Nicholas Winterton.

14 Shaw (2002), Appendix 2, Interview B, lines 80–5.

15 Shaw (2002), Appendix 2, Interview A, line 433.

16 This statement was made by Jackie Ballard (Shaw 2002, Appendix 2, Interview B, lines 94–5, p. 326). Another female Labour MP expresses this contradictory attitude, at first claiming that '*we're doing things differently and we know we're doing things differently*' and that '*we have to hold our nerve and not turn into the men*' but then stating that '*I think gradually we'll be sucked into behaving the way they* (the men) *behave because that's what they want, the establishment* (Shaw (2002), Appendix 2, Interview A, p. 321, lines 433, 439–40, 459–61).

17 The observation that women are 'interlopers' who are more subject to the negative effects of gender stereotyping can be related to Kanter's (1977) idea of tokenism, and Yoder's (1991: 183) observation that studies of tokenism in gender inappropriate occupations have found that women 'experience performance pressures, isolation, and role encapsulation, but men do not'.

18 Shaw (2002), Appendix 2, Interview D, lines 92–4.
19 Shaw (2002), Appendix 2, Interview A, lines 255–75, 400–8.
20 The critical mass theory claims that a qualitative shift will automatically take place in an institution when women's representation reaches about 30 per cent (Kanter, 1977). It is a very influential theory even though many researchers (e.g. Yoder, 1991, Kathlene, 1994) have shown that simply increasing the numbers of a minority does not eradicate sexism.
21 Shaw (2002), Appendix 2, Interview B, lines 38–40.
22 Shaw (2002), Appendix 2, Interview B, lines 187–94.

References

Ayala, S. P. De (2001) 'FTAs and Erskine May: Conflicting need?'. *Journal of Pragmatics.* 33, 143–69.

Bourdieu, P. (1991) *Language and Symbolic Power.* Cambridge: Polity and Blackwell.

Bucholtz, M. (2003) 'Theories of discourse as theories of gender: Discourse analysis in language and gender studies' in Holmes, J. and Meyerhoff, M. (eds) *The Handbook of Language and Gender.* Oxford: Blackwell, 43–68.

Cameron, D. (2003) 'Gender and language ideologies' in Holmes, J. and Meyerhoff, M. (eds) *The Handbook of Language and Gender.* Oxford: Blackwell, 447–67.

Childs, S (2000) 'The new Labour women MPs in the 1997 British Parliament', *Women's History Review.* 9 (1), 55–73.

Childs, S. (2004) 'A feminised style of politics? Women MPs in the House of Commons'. *British Journal of Politics and International Relations.* 6 (1), 3–19.

Christie, C. (2003) 'Politeness and the linguistic construction of gender in parliament: An analysis of transgressions and apology behaviour'. *Sheffield Hallam Working Papers: Linguistic Politeness and Context.* http://www.shu.ac.uk/wpw/politeness/christie.htm.

Dahlerup, D. (1988) 'From a small to a large minority: Women in Scandinavian polities'. *Nordic Political Science Association.* 11 (4), 275–98.

Eckert, P. (1998) 'Gender and sociolinguistic variation' in Coates, J. (ed.) *Language and Gender: A Reader.* Oxford: Blackwell, 64–75.

Eckert, P. and McConnell-Ginet, S. (1992) 'Communities of Practice: Where language, gender and power all live' in Hall, K., Bucholtz, M. and Moonwomon, B. (eds), *Locating Power: Proceedings of the Second Berkeley Women and Language Conference*, Berkeley Women and Language Group. Berkeley, CA, 88–99.

Eckert, P. and McConnell-Ginet, S. (1999) 'New Generalisations and explanations in language and gender research'. *Language and Society.* 28 (2), 185–201.

Edelsky, C. and Adams, K. L. (1990) 'Creating equality: Breaking the rules in debates'. *Journal of Language and Social Psychology.* 9 (3), 171–90.

Fairclough, N. (1992) *Discourse and Social Change.* Cambridge: Polity Press.

Freed, A. (1996) 'Language and gender in an experimental setting' in Bergvall, V., Bing, J. and Freed, A. (eds) *Re-thinking Gender and Language Research: Theory and Practice.* London and New York: Longman.

Furnow, M. M. and Cook, J. A. (1991) *Beyond Methodology: Feminist Scholarship as Lived Research.* Bloomington and Indianapolis: Indiana University Press.

Gal, S. (1991) 'Between speech and silence: The problematics of research on language and gender' in di Leonardo, M. (ed.), *Gender at the Crossroads of Knowledge: Feminist Anthropology in the Postmodern Era.* Berkeley, CA: University of California Press, 175–203.

Harris, S. (2001) 'Being politically impolite: Extending politeness theory to adversarial political discourse'. *Discourse Studies.* 12 (4), 451–72.

Holmes, J. (1992) 'Women's talk in public contexts'. *Discourse and Society.* 3 (2), 121–50.

Hymes, D. (1972) 'Toward ethnographies of communication: The analysis of communicative events' in Giglioli, P. (ed.) *Language and Social Context.* Harmondsworth: Penguin, 21–44.

Hymes, D. (1974) *Foundations in Sociolinguistics: An Ethnographic Approach*. Philadelphia: University of Pennsylvania Press.

Kanter (1977) *Men and Women of the Corporation*. New York: Basic.

Kathlene, L. (1994) 'Power and influence in state legislative policy making: The interaction of gender and position in committee hearing debates'. *American Political Science Review*. 88 (3), 560–76.

Lovenduski, J. (1996) 'Sex, gender and British politics' in Lovenduski, J. and Norris, P. (eds) *Women in Politics*. Oxford: Oxford University Press, 3–18.

May, T. E. (1989) *Erskine May's Treatise on the Law, Privileges, Proceedings and Usage of Parliament*. London: Butterworths.

Mitchell, J. (2000) 'New parliament, new politics in Scotland'. *Parliamentary Affairs*. 53 (3), 605–21.

Ochs, E. (1992) 'Indexing gender' in Duranti, A. and Goodwin, C. (eds) *Re-thinking Context: Language as an Interactive Phenomenon*. 335–58.

Puwar, N. (2004) 'Thinking about making a difference'. *British Journal of Politics and International Relations*. 6 (1), 65–80.

Sacks, H., Schegloff, E. A. and Jefferson, G. (1974) 'A simplest systematics for the organization of turn-taking in conversation'. *Language*. 50, 696–735.

Shaw, S. (2000) 'Language, gender and floor apportionment in political debates'. *Discourse and Society*. 11 (3), 401–18.

Shaw, S. (2002) *Language and Gender in Political Debates in the House of Commons*. Unpublished PhD thesis: University of London.

Smith, D. (1990) *Texts, Facts and Femininity: Exploring the Relations of Ruling*. London: Routledge.

Stacey, J. (1988) 'Can there be a feminist ethnography?'. *Women's Studies International Forum*. 11, 21–7.

Walsh, C. (2000) *Gender, Discourse and the Public Sphere*. Unpublished PhD thesis: Sheffield Hallham University.

Walsh, C. (2001) *Gender and Discourse: Language and Power in Politics, the Church and Organisations*. London: Longman.

West, C. and Zimmerman, D. H. (1987) 'Doing Gender'. *Gender and Society*. 1, 125–51.

Wodak, R. (2003) 'Multiple identities: The roles of female parliamentarians in the EU parliament' in Holmes, J. and Meyerhoff, M. (eds) *The Handbook of Language and Gender*. Oxford: Blackwell, 573–99.

Yoder, J. (1991) 'Re-thinking tokenism: Looking beyond numbers'. *Gender and Society*, 5, 178–92.

24

"Doing Femininity" at Work: More than Just Relational Practice

Janet Holmes and Stephanie Schnurr

Source: *Journal of Sociolinguistics* 10(1) (2006), pp. 31–51. Reprinted with permission of Wiley-Blackwell.

Introduction

Researchers in the area of language and gender have recently begun to examine the 'multiplicity of experiences of gender' (Eckert and McConnell-Ginet 2003: 47) in different social contexts and communities of practice. A number of researchers, for example, have explored the concept of masculinity, and indeed 'masculinities' (Connell 1995; Cameron 1997; Edley and Wetherell 1997; Johnson and Meinhof 1997; Kiesling 1998, 2004; Bucholtz 1999; Meân 2001; Coates 2003; Bell and Major 2004). Some attention has also been paid to 'the multiplicity of…femininities' (Eckert and McConnell-Ginet 2003: 48), that is, the dynamic and diverse ways in which people construct different kinds of femininity in social interaction in different contexts (e.g. Okamoto 1995; Livia and Hall 1997; Cameron 1997, 1998; Coates 1997, 1999; Cameron and Kulick 2003). This paper contributes to this enterprise by analysing some of the ways in which people construct and negotiate different femininities in white-collar New Zealand workplaces.

Femininity is an ambiguous concept with complex associations. It could even be argued that 'femininity' has been treated as something of a dirty word in gender studies, associated, from a feminist perspective, with a rather dubious set of behaviours. Most obviously, acting 'feminine' conjures up politically incorrect 'frilly pink party dresses'; femininity is associated with demureness, deference, and lack of power and influence (as discussed in Eckert and McConnell-Ginet 2003: 16ff, 184ff; see also Lakoff 2004). Femininity invokes a stereotype, and it is a negative one for many feminists, and a problematic and uncomfortable one for many academic women.[1] Discussing this issue, Mills (2003) implicitly subscribes to this negative attitude: 'one of the many important advances made by feminism is to open up within the notion of what it means to be a woman a distinction between femininity and femaleness, so that one can be a woman without considering oneself to be (or others considering one to be) feminine' (Mills 2003: 188). Accepting such a claim entails subscribing to the view that 'feminine' and 'femininity' are dirty words which must be replaced by the euphemisms 'female' and 'femaleness'. But is this necessary? We argue that 'feminine' can be reclaimed as a positive attribute.

In contesting the denigration and rejection of the words 'feminine' and 'femininity', it is important to note that the basis for this negative stereotype is the *exaggeration* of features which are associated with the construction by women of a normative gender identity. The exaggeration evokes derision. As Mills herself notes, in the media 'the representation of stereotypically feminine women is rarely presented ... without mockery or ridicule' (2003:187).[2] But this should not mean that the enactment of normatively feminine behaviour should be a cause for embarrassment and apology by professional women (or men) in the workplace.

In what follows, we attempt to re-present the notion of femininity as a positive rather than a negative construction in workplace interaction. We analyse a number of specific examples which illustrate the negotiation of a range of femininities at work. We draw on the notion of a gendered community of practice (Holmes and Stubbe 2003a), in which certain kinds of gender performance are perceived as 'unmarked' (Ochs 1992: 343), or ' "normal" behaviour' (Kiesling 2004: 234), while others are regarded as marked or 'emphasised' (Connell 1987: 187). Building on the notion that – through their association with particular roles, activities, traits, and stances – certain socio-pragmatic, discursive and linguistic choices, or ways of speaking, 'index' (Ochs 1992, 1996) or culturally encode gender (Cameron and Kulick 2003: 57), we explore the different ways of 'doing femininity' identified in our workplace data.

In a recent paper examining the ways in which authority is constructed in workplace interaction, Kendall (2004) suggests that gender identity is often irrelevant in the workplace. She argues that in everyday interaction people focus on role construction rather than gender identity: 'women and men do not generally choose linguistic strategies for the purpose of creating masculine or feminine identities' (2004: 56) ... 'situations in which women and men consciously choose language options to create femininity and masculinity are rare' (2004: 76). Certainly gender is not frequently a *conscious* focus of identity performance at work (but see Hall 1995, 2003; Besnier 2003). Nonetheless, the distinction between two types of social identity is not always easy to make, especially when particular linguistic features are associated with more than one kind of identity (e.g. masculinity and leadership, femininity and subordination/server status). As Cameron and Kulick note, in some cases 'the same way of speaking signifies both a professional identity and a gendered identity, and in practice these are difficult to separate: the two meanings coexist, and both of them are always potentially relevant. The actual balance between them is not determined in advance by some general principle, but has to be negotiated in specific situations' (2003: 58).

In our view, then, gender is relevant at some level in every workplace interaction, an ever-present influence on how we behave, and how we interpret others' behaviour, even if our level of awareness of this influence varies from one interaction to another, and from moment to moment within an interaction.[3] We are always aware of the gender of those we are talking to, and we bring to every workplace interaction our familiarity with societal gender stereotypes, and the gendered norms to which women and men are expected to conform (Eckert and McConnell-Ginet 2003: 87). Workplaces are simply one of many sites for gender performances which have the potential to strengthen the 'gender order' (Connell 1987); and while in some professions 'doing gender' is quite central to workplace performance, in all workplaces individuals unavoidably enact gendered roles, adopt recognisably gendered stances, and construct gender identity in the process of interacting with others at work.

In addition, there are situations in which people exploit their audience's familiarity with stereotypical concepts of femininity or masculinity in a more conscious fashion for particular effect, as we illustrate below. The concept of 'double voicing' (Bakhtin 1984) is relevant here, accounting for the ways in which speakers mingle components of different styles for particular effect. Talk which indexes gender in exaggerated or over-emphatic ways may be manipulated for the purpose, for instance, of parodying and even subverting established workplace norms and expectations about appropriate ways for professional employees to behave at work. The ability to interpret and appreciate the social meaning of such gender performances depends inevitably on recognition of what constitutes an unmarked gender performance or 'unmarked behaviours for a [particular] sex' (Ochs 1992: 343) in a particular community of practice. The first section of the analysis addresses, therefore, the issue of the construction of unmarked femininity in particular communities of practice.

The data we draw on was collected by the Wellington Language in the Workplace (LWP) Project (see www.vuw.ac.nz/lals/lwp; Holmes and Stubbe 2003b). The Project includes material from a wide variety of New Zealand workplaces, and uses a methodology which allows workplace interactions to be recorded as unobtrusively as possible. The LWP corpus currently comprises over 2,500 workplace interactions, involving around 400 participants. In this paper, we draw on data from white-collar professional workplaces in order to explore the ways in which workplace participants, and especially workplace managers, construct complex femininities in different discourse contexts within particular communities of practice.

'Doing Femininity' in a Feminine Community of Practice

We begin by considering what it means to behave in a normatively feminine way in a recognisably feminine community of practice. Holmes and Stubbe (2003a) explored the notion of 'gendered' workplaces, and examined some of the discourse features which people use to characterise the organisational culture of different workplaces as being relatively more 'feminine' or 'masculine'. Describing workplaces in this way does not indicate that everyone in a particular workplace behaves in a consistently gendered manner; rather these labels act as a shorthand, indicating the expectations and constraints on gender performances in some contexts in those workplaces.[4] Indeed our analyses demonstrate that the characteristics stereotypically associated with such generalisations are often inaccurate, and that day-to-day interactions in particular communities of practice typically challenge the generalisations. Nevertheless, it was clear that those participating in our research, as well as members of the wider New Zealand community, were very willing to identify some workplaces as particularly feminine and others as very masculine. And such perceptions inevitably affect expectations about appropriate behaviour including ways of speaking. IT companies and manufacturing organisations typically tended to be labelled as more masculine workplaces, while organisations (and especially government departments) which dealt directly with clients, or with people-oriented, social issues, or with education, tended to be perceived as more feminine places to work.

Within such workplaces people draw from a range of linguistic and discursive resources to construct their identities as 'professionals' in workplace interaction, and to negotiate particular pragmatic functions, such as giving directives, criticising, disagreeing, approving, and so on. Their choices index particular stances (e.g. authoritative, consultative, deferential) which construct not only their particular professional identities or roles (e.g.

manager, team leader, support person), but also their gender positioning (see, for example, Holmes, Stubbe and Vine 1999; Holmes and Stubbe 2003a; Kendall 2003, 2004). This is the most obvious way in which people enact conventional gender identities at work – through linguistic and discursive choices which indirectly index normative femininity whilst also instantiating a particular professional relationship. Example 1 illustrates this in a community of practice described by its members, as well as by outsiders, as a very feminine community of practice:

Example 1[5]
Context: Ruth is the department manager. Nell is a policy analyst. Nell has prepared an official letter on which Ruth is giving her some feedback.[6]

1	RUTH:	it's **actually** quite **I mean** it's
2		it's well written [inhales] I **just** have
3		I **just** think the approach is **could**
4		should be a bit different in terms of see like
5		the organisation wouldn't
6		we wouldn't usually say something like this
7		that **I mean** it's true but um we should **probably**
8		put in there that um the organisation has
9		what we did **actually** in terms of
10		providing advice on other avenues of funding
11		// but\ what the organisation =
12	NELL:	// mm\
13	RUTH:	= provides is a policy advice organisation
14		and does not have um ++
15		they **actually** have only limited funding for
16		sponsorship + (and) I've **just** realised though
17		that this is (like) that they go in a couple of weeks
18		it **might** have been worth talking to Stacey
19		about um funding through
20		**I think** it's through [*name of funding agency*]
21		( ) last year we got funding for [tut] a someone
22		from [*name of organisation*] to attend
23		an international conference [drawls]:in: India
24		**I think** + I **can't remember exactly** the criteria
25		but there is a fund there and it **may might** be **a bit** late
26		but **just I mean** Stacey knows the contacts
27		and I **think** it's in [*name of funding agency*]
28		and whether or not it's worth having a talk to them about…

Ruth wants Nell to make some amendments to the letter, and the interaction is clearly potentially face threatening. Ruth's strategy for conveying her critical comments and her directives entails the use of a range of classic face-saving mitigation devices. In this short interaction, she uses a variety of hedges and minimisers (in bold above): *could, may, might, probably, just* (2), *actually* (3), *I mean* (3) and *I think* (5), and approximators, *a bit, I think it was, I can't remember exactly*, etc. These devices minimise the force of the face-threatening implicit criticisms and directive speech acts, and pay attention to Nell's face needs (Brown and Levinson 1987).[7]

Ruth also minimises the critical implications of her comments by emphasising the positive. So she begins by highlighting the fact that Nell's version of the letter is fine, *it's well written* (line 2). She also acknowledges that what Nell has said is true (line 7), but comments that it is not the *usual* way of doing things in the organisation. The shift from *the organisation* (line 8) to the use of the pronoun *we* (line 9) which is strategically ambiguous between exclusive and positively polite inclusive meaning (*we wouldn't usually say something like this*), allows Ruth to suggest that she and Nell are working on this together, thereby again saving both interlocutors' faces in a potentially tricky situation. On this interpretation, mitigation is clearly at the core of this array of strategies.

From an analyst's perspective, this is normatively feminine talk, characterised by features which have been described in decades of language and gender research (e.g. see Tannen 1993, 1994a, 1994b; Crawford 1995; Holmes 1995; Aries 1996; Coates 1996; Wodak 1997; Talbot 1998; Romaine 1999). In this section of her interaction with Nell, Ruth is making use of linguistic, pragmatic and discursive devices which signal considerateness and positive affect, stances associated with femaleness and feminine identity in New Zealand society. These are, of course, just some of the available strategies for fulfilling her role as manager, and in other contexts she draws on more confrontational, authoritative, and direct strategies to achieve her goals (see, for example, Holmes and Stubbe 2003b: 49). Example 1 serves, however, to illustrate an interaction in which a middle-class professional woman performs her managerial role in a way which also constructs a conventionally feminine gender identity. It also serves as a linguistic instantiation of classic 'relational practice' (Fletcher 1999), that is, off-record, other-oriented behaviour which serves to further workplace goals. In Fletcher's analysis relational practice is paradigmatically women's work, and thus a quintessential example of 'doing femininity' at work. In the community of practice in which these women worked, this gender performance was unremarkable and 'unmarked'. Being normatively feminine in this community of practice did not arouse derision, and nor did it require apology.

Importantly, however, the perception of such behaviour as acceptable and unmarked held true for professional women in many of the white-collar workplaces in which we recorded. Doing feminine gender using the kinds of strategies and linguistic devices described above was typically perceived as unmarked, as simply one component of performing their professional identity in particular interactions in a very wide range of communities of practice. Feminine behaviour, in other words, was regarded as normal behaviour in such contexts, and hence can be re-classified positively rather than derided.

When men 'do femininity' at work, however, the perceptions of, and reactions to, their behaviour are much more complex. For example, in our data, when men made use of discourse strategies and linguistic devices associated with normatively feminine behaviour, the responses varied significantly on different occasions in different communities of practice. In a relatively feminine community of practice, the use by a male of linguistic markers of considerateness and concern for the addressee's face needs, such as those identified in Example 1, when used in a similar professional context, occasioned no comment. Indeed, our ethnographic observations and interviews, indicate that such behaviour was regarded as normal, appropriate and unmarked.

An example of such normatively feminine behaviour by a male in a department with education as its core business, is provided in Holmes and Stubbe (2003b: 32). Giving a directive to a subordinate, Len, the manager, uses a range of mitigating strategies, including hedges, modalised interrogatives, minimisers, and hesitations, devices which very closely match those used by Ruth in Example 1. In the context where he works, this linguistic behaviour was considered perfectly appropriate; it did not attract comment as 'marked' in any respect, and his colleagues clearly regarded his linguistic and discursive style as unremarkable.

Example 2 illustrates the same pattern in a different community of practice. It is taken from a meeting in one section of a large organisation; the section has specific responsibility for meeting the needs of the organisation's clients. Smithy, the male project manager, engages in facilitative behaviour by drawing the attention of the chair to a contribution which merits praise:[8]

Example 2

Context: Large project team meeting in commercial organisation. The project manager, Smithy, is reporting on the project's progress to the section manager, Clara.

```
1   SMITHY:   um service level team to produce
2             a strategy document they've done(.)
3             um Vita was to meet with I S to determine er
4             an implementation plan for the recording device
5   VITA:     yes done it +
6   SMITHY:   [parenthetical tone] Vita's done a um work plan
7             just for that// um implementation\ and that
8   CLARA:    great//that'll make the plan easier\
9   SMITHY:   we can feed// (out what) you want\
10  VITA:     // haven't actually\(heard anything ...)
11  SMITHY:   Vita's going to meet with Stewart
12            to determine how 0800 numbers
13            come in to the call centre
```

In lines 1–4, Smithy reports on what the team agreed Vita should do by this meeting, and in line 5, Vita confirms that she has indeed accomplished the specified task. Since Clara, the Department manager, makes no immediate response. Smithy proceeds to 'prime' Clara to provide positive feedback to Vita (*Vita's done a work plan just for that implementation*, lines 6–7). Clara responds appropriately in line 8 with a positive and appreciative comment, and Smithy then continues with the next item. Smithy's facilitative move is made extremely discreetly, and Clara picks up his cue without missing a beat. This is a nice example of relational practice – subtle, backgrounded discursive work, attending to collegial relationships and ensuring that things run smoothly. Relational practice is quintessentially gendered as 'feminine' in Fletcher's (1999) book *Disappearing Acts*, in which she argues that relational skills are typically associated with women, and hence Smithy's behaviour in Example 2 could be characterised as 'doing femininity'. This is just one of many similar examples of Smithy's style of workplace interaction which attracts no comment, and appears to be regarded as normal and unremarkable behaviour in context, even in this somewhat less feminine community of practice.

In neither Len's workplace nor Smithy's, then, does their use on occasion of a normatively feminine style of discourse seem out of place, and nor does it attract comment as 'marked' in any respect. Using linguistic features and discourse strategies which attend to relational aspects of the interaction, and index normative femininity, is perfectly acceptable as a way of performing aspects of one's professional identity within these communities of practice. In other words 'doing femininity' is unmarked behaviour in such contexts, whether it is performed by a man or a woman. Thus defined, normative femininity can be regarded positively rather than treated as the focus of ridicule.

'Doing Femininity' in a Masculine Community of Practice

There are however, workplace contexts where using a feminine style can evoke a very much less positive response. Especially in relatively masculine communities of practice, the effective use of a normatively feminine style was a much more complex and even hazardous enterprise. And men, in particular, tended to be the target of negative comment for using stylistic features which conventionally index femininity.

So, for example, the discursive behaviour of members of an IT team in a big commercial organisation contrasted sharply with the norms of the places where Ruth, Len and Smithy worked. There was, for instance, scarcely any conventional small talk among team members before or after meetings. Pre-meeting talk tended to be business-oriented, a chance to update on work which team members were doing together in other contexts. In the six meetings of this team that we videotaped in full, there is scarcely a single topic that is not directly related to some aspect of the team's work. And the humour among these team members was predominantly aggressive and sarcastic, and sometimes undeniably sexist (e.g. with references to nagging wives, and heavy drinking with the boys).[9] Over 90 percent of the humorous comments which occurred in one meeting, for instance, were sarcastic and negative jibes, intended to put down the addressee or to deflate them. Behaviour which was perceived as 'soft' or conventionally 'feminine' elicited a very different reaction in this community of practice from the way it was treated by Ruth's colleagues and in Len's workplace, as Example 3 demonstrates:

Example 3[10]

Context: Six men in a regular meeting of a project team in a large commercial organisation. They are discussing a technical issue related to a project for some clients. Callum's colleagues pretend to be horrified that he has actually talked face-to-face with the clients.

```
 1  BARRY:    but we can we can kill this// particular action\ point
 2  MARCO:    //well yep\ you can kill
 3            this particular action point
 4  BARRY:    and you// guys\
 5  CALLUM:   //are\ you sure +++ I took the opportunity
 6            of talking with some of the users
 7  BARRY:    what again? [laughs] // [laughs]\
 8  MARCO:    // not again what are you doing talking to them\
 9  BARRY:    [laughs]: go on// Callum come on\
10  MARCO:    //[laughs]\
11  CALLUM:   and th- and they th- ++
12  MARCO:    they've still got// issues\
13  CALLUM:   //(I I I)\ well + I don't think they're sure? +
14            ( ) if they're really issues or not
```

The group of men here make fun of Callum for engaging voluntarily in 'communicative' behaviour with clients. Using stereotypically masculine language, Barry and

Marco suggest that a proposed action, namely dealing with a specific technical issue, be *killed*, that is, dropped (lines 1–3), since it is peripheral to the main project. Callum interrupts with a protest, using a question *are you sure* (line 5), rather than a more aggressive form of challenge. Even so, the three-second pause suggests that his comment causes surprise. He goes on to point out that the proposed action emerged from his discussions with the people who will be using the programme (lines 6–7). Barry and Marco then proceed to mock Callum, ridiculing the notion that he should actually 'talk', that is verbally communicate face-to-face, with clients. Barry's tone of voice in his question *what again?* (line 7) conveys mocking astonishment, and Barry's *Callum come on* (line 9) is drawled with a rise-fall intonation indicating sardonic incredulity. Callum persists, despite the mockery, and maintains his relatively feminine approach, *I don't think they're sure? if they're really issues or not* (lines 13–14) with a high rising terminal on *sure*, a feature coded as feminine in New Zealand speech. He is also reporting behaviour that is stereotypically feminine, namely, these people don't know what they think, thus risking tarring himself with the same brush by association.

This short excerpt illustrates how this group of professional IT experts construct themselves as a very masculine community of practice; both in content (e.g. *kill this point*) and style: they contest each other's statements very directly, and the floor is a competitive site where they interrupt one another freely. In this context, Callum's verbal behaviour is clearly 'marked'. The underlying (only slightly facetious) assumption is that 'real men' (and especially computer experts) do not ever actually talk face-to-face with clients; talking to clients is rather the responsibility of the support staff at the user interface, many of whom are, unsurprisingly, women. Indeed, contributing more than the minimal amount of talk seems to be generally regarded as relatively feminine behaviour within the culture of this IT project team, where the most senior participant in the team meetings contributes the least talk. In this exchange, then, the team members imply that Callum has behaved in an unmasculine way, and mock his conventionally feminine approach.

Example 4 provides another suggestive illustration of the kind of response elicited by normatively feminine behaviour in a relatively masculine community of practice. It is an excerpt from an interaction between members of the senior management team in Company S, a community of practice similar in some ways to the IT team described above. Many of the norms for interaction between the all-male members of this team are stereotypically masculine, with relational practice expressed through contestive humour, jocular insult, and extensive competitive teasing (see Schnurr 2009). During the period that we recorded, a new member of the team, Neil, was being inculcated into the team culture, the normal 'way we do things around here' (Bower 1966, cited in Clouse and Spurgeon 1995: 3), often through teasing and sarcastic comment on features of his behaviour which were regarded as inappropriate in the context of the team's usual ways of interacting. On one occasion, for instance, he took seriously a negative critical response to his excuse for not being able to attend a meeting. It was clear from the reactions of others, as well as the subsequent discourse, that the criticism was intended as jocular. But Neil misinterpreted Shaun's tone, and responded in a way that the other team members clearly regarded as inappropriately fulsome. Our observations and analyses in this rather masculine community of practice suggest that one dimension of this inappropriateness was the association of apologetic and mitigating language with relatively feminine ways of talking.

Example 4

Context: Meeting of the senior management team in middle-sized IT company. Neil apologises
for not being able to attend the first monthly staff meeting to which he has been invited.

```
 1   SHAUN:   okay but I think it's important
 2            you do go to the staff meeting
 3            and get introduced
 4   NEIL:    yeah .........
 5            er I can't do it today unfortunately I've
 6            I've already booked in some time
 7            with someone else this afternoon
 8            but the next one I can come along to yeah
 9   SHAUN:   we'll think about it
10   NEIL:    pardon
11   SHAUN:   we'll think about it
12   NEIL:    //[laughs]\
13   SHAUN:   //we don't take kindly to \ being rejected
14   NEIL:    oh I'm sorry I've got a yeah got a meeting
15            this afternoon which I can't get out of
16            if I'd have known I would've changed it yeah
17   SHAUN:   what is our formal position on Neil (5)
```

Neil needs to be introduced to the wider staff of the organisation (lines 1–3). The fact that
he is not free to attend (lines 5–8) provides an opportunity for Shaun to tease him for
rejecting their invitation (lines 9,11,13). Neil does not recognise that he is being teased,
and he responds seriously to Shaun's comment *we don't take kindly to being rejected* (line
13), with an elaboration of his excuse (lines 14–16). His response is marked by a number
of appeasement devices (e.g. apology, excuse; he even claims he would have changed his
appointment if he had known that he was expected to attend the staff meeting (line 16)).
Shaun does not respond, however, to Neil's attempt at appeasement; rather he replies in a
very challenging tone with a confrontational, direct attack on Neil's status: *what is our formal position on Neil* (line 17).

Neil's inappropriately elaborate apology could be regarded as overly conciliatory, a
stance strongly associated with more feminine styles of interaction. It clearly marks him
as an outsider to the team, a team which our ethnographic data indicates forms a very
close-knit community of practice, with a number of normatively masculine norms of
interaction, as mentioned above. Clearly then, ways of talking which conventionally
index femininity can function as unmarked in some communities of practice, while the
same discourse strategies and linguistic features may be perceived as marked and com-
ment-worthy in others. We turn now to the discussion of a rather different way in which
women may exploit gendered norms of interaction at work, drawing on the conventional
indices of femininity for particular, and sometimes subversive, purposes.

Exploiting Normative Femininity

The extensive exploration of style and styling in the speech of those from a diverse range of
social, ethnic and gender backgrounds (e.g. Bell 1999, 2001; Bucholtz 1999; Johnstone
1999, 2003; Rampton 1999, 2003) provides a useful framework for discussing the ways in
which some New Zealand women exploit features of normative and even stereotypical

femininity in workplace interaction. As these researchers note, Bakhtin's (1984) concept of 'double voicing' provides a way of accounting for the mingling of stereotypical components of another style with 'habitual speech patterns' to 'generate symbolically condensed dialogues between self and other' (Rampton 1999: 422). In particular, this approach provides a way of describing how professional women in the workplace make strategic use of linguistic features associated with stereotypical femininity to parody, and thus implicitly contest and 'trouble' the images of women and the gender categories that such features support and maintain (Butler 1990; Bell, Binnie, Cream and Valentine 1994: 31; Jones 2000).

In our data, this particular kind of double voicing, namely the 'strategic use of an ingroup variety' (Johnstone 1999: 514), was observable in the behaviour of senior women who were secure in their professional identity.[11] This strategy allowed them to make use of features which might otherwise be misinterpreted as 'serious' rather than ironic. Traditionally, the concept of leadership has been associated with dominant, hegemonic masculinity: 'what counts as leadership, the means of gaining legitimacy in leadership, and so on, are male dominated in most organizations' (Hearn and Parkin 1988: 27). Consequently, 'the language of leadership often equates with the language of masculinity' (Hearn and Parkin 1988: 21). We found that effective women leaders typically drew skilfully and competently on a wide range of discourse strategies, some regarded as indexing conventional masculinity, and some as enacting normative femininity, to accomplish both their transactional and relational goals (Holmes 2000; Stubbe, Holmes, Vine and Marra 2000).

Jill, for example, is a company director in a small IT company, and the chair of the company Board. She appears to enjoy her position as a woman in the predominantly masculine world of IT (Trauth 2002), as evidenced by many aspects of her behaviour (see Schnurr forthcoming). Our recordings indicate that Jill makes use of a wide range of interactional strategies and ways of talking, including some which can be regarded as normatively feminine, constructing her female gender in a conventional, unmarked and unselfconscious way within a range of workplace interactions, while at other times she draws on more conventionally masculine strategies. So, at times she uses conventionally polite discourse, standard relational practice in Fletcher's (1999) sense, apologising for interrupting a subordinate, for instance, *can I be a real pain and interrupt you again*, and making use of a variety of facilitative and supportive strategies in running a meeting. At other points, she uses more direct and forceful strategies, interrupting small talk to start a meeting, for instance, and firmly asserting the need to move on to the next point on the agenda.

In addition, however, Jill strategically 'does femininity' on occasion, in a self-aware and ironic fashion that both exploits and parodies gender stereotypes. On such occasions, instead of playing down or minimising areas of difference in gender display in her male-dominated workplace, as senior women often do, she emphasises her femininity in a variety of ways, lampooning stereotypical features of gender performance. In Example 5, for instance, she plays up her helplessness and ignorance (albeit, importantly, with an ironic element of self-parody):

Example 5[12]

    Context: Jill, chair of the Board of an IT company, has had a problem with her computer and has consulted Douglas, a software engineer, for help. Returning to her office, she reports her experience to her colleague, Lucy, a project manager in the company.

1   JILL: [*walks into room*] he just laughed at me
2   LUCY: [laughs]: oh no:
3   JILL: he's definitely going to come to my aid
4   but ( ) he just sort of laughed at me

5	LUCY:	[laughs]
6	JILL:	(and then) I've got this appalling reputation
7		of being such a technical klutz and// ( )\
8		sometimes look it's not *me* +
9	LUCY:	//[laughs]\
10	JILL:	I work with what I've got +// ( )\
11	LUCY:	//I know\ it's the tools you've been prov//ided\
12	JILL:	//that's\ right +++

In this exchange, Jill constructs an image of herself as a stereotypical female: as technically ignorant and incompetent, a *technical klutz* (line 7) in the area of the organisation's specialisation, computer technology. She describes how her ignorance elicited laughter from the technical guy who was assisting her (lines 1, 4). Although she laughingly refutes the implication of incompetence, by blaming her tools (lines 8, 10), this excuse is clearly tongue-in-cheek or ironic, since *technical klutz* is an identity she regularly adopts, playing up the stereotypically feminine role of incompetent ignoramus in the IT area.[13] The exaggerated intonation and high pitch with which lines 8 and 10 are delivered further underline Jill's parodic intent.

Our extensive observational data indicate that Jill is a confident and competent member of this professional organisation, and this, along with her sardonic tone, supports an ironic (and even subversive) reading of her construction of a stereotypical, ultra-feminine, identity. In other words, we could interpret Jill's gender performance here not as reinforcing the predominantly masculine norms of her IT community of practice, but rather as troubling and contesting the assumptions underlying them. By refusing to treat IT incompetence as a serious matter, she implicitly questions the validity of the hegemonic stereotype which discounts the competence of women who are technically unsophisticated. Like the American adolescent girls Eder researched, Jill here parodies 'traditional norms about feminine behaviour' (1993: 25), and, as a demonstrably intelligent woman and competent manager, implicitly contests them, thus transforming their role as unquestioned and unquestionable reference points.

Unlike some women in IT workplaces in which we have observed, Jill does not appear to feel any pressure to pretend that she is no different from a man. So, for example, in response to a comment from her colleague Lucy that by not having a computer monitor she will have space for a pot plant, she comments humorously to a male colleague *you can tell the girly office can't you*. Jill's use of the term *girly* here is superficially problematic since it appears to dismissively endorse an ideology which denigrates women's preferences. Analysing a narrative in which a woman, Meg, uses the term *girl* in just such an oppressive way, Coates (1997: 310) comments that Meg 'presents herself as colluding in a world view that denigrates and trivializes women'. But Jill's usage here is different. Firstly she is talking about herself, and secondly, the comment is in no way apologetic in tone. Drawing on Bakhtin's (1984) concept of 'double voicing', an ironic reading is thus possible, a reading which is much more consistent with Jill's confident gender performance in this male-dominated community of practice. So, for instance, she and Lucy take responsibility for the kitchen renovations, discussing paint and cushions with no sense that they need to reject such a stereotypically feminine task. Although she holds a powerful leadership position, Jill enacts her feminine identity with good-humoured assurance, alongside an intelligent awareness of the dominant societal gender stereotypes. Thus her use of the term *girly office* can be interpreted as indicating her awareness of her male colleagues' gender stereotypes, along with an implicit contestation and troubling of those views. By unapologetically embracing the concept of a feminine space at work, and indicating its acceptability, this powerful woman implies that she sees no contradiction between being statusful and being feminine in this community of practice.

In another workplace the boss is known as 'Queen Clara', and addressed and referred to by her staff with good-humoured irony as 'your royal highness'. Clara, like Jill, is perfectly secure both with her professional and her gender identity, and draws comfortably on the full panoply of available discourse strategies, including those conventionally regarded as masculine, to do authority when appropriate (see, for example, the 'screen-dumps' example in Holmes and Marra 2002b: 391). Equally, Clara frequently behaves in normatively feminine ways without any sense that this is inappropriate to her high status in the organisation.

It is possible that Clara and Jill, as senior women who refuse to conform to the conventionally masculine norms associated with leadership (Ely 1988; Hearn and Parkin 1988; Geis, Brown and Wolfe 1990; Maher 1997; Sinclair 1998), are effectively contesting the related widespread expectation that workplaces (and especially those concerned with technology and IT) should be regarded as uncompromisingly masculine domains (cf. Tannen 1994b; Trauth 2002; Kendall 2003), where male patterns of interaction serve as the unmarked model. Their secure attitude to the performance of their gender identity in the workplace appears to free up these women to enjoy and exploit stereotypical, and even hyperbolic ways of 'doing femininity'. Clara and Jill seem to revel in semi-facetiously and parodically 'doing femininity' in the more off-record, peripheral aspects of their managerial roles, but they also draw on both normatively masculine and feminine discourse resources in the course of their everyday workplace interactions. As women who are secure in their professional identities, it seems that they do not to need to downplay the fact that they are female or minimise gender differences in aspects of their behaviour in order to ensure they are taken seriously.

Conclusion

This paper has explored certain aspects of gender performance in the workplace. We have discussed different femininities or ways of 'doing femininity', and suggested that workplace interaction provides opportunities not only for indexing normative femininity, a kind of gender performance which has been associated with 'relational practice' (Fletcher 1999), but, also for parodying, contesting, and troubling gendered workplace expectations and assumptions.

We have shown that the use of familiar and normative discourse resources for indexing femininity by both women and men may elicit different responses in different contexts within different communities of practice. We have suggested that, especially in relatively feminine communities of practice, such performances are frequently treated as 'unmarked behaviours' (Ochs 1992: 343), not just for women but for either sex. Indeed, in many contexts within such communities of practice, the ability to discursively index conventional femininity is regarded as an asset, and skill in adopting a feminine stance is positively construed. There is no evidence here for the negative conception of femininity which pervades much of the discussion of this concept. Feminine behaviour is regarded as normal and assessed positively in many contexts within such communities of practice.

On the other hand, we identified relatively low tolerance for aspects of behaviour perceived as normatively feminine in some contexts, and especially by men engaged in transactional, task-oriented interaction in more masculine communities of practice. Features which are conventionally associated with femininity may thus attract negative comment or derision in particular workplace interactions, within particular workplace cultures. Though often expressed in covert and implicit ways, such negative reactions could be regarded as evidence of sexism in such workplaces.

More positively, identifying particular types of behaviour as markedly feminine, also opens up the possibility for exploitation, and through a kind of 'double-voicing', for parody and ironic self-quotation. Language can be used not only to enact and reinforce conventional gender positioning, the 'gender order', but also to subvert unacceptable socio-cultural norms, and contest restrictive concepts of professional identity at work. Hence, some senior women in our data deliberately exploit feminine stereotypes, consciously parodying conventional notions of how women should behave in the workplace (cf. Koller 2004).

In conclusion, while professional identity might appear the most obviously relevant aspect of social identity in workplace interaction, the analysis in this paper demonstrates that people also discursively manage and interpret complex gender identities through workplace talk. Moreover, we suggest that our analysis provides a basis for recasting the concepts 'feminine' and 'femininity' in a more positive light, reclaiming the potential for women and men to behave in feminine ways, and make constructive but unremarkable use of conventionally feminine discourse strategies, 'even' at work.

Notes

The content of this paper was first presented at IGALA 3, the 3rd Biennial Conference of the International Gender and Language Association held at Cornell University, June 5–7, 2004. We thank those who attended and contributed to the discussion which has informed our revision. We thank those who allowed their workplace interactions to be recorded, and other members of the Language in the Workplace Project team who assisted with collecting and transcribing the data. We also thank Meredith Marra and Emily Major for much-appreciated assistance with editing and preparing this paper for publication. Finally we are indebted to the editors and the three anonymous reviewers who provided detailed and valuable feedback which has resulted in a much improved paper.

1 In this the concept of 'femininity' contrasts significantly with the concept of 'masculinity', which is regarded positively. As Kiesling (2004: 230) points out 'studying masculinity allows the discussion of idealizations of manhood that no man may actually fulfill'.

2 Mills (2003:186–8) describes changes in feminist analyses of femininity over the last decade, and especially the ironisation of femininity which has been the focus of work by Liladhar (2001). The concept of ironising a 'feminine' performance is explored below. See also Clift (1999).

3 This approach is endorsed by a number of other analysts, for example, West and Fenstermaker (1995), Martín Rojo (1998), Stokoe and Weatherall (2002), Stokoe and Smithson (2002), Kitzinger (2002).

4 This point is more fully explored in Holmes and Meyerhoff (2003), Holmes and Stubbe (2003a), and Holmes (2006).

5 This example is discussed in more detail in the context of an analysis of leadership strategies in Holmes, Schnurr, Chiles and Chan (2003). Tina Chiles, in particular, contributed to the analysis of this example.

6 See Transcription Conventions 1, p. x.

7 We are not suggesting that indirectness should always be construed positively (or directness negatively). There are obviously occasions when indirectness can be unhelpful and

counter-productive (see Holmes in press chapter 2). Such assessments can only be made in context; they require attention to participants' reactions, and often to the longer-term outcomes of an interaction insofar as these can be derived from the ethnographic detail collected in workplaces where we recorded.

8   This example is also discussed in Holmes and Marra (2004: 388), a paper which focuses on the range of linguistic and discursive strategies which may instantiate Fletcher's (1999) concept of 'relational practice'.

9   See Holmes and Marra (2002a) for a fuller description and exemplification, and Baxter (2003: 145) for a description of a very similar community of practice in the British context.

10   This example is used to illustrate a different point in Holmes (2005: 53).

11   Tew (2002: 78ff) discussing the work of Cixous and Kristeva, notes the importance they attach to identifying elements of ' "a different voice" ... in the ordinary everyday discourses of women and other subordinated social groups', as one means of starting to disrupt the hegemony of 'phallocentric codes and rules' (2002: 81–82). Parody constitutes one such element.

12   This example is also discussed in Schnurr (forthcoming) and in Holmes and Schnurr (2005) where it is used to illustrate the way Jill uses humour in the workplace.

13   See Clift (1999: 543) on self-deprecating irony, and also on 'the affiliative qualities of irony'. See also Johnstone (2003: 204–5) who describes how being southern and sounding southern as resources for some Texan women, can be used sometimes 'for very specific fleeting purposes (such as selling a business service to a man who wants you to flirt)'.

References

Aries, Elizabeth. 1996. *Men and Women in Interaction*. Oxford: Oxford University Press.

Bakhtin, Mikhail. 1984. *Problems in Dostoevsky's Poetics*. Minneapolis: University of Minnesota Press.

Baxter. Judith. 2003. *Positioning Gender in Discourse: A Feminist Methodology*. Chippenham: Macmillan Palgrave.

Bell, Allan. 1999. Styling the other to define the self: A study in New Zealand identity making. *Journal of Sociolinguistics* 3: 523–41.

Bell, Allan. 2001. Back in style: Reworking audience design. In Penelope Eckert and John R. Rickford (eds.) *Style and SociolinguisticVariation*. Cambridge: Cambridge University Press. 139–69.

Bell, Allan and George Major. 2004. 'Yeah right': Voicing kiwi masculinity. Paper presented at the New Zealand Language and Society Conference, Massey University, Palmerston North, NZ.

Bell, David, Jon Binnie, Julia Cream and Gill Valentine. 1994. All hyped up and no place to go. *Gender, Place and Culture* 1: 31–47.

Besnier, Niko. 2003. Transgenderism and language use in Tonga. In Janet Holmes and Miriam Meyerhoff (eds.) *Handbook of Language and Gender* Oxford: Blackwell. 279–301.

Brown, Penelope and Stephen C. Levinson. 1987. *Politeness. Some Universals in Language Usage*. Cambridge: Cambridge University Press.

Bucholtz, Mary, 1999. You da man: Narrating the racial other in the production of white masculinity. *Journal of Sociolinguistics*. 3: 443–60.

Butler, Judith. 1990. *Gender Trouble: Feminism and the Subversion of Identity*. New York: Routledge.

Cameron, Deborah. 1997. Performing gender identity: Young men's talk and the construction of heterosexual masculinity. In Sally Johnson and Ulrike Hanna Meinhof (eds.) *Language and Masculinity*. Oxford: Blackwell. 47–65.

Cameron, Deborah. 1998. 'Is there any ketchup Vera?': Gender, power and pragmatics. *Discourse and Society* 9: 435–55.

Cameron, Deborah and Don Kulick. 2003. *Language and Sexuality*. Cambridge: Cambridge University Press.

Clift, Rebecca. 1999. Irony in conversation. *Language in Society*. 28: 523–54.

Clouse, R. Wilburn and Karen Spurgeon. 1995. Corporate analysis of humor. *Psychology – A Quarterly Journal of Human Behaviour* 32: 1–24.

Coates, Jennifer. 1996. *Woman Talk. Conversation Between Women Friends*. Oxford: Blackwell.

Coates, Jennifer. 1997. Competing discourses of femininity. In Helga Kotthoff and Ruth Wodak (eds.) *Communicating Gender in Context*. Amsterdam and Philadelphia, PA: John Benjamins. 285–314.

Coates, Jennifer. 1999. Changing femininities: The talk of teenage girls. In Mary Bucholtz, A. C. Liang and Laurel A. Sutton (eds.) *Reinventing Identities*. New York: Oxford University Press. 123–44.

Coates, Jennifer. 2003. *Men Talk*. Oxford: Blackwell.

Connell, Robert W. 1987. *Gender and Power: Society, the Person and Sexual Politics*. Stanford, CA: Stanford University Press.

Connell, Robert W. 1995. *Masculinities*. Berkeley, California: University of California Press.

Crawford, Mary. 1995. *Talking Difference, On Gender and Language*. London: Sage.

Eckert, Penelope and Sally McConnell-Ginet. 2003. *Language and Gender*. Cambridge: Cambridge University Press.

Eder, Donna. 1993. 'Go get ya a French!' Romantic and sexual teasing among adolescent girls. In Deborah Tannen (ed.) *Gender and Conversational Interaction*. Oxford: Oxford University Press. 17–31.

Edley, Nigel and Margaret Wetherell. 1997. Jockeying for position: The construction of masculine identities. *Discourse and Society* 8: 203–17.

Ely, Robin. 1988. Attitudes toward women and the experience of leadership. In Suzanna Rose and Laurie Larwood (eds.) *Women's Careers. Pathways and Pitfalls*. New York: Praeger. 65–81.

Fletcher, Joyce K. 1999. *Disappearing Acts. Gender, Power, and Relational Practice at Work*. Cambridge, MA: MIT Press.

Geis. Florence, Virginia Brown and Carolyn Wolfe. 1990. Legitimizing the leader: Endorsement by male versus female authority figures. *Journal of Applied Psychology* 20: 943–70.

Hall, Kira. 1995. Lip service on the fantasy lines. In Kira Hall and Mary Bucholtz (eds.) *Gender Articulated: Language and the Socially Constructed Self*. New York: Routledge. 183–216.

Hall, Kira. 2003. Exceptional speakers: Contested and problematized gender identities. In Miriam Meyerhoff and Janet Holmes (eds.) *Handbook of Language and Gender*. Malden, MA: Blackwell. 352–80.

Hearn. Jeff and P. Wendy Parkin. 1988. Women, men, and leadership: A critical review of assumptions, practices, and change in the industrialized nations. In Nancy Adler and Dafna Izraeli (eds.) *Women in Management Worldwide*. London: M.E. Sharpe. 17–40.

Holmes. Janet. 1995. *Women, Men and Politeness*. London: Longman.

Holmes, Janet. 2000. Women at work: Analysing women's talk in New Zealand workplaces. *Australian Review of Applied Linguistics (ARAL)* 22: 1–17.

Holmes, Janet. 2005. Power and discourse at work: Is gender relevant? In Michelle Lazar (ed.) *CDA and Gender*. London: Palgrave. 31–60.

Holmes, Janet. 2006. *Gendered Talk at Work: Constructing Gender Identity Through Workplace Discourse*. Oxford: Blackwell.

Holmes, Janet and Meredith Marra. 2002a. Over the edge? Subversive humour between colleagues and friends. *Humor* 15: 1–23.

Holmes, Janet and Meredith Marra. 2002b. Humour as a discursive boundary marker in social interaction. In Anna Duszak (ed.) *Us and Others: Social Identities across Languages. Discourses and Cultures*. Amsterdam.The Netherlands: John Benjamins. 377–400.

Holmes, Janet and Meredith Marra. 2004. Relational practice in the workplace: Women's talk or gendered discourse? *Language in Society* 33: 377–98.

Holmes, Janet and Miriam Meyerhoff. 2003. Different voices, different views: An introduction to current research in language and gender. In Janet Holmes and Miriam Meyerhoff (eds.) *Handbook of Language and Gender*. Oxford: Blackwell. 1–17.

Holmes, Janet and Stephanie Schnurr. 2005. Politeness, humour and gender in the workplace: Negotiating norms and identifying contestation, *Journal of Politeness Research* 1:121–49.

Holmes, Janet, Stephanie Schnurr, Tina Chiles and Angela Chan. 2003. The discourse of leadership. *Te Reo* 46: 31–46.

Holmes, Janet and Maria Stubbe. 2003a. 'Feminine' workplaces: Stereotypes and reality. In Janet Holmes and Miriam Meyerhoff (eds.) *Handbook of Language and Gender*. Oxford: Blackwell. 573–599.

Holmes, Janet and Maria Stubbe. 2003b. *Power and Politeness in the Workplace. A Sociolinguistic Analysis of Talk at Work*. London: Longman.

Holmes, Janet, Maria Stubbe and Bernadette Vine. 1999. Constructing professional identity: 'Power' in policy units. In Srikant Sarangi and Celia Roberts (eds.) *Talk, Work and Institutional Order. Discourse in Medical, Mediation and Management Settings*. Berlin: de Gruyter. 351–85.

Johnson, Sally and Ulrike Hanna Meinhof (eds.). 1997. *Language and Masculinity*. Oxford: Blackwell.

Johnstone, Barbara. 1999. Uses of Southern-sounding speech by contemporary Texas women. *Journal of Sociolinguistics* 3: 505–22.

Johnstone, Barbara. 2003. Features and uses of Southern style. In Stephen J. Nagle and Sara L. Sanders (eds.) *English in the Southern United States*. Cambridge: Cambridge University Press. 189–207.

Jones, Deborah. 2000. Gender trouble in the workplace: 'Language and gender' meets 'feminist organisational communication'. In Janet Holmes (ed.) *Gendered Speech in Social Context: Perspectives from Gown and Town*. Wellington, NZ: Victoria University Press. 192–210.

Kendall, Shari. 2003. Creating gendered demeanours of authority at work and at home. In Janet Holmes and Miriam Meyerhoff (eds.) *Handbook of Language and Gender*. Oxford: Blackwell. 600–23.

Kendall, Shari. 2004. Framing authority: Gender, face and mitigation at a radio network. *Discourse and Society* 15: 55–79.

Kiesling, Scott Fabius. 1998. Men's identities and sociolinguistic variation: The case of fraternity men. *Journal of Sociolinguistics* 2: 69–99.

Kiesling, Scott Fabius. 2004. What does a focus on 'men's language' tell us about language and woman's place? In Mary Bucholtz (ed.) *Language and Woman's Place: Text and Commentaries*. Oxford: Oxford University Press. 229–36.

Kitzinger, Celia. 2002. Doing feminist conversational analysis. In Paul McIlvenny (ed.) *Talking Gender and Sexuality*. Amsterdam, The Netherlands: John Benjamins. 163–93.

Koller, Veronika. 2004. Businesswomen and war metaphors: 'Possessive, jealous and pugnacious'? *Journal of Sociolinguistics* 8: 3–22.

Lakoff, Robyn Tolmach. 2004. Language and woman's place revisited. In Mary Bucholtz (ed.) *Language and Woman's Place: Text and Commentaries*. Oxford: Oxford University Press. 15–28.

Liladhar, Janine. 2001. Making, unmaking and re-making femininity. Unpublished PhD thesis. Sheffield: Sheffield Hallam University.

Livia, Anna and Kira Hall (eds.). 1997. *Queerly Phrased: Language, Gender, and Sexuality*. New York: Oxford University Press.

Maher, Karen. 1997. Gender-related stereotypes of transformational and transactional leadership. *Sex Roles: A Journal of Leadership* 37: 209–26.

Martín Rojo, Luisa. 1998. Intertextuality and the construction of a new female identity. In Mercedes Bengoechea and Ricardo J. Sola Buil (eds.) *Intertextuality/Intertextualidad*. Alcalá de Henares. Spain: Universidad de Alcalá de Henares. 81–98.

Meân, Lindsey. 2001. Identity and discursive practice: Doing gender on the football pitch. *Discourse and Society* 12: 789–815.

Mills, Sara. 2003. *Gender and Politeness*. Cambridge: Cambridge University Press.

Ochs, Elinor. 1992. Indexing gender. In Alessandro Duranti and Charles Goodwin (eds.) *Rethinking Context: Language as an Interactive Phenomenon*. Cambridge: Cambridge University Press. 335–58.

Ochs, Elinor. 1996. Linguistic resources for socializing humanity. In John J. Gumperz and Stephen C. Levinson (eds.) *Rethinking Linguistic Relativity*. Cambridge: Cambridge University Press. 407–38.

Okamoto, Shigeko. 1995. 'Tasteless' Japanese: Less 'feminine' speech among young Japanese women. In Kira Hall and Mary Bucholtz (eds.) *Gender Articulated: Language and the Socially Constructed Self*. New York: Routledge. 297–325.

Rampton, Ben. 1999. Styling the other: Introduction. *Journal of Sociolinguistics* 3: 421–7.

Rampton, Ben. 2003. Hegemony, social class and stylisation. *Pragmatics* 13: 49–83.

Romaine, Suzanne. 1999. *Communicating Gender*. London: Lawrence Erlbaum.

Schnurr, Stephanie. 2009. *Leadership Discourse at Work: Interactions of Humour, Gender and Workplace Culture*. London: Palgrave Macmillan.

Sinclair, Amanda. 1998. *Doing Leadership Differently. Gender, Power and Sexuality in a Changing Business Culture*. Melbourne, Australia: Melbourne University Press.

Stokoe, Elizabeth H. and Janet Smithson. 2002. Gender and sexuality in talk-in-interaction: Considering conversation analytic perspectives. In Paul McIlvenny (ed.) *Talking Gender and Sexuality: Conversation, Performativity and Discourse in Interaction*. Amsterdam: John Benjamins. 79–109.

Stokoe, Elizabeth H. and Ann Weatherall. 2002. Gender, language, conversation analysis and feminism. *Discourse and Society* 13: 707–13.

Stubbe, Maria, Janet Holmes, Bernadette Vine and Meredith Marra. 2000. Forget Mars and Venus, let's get back to earth: Challenging stereotypes in the workplace. In Janet Holmes (ed.) *Gendered Speech in Social Context: Perspectives from Gown and Town*. Wellington, NZ: Victoria University Press. 231–58.

Talbot, Mary. 1998. *Language and Gender. An Introduction*. Malden, MA: Polity Press.

Tannen, Deborah (ed.). 1993. *Gender and Conversational Interaction* Oxford: Oxford University Press.

Tannen, Deborah. 1994a. *Gender and Discourse*. London: Oxford University Press.

Tannen, Deborah. 1994b. *Talking from 9 to 5*. London: Virago Press.

Tew, Jerry. 2002. *Social Theory, Power and Practice*. Basingstoke: Palgrave.

Trauth, Eileen. 2002. Odd girl out: An individual differences perspective on women in the IT profession. *Information Technology and People* 15: 98–118.

West, Candace and Sarah Fenstermaker. 1995. Doing difference. *Gender and Society* 9: 8–37.

Wodak, Ruth (ed.). 1997. *Gender and Discourse*. London: Sage.

25

Communities of Practice at Work: Gender, Facework and the Power of *Habitus* at an All-Female Police Station and a Feminist Crisis Intervention Center in Brazil

Ana Cristina Ostermann

Source: *Discourse & Society* 14(4) (2003), pp. 473–505. Reprinted with permission of SAGE.

Introduction

[...]

In the past 10 years, there has been an increasing interest in considering a complexity of issues involved in 'doing' gender in language (Bergvall, 1999; Eckert and McConnell-Ginet, 1992, 1995, 1999; Stokoe, 1998). Eckert and McConnell-Ginet's article 'Think practically and look locally: Language and gender as a community-based practice' (1992) was influential in shifting the focus of language and gender research to *diversity* (Bing and Bergvall, 1996). The essay criticized the binarism of 'women's style' and 'men's style'. Building upon the social theory of learning offered by Lave and Wenger (1991), with their introduction of the concept of 'community of practice', Eckert and McConnell-Ginet argue that gender identity too is negotiated through the individuals' participation in 'communities of practice' (CofP). They use CofP to stress 'the learning and mutability in gendered linguistic displays across groups', thus assuming *intra*gender differences as natural, rather than deviant (Bergvall, 1999). The concept of CofP assumes that gender is 'occasioned' within interaction (Stokoe, 1998) and thus in order to understand gender one has to look at the 'situatedness' of talk.

Following the anti-essentialist feminist body of research on language and gender discussed earlier, the current study attends to the multiple characterizations of 'women's language', or to borrow Butler's (1990) words, it 'troubles' the essentialist definitions of women's language. In this study I comparatively analyze the discursive practices of professionals in two parallel institutions created to address violence against women in Brazil: a unit of an all-female staffed police station (*Delegacia da Mulher*) and of a feminist non-governmental crisis intervention center (*CIV Mulher*) in their interactions with victims of domestic violence. The selection of these two settings was motivated by a desire to understand whether and how linguistic practices of female professionals are constructed to reflect and constitute those groups as communities of practice.

The current study aims at understanding how talk in these all-women organizations shapes and is shaped by the services they provide as well as by other factors such as the professionals' 'situatedness' (social class, education, life experience) and by how they position themselves towards their jobs, domestic violence, and victims of violence in the home sphere. This study also attempts to bridge an interdisciplinary gap by bringing analytical tools provided by the discipline of linguistics to the study of these settings. Previous studies have raised criticism about the practices employed at both the *Delegacias da Mulher* and feminist crisis intervention centers in Brazil (e.g. Azevedo, 1985; Chauí, 1984; Hautzinger, 1998; Nelson, 1996; Paoli, 1984; Sorj and Montero, 1984). Such studies, however, have only examined these settings ethnographically, none focusing linguistically on the spoken interactions between professionals and victims. When scattered comments on interactional behavior are present, they are without specific linguistic evidence; e.g. '[She] asked with a note of sarcasm [...]' (Nelson, 1997: 122); '[T]heir resentment often manifested itself in a patronizing or condescending treatment of women' (Nelson, 1997: 122).

In contrast, the present investigation assumes that social practices are realized in language *in* interaction and that spoken interaction is indeed a type of *action* creating or maintaining relations of power. Close investigation of the dynamics of recorded and transcribed spoken interaction of professionals and victims (such as turn taking and turn design, topic change, pauses, among others) as carried out in the current study can help us understand the impact of setting on the interactions, and on whether the opposing ideological stances of the two settings are created and reinforced within the institutions' discursive practices.

Face and Politeness in Reporting Domestic Violence

Disclosing and describing to strangers the violence that takes place in the private sphere of one's home constitutes a potential threat to one's public image or *face*. This holds even when those strangers are professionals whose job involves dealing with cases of domestic violence on an everyday basis. It is potentially face-threatening for the victim because it places her in an emotionally vulnerable position. In fact, the creation of unique specialized types of settings to deal with these issues in Brazil – female police stations and crisis intervention centers – to some extent constitutes a redressive type of action to potentially face-threatening encounters of this kind. As a result, one might expect that in dealing with victims, professionals in both settings will try to be sensitive to the victim's public image by making use of linguistic strategies to minimize the threat these encounters pose to the latter.

Originally introduced by Goffman (1955), the concept of *face* is generally understood in sociology and linguistics as 'the negotiated public image, mutually granted each other by participants in a communicative event', and it is located in the very flow of our daily communication (Scollon and Scollon, 1995). It is the 'positive social value' that individuals want to create and/or maintain to themselves (Goffman, 1955: 213). But interactants usually aim not only at maintaining their own face, but also that of their communicative partners, and in order to maintain both their own and their partners' face, interactants employ a variety of linguistic strategies; i.e. they do *facework* (Goffman, 1955). Thus, face-work refers to specific types of actions that interactants perform so as 'to keep interaction flowing smoothly' and to maintain their positive social persona (K. Tracy and Tracy, 1998: 227). In other words, whereas face has to do with the 'socially situated identities people claim or attribute to others', facework refers to the specific 'communicative strategies' that are used for the realization and maintenance of those identities (K. Tracy, 1990: 210).

One area of interactional sociolinguistics analysis in which one can investigate facework (or lack of) – and the implications of those in establishing systems of solidarity, deference, etc. – is 'turn taking' and 'turn design' (e.g. Brown and Levinson, 1983; Holmes and Stubbe, 1997; Scollon and Scollon, 1995). For instance, the provision of continuers or backchannels such as *mm*, *mhm*, and *yeah*, and the design of previous turn-related questions and/or comments might reflect 'politeness, or sensitivity to the needs of others' (Holmes, 1995: 37). Continuers, in particular, as Holmes argues, constitute a more obvious positive politeness strategy, because they encourage the speaker to continue her train of thought. Questions and previous-turn topic-related comments function as a means to engage partners in conversation. They constitute 'supportive elicitation', because they also function to encourage further talk from the other participant (Holmes, 1995: 56).

Holmes (1995) claims that women in general seem to be more attentive to their partners' conversational needs through their turn-taking behavior. In her analysis of cross-gender differences, the author empirically demonstrates how females' and males' interactive patterns differ and how such differences reflect the speakers' different social orientations. The author shows that in contrast to males, females tend to provide more encouraging responses to their interlocutors – as, for instance, continuers – and that such responses are 'placed to be non-disruptive' in manner so as to guarantee the smooth flow of conversation (Holmes, 1995: 31). The questions designed by females also tend to encourage the other speaker to talk more. These interactional patterns contribute to 'establish[ing] and maintaining solidarity or "connection"' (Chodorow, 1974, in Holmes, 1995: 31). Abrupt topic changes initiated by the next speaker, in contrast, show lack of interest in the current speaker's topic, and thus pose a threat to her face (i.e. to her want of having her wants appreciated by the others).

As pointed out above, the current study departs from the trend of *inter*gender analysis for it explores instead *intra*gender differences across the groups of female professionals in the two institutional settings under analysis here, in their relationship with female clients.

Data for the Current Study

The data analyzed here comprise 26 audio-taped *first-time* encounters between professionals and clients at a unit of *Delegacia da Mulher* and of *CIV Mulher*, both located in Cidade do Sudeste, Southeastern Brazil.[1] In total there are 13 interviews per setting involving three different professionals in each institution – three *triagistas* at *CIV Mulher* and three police officers (also known as *frentistas*) at the *Delegacia da Mulher*. The interactions recorded were limited to those involving female victims of violence in the home sphere, and violence that had been inflicted by someone of the opposite sex with whom they were or had been intimate (boyfriends, partners, husbands).

In addition, the final data corpus collected comprises:

- notes taken during recorded encounters;
- ethnographic notes on the settings and their personnel;
- information contained in the documents generated during the encounters between professionals and victims;
- information obtained through e-mail exchanges with some of the professionals.

It is important to point out, however, that the transcribed recorded interactions represent the major data source for the analysis of talk. Ethnographic notes on the settings, personnel and encounters, and written information recorded in the victims' personal files at *CIV Mulher* and in the police reports at the *Delegacia da Mulher* are used as secondary sources of information, serving as resources to explain some of the linguistic practices observed.[2]

Landscapes and Portraits:[3] Settings and Personnel

The creation of the first *Delegacias da Mulher* in Brazil in 1985 was grounded on the essentialist assumption that female police officers would be 'naturally' better suited to deal with violence against women than their male counterparts, and that the general male-dominated environment of the regular police stations was not conducive to women's reports of violence against themselves (Nabucco, 1989; Nelson, 1996, 1997). The creation of an all-woman staffed delegacia represented an attempt to 'humanize [...] the police after decades of military rule' (Station, 1989: 69).

But previous to, and of crucial influence on the creation of these specialized police stations in Brazil were feminist groups and organizations that began to form in the 1980s, after years of authoritarian government, to address the problem of violence against women (Hautzinger, 1997). The main objectives of these groups were to break the isolation of women who suffered gendered violence, raise consciousness among them that the oppression they suffered at home was a shared and gendered one, help empower victims by offering psychological and legal support, and help in reporting the violent incidents to the police (Azevedo, 1985; Chauí, 1984; Nelson, 1996, 1997: Sorj and Montero, 1984). Among these groups was the unit of *CIV Mulher* investigated in this study.

Delegacia da Mulher Unit and its Personnel

Despite functioning in a mansion-size rented house, a walk inside the *Delegacia da Mulher* in Cidade do Sudeste reveals its poor physical condition. In the waiting room, where the victims sit in chairs arranged in rows, lies a clay water filter from which water is drunk in re-used yogurt pots. In the yard, the grass grows without care. The water rots green in the backyard pool, creating worry among the staff that it could become a breeding ground for mosquitoes carrying *dengue* – a disease of general concern in that region of the country. In fact, lack of resources, such as office supplies, interferes with the efficacy

of the *Delegacia's* work. At the time of my data collection, the state was no longer providing the *Delegacia* with postage stamps. Because of that, victims had to make an extra trip
back to the precinct to fetch a stamp[4] so that a summons could be actually sent to the
perpetrators.

The *Delegacia* is open from 8:30am to 6pm, Monday through Friday, and I do not
remember having ever seen it without clients. The officers have an hour and a half for
lunch everyday, and during this time, BOs (*boletins de ocorrência* or 'police reports') are
carried out by one of the frentistas. For the greater part of their eight working hours,
those in charge of making BOs are seeing victims and producing reports. Because eight
hours of making BOs is felt as too stressful by the officers, they occasionally ask to switch
into paperwork tasks so that they can 'unwind a bit'.

To enter the police force, applicants must pass a battery of public exams. Once they have
passed these exams, police officers who will end up in charge of producing BOs are required
to attend the state police academy for three months. Their training involves learning how
to do BOs, shooting lessons, and some basic knowledge of criminal law. Discussion about
handling domestic violence, or even the more general issues involving violence against
women, are not part of their training; '[that training] is for the *delegadas* (chief police
officers) but not for lower rank police officers', says Alessandra, one of the frentistas.

Once the police academy is over, officers are assigned to work anywhere in the state,
and for females, the likelihood of being posted to a *Delegacia da Mulher* increases. This
generates much dissatisfaction among many; after all, they never asked to do such specialized type of police work or received any training for it.

At the time of the data collection, the three police officers in charge of producing BOs
and, thus, of having first-time encounters with victims were Elisete, Alessandra and Maria.
The three officers are upper-working and lower-middle class single mothers, two of them
having suffered some type of violence in their domestic sphere. Alessandra lived at the
Delegacia da Mulher unit in Cidade do Sudeste and away from her son who was being
raised by Alessandra's parents. Elisete lived with her parents, who also helped her with raising her child. Finally, Maria lived with her daughter whom she raised on her own. Both
Alessandra and Maria quit school after obtaining high-school degrees. Despite some financial difficulties, among the three officers studied here, Elisete was the only one who had
continued studying after high school, having actually managed to obtain a bachelor's degree
(Public Relations). None of them had chosen to work at the *Delegacia da Mulher* and the
three of them showed dissatisfaction with the work they did at the unit. One of them,
Alessandra, had already had three transfer requests denied.

Elisete was especially prominent among her colleagues in complaining about emotional stress at work. She was also aware that the lack of training and of 'natural aptitude',
as well as lack of support from the state were part of the problem:

> Many of us quit. We don't have the aptitude for this. Because we're not prepared for this.
> We're not naturally gifted for this. We don't have any external support out of here. [...] A
> good number of us comes here because we were assigned here, not because we asked to be
> here. [...] Look who's here since the beginning? The work demands too much from us.
> We're not prepared for this.

Moreover, the officers believed that the work done at the *Delegacia da Mulher* was not the
work of 'real' police officers: 'It's not the type of work that gives me pleasure', says Elisete.

Elisete's reasons for dissatisfaction with her job and work environment also became a
justification for the quality of her interactions with the victims: 'That's why many times

we "lose our patience." [...] Ai, girl (addressing me). I'm stressed out. Nine years listening to, other people's problems drives anyone crazy.'

Alessandra, the other officer, frequently showed disapproval about the choices victims make, claiming that they [the victims] change their partners so often, 'that sometimes they don't even know the last name of their current partners.' 'It's a complete lack of commitment!', she said. Alessandra also clearly revealed unawareness about the complexities of issues involved in domestic violence, especially with regards to its recurring cycle:

> Even a woman who was broken into pieces still comes with her wedding band on her finger and her last name as if they were a trophy. Sometimes they let themselves get beaten up just to save their marriage. If they insist that you use their married name it's because they want to fix their relationship, not to give it an end.

Alessandra also thought that the *Delegacia da Mulher* actually gave and listened 'too much' to the victims. In regular precincts, as opposed to the *Delegacias da Mulher*, she says, 'the victim has to stand up by the counter while the report is being made'.

Finally, it is important to mention that none of the officers recorded for this study considered themselves feminist.

CIV Mulher Unit and its Personnel

'Gone are the times when we were just a bunch of women "doing CIV" *no fundo do quintal* ("in the backyard"),' says the CIV coordinator during a staff meeting, as she recalls the times when CIV had no physical setting. It once was just a group of volunteer women and their briefcases, traveling back and forth to the city's different districts to spread the seeds of awareness about violence against women. Almost two decades after its creation, the group *CIV Mulher* is no longer just a group with a feminist agenda; it now consists of a physical setting, a group of paid professionals, and a defined set of working practices.

At the time of the data collection *CIV Mulher* operated with three psychologists, two lawyers, an anthropologist, and two receptionists who alternated shifts. CTV is open from 9 AM to 5 PM, Monday through Friday. However, the staff are not there throughout, some of them not working full-time at CIV, as discussed below. *Triagens*, i.e. first-time encounters between CIV professionals and victims, occur three times a week and only in the afternoons. During other times, victims are seen only for follow-up appointments (with lawyers and psychologists). Some weekdays are reserved for general staff meetings, and other project meetings (e.g. an AIDS prevention campaign among women).

There is no specific training to become a *triagista* at *CIV Mulher*. Learning how to conduct a first encounter with victims comes from observing more senior staff do it. According to CTV coordinator, Tânia, the *triagistas* also largely draw on skills acquired in their own field of professional training such as psychology and anthropology.

The three *triagistas* recorded for this study were Fernanda, Ivone, and Tânia, all established middle- and upper-middle class graduated professionals. Ivone is a clinical psychologist with a graduate certificate in family and couple's therapy, working part-time and with her private practice. By the time of the data collection, Ivone had been working at CIV for 10 years.

Ivone sees her role in the first encounter with a victim as a moment:

> to welcome her [the victim], to release her tension, to show her that violence against women is a social problem and that there are solutions to the problem the client tells, to inform her of what CIV can offer her, to collect a complete history about her current relationship, and of previous relationships.

She also thinks that in order to be able to help a woman who seeks CIV, the *triagista* needs to create empathy. According to her, empathy is one of the ways to help the client 'mobilize her own resources, since the actual solution lies in her hands'.

Fernanda is also a clinical psychologist and holds a graduate certificate in psychodrama. She started at CIV in 1996, first as an unpaid volunteer and a year later signed a contract as a paid professional. She sees her role as a *triagista* as someone who 'welcomes the client's complaints', and who 'helps her organize her thoughts'. Moreover, following the same practice as Ivone, Fernanda reveals the importance of empathy with a client: 'The ideal triagem is when you're able to create some type of bonding with her [the client].'

Like Ivone, Fernanda also believes that her work at CIV has helped to improve herself professionally as well as personally:

> It's gratifying to be always learning from these women's stories, each of them triggering a need for an internal review in myself. [...] Each woman who sits in front of me represents a new book that I try to read, that stirs up my concepts and values. [...] My growth never stops.

Finally, there is Tânia, the coordinator of CIV, who holds a bachelor's degree in social sciences and a master's degree in anthropology. She has been working with CTV since its beginning, being one of the proponents of its creation. Tânia is married, has three children, and has lived in Cidade do Sudeste for almost 30 years. Certainly a character of some prominence in Cidade do Sudeste, Tânia is known by and has easy access to intellectual and political circles. She has taught for a few years at one of the local universities, and has a long history as a feminist activist in Cidade do Sudeste, being frequently invited to give interviews to the local TV channel and newspapers, as well as to speak at political and intellectual events.

Tânia regards the *triagista* as 'the most important figure at CIV', According to her, the *triagista* builds the connection with the women who seek CIV, and this connection is what will guarantee the type of work the institution wants to develop with the victims.

Professionals' Response Types to Victims' Turns of Talk

In order to investigate the overall pattern of the response types to the victims' turns by the professionals in each setting, a quantitative analysis was conducted. After looking at all responses provided by the professionals to the victims' turns of talk, four types of response types were identified in both settings:

1 *Silence:* when the professional does not take a turn after the victim reaches a *transitional relevance place* (i.e. classical moment for change of speakers) (Sacks et al., 1974). As a result, after a moment of silence, the victim self-selects a turn of talk and continues speaking.

2 *Continuers:* vocalization of backchannels such as *mhm, mm, uh, aham*, which are uttered by the professional to pass up her turn to talk, and thus encourage the victim to continue talking.
3 *Topic-related responses:* these are turns that are actually taken by the professional, and whose content is topic related to the victim's preceding turn.
4 *Topic change responses*, which again are turns taken by the professional, but their content diverges from anything the victim has uttered in the immediately preceding turn.

Figure 1 thus displays the overall pattern of the professionals' turns in response to the victims' utterances.

A contingency analysis was carried out to compare the four types of responses at *Delegacias da Mulher* (DDM) and *CIV Mulher* (CIV), and was adjusted for the number of professionals in each setting. The results pointed out a highly significant difference in the proportions of the four types of responses in the two settings ($p = .00018$). As shown in Figure 1, the professionals' response types are similar in some aspects and contrastive in others. They are similar insofar as *topic-related response* is the major type of response produced by professionals in both settings, accounting for 41 percent of the officers' responses, and 58 percent of the *triagistas'* responses. That seems to be in accordance with interactions in general; that is, a great number of responses necessarily have to be topic connected to previous turns so as to ensure some degree of cohesiveness in the interaction, and thus also guarantee some degree of smoothness in its development. However, the percentage of topic-related responses differs considerably with CIV including 17 percent more than DDM (58 versus 41%).

On all other accounts the two settings differ. At CIV, the second major type of response is *continuers*, accounting for 29 percent of the *triagistas'* responses. In contrast, at DDM both *silence* and *topic change response* stand closely as the second and third second major types of responses, accounting for nearly a third and a quarter respectively of all responses. *Continuers* at DDM represent the least used type of response by officers. Thus, whereas *silence* and its close competitor *topic change response* represent the top second major choices at DDM, they account for the two least preferred choices at CIV.

These results point to the general facework strategies used at CIV and DDM. That is, interactions at CIV are geared towards more solidarity, with the *triagistas* providing more continuers, which function to encourage the victims to develop their stories. This strategy also builds more cooperativeness in the encounters. Change in topics, even though necessary for the advancement of any interaction, falls into the least preferred category of response provided by the *triagistas*, immediately followed by silence.

The prevalence of both *silences* and *topic change responses* at DDM suggests that the encounters in that setting are less cooperative, and that the smooth flow of the interactions seems to be more easily at risk, thus creating more opportunities for turn-taking violations, which constitute face-threatening events in themselves. For example, both silence and topic change may indicate a lack of interest in the victim's contributions, thus threatening her face.

But as Gal (1995) argues, one has to look at the 'situatedness of talk', here understood as the use of these responses in their discursive contexts. In other words, one has also to investigate the complexities involved in the use of one or another response in the flow of interaction. Silent responses, in particular, have multiple meanings; they can be 'powerful' or 'disempowering' (Mendoza-Denton, 1995), and are far more complex

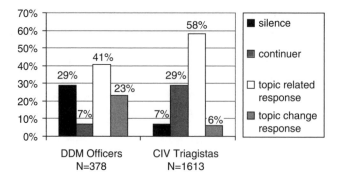

Figure 1   Professionals' response types

than simple frequencies might show (Gal, 1995; Lakoff, 1995; Mendoza-Denton, 1995). In order to be understood silence has to be contextualized; 'only by contextualizing a silence can we come closer to an understanding of its meaning' (Mendoza-Denton, 1995: 60). As Gal (1995: 172) puts it, 'Silence [...] gains different meanings and has different effects within specific institutional and cultural contexts, and within different linguistic ideologies.'

Silence might also be connected to other forms of power in discourse such as *topic control* (Matoesian, 1993; Mendoza-Denton, 1995; West and Zimmerman, 1983). Whereas a victim might be made to speak by the professional's *non-responses*, she may be silenced by the imposed *topic change responses*. In other words, topic change responses may force the other speaker to follow new content, not chosen by her.

Thus, in the next sub-section, I contextualize the professionals' *silent* and *topic change responses* within a discursive level of analysis, investigating where and how they occur. More specifically, I examine how these two types of responses might work in subtle and connected ways so as to construct discourse as 'a site for the reproduction of power relations' (Matoesian, 1993; Mendoza-Denton, 1995). Moreover, I comparatively analyze *silence* and *topic change* at DDM and CIV so as to show the complexities that are not reflected in their frequencies of use.

Silence and Topic Change at DDM: Control, Distance and Dismissal

This section explores how *silence* and *topic change* are used as responses by the police officers at DDM, and argues that these two types of responses are used as a means to control the victims' contributions to the interaction, and to create distance between the participants. Their combined usage, in particular, creates what Bucholtz and Hall (1995: 9) have called 'the paradox of hegemony and control;' i.e. that in their encounter with the police officers at DDM, victims are at the same time 'silenced' and made to speak (Bucholtz and Hall, 1995; Lakoff, 1995).

As will become evident from the analysis, what seems to be most problematic about silence as a type of response by the police officers is its cumulative effect across several turns. Excerpt 1 below takes place at the very beginning of the encounter between police officer (PO) Alessandra and victim Pulsina.

Excerpt 1 [DDM11-AP]

1	*((Victim comes into the cubicle with her one-year-old*
2	*daughter.))*
3	*((Officer puts the forms into the typewriter and types in the*
4	*number for the next report.))*
5	PO ALESSANDRA:	Que que tá acontecendo?
6		*What's happening?*
7	PULSINA:	É assim, ele é::– nós nos conhecemos há:: cinco
8		anos. Estamos juntos há quatro, e é casado um um
9		ano só.
10		*It's like this, he is– we met five years ago.*
11		*We've been together for four, and married for one*
12		*one year.*
13		(0.9)
14	PULSINA:	E:: ela acabou de fazer um aninho, tá. E nós vi-
15		a::h ficamos separados durante o tempo que a
16		gente– que eu tava grávida, e:: mudamos em final
17		de fevereiro. Em março ele chegou um dia em casa
18		é:: me dizendo que usava drogas há mais de doze
19		anos. Ou seja, ele usou a gravidez dela
20		inteirinha.
21		*And she has just turned one, right. And we liv-*
22		*ah were separated during the the time when we*
23		*were– when I was pregnant, and moved at the end*
24		*of February. In March he came home one day uh*
25		*telling me that he had been using drugs for more*
26		*than twelve years. That is, he used drugs during*
27		*my entire pregnancy.*
28		(1.2)
29	PULSINA:	E sempre, na gravidez– quando ela tava na minha
30		barriga, ele sempre:: chegava em casa de manhã::
31		ou bêbado::– eu achava que era só bêbado, né. E
32		não era.
33		*And always, during the pregnancy– when she was*
34		*in my tummy, he always got home in the morning or*
35		*drunk–I thought it was just drunk, right. And*
36		*it wasn't.*
37		(1.6)
38	PULSINA:	E sempre agressivo. Sempre agressivo. Qualquer
39		coisinha assim. Essa semana ela caiu duas vezes,
40		tava começando a andar sozinha. E:: CAIU do lado
41		dele, né. Aí ele:: acho que começa a se sentir
42		culpado. ele diz que sou eu, começa a gritar, me
43		agredir ((começa a chorar enquanto fala)), ontem
44		quase quebrou meu bra::ço ((entonação subindo))
45		*And always aggressive. Always aggressive. Any*
46		*little thing like that. This week she fell down*
47		*twice, she was beginning to walk on her own. And*
48		*she FELL next to him, right. And he I think he*
49		*begins to feel guilty, he says that it's me,*
50		*begins to yell, to hit me ((begins to cry while*
51		*speaking)), yesterday he almost broke my arm*
52		*((rising intonation))*

53		(1.1)
54	PULSINA:	Entendeu? É sempre assim. B hoje ele:: saiu com
55		um amigo dele– ele não tern na- – faz tempo que
56		eu tô falando pra ele pra tirá de cópia do
57		cadeado pra mim. Então ele sai, e ela quer
58		passear na rua, e eu não tenho chave porque eu tô
59		trancada dentro de ca::sa. ((entonação subindo))
60		*Do you understand? It's always like this. And*
61		*today he went out with a friend of his– he*
62		*doesn't have any- – it's been long that I've*
63		*been telling him to make a copy of the key for*
64		*me. Then he leaves, and she wants to go for a*
65		*walk on the street, and I don't have the key*
66		*because I'm locked inside the house, ((rising*
67		*intonation))*
68		(0.8)
69	PULSINA:	{Ele sai pro trabalho e eu tenho que tá em casa.}
70		Ele NUNCA sai comigo. Então na hora que ele
71		chegou em casa, eu disse, 'Poxa vida. Onde você
72		tava, eu pedi pra você vir mais cedo. Pra você XX
73		com ela pra ela não ficá–' Porque eu tava ainda
74		com ela no colo, né. Ele falõ assim, 'É sua
75		obrigação. O problema é teu, porque não sei o
76		quê.' Começou a me xingá, eu gritei {pra ele
77		falá} mais baixo, né. Nisso ela acordou, aí ele
78		ficô– a gente tá com um monte de conta atrasada,
79		pedimo dinheiro emprestado pro um amigo dele, e
80		ele tinha ido pegá. E saiu depois pra
81		[bebê com esse cara.]
82		*{He takes off for work and I have to be at home.}*
83		*He NEVER goes out with me. Then at the time he*
84		*arrived home, I said. 'For God's sake. Where were*
85		*you, I asked you to come home earlier. So that*
86		*you would XX with her so that she doesn't get–'*
87		*Because I was still holding her, right. He said*
88		*like, 'It's your obligation. The problem is*
89		*yours, and stuff like that.' He began to blame*
90		*me, and I yelled {at him to lower} his voice,*
91		*right. At this moment she woke up, the he got–*
92		*we have lots of overdue bills, we borrowed some*
93		*money from a friend of his, and he had gone to*
94		*pick it up. And left right after to*
95		*[drink with this guy.]*
96	PO GENI:	[Alessandra?]
97		*[Alessandra?]*
98		PO ALESSANDRA: Oi.
99		*Yes.*
100	PULSINA:	E chegou alto.
101		*And got home drunk.*
102	PO ALESSANDRA:	((Stands up and leaves the cubicle.))
103	CHILD:	((Vocalizes something.))
104	PO ALESSANDRA:	((Returns to the cubicle after 56 seconds.))
105	PO ALESSANDRA:	A::h. E pegá às sete e meia. ((falando ainda com

106		a outra policial))
107		*Oh. And start at seven-thirty.*
108		(*(finishing her conversation with the other*
109		*officer))*
110		(0.8)
111	Po Alessandra:	Isso. Continua.
112		*All right. Continue.*

After the police officer's classic opening question 'What's happening?', the victim produces six turns (ll. 7–12, 14–27, 29–36, 38–52, 54–67 and 69–95) which end at transition-relevant places and the police officer offers no response. Her sixth turn is overlapped by another officer's speech. Note that in two turns Pulsina's turn-relevant places are marked with rising intonation (ll. 44/52; 59/66–7), followed by pauses (ll. 53 and 68). At the end of her fourth turn (ll. 43/50–1), Pulsina begins to cry, and after an absence of response of any kind from the police officer, she begins her next turn asking the police officer: 'Do you understand?'. One cannot argue for the victims' actual 'intentions' in asking such a question; 'do you understand' might be simply a rhetorical question, or an actual acknowledgement elicitor. However, independent of the victim's intentions with such a question, the police officer continues to opt out from any type of response. The communicational burden of the continuation of the interaction is left entirely to the victim.

As discussed earlier, the provision of continuers in interactions functions so as to encourage the current speaker to continue developing her train of thought. Ironically, as we can see in the excerpt above, silence also generates more talk from the current speaker. However, the crucial difference between these two strategies is that, whereas continuers 'encourage' the current speaker to develop her thoughts, silence actually 'forces' her to do so. Moreover, whereas continuers acknowledge recipiency, show active listernership, and pass up the opportunity to take a turn of talk (Clark and Schaefer, 1989; Schegloff, 1981), thus ensuring some degree of cooperation in maintaining the conversation flow (Holmes, 1995; Holmes and Stubbe, 1997; Lakoff, 1995), silence might become a means of control over the interaction. In fact, that the control of the interaction is in the hands of the police officer in the exchange above is further evidenced by police officer Alessandra's use of the imperative after the interruption by another officer, 'All right. Continue' (ll. 111–12), which consists of an unusual strategy to foster talk in ordinary conversation.

Another form of control over the interaction is the professionals' dismissal of the victims' topics under development, by following up her turn with changes in topics, as discussed next.

Excerpt 2 [DDM7-AS]

1	Po Alessandra:	Que que aconteceu?
2		*What happened?*
3	Sandra:	É que o meu ex-marido saiu de casa, né?
4		*It's that my ex-husband left home, right?*
5	Po Alessandra:	É marido ou amásio?
6		*Is it husband or common-law?*
7	Sandra:	Não, é meu ex-marido–é:: a gente se se ajuntô.
8		No, *it's ex-husband– uh we we lived together.*
9	Po Alessandra:	Era amásio.
10		*It was common-law.*

11	SANDRA:	É. Então ele foi embora. Aí:: ele de- –; ele não
12		deixou muita coisa, né. Então aí foi– aí ele não
13		dá nada pros menino. Aí quando foi sábado, ele
14		foi lá, buscou a televisão. Ele me ameaçou. Ele
15		falou que se eu falasse alguma coisa, que se eu
16		fosse atrás dos meus direito, que ele ia– que
17		ele ia fazê– que ele ia me matá. Aí:: e eu
18		queria que ele devolvesse essa televisão de
19		volta, porque é a única coisa que eu tenho pros
20		menino. Pros menino vê::
21		*Yeah. Then he left So he le- – he didn't leave*
22		*much behind, right. So then it was– then he*
23		*doesn't give anything to the boys. Then when it*
24		*was Saturday, he went there, to get the TV. He*
25		*threatened me. He said that if said anything,*
26		*that if I went after my rights, that I he would–*
27		*that he would do– that he would kill me. Then I*
28		*wanted him to return the TV back, because it's*
29		*the only thing that I have for my boys.*
30	Po ALESSANDRA:	Onde você mora?
31		*Where do you live?*
32	SANDRA:	Eu moro no Bairro Noel. Aí só que eu tô ficando
33		na casa da minha mãe, e só não tô indo lá porque
34		ele falou [que se eu se eu–]
35		*I live in Bairro Noel. So it's just that I'm*
36		*staying at my mother's house, and I'm just not*
37		*going there because he said [that if I if I–]*
38	Po ALESSANDRA:	[ELE RESPONDS] algum processo?
39		*[DOES HE HAVE] any court process*
40		*against him?*
41	SANDRA:	Não, ele minca respondeu.
42		*No, he never did.*
43	Po ALESSANDRA:	((Espirra.)) Pode continuar.
44		*((Sneezes.)) You can continue.*

Upon the police officer's opening question (ll. 1–2), the victim begins to report the facts by disclosing that her husband has left home (ll. 3–4), to which the officer follows up with a previous-turn topic-related response (ll. 5–6). This response in the format of a question consists of an 'other-initiated repair' (Schegloff et al., 1977); which consists of a type of correction or clarification that is initiated by the other speaker; in this case, initiated by the police officer Alessandra. That is, Alessandra asks the victim to clarify if the alleged husband is actually a husband or a common-law partner (ll. 5–6). The victim's 'not-yet on-target' response (ll. 7–8) is further repaired by the officer in ll. 9–10, to which the victim agrees (ll. 11/21).

Having clarified her marital status, in ll. 11–29 the victim goes back to respond to the officer's initial question. Her extended turn is met by an unrelated question by the officer, i.e. where she resides (ll. 30–1), to which the victim promptly responds, and goes on to develop reasons for why she is currently living at that specific place (ll. 32–37). Her turn is overlapped by the officer with another topic-change question (ll. 38–39) before the victim actually reaches a transition-relevant place, and at the exact moment in which she manages to bring back the topic about her former partner (ll. 33–4/36–7).

Like silent responses, then, topic change responses seem to become even more 'effective' as a strategy of control over the interaction at DDM when they are cumulative, as shown above. As the victim attempts to put her thoughts coherently together so that she can report the facts accordingly, her delivery is successively disrupted by the officer's topic-change responses[5]. Such unilateral topic changes inhibit the production of the victim's account.

Silence at CIV: Challenging the Victim

In contrast to DDM, the overall distribution of silences at CIV not only tends to happen more rarely (representing one of the two least preferred, or 7 percent of all responses in that setting), but also irregularly over the interactions. That is, instead of happening cumulatively, or in clusters, silence as a type of response by the CIV professionals is characterized by *single* occurrences among several other surrounding responses which consist of continuers, and topic-related comments or questions, as illustrated in the exchange below. Excerpt 3 below takes place between *triagista* Fernanda and victim Maria Luisa.

Excerpt 3 [CIV15-FML]

248	MARIA LUISA:	Aí eu fui tomando bronca dele, eu fui ficando com
249		raiva dele. Ele trazia um doce pra filha dele, e
250		[não trazia pro meu filho]
251		*Then I began to feel upset at him, I was feeling*
252		*anger towards him. He would bring sweets for his*
253		*daughter, and*
254		*[didn't bring to my son]*
255	CIV-FERNANDA:	[Fazia diferença entre os dois.]
256		*[He created a difference between the two.]*
257	MARIA LUISA:	Não. Ele não trazia pro meu filho.
258		*No. He didn't bring for my son.*
259	CIV-FERNANDA:	mhm
260		*mhm*
261	MARIA LUISA:	E quando o Rodrigo pedia pra ele, ele dizia
262		assim, 'Ah, vai comprar. Manda seu pai comprar.'
263		*And when Rodrigo would ask him, he would say,*
264		*'Oh, you go buy it. Tell your dad to buy.'*
265		(1.4)
266	MARIA LUISA:	Então eu fui tomando bronca dele, eu fui tomando
267		raiva. Eu não sentia mais nada por ele. Até
268		quando ele piscava eu morria de ódio.
269		*Then I began to feel upset at him, I was building*
270		*anger towards him. I didn't feel anything anymore*
271		*towards him. Even when he blinked I was burning*
272		*in anger.*
273	CIV-FERNANDA:	Tá.
274		*OK.*
275	MARIA LUISA:	Então eu ia levando porque eu não podia sair. Não
276		podia pagar alugue::l, [eu não podia–]
277		*So I was coping with it because I couldn't leave.*
278		*I couldn't pay rent, [I couldn't–]*

279	CIV-FERNANDA:	[Você tava] sem condições
280		financeiras de tomar uma outra decisão=
281		*[You had no financial*
282		*conditions to make another decision=*
283	MARIA LUISA:	=sem condições. Então eu não podia sair pra lugar
284		nenhum=
285		*=no conditions. So I couldn't go to anywhere=*
286	CIV-FERNANDA:	=mhm=
287		=mhm=

In the exchange above, the single silent response produced by the *triagista* (l. 265) happens in an environment in which the triagista not only shows herself to be an active listener (by providing continuers, as in ll. 259–60 and 273–4), but also an active participant by collaboratively 'turn co-constructing' (Clark and Schaefer, 1989; Lerner and Takagi, 1999) with the victim (ll. 255–6 and 279–82). Thus, when silence occurs it does not seem to reflect a general pattern of disruption or disregard.

However, two or more consecutive silent responses by the *triagista* occur in special moments in the interaction. In Excerpt 4, these are the moments in which the victim's beliefs or actions are challenged by the *triagista;* that is, when the victim is challenged to reflect back – as opposed to just continue reporting facts.

Excerpt 4 takes place between *triagista* Ivone and victim Geni. Geni has been both psychologically and physically abused multiple rimes by her husband. She has had two miscarriages which, according to her, have been diagnosed as a result of psychological and physical distress from fights at home. Her husband has developed symptoms of sexual impotence, and blames his impotence on her, abusing her both verbally (calling her both 'frigid' and 'slut') and physically. According to Geni, he has unfairly accused her so many times that she ended up actually 'sleeping' with another man three days before she went to CIV.[6] Geni reveals that she is dealing with a great amount of guilt which seems to be somewhat increased by her religious beliefs – at various moments in the interview she claims having 'stepped on Christ's blood,' and thus that she 'will never be forgiven for that'. She has been expelled from her house by her husband, and believes she will be also expelled from the church for what she has done. She cries at several moments in the interview.

Excerpt 4 [CIV20-IG]

368	GENI:	É eu falei– as criança ouviu né, aí ele pôs as
369		criança contra mim, né. Que eu dormi com outro
370		homem.
371		[Aí ele falou as-]
372		*Yes I said– the(pl.) kid heard right, then he*
373		*put the(pl.) kid against me, right. That I slept*
374		*with another man.*
375		*[Then he said li-]*
376	CIV-IVONE:	[Ele falou isso] pras crianças.
377		*[He said that] to the kids.*
378	GENI:	Aí ele falou assim. 'Você pecou, você pode sumir
379		da minha vida. Some que eu não quero você nem
380		pintada de ouro. Você pecou, você se sujou, você
381		é imunda, porca. E some que senão eu nem sei o
382		que eu sou capaz de fazer com você.'
383		*He said like, 'You sinned, you can disappear from*

384		*my life. Disappear because I don't want you not*
385		*even in gold. You sinned, you became dirty, you*
386		*are filthy, a pig. And disappear because I don't*
387		*even know what I might do to you.'*
388	Civ-Ivone:	E você pensa como ele, que você pecou, que você é
389		imunda, porca também?
390		*And do you think like him, that you sinned, that*
391		*you're filthy, a pig too?*
392	Geni:	Nem sei.
393		*I don't even know.*
394		(2.2)
395	Geni:	Nem sei. ((Chora.))
396		*I don't even know. ((Cries.))*
397		(3.5)
398	Geni:	Porque depois que eu cheguei neste ponto agora.
399		*Because after I got to this point now.*
400	Civ-Ivone:	Que será que aconteceu, o Geni, que você nunca
401		procurou ajuda ANTES.
402		*What might have happened, Geni, that you never*
403		*looked for help EARLIER.*
404	Geni:	Eu tinha dó, muita dó dele. Toda vez que ele me
405		que ele me agredia, eu tioha muita dó dele. Eu
406		achava que se eu procurasse a polícia pra ele,
407		ele poderia vingá de mim depois, que ele– que
408		nem, tá com uns quinze, vinte dias, a irmã dele
409		mais nova, tirou minha menina de mim, levou pra
410		casa dela. Deu pra fazer pra mim pra achar onde
411		ela tava. E ela disse que ia tomá de mim minha
412		filha. ((Ivone, enquanto isso, procura papel
413		higiênico, mas não consegue encontrar.))
414		*I felt sorry, very sorry for him. Every time that*
415		*he hit me, I felt sorry for him. I thought that*
416		*if I sought help from the police against him, he*
417		*could take revenge on me later on, that he–*
418		*like, it's been fifteen, twenty days, his younger*
419		*sister, took my daughter from me, took to her*
420		*place. It took a lot of trouble for me to find*
421		*out where she was. And she said that she would*
422		*take my daughter from me. ((Ivone, meanwhile,*
423		*looks for toilet paper for Geni's tears, but*
424		*cannot seem to find it.))*

In the exchange above, after the victim reports her husband's insults against her (ll. 368–74 and 378–87), *triagista* Ivone challenges the victim by asking her if she too believes these accusations (ll. 388–91). The victim's first response is to claim not to know it (ll. 392–3), which is followed up with silence from the *triagista* (l. 394). The victim goes onto reiterate her response (ll. 395–6), which is again followed by silence from the *triagista* (l. 397), thus passing on the turn of talk back to the victim, and perhaps inviting her to elaborate her thoughts further. What seems to further evidence this as a critical challenging moment in the interaction is the *triagista's* new question in ll. 400–3, in which she asks the victim about the reasons for not having sought help before, to which the victim finally responds more elaborately (ll. 404–24).[7]

Contextualization of Topic Change at CIV

Finally, topic change responses at CIV are crucially different from those at DDM in two important ways. First, when topic changes occur at CIV they are marked by some additional linguistic features; i.e. they are contextualized by some type of 'cue' (Gumperz, 1982). One of these cues is the use of the *victim's first name* as a vocative (see Ostermann, 2000, for detailed discussion of vocatives). Other cues that contextualize topic change (by actually prefacing it) are: (1) discourse markers such as *tá*, and *então tá* (similar to 'OK' and 'So, OK' in English); (2) metacomments such as *me diz uma coisa* (similarly to 'tell me something' in English); and (3) metacomments that refer back to a topic raised by the victim earlier in the encounter, such as *você falou antes que...* ('you said earlier that...'), as the following excerpts illustrate.

Excerpt 5 [CIV19-FK] *Tá* **as a contextualization cue for topic change**

487	KÊNIA:	[Então] eu não consigo misturá.
488		*[So] I don't like to mix things.*
489	CIV-FERNANDA:	[mhm]
490		*[mhm]*
491	KÊNIA:	[Né.] Criança é uma coisa, adulto é outra.
492		*[Right.] A child is something, an adult is another.*
493	CIV-FERNANDA:	**Tá.** hhh por essa postura que ele teve ontem, você
494		acha, que ele tá predisposto à separação::, ou
495		que é MAIS uma das crises de você::s e::, [da
496		parte]
497		*OK. hhh because of this attitude that he had*
498		*yesterday, do you think, that he is willing to*
499		*separate, or that is ONE more of your(pl.) crises*
500		*and, [from his]*

Excerpt 6 [CIV20-IG] *Me diz uma coisa* **as a contextualization cue for topic change**

1164	GENI:	Ele fala disso desde que a gente casou. Que eu tô
1165		pondo roupa de puta, roupa de galinha. Isso aí
1166		pra mim:: me machuca por dentro.
1167		*He says this since we got married. That I'm*
1168		*wearing whore's clothes, slut's clothes. This*
1169		*type of thing for me, it hurts me inside.*
1170	CIV-IVONE:	**Me diz uma coisa.** Na família dele, tem alguém que
1171		tem problema menta::l ((entonação subindo))
1172		*Tell me something. In his family, is there anyone*
1173		*who has mental problems*
1174	GENI:	Ah eu não sei. ((Continua.))
1175		*Ah I don't know. ((Continues.))*

Excerpt 7 [CIV22-IH] *Você disse que...* **as a contextualization cue for topic change**

317	CIV-IVONE:	[Vocês tinham] uma boa vida sexua::l [ou ele–]
318		*[Did you(pl.) have] a good sexual life [or he–]*
319	HELENA:	[Tinha.]
320		Tinha. Só que com as brigas foi foi se espaçando,
321		as relações. Inclusive ele fala fala palavras de
322		baixo calão na frente da minha mãe. Na frente dos

323		meus fi::lhos. Né. E:: tá sendo MUTTO humilhante,
324		muito difícil. Tenho procurado evitar discussões
325		SÉRIAS, mas chega uma hora que a gente também se
326		desequili::bra=
327		*[We did.]*
328		*We did. But with the fights it was was getting more*
329		*rare, the sexual relations. IN fact, he says says*
330		*names in front of my mother. In front of my kids.*
331		*Right. And it's been TOO humiliating, very*
332		*difficult I've been trying to avoid serious*
333		*arguments, but it gets to a point that we also*
334		*lose control=*
335	Civ-Ivone:	=mhm::
336		*=mhm*
337	Helena:	E:: e tá assim.
338		*And and it's like this.*
339	Civ-Ivone:	**Você falou que** ele foi alcóolatra e não é mais. O
340		que é não ser mais
341		alcóolatra. [Ele bebe como agora?]
342		***You said that*** *he was an alcoholic and is not*
343		*anymore. What is it not to be an alcoholic.*
344		*[How does he drink now?]*
345	Helena:	[Não ser mais–] Ele bebe ah:: no final de
346		sema::na, duas cerve::ja. ((Continua.))
347		*[Not to be–] He drinks uh on the weekends, two*
348		*beers.((Continues))*

As can be seen in the examples above, these 'contextualization cues' function as a signal to the interlocutor that a change in topics is in order. They help towards the smoothness of the interaction (and thus do facework) for showing care to avoid abrupt, non-signaled topic changes.

Finally, in addition to being contextualized, topic change at CIV is not characterized as recursively happening across several turns. Similar to silent responses at CIV, besides being one of the two least preferred responses, topic change is also characterized as being scattered along the interaction.

[…]

Final Considerations

Perhaps from force of occupational habit, perhaps by virtue of the calm that is acquired by every important man who is consulted for his advice and who, knowing that he will keep control over the situation, sits back and lets his interlocutor flap and fluster, perhaps also in order to show off to advantage the character of his head (which he believed to be Grecian in spite of his whiskers), while something was being explained to him, M. de Norpois maintained an immobility of expression as absolute as if you had been speaking in front of some classical – and deaf – bust in a museum. (Marcel Proust, *A la recherche du temps perdu*, in Pierre Bourdieu, 1977: 645)

Although Pierre Bourdieu cites a male character in the above quotation, his claim surely applies to the display of power more generally and illustrates one of his fundamental claims – that language is not only a means of communication or knowledge but also a means of power. The analysis as carried out in this study has shown that the encounters at DDM are overwhelmingly characterized by the police officers' high degree of control over the interactions as well as distance from the victims. Police officers clearly attend less to the victims' needs and wants (i.e. their face) by providing minimal or no feedback when the victims report their problems. In contrast, professionals at CIV place special emphasis on diminishing the obvious distance that exists between them and the victims as well as on lessening the degree of face threat that an encounter of such a kind might pose to the latter.

As regards the findings presented here, further questions arise. According to Brown and Levinson (1987), it is usually the case that one's failure (or lack of concern) to do facework to protect her interlocutor's face (such as by abruptly changing topics or failing to provide her with active listenership) also threatens one's own face, or to borrow Bayraktaroglu's (1991) words, it 'taints' her face. If this is so, why wouldn't the police officers also fear losing their own face? Possible answers lie in Brown and Levinson's (1987) own theory. The authors explain that a speaker might decide not to redress her acts when she is 'vastly superior in power' to her interlocutor. Another possibility, as the authors go on to say, is that in doing so, she (in this case the DDM police officer) might secure audience support for herself (Brown and Levinson, 1987). The police officers obviously hold some power over the context of reporting violence; i.e. they are gate-keepers over the production (or not) of the official document that will 'validate' actions as criminal acts. But whose support might the police officers be wanting to achieve for themselves?

The power of *habitus* in the construction of communities of practice

Two interrelated concepts become crucial here in attempting to interpret the linguistic phenomena found in this investigation. These are the concepts of '*habitus*' (Bourdieu, 1977, 1991) and of 'community of practice' (Eckert and McConnell-Ginet, 1992). Bourdieu defines *habitus* as a set of embodied dispositions to language and situations of interaction and to perceptions of the world which define for a particular speaker the linguistic strategies that are 'adapted to his [sic] particular chances or profit, given his [sic] competence and authority' (Bourdieu, 1977: 655). Discourse, according to Bourdieu, is thus a 'symbolic asset' (p. 651) which is acquired and conditioned by social, economic and political factors which in their turn essentially consist of relations of power.

Most importantly, *habitus* represents the practices that are involved in structuring a person's world and her place in it (Murray, 1990). And it is specifically this aspect of *habitus* that is related to the concept of communities of practice. Thus, it is these situated, 'occasioned' (Stokoe, 1998) communities of practice in which groups mutually engage in specific activities and in somewhat intensive ways, that give rise to a particular set of socially shared – linguistic and non-linguistic – practices.

The 'communities' that inhabit, reproduce and shape the institutions looked at in this study do not share the same practices in their interactions with victims of domestic violence. The police officers, as we know by now, are not just 'females'. They are female workers within a traditionally male-dominated system (and still primarily ruled by males), the State civil police force. They are also females of the upper-working class/lower-middle class. They are single parents, some of them relying on their parents' labor and financial support to be able to raise their own children. All are females who have been placed in a working environment which, despite presenting some recognized advantages to them, was not a work setting of their choice. In addition, they have received no training (sensitivity or otherwise) to work with the type of clientele and crimes they encounter. Furthermore, despite the close personal experience with abuse some have had in the home sphere, the police officers at the *Delegacia* claim as well as work towards not identifying themselves with the victims.

Similarly, the professionals at CIV are not only females. They are white, established middle class and upper-middle class professionals who hold university degrees, and who have specifically chosen to volunteer/work at CIV by identifying themselves with the philosophy of the institution and the types of services it offers. They are also involved in a sizzling intellectual environment where gender-related issues are a constant theme. Equally important, as two of the main *triagistas* are psychologists themselves, they not only have specialized training for conducting interactions but also external professional support. Finally, as we also have seen, in contrast to the officers at DDM, the professionals at CIV are able (and want) to identify with the lives of the many women who seek their service.

It is within such contexts that we can now reconsider the sharply differing discursive practices we identified in the two institutions. Although not necessarily explicitly recognized by the professionals in each setting, the police officers' situatedness is much closer to the victims they serve than is that of the professionals at CIV. For the *triagistas* at CIV, however, the perceived similarity they see between their own lives and those of the victims' (probably resulting from their feminist philosophy of action) actually consists only of a 'slice' of life – a slice that is limited to their shared 'female' status in society. Overall, there is much less about the CIV *triagistas*' situatedness that is similar to the victims'.

As discussed earlier, CIV professionals identify themselves with a feminist profile of action and participate in a community (or perhaps several communities) that share such a profile. In employing interactional strategies that approximate themselves to the victims and that advance the profile of the institution they constitute, CIV staff also gain status within their own community. They gain acceptance and strengthen their membership in that community of practice, or in Bourdieu's words, in that 'symbolic market'.

The *Delegacia da Mulher* is embedded within a different contextual system and symbolic market. Recall here that the creation of the *Delegacias da Mulher* in Brazil assumed an essentialist view of gender. Women were seen as 'naturally' more suitable for engaging in interactions with victims of domestic violence, a position the female staff explicitly deny.

So I return here to the question I raised earlier. The police officers' distancing and controlling interactional strategies, demonstrated through the analysis here and through analyses elsewhere (Ostermann, 2000, 2002, 2003), are certainly not the only strategies with which they are competent. They were just as able to engage in interactions with me and some of their peers that exhibited a great degree of solidarity. However, in their interactions with victims they deny, occlude these strategies, as they are not 'valuable' for them in the symbolic market of their *habitus*. They are the 'expected' strategies from them, but unless they defy the ideology that these are 'the only' attributes they have as female police officers, they cannot compete with their male counterparts for positions outside the *Delegacia da Mulher*. It seems that in the police system symbolic market, a more affiliative way of relating to the female clientele might in fact work against the female police officers and their aims. They might reify the essentialist ideology that affiliative interactions are 'natural' to women, or perhaps worse, that is *all* females can offer in the police system, and thus confine them to work settings where they do not wish to be.

Finally, it is also important to point out the potential contribution of the findings presented here to broadening our understanding of the links between language and gender; in particular, to bearing a part in the body of research interested in 'exploding the gender dichotomy' (Stokoe, 1998) by questioning homogeneous definitions of the 'female' gender in its relationship to language. It becomes clear from this investigation that the interactional styles we have studied cannot by any means be collapsed within a single category called *female speech*. The females whose interactional practices were characterized here are better understood as members of distinctive 'communities of practices' (Eckert and McConnell-Ginet, 1992, 1998), with distinctive ideologies and power relations, and that clearly present differing ways of carrying out their professional activities and, of course, their ways of interacting. The findings suggest that gender does not predict interactional patterns; instead these interactional patterns are best understood as reflecting the gendered communities of practice from which the professionals are drawn.

Notes

Earlier drafts of this article have received thoughtful comments and suggestions from Deborah Keller-Cohen, Lesley Milroy, Robin Queen, Sueann Caulfield, Teun A. van Dijk, and an anonymous reviewer. I am thankful to all of them. Any remaining errors are of course my own. The larger research project from which this article draws was generously supported by American Association of University Women (AAUW), Center for the Education of Women (CEW), Rackham School of Graduate Studies at the University of Michigan, Department of Linguistics at the University of Michigan, Coordenação de Aperfeiçoamento de Pessoal de Ensino Superior, Brazil (CAPES), Fundação de Amparo a Pesquisa do Estado do Rio Grande do Sul, Brazil (FAPERGS), and Programa de Pós-Graduação em Lingüística Aplicada da Universidade do Vale do Rio dos Sinos (PROENPE n°.: 41.00.006/01–0).

1   In order to preserve the anonymity of the participants in this study, all personal names, name of the city, names of hospitals, streets and other locations, as well as names of the local newspapers have been replaced by fictitious ones.
2   All the spoken data were transcribed by the author using transcription conventions adapted from Du Bois et al. (1992).
3   I borrow the word 'portraits' from McElhinny's (1993) ethnographic dissertation chapter.
4   Following my practice with CIV, I proposed to the Delegada that I write a letter to local companies to request stamp donations, an idea she quickly refuted, claiming that "the State wouldn't like to show publicly its bankruptcy" (my translation).
5   Frequent topic change at the DDM seems to have a pervasive effect in the overall coherence of the narratives produced by the victims. Narratives produced by the victims at DDM were always considerably less understandable to me, a non-participant observer, than those at CIV.
6   It is not clear from the interaction whether she and this man have had any type of sexual relationship. The victim just refers to the encounter as 'sleeping' and 'spending the night' with him, and the two expressions are ambiguous in Brazilian Portuguese as to whether they refer to the act of sleeping or having sexual intercourse.
7   Some of consecutive silent responses by the triagistas at CIV are explained by the fact that the triagistas occasionally return to taking notes (which for its most part is a silent act; not always captured in the recording or in my field notes), and thus respond with silence – even though many times explicitly showing acknowledgement by the note-taking act itself. Moreover, nodding, another silent type of acknowledgment, was not registered in my field notes every time it occurred – even though my notes report a general tendency for nodding at CIV.

Transcription Conventions

Transcription conventions are given on p. x. In addition:

1 Each turn in the transcript is followed by free translations of the original Portuguese notated in italics.

2 Sound elongation, notated ':::' in the transcripts in Portuguese, is not reproduced in the English translations as it is not always obvious where the corresponding elongation would take place in the English version.

3 When referring the reader to specific lines in the transcript, the following conventions apply: e.g. *lines 3–7* refer to stretches in the interaction that include original Portuguese and English translation which run from lines 3 to *7*; *lines 3/7* refer to a specific element in the transcript, such as a discourse marker, which is found in line 3 in the original Portuguese and in line *7* in the English gloss.

References

Azevedo, M. A. (1985) *Mulheres Espancadas: A Violência Denunciada*. São Paulo, Brazil: Cortez.

Bayraktaroglu, A. (1991) 'Politeness and Interactional Imbalance', *International Journal of the Sociology of Language* 92: 5–34.

Bergvall, V. L. (1999) 'Toward a Comprehensive Theory of Language and Gender', *Language in Society* 28: 273–93.

Bing, J. M. and Bergvall, V. L. (1996) 'The Question of Questions: Beyond Binary Thinking', in V. L. Bergvall, J. M. Bing and A. Freed (eds) *Rethinking Language and Gender Research*, pp. 1–30. New York: Longman.

Bourdieu, P. (1977) 'The Economics of Linguistic Exchanges', *Social Science Information* 16: 645–68.

Bourdieu, P. (1991) *Language and Symbolic Power* (trans. G. Raymond and M. Adamson). Cambridge: Polity Press.

Brown, P. and Levinson, S. C. (1987) *Politeness: Some Universals in Language Usage*. Cambridge: Cambridge University Press.

Bucholtz, M. and Hall, K. (1995) 'Introduction: Twenty Years after Language and Woman's Place', in K. Hall and M. Bucholtz (eds) *Gender Articulated: Language and the Socially Constructed Self*, pp. 1–24. New York: Routledge.

Butler, J. (1990) *Gender Trouble: Feminism and the Subversion of Identity*. New York: Routledge.

Chauí, M. (1984) 'Participando do Debate Sobre Mulher e Violência', in M. Chauí, M. C. Paoli and P. Montero SOS-Mulher (eds) *Perpspectivas Antropológicas da Mulher 4*, pp. 23–62. Rio de Janeiro. Brazil: Zahar Editores.

Clark, H. H. and Schaefer, E. F.(1989) 'Contributing to Discourse', *Cognitive Science* 13: 259–94.

Du Bois, J. W., Schuetze-Coburn, S., Paolino, D. and Cumming, S. (eds) (1992) *Discourse Transcription*. Santa Barbara, CA: University of Santa Barbara.

Eckert, P. and McConnell-Ginet, S. (1992) 'Think Practically and Look Locally: Language and Gender as Community-Based Practice', *Annual Review of Anthropology* 21: 461–90.

Eckert, P. and McConnell-Ginet, S. (1995) 'Constructing Meaning, Constructing Selves: Snapshots of Language, Gender, and Class from Belten High', in K. Hall and M. Bucholtz (eds) *Gender Articulated: Language and the Socially Constructed Self*, pp. 469–507. New York: Routledge.

Eckert, P. and McConnell-Ginet, S. (1999) 'New Generalizations and Explanations in Language and Gender Research', *Language in Society* 28: 185–201.

Gal, S. (1995) 'Language, Gender, and Power: An Anthropological Review', in K. Hall and M. Bucholtz (eds) *Gender Articulated: Language and the Socially Constructed Self*, pp. 169–82. New York: Routledge.

Goffman, E. (1955) 'On Face-Work: An Analysis of Ritual Elements in Social Interaction', *Psychiatry: Journal for the Study of Interpersonal Processes* 18: 213–31.

Gumperz, J. J. (1982) *Discourse Strategies*. New York: Cambridge University Press.

Hautzinger, S. (1997) '"Calling a State a State": Feminist Politics and the Policing of Violence Against Women in Brazil', *Feminist Issues*, 15(1–2): 3–30.

Hautzinger, S. (1998) 'Machos and Policewomen, Battered Women and Anti-Victims: Combating Violence Against Women in Brazil', unpublished PhD dissertation, Johns Hopkins University, Baltimore.

Holmes, J. (1995) *Women, Men and Politeness*. London: Longman.

Holmes, J. and Stubbe, M. (1997) 'Good Listeners: Gender Differences in New Zealand Conversation', *Women and Language* 20(2): 7–14.

Lakoff, R. (1995) 'Cries aud Whispers', in K. Hall and M. Bucholtz (eds) *Gender Articulated*, pp. 25–50. New York: Routledge.

Lave, J. and Wenger, E. (1991) *Situated Learning*. New York: Cambridge University Press.

Lerner, G. H. and Takagi, T. (1999) 'On the Place of Linguistic Resources in the Organization of Talk-in-Interaction: A Co-Investigation of English and Japanese Grammatical Practices', *Journal of Pragmatics* 31(1): 49–75.

Levinson, S. C. (1983) *Pragmatics*. Cambridge: Cambridge University Press.

Matoesian, G. M. (1993) *Reproducing Rape: Domination Through Talk in the Courtroom*. Cambridge: Polity Press.

McElhinny, B. S. (1993) 'We All Wear Blue: Language, Gender and Police Work', unpublished PhD, Stanford University, Stanford, CA.

Mendoza-Denton, N. (1995) 'Pregnant Pauses', in K. Hall and M. Bucholtz (eds) *Gender Articulated*, pp. 51–66. New York: Routledge.

Murray, K. (1990) *Life as Fiction*. Victoria, Australia: University of Melbourne.

Nabucco, A. (1989, April 30) 'Aumentam os casos de estupro em um quadro geral de violência familiar', *Diário Popular*, pp. 12–13.

Nelson, S. E. (1996) 'Constructing and Negotiating Gender in Women's Police Stations in Brazil', *Latin American Perspectives* 23, no. 1(88): 131–48.

Nelson, S. E. (1997) 'Policing Women: Race, Class and Power in the Women's Police Stations of Brazil', unpublished PhD, University of Washington, Washington.

Ostermann, A. C. (2000) 'Reifying and Defying Sisterhood: Communities of Practice at Work at an All-Female Police Station and a Feminist Crisis Intervention Center in Brazil', unpublished PhD, University of Michigan, Ann Arbor, MI.

Ostermann, A. C. (2002) 'A Ordem Interacional: A Organização do Fechamento de Interações entre Profissionais e Clientes em Instituições de Combate à Violência Contra a Mulher', *ALFA: Revista de Lingüística* 46.

Ostermann, A. C. (2003) 'Localizing Power and Solidarity: Pronoun Alternation at an All-Female Police Station and a Feminist Crisis Intervention Center in Brazil', *Language in Society* 32(3): 351–81.

Paoli, M. C. (1984) 'Mulheres: Lugar, Imagem, Movimento', in M. Chauí, M. C. Paoli and P. Montero SOS-Mulher (eds) *Perspectivas Antropológicas da Mulher* 4, pp. 63–100. Rio de Janeiro, Brazil: Zahar Editores.

Sacks, H., Schegloff, E. A. and Jefferson, G. (1974) 'A Simplest Systematics for the Organization of Turn-Taking for Conversation', *Language* 50(4): 696–735.

Schegloff, E. A. (1981) 'Discourse as an Interactional Achievement: Some Uses of "uhuh" and Other Things that Come between the Sentences', in D. Tannen (ed.) *Analyzing Discourse: Talk and Text*, pp. 71–93. Washington, DC: Georgetown University Press.

Schegloff, E. A., Jefferson, G. and Sacks, H. (1977) 'The Preference for Self-Correction in the Organization of Repair in Conversation', *Language: Journal of the Linguistic Society of America* 53: 361–82.

Scollon, R. and Scollon, S. W. (1995) *Intercultural Communication: A Discourse Approach*. Cambridge, MA: Blackwell.

Sorj, B. and Montero, P. (1984) 'SOS-Mulher e a Luta Contra a Violência', in M. Chauí, M. C. Paoli and P. M. SOS-Mulher (eds) *Perspectivas Antropológicas da Mulher 4*, pp. 101–8. Rio de Janeiro, Brazil: Zahar Editores.

Station, E. (1989, November) 'Partners Against the Crime: Brazil's Police Work with Women to Fight Domestic Violence', *Ms.* 18: 69–70.

Stokoe, E. H. (1998) 'Talking about Gender: The Conversational Construction of Gender Categories in Academic Discourse', *Discourse & Society* 9: 217–40.

Tracy, K. (1990) 'The Many Faces of Facework', in H. Giles and W.P. Robinson (eds) *Handbook of Language and Social Psychology*, pp. 209–26. Chichester: Wiley.

Tracy, K. and Tracy, S. (1998) 'Rudeness at 911: Reconceptualizing Face and Face Attack', *Human Communication Research* 25: 225–51.

West, C. and Zimmerman, D.H. (1983) 'Small Insults: A Study of Interruptions in Cross-Sex Conversations Between Unacquainted Persons', in B. Thorne, C. Kramarae and N. Henley (eds) *Language, Gender and Society*, pp. 103–17. Rowley, MA: Newbury House.

26

Trial Discourse and Judicial Decision-Making: Constraining the Boundaries of Gendered Identities

Susan Ehrlich

Source: Judith Baxter (ed.), *Speaking Out: The Female Voice in Public Contexts*. London: Palgrave (2006), pp. 139–58. Reprinted with permission of Palgrave Macmillan.

Introduction

Recent formulations of the relationship between language and gender, following Butler (1990), have emphasized the performative aspect of gender. Under this account, language is one important means by which gender – an ongoing social process – is enacted or constituted; gender is something individuals *do* – in part through linguistic choices – as opposed to something individuals *are* or *have* (West and Zimmerman, 1987). While the theorizing of gender as 'performative' has encouraged language and gender researchers to focus on the agency and creativity of social actors in the constitution of gender, to my mind there has been less emphasis placed on another aspect of Butler's framework – the 'rigid regulatory frame' (Butler, 1990) within which gendered identities are produced – that is, the limits and constraints on speakers' agency in constructing such identities. This emphasis on the 'performative' aspect of Butler's work, rather than on her discussions of the regulatory norms that define and police normative constructions of gender, may arise because, as Cameron (1997) suggests, philosophical accounts of Butler's 'rigid regulatory frame' often remain very abstract. For Cameron (1997: 31), too often in feminist philosophical discussions, 'gender … floats free of the social contexts and activities in which it will always be … embedded,' obscuring the fact that the routine enactment of gender is often, perhaps always, subject to what she calls the 'institutional coerciveness' of social situations. In other words, cultural norms (i.e. Butler's rigid regulatory frame) make certain performances of gender seem appropriate and intelligible; in Butler's (p. 49) words, they 'congeal over time to produce the appearance … of a natural kind of being.' These same cultural norms render other performances of gender inappropriate and unintelligible and at times subject to social and physical penalties and sanctions (e.g. homophobia, gay-bashing, the 'fixing' of intersexed infants).

By examining data from a public institution, a Canadian sexual assault trial, I demonstrate how culturally dominant notions of male and female sexuality can impose constraints on the formation of participants' gendered identities. Moreover, I show how the gendered identities ascribed and assigned to individuals can depart from the identities individuals intend to claim or adopt.

Significant to an investigation of 'talk' in trial contexts is the fact that interpretations and understandings of the talk are discernable not only in the talk's local discourse (i.e. in the trial), but also in the non-local assessments and judgments of non-speaking recipients (i.e. juries and/or judges). Thus, while the Crown attorney (i.e. the lawyer representing the state) in the sexual assault trial 'talk' described later represented the complainant as *resisting* her perpetrator of sexual assault to the extent possible, judges at both the trial level and the appeal level represented the complainant as *participating* in consensual sex with the accused.[2] Put somewhat differently, the gendered sense-making framework, or *discourse*, that the judges imposed on the events in question departed quite dramatically from the gendered sense-making framework, or discourse, invoked by the Crown attorney in her questioning of the complainant. Through her questioning of the complainant, the Crown attorney allowed a feminist understanding of sexual violence to emerge: one that acknowledged the unequal power dynamics that can shape and restrict women's behavior in the face of men's sexual violence. Yet such an understanding of the complainant's behavior failed to find its way into the judicial decisions of the trial judge or the appeal judge. Indeed, the fact that it was not recognized in these judicial decisions is illustrative, I suggest, of the way that dominant, androcentric discourses (i.e. Butler's rigid regulatory frame) can render certain performances of gender as unintelligible and incoherent. Thus, this chapter considers the notion of 'the female voice' to the extent that it demonstrates the way a feminist perspective, when manifest in a public context, can be distorted or rendered invisible by the androcentric discourses that often dominate in these contexts.

The Participant Structure of Trial Discourse

In describing trial practices, Hale and Gibbons (1999: 203) make a useful distinction between 'two intersecting planes of reality' in the courtroom: the reality of the courtroom itself – what they call the 'courtroom reality' – and the reality that comprises the events under investigation in the courtroom – what they call the 'external reality.' In the court's representation of this 'external reality,' visual images (e.g. photographs, diagrams) and physical entities (e.g. weapons, clothing) are often introduced as evidence, but Hale and Gibbons (1999: 203) remark that 'by far the most common representation of this other reality [the external reality] is ... through testimonial evidence which consists of descriptions of the events by witnesses – versions of the second reality presented through language.' That is, within the context of legal adjudication processes, language is the primary means by which witnesses and lawyers convey information about the events that are the subject of a court's deliberations. And, while much of the courtroom language representing this 'external reality' ostensibly occurs between lawyers and witnesses – that is, it is dyadic – the participant structure of the speech event of the trial is in fact more complex than this. Given that the primary target of courtroom interactions between lawyers and witnesses is a third-party, overhearing recipient – a judge and/or jury – trial talk is more accurately characterized as multi-party (Drew, 1985; Cotterill, 2003). One way of conceptualizing this multi-party structure is by appealing to Goffman's

(1981) notion of the 'gathering.' According to Goffman (1981: 136), 'interactional facts' have to be considered in relation to 'the full physical arena in which persons present are in sight and sound of one another' – what Goffman labeled a 'gathering.' Put somewhat differently, Goffman (1981) argued that the two-person, face-to-face, speaker-hearer model is too crude a construct to account for significant aspects of talk-in-interaction given that speakers will alter how they speak and/or what they say 'by virtue of conducting their talk in visual and aural range of non-participants' (Goffman, 1981: 136). These 'non-participants,' according to Goffman, can include unratified recipients such as bystanders or eavesdroppers as well as ratified recipients. Within the courtroom context, judges and juries constitute ratified recipients, and for Levinson (1988), who elaborates on Goffman's framework, they are the 'indirect target' of trial talk.

For my purposes here, what is important is Goffman's recognition that participants who are not actively and directly participating in an interaction may nonetheless influence many of its properties. While Goffman talks explicitly about how speakers may alter their linguistic identities under the influence of unratified indirect recipients of talk (e.g. bystanders), in this paper I am interested in how ratified indirect recipients of talk, that is judges in trial contexts, may influence and control the (gendered) meanings and interpretations assigned to speakers' linguistic identities. I shall argue that, in order to understand the complexity of gendered identities and, in particular, the way they can be constrained by cultural norms (i.e. Butler's rigid regulatory frame); we need to be attentive to the work of indirect recipients within an interaction or, in Goffman's (1981: 136) words, to 'the full physical arena in which persons present are in sight and sound of one another.'

Data

The data analyzed here come from a Canadian criminal trial involving sexual assault: Her Majesty the Queen v. Ewanchuk, 1995. The case involved a sexual assault that took place during a job interview between the accused (also referred to as the defendant) and the complainant (also referred to as the plaintiff), a 17-year-old woman who ultimately charged the man with sexual assault. The accused was a carpenter and wished to hire individuals who would sell his work for him. While the complainant suggested that her job interview be held in a mall, the accused expressed a preference for more privacy and proposed instead that the interview take place in his van. The interview was conducted in a polite, business-like fashion, according to the complainant's testimony. During the interview the complainant left the door of the van open because she was hesitant about discussing the job offer in his vehicle. After the job interview, the accused invited the complainant to see some of his work in his trailer (i.e. caravan) which was attached to the van. Again, according to the complainant's testimony, she purposely left the trailer door open out of fear of being alone with the accused in a confined space, but the accused ignored her efforts and closed and locked the door. The accused initiated a number of incidents with the complainant that involved sexual touching, with each incident becoming progressively more intimate than the previous. The complainant said that she complied with many of his requests out of fear that any resistance would prompt the accused to become more violent. However, when his touching progressed to the complainant's breast, she used her elbows to push him away and said 'no.' The accused resumed his sexual touching and began to massage the complainant's inner thigh and pelvic area, at which point the complainant again said 'no.' The accused resumed his advances by grinding his pelvis into hers, touching her vaginal area and placing his penis on the complainant's pelvic area under her shorts. He stopped after the complainant said 'no' a third time. After these incidents, the accused opened the door of the trailer at the complainant's request and the complainant left the trailer. She later charged the accused with sexual assault.

The trial judge acquitted the accused of sexual assault relying on the defense of 'implied consent' and the Alberta Court of Appeal upheld this acquittal. The Supreme Court of Canada overturned this acquittal and entered a conviction of sexual assault for the accused. In what follows, I analyze data from the 1995 trial, the 1995 decision of the trial judge and the 1998 decision of the Alberta Court of Appeal. In particular, I contrast two sets of data from this case: excerpts from direct recipients' talk, that is question-answer sequences between the Crown attorney and the complainant, *and* excerpts from indirect recipients' discourse, that is the judges' decisions. Specifically, looking beyond the face-to-face aspects of communication to the discourse of indirect recipients allows us to consider the regulatory norms – that is, Butler's rigid regulatory frame – and the constraints they can impose on identities.

Question-Answer Sequences in Trial Discourse

Like other types of institutional discourse, courtroom discourse has been the subject of much research over the past two decades – research that, among other things, has highlighted its asymmetrical character. As others have noted about courtroom discourse (e.g. Atkinson and Drew, 1979; Walker, 1987; Conley and O' Barr, 1998), differential participation rights are assigned to participants depending on their institutional roles; that is, questioners in legal contexts have the right to initiate and allocate turns by asking questions of witnesses but the reverse is not true. And, such differential participation rights, it has been argued, bestows considerable conversational power and control upon the participant who is sanctioned to ask questions (Hutchby and Wooffitt, 1998). For example, in discussing doctor-patient interaction, Drew and Heritage (1992) note that the question-answer pattern that characterizes most such interactions not only allows doctors to gather information from patients, but can also result in doctors directing and controlling talk: introducing topics, changing topics, and selectively formulating and reformulating the terms in which patients' problems are expressed. Similar claims have been made about lawyers in their role as questioners in the courtroom. However, given the *adversarial* nature of courtroom discourse within the Anglo-American common law system and the *legally sanctioned* power of lawyers to ask questions, lawyers may exercise even more conversational control than doctors in their respective institutional settings.

Adversarial dispute resolution, of which trials are a notable example, requires that two parties come together formally, usually with representation (e.g. lawyers), to present their (probably different) versions of the dispute to a third party (e.g. judge, jury, tribunal) who hears the evidence, applies the appropriate laws or regulations, and determines the guilt or innocence of the parties. Lawyers have as their task, then, convincing the adjudicating body that their (i.e. their client's) version of events is the most credible, or in Capps' and Ochs' (1995) terms, 'the official story.' Apart from making opening and closing arguments, however, lawyers do not themselves testify. Thus, through the posing of questions, lawyers must elicit from witnesses testimony that will build a credible version of events in support of their own clients' interests in addition to testimony that will challenge, weaken, and/or cast doubt on the opposing parties' version of events. Atkinson and Drew (1979: 70) note that while trial discourse is conducted predominantly through a series of question-answer sequences, other actions are accomplished in the form of such questions and answers. For example, questions may be designed to accuse witnesses, to challenge or undermine the truth of what they are saying, or, in direct examination, to presuppose the truth and adequacy of what they are saying.

Direct examination of the complainant

In contrast to the adversarial, combative nature of cross-examination, direct examination, that is the questioning of one's own witness, has been characterized by both legal practitioners and scholars as supportive and cooperative (e.g. Woodbury, 1984; Barry, 1991; Maley, 1994). According to Cotterill (2003: 129), direct examination 'represents an initial, dominant narrative statement, which is then responded to, challenged and sometimes subverted in cross-examination questioning.' Because the emphasis in direct examination is on developing new information, open-ended questions tend to be more frequent in direct examination. Moreover, Woodbury (1984: 211) suggests that open-ended questions have a strategic function as well: they allow witnesses to construct extended narratives that 'give an authentic ring to testimony' and convey to third-party recipients (e.g. judge and/or jury) that lawyers are trusting of their witnesses. Indeed, Harris (2001: 68) argues that lawyers must exercise a high degree of control over *all* witnesses, but that the strategies required to do this differ depending on whether the witness is 'friendly' or 'hostile.'

Because the varying versions of events that emerge in trial discourse are determined to a large extent by the questions that lawyers ask of witnesses (e.g. their controlling of witnesses' topics, their selective reformulations of witnesses' prior answers, etc.), Cotterill (2003: 149) argues that courtroom narratives are best characterized as 'dual-authored texts,' 'with the emphasis on the voice of the lawyer as the primary and authoritative teller.' Due to the 'dual-authored' nature of courtroom narratives, in what follows I analyze question-answer sequences between the Crown attorney and the complainant using the analytic framework of Conversation Analysis, broadly conceived. Conversation Analysis is fundamentally concerned with the sequential analysis of utterances, that is 'how utterances are designed to tie with, or 'fit' to, prior utterances and how an utterance has significant implications for what kinds of utterances should come next' (Wooffitt, 2001: 54). I adopt this approach to question-answer sequences in the direct examination of the complainant because the nature of the questions asked by the Crown attorney has significant implications for what kinds of utterances come next, specifically the kind of testimony the complainant produces and the kind of discursive identity she projects.[2]

In the direct examination of the complainant in the Ewanchuk case, the Crown attorney typically began by asking a broad Wh-question (e.g. 'What happened then?'), that is a Wh-question that allowed the complainant to construct an extended narrative. In response to this broad Wh-question, the complainant would provide an answer that described an event or a series of events. Immediately following such an answer, the lawyer would ask a more narrow Wh-question, that is a Why-question that attempted to elicit more specific information: the plaintiff's motivation for performing a particular action that she had described. For example, in (1) below, the Crown attorney begins by asking a broad Wh-question about the events that transpired once the plaintiff reached the defendant's van. The plaintiff's answer is followed by a more narrow Wh-question – a Why-question inquiring about the plaintiff's motivation for suggesting that she and the defendant talk inside the mall, as opposed to in his van. What emerges in the answer to the Why-question is the complainant's desire to talk to the defendant in a public place.[2]

> Q: Was he inside the van or trailer when you first got there?
> A: I believe he was inside the van, but – he might have stepped out to meet me.
> Q: What happened once you got there?
> A: I asked him if we could go inside the mall, have a cup of coffee and talk about whatever.
> → Q: Why did you want to go inside the mall to talk?
> A: Because it was – it was a public place. I mean, we could go in and sit down somewhere and talk.

According to Woodbury (1984: 211), the narrow Wh-questions that follow broad Wh-questions in direct examination serve a narrative function. Since it is important that lawyers and witnesses co-construct 'a coherent and maximally detailed account' for the sake of third-party recipients, Woodbury maintains that narrow Wh-questions allow witnesses to elaborate on details that contribute to the coherence of the narrative. But, what is it that determines the *kind* of details that will make a narrative cohere? Why, for example, does the Crown attorney in the Ewanchuk case follow up her broad Wh-questions with Why-questions that probe the plaintiff's reasons for performing certain actions in the series of events under question?

It is my contention that the narratives elicited from the complainant through the Crown attorney's questions cohered as feminist narratives. That is, the Crown attorney allowed a feminist understanding of sexual violence to emerge in the complainant's testimony. In particular, it became clear through the question-answer sequences of the Crown attorney and the complainant that the threat of men's sexual violence can create an asymmetrical power relationship between men and women which, in turn, can shape and restrict women's efforts to resist their perpetrators. Consider examples (1)–(5) below which all come from the direct examination of the complainant (I have repeated example (1) below), and all contain a Why-question from the Crown attorney that asks why the complainant has performed a particular action. The answers elicited by these questions (italicized below) reveal the strategic nature of the complainant's actions; that is, the particular actions the Crown attorney asks about are represented by the complainant as ways she attempted to discourage the accused's sexual advances.

Example 1
Q: Was he inside the van or trailer when you first got there?
A: I believe he was inside the van, but – he might have stepped out to meet me.
Q: What happened once you got there?
A: I asked him if we could go inside the mall, have a cup of coffee and talk about whatever.
→ Q: Why did you want to go inside the mall to talk?
A: *Because it was – it was a public place. I mean, we could go in and sit down somewhere and talk.*

Example 2
Q: What happened then?
A: He said, Why don't we just talk inside the van here. And he sat into his driver's seat, and I opened the door, and I left the door open of the passenger seat and I sat down there.
→ Q: And why did you leave the door open?
A: *Because I was still very hesitant about talking to him.*

Example 3

Q: What happened after you agreed to see some of his work?

A: He went around to – no, first, he said, Okay, I'd like to pull the van into the shade. It was a hot day, and there was cars that were *parked under the shade for an shade of a tree* [*sic*], I believe, and he got out, and he went and he stepped inside, and he said, Come on up and look. So I stepped up Inside, took about two steps in, I didn't, like, walk around in it. And then he went to the door, closed it, and locked it.

(some intervening turns)

Q: Had you expected him to lock the door?

A: Not at all. I left the door completely wide open when I walked in there for a reason.

→ Q: And what was that reason?

A: *Because I felt that this was a situation that I shouldn't be in, that I – with anybody to be alone in a trailer with any guy with the door closed.*

Example 4

Q: Did you talk about other things while you were sitting in front of the van?

A: Yes. He asked – we talked a little bit more on a personal level.

Q: What do you mean by that?

A: I believe I told him that I was living on my own. Well, not totally on my own. There was about three other people living there and that I had a boyfriend.

→ Q: Why would you tell him those things?

A: *Because I felt that he should know because I just – I felt – I felt that he might feel a little more threatened if I had said that.*

Example 5

Q: What happened after you talked about your personalities?

A: We were still mentioning a lot of personal things. Like I was still mentioning that I had a boyfriend. I believe I said his name.

Q: What was his name?

A: His name was Allan.

(some intervening turns)

→ Q: Why were you mentioning your boyfriend Allan?

A: *Because, like I said, I felt like if he ever – if – it might prevent him from going beyond any more touching.*

In example (1), when asked why she suggested going inside the mall, the complainant explains that it was a *public* place. (Presumably, sexual advances are less likely to occur in public places.) In examples (2) and (3), when asked why she left the doors open to the front of the van and the trailer, respectively, the complainant explains that she was 'hesitant' about talking to the accused alone 'with the door closed.' In examples (4) and (5), when asked why she was mentioning her boyfriend, Allan, the complainant explains that she wanted the accused to feel 'threatened' and that she wanted to 'prevent him from going beyond any more touching.' Clearly, what the Crown attorney succeeds in eliciting in asking these particular Why-questions is a sense that the complainant is not passive, but rather is actively attempting to create circumstances that will discourage the accused's sexual advances.

Examples (6)–(9) are somewhat different from (1)–(5), as the Crown attorney does not ask questions about actions intended to discourage and/or prevent the accused's sexual advances, but rather asks about actions that could be construed as preambles to consensual sex.

Example 6

Q: Did he say anything when he locked the door?

A: He didn't say anything about the door being locked, but he asked me to sit down. And he sat down cross-legged.

Q: What did you sit on?

A: Just the floor of the trailer.

→ Q: Now, why did you sit down when he asked you to sit down?

A: *Because I figured I was in this trailer, the door was locked, he was not much more than this stand is away from me here, probably only a couple of feet away from me. I felt that I was in a situation now where I just better do what I was told.*

Example 7

Q: And what happened then?

A: He told me that he felt very tense and that he would like to have a massage, and he then leaned up against me with his back towards me and told me to rub his shoulders and I did that.

Q: And up to the time he told you he was tense and wanted a massage, had the two of you talked about you giving him a massage?

A: I believe all he had said right before that is that he liked to have them, and he was tense feeling and that was all.

Q: Had you ever offered to give him a massage?

A: No.

Q: Did you want to give him a massage?

A: No.

(some intervening turns)

→ Q: If you didn't want to give him a massage at that point in time, why did you touch his shoulders?

A: *I was afraid that if I put up any more of a struggle that it would only egg him on even more, and his touching would be more forced.*

Example 8

Q: And what happened then?

A: Then he asked me to turn around the other way to face him, and he said he would like to touch my feet or he would like to massage my feet, so I did. And he was just touching my feet.

Q: Did you want him to massage your feet?

A: No.

→ Q: Why did you turn around?

A: *Because I guess I was afraid. I was frozen. I just did what he told me to do.*

Q: Did he ever ask you if you would like him to massage his feet – your feet?

A: No, he just said, Turn around I'm going to.

Q: What happened after you turned around?

A: He was massaging my feet, but he didn't stay there. He was moving up my leg more toward my inner thigh, my pelvic area, and then he'd move back again, and then he'd move back up again, and *I just sat there, and I didn't – I didn't do anything. I didn't say anything. I knew something was going to happen, and I didn't want to fight. I didn't want to struggle. I didn't want to scream, because I felt that that would just egg him on more.*

Example 9

Q: And what happened when he reached to hug you?

A: He just did, and I, at this time, I was trying really hard not to cry. I had been wiping my eyes when he was on top of me when he couldn't see me, and I just…. I just responded by just lightly putting my arm on him when he hugged me because I was afraid that he would think I was really scared, and that I would leave there telling people.

→ Q: And why were you worried about him thinking that?

A: *Because I didn't think that he would stop there, that it would get worse, and it would be more brutal.*

Put somewhat differently, in examples (6)–(9), the Crown attorney asks why the complainant complies with the accused's requests: in (6), why she sits down when asked; in (7), why she begins to massage the accused when asked; in (8), why she turns around to face the accused when he asks to massage her feet; and, in (9), why her fear of the accused leads her to reciprocate his hug. In response to these questions, the complainant says a variety of things: that she was afraid; that she felt she should do what she was told; that she feared if she did not comply with the accused's requests or if she put up a struggle that she would 'egg him on even more,' 'his touching would be more forced,' and 'it would be more brutal.' Indeed, such responses reflect strategies that many victims of sexual violence employ to prevent more prolonged and extreme instances of violence. As researchers on violence against women have asserted, submitting to coerced sex or physical abuse can be 'a strategic mode of action undertaken in preservation of self' (Lempert, 1996: 281). That is, if physical resistance on the part of victims can escalate and intensify violence, as some research shows (e.g. Dobash and Dobash, 1992) and many women (are instructed to) believe, then submission to coerced sex is undoubtedly the best strategy for survival. Significant about the Crown attorney's questioning in (6)–(9) is the fact that her questions allow the complainant's actions to be revealed as strategies of resistance, rather than as precursors to consensual sex. In fact, all of the Crown's why-questions highlighted in examples (1)–(9) function to elicit responses that emphasize the complainant's active deployment of strategies meant to discourage and resist the accused's escalating sexual violence. Put another way, the complainant's actions were contextualized within a framework, or discourse, that acknowledged the potential structural inequalities that characterize male-female sexual relations and the effects of such inequalities on women's strategies of resistance. We will see in the next section that, by contrast, the trial judge and the appeal judge contextualized the complainant's actions within an alternative framework or discourse – one that erased the unequal Dower dynamics of male–female sexual relations and, concomitantly, construed coerced sex as consensual sex.

Judges' Discourse

As stated in a previous section, the trial judge's decision to acquit the accused in this case was appealed to the Alberta Court of Appeal, where the acquittal was upheld, and then to the Supreme Court of Canada, where the acquittal was overturned. In this section, I discuss both the decision of the trial judge and the Alberta Court of Appeal judge, including the defense both judges invoked in acquitting the accused – 'the defense of implied consent.'

The first noteworthy aspect of both of these decisions, given that the Crown attorney and the complainant depicted the complainant as attempting to discourage and resist the accused, was the consistent representation of sexual relations between the accused and the complainant as consensual sex. Consider the following excerpt from the trial judge's decision, at a point when the judge is describing the 'facts' of the case:

Example 10

```
 1  B [the complainant] told A [the accused] that she was an open,
 2  friendly and affectionate person; and that she often liked to touch
 3  people. A told B that he was an open, friendly and affectionate
 4  person; and that he often liked to touch people. A and B talked.
 5  They touched each other. They hugged. They were sitting on the
 6  floor of the trailer and they were lying on the floor of the trailer.
 7  A told B that he would like a body massage, and B gave A a body
 8  massage. For the body massage, A sat in front of B so that B could
 9  massage A's back. They later exchanged places so that A could give
10  B a body massage. B later lay on her back, and A gave B a foot
11  massage. After the foot massage, A massaged B's bare legs and he
12  massaged her bare inner thighs. During this period of two and one
13  half hours, A did three things which B did not like. When A was
14  giving B a body massage, his hands got close to B's breasts. B said
15  "No", and A immediately stopped. When B and A were lying on
16  the floor, A rubbed his pelvic area against B's pelvic area. B said
17  "No", and A immediately stopped. Later on A took his soft penis
18  out of his shorts and placed it on the outside of B's clothes in her
19  pelvic area. B said "No", and A immediately stopped.
20  During all of the two and one half hours that A and B were
21  together, she never told A that she wanted to leave. When B
22  finally told A that she wanted to leave, she and A simply walked
23  out of the trailer.
```

(from Reasons for Judgment (Moore, J., C.Q.B.A.),
November 10,1995)

These same 'facts' are confirmed by the Alberta Court of Appeal judge in his support of the trial judge's 'doubts about consent.'

Example 11

Yet, if review of the evidence that supports the trial judge's doubts about consent in this case is called for, it may be found in the following. The advances that are now said to be criminally assaultive were preceded by *an exchange of consensual body massages, partially on the floor of the trailer, hugs and assurances of trust and restraint....* Beyond that (and somewhat inconsistent with an appellate profile of Ewanchuk as a relentless sexual predator) every advance he made to her stopped when she spoke against it. (from Reasons for Judgment of Honourable Mr. Justice McClung, February 12, 1998)

In general, these descriptions of what transpired between the accused and the complainant – with the exception of the descriptions of the three times that the complainant said 'no' – emphasize the consensual, mutual and reciprocal nature of their sexual relations. Indeed, the appeal judge states quite explicitly that the hugs and the body massages were reciprocal (i.e. 'an exchange') and 'consensual' (in italics above). Particularly striking is the fact that both judges represent as consensual and reciprocal events that the Crown attorney and the complainant depicted as coerced sex. That is, on many occasions – and this is exemplified in examples (6)–(9) – the complainant said she complied with the accused's wishes out of fear that his violence would otherwise escalate. Yet, the judges represent these events as ones that the complainant engaged in without coercion. For example, in line 5 of example (10), the trial judge states that the complainant and the accused hugged each other in a reciprocal way (i.e. 'They hugged') whereas in example

(9) the complainant says that she responded to the accused's hug out of fear, that is 'because [she] was afraid that he would think [she] was really scared' which in turn would lead to even greater brutality. Likewise, in lines 7–8 of (10), the judge states simply that the complainant gave the accused a body massage in response to his request (i.e. 'A told B that he would like a body massage, and B gave A a body massage'); yet in example (7) the complainant says that she agreed to massage the accused only because she 'was afraid that if [she] put up any more of a struggle that it would only egg him on even more and his touching would be more forced.' Finally, we see that in lines 11–12 of (10), the judge states the accused massaged the complainant's bare legs and inner thighs, as if this were a consensual act (i.e. 'After the foot massage, A massaged B's bare legs and he massaged her bare inner thighs'); but in example (8) the complainant says that she complied with the accused's massages because she did not want to 'egg him on more.' In sum, despite the fact that the complainant conveyed in her direct testimony that she had little choice but to comply with the accused's sexual advances, the judges' decisions failed to qualify or modify the sexual advances in such a way. Indeed, there is a sense in both decisions that the complainant's consent was freely given. By contrast, it is noteworthy that in the decision of the Supreme Court of Canada, there are many descriptions of the 'facts' that acknowledge the coerced nature of the sexual contact between the accused and the complainant, for example 'At some point the accused said that he was feeling tense and asked the complainant to give him a massage. The complainant complied, massaging the accused's shoulders for a few minutes.' 'The complainant did not want the accused to touch her in this way, but said nothing as she was afraid that any resistance would prompt the accused to become violent.' (from 1999 decision of the Supreme Court of Canada, Her Majesty the Queen v. Ewanchuk).

In previous work on the language of Canadian sexual assault trial judgments, Coates, Bavelas, and Gibson (1994) noted that judges recognized resistance on the part of complainants only when it took the form of persistent physical struggle. Coates et al. (1994: 195) elaborate: 'The language of appropriate resistance seemed to us to be drawn from male-male combat between equals, where continued fighting is appropriate, rather than from asymmetrical situations… where physical resistance would lead to little chance of success and a high probability of further harm.' While the excerpts from the judges' decisions do not seem to deem physical struggle as the only appropriate form of resistance, they do seem to require that resistance at least take the form of verbal refusal. For example, based on lines 14–19 of example (10), it seems that verbal refusals are the only indicators or signals that the trial judge recognizes as resistance on the part of the complainant. That is, although the Crown attorney is successful in eliciting testimony (for example, (1)–(9)) that depicts the complainant as attempting to discourage and resist the accused in a variety of ways – including submitting to coerced sex, the trial judge appears to only perceive her resistance on the three occasions that she said 'no' to the accused.

The defense of implied consent

Under Canadian criminal law, an accused will be found guilty of sexual assault if the Crown attorney proves beyond a reasonable doubt that the complainant did not (or could not) consent to the acts. As stated earlier, the trial judge did not find the accused guilty of sexual assault, but rather acquitted the accused, relying on the defense of 'implied consent.' The Alberta Court of Appeal upheld this acquittal and the defense. For both of these judges, then, the complainant was considered to have *implied* consent; moreover, the Alberta Court of Appeal judge defined implied consent as 'consent by conduct.' One of the questions that arises from these judgements concerns the kind of 'conduct' that these judges deemed as signaling consent. Both the trial judge and the Court of Appeal judge found that the complainant was a 'credible witness' (from the trial judge, Moore) and that she was genuinely afraid of the accused: 'Certainly the complainant was afraid of Ewanchuk as the trial judge found' (from the Court of Appeal judge, McClung). However, both judges also commented in their decisions that she did not communicate her fear to the accused. Consider the follow excerpt from the trial judge's decision:

Example 12
All of B's [the complainant's] thoughts, emotions and speculations were very real for her. However, she successfully kept all her thoughts, emotions, and speculations deep within herself. She did not communicate most of her thoughts, emotions and speculations....Like a good actor, she projected an outer image that did not reflect her inner self. B did not communicate to A by words, gestures, or facial expressions *that she was 'frozen' by a fear of force.* B did not communicate that *she was frozen to the spot,* and that fear prevented her from getting up off the floor and walking out of the trailer.

The picture that emerges from this description of the complainant is that she was 'frozen to the spot' and 'that she was "frozen" by a fear of force' (italicized above), yet she kept her emotions and feelings hidden from the accused. And, on the basis of this type of 'conduct,' the trial judge acquitted the accused, suggesting that the complainant's conduct *implied* consent. Given that the accused would have to draw inferences in order to understand the complainant as 'implying' consent, one wonders what kind of cultural background knowledge these inferences would rely upon. In other words, what kind of cultural assumptions might give rise to the inference that concealing emotions and being frozen to the spot conveys consent? What becomes clear from questions such as these is the ideological nature of the cultural assumptions that the accused is understood to rely upon in drawing such an inference. That is, by ruling that a woman who is emotionless and frozen to the spot *is implying* consent, the judges are invoking assumptions about women's lack of agency and passivity in the course of 'normal' heterosexual sex. As Cameron and Kulick (2003: 36) remark about such societal assumptions, 'the denial of sexual agency to women means that saying "yes" to sex (or initiating it) is disapproved of. Nice girls should demur coyly in order to demonstrate that they are not sluts or nymphomaniacs, but this is a ritual, formulaic gesture and men should not be deterred.' Clearly, the accused in Her Majesty the Queen v. Ewanchuk was not deterred by the complainant's emotionless and frozen demeanor (indeed, not even by her three verbal refusals); and, such behavior was authorized by the trial judge and the Alberta Court of Appeal judge presumably because of the weight of cultural beliefs that equate a woman's sexual passivity with consent.

Conclusion

Recent approaches to language and gender, while emphasizing the agency and creativity of speakers in constructing gendered identities, have paid less attention to the normative discourses (i.e. Butler's rigid regulatory frame) that police and regulate the intelligibility of such identities. In this paper, I have suggested, following Goffman (1981), that a full understanding of identity construction requires looking beyond the face-to-face aspects of interaction to what Goffman calls the 'gathering.' Put somewhat differently, I have used a sexual assault trial to demonstrate how participants who are not directly and actively involved in an interaction can nonetheless influence the meanings and understandings that are assigned to that interaction. More specifically, I have attempted to show how the identity *imposed* upon the complainant in this sexual assault case – as a participant in consensual sex – departed quite dramatically from her identity – as a victim of coerced sex – as it was co-constructed in her direct testimony.

Capps and Ochs (1995: 21) argue that adjudicators in legal cases never determine the truth of a case; rather, 'on the basis of divergent versions of events, jury members [and adjudicators] construct a narrative that is plausible and coherent in their eyes. ... In this sense rendering a verdict is analogous not to ascertaining the facts of a case but to determining an official story.' While there are undoubtedly many factors contributing to the determination of an 'official story,' I am suggesting here that a crucial determining factor, especially in the context of a sexual assault trial, is the intelligibility – or lack thereof – of participants' 'performances' of gender. Indeed, in the judicial decisions analyzed so far, the version of events endorsed by the trial judge and the Court of Appeal judge relied upon a very particular understanding of gender and sexuality – one that viewed women's verbal refusals as necessary to resistance and equated women's lack of physical responsiveness with consent. As demonstrated before, the Crown attorney and complainant invoked an alternative, feminist sense-making framework in this trial – one that viewed submission to coerced sex as a way for the complainant to resist more extreme and prolonged instances of violence. Yet, this alternative way of assigning meaning to the events in question did not seem to resonate with the sense-making frameworks of the trial judge and the Alberta Court of Appeal judge. McConnell-Ginet (1988, 1989) has argued that counter-hegemonic viewpoints or discourses may encounter difficulty functioning as background knowledge in linguistic exchanges that do not take place among familiars (McConnell-Ginet, 1988: 92). In other words, because the Crown attorney's discursive strategy involved a feminist understanding of sexual assault, it had difficulty surviving as a contextualizing framework within a public institution, such as a trial. Rather, this trial – or at least crucial and defining aspects of it – relied on dominant, androcentric background assumptions (i.e. Butler's rigid regulatory frame) to inform and constrain its interpretation of events.

Notes

I thank Judith Baxter for valuable comments on a previous version of this paper. The research for this article was funded, in part, by a Regular Research Grant from the Social Sciences and Humanities Research Council of Canada, grant # 410–2000–1330.

1 Within the Canadian criminal justice system, Crown attorneys represent the state and complainants assume the role of witnesses for the state. That is, complainants are not *directly* represented by Crown attorneys.

2 The arrows within the transcripts point to narrow Wh-questions asked by the Crown attorney.

3 In previous work on the language of sexual assault trials (Ehrlich, 2001), I have argued that defense lawyers strategically invoke the 'utmost resistance standard' in trial discourse as a way of undermining the credibility of complainants. Until the 1950s and 1960s in the United States, the statutory requirement of utmost resistance was a necessary criterion for the crime of rape (Estrich, 1987); that is, if a woman did not resist a man's sexual advances to the utmost then the rape was said not to have occurred. While the 'utmost resistance standard' is no longer

encoded in legal statutes in the United States or Canada, the adjudication of sexual assault cases often relies on such a principle. Moreover, given that this standard has found its way into trial discourse, it is possible that the Crown attorney's questioning of the complainant in the Ewanchuk case anticipated, and was designed to counteract, such a strategy on the part of Ewanchuk's lawyer.

References

Atkinson, J. M. and Drew, P. (1979) *Order in Court*. London: Macmillan Press.

Barry, A. (1991) 'Narrative style and witness testimony', *Journal of Narrative and Life History*, 1:281–93.

Butler, J. (1990) *Gender Trouble: Feminism and the Subversion of Identity*. London: Routledge.

Cameron, D. (1997) 'Theoretical debates in feminist linguistics: Questions of sex and gender', in R. Wodak (ed.), *Gender and Discourse*, pp. 21–36. London: Sage.

Cameron, D. and Kulick, D. (2003) *Language and Sexuality*. Cambridge: Cambridge University Press.

Capps, L. and Ochs, E. (1995) *Constructing Panic: The Discourse of Agoraphobia*. Cambridge, MA: Harvard University Press.

Coates, L., Bavelas, J., and Gibson J. (1994) 'Anomalous language in sexual assault trial judgements', *Discourse & Society*, 5:189–206.

Conley, J. and O'Barr, W. (1998) *Just Words: Law, Language and Power*. Chicago: University of Chicago Press.

Cotterill, J. (2003) *Language and Power in Court: A Linguistic Analysis of the O.J. Simpson Trial*. London: Palgrave Macmillan.

Dobash, R. E. and Dobash, R. P. (1992) *Women, Violence and Social Change*. London: Routledge.

Drew, P. (1985) 'Analyzing the use of language in courtroom interaction' in T. A. van Dijk (ed.), *Handbook of Discourse Analysis* (volume 3), pp. 133–47. New York: Academic Press.

Drew, P. and Heritage, J. (1992) 'Analyzing talk at work: An Introduction', in P. Drew and J. Heritage (eds), *Talk at Work: Interaction in Institutional Settings*, pp. 3–65. Cambridge: Cambridge University Press.

Ehrlich, S. (2001) *Representing Rape: Language and Sexual Consent*. London: Routledge.

Estrich, S. (1987) *Real Rape*. Cambridge, Massachusetts: Harvard University Press.

Goffman, E. (1981) *Forms of Talk*. Philadelphia: University of Pennsylvania Press.

Hale, S. and Gibbons, J. (1999) 'Varying realities: Patterned changes in the interpreter's representation of courtroom and external realities', *Applied Linguistics*, 20: 203–20.

Harris, S. (2001) 'Fragmented narratives and multiple tellers: Witness and defendant accounts in trials', *Discourse Studies*, 3: 53–74.

Hutchby, I. and Wooffitt, R. (1998) *Conversation Analysis*. Oxford: Polity Press.

Lempert, L. (1996) 'Women's strategies for survival: Developing agency in abusive relationships', *Journal of Family Violence*, 11: 269–89.

Levinson, S. C. (1988) 'Putting linguistics on a proper footing: Explorations in Goffman's concepts of participation', in P. Drew and A. Wooton (eds), *Erving Goffman: Explorations in the Interactional Order*, pp. 161–228. Oxford: Polity Press.

Maley, Y. (1994) 'The language of the law', in J. Gibbons (ed.), *Language and the Law*, pp. 11–50. London: Longman.

McConnell-Ginet, S. (1988) 'Language and gender', in F. Newmeyer (ed.), *Linguistics: The Cambridge Survey*, Volume IV, pp. 75–99. Cambridge: Cambridge University Press.

McConnell-Ginet, S. (1989) 'The sexual (re)production of meaning: A discourse-based theory', in F. Frank and P. A. Treichler (eds), *Language, Gender, and Professional Writing*, pp. 35–50. New York: Modern Language Association of America.

Reasons for Judgment (Moore, J., C.Q.B.A.), November 10, 1995, Queen v. Ewanchuk.

Reasons for Judgment of the Honourable Mr. Justice McClung, February 12, 1998, Queen v. Ewanchuk.

Walker, A. G. (1987) 'Linguistic manipulation, power and the legal setting', in L. Kedar (ed.), *Power through Discourse*, pp. 57–80. Norwood, New Jersey: Ablex.

West, C. and Zimmerman, D. (1987) 'Doing gender', *Gender and Society*, 1:25–51.

Woodbury, H. (1984) 'The strategic use of questions in court', *Semiotica*, 48:197–228.

Wooffitt, R. (2001) 'Conversation analysis', in M. Wetherell, S. Taylor and S. Yates (eds), *Discourse as Data*, pp. 49–92. London: Sage Publications.

Part VI

Language, Gender, and Sexuality

One of the key stimuli to fresh thinking about gender has been the new field of queer linguistics. This new field "has the sexual and gender deviance of previous generations at its centre" (Hall 2003: 354). Language in queer linguistics is studied from the twin perspectives of gender and sexuality, so research focusing on the language of gay, lesbian, bisexual, and transsexual communities is at its heart. The notion of gender as fluid and multiple is intrinsic to queer linguistics, since binary categories like *man/woman* are unhelpful when studying communities like these.

The first paper in this section is Hideko Abe's "Lesbian Bar Talk in Shinjuku, Tokyo." Abe investigates the naming and identity-construction of lesbian women in Tokyo and the linguistic patterns typical of their interactions. These women self-identify as belonging to two different groups: *rezubian* and *onabe*. *Rezubian* are women who are attracted to women and who identify as female; *onabe*, by contrast, are women who are attracted to women but whose social and emotional identity is male. These two groups are catered for by two different kinds of bar: *rezubian* bars and *onabe* bars. Abe's fieldwork involved frequent visits to these bars in a small area of Tokyo over a 10-month period. She did not record interactions in the bars, partly because of the noise (loud music was played in all of them), but mainly because the owners and their employees did not agree to recordings being made. Instead she conducted interviews with customers, owners, and employees; she made detailed field notes; and she also corresponded with some employees by email. Among other things she analyzed pronoun usage. In Japanese, first-person pronouns are gendered (just like third-person pronouns in English: *he/she*). Abe established that the general pattern was that *rezubian* use the first-person pronoun *watashi* (a pronoun available to both women and men) while *onabe* use *jibun* (a reflexive pronoun associated with men in sports or the army). But the same speaker can use multiple first-person forms depending on the context, demonstrating the fluidity of lesbian identity in this community. Research like this shows very clearly how constricting a binary approach can be. Here, all the people being studied are biologically women, but some identify as female and some as male. It would be all too easy to expect that first-person-pronoun usage would correlate neatly with these two kinds of gay woman, but Abe's research shows that this is not the case.

Language and Gender: A Reader, Second Edition. Edited by Jennifer Coates and Pia Pichler.
© 2011 Blackwell Publishing Ltd except for editorial material and organization. © 2011 Jennifer Coates and Pia Pichler. Published 2011 by Blackwell Publishing Ltd.

In the next paper, "Boys' Talk: Hindi, Moustaches, and Masculinity in New Delhi," Kira Hall explores the way in which language, masculinity, and social class intersect. This paper arises from research carried out in New Delhi, India, and again involves two different kinds of lesbian: those who identify as female and refer to themselves as lesbian, and those who identify as male and who refer to themselves as "boys." These women were involved in an outreach program designed for "women who are attracted to women," run by a New Delhi NGO whose aims include educating the public about sexual diversity and HIV/Aids. As Hall shows, the program tries to persuade the participants that being a woman and being attracted to other women is perfectly "normal." However, while some of the women aligned themselves with this (more western, social constructionist) stance, others aligned themselves with a more traditional, working-class idea of sexual desire as intrinsically heterosexual. They therefore insisted on being addressed as "boys" and were insulted if referred to as women. They aspire to "a semiotics of masculinity which has sexual reassignment surgery as its endpoint." Hall's delicate analysis shows how they code-switch between English (the language of the educated elite and of the imperial oppressor) and Hindi (an Indian language connoting tradition and a more working-class image) to signal these allegiances. Understandings of masculinity and of the links between language, social class, masculinity, and sexuality are continually contested in the interactions she observed.

William Leap's paper, "Queering Gay Men's English," explicitly addresses the question "What do queer theories have to offer researchers of gender and language?" He presents a critique of his own earlier work on Gay English (in particular his book *Word's Out*, Leap 1996), which he describes as "identity-centred linguistic inquiry." In this paper he carries out an analysis of the narrative of a young gay South African from a Black township outside Cape Town who is trying to make sense of his own life and where he stands in relation to his sexuality and his ethnicity. Leap takes the position in this paper that identity-formation is a product of the speaker's linguistic practices and that, following Butler (1990), gender is constantly "in formation." Leap argues that life-story narratives are "queer texts," and that Bob's narrative is not only a version of a coming-out story but can only be fully understood if contextualized both socially and politically. Unlike the gay men Leap studied in the USA, Bob does not tell a story of coming out to his family (on the contrary, he claims that his brother would kill him if he did), but has to wrestle with the conflicting norms of his township (which sees homosexuality as involving men-who-want-to-be-women and who dress in drag) and of the city (where a more North Atlantic view of gay identity prevails). (There are clear parallels here with the conflicting norms expressed by the lesbians in Hall's paper.) The conflicting norms confronted by Bob are associated with conflicting ethnicities: in his struggle to express himself, Bob aligns himself with the white norms of the city center and the university, rather than the norms of the Black township where he lives. Bob's is thus a story about ethnicity as much as it is a story about gender and sexuality.

In the fourth paper, Rusty Barrett's "Indexing Polyphonous Identity in the Speech of African American Drag Queens," the focus is again on gay men, but on a very particular subgroup of gay men – drag queens. Like female impersonators, drag queens dress in women's clothes and entertain people in clubs and bars, but unlike female impersonators, who are straight, drag queens are gay. The drag queens that Barrett's paper concentrates on are "glam queens," that is glamour-oriented drag queens who aim to produce a physical representation of hyperfeminine womanhood. He explores the way that speakers draw on a multiplicity of identities, and in particular shows how the drag queens he studied use language to index their identities as African Americans and gay men, as well as drag queens. Speakers exploit different speaking styles, switching between white-woman style, African American Vernacular English (AAVE), and gay male speech. The white-woman style indexes "ideal" feminine behavior and contrasts with other styles: in their performances, drag queens will use a stereotypically feminine speaking style but will deliberately subvert this by using taboo words or by switching into a stereotypically masculine voice. As Barrett puts it: "the polyphony of stylistic voices and the identities they index serve to convey multiple meanings..."

The last paper in this section is Marisol del-Teso-Craviotto's "Language and Sexuality in Spanish and English Dating Chats." Del-Teso-Craviotto collected a large corpus of material from internet chatrooms. She included both English- and Spanish-speaking sites, but all sites studied were dedicated to online dating, both gay and straight. The final corpus involved 45 extracts from online dating interactions, each lasting 30 minutes. Del-Teso-Craviotto explores the idea of "desire" and its linguistic manifestations (a theme which some researchers consider central to any discussion of language and sexuality – see Kulick 2000, 2003; Eckert 2002; Cameron and Kulick 2003). She uses Conversation Analytic methods to transcribe and analyze her data, and shows how participants adopt a play frame in their interactions. The play frame is multi-functional: it alleviates the tension associated with engaging in erotic conversations in the public domain, it allows participants "to establish a safe distance between their real (critical) selves and their virtual (enjoying) selves," and also it creates a safety net in that participants can retreat to an "only joking" position. She analyzes her data extracts to show how certain discourse features – laughter, colloquial or childish speech styles, wordplay, and exploiting the alter ego of their online persona – contribute to the expression of sexual desire.

Research exploring the intersection of language, gender, and sexuality is a fast-growing area, as the spate of recent publications attests (for example, Campbell-Kibler et al. 2002; Cameron and Kulick 2003; Bucholtz and Hall 2004; Morrish and Saunston 2007; Saunston and Kyratzis 2007; Baker 2008). Case studies like the ones included in this section have been invaluable not only in breaking the stranglehold of simplistic understandings of gender but also in opening up research to non-English-speaking cultures. The new focus on language and sexuality has also served to problematize heterosexuality, and to make more visible the way language is used to impose heteronormativity. The aim of queer theory to disentangle sexuality from gender has proved to be less achievable. As the papers in this section illustrate, gender and sexuality are very closely intertwined – in particular, and as the papers by Kiesling and by Cameron in Part IV illustrate, dominant norms of masculinity are intrinsically heterosexual. As Cameron and Kulick (2003: 141) put it: "Since desiring subjects and desired objects are never genderless, you cannot 'do sexuality' without at the same time 'doing gender.'"

References

Baker, P. (2008) *Sexed Texts: Language, Gender and Sexuality.* London: Equinox.

Bucholtz, Mary and Hall, Kira (2004) "Theorizing identity in language and sexuality research," *Language in Society* 33, 469–515.

Butler, Judith (1990) *Gender Trouble: Feminism and the Subversion of Identity.* New York: Routledge.

Cameron, Deborah and Kulick, Don (2003) *Language and Sexuality.* Cambridge: Cambridge University Press.

Campbell-Kibler, Kathryn, Podevsa, Rob, Roberts, Sarah J., and Wong, Andrew (eds) (2002) *Language and Sexuality: Contesting Meaning in Theory and Practice*. Stanford, CA: CSLI Publications.

Eckert, Penelope (2002) "Demystifying sexuality and desire," pp. 99–110 in Kathryn Campbell-Kibler, Rob Podevsa, Sarah J. Roberts, and Andrew Wong (eds) *Language and Sexuality: Contesting Meaning in Theory and Practice*. Stanford, CA: CSLI Publications.

Hall, Kira (2003) "Exceptional speakers: contested and problematised gender identities," pp. 353–80 in Janet Holmes and Miriam Meyerhoff (eds) *The Handbook of Language and Gender*. Oxford: Blackwell.

Kulick, Don (2000) "Gay and lesbian language," *Annual Review of Anthropology* 29, 243–85.

Kulick, Don (2003) "Language and desire," pp. 119–41 in Janet Holmes and Miriam Meyerhoff (eds) *The Handbook of Language and Gender*. Oxford: Blackwell.

Leap, William (1996) *Word's Out: Gay Men's English*. Minneapolis: University of Minnesota Press.

Morrish, Liz and Saunston, Helen (2007) *New Perspectives on Language and Sexual Identity*. London: Palgrave Macmillan.

Saunston, Helen and Kyratzis, Sakis (eds) (2007) *Language, Sexualities and Desires: Cross-Cultural Perspectives*. London: Palgrave.

Recommended Further Reading

Abe, Hideko (2010) *Queer Japanese: Gender and Sexual Identities through Linguistic Practice*. London: Palgrave Macmillan.

Cameron, Deborah and Kulick, Don (2003) *Language and Sexuality*. Cambridge: Cambridge University Press.

Cameron, Deborah and Kulick, Don (2006) *Language and Sexuality: A Reader*. London: Routledge.

Campbell-Kibler, Kathryn, Podevsa, Rob, Roberts, Sarah J., and Wong, Andrew (eds) (2002) *Language and Sexuality: Contesting Meaning in Theory and Practice*. Stanford, CA: CSLI Publications.

Harvey, Keith and Shalom, Celia (eds) (1997) *Language and Desire: Encoding Sex, Romance and Intimacy*. London: Routledge.

Leap, William and Boellstorff, Tom (eds) (2004) *Speaking in Queer Tongues: Globalisation and Gay Language*. Chicago: University of Illinois Press.

Livia, Anna and Hall, Kira (eds) (1997) *Queerly Phrased: Language Gender and Sexuality*. Oxford: Oxford University Press.

Morrish, Liz and Saunston, Helen (2007) *New Perspectives on Language and Sexual Identity*. London: Palgrave Macmillan.

Saunston, Helen and Kyratzis, Sakis (eds) *Language, Sexualities and Desires: Cross-Cultural Perspectives*. London: Palgrave.

Wood, Kathleen (1999) "Coherent identities amid heterosexist ideologies: deaf and hearing lesbian coming-out stories," pp. 46–63 in Mary Bucholtz, A. C. Liang, and Laurel Sutton (eds) *Reinventing Identities: The Gendered Self in Discourse*. Oxford: Oxford University Press.

27

Lesbian Bar Talk in Shinjuku, Tokyo

Hideko Abe

Source: Originally published in a longer version as pp. 205–21 of Shigeko Okamoto and Janet Shibamoto-Smith (eds), *Japanese Language, Gender and Ideology: Cultural Models and Real People*. Oxford: Oxford University Press, 2004. Reprinted with permission of Oxford University Press.

This chapter focuses on the relationship between identity and language use observed among women at lesbian bars in Shinjuku, Tokyo. I chose lesbian bars as a setting for ethnographic linguistic study because lesbians, in contrast to gays, have been generally underrepresented in Japanese studies. Watanabe (1990) argues that lesbianism in Japan has historically been marginalized and is much less well documented than male homosexuality. As Moonwomon-Baird puts it, 'Lesbian practice is regarded as marked behavior, but goes unremarked much more than is true of gay male practice, even in this era of both friendly and hostile societal discourse on queers' (1997: 202).

This study discusses two issues: (1) naming and identity construction in discourse and (2) linguistic behaviour and interaction at lesbian bars. In the first part of this chapter, I examine how certain terms of social categorization are used to differentiate one individual's identity from others and how the social spaces of lesbian bars help individuals construct, renew, or vitalize their identities. Then I discuss how lesbian speech at bars tends to contain extensive use of masculine forms with wide contextual and individual variation. As I will discuss later, these two phenomena are crucial to understanding the relationship between Japanese lesbian identities and linguistic practice.

Method and Data Collection

Tokyo's Shinjuku Ni-choome 'the Second Block', an area as small as 300 meters by 400 meters, is often referred to as the world's largest gay town. It was formerly a district inhabited by Japanese female prostitutes who served American personnel during the Occupation after World War II. According to a recent gay travel guide, there are 217 gay bars in Ni-choome. By contrast, there are 12 lesbian bars in Ni-choome and one in Sanchoome 'the Third Block' in Tokyo, four in Osaka, and one each in Kyuushuu and Hokkaido.

The fieldwork for this study was conducted between September of 1999 and June of 2000 in the Shinjuku area of Tokyo. I visited lesbian bars almost every week, spending at least two to three hours as a customer and researcher at each bar. I also corresponded with employees via e-mail. In total, there are 13 lesbian bars in Shinjuku, and I visited 12

Language and Gender: A Reader, Second Edition. Edited by Jennifer Coates and Pia Pichler.
© 2011 Blackwell Publishing Ltd except for editorial material and organization. © 2011 Jennifer Coates and Pia Pichler. Published 2011 by Blackwell Publishing Ltd.

of them; I spent considerable time at some, and others I visited only once. Not all lesbian bars are the same; some target older middle-class professional women while others target younger nonprofessional women, both middle- and working-class. However, some bars have both types of women. All employees of the bars are lesbians.

Whenever I visited a bar for the first time, I arrived at opening time so that I could be the first customer and spend time alone with the owner or the manager of the bar to explain my research. This is when I asked for permission to take field notes. I was allowed to have a notebook in front of me and to make notes at any time. Often employees jokingly said to me, 'a *mata nan ka kaiteru*', 'she's writing something again' while they were serving other customers. I conducted interviews with owners and employees but also interacted with other customers, all of whom knew of my research project. I did not tape-record interactions at bars, nor did I conduct interviews outside the bars. There are two reasons for not recording the interactions. The first is that there was always loud music playing at the bars, which would have made recording almost impossible. Second, and more important, the bar owners and employees did not agree to recording. The reason was clear. In most bars, women are anonymous and it was important that they be allowed to remain so. My sources of data thus are (1) interviews, (2) field notes, (3) articles from magazines, and (4) e-mail messages.

Naming and Identity Construction in Discourses at Lesbian Bars

The definition of the community served by lesbian bars turned out to be broader than I had expected. While some owners and employees described their businesses as places that catered only to a female clientele, some welcome *onabe* and *nyuu haafu* 'transsexual/transgendered people' and even gay male friends of customers or employees. Owners and employees generally assume that female clientele are homosexual or bisexual but welcome others. During my visit to one bar, I encountered a situation in which a *jooren*, 'regular customer' brought her friend and introduced her to the owner and employees as a *nonke*, 'straight'. It appears that a customer's sexuality has to be stated explicitly if she or he is straight.

I found it crucial to differentiate between a lesbian bar and an *onabe* bar. The word *onabe*, 'pan', which is parallel to *okama*, 'pot', meaning male homosexuals, is often used to refer to lesbians in a broad sense, but the two words, lesbian and *onabe*, are not the same (Valentine 1997), as is clearly demonstrated in example (1). In this example, the manager (A) of a lesbian bar is talking about her sexuality.

(1) *Yoosuru nijishoteki ni wa dooseeaisha tte koto ni narimasu ne. Onabe to chigau no wa, jibun no josee to yuu see o mitometa ue de, josee ga suki tte yuu.*

'Anyway, I am a homosexual by the dictionary definition. How I am different from *onabe* is that I accept my sex as female and like women'.

Another employee (B) at a different lesbian bar contends that a lesbian is a woman who feels comfortable with her female body (in other words, with her biologically female sex) and who chooses a woman as a partner. Unlike straight women, her identity as a woman is constructed through a relationship with another woman. However, according to this employee, an *onabe* loves women and chooses a woman as a partner, but an *onabe's* social and emotional identity is male. Thus, both the concept of *onabe* and that of lesbian challenge the conventional heterosexual gender arrangement, yet her explanation remains restricted within the binary 'woman'/'man'.

The same employee (A) explains the difference between *onabe* and *rezu* (or *rezubian*), 'lesbians', in example (2).

(2) *Chigaimasu ne. Ishikiteki ni mo. Kore wa yoku iwareru n desu kedo, <u>onabe san</u> wa, <u>rezu</u> <u>no ko</u> to wa tsukiattari, anmari shinai n desu yo. Sore wa, <u>onabe san</u> wa jibun ga otoko to shite miraretai tte yuu no ga aru kara, onna o suki na <u>rezu no ko</u> to wa, tsukiaenai.*

'Yes, we are different. Consciously as well. People often say this – *onabe* do not date lesbians. Because they want to be seen as men, they cannot date a lesbian who likes women'.

It is significant that the speaker added *-san* 'Ms./Mr.' to *onabe* and *ko* 'child' to *rezu*. The former emphasizes the distance between the speaker and the referent, while the latter constructs an intimate or friendly relationship. This kind of identity construction through naming is also found in other interviews.

Onabe bars, then, are butch-type bars where staff members usually wear men's clothes and work as hosts. There are three *onabe* bars in Tokyo (Valentine 1997). Customers at *onabe* bars are usually half lesbians and half *nonke* 'stright women'. According to many employees of *rezubian* bars, these bars are places where customers, who may be *onabe* or lesbians, and employees are on equal terms, whereas in *onabe* bars employees are there to serve customers. They also suggest that customers who are tired of *onabe* bars may move on to host bars, where young straight men serve women.

Nine of the 13 lesbian bars accept only women, including heterosexuals, *onabe*, and *nyuu haafu*. In example (3), a manager (C) of another lesbian bar talks about her clientele.

(3) *Toriaezu, rezu no okyaku sama ga taihan nan desu kedo, rezu ja nai <u>ko</u> mo iru n desu ne. Rezu wa rezu de kakusazu ni, soo ja nai ko mo tanoshiku. Betsu ni itsu mo rezu no wadai bakkari tte wake nai kara. Dansee wa ne, watashi no hontoo ni goku shitashii <u>homo</u> no <u>kata</u> to ka, soo yuu hito dake desu ne. Yappari onna no ko ga dansee no me o ki ni shinai de kiraku ni nomeru tte koto de, kihonteki ni dansee wa dame desu. <u>Onabe no ko</u> to ka <u>nyuu haafu</u> no <u>ko</u> to ka kiraku ni asobi ni kite kureru shi, <u>futsuu</u> no onna no <u>ko</u> datte ii shi. Mattaku <u>futsuu</u> no <u>otoko</u> wa dame. Dono janru ga doo ka ja nakute, mainoritii de zenzen oorai. Soo soo, guroobaru na imi de nan de mo oorai.*

'Anyway, the majority of our customers are lesbians, but there are some who aren't. For lesbians, they don't have to hide their identity. Nonlesbians can have a good time here too. We don't talk only about lesbianism, you know. As for male customers, only a few close homosexual friends of mine can come here. As a rule, we don't allow male customers because we want to provide a place where women feel comfortable drinking without worrying about men's eyes. People who are *onabe* or *nyuu haafu* come here as well. Ordinary [meaning heterosexual] women are also welcome. But ordinary men are not welcome here. I'm not categorizing people, but as long as they are a minority, they're totally welcome. Yes, anybody in a global sense is welcome'.

Whereas speaker (A) in example (2) added -*san* to *onabe*, speaker (C) uses the term *ko* 'child/young person' (instead of *hito* or *kata*, two terms for 'person'), as in *onabe no ko* 'a young *onabe*' and *nyuu-haafu no ko* 'a young *nyuu haafu*'. This shift indicates that onabe are here treated as in-group members (customers). This use of *ko* is a reflection of the fact that the majority of customers are in their twenties (younger than the owners or employees) and also that employees want to sound more inclusive and intimate. The alternative words, *hito* or *kata*, are more formal and distant. Interestingly, the women I interviewed never use *ko* to refer to men; instead they use *dansei* 'men' or *otoko* 'men' or even *homo no kata* 'homosexuals'. Otherness is emphasized by non-use of *ko*.

Linguistic Behavior and Interactions at Bars

In this section, I discuss several linguistic features found in interactions at lesbian bars among employees as well as between employees and customers.

First-person pronouns

Previous studies have claimed that the use of first- and second-person pronouns exhibits the most gender-differentiated characteristics of the Japanese language. Ide (1979) asserts that the first-person pronouns *watakushi* and *watashi* are used by both sexes, the forms *boku* and *ore* (standard) as well as *wagahai* and *washi* (nonstandard) are used exclusively by men, and the forms *atakushi* and *atashi* (standard) as well as *atai* and *uchi* (non-standard) are used by women. Kanamaru (1997) claims that *jibun* is also a masculine form. *Jibun* is a reflexive pronoun; its use as a personal pronoun is relatively old-fashioned and is often associated with men in sports or in militaristic groups such as the *jieetai* 'self-defense army' or the police force. It is clear that these options for first-person pronouns reflect the strong sense of an idealized form of women's and men's speech. However, the choice of personal pronouns is not as categorical as was once believed. Women in different parts of Japan may have different options and women in different parts of the age spectrum may use different forms.

An example from the bisexual and lesbian magazine *Anise* (Hagiwara 1997) gives some insight into the use of first-person pronouns among lesbians, *onabe*, and transsexuals. Examples (4)–(7) are drawn from the magazine transcript of a panel discussion among six people, two self-identified female-to-male transsexuals (T1 and T2), two self-identified *onabe* (O1 and O2), and two self-identified lesbians (L1 and L2). They are talking about their gender.

(4)　T1:　*Boku wa rezubian ga kirai nan ja nakute, rezu ikooru onna, jibun ga onna ni*
　　　　　mirareru no ga iya datta.
　　　　　'It is not that I dislike lesbians, but lesbian means a woman. I didn't want to be perceived as a woman'.

　　　O2:　*Jibun mo yoku rezu tte iwarete 'jibun wa otoko nan da' tte tomodachi to kenka*
　　　　　shimashita.
　　　　　'I was also told that I'm a lesbian. I used to fight with my friends for saying that I'm a man'.

(5)　T2:　*Boku wa nenrei ga agareba penisu ga haete kuru mon da to omotte ita, n desu yo.*
　　　　　'I believed that once I got older, I would grow a penis'.

(6) L1:   *Watashi* wa monogokoro tsuita toki kara, zutto onna no ko ga suki datta. Otoko to
          ka onabe ni naritai tte kimochi mo atta kedo, seken no hito wa otoko na no ka onna
          na no ka waketagaru n da yo ne. Ippan shakai de wa joshi toire ni wa hairenai
          shi.
          'Ever since I was a child, I always liked girls. There was a time when I wanted to
          be a man or *onabe*. People want to categorize themselves into men or women. In
          this society, I can't use a public women's bathroom'.

      L2:   *Watashi* wa joshi toire ni hairu yo.
          'I use a women's bathroom'.

(7) O2:   *Jibun* mo danjo to ka kangaenai hoo nan desu yo.
          'I tend not to think about if someone is a man or woman'.

The three groups of speakers use first-person pronouns distinctively; the transsexuals
use *boku*, the *onabe* use *jibun*, and the lesbians use *watashi* almost uniformly. It is as if
there is a rule for them to use a different personal pronoun depending on their own
identity (at least in this context).

The use of first-person pronouns shown in examples (4)–(7), however, does not
mean that each speaker uses the same pronoun no matter what context s/he is in.
Further analysis suggests that speakers negotiate gendered speech norms in each context. This negotiation becomes more apparent if we examine examples in which a
speaker shifts the use of pronoun forms, which is frequently observed at lesbian bars.
In fact, one of the participants in the panel discussion (Ll) is an employee at a lesbian
bar I often visited, where I observed her use of *jibun*. Moreover, I observed the use
of several first-person pronouns at lesbian bars: *watashi, atashi, ore, washi, and jibun*,
with the same speaker using multiple first-person pronouns depending on the context. One of the first questions I often asked at bars concerned the use of personal
pronouns. Younger employees in their early twenties exclusively listed *jibun* 'oneself'
(a form commonly considered masculine) as their favorite first-person pronoun. One
employee explained that she uses the term because *watashi* and *atashi* exhibit too
much femininity, but she does not want to use *boku* or other 'masculine' first-person
pronouns because she is not a man. She said that she refuses to *dooitsuka-suru* 'merge
and identify' with men. An employee at a different bar argued, 'Why do I need to use
boku? I don't even like men'. Her use of *jibun* is illustrated in example (8).

(8)   *Kutte nee, jibun wa. Nan da, nan ni mo nee jan.*
      'I haven't eaten. What! There's nothing left'.

This employee was 21 years old and had been working at the bar for several months.
Asked by her female supervisor if she had eaten something before coming to work, she
replied, using *jibun*. During the course of the evening, this young employee maintained
the use of *jibun* irrespective of whether she was talking to her coworkers or to customers.
As she puts it, for her, *jibun* is the most neutral personal pronoun available. The use of
jibun was observed at all the bars in my study.

However, at a bar down the street I observed a quite different interaction. The
employee in example (9) was 20 years old and had been working almost a year. When I
entered, there was nobody but her in the bar. We introduced ourselves and started talking about various things such as why she started working there and whether she enjoyed
working at the bar. When I noticed her using *jibun* in our interaction, I asked the reason

for her choice. Her answer was that she did not want to sound too feminine by using *watashi* or *atashi*. She added that *jibun* was her favorite term and that she did not use other 'masculine' personal pronouns, unlike her boss, who uses *washi*. It is interesting to note that *washi* presents a more 'masculine' nuance to her than *jibun*. However, her answer does not reflect her actual speaking practices. She and I had been talking alone for more than two hours when the telephone rang. The caller was a regular customer, whom this employee knew very well. The employee explained to me that there had been a party at the bar the night before during which this customer got drunk and did some crazy things that upset the employees and other customers, but the customer claimed that she did not remember anything. The employee did not believe she had forgotten. The employee's side of the conversation was as follows.

(9) *Omee na, fuzaken na yo, <u>ore</u> oko-ru yo.*
      'Are you kidding? I'll get mad at you'.

      Jaa, A-san ni kiite mi na yo.
      'Then, ask A'.

      Anne, soo da yo, anta, minna ni meewaku kaketa n da kara.
      'You bothered everyone'.

      <u>Ore</u> sugee koshi itai man. Koshi ni kita yo.
      'As for me, my lower back hurts. It really hurts'.

Here we see the employee's shift from *jibun* in her conversation with me to *ore* in her interaction with her customer. In the first instance of *ore*, the speaker is expressing her anger or frustration and thus is very emotionally involved. In the second instance, she is describing how much pain she has now thanks to the customer. The use of *ore* in this example as opposed to her previous use of *jibun* exhibits negotiation of multiple identity positions in relation to different contexts. For her, *jibun* is used in more formal settings of interaction, such as an interaction with a relatively new customer who is also a researcher, but *ore* is her preferred choice in more intimate and emotional contexts.

The use of *boku* is quite different. The speaker in example (10) is a lesbian customer in her mid thirties who works at a computer graphics company. She and I had been discussing the use of first-person pronouns for a while and I had noticed that she used *atashi* in our conversation. When I asked if she ever used different first-person pronouns, she answered by saying:

(10) *<u>Atashi</u> wa kyosee o haru toki, '<u>boku</u>' o tsuka-u.*
      'I (*atashi*) use I (*boku*) when [I] make a false show of power'.

She added that she uses *boku* in arguments at her workplace with her male boss, who may suspect that she is lesbian, and claims that this helps her situate herself at the boss's level. Here the speaker explicitly recognizes the forcefulness attached to 'masculine' forms. She also expressed the belief that the 'feminine' first-person pronoun, *atashi*, did not make her strong. However, in explaining the use of *boku* the speaker used the term *kyosee* 'false show of power', literally, *kyo* 'emptiness' + *see* 'power, force', which implies merely a superficial or even empty power.

Second-person Pronouns

Second-person pronouns are also considered highly gendered, but to a lesser degree than first-person pronouns. Many researchers identify two forms (*anata* and *anta*) for women and five or more forms (*anata, anta, kimi, omae, kisama, otaku,* and *temee*) for men (Ide 1979; Kanamaru 1997). However, actual uses of second-person pronouns do not necessarily conform to these gender classifications.

I found two types of second-person pronouns at the bars I studied: *anta* and *omee*. The frequency of these two terms is not high, since speakers generally prefer to use nicknames or first names. *Anata* 'you', a more formal second-person pronoun, is almost never used. The use of *omee*, a very casual 'masculine' second-person pronoun, is found among close friends at bars, between employees and customers, and between customers. In example (9), the speaker used both *anta* and *omee* in criticizing one of her customers. *Omee* is used to express the employee's extreme rage toward the customer (*omee no, fuzaken na yo*), whereas *anta* accompanies an attempt at persuasion (*soo da yo, anta, minna ni meewaku kaketa n da kara*). Thus, the shift between the two pronouns reflects the change in her emotional state.

The customer (in 10) who uses *boku* in arguments with her boss also told me that she uses *omee* when she argues with close male friends, adding that *omee* has a certain forcefulness that cannot be expressed by *anta* or *omae*, a term that is stereotypically associated with male speakers. The speakers in these examples both assert that *omee* helps them argue more persuasively. Both speakers are manipulating the pragmatic meaning (forcefulness) attached to the term *omee*.

Commands and requests

Other linguistic forms that are often associated with gender roles are found in commands and requests. For instance, the use of bald imperative verb forms, such as *tabero* 'eat', is generally considered to indicate that the interlocutor is not in a superior position and also that the speaker is a man. This type of imperative is traditionally categorized as a 'masculine' form (Martin 1975). Tohsaku (1999: 43) notes that this type of imperative form 'sounds very blunt and harsh' and says that female speakers should not use it at all.

Despite this prescription, example (9) includes strong imperative forms. The first negative imperative, *fuzaken na* 'don't mess with me', can be articulated differently in different contexts, from the most formal *fuzakenai de kudasai*, to *fuzakenai de*, to the very informal *fuzakeru na*. The assimilation and reduction of *-ru* (in *fuzakeru na*) to *-n* (in *fuzaken na*) indexes even stronger roughness or toughness. As noted earlier, the speaker in this example is extremely angry and emotionally involved.

Sentence-final particles

The last linguistic feature I discuss here is sentence-final particles. The functions of these forms have been identified as (1) indicating the speaker's emotions and attitudes such as doubt, caution, and confirmation (Martin 1975: 914, Makino and Tsutsui 1986: 45); (2) encouraging rapport between speech participants (Makino and Tsutsui 1986: 45); (3) achieving a close monitoring of the feelings between speech participants (Maynard 1987: 28); and (4) expressing one's own masculinity and/ or femininity (Makino and Tsutsui 1986: 49). Traditional gender classification of sentence-final particles suggests three types: (1) feminine forms, which are said to be predominantly used by female speakers (e.g., *wa* with a rising intonation, *na no/na no ne, kashira*); (2) masculine forms, used by male speakers (e.g., *zo/za, da, da yo*); and (3) neutral forms, used by both women and men (e.g., *yo ne, ka no*). As Okamoto (1995: 301) argues, the traditional classification should be understood as a reference point rather than a description of actual use.

The actual use of sentence-final particles at the lesbian bars bears this point out. The most frequently used sentence-final particles are *yo* and its variations such as *da yo* and *da yo ne*. For example, in (11) an employee and a few customers are chatting while looking at a magazine article, which describes an *onabe* bar.

(11) CUSTOMER: *Kore otoko <u>da yo</u>, hakkiri itte.*
                 'This is a man, frankly speaking'.

      EMPLOYEE: *Kurabete moraitaku nai ne.*
                 'I don't want you to compare me with this guy'.

The customer points out that the figure in the picture in the magazine looks like a man. She uses *da yo* in this utterance. As mentioned earlier, in the conventional classification, *da yo* is regarded as a masculine form. Yet it seems that this form is used more commonly used by many women than it used to be (Abe 2000). Thus, it is possible that this form is neutral for this speaker.

Other conventional masculine forms are found in example (12). Here younger employees, who typically refer to themselves as *jibun*, are talking with some customers in their thirties. Two of them are trying to remove a spot from the surface of a toy.

(12) EMPLOYEE: *Kosutte mo torenee n <u>da</u>.*
                 'We can't get rid of it even by rubbing'.

      CUSTOMER: *Nani ka iro ga chiga-u <u>zo</u>.*
                 'Hey, the color is somehow different!'

The employee uses *da*, a (moderately) masculine form, and the customer uses *zo*, which is often classified as strongly masculine. In addition, the 'rough' negative form, *nee*, is used instead of *nai*. Moreover, the speaker uses *kuu* 'to eat' instead of *taberu* 'to eat'. The latter is a standard form of the verb, while *kuu* suggests 'masculine' speech. This speaker elsewhere uses the plain interrogative form *ka* (verb + *ka*) in *Ureshii ka* 'are you happy?' and *Nomu ka* 'do you want to drink?' another construction associated with 'masculine' speech. This type of question form is usually considered too strong and rude for women to use.

In sum, these speakers are rejecting the forms that they feel are too feminine, while adopting masculine or neutral forms. Their use of masculine forms, however, does not mean that lesbians want to be identified as men, as the discussion on the difference between lesbian and *onabe* clearly demonstrates, nor is it simply a case of butch lesbians speaking like men. On the other hand, even though they may consider themselves women (also indicated earlier in their comparison of lesbians and *onabe*), they are not using stereotypical feminine forms. I argue, therefore, that their linguistic choices indicate that they are marking their difference in speech, which, they believe, supports their identities as lesbians. Speakers use masculine speech styles in a complex way in order to express a variety of context-dependent meanings related to their lesbian identities and relationships.

References

Abe, Hideko (2000) *Speaking to Power: Japanese Women and their Language*. Munich: Lincom Europa.

Hagiwara, Mami (ed.) (1997) 'Sexuality'. *Anise* 3: 24–7.

Ide, Sachiko (1979) *Onna no kotoba, otoko no kotoba*. [*Women's language, men's language.*] Tokyo: Nihon Keizai Tsushinsha.

Kanamaru, Fumi (1997) 'Ninshoo daimeeshi/koshoo' [Person pronouns and address terms]. In S. Ide (ed.) *Joseigo no sekai* [*The world of women's language*]. Tokyo: Meiji Shoin. Pp. 15–32.

Makino, S. and Tsutsui, M. (1986) *A Dictionary of Basic Japanese Grammar*. Tokyo: Japan Times.

Martin, Samuel (1975) A reference grammar of Japanese. New Haven: Yale University Press.

Maynard, Senko Kumiya (1987) *Japanese Conversation: Self-Contextualisation through Structure and Interactional Management*. Norwood, NJ: Ablex.

Moonwomon-Baird, Brich (1997) 'Toward the study of lesbin speech'. In Anna Livia and Kira Hall (eds) *Queerly Phrased: Language, Gender and Sexuality*. New York: Oxford University Press.

Tohsaku, Yasu-Hiko (1999) *Yookoso: Continuing with Contemporary Japanese*. Boston: McGraw-Hill College.

Valentine, James (1997) 'Pots and pans: identification of queer Japanese in terms of discrimination'. In Anna Livia and Kira Hall (eds) *Queerly Phrased: Language, Gender and Sexuality*. New York: Oxford University Press.

Watanabe, Mieko (1990) *Uuman Rabingu* [*Women Loving*]. Tokyo: Gendai Shokan.

Okamoto, Shigeko (1995) 'Tasteless Japanese: Less "Feminine" Speech among Young Japanese Women'. In Kira Hall and Mary Bucholtz (eds) *Gender Articulated: Language and the Socially Constrcted Self*. New York: Routledge.

28

Boys' Talk: Hindi, Moustaches and Masculinity in New Delhi

Kira Hall

Source: P. Pichler and E. Eppler (eds), *Gender and Spoken Interaction*. London: Palgrave (2009), pp. 139–62. Reprinted with permission of Palgrave Macmillan.

Introduction

Since the 1990s, scholars working within the area of language and gender have increasingly considered the ways in which masculinity informs and structures everyday language practice. While the paradigms that frame scholarship on language and masculinity differ, with early studies focusing on differences between men's talk and women's talk (e.g., Johnstone 1990; Tannen 1990) and later studies seeking to explain how men's talk is produced performatively through appeal to ideologies of gendered language (e.g., Cameron 1997), the research has left us with a trove of data regarding linguistic possibilities for the enactment of masculinity. Whether explicating the homophobic story-telling strategies of male friends in Britain (Coates 2007), the use of sentence-final particles by white-collar Japanese men (SturtzSreetharan 2006), or employments of the address term *dude* among American college-aged men (Kiesling 2004), linguistic research on masculinity has decisively demonstrated that 'maleness' is as much gained as it is given, with speakers reproducing, and often exploiting, ideological links between form and meaning in the production of a gendered subjectivity. The burgeoning body of literature on women's appropriation of purportedly masculine forms of discourse has offered a kind of proof for this theoretical position, establishing the floating and hence endlessly flexible nature of the linguistic sign (e.g., Queen 2005; Matsumoto 2002; Tetreault 2002; McElhinny 1995).

Linguistic research on social class, in contrast, has been less forthcoming in considering the category's ideological dimensions. Because socioeconomic realities such as educational access so clearly constrain the potential for certain kinds of linguistic appropriation, researchers have tended to focus on class as given instead of gained, viewing it as a stable and even quantifiable designation that precedes interaction. Certainly, speakers from divergent class backgrounds do not always share common ground when it comes to discursive meaning-making, including the sociolinguistic making of femininity and masculinity. It is therefore imperative that discourse analysts continue to recognise the possibility of class-based semiotic dissonance. But social class is also vulnerable to discursive appropriation, particularly when different class positions come to be associated with specific ways of talking. In short, the linguistic indices of class, like those of masculinity, are also in some sense flexible. Most critically for the current discussion, the linguistic forms that index social class can be used as a resource for establishing one's positionality with respect to other social categories, such as gender and sexuality.

This is precisely the case for female participants within the Hindi- and English-speaking New Delhi non-government organisation that is the subject of this study. Founded in 1994 and initially funded by the North American-based Ford Foundation, this NGO, hereafter called the Center, seeks to educate the public on HIV/AIDS and sexual diversity through the sponsorship of a number of outreach programmes. The programme under discussion, a support group designed for 'women who are attracted to women', brings together diverse middle-class participants who orient to distinct class-based sexualities: namely, 'lesbian' and 'boy'. While lesbian-identified women in the support group orient to the same-sex models of sexual attraction associated with the West, male-identified women (or 'boys', as they later came to call themselves) orient to the other-sex models of gender eroticism long associated with rural India, aspiring to a semiotics of masculinity that has sexual reassignment surgery as its endpoint. There are no isolatable demographic factors that clearly distinguish the socioeconomic status of lesbians from that of boys, and yet both of these identity positions are established interactively through appeal to ideologies of social class (see also Pichler, this volume).

The linguistic and ethnographic data I discuss in this chapter suggest that lesbians and boys participating in the support group not only have very different relationships to masculinity, they also exhibit different understandings of how masculinity may be invoked in spoken interaction. For many lesbian-identified speakers, the very use of Hindi for discussions of sexuality is read as indexical of a kind of masculine vulgarity, an interpretation that has serious consequences for those boys who, although bilingual, typically discuss sexuality in Hindi when first joining the group. Veteran members prefer to use English in group discussions, a language they associate with progressive ideas, particularly in the realm of gender and sexuality. But English carries a very different meaning within the predominantly Hindi-speaking classes, where its usage, because of a variety of complex postcolonial and nationalist processes, is often associated with prudishness if not effeminacy (see Gupta 2002). Hindi is thus easily embraced by boy-identified speakers as indexical of a masculinity that is antagonistic to elite ideas about female sexuality, providing a resistant rallying tool for speakers whose understanding of self is dismissed by some Center participants as rudely vernacular. This chapter thus argues for a deeper consideration of the discursive alliance between language, masculinity, and social class (see also Livia 2004), holding along with other authors in this collection that the linguistic performance of gender, like that of other social categories, is always relationally produced and interpreted. My argument is not simply that linguistic constructs of masculinity vary over time, nationstate, and class, although this observation is assumed for the analysis I offer here. Rather, I aim to illustrate how the articulation of masculinity, while importantly influenced by ideological linkages within these larger parameters, is likewise a product of everyday interaction, emergent within localised negotiations of the relationship between form and meaning.

Data and Methodology

This chapter additionally asserts the importance of ethnographic methodology for the study of gender and spoken interaction. Specifically, I seek to illuminate what sociolinguists can gain by examining masculinity and femininity ethnographically as emergent within interaction. My discussion of the conversational excerpts selected for analysis below is thus informed by a much greater body of data that includes several months of fieldwork among boys and lesbians during the autumn of 2000, the spring of 2001, and the spring of 2007. In my research among these two groups inside and outside of the Center, I acted as participant observer in daily gatherings and events, wrote extensive fieldnotes, collected over 50 hours of audio and video recordings of conversational interaction, and conducted 20 ethnographic interviews with administrators, employees and group members, many of which involved the elicitation of individual coming-out narratives. This research was in turn informed by a number of extended fieldwork visits over the preceding decade among groups associated with sexual and gender alterity in various areas of northern India, among them *hijras* in Banaras (see Hall 1997; Hall and O'Donovan 1996) and *kotis* in New Delhi (see Hall 2005). The combined body of ethnographic data has helped me puzzle out the social meaning of certain aspects of the linguistic data that is not transparently accessible through a study of isolated conversational examples. The diachronic and ever-shifting nature of the bilingual data I collected at the Center has compelled me to think through the ways in which the links between language and masculinity emerge over time as a product of localised discursive exchange.

The issue of temporality is critical to the way I approach my analysis of the spoken data. The male-identified women who came to the Center in response to a local advertisement campaign were quickly socialised into new patterns of expression that relied on an ideological understanding of English as the appropriate language for discussions of sexuality, whether these discussions involved sexual practice, sexual desire or sexual identity. Veteran group members, most of whom had come to identify as lesbian within the context of this transnationally funded NGO, viewed Hindi as unsuitable for the expression of a progressive sexuality. For them, the use of Indian languages in sexual discursive domains was backwards, rude and just plain vulgar, an interpretation that appears to be shared by many multilingual speakers of the educated Indian middle class more generally (cf. Puri 1999). In Center meetings, group members would manage their verbal discomfort with Hindi by offering novices a sexualised English lexicon to use in its place. Over time, the boys began to shift their language style toward that of their lesbian peers, using English when voicing sexual concerns and reserving Hindi for domains of talk thought to be more traditional (see Bucholtz and Hall 2008a). In short, English came to hold sociosexual capital for its Center users: Both boys and lesbians learned to employ it as a resource for the expression of a sexually progressive self. I thus observed a rather accelerated process of language shift in this localised environment over the course of my fieldwork, not only in the way novices oriented to Hindi and English at the ideological level, but also in the specifics of their Hindi-English codeswitching practices.

Yet this is not the whole story. The group's dichotomous mapping of English and Hindi onto progressive and traditional domains of talk, respectively, intersected with a number of other ideological polarisations: among them, upper class vs. lower class, femininity vs. masculinity, and lesbian vs. boy. The use of one language as opposed to the other in Center meetings thus accomplished important ideological work, indexing the speaker's position with respect to these polarisations.

The two excerpts I analyse below are taken from a recording of a one-hour Center support group meeting in March of 2001, four months after I began my fieldwork at the Center. With so many boys still hoping for sexual reassignment surgery, Liz,[1] a British expatriate who was instrumental in establishing the support group, had decided to act as facilitator for a discussion on the topic of masculinity. Her plan for the meeting, as she described it to me the night before, was to introduce the group to the idea that masculinity is a social construct, not a biological fact. If the boys could just understand that masculinity is available to women as well as men, she asserted, they might be able to avoid the more extreme consequences of surgery. Although Liz's activism was motivated by concern for the boys' well-being – for example, she talked with me at length about the financial, physical and psychological burdens associated with a surgical solution that remains dangerous – her position was also uncomfortably allied with dominant Western discourses on sexual alterity, particularly in its assumption that same-sex desire is a viable, or in this case even preferable, substitute for surgically enabled cross-sex desire. Her position was further complicated by the fact that many of the boys had adopted what she and her feminist-identified Indian peers considered to be a sexist understanding of gender relations, desiring servile, stay-at-home wives who managed the women's work associated with traditional India. Yet for the boys, some of whom had even made an ethical decision to delay all sexual contact with their girlfriends until after transition, the same-sex eroticism associated with European and American models of gay and lesbian identity was unthinkably foreign, if not repulsive. Indeed, group members would often enact this repulsion iconically in their everyday pronunciations of the English word 'lesbian', grimacing in disgust while loudly mimicking stereotypically Western pronunciations of the initial /l/ and medial /z/. Simply put, the boys' use of phonetic mockery works as a distancing mechanism, bracketing off the term as alien to what would otherwise be everyday discourse.

I offer these brief ethnographic details as a means of contextualising the discursive polarisations that occur in the data, where the boys use Hindi to reject Liz's constructivist take on gender identity and assert a biological one in its place. My understanding of the term *context* is thus much broader than what is asserted in those forms of discourse analysis that limit inquiry to the immediate spoken text, such as conversation analysis (CA). Susan Speer (2005: 101), for instance, in an important critique of how language and gender researchers have misused the top-down concept of hegemonic masculinity, characterises everything but the immediate materialisation of turns and sequences as 'beyond the talk' and hence analytically irrelevant. Bethan Benwell and Elizabeth Stokoe (2006: 68) echo this perspective in their critique of what they group together as 'performativity/constructionist accounts' of gender in everyday conversation.[2] But for me, a linguistic anthropologist who makes use of ethnographic methods, the conversations that precede and follow a given stretch of talk – whether distanced by days, months, or even years – are just as crucial for understanding the localised ways in which speakers orient to abstract concepts such as masculinity.

The conversation I analyse below is thus just one piece of a much larger ethnographic puzzle, positioned alongside, for instance, a conversation I had three months earlier with Nanhi and her good friend Jess, both of whom are veteran participants in the Center support group. The two had taken me to a sweet shop in Delhi's Bengali Market after a group meeting to experience golgappa, the delicately deep-fried dough bubble that releases an electrifying green liquid of mint, lime, and chilli. It was on a busy street corner outside of the shop, after popping in the fourth or fifth crisp and experiencing yet another burst of what can only be described as gustatory bliss, that I first became aware of the ideological significance of Hindi and English for the local construction of sexual identity. Jess, perhaps inspired by her own experience with what is popularly known in Delhi as India's sexiest snack, began to relay a series of humorous stories about past lovers who had made the 'mistake' of using an Indian language during a romantic encounter. In her dramatisation of their linguistic blunders – the college roommate who slipped a love letter in her pocket that was written entirely in Panjabi; the ex-girlfriend whose use of Hindi in bedroom sex talk precipitated a break-up; and finally, the current lover who likes to translate passionate English phrases into Hindi for humorous effect – I got my first inkling of the language ideologies that inform and in many ways structure Hindi-English code choice practices at the Center.

An analytic consideration of ideology is thus not always 'top-down' and 'macro-level', as Speer (2005: 15) suggests in her critique of the many forms of discourse analysis that utilise the theoretical insights of poststructuralism. Linguistic anthropologists engaged in ethnography seek to uncover the more localised ideologies that inform language practice, viewing conversation as a product of historical and cultural specificity. Some understandings of masculinity may indeed be culturally dominant, achieving a level of hegemony that circulates through and around this specificity. But the social meaning behind the use of particular linguistic forms in everyday conversation can only be determined by attending to the local worlds of discourse that control meaning-making. If we truly want to avoid imposing our own categories of analysis onto the conversations we study, as Speer rightly asserts, we must consider how the participants themselves interpret the relationship between form and meaning. For a linguistic anthropologist like myself, these interpretations are best uncovered through ethnography, a research methodology that views a given instance of talk as just one episode in a much larger interactive history. Masculinity may indeed be produced in the turns and sequences of conversational immediacy, but we cannot possibly recognise it unless we first understand the cultural context that informs its interpretation.

Boys' Talk

By the time the meeting under discussion took place, many of the boys had come full circle in their relationship to Center discourses on sexual identity. Although they had initially allied themselves with the understanding of female-to-female attraction espoused by group leaders, grateful to be able to share their sense of sexual marginalisation with open-minded others, they later became much more aware of the differences between themselves and their lesbian friends, and more poignantly, of the social hierarchies that inform and structure these differences. Their code choice patterns parallel this progression. The boys had initially learned to orient to English as the appropriate language for sex talk in weekly support groups, adopting the codeswitching styles of their more veteran peers. But they eventually became much more critical of the prominence and prestige given to English in this interactive style. Likewise, they began to reject the related perception that Hindi-inflected sexuality was necessarily vulgar, an idea that circulated at the Center, for instance, in the condescending use of the derogatory slang term *vernac* for Hindi-speaking participants. The term, which is thought to have originated among Delhi and Mumbai college students in tandem with the North Indian term *HMT* (Hindi Medium Type), literally references a student educated in a regional Indian language as opposed to English. But it carries a much more insidious meaning in elite popular culture, where it is used to characterise speakers as backwards, unsophisticated, provincial, unfashionable and just plain crude (see Devraj 2005).

This is the context that Liz unknowingly walked into as group facilitator on that March day, unaware that her brazenly postmodern solution for boy identity would trigger a network of ideological alliances and contrasts that would make her project impossible. Because masculinity is the domain of boys, not lesbians, group participants immediately saw Liz's authoritative self-positioning as suspect. 'What do *you* know about masculinity?' Jess shouts from her lounging position on the couch after Liz announces the topic for the day.³ In the fifty-five minutes of conversation that follows, lesbian and boy participants fight for semantic ownership of the concept, with the former defining it as social and the latter as physical. But in contrast to previous meetings where participants unquestioningly oriented to English as the appropriate medium for discussion, the boys in this meeting make use of Hindi, a resource that is better suited to their own understanding of masculinity.

The ideological schism between Hindi and English emerges gradually throughout the course of the discussion, as lesbians and boys register divergent positions on sexuality through the use of two separate languages. As revealed in the opening lines of Extract 1 below (lines 1–24), Liz remains faithful to the plan she voiced to me the night before, proposing a series of repetitive questions that present masculinity as a frame of mind, not a biological reality. But when she later in the same excerpt tries to make her point by characterising Jess as 'a woman' who is 'attracted to other women' (lines 31–4), interpellating her through the terms of lesbian identity instead of boy identity, Jess answers with an alternative understanding of sexuality that relies on Hindi for its emotional force (lines 35–40). [A key to the transcription conventions is located on page x.]

(1) Extract 1. *She calls me* woman!
(English is in standard font, Hindi in italics)

```
 1  LIZ:        You- is there no room to be (.) femini-
 2              to be a female (.) but masculine.
 3              to be female [but (.) to be masculine.]
 4  BARBARA:              [That's really-        ] that's
 5              just the opposite of the masculine?
 6              I suppose?
 7  LIZ:        No to be female and to be masculine.
 8              Is there no [room for it.]
 9  BARBARA:               [That's not  ] a way,
10              You make that all up (.) opposite things,
11              then (you're still a woman),
12  LIZ:        No I'm not saying whether it becomes
13              permanent,
14              I'm saying for the individuals in this group.
15              today.
16              who we are (.) sitting with.
17              Is there no room to be a fe:male
18              and yet to be: (.) masculine.
19              in that role.
20              to ↑ be: like that.
21  JESS:                          I th[ink  ]-
22  LIZ:                              [Why] doesn't society
23              allow for that.
24                Why can't we be like tha[t.   ]
25  JESS:                                [Well] because
26              that's -ss uh one of those things,
27              You have to follow a pattern.
28              You're a woman so you have to
29              ↑[BE:::  this this this] this.
30  LIZ:        [Yeah but ↑WHY::. ]     Why?
31              You're- you're also- you're a woman,
```

32		but you are attracted to other women.
33		That's not acceptable to society,
34		but you are being like that,
→35	JESS:	<quietly, rapidly> <*gālī detī hai.*
36		*mujhe* woman [*boltī hai.*]>
37	LIZ:	<falsetto> <[↑Well just]> [[feh-]]
38	JESS:	<loudly, rapidly> <[[*gālī*]] *detī hai.*
39		woman *boltī hai mujhe.*
40		*tereko abhī āg lagtī hū̃ maī.>*
41	SARVESH:	[<laughs>]
42	PRITI:	[<laughs>]
43	BIJAY:	[<laughs>]
44	LIZ:	<rapidly> <NO. GUYS.>
45		I'm just asking the question, (.) basically.

> ### *Hindi translation* (for lines 35–40)
>
> JESS: <quietly, rapidly> <*She insults me.*
>
>   *She calls me* woman!>
>
> LIZ: <falsetto> <↑Well just> feh-
>
> JESS: <loudly, rapidly> <*She insults me.*
>
>   Woman *she calls me!*
>
>   *Now you think I'm fire (to burn you alive)?>*

As a regional language that has become ideologically associated with both tradition and anti-elitism through divergent strands of Hindu nationalism, Hindi serves as a likely conduit for a localised expression of identity that challenges the ideas of a globalised English-speaking elite. Jess exploits these associations in her response in lines 35–40, using Hindi to assert her allegiance to a polarised model of sexual alterity that is more in sync with traditional India. Appealing to the boy belief that only men can love women, Jess takes on the positionality of a man and objects to having been wrongly categorised as a 'woman': *gālī detī hai. mujhe* woman *boltī hai. gālī detī hai.* woman *boltī hai mujhe.* 'She insults me. She calls me woman! She insults me. Woman *she calls me!*' Although it may seem surprising that it is Jess who here introduces Hindi into the discussion, given her distaste for ex-girlfriends who discuss sex in Indian languages, her use of Center rhetoric is not always consistent with how she self-identifies. Jess gave up her dream of undergoing sexual reassignment surgery shortly after joining the group, but she continues to maintain an uncomfortable relationship to the same-sex requirement associated with lesbianism, still identifying first and foremost as a boy. This identification materialises here in the particularities of conversational address: Jess directs her response not to Liz but to her fellow boys, referencing Liz in the third person and thus positioning her as conversational outsider. But because this expression of disalignment is articulated in Hindi, the language itself emerges concurrently as indexical of boy identity, setting into motion the ideological associations that control the remainder of the discussion.

Yet Jess's response is not merely about her alignment with a subaltern form of sexual identity; it is also a performance of the masculinity that is required by it. In this excerpt and throughout the discussion, Jess and her friends find in Hindi a resource for the expression of an authentic masculinity that opposes the fictitious characterisation of masculinity suggested by Liz's appeal to social constructionism. For the boys, maleness is an essential aspect of their understanding of self, not a constructed one, a point underscored by Jess in her decisive rejection of the membership category *woman*. And yet Jess's contribution, in part because of the extremeness of its articulation, is very much recognised as a performance of masculinity by her fellow boys, who respond with uproarious laughter (lines 41–3). In fact, all of the adversarial uses of Hindi I analyse in this excerpt are delivered in good fun. The boys and lesbians discussed in this chapter are all close friends, even if their positions on sexual identity differ. To borrow from Pia Pichler's (2006) recent work on the use of teasing among British Bangladeshi girls, Jess is displaying a kind of playful 'toughness' in this excerpt. This stance is forwarded by the use of paralinguistic features that are stereotyped as masculine in Hindi-based popular media: for instance, Jess's use of rapid speech and increasing volume recalls the menacing voice of a Bollywood villain, countering the measured and steady delivery of her English-speaking interlocutor.

Jess's contribution thus contrasts starkly with the discourses of politeness popularly associated with educated elites, represented here in the voice of Liz. Jess's final line comes across as particularly intense in this regard, when she produces the highly adversarial phrase *tereko abhī āg lagtī hū maī* 'Now you think I'm fire (to burn you alive)?' (line 40). These fighting words, which conjure a threatening image of the Hindu death ritual of cremation, reframe Liz's earlier characterisation not as a passive mistake but as a calculated act of aggression meant to stir Jess's ire. Jess's use of Hindi instead of English for this adversarial response thus calls into play a matrix of language ideologies that predate and inform the immediate text, among them associations of Hindi with lower class impoliteness, with authentic Indianness, and even with the display of stereotypically masculine emotion, such as anger. While these associations may be discoverable as higher level ideologies through a close analysis of popular media texts – for instance, in the Hindi-English code-switching patterns that govern Bollywood film or in the pro-Hindi discourses that surface in Hindu nationalist politics – they are also importantly ideologies that surface in group members' own metalinguistic commentaries regarding language practice, a fact readily determined through ethnographic interviews and participant observation.

Interestingly, the more temporary subject positions that emerge within the interaction coordinate with the ideological contrasts that distinguish lesbian and boy identity. Of particular salience in this regard is the way in which Liz materialises as 'questioner' throughout the discussion, as she frames her ideas in the form of inquiries so as to bring the boys to her own understanding of masculinity. In the confines of this short excerpt, for example, Liz asks nine questions in shotgun style, three times rejecting the answers of her interlocutors outright with a definitive 'no' (lines 7, 12, 44). In fact, her questioning routines often leave little room for any kind of reply, as when she interrupts Jess in two places with a pair of successive questions (line 22; line 30):

Extract 1 (Lines 17–24)
```
17  LIZ:   Is there no room to be a fe:male
18         and yet to be: (.) masculine.
19         in that role.
```

    20   to ↑b<u>e</u>: like that.
    21   JESS: I th [ink   ]-
→22   LIZ: [Why] doesn't society
    23   allow for that.
    24   Why can't we b<u>e</u> like tha [t.   ]

Extract 1 (Lines 27–30)
    27   JESS: You have to follow a p<u>a</u>ttern.
    27   You're a woman so you have to
    28   ↑[BE::: this this this   ] this.
→30   LIZ: [Yeah but ↑WHY::.]   Why?

This questioning style often provokes a kind of interactional resistance on the part of the boys, who do not so easily assume the complementary subject positions of either interruptee or respondent. This reaction materialises here in line 28 when Jess, immediately after the onset of Liz's interruption, raises her voice, lengthens her pronunciation of the word *be*, and then uses repetition ('this this this] this') to sustain her turn through the duration of Liz's interrupting question.

Jess's switch into Hindi in lines 35–40, then, is perhaps precipitated as much by the style of Liz's talk as it is by the content. By articulating an adversarial stance in Hindi, Jess is at the very least able to gain exclusionary control of the conversational floor and thus challenge the interactional role that has been imposed upon her:

Extract 1 (Lines 35–45)
    35   JESS: <quietly, rapidly> <g<u>ā</u> l<u>ī</u> det<u>ī</u> hai.
    36   mujhe wom<u>a</u>n [bolt<u>ī</u> hai.]>
    37   LIZ: <falsetto> <[↑well just]> [[feh-]]
    38   JESS: <loudly, rapidly> <[[g<u>ā</u>l<u>ī</u>]] det<u>ī</u> hai.
    39   wom<u>a</u>n bolt<u>ī</u> hai mujhe.
    40   tereko abh<u>ī</u> <u>ā</u>g lagt<u>ī</u> h<u>ũ</u> mai.>
    41   SARVESH: [<laughs>]
    42   PRITI: [<laughs>]
    43   BIJAY: [<laughs>]
    44   LIZ: <rapidly> <NO. GUYS.>
    45   I'm just asking the question (.) basically.

> *Hindi translation* (for lines 35–40)
>
> JESS: <quietly, rapidly> <*She insults me.*
>
>   *She calls me* woman!>
>
> LIZ: <falsetto> <↑Well just> feh-
>
> JESS: <loudly, rapidly> <*She insults me.*
>
>   Woman *she calls me!*
>
>   *Now you think I'm fire (to burn you alive)?*>

The success of Jess's challenge is facilitated by the fact that Liz is only semi-fluent in Hindi, and she is simply unable to maintain control of the interaction in a language she can only partially understand. Although she recognises that her words have incited

Jess's reaction, objecting with an uncharacteristic use of falsetto (line 37), she does not appear to realise that her own conversational practices may have contributed to its intensity. Indeed, she ultimately comes to embrace the very interactional identity that is the source of the trouble, calling a halt to the boys' laughter and defending her comments as 'just asking': '<rapidly> <NO. GUYS.> I'm just asking the question, (.) basically.' (lines 44–5).

If we were to apply the classic CA question 'why this utterance now?' (Schegloff and Sacks, 1973: 299) to Jess's use of Hindi, then, we would need to consider at least two analytic possibilities. The first of these, discoverable through ethnographic methodology, argues that the boys' own language ideologies regarding Hindi and English control the codeswitch, in that Hindi has become indexical of a variety of qualities that sync with boy identity. The second, discoverable in large part through an analysis of turns and sequences in a single excerpt, explicates how the use of Hindi establishes an adversarial floor that reverses an unwelcomed conversational asymmetry. I suggest here that neither of these approaches is by itself sufficient for a holistic analysis of the workings of identity in interaction. That is, as Mary Bucholtz and I have discussed in a pair of recent articles (Bucholtz and Hall 2008b, 2005), the identities that emerge at the interactional level – e.g., questioner vs. respondent, interrupter vs. interruptee – often link up in profound ways to the more durable subject positions that move across texts, such as lesbian and boy. As Elinor Ochs (1992) argues in her early discussion of direct vs. indirect indexicality, the association between a linguistic form and a particular social identity is rarely direct; rather, the structural and ideological levels of discourse are mediated by the kinds of stances that speakers take in interaction.

The asymmetry between questioner and respondent that materialises in this group meeting, for instance, is highly reminiscent of power asymmetries associated with teacher–student interaction in the Indian classroom. The Indian educational system has long received extensive criticism for its reliance on rote learning (cf. N. Kumar 2002; Alexander 2001; Clarke 2001; K. Kumar 1988), a teaching method that often uses rapid-fire question–answer routines to test memorisation. But the teacher–student relationship, in that it is emblematic of a class-based intellectual asymmetry, is itself reminiscent of broader asymmetrical relationships forged through British colonialism and its postcolonial aftermath: for instance, between elites and non-elites, English speakers and Hindi speakers, and even, from the standpoint of local identity categories at this New Delhi NGO, lesbians and boys. There is much ethnographic evidence that the boys themselves associate these higher level identity categories with the interactional identities that habitually emerge in group meetings, beginning with the quite basic finding that they often tease lesbian group facilitators for sounding not only 'teacher *jaise*' (teacher-like) but also formal, uptight and feminine, all qualities they ascribe to the English language as well as to the elites who speak it. In other words, in order to understand how speakers themselves interpret interaction – or in this case, the asymmetrical questioning practices that originate from Liz's role as facilitator – we must isolate the ideological linkages that imbue such practices with social meaning. From the standpoint of linguistic anthropology, this undertaking will require us to go beyond the immediate text and consider the localised sociocultural contexts in which it is embedded.

Hindi operates throughout the discussion as a parallel discursive universe of sorts, in that the boys employ it to develop an alternative conceptualisation of masculinity that is more in line with boy concerns. Specifically, while Liz and her lesbian-identified friends work to convince the boys that masculinity is a matter of attitude, the boys develop in Hindi a counter-discussion that positions masculinity as a matter of physicality. The initiation of this practice within the meeting follows a conversational floor that disallows their contributions. Throughout the hour of discussion, the boys frequently try to challenge Liz's insistence that masculinity is a social phenomenon by introducing male attributes that are in their perception incontrovertibly biological, among them facial hair, broad shoulders, height, and perhaps most critically in terms of sexual reassignment surgery, the penis. But when Liz repeatedly dismisses their contributions for being about 'men' instead of 'masculinity', they find in Hindi a medium that better addresses the disconnect they are all experiencing between their bodies and their male identification.

In the remaining pages, I analyse one additional example as paradigmatic of this code-switching pattern. The exchange takes place directly after a discussion in which Liz has overtly expressed her opposition to sexual reassignment surgery, claiming – to the boys' profound puzzlement – that 'even a penis can be socially constructed'. Growing increasingly frustrated at the boys' inability to understand her point that masculinity need not be the exclusive property of males, Liz once again asks them to come up with attributes that they perceive to be 'masculine' and not 'male':

Extract 2. I don't have a bloody moustache!
(English is in standard font, Hindi in italics)

1	LIZ:	I'm not talking about m<u>a</u>le.
2		I'm talking about m<u>a</u>sculine.
3		I'm not saying [what about m<u>e</u>n.]
4	BARBARA:	[Yeah but but-]
5		within e::h woman. woman. [[woman.]]
6	LIZ:	[[N<u>o</u>:, I'm]] just
7		saying masculine just (.) ↑in general what
8		[masculine is.]
9	BIJAY:	[masculine r<u>ea</u>]lly re[[fers]] to.
10	LIZ:	[[I'm just saying]]
11	JESS:	<laughs> <Mascu[line?>]
12	LIZ:	[M<u>as</u>]culine.
13	JESS:	Masculine.
14	LIZ:	M<u>a</u>sculine.
15		What<u>e</u>ver.
16		Wh-what comes to mind when you hear
17		mascu[line.]
18	JESS:	[A bike?]
19	NANHI:	A::nd, (1.3) Liz?=
20		<Liz is talking to the employee making chai>
21	PRITI:	=Shave,
22	BIJAY:	<quietly> <Moustache.>
23		(2.9)
→ 24	SARVESH:	*baṛī kośiś kī yār.*
25		I don't have bloody moustache [no.]
26	NANHI:	[*tū ṭhīk hai*].
27	SARVESH:	↑ *cup.*
28		<laughs> <*(xxx) vah boltī hai.*>
29		<Liz returns to the conversation>
30	LIZ:	Keep raising them.=
31	BIJAY:	<singing> =<↑ *Oo::h*>
32		(1.7)
33	SARVESH:	<deeply, loudly> <*hai mere bac↓ ce↑:::*>

> | | *Hindi translation* (for lines 24–33) |
> |---|---|
> | SARVESH: | *I really tried, yaar.* |
> | | I don't have bloody moustache   [no.   ] |
> | NANHI: | [*You're okay.*] |
> | SARVESH: | ↑*Shut up.* |
> | | \<laughs> \< *(xxx) She says.*> |
> | | \<Liz returns to the conversation> |
> | LIZ: | Keep raising them.= |
> | BIJAY: | \<singing> =\<↑ *Oo :: h*> |
> | | (1.7) |
> | SARVESH: | \<deeply, loudly> \<*Hey my child, it is I!*> |

In contrast to Extract 1, the switch to Hindi in this excerpt is facilitated by Liz's unexpected departure from the conversation (she begins talking to a kitchen employee), an act that frees the floor from the interactive constraints imposed by her role as facilitator. As soon as the boys perceive that her attention is directed elsewhere – namely, when she fails to answer Nanhi's call (line 19) – they begin to introduce attributes that bring the discussion back from bikes to biology, with Priti introducing 'shave' (line 21) and Bijay 'moustache' (line 22). The boys then experience an unusually long pause of 2.9 seconds, particularly given Liz's propensity to interrupt their talk with rapid-fire successive questions. It is at this point that Sarvesh establishes a Hindi-speaking floor through a personal admission of her physical inability to grow a 'bloody moustache': *barī kośiś kī yār*. '*I really tried, yaar*' (line 24). As with Jess's initiation of Hindi in Extract 1, Sarvesh's contribution immediately registers a challenge to the formality of Liz's regimented question-answer style. Particularly notable in this respect is Sarvesh's use of the address term *yār* ('friend', 'buddy', 'pal'), a form used especially among young people in situations of informality and camaraderie.

Hindi is activated here as a resource for discussing the physical aspects of masculinity that stand between boy and man. The boys feel that they already possess the attributes of social masculinity that are of interest to Liz, conceptualising themselves for the most part in male terms. Indeed, many of them voice this self-conceptualisation overtly in this discussion through the use of grammatically masculine self-reference. But what Jess, Sarvesh, Priti and Bijay do not possess are the attributes of physical masculinity ideologically associated with Indian manhood, such as moustaches. Liz's decision to structure the conversation around social constructionism thus makes little sense to the boys, who instead want to discuss what they can do to acquire the essential technologies of male virility. The emergence of a Hindi-speaking floor gives them the opportunity to do just that, providing an alternative verbal space to debate, for instance, their successes and failures at growing facial hair.

Yet the boys' interactive practices also bring about new indexical links between Hindi and indigenous forms of maleness, precisely by exploiting already existent ideologies of both masculinity and language. As a case in point, consider the exchange that develops around the attribute 'moustache'. Without any understanding of the larger context in which Bijay's and Sarvesh's comments are embedded, we could easily hypothesise that Bijay's registering of the moustache as a male attribute (line 22), along with Sarvesh's subsequent admission of her failed attempt at growing one (line 24), quite simply reflects their desire to pass more convincingly as men. But if we were to know how the moustache operates socioculturally in contemporary India, as well as how the boys themselves orient to it as a marker of masculinity, we would want to analyse their comments in a much more complex way. The moustache looms large in the Indian imagination as a marker of ideal masculinity, so much so that the women I interviewed in Delhi claim that at least 90 per cent of Indian men wear one. Moustaches, when groomed appropriately, are seen as indexical of both prestige and courage. Indeed, in the state of Madhya Pradesh, the Indian police force, after determining that 'moustachioed constables' receive more respect from civilians (BBC News 2004), recently began a programme that pays policemen thirty rupees per month just for growing one. Venerated in the popular Hindi proverb *much nahī kuch nahī* 'no moustache, no nothing', the moustache stands as one of India's most important markers of sexual virility. This fact might explain, for example, why a recent report on violence against women in northern India points to the high rate of moustache-wearers in Uttar Pradesh as evidence for the fact that the state is a 'stronghold of patriarchy' (MASVAW 2007: 2).

Yet critically, the Indian moustache is also ideologically associated with a class position that is definitively *not* elite. Although once a status marker comfortably situated in upper as well as lower tiers of class and caste hierarchy, particularly before the advent of British colonialism, the moustache appears to have been losing its appeal among globalised urban elites in Delhi and Bombay. Most of the middle class men and women I knew at the Center were no exception, viewing the moustache as a preoccupation of the uncultured urban classes. For many of them, a moustache was the opposite of modern, an anti-fashion, of sorts, better situated on the face of a pagari-wearing Rajput from the countryside of Rajasthan. A number of scholars and social commentators have attributed the anti-moustache shift to the influential Bollywood film industry, given that almost all of the most popular stars under the age of 40 do not wear them (e.g. Kala 2007; Dwyer 2000). Moreover, while the heroes of Bollywood narratives are typically clean-shaven, their enemies often display bold moustaches of varying shapes and sizes.

Whatever the cause for the moustache's decline among urban elites, the class division over this issue connects up in significant ways with globalisation. Shortly before the advent of my fieldwork, the media had even popularised this connection in its handling of the now infamous Indian Airlines' grounding of a 33-year veteran employee for refusing to shave off his large handlebar moustache. When a spokesperson for this Delhi-based air carrier backed up the decision by asserting that 'some passengers could be unnerved by such a striking facial feature' (BBC News 2002), the company registered its commitment to a sense of fashion that was not Indian, but decisively global. The rise of the clean shave as a new marker of Bourdieuian distinction (Bourdieu 1984) might also be behind why many of the boys confess a 'secret' love for the film stars of the less globalised Tamil-language Kollywood industry, who unlike their Bollywood counterparts, almost always sport hefty upper-lip facial hair.

Without a consideration of these sorts of ethnographic specificities, we would be unable to see a relationship between Bijay's quietly spoken suggestion of the attribute 'moustache' and Sarvesh's subsequent introduction of a Hindi-speaking floor. Like the activity of 'winking' in Clifford Geertz's (1973) oft-quoted discussion of ethnographic methodology, we can determine the social meaning of linguistic practices such as these only if we engage in the kind of 'thick description' that enables us to distinguish a wink from a twitch. I assert here that both of these conversational 'winks' are ideologically related. In short, both practices index an orientation to indigenous models of sexuality that oppose the sensibilities of globalised elites. The boys are acutely aware that many English speakers at the Center denigrate moustache wearers and Hindi speakers as similarly 'vernac', and they here embrace both practices in order to establish an oppositional class position that better aligns with the masculinity they wish to project. Moustaches and Hindi thus emerge as jointly indexical of the more traditional understanding of masculinity that is core to boy identity.

Yet this emergence is ultimately dependent upon the structural particularities of the interaction itself. This observation is again exemplified by the final line of the above example, where Sarvesh enacts an extremely adversarial stance in response to Liz's attempts to regain a more regimented English-speaking floor: *haĩ mere bac↓ ce↑::: 'Hey my child, it is I!'* (line 33). (The pragmatic effect of this expression, which is not altogether clear from the translation, is something like: 'Who do you think you are? It will take you several generations to reach my level!') This classically hierarchical putdown is precipitated by Liz's return to the conversation: Instead of acknowledging the boys' concerns, her actions work to disrupt, or otherwise ignore, the more solidarity-oriented Hindi-speaking floor. Most notably, she places the boys back into the interactional role of respondent, ordering them to come up with more masculine attributes ('keep raising them', line 30). Sarvesh's response thus works to reverse this unwanted conversational asymmetry, if only momentarily, by putting herself into the role of adult and Liz into that of child. Yet in terms of the larger discussion, the response also works to establish Hindi as the preferred medium for the enactment of combative oneupmanship. The hierarchical use of Hindi in this excerpt, far from isolated, is just one of many instances where the boys employ the language for adversarial stance-taking. And because this kind of stance-taking is itself ideologically associated with male speakers – a connection made here by Sarvesh's uncharacteristic use of a low-pitched voice – Hindi emerges by association as indexical of masculinity more generally.

Conclusions

My primary argument in this chapter has been concerned with the way in which masculinity emerges in interaction through a confluence of structural and ideological factors. I have suggested that group members, bilingual in Hindi and English, are continually in the process of negotiating new indexical links between language, masculinity and sexuality. While these negotiations materialise through and against dominant metalinguistic understandings of English and Hindi, the specifics of this materialisation emerge within daily interaction at the Center and related environs, where Hindi and English increasingly come to occupy antagonistic ideological endpoints with respect to the articulation of sexuality. The interactional subject positions that emerge from the turns and sequences of conversational immediacy are thus situated within locally bound ideologies regarding the relationship between language and identity.

This brings us back to that bugbear of a concept that in many ways motivated the writing of this chapter: social class. Language and gender researchers, particularly those influenced by the paradigm of performativity, have long challenged static conceptualisations of gender, race and sexuality by treating these categories as ideological instead of fixed. Scholarship written within this tradition does not deny the existence of social hierarchy, but rather gives discourse a central role in its production. Yet the same body of scholarship has been much more reluctant to view social class as having discursive fluidity, often working from the assumption that class is a stable designation that precedes, and in many ways predicts, how speakers speak. This is not without good reason, given that the material reality of social class in many ways determines the possibilities of talk, particularly given the relationship between socioeconomic status and educational access. In northern India, to name but one relevant example, competency in English is importantly reliant on whether speakers have attended Hindi-medium or English-medium schools. Indeed, the 'medium' divide, forged through economic liberalisation, has produced a new category of identity within the Indian middle classes (LaDousa 2006), a development no doubt intensified by the hefty price tag associated with English-medium education.

But the lesbians and boys associated with the group, in that they share the ability to converse fluently in both Hindi and English, do not generally distinguish themselves along the lines of medium, viewing themselves, for the most part, as socioeconomic equals. Their divergent uses of the two languages in the above data are thus motivated primarily by ideological orientation, not material constraint. Specifically, Center boys orient to a semiotics of lower classness in order to oppose what they perceive to be an elite and un-Indian conceptualisation of sexual identity. In contrast, Center lesbians, although not well represented in the data discussed here, appropriate the linguistic resources of upper classness as a means of positioning their identity as globally progressive. It is not only masculinity that is emergent in group interactions, then, but also social class. Indeed, these two orientations materialise in the data as ideological bedfellows, mutually indexed by the same set of linguistic resources. That is, the adversarial stance-taking that indexes boy masculinity – here developed through, for example, the use of verbal oneupmanship, Bollywood villain intonation, exclusionary uses of the solidarity address term *yār*, and most critically, Hindi – also works to index a non-elite class position, particularly through its defiance of upper class norms of politeness.

The Center thus provides the globalised local context in which tensions around sexual identity, social class, language and postcolonialism take form. A British woman acts as an intermediary between the Ford Foundation's mission to address the AIDS epidemic and the identity concerns of the middle classes. But in the course of this mediation, she brings to the conversational table Western understandings of masculinity and sexuality. Some participants, particularly those whose understanding of self cannot be reconciled with Western ideologies of social constructionism, are inspired to rebellion; others come to embrace the identities put before them. NGOs like the Center, by providing access to global identities of masculinity and sexuality, offer their members a powerful kind of sociosexual mobility. But because this mobility is dependent upon ideological transformation, such spaces are also changing the very process through which masculinity is recognised and reproduced.

Notes

This article includes excerpts from a much longer, as yet unpublished, manuscript entitled 'Masculinity under *Fire* in New Delhi.' I am very grateful to the editors of this volume, Pia Pichler and Eva Eppler, for their encouragement and insightful suggestions. [...] I am also indebted to a number of friends, students and colleagues who have helped me think through various ideas expressed in this chapter, particularly Mary Bucholtz, Donna Goldstein, Chaise LaDousa, Sujata Passi, Joshua Raclaw, Betu Singh and Ved Vatuk. Above all, I would like to offer my heartfelt thanks to the lesbians and boys who agreed to participate in this study, and who gave me many months of unforgettable Delhi-style fun.

1 Because the decision to participate in this organisation carries significant personal risk for the individuals involved, I have chosen to use pseudonyms for the group title as well as for the boys and lesbians discussed in this article. I have tried to select pseudonyms that in some way convey the spirit of the actual names, with particular attention to connotations of gender, formality, and/or linguistic origin.

2 In their review of language and gender research, Benwell and Stokoe conflate a number of theoretical perspectives that are usually viewed as intellectually distinct by social theorists, most notably social constructionism and gender performativity.

3 I have chosen to refer to individuals with the pronoun that they themselves prefer. For instance, while Jess, Sarvesh and Priti usually use the feminine first person when speaking Hindi, Bijay always uses the masculine.

References

Alexander, Robin (2001) *Culture and Pedagogy*. Oxford: Blackwell.

BBC News (2002) No bar on handlebar moustaches. *BBC News*. February 8. http://news.bbc.co.uk/2/hi/south_asia/1809171.stm (accessed 1/15/2008).

BBC News (2004) Indian police given moustache pay. BBC News. January 13. http://news.bbc.co.uk/2/hi/south_asia/3392809.stm (accessed 1/15/2008).

Benwell, Bethan and Stokoe, Elizabeth (2006) *Discourse and Identity*. Edinburgh: Edinburgh University Press.

Bourdieu, Pierre (1984) *Distinction: A Social Critique of the Judgment of Taste*. Cambridge, MA: Harvard University Press.

Bucholtz, Mary and Hall, Kira (2005) Identity and interaction: a sociocultural linguistic approach. *Discourse Studies* 7(4–5): 585–614.

Bucholtz, Mary and Hall, Kira (2008a) All of the above: from paradigms to coalitions in sociocultural linguistics. *Journal of Sociolinguistics* 12 (4): 401–31.

Bucholtz, Mary and Hall, Kira (2008b) Finding identity: theory and data. *Multilingua* 27(1–2): 151–63.

Cameron, Deborah (1997) Performing gender identity: young men's talk and the construction of heterosexual masculinity. In Johnson, S. and Meinhof, U. H. (eds.) *Language and Masculinity*. Oxford: Basil Blackwell. 47–64.

Clarke, Prema (2001) *Teaching and Learning: The Culture of Pedagogy*. New Delhi: Sage.

Coates, Jennifer (2007) 'Everyone was convinced that we were closet fags': the role of heterosexuality in the construction of hegemonic masculinity. In Saunston, H. and Kyratzis, S. (eds.) *Language, Sexualities, Desires: Cross-cultural Perspectives*. New York: Palgrave Macmillan. 41–67.

Devraj, R. (2005) Vern, vernie, vernac. *Dick and Garlick: Notes on Indian English, Hinglish, Slang, and Popular Culture*. May 23. http://dickandgarlick.blogspot.com/2005_05_01_archive.html (accessed 1/15/08).

Dwyer, Rachel (2000) Bombay Ishtyle. In Bruzzi, S. and Gibson, P. C. (eds.), *Fashion Cultures: Theories, Explorations, and Analysis*. New York: Routledge. 178–90.

Geertz, Clifford (1973) Thick description: toward an interpretive theory of culture. *The Interpretation of Cultures: Selected Essays*. New York: Basic Books. 3–30.

Gupta, Charu (2002) *Sexuality, Obscenity, and Community: Women, Muslims, and the Hindu Public in Colonial India*. New York: Palgrave Macmillan.

Hall, Kira (1997) 'Go suck your husband's sugarcane!': hijras and the use of sexual insult. In Livia, A. and Hall, K. (eds.) *Queerly Phrased: Language, Gender, and Sexuality*. New York: Oxford University Press. 430–60.

Hall, Kira (2005) Intertextual sexuality: parodies of class, identity, and desire in liminal Delhi. *Journal of Linguistic Anthropology* 15(1): 125–44.

Hall, Kira and O'Donovan, Veronica (1996) Shifting gender positions among hindi-speaking hijras. In Bergvall, V., Bing, J., and Freed, A. (eds.) *Rethinking Language and Gender Research: Theory and Practice*. London: Longman. 228–66.

Johnstone, Barbara (1990) *Stories, Community, and Place: Narratives from Middle America*. Bloomington: University of Indiana Press.

Kala, Arvind (2007) A moustache divide. *The Times of India*. June 16. http:// timesofindia.india-times.com/Opinion/Editorial/A_moustache_divide/rssarticle show/2126822.cms (accessed 2/1/2008).

Kiesling, Scott F. (2004) Dude. *American Speech* 79(3): 281–305.

Kumar, Krishna (1988) Origins of India's 'textbook culture.' *Comparative Education Review* 32(4): 452–64.

Kumar, Nita (2002) Children and the partition. In Kaul, S. (ed.) *The Partitions of Memory: The Afterlife of the Division of India*. Bloomington: Indiana University Press. 269–302.

LaDousa, Chaise (2006) The discursive malleability of an identity: a dialogic approach to language 'medium' schooling in North India. *Journal of Linguistic Anthropology* 16(1): 36–57.

Livia, Anna (2004) Language and Woman's Place: picking up the gauntlet. In Bucholtz, M. (ed.) *Language and Woman's Place: Text and Commentaries*. New York: Oxford University Press.

MASVAW (2007) A journey towards justice: men's action for stopping violence against women. *Men's Action for Stopping Violence Against Women*. http://www. sahayogindia.org/ (accessed 1/20/2008).

Matsumoto, Yoshiko (2002) Gender identity and the presentation of self in Japanese. In Benor, S., Rose, M., Sharma, D., Sweetland, J., and Zhang, Q. (eds.) *Gendered Practices in Language*. Stanford, CA: CSLI Publications. 339–54.

McElhinny, Bonnie (1995) Challenging hegemonic masculinities: female and male police officers handling domestic violence. In Hall, K. and Bucholtz, M. (eds.) *Gender Articulated: Language and the Socially Constructed Self*. New York: Routledge. 217–44.

Ochs, Elinor (1992) Indexing gender. In Duranti. A. and Goodwin, C. (eds.) *Rethinking Context: Language as an Interactive Phenomenon*. Cambridge: Cambridge University Press. 335–8.

Pichler, Pia (2006) Multifunctional teasing as a resource for identity construction in the talk of British Bangladeshi girls. *Journal of Sociolinguistics* 10(2): 225–49.

Puri, Jyoti (1999) *Women, Body, Desire in Post-Colonial India: Narratives of Gender and Sexuality*. New York: Routledge.

Queen, Robin (2005) 'How many lesbians does it take …': jokes, teasing, and the negotiation of stereotypes about lesbians. *Journal of Linguistic Anthropology* 15(2): 239–57.

Schegloff, Emanuel A. and Sacks, Harvey (1973) Opening up closings. *Semiotica* 8(4): 289–327.

Speer, Susan (2005) *Gender Talk: Feminism, Discourse, and Conversation Analysis*. New York: Routledge.

SturtzSreetharan, Cindi L. (2006) 'I read the nikkei, too': crafting positions of authority and masculinity in a Japanese conversation. *Journal of Linguistic Anthropology* 16(2): 173–93.

Tannen, Deborah (1990) *You Just Don't Understand: Women and Men in Conversation*. New York: Ballentine Books.

Tetreault, Chantal (2002) 'You call that a girl?': borderwork in a French city. In Benor, S., Rose, M., Sharma, D., Sweetland, J., and Zhang, Q. (eds.) *Gendered Practices in Language*. Stanford, CA: CSLI Publications. 237–54.

29

Queering Gay Men's English

William L. Leap

Source: Kate Harrington et al. (eds), *Gender and Language Research Methodologies*. London: Palgrave (2008), pp. 283–96. Reprinted with permission of Palgrave Macmillan.

What do queer theories have to offer researchers of gender and language? As Sauntson (2008) explains, the utility of the queer position seems limited, given that queer theories do not always use gender identity as the entry point for their discussion. In contrast, in language and gender research, the identity of the (speaking) subject is often named from the outset, a goal of the inquiry being to explore the language use of that subject in various domains.

Identity-centred linguistic inquiry was the approach to language and gender research taken in *Word's Out: Gay Men's English* (Leap, 1996, hereafter WO). The first section of this paper uses key arguments from queer theory to disclose weaknesses in WO's identity-based discussion of gay English text-making. The remainder of the paper considers what a description of 'gay men's English' might entail, if the 'identity' of the speaking subject were *not* named at the outset of inquiry while WO's other interests in language and gendered practices 'at the site' were maintained. Taken together, this chapter addresses key concerns that queer theory brings to the study of gender and language, including:

1 Gender is not a static construction but is always in formation.
2 Linguistic practices provide sites for those formations; they do not simply index a gendered presence that enters the social moment already constructed.
3 Gendered identity builds on understandings of normality and difference that are reflected in sexual, racial, ethnic and/or class-related identities.
4 Meanings of gender are expressed through linguistic practice, but these expressions are not limited to any single feature of linguistic practice.

Word's Out Was Not a 'Queer Text'

For years, studies of gay men's English were largely confined to discussions of gay-related vocabulary. Descriptions of gay men's language use in social settings were concerned with social practices – dynamics of public sex, social organisation of gay commercial venues, gay folklore, the rhetoric of homophobia. Linguistic data provided evidence for these larger concerns, but were not the focus of discussion in their own right.

My intent in writing WO was to demonstrate that gay men's English was not limited to erotic vocabulary, 'camp' expressions and other features of the so-called 'lavender lexicon' – the impression presented in much academic and popular literature at that time. In contrast, I used a close reading of gay men's conversations, oral narratives and written sources to argue that gay men's English should be described in terms of the linguistic practices – for example, turn-taking, style-shifting, lexical choices, narrative organisation, integration of affect – that enable gay men's communication, as gay men, within the linguistic moment. Frequently, the 'gay content' associated with gay English texts is not explicitly marked, but emerges through speaker/listener co-construction as the text-making unfolds. Similarly, while gay men's English is often found in contexts dominated by other forms of gay visibility, it is also evidenced in settings where explicit statements of sexually transgressive themes are actively discouraged, and where gay presence itself is a form of risk-taking. Speakers and listeners adjusting their linguistic practices accordingly, and how those adjustments are negotiated, were also addressed in WO.

In short, WO describes gay men's English as a type of linguistic work associated with a particular category of speaking subject. WO never argued that the linguistic practices associated with the speaking subject were 'inherently' gay or unique to gay text-making; examples show how different forms of language use gained this attribute through association with gay-identified speakers and messages at the site. And, as noted, gay-related messages themselves are often products of the linguistic moment, and not necessarily encoded directly in the text. Here, as Kulick (2000) and others correctly observe, the argument in WO took on a certain circularity: the 'source' of the 'gayness' of gay men's English is the gay identity claimed by one or more of the speaking subjects, yet linguistic practices are one of the primary means through which speakers construct and proclaim gay identity in public and private settings.

Admittedly, WO did not address this circularity. Having already named the identity of the speaking subject at the outset of the analysis, the chapters described how the named speaking subjects used English in conversation and other social action in the given setting. So if the logic was circular, the research task was unquestionably linear in its analytical direction. Invoking what Spivak (1993) has termed the 'risk' of 'strategic essentialism', WO made some claims about gay men's language use, illustrated those claims with examples of conversation and narrative, and opened this argument to critical discussion.

Naming the subject (i.e., as 'gay men') imposed limitations on WO's argument, however. For example, when I organised material for the book, discussions of the English language use of African-American, Hispanic or other same-sex identified men of colour that are available today were just beginning to appear in print. WO's examples drew heavily on research and personal experiences that were almost exclusively nested within urban US settings and within domains of whiteness, and that placed considerable restriction on the understandings of male sexual sameness that informed WO's discussion of gay men's English.

From a queer theoretical perspective, this focus was highly objectionable. Queer theory stresses that gender is closely tied to assumptions of normativity that assign value to all forms of subject position within the social setting. In fact, particular claims to gender have become so closely connected with claims to race and class that '[i]n the US today, the dominant image of the typical gay man is a white man who is financially better off than most everyone else', while the primary themes in the nation's 'gay rights agenda' – same-sex marriage, equal access to military service – remain detached from 'supposedly non-gay issues such as homelessness, unemployment, welfare, universal health care, union organising, affirmative action and abortion rights' (Berube, 2001: 234, 235). WO could have used gay men's English as an entry point for exploring the workings of normativity. But to do this, the discussion would need to examine language use outside the domains of gay experience and outside the domains of whiteness; WO did not do this. And even though the volume's focus on whiteness is acknowledged in the introductory chapter (1996: xviii–xix), how whiteness (and white privilege) may help shape gay men's gendered stances, linguistic practices, and the expressions of these stances and practices 'at the site' are not addressed.

Nor did WO consider the extent to which assumptions about masculinity influenced gay men's linguistic practices, even though some of the elements of gay men's text-making resemble features of an English language-based linguistic masculinity (Coates, 2003; Cameron, 1997). The presence of these features strengthens gay English connections to broader patterns of normativity in US society, and WO acknowledged the possibility of such a connection (1996: xi). Yet, despite the whiteness of the speaking subject being acknowledged, the implications of this alliance remained unexamined in the book's examples.

Queering Gay Men's English: An Example from Cape Town, South Africa

But what would a discussion of 'gay men's English' look like, if the identifiers particular to the speaking subject were *not* named at the outset of the inquiry – if the analysis treated identity formation as a product of the speaker's linguistic practices rather than the foundation on which they are based? Such an inquiry builds on queer theory's assertion (point 1, above) that gender is a point of reference constantly in formation, that is, 'an ongoing discursive practice…open to intervention and resignification' (Butler, 1990: 33). This 'ongoing discursive practice' unfolds within particular moments of social interaction, and a queer-centred exploration of gay men's English would focus attention on the social interaction and the moment where it unfolds, tracing claims to gendered (and other) identity as they unfold within that setting.

Bucholtz and Hall (2004) proposed a framework for such inquiry in their discussions of 'tactics of intersubjectivity' (see Sauntson 2008). Rather than looking at language use in formal terms, their framework focuses on forms of conversational practice as embedded within different categories of social interaction, each of which helps speakers establish claims to a subject position at the site, as gendered persons and in other ways.

In the following paragraphs, I consider the intersubjective formation of gendered identity in the context of story-telling – specifically, as part of the telling of a life-story narrative.[1] I use *life-story narrative* to refer to what Linde (1993: 20) terms 'oral units of social interaction', whose details are culled from a larger, more inclusive inventory of interrelated 'stories and associated discourse units' that are:

> told by an individual during the course of his/her lifetime [and] have as their primary evaluation a point about the speaker, not a general point about how the world is. (ibid.: 20–1)

The speaker-centred, highly reflective focus of these narratives makes them an especially useful resource in language and gender research. Moreover, life stories are accessible to researchers; people are often willing to tell stories about themselves, even when they may be reluctant to talk about other issues facing them in daily life. Heavily gendered moments figure prominently in life-story narratives: for gay men, such moments include 'coming out' experiences, the discovery of key sites in the urban terrain, 'how I met my boyfriend', as well as descriptions of face-to-face encounters with homophobia. Life stories then provide entry points to further discussion.

Life stories are also of interest to speakers themselves, who often use the telling of a story (whether in an interview or a context of everyday life) as an occasion for working through conflicting assumptions of identity and proposing claims to subject positioning which can then be evaluated, and accepted or rejected, by other participants in the story-telling. The enduring popularity of life stories rests, in part, with the way that speakers can vary their subject position in the story line without disrupting the overall coherence of the narrative.

'Bob's story' is an example of a life-story narrative, where the speaker's sexuality and other components of his subject position are very much in formation and where the details of that formation are key elements in the linguistic work of the story-telling. In this story, Bob, an 18-year-old Black African man, describes his first visit to a gay club in the City Centre of Cape Town, South Africa, and situates that visit within competing meanings of masculinity, homosexuality and racial status in the final moments of apartheid.

The interview took place in May 1996; the interviewer, Mfume, was a 21-year-old Black African woman. Bob and Mfume were good friends and students at the University of Cape Town at this time; Mfume was enrolled in a seminar I was teaching at UCT. She conducted this interview as part of a class project, and, with Bob's consent, agreed to have the text reproduced here.

The incident at the City Centre gay club took place in July 1995. At that time, Cape Town's City Centre, which had been a white-only terrain under apartheid, had been officially desegregated, and people of Colour now had access to the City Centre's public spaces and commercial terrains, gay clubs included. Even so, white mistrust of Coloured and Black intention and other legacies of apartheid tradition were still in evidence, as Bob's story indicates. The personal experiences that his story describes are infused with social themes, only one of which has to do with male-centred, same-sex desire.

Background: Life Stories as Queer Texts

Life-story narratives are 'queer texts' in the sense of the four points introduced in the opening section of this chapter. They are created in specific moments of social interaction. Their construction enunciates speakers' claims to gendered and other forms of social identity, yet the process of construction does not require that those claims already be formed. Instead, telling these stories becomes a context for (ex)pressing those claims, especially when events in those stories are framed in relation to broader expectations of power and authority. Understandably, Plummer has argued, 'we live in a world of sexual stories' and we reveal 'who we are through accounts of our identity struggles' (1995: 5).

But life stories are not self-contained statements, by any means. These stories have often been told before, and telling them again brings that history into the narrative moment. They are constantly revised and updated as a consequence of retelling, and in response to new events and new discoveries about older and familiar experiences. In other words, while life stories may appear scripted, in some sense, they are also texts in formation, and understanding how these stories are constructed is as important to life-story analysis as is understanding the basics of the story line.

Accordingly, rather than emphasising the life story's formal detail, more recent interests examine the internal form of the text as part of the speaker's engagement with memory, value and voice, within the historical and social moment, and beyond (James, 2000; Portelli, 1993; Kleinman, 1988). Under this framework, life stories cease to be sites of coherence, and become statements of assumption, contradiction and omission, features that provide opportunities for the active engagement of the audience in the development of the narrative.

Bob's story

Speaker: Bob; Interviewer: Mfume
> [MFUME: *When did you come out?*]
> I haven't really come out. The question should be when did I get into the scene. I've known about myself ever since I was in Standard 7. I'd gone through some literature about it, but I've never had the guts to practice it. Until I almost committed suicide. I had to stop fighting with myself. Then I came back to varsity. I used to stay in [a men's residence hall at UCT]. They had this poster about this place [names the club]. Then I decided to go there, but they didn't allow me to come in. I didn't know anything about clubbing at that stage. I was just a nerd. Clubs sounded far and weird. [Mfume: *Why far?*]
>
> Because of where I lived I had a funny perception about what went on there. I thought people would just grab you and do things to you.

> [MFUME: *So after you went there and they didn't let you in?*]
> I went to Foreplay.[2] It's not really a life you know, it's a game. There are some funny rules you have to play by. I met a stranger at a porno shop. I was very much into cruising then. I wouldn't like to go further into that. He gave me this list, a brochure, a list of all these clubs and bars, and after that I tried Foreplay.

> [MFUME: *Why didn't they let you in at (names club)?*]
> They said members only. I actually went early, before they opened for the night. I stood at the door and they had the chairs on the tables and I think they were getting ready to open. I stood there and the manager came running, looked at me strangely like I was some kind of thief. Maybe not a thief but somebody who had invaded some kind of territory. But then I heard about ABIGALE.[3] I decided then, I don't know, through some literature, oh! it was through the UCT Diary so I decided to find out about these people.

Bob's story: Useful Fictions of Incompleteness

At first reading, and without paying attention to contextual details, Bob's story is very much about competing expectations of masculinity, and his efforts to locate himself within that contested terrain of those expectations. Importantly, and contrary to older claims about life-story construction, his efforts are not presented in terms of a strict chronology, nor is the context of these experiences fully described. In fact, Bob's story-telling assumes that listeners will recognise the defining themes in recent South African cultural and political history, particularly the ways that apartheid rule used meanings of *place* to draw distinctions between, for example, male and female bodies, Black, Coloured and white bodies, authoritative and powerless bodies, and to assign value to locations that have ties to white, masculine authority. So Bob does not clarify the apartheid-related meanings of phrases like *township, City Centre, where I lived* (see below), *thief, invad[er] of some kind of territory*, and Mfume did not ask Bob to explain these. Both being Black South Africans, township residents by birth, and residents of the Cape Town area during the indicated time period, such clarification was not necessary. In effect, Bob's story-telling did not produce a static, self-contained narrative, but a text in formation, whose details were deeply dependent on his interaction with Mfume during the story-telling, on the particulars of historical moment within which the story-telling was taking place, and on his lingering memories of apartheid rule.

It is doubtful that Bob would tell this story in similar terms to another audience, or at a later point in his life. Alterations would not, however, mean that earlier versions of the story were defective. If, as queer theory claims, gender (and other formations related to normativity) are always *in* formation, then stories like Bob's where formations of gender are described will *themselves* be contingent, never emerging in final form. In this sense, lifestory narratives resemble what Laclau (1996: 53) terms an *empty signifier*. That is, they contain inconsistent references, gaps in information, and other shortcomings; yet their value as statements of personal meaning encourages speakers and listeners to proceed as if the narratives contained no such 'flaws'. The fiction of completeness that surrounds these narratives resembles 'the appearance of substance, of a natural sort of being' that Butler (1990: 33, and see note 1) associates with gender and this may be one reason why speakers use life-story narratives to answer questions about their gender (and other) identity when such questions are raised by others (or themselves).

Escaping Township Homosexuality

One of the topics where Mfume did ask questions concerned township homosexuality. This is an area with which she may have been familiar, but one on which she wanted to hear Bob's point of view. And contrary to the image of the naïve and uninformed subject that he presented in the opening segment of his story, Bob's responses to Mfume's questions revealed that he knew a lot about the township 'scene' and that what he 'knew about himself' while living at home was shaped by this information as well as by the literature that he read.

Bob never identifies himself as a Black South African in this text, however. In one sense, he did not need to do so: the fact was already foregrounded in the assumptions of emplacement and embodiment that surrounded Bob's and Mfume's presence in the narrative moment. By treating 'Blackness' as the unmarked racial reference, Bob's discussion becomes dominated by references to whiteness. That message is underscored by references to locations where forms of normativity may be contested, but never entirely undermined. These locations include: the secondary school classroom, the university, the college residence hall – and the gay dance club. His discomfort with these sites marks him as different, and marks his story as a narrative about difference, even if the specifics of difference have yet to be named.

Bob began to engage the tensions of normativity and difference once he discussed his unfamiliarity with the club scene: *Clubs sounded far and weird*, he noted, and when Mfume asked *Why far?*, Bob responded: *Because of where I lived. Where I live(d)* is a South African township English phrasing that dates from the apartheid period, when 'persons of colour' were officially assigned to a single residence, whose location was then indicated on the speaker's identity documents; any deviation from this violated the state's efforts to enforce racial segregation and made the individual subject to legal action. Because township residents often had to leave home to seek employment or for other reasons, township English speakers distinguished *where I live*, the official address, from *Where I stay*, the residence the speaker occupies for a shorter period of time. Thus, by using *where I lived* to frame his answer to Mfume's question, Bob makes clear his sense of the *weird*ness of city centre gay clubs, and his *funny perception about what went on there* was based on his understandings of male homosexuality as practiced in his home township. In effect, without employing explicit references to do so, Bob's remarks are 'queering' the City Centre's gay terrain: that is, he is using township perspectives as a benchmark against which City Centre-related assumptions of white gay masculinity can then be exposed.

During a later part of the discussion, Bob turned his queer gaze onto the assumptions structuring township-based homosexuality. He explained to Mfume that township homosexuality is dominated by *people who are into cross-dressing … drag queens*. He continued:

BOB: …They wear make-up and stuff …They're trying to be women. I really hate that, you know. People think that if you are gay then it means you are trying to be a woman … To white people they just think of you as a guy attracted to other guys. In black communities they'll go so far as determining your taste. In the townships they're very cliquey. They associate you with a group…. They are very forward there. They just start fiddling with you. They grab you by force. At [city centre clubs] they're very snobbish, so they have restraint. And in townships they're very nosy so they've got to know even what you do in bed.

MFUME: So privacy's important to you?

BOB: Yes, and there's not much of it in the townships. At least if I go to [city centre clubs] no one knows me.

MFUME: Did you know a lot of gay people in [home township]

BOB: No. I couldn't even think of practicing it. Maybe it was one of the reasons I wanted to be out of [home township], so I could start practicing this thing.

Mfume then asked more pointedly why Bob couldn't *practice this thing* in his home township:

BOB: My family of course. My brother would have killed me. Literally. And my mother would have disowned me.

MFUME: Did your mother ever make comments that made you believe that?

BOB: Ja, lots of things like: 'If someone ever did that, I wouldn't even let them into my house.'

MFUME: And your brother?

BOB: When I came home in first term, he asked me if I had a girlfriend. I said 'No,' and he said; 'Why? You're a man. I just hope you're not queer because those white universities have all these facilities for people to practice homosexuality. It's easy there. No one gives a damn in white universities.'

As these remarks suggest, one of Bob's reasons for leaving his home township and *coming to varsity*, was to find an alternative to the assumptions regarding Black (heterosexual) masculinity that are widely maintained within the township 'scene'. Another reason was to escape the surveillance of family and close friends whose distaste for homosexuality (and especially its ties to whiteness) resembles anti-gay discourses widely articulated throughout sub-Saharan Africa (Epprecht, 2004; Aarmo, 1999; Murray, 1998).

Indeed, while leaving his home township allowed Bob to get away from township-defined homosexuality and the ever-watchful supervision of his family, it also meant that he was moving out of a historically Black-proclaimed terrain and into an area that had been heavily inscribed for whiteness. The sites where Bob hoped to find homosexual opportunities that were more to his liking were historically white locations; and, in this sense, what Bob's brother reportedly said about *white universities having facilities for people to practice homosexuality* was quite accurate. And for a time, as Bob discovered, *no one gives a damn in white universities* or in any other white locations, especially if the would-be subject is a person of colour. What he would learn about the city centre scene, and about the assumptions regarding white-defined masculinity that are widely maintained there, he would have to learn for himself.

Not Exactly a Coming Out Story

In some ways, then, what Bob's story describes is akin to the coming out experience that figures prominently in gay men's life stories in North Atlantic settings (Leap, 1996; Liang, 1997). These stories also resemble the heroic narratives described by Campbell (1949). In this framework, coming out unfolds as a journey that takes the subject into unfamiliar, mysterious terrain. There the subject is confronted by a series of demanding challenges related to sexual (and related) identity, some of which the subject transcends, others of which present temporary setbacks. Usually, the subject engages with the challenges alone, and this increases their difficulty. But the subject perseveres, and is ultimately able to make a public affirmation of sexual orientation. This may restore relations with family or friends, or further widen the distance between them. Either way, the story ends with the triumphant ending of the subject's journey – self-acceptance, articulation, visibility – even if the subject has now come to the threshold of a new journey, and equally unfamiliar terrain.

Similarly, Bob first presents himself as uninformed and inexperienced about aspects of homosexual life, and explains the failure of his first visit to a gay club in terms of his own naiveté: *I didn't know anything about clubbing at this stage. I was just a nerd. Clubs sounded far and weird.* Even so, being refused entrance to the city centre gay club did not render him powerless. Bob went on to make contact with (presumably gay) men at other locations in the city centre, and eventually found his way to a bookstore that was a popular meeting place for same-sex identified white men and men of colour. He learned, in the process, that *there [were] some funny rules that you have to play by*, and people like *the stranger at the porno shop* helped him master these. Still, Bob remains the primary actor, the source of initiative, the subject of a largely self-managed socialisation. Thus, just as he moved from the gay clubs to the porno shop and other City Centre locations, then he moved on to Foreplay. And then he *heard about ABIGALE… and decided to find out about those people*, which broadened his contacts with the Cape Town area gay resources, and added a political dimension to his 'coming out' experience.

In other ways, however, this example does not fit so easily into the North Atlantic based 'coming out' story framework. For one thing, his relationship with Mfume excepted, the disclosure of sexual orientation to family and friends, always a key event in North Atlantic narratives, is not attested here. We don't know whether Bob has ever told his family, and, given his remarks, it seems unlikely that he would ever do so.

Moreover, while this is a narrative about Bob's experience, as a sexual subject, it also addresses issues of normativity that are much broader than Bob's own life story and more complex than a disclosure of personal sexual preference. Township homosexuality, with its assumption that all sexuality is framed in terms of 'men' or 'women,' and its emphasis on cross-dressing and other obligations of taste, contrasts with City Centre gay sexuality, defined in terms of *guy[s] attracted to other guys*, and framed within a commercial geography rather than networks of kinship and friendship ties. The racialised messages embedded within this contrast connect these competing forms of sexual sameness to the workings of apartheid technology and the regulation of South African society that this technology enabled.

Thus, from a township perspective, homosexuality emerges in Bob's text as either a Black construction, and therefore local and familiar, or as something that is white, alien, and linked to oppressive rule. These assumptions of normativity did not vanish as apartheid rule transitioned to democratic government. Access to City Centre gay geography made the 'alien terrain' accessible, but did not erase its associations with whiteness. Thus Bob's first visit to the City Centre gay terrain found him labelled *a thief...somebody who had invaded some kind of territory*. And this forces him to find City Centre territory where he is not judged out of place. The cruising locations, where white men and men of colour could meet and negotiate private liaisons, were much more accepting in that regard; this is where he learned the *funny rules you have to play by*.

Ironically, Bob's dislike of township homosexuality had to do with the township's treatment of the homosexual person as if he were a commodity – something that may be acquired, exchanged, used and discarded without regard for the person's well-being:

> In black communities they'll go so far as determining your taste … They are very forward there. They just start fiddling with you. They grab you by force.

The City Centre gay venues provided a space of escape from township experience, yet they also imposed a different type of commodification. Here, while the object of desire is still a 'pawn' in the game of public sex, the object is now defined in racialised as well as sexualised terms. And here, even though Bob *wouldn't like to go further into that*, the object can claim a position of agency, both by *becoming very much into cruising* and ultimately by seeking out ABIGALE and anchoring his homosexuality in terms of an anti-apartheid-related politics. Neither actions were open to him within the township setting, and both of them become attempts to undermine the authority of the township/City Centre and Black/White binaries.

Certainly, 'coming out' themes are deeply embedded in this work; but to summarise the whole of Bob's experiences with this label would divert attention from the dynamics of social and political settings in favour of context-free psychological themes. If queer theories intend to 'investigate … the underlying preconditions of gender identity, and how they are enacted and formulated in discourse', as Sauntson (2008) explains, attention to social and political setting cannot be ignored.

Is Bob's Story a Gay English Text?

Given how much can be learned about Bob's story if we add a queer theory perspective and refuse to 'name the subject' in advance of the analysis, it seems worthwhile to ask whether anything is gained here by labelling Bob's story as a gay English text. Indeed, Bob's story is not a narrative about 'gay experience' as such. The discussion of 'identity' is heavily inflected with issues of racial and class tension, not confined solely to a male-oriented same-sex attraction, and the understanding of homosexuality on which the discussion is based is not constrained by North Atlantic, and increasingly transnational, constructions of sexual privilege. And Bob does not refer to himself as a 'gay man' or as any other sexual category. In this sense, referring to Bob's story as a 'gay English text' is misleading. It mistakenly implies that a single, fixed identity anchors the issues addressed in this narrative, and that the linguistic practices that enable text-making are oriented in terms of a similar, singular focus.[4]

A text where gay English is refused?

At the same time, Bob's story is, in part, a narrative about 'gayness'. The narrative displays his repeated attempts to engage with meanings of 'gay identity' that circulate within the contexts of the City Centre, and with the comparable sexual meanings confronting him in the township settings. When access to one component of township or City Centre terrain was denied, Bob turned to other locations and the meanings of sexual subjectivity which were possible in those settings. The intersubjectively constructed language of the narrative – including Mfume's sequencing of the narrative through her questions, and both participants' repeated reliance on implicit meanings at key points to mark key moments in the narrative – captures this ongoing engagement. None proved to be satisfactory, however, and, hearing about ABIGALE, Bob shifted focus, away from township and the City Centre, towards a more politicised, Black/Coloured affirming, sexualised terrain. Bob's remarks do not indicate whether this multi-layered, politicised subject position will also become a foundation for further exploration, rather than a fixed identity; given the overall direction of the narrative, such an outcome would not be surprising.

In this sense, Bob's story could be called a 'gay English text' provided we make clear that in this instance, gay English usage shows how gay identity was engaged and then rejected, that is, this is a 'gay English text' where gay English itself is ultimately refused. This is a very different meaning of 'gay English text' from that found in North Atlantic settings, where linguistic practices encode gay experience more directly and more consistently throughout the text.

A text whose language affirms gender as a flexible accumulation?

If there is a dominant or centralising theme in Bob's story, I suggest that it rests in Bob's struggle to claim a particular position of masculinity and to fashion a text where linguistic practices capture these gendered claims. Multiple meanings of 'masculinity' are attested in these texts, including his family's assumptions about hetero-manliness, township-centred expectations of M-to-F (male-to-female) cross-dressing and transgender performance, urban attraction of gay opportunity and gay privilege, and Black political masculinity; tensions between Blackness and whiteness and other forms of opportunity and privilege lend further texture to these meanings.

To say that Bob's story is merely about gender is limiting, however. Here, gender as relevant to this text is not singular, fixed and stable, but has been fashioned along lines that resemble the processes of flexible accumulation that characterise commodity production (Harvey, 1989), citizenship (Ong, 1999) and other dominant themes in late modernity. I have suggested (Leap, 2003, and elsewhere) that the differences in linguistic practices associated with gendered text-making in various late modern settings can be read productively in terms of these accumulation processes. Perhaps it is time to consider 'gay men's English' as a particular expression of those processes, even if at times the processes and their outcomes are not so flexibly expressed.

Conclusions: How Queer Theory Can Be Helpful for Studies of Language and Gender

Queer theory may appear to be a mode of inquiry that is detached from real-world experience. But the discussion in this chapter suggests that this appearance may be misleading, at least in so far as language and gender studies are concerned. Queer theory's interests in the decentring of subject position and in the non-specificity of theory provide helpful constraints for researchers interested in understanding how meanings of gender become constructed, negotiated and contested through forms of linguistic practices. Besides asking *who* is speaking, and *how* they invoke language to express gendered meanings, queer theory insists that the inquiry disclose connections between gender and other forms of social location that are being addressed within the social moment. This requires a close reading of text, and careful consideration of speaker biography and speaker intention, but it also requires social and historical perspectives that extend far beyond the textual boundary.

Other approaches to discourse analysis argue in favour of attention to contextualisation and archive in studies of text (Blommaert, 2005). Missing in Blommaert, and in other treatments of discourse analysis, is an insistence that gender be a foregrounded category in the discussion. Queer theory may not always foreground discussions of gender, but it does not allow gender to be pushed into the sidelines so that a-historical, highly generic political process can move into centre stage. By keeping the subject out of the discussion, initially, and by inviting researchers to trace how speakers bring the subject into the text – or, in the sense of Bob's story, how speakers may refuse to do so – queer theory enriches the understandings of language and gender that other modes of critical inquiry currently provide.

Notes

1 Story-telling and conversation are similar in certain ways. Story-telling involves exchange between the narrator and other participants in the event, as shown in Mfume's questions to Bob and Bob's shaping his narrative in response to them. Importantly, in oral narrative, one speaker (the narrator) is the dominant voice in the turn-taking and that status is usually not contested. In other genres of everyday conversation, such assertions of privilege would probably be contested.

2 A Cape Town City Centre adult bookstore.

3 Lesbian/gay activist organisation, specifically for persons of colour.

4 Orthodox queer theorists would likely respond here that no such text, whether South African or North American in basis, would be oriented in terms of such fixed identity. I suggest that such orientation *guides* some men's stories of, e.g., their attempts to negotiate a pathway through 'a desert of nothing' and toward an oasis of gay identity (Leap, 1996: 125–39). The foregrounding of sexuality over other aspects of speaker subject position may well be a marker of privilege, but it is still a narrative style attested in the North Atlantic terrain.

References

Aarmo, M. (1999) 'How homosexuality became "un-Africa": the case of Zimbabwe'. In Blackwood, E. and Wieringa, S. (eds) *Same-Sex Relations and Female Desires: Transgender Practices across Cultures.* New York: Columbia University Press. 255–80.

Berube, A. (2001) 'How gay says white and what kind of white it says'. In Rasmussen, B., Klineberg, E., Mexica, I. and Wray, M. (eds) *The Making and Unmaking of Whiteness.* Durham, SC: Duke University Press. 234–65.

Blommaert, Jan (2005) *Discourse: A Critical Introduction.* Cambridge: Cambridge University Press.

Bucholtz, Mary and Hall, Kira (2004) 'Theorising identity in language and sexuality research. *Language in Society* 33: 469–515.

Butler, Judith (1990) *Gender Trouble: Feminism and the Subversion of Identity.* New York: Routledge.

Cameron, Deborah (1997) 'Performing gender identity: young men's talk and the construction of heterosexual masculinity'. In Johnson, S. and Meinhof, U (eds) *Language and Masculinity.* Oxford: Blackwell. 47–65.

Campbell, J. (1949) *The Hero with a Thousand Faces.* Princeton: Princeton University Press.

Coates, Jennifer (2003) *Men Talk: Stories in the Making of Masculinities.* Oxford: Blackwell.

Epprecht, Mark (2004) *Hungochani: The History of a Dissident Sexuality in Southern Africa.* Montreal: McGill-Queen's University Press.

Harvey, D. (1989) *The Political-Economic Transformation of Late Twentieth Century Capitalism: The Condition of Post-modernity.* Oxford: Blackwell.

James, D. (2000) *Dona Maria's Story: Life, History, Memory and Political Identity.* Durham, NC: Duke University Press.

Kleinman, A. (1988) *The Illness Narrative: Suffering, Healing and the Human Condition.* New York: Basic Books.

Kulick, Don (2000) 'Gay and lesbian language'. *Annual Review of Anthropology* 29: 243–85.

Laclau, E. (1996) *Emancipation(s).* London: Verso.

Leap, William (1996) *Word's Out: Gay Men's English.* Minneapolis: University of Minnesota Press.

Leap, William (2003) 'Language and gendered modernity'. In Holmes J. and Meyerhoff, M. (eds) *The Handbook of Language and Gender.* Oxford: Blackwell. 401–22.

Liang, A. (1997) 'The creation of coherence in coming-out stories'. In Livia, Anna and Hall, Kira. *Queerly Phrased: Language Gender and Sexuality.* New York: Oxford University Press. 287–309.

Linde, C. (1993) *Life Stories: The Creation of Coherence.* New York: Oxford University Press.

Murray, S. (1998) 'Sexual politics in contemporary Southern Africa'. In Murray, S. and Rosco, W. (eds) *Boy-Wives and Female Husbands: Studies in African Homosexualities.* New York: St Martin's Press. 243–53.

Ong, A. (1999) *Flexible Citizenship: The Cultural Logics of Transnationality.* Durham, NC: Duke University Press.

Plummer, Ken (1995) *Telling Sexual Stories.* London: Routledge.

Portelli, A. (1993) *The Death of Luigi Trastulli and Other Stories: Form and Meaning in Oral History.* Albany: SUNY Press.

Saunston, Helen (2008) 'The contribution of queer theory to gender and language research'. In Kate Harrington et al. (eds) *Gender and Language Research Methodologies.* London: Palgrave Macmillan.

Spivak, G. (1993) 'In a word: Interview'. In *Outside the Teaching Machine.* New York: Routledge. 1–24.

30

Indexing Polyphonous Identity in the Speech of African American Drag Queens

Rusty Barrett

Source: Mary Bucholtz, A. C. Liang, and Laurel A. Sutton (eds), *Reinventing Identities*. Oxford: Oxford University Press (1999), pp. 313–31. Reprinted with permission of Oxford University Press.

In this paper, I examine the presence and use of a "white-woman" style of speaking among African American drag queens (hereafter AADQs). I hope to demonstrate that a close examination of this language use suggests an ambivalent, sometimes critical, sometimes angry, view of whiteness that does not lend itself to a simplistic explanation of "wanting to be white." After discussing the issue of drag itself, I will discuss the ways in which AADQs create a "white-woman" linguistic style. However, this style of speaking is only one voice used by AADQs. The complete set of linguistic styles together index a multilayered identity that is sometimes strongly political with regard to issues of racism and homophobia.

Drag

Before discussing the issue of drag, it is important to distinguish drag queens from other transgender groups, such as transsexuals, transvestites, cross-dressers, and female impersonators.[1] Transsexuals are individuals who feel that their gender identity does not correspond to the sex that they were assigned at birth. Many (but not all) transsexuals undergo hormone treatment or "sex-reassignment" surgery as means of altering their physical appearance to match that typically associated with their gender identity. Transsexuality and homosexuality are independent issues, and transsexuals may be heterosexual, homosexual, bisexual, or asexual (cf. MacKenzie 1994). In contrast, drag queens do not identify themselves as having female gender (that is, they do not see themselves as women).

Unlike transsexuals, transvestites identify with the gender corresponding to their assigned sex. The terms *transvestite* and *cross-dresser* refer to anyone who wears clothing associated with the other gender. The term *transvestite* does not necessarily refer to an individual who fully crosses gender roles, and it may be used for situations such as a man wearing women's undergarments under traditional "male" clothing. Studies have suggested that between 72 and 97 percent of male transvestites are heterosexuals (Bullough

Language and Gender: A Reader, Second Edition. Edited by Jennifer Coates and Pia Pichler.
© 2011 Blackwell Publishing Ltd except for editorial material and organization. © 2011 Jennifer Coates and Pia Pichler. Published 2011 by Blackwell Publishing Ltd.

and Bullough 1993). In contrast, *drag queen* refers almost exclusively to gay men (with *drag king* referring to lesbian cross-dressers).

The term *female impersonator* is very similar to *drag queen*, although (like *transvestite* and *cross-dresser*) it may be used to refer to heterosexuals. Female impersonators are professional cross-dressers who typically focus their performances on creating a highly realistic likeness of a famous woman (such as Diana Ross, Cher, Reba McEntire, or Madonna). Glamour-oriented drag queens (or "glam queens") often produce a physical representation of hyperfeminine womanhood that is quite similar to that of female impersonators. The performances of female impersonators generally build on their ability to "pass" as women, however, and drag queens usually make no pretense about the fact that they are (gay) men, even though they may present a realistic *image* of a particular type of woman (cf. Fleisher 1996:14–15). Also, female impersonators generally perform for the amusement of heterosexuals, whereas drag queens perform for lesbian and gay audiences. Although both female impersonators and drag queens may produce highly similar external conceptions of femininity, the intent and attitude behind their performances are quite different.

All the drag queens in this study are glam queens. They typically go to great lengths to produce a highly feminine image. In addition to wigs, makeup, and "tucking" (hiding one's genitals), drag queens often use duct tape to push their pectoral muscles closer together to give the impression of cleavage. Glam queens almost always wear high-heeled shoes and shave their arms, legs, chest, and (if necessary) back. The dresses worn by glam queens are quite extravagant, often covered in beads or sequins. Many dresses do not have sleeves or have high slits to make it clear that the wearer is not trying to hide masculine features under clothing. Jewelry is almost always worn, especially large earrings and bracelets. The overall goal is to produce an image of hyperfemininity that is believable – an image that could "pass" for a woman. The ideal of glam drag is to be "flawless," or to have no visual hints of masculinity that could leave one open to being "read" (insulted; see also Morgan, 1999).

The drag queens I studied are professional entertainers who work primarily in gay bars. In order to become a full-time professional, a drag queen must achieve a certain degree of exposure, usually by working without pay or by winning beauty pageants. Thus, to become a professional, a drag queen must prove that she is sufficiently flawless.[2] Drag queens who are not flawless may be viewed as "messy": lacking professionalism both in the image produced and in the demeanor presented in the bar. Thus, a *messy* queen is often one who is unsuccessful at presenting an image of "proper" femininity (both in speech and poise). The term *messy* may also be used for queens who cause problems by spreading gossip or getting into trouble through drugs, alcohol, theft, or prostitution. A messy queen has little chance for success as a professional performer because she is unable to convey a convincing image of femininity both on stage and during interactions in the bar.

Feminist scholars have argued that drag is inherently a misogynistic act, primarily because they feel that it represents a mockery of women or, at the very least, a highly stereotyped image of femininity and womanhood (Ackroyd 1979; Frye 1983; Lurie 1981; Raymond 1994, 1996; Williamson 1986). It has also been argued that drag is a way of reinforcing a performer's masculinity by demonstrating that he is not actually a woman but that he is able to control the qualities associated with women (Gilbert 1982; Showalter 1983). Because the goal of glam drag is to produce an outward appearance indistinguishable from that of a "real" woman, humor in the performance of glam drag is not derived from the performer's inability to "be" a woman but from the virtuoso performance itself.

The argument that drag is primarily a mockery of women relies on the stereotyped perception of drag queens displaying "big tits, fat tummies, wobbly hips and elaborate hair-dos" (Williamson 1986:48) that "draw hoots and howls in audiences of mostly men" (Raymond 1996:217). With the exception of elaborate hairstyles, this stereotyped image of drag has very little to do with the reality of the gay drag performances included in this study. The drag performers I studied do not intend to produce laughter through their appearance. As Edmund White has argued, drag (at least among gays) "is an art of impersonation, not an act of deception, still less of ridicule" (1980:240). These arguments against drag often confuse gay drag queens with the sort of transvestite shows produced by straight (usually white and wealthy) men as a sort of male bonding experience, even though the latter (often including hairy men wearing exaggerated false breasts and rear ends) are quite different in both content and intent.

More recently, commentators (Butler 1990, 1993; Feinberg 1996; Fleisher 1996; Hilbert 1995) have critiqued this perspective not only because it views all forms of transgender behavior as male homosexual activities but also because it places women at the center of male homosexuality. These scholars argue that drag is not "about" women but rather about the inversion or subversion of traditional gender roles. These scholars often praise drag queens for demonstrating that gender displays do not necessarily correlate with anatomical sex and typically see drag as a highly subversive act that deconstructs traditional assumptions concerning gender identity. Butler, for example, argues that drag exposes the imitative nature of gender, showing that gender is an "imitation without an origin" (1990:138). Rather than viewing drag as an imitation of women, queer theorists usually glorify it as a highly political deconstructive force working to undermine gender assumptions.

Drag queens themselves also adamantly reject the notion that drag mocks women. They distinguish their performances from those of heterosexual men (who, in their view, clearly *do* mock women). For example, the nationally known AADQ singer RuPaul was angry and offended when she had to copresent an MTV music award with Milton Berle, an older heterosexual comedian known for using drag in his humor. She reports in her autobiography that problems between her and Berle began when he insulted her backstage (RuPaul 1995). The problems continued onstage as well, resulting in an argument that was aired on live television. According to RuPaul, the producers of the program did not realize that there was no connection between her status as a drag queen and Berle's use of women's clothing to produce humor at women's expense. As she describes it, "They didn't get that my take on drag is all about love, saying that we are *all* drag queens. It's certainly not about putting women down. And it's not about being the butt of a bunch of cheap dick jokes" (1995:181).

In addition, drag queens sometimes see themselves as fighting against gender oppression in general, a cause that many feel should garner support rather than disdain from feminists. And despite the role of drag queens in the gay liberation movement (cf. Duberman 1993; Marcus 1992), many gay men openly express scorn for drag queens. Hapi Phace, a New York drag queen interviewed by Julian Fleisher (1996), points out, "The thing that you have to remember is that as drag queens we have a lot of the same issues as feminists in our own dealings with the gay community. To gay men, we're considered 'women.' We get to see a lot of the misogyny in gay men" (Fleisher 1996:33–34). This view sees drag performers (both kings and queens) as part of a larger set of individuals persecuted by an intolerant society for their deviance from prescribed gender norms. As Leslie Feinberg argues, "it's really only drag performance when it's transgender people who are facing the footlights ... the essence of drag performance is not impersonation of the opposite sex. It is the cultural presentation of an oppressed gender expression" (1996:115). In other words, drag is not intended as a negative portrayal of "women" but rather is an expression of a particular gender performance (cf. Butler 1990) – a performance by those who are themselves oppressed by the forces of patriarchy.

Part of the fascination with drag is its ability to cause such diverse reactions in different contexts and with different audiences. In some instances, cross-dressing is used as a weapon of misogyny and even homophobia. In other contexts, drag may serve to question the rigidity of prescriptive gender roles, acting as a tool of liberation. One of the main functions of drag performance is to expose the disunity between perceived or performed identity and underlying "authentic" biographical identity. The "meaning" of drag is often created by audience members in their individual attempts to reconnect their physical perceptions of the performance with their personal assumptions concerning social identity and gender categories. Many drag queens argue that they are not really trying to "achieve" any great social message but are merely expressing their personal identity (which happens to involve cross-dressing).

The celebration and even glorification of drag by queer theorists such as Butler might be seen as exploiting drag-queen identity for the sake of theoretical deconstruction of gender categories. Like the feminist view of drag as inherently misogynistic, the view that drag is inherently subversive imposes a unidimensional meaning on the personal identity of a particular group. But there are certainly cases in which drag-queen performances are clearly misogynistic. As Miss Understood, another of Fleisher's interviewees, argues, "I think that men in general are pretty misogynist. Men are sexist all the time and if drag queens are men, of course there's going to be sexist things coming out of their mouths" (Fleisher 1996:32). Although drag queens may be misogynistic at times, their personal identity as drag queens does not make them *de facto* sexists. In many cases, they may be viewed as highly subversive. Thus neither the view of drag as inherently subversive nor as inherently misogynistic is "correct." Rather, drag queens are individuals whose social identity no more determines their political stance than any other aspect of their personal identities, such as gender, class, or ethnicity. Indeed, the performances by AADQs considered here generally focus on other aspects of identity (such as sexual orientation, ethnicity, and class) rather than on the issue of cross-dressing itself.

Polyphonous Identity and Acts of Performed Identity

Historically, sociolinguistic studies have tended to view identity monolithically, often assuming a one-to-one relationship between language use and membership in some identity category (usually based on class, race, or sex). Speakers were "allowed" only a single identity that was typically mapped onto a particular identity category. Those who did not fit the norms of language usage were implicitly viewed as possessing a "failed" identity, as with William Labov's (1972) *lames* or Peter Trudgill's (1983) concept of *conflicting identity*. Thus the fact that some speakers could not easily be classified into a particular identity category on the basis of their language usage was seen as a problem with the speaker rather than a problem in the research paradigm.

As Marcyliena Morgan (1999) points out, Labov's focus on unemployed adolescent boys in his study of African American Vernacular English (hereafter AAVE) has contributed to stereotypes of what constitutes a "real" African American identity. Sociolinguistic research has typically perpetuated the myth that one must speak AAVE (and must usually be a heterosexual male) to qualify as a "true" African American, leaving many African Americans classified as "lames" or simply ignored. This myth of what constitutes African American identity is especially relevant to African American gay men. Because of the combined forces of racism in the white gay community (cf. Beame 1983; Boykin 1996; DeMarco 1983) and homophobia in the African American community (Boykin 1996; hooks 1989; Monteiro and Fuqua 1994), African American gay men are often pressured to "decide" between identifying with African Americans or with white gay men (Peterson 1992; Simmons 1991; Smith 1986; Tinney 1986). Due to the stereotypical view that AAVE is somehow tied exclusively to young heterosexual men and is a strong marker of masculinity (cf. Harper 1993; Walters 1996), the use of "Standard" English by African American gay men (including drag queens) contributes to the argument that they have somehow abandoned the African American community by identifying themselves as gay. Thus simplistic conceptions of the relationship between language and identity in sociolinguistic research may serve to reinforce the racism and homophobia prevalent in American society.

More recently, as studies in language and gender have moved to a practice-based approach (Eckert and McConnell-Ginet 1992), it has become clear that identities based on categories such as gender, class, and ethnicity are often enmeshed in very complex ways. Expressions of gender are simultaneously expressions of ethnicity (Bucholtz 1995; Hall 1995) and of class (Bucholtz 1999; McElhinny 1995; Woolard 1995). Hence the concept of a prescriptive norm for "women's language" is often a reflection of ideology concerning not only gender but also race and class.

Given the complex relationship between linguistic form and ideologies of gender, class, race, and ethnicity, one would expect speakers to attune their linguistic performances to their personal stance toward gender and other ideologies. Speakers may heighten or diminish linguistic displays that index various aspects of their identities according to the context of an utterance and the specific goals they are trying to achieve. Thus a speaker may use the indexical value of language (cf. Ochs 1992) to "position" (Davies and Harré 1990) the self within a particular identity at a particular interactional moment. This practice implies that speakers do not have a single "identity" but rather something closer to what Paul Kroskrity (1993:206 ff.) has called a "repertoire of identity," in which any of a multiplicity of identities may be fronted at a particular moment. In addition, at any given moment speakers may also convey more than one particular "categorical" identity. For this reason I have chosen the term *polyphonous identity* rather than *repertoire* to convey the idea that linguistic displays of identity are often multivoiced or heteroglossic in the sense of Mikhail Bakhtin (1981, 1984). Thus speakers may index a polyphonous, multilayered identity by using linguistic variables with indexical associations to more than one social category. In the case of AADQs, speakers typically use language to index their identities as African Americans, as gay men, and as drag queens. Through style shifting, the linguistic variables associated with each aspect of identity may co-occur, creating a voice simultaneously associated with several identity categories (cf. Barrett 1998).

One important distinction between the language of drag-queen performances and many other forms of language is that although drag queens use language to index "female" gender, they do not generally see themselves as "women." Thus they perform an identity (as a "woman") that they may see as distinct and separate from their own biographical identity. Sociolinguistic theory has not traditionally made a distinction between a performed identity and those identities associated with the social categorization of the self. In her analysis of drag, Butler (1990) points out that, in addition to the traditional distinction made between sex and gender, drag creates the need for a third category, performance. Although gender performance often corresponds directly with gender identity, cases such as drag require an understanding that performed gender may differ from self-categorized gender identity. The majority of drag queens maintain "male" gender identity alongside "female" gender performance. Indeed, perhaps the strongest distinction between drag queens and transsexuals is the distinction between performance and identity, in that transsexuals typically maintain a gender identity that corresponds to their gender performance (but may not correspond to anatomical sex), whereas the gender performance of drag queens typically does not correspond to either gender identity or anatomical sex.

The distinction between performance and identity has not been utilized in sociolinguistic research, but it is potentially crucial, for the linguistic manifestations tied to performance are likely to be quite different from those related to personal identity. In identity performance, out-group stereotypes concerning the behavioral patterns of the group associated with the performed identity are likely to be more important than actual behavior or the group's own behavioral norms (Hall 1995). Audience assumptions and expectations may crucially help to coconstruct a performance that successfully conveys a particular identity regardless of the accuracy of the linguistic performance when compared to the behavior of "authentic" holders of the identity in question (Preston 1992). Thus the language used in a performed identity is likely to differ from the actual speech of those who categorize themselves as having that identity.

In addition to differences in linguistic form, a performed identity and a self-categorized identity are associated with different social factors. Robert Le Page and Andrée Tabouret-Keller (1985) offer four conditions that must be met if one is successfully to match the behavior of groups with which one wishes to identify: (1) identification of the groups; (2) access to the groups; (3) motivation to join them and reinforcement from group members; and (4) ability to modify one's behavior. Although these conditions may be necessary for the creation of identity based on self-categorization, they may not be required for the creation of a successful performed identity. For the sake of performance, it may be sufficient simply to identify the groups in question and to have the ability to modify one's behavior. One does not necessarily need access to the groups and one certainly does not need motivation to join the groups. In fact, in many cases performance may be used as a means to actually create distance from the group in question (as in the case of blackface). Reinforcement from the group is likely to be absent, and indeed, the performance may cause revulsion of members of the group itself (as with some feminist responses to drag). It is likely that in performing identity, reinforcement from the audience or listener will be more important than the actual behavior of the group being imitated; as with the mocking use of an ethnic dialect, performed identities may actually reflect disdain for the imitated group. Speakers in performance need only adjust their linguistic behavior to the extent necessary to index the identity in question. Such an adjustment may in fact be quite slight, possibly even consisting only of the use of specific lexical items (cf. Preston 1992).

Performances by AADQs are often judged (by audiences and other drag queens) on the basis of *realness*, or the ability to seem to be or "pass" (cf. Bucholtz 1995) as a "real" woman. In order to be "flawless," a drag queen must be "real": Her performance must plausibly lead (usually straight) outsiders to assume that she is anatomically female. Any response (whether reinforcement, rejection, or simply acknowledgment) from actual women is unimportant in the creation of a successful performance. What matters is the response of other gay men and drag queens, who base their judgment not on the actual behavior of women but rather on stereotyped assumptions concerning "feminine" behavior. The performer will also base her performance on stereotypes (and on her assumptions concerning the stereotypes held by the audience). These stereotypes may sometimes reflect the misogynist attitudes and sexist assumptions of the performer.

Traditional studies of performance have stressed the performer's responsibility to demonstrate communicative competence before an audience (cf. Bauman 1977; Briggs 1988; Hymes 1981). In drag performances, the performer must be able to produce a "real" feminine speech style or a feminine way of speaking that would sound convincing to someone who did not know that the performer was actually anatomically male. Ironically, the success of drag also depends on making the audience aware that this performance is indeed "false" in some sense (that is, the audience must be reminded that the performer is biologically male). Because a successful drag performance is one in which the audience accepts that the performer could pass as a woman, the audience must be occasionally reminded that the performer is indeed *performing* rather than claiming a female identity. Thus, although glam queens present an external image of exaggerated femininity, they also use language both to create and to undermine this surface image. For example, drag queens frequently use a stereotypically "feminine" speaking style, but a stereotypically "masculine" voice may break through during the performance, creating a polyphonous and often ambiguous performed identity.

Within the performances of AADQs in particular, a crucial aspect of communicative competence is the rhetorical device of signifyin(g) (Abrahams 1976; Gates 1988; Mitchell-Kernan 1972; Smitherman 1977). In signifying, the full intended meaning of an utterance does not rest solely on referential meaning. Rather, an utterance is valued because of its ability to index an ambiguous relationship between the signifier and the signified. Thus the signifier does not simply correspond to a particular concept but indexes a rhetorical figure or skill at verbal art. In signifying, a speaker draws attention to language itself, particularly to her or his skill at using language creatively. Specific attention to language (rather than referential content) may be created through a variety of devices, including the creation of polysemy or ambiguity, the creative use of indirection (Morgan 1991), and the contrastive use of a particular style, as in reading dialect (Morgan, 1999). Signifying relies on the listener's ability to connect the content of an utterance to the context in which it occurs and specifically to sort through the possible meanings and implications of an utterance and realize both the proper meaning and the skill of the speaker in creating multiple potential meanings.

Successful performances by AADQs typically include cases of signifying. A highly effective instance of signifying is sometimes picked up by other drag queens for use in their own performances. Example (1) has been used fairly widely by various AADQs in Texas:

(1) DRAG QUEEN: Everybody say "Hey!"
    AUDIENCE: Hey!
    DRAG QUEEN: Everybody say "Ho!"
    AUDIENCE: Ho!
    DRAG QUEEN: Everybody say "Hey! Ho!"
    AUDIENCE: Hey! Ho!
    DRAG QUEEN: Hey! How y'all doin?

This example draws on the form of a call-response routine, a rhetorical trope sometimes associated with African American sermons and often used in drag performances. The example relies on the polysemy of the word *ho* as both an "empty" word frequently used in call-response routines by drag queens and as an equivalent of *whore*. After leading the audience into the chant and getting them to yell "Hey! Ho," the drag queen reinterprets the word *ho*, taking the audience's chanting of *ho* as a vocative. The polysemy is dependent on the connection between the utterance and the context. Performances of AADQs contain numerous examples of signifying, in many of which the polysemy is achieved through the juxtaposition of language styles or social dialects.

White Women's Language among AADQs

Marjorie Garber (1992) notes that there is a long tradition of simultaneous movement across lines of both gender and race/ethnicity. For AADQs, the move to perform female gender is often accompanied by a simultaneous movement across lines of race and class. Sometimes an AADQ will openly state that she is actually white. For example, The Lady Chablis, a Savannah drag queen made famous in John Berendt's (1994) *Midnight in the Garden of Good and Evil*, often refers to herself as a "white woman." Berendt describes one of her performances as follows: " 'I am not what I may appear to be,' she will say with apparent candor, adding, 'No, child, I am a heterosexual white woman. That's right, honey. Do not be fooled by what you see. When you look at me, you are lookin' at the Junior League. You are lookin' at an uptown white woman, and a pregnant uptown white woman at that' " (Berendt 1996:14). As a "pregnant uptown white woman," The Lady Chablis moves from being a gay African American who is biologically male and from a working-class background to being upper-class, white, heterosexual, and female. In her autobiography, The Lady Chablis refers to herself and a close circle of friends as the Savannah League of Uptown White Women (or SLUWW). SLUWW was formed "to honor the belief that all of us [the league members] is entitled to spend our days sitting up under hairdryers, going to lunch, and riding around town shopping – *all at somebody else's expense*" (1996:173; original emphasis). She defines an "uptown white woman" as "the persona of a classy, extravagant, and glamorous woman – big car, big rings, etc.," adding parenthetically, " *(This term can be used for all women regardless of color)*" (1996:175; original emphasis). The term *white woman* refers primarily to a class rather than an ethnic distinction and also collapses the categories of ' "real" women' and 'drag queens'. Thus each of us has the potential to become an "uptown white woman," no matter what our sexual, racial, ethnic, or gender identity may be. Instead of suggesting a category based on sex or race, *white woman* indexes a prevailing ideology of gender, class, sexuality, and ethnicity that enforces a particular view of what constitutes "femininity" in US culture.

The combination of particular identity stances (white, rich, female, and heterosexual) works to produce a cultural conception of what constitutes the feminine ideal. This ideal femininity is often associated with the idea of being a "lady." As Esther Newton (1979:127) notes, "Most female impersonators aspire to act like 'ladies,' and to call a woman a 'lady' is to confer the highest honor." The "white-woman" style of speech as used by AADQs represents a stereotype of the speech of middle-class white women, of how to talk "like a lady." This stereotype is closely tied to Robin Lakoff's notion of "women's language" (WL), which also depicts a stereotype of white middle-class women's speech, a fact that Lakoff herself recognized (1975:59). Mary Bucholtz and Kira Hall (1995) have noted the pervasiveness of WL as a hegemonic notion of gender-appropriate language. Because it is such a strong symbol of ideal femininity,

WL is a powerful tool for performing female identity. For example, Lillian Glass (1992) reports that she used Lakoff's (1975) *Language and Woman's Place* in speech therapy with a male-to-female transsexual to produce gender-appropriate language use. Similarly, Jennifer Anne Stevens (1990) presents many of the features of WL in her guidebook for male-to-female transgenders. In addition to discussing issues of hormones and offering tips on choosing makeup and clothing, Stevens presents details about creating a feminine voice. Many elements of Lakoff's WL are included in the features of feminine speech that Stevens suggests, including tag questions, hedges, the use of "empty" adjectives, the absence of obscenities, and the use of intensive *so*.

Because of the power of WL as a stereotype of how middle-class white women talk (or "should" talk), I will use it as a basis for discussing the "white-woman" style of AADQs' speech. Here my use of the term *white-woman style* is intended to reflect this stereotyped representation rather than the real behavior of any actual white women.

Lakoff summarizes the main characteristics of WL as follows:

1 Women have a large stock of words related to their specific interests, generally relegated to them as "woman's work": *magenta ... dart* (in sewing), and so on.
2 "Empty" adjectives like *divine, charming, cute.*
3 Question intonation where we might expect declaratives: for instance, tag questions ("It's so hot, isn't it?") and rising intonation in statement contexts ("What's your name, dear?" "Mary Smith?").
4 The use of hedges of various kinds. Women's speech seems in general to contain more instances of "well," "y'know," "kinda," and so forth.
5 Related to this is the intensive use of "so." Again, this is more frequent in women's than men's language.
6 Hypercorrect grammar: Women are not supposed to talk rough.
7 Superpolite forms: Women don't use off-color or indelicate expressions; women are the experts at euphemism.
8 Women don't tell jokes.
9 Women speak in italics [i.e., betray the fear that little attention is being paid to what they say]. (1975:53–6)

Of these nine elements of WL, AADQs utilize only the first six. Several of these, such as the use of precise color terms and "empty" adjectives, overlap with gay male speech. However, AADQs typically distinguish between the two styles. For example, the "empty" adjectives in the gay-male style of speaking are characteristically "gay," such as *flawless, fierce, fabulous,* and so on. In the "white-woman" style, the empty adjectives are more similar to those discussed by Lakoff. For example, in (2a) an AADQ asked why I was studying "drag language." When told that I was a linguist, she responded with *Oh, really, that's cute*, where *cute* seems fairly devoid of meaning. Example (2b), also from a Texas AADQ, provides further instances of intensifiers and "empty" adjectives (*really* and *cute*). (Note also the use of intensive *so* in example (2b).)[3]

    (2a) A: ... drag language? What is ...
           B: He's a linguist ... linguistic.
           A: ((overlap))My brain is dead.
           A: Oh really ... that's *cute.*

(2b)   Oh, my, my … I lost a ring y'all and I am <u>vixed</u> [= vexed]
<u>Really</u> vixed, because …
I have no idea where it is and I just bought that little ring and it's
<u>so cute</u>.

Example (3) is taken from an interview with RuPaul on "The Arsenio Hall Show." This example demonstrates the use of final high intonation on declarative sentences (Lakoff's second characteristic of WL. Where H = high intonation, L = low intonation, H* = pitch accent):

(3) L   H   L   H*   L
You guys, I wish there was a camera so I could remember
H*   L   H
all the love you're sending to me
L   H
and the ..
L   H
the love energy from over here.
L   H*   L
You're absolute the best.

In these examples, AADQs use careful, "Standard" English phonology. In other words, they use "correct" prescriptive pronunciations as opposed to phonological features stereotypically associated with AAVE. This "white-woman" style is the most common speaking style among AADQs, and the ability to use this style is considered vital to the success of AADQs' performances. The use of this style also distinguishes AADQs from other African American gay men. Thus it functions both to index stereotypes of white femininity and to construct a unique drag-queen identity that appropriates and reworks the symbols of "ideal" femininity.

Performing Polyphonous Identity

Although the use of the white-woman style of speaking is closely tied to ideals of expected feminine behavior, AADQs do not use it exclusively. If such speakers actually wanted to be white, one would expect them to use white women's speech in an attempt to gain the social standing afforded to white women. Frequently, however, they use the "white-woman" style as a type of dialect opposition (Morgan 1999) in which this style is contrasted with other styles of speaking, primarily AAVE, to highlight social difference. In fact, the use of white women's speech among AADQs is itself a type of signifying. It indexes not only the social status or identity of white women but also the ability of a particular AADQ to use the "white-woman" style effectively. Most of the remaining examples are cases of polysemy created through dialect opposition, reflecting the ambiguity of signifying. These examples demonstrate that although the "white-woman" style is a vital characteristic of AADQs' identity, its use does not imply an underlying desire to be white. Rather, the white-woman style is one of numerous stylistic voices related to drag-queen identity and is used to create specific personas and changing identities throughout the course of a performance. Other stylistic choices, such as AAVE or gay male speech, are used to "interrupt" the white-woman style, to point out that it reflects a performed identity that may not correspond to the assumed biographical identity of the performer.

As noted earlier, AADQs do not adopt the last three characteristics of WL (avoiding off-color expressions, not telling jokes, and speaking in italics). Although all of the features of WL are related to "acting like a lady," these three are perhaps the most important keys to "ladylike" behavior. Lakoff notes that they may indicate that women realize "that they are not being listened to" (1975:56). One major difference between the "ladylike" behavior represented by WL and the behavior of AADQs is that "ladies" do not make themselves the center of attention, whereas drag queens often do little else. AADQs sometimes flaunt the fact that they do not meet the standard of proper middle-class women's behavior by using obscenities strategically. In example (4), a drag queen points out that she is not supposed to use words like *fuck* and *shit*, accentuating the fact that she deviates from the prescribed linguistic behavior of middle-class white women:

(4) Are you ready to see some muscles? [audience yells].... Some dick?
     Excuse me I'm not supposed to say that ...
     words like that in the microphone ...
     Like shit, fuck, and all that, you know?
     I am a Christian woman.
     I go to church.
     I'm *always* on my knees.

The statement *I'm always on my knees* is an instance of signifying in that it conveys double meaning. In the context of the utterance, it suggests that the speaker prays all the time. Because it is spoken by a drag queen in a gay bar, however, it also insinuates that she frequently performs oral sex on other men. The failure to have an ideal "ladylike" way of speaking (the use of obscenities) is paralleled in the failure to have appropriate "ladylike" sexual behavior. Here, the white-woman style co-occurs with obscenities that suggest the "falseness" of the performed white-woman identity. By creating two contrasting voices within a single discourse, the performer plays off of the disjuncture between performed ("female") and biographical ("male") identity.

In example (5), a Texas AADQ moves from speaking fairly "Standard" English in a high-pitched voice to using an exaggerated low-pitched voice to utter the phrase *Hey what's up, home boy* to an African American audience member. This monologue occurred in a gay bar with a predominantly white clientele. The switch serves to reaffirm the fact that the AADQ is African American and biologically male while simultaneously creating a sense of solidarity with the audience member to whom it is addressed. (Note: *a butt-fucking tea* is anything that is exceptionally good.)

(5) Please welcome to the stage, our next dancer.
     He is a butt-fucking tea, honey
     He is hot.
     Masculine, muscled, and ready to put it to ya, baby.
     Anybody in here (.) hot (.) as (.) fish (.) grease?
     That's pretty hot, idn't it?
     ((Switch to low pitch)) Hey what's up, home boy? ((Switches back))
     I'm sorry that fucking creole always come around when I don't need it.

The speaker apologizes with *that fucking creole always come around when I don't need it*, but the word *creole* is pronounced with a vocalized /1/, and the verb *come* is spoken without the "Standard" English /+s/ inflection. Thus, in apologizing for her use of AAVE (or "creole"), she continues to include features characteristic of AAVE in her speech (just as the apology for using an obscenity in example (4) involved the continued use of obscenities). This helps shape the statement as a form of signifying by implying that what is spoken does not really convey the full meaning of the utterance. The speaker's continued use of AAVE suggests that she has no intention of actually switching totally into "Standard" English (or of totally giving in to the performed white-woman identity symbolized by that variety of English).

Unlike the previous examples, example (6) is not typical of AADQs' performances. I include it here because it deals with a complex set of issues revolving around white stereotypes of African Americans. In this example, performed in an African American gay bar, an AADQ uses the "white-woman" style in acting out an attack on a rich white woman by an African American man. Acting out the rape of any woman is a misogynistic act; yet although this misogyny should not be excused, it is important to note that the main impetus for this piece of data is anger concerning the myth of the African American rapist. As Angela Davis has pointed out (1983), fraudulent charges of rape have historically been used as excuses for the murder (by lynching) of African American men. Because it is based on the racist stereotype of African Americans as having voracious sexual appetites, the myth of the African American rapist operates under the false assumption that rape is a primarily sexual act (and not primarily an act of violence). It assumes that all African American men are desirous of white women and are willing to commit acts of violence in order to feed this desire. The fact that this assumption has no basis is especially heightened in the context of African American gay men, who may not be desirous of *any* women. Nevertheless, the patrons of the bar must continuously deal with the ramifications of the myth of the Black rapist, including unfounded white fears of violence. Lines 1 through 21 present the attack on the white woman, in which the AADQ, in interaction with a male audience member who assists in the scene, uses the "white-woman" style alternating with AAVE as she moves in and out of the persona of a white woman:

(6) 1 I'm a rich white woman in {name of wealthy white neighborhood}
     2 and you're going to try to come after me, OK?
     3 And I want you to just...
     4 I'm going to be running, OK?
     5 And I'm gonna fall down, OK? OK?
     6 And I'm just gonna . . look at you ...
     7 and you don't do anything.
     8 You hold the gun ...
     9 Goddamn- he got practice. [audience laughter] <obscured>
    10 I can tell you're experienced.
        [The audience member holds the gun, but so that it faces down, not as if he were aiming it]
    11 OK hold it.
    12 You know you know how to hold it, don't play it off ...
    13 Hold that gun ... Shit ... Goddamn ..
    14 [Female audience member]: Hold that gun!
    15 That's right fish! Hold that gun! Shit!
    16 OK now, y'all, I'm fish, y'all, white fish witch!
    17 And I'm gonna be running cause three Black men with big dicks chasing me!

18 [Points to audience member] He's the leader, OK?
19 Now you know I gotta fall, I want y'all to say, "Fall bitch!"
20 [Audience]: Fall bitch!
[The AADQ falls, then rises, makes gasping sounds, alternating with "bum-biddy-bum" imitations of the type of music used in suspense scenes in movies and TV shows]
21 Now show me the gun!
[The audience member holds up the gun and the AADQ performs an exaggerated faint]

It is interesting to note that the man holding the gun does not "do anything" (lines 7–8). Despite the AADQ's insinuation that he is "experienced" (line 10), the audience member fails to hold the gun correctly until a woman in the audience yells at him (line 14). The "white woman" pretends that "Black men with big dicks" are chasing her through the park (line 17) and faints on seeing the man with the gun (line 21). Thus, the African American man is basically passive throughout the exchange and the "white woman" reacts primarily based on fear fed by racism.

In the remainder of the segment, the corollary to the myth of the African American rapist is presented, the myth of the promiscuity of the African American woman (Davis 1983:182). In lines 22 through 26, the same scene is acted out with an "African American woman" (speaking primarily in a tough, streetwise "bangee girl" style of AAVE) rather than a "white woman." The "African American woman," on seeing the large feet of the man with the gun (which implies he has a large penis as well), consents to having sex with him, saying that the gun is unnecessary (lines 25–6):

22 Now this Black fish ...
23 <obscured> Black men's running after her ..
24 I ain't no *boy*! Fuck y'all! Fuck y'all mother fuckers!
[AADQ looks at the gun]
25 You don't have to use that baby, I see them size feet.
26 Come on! Come on!

To focus only on the inescapable misogyny of this example is to miss its political complexity. The performance also touches all aspects of the myth of the African American rapist, the racist assumptions concerning both the "pure and fragile nature" of white women as "standards of morality" and the "bestial nature" of African American women and men. In this highly political performance, the drag queen moves in and out of the personas of narrator, director, and actor in the drama she is creating. She performs a variety of identities indexed by a variety of linguistic styles to undermine a variety of stereotypes and prejudices that are all too familiar to her audience.

Conclusion

The examples discussed above suggest that the use of white women's speech by AADQs cannot be interpreted as simply reflecting a desire to be white. The femininity associated with speaking like a "white woman" simultaneously indexes a set of class, gender, and ethnic identities associated with the ideology of what constitutes "ideal" feminine behavior. Although the "white-woman" style is sometimes emblematic of status, it is also used in combination with other stylistic choices to highlight a variety of more critical attitudes toward whiteness. Thus the appropriation of aspects of dominant culture need not necessarily indicate acceptance of its dominating force. Rather, this appropriation can serve as a form of resistance (Butler 1993:137). Indeed, in some cases the appropriation of white women's language does succeed in undermining racist and homophobic assumptions associated with the dominant culture. But arguments concerning the misogyny of drag cannot be brushed aside simply because drag is sometimes subversive. Although the examples in this chapter suggest a form of resistance toward racism and homophobia, they do little to call into question the sexism in American society. The performances of AADQs should not be understood simply as "subversive" or "submissive" with regard to dominant hegemonic culture. The polyphony of stylistic voices and the identities they index serve to convey multiple meanings that may vary across contexts and speakers. A full understanding of a phenomenon such as drag requires that we follow the advice of Claudia Mitchell-Kernan and "attend to all potential meaning-carrying symbolic systems in speech events – the total universe of discourse" (1972:166).

Notes

This chapter is dedicated to the memory of Grainger Sanders (1954–1994). Grainger inspired this research and assisted both in collecting data and in shaping my understanding of AADQs. I could never have thanked him enough. Additional thanks to Gregory Clay, Kathryn Semolic, and Keith Walters. An earlier version of this chapter (Barrett 1994) was presented at the Third Berkeley Women and Language Conference. For different but complementary analyses of some of these data, see also Barrett (1995, 1998).

1 The terms *transgenderist* and *transgender(ed) person* are often used as umbrella terms for members of these different groups. They are sometimes seen as alternatives to terms with medical connotations, such as *transvestite* and *transsexual.*
2 Following community norms for polite reference, I use *she* to refer to drag queens when they are in drag.
3 Transcription conventions are as follows:

< >	obscured material
[]	text-external information
{}	segment removed from data to ensure anonymity
italics	emphasis
H	high intonation (see McLemore 1991)
L	low intonation
H*/L*	pitch accent
(.)	short pause forming separation between words
…	longer pause (more periods indicate greater length)
underlining	material under discussion

References

Abrahams, Roger D. (1976). *Talking black.* Rowley, MA: Newbury House.
Ackroyd, Peter (1979). *Dressing up—Transvestism and Drag: The History of an Obsession.* New York: Simon & Schuster.
Bakhtin, Mikhail M. (1981). *The dialogic imagination.* Ed. Michael Holquist. Trans. Caryl Emerson and Michael Holquist. Austin: University of Texas Press.

Bakhtin, Mikhail M. (1984). *Problems of Dostoevsky's Poetics.* Ed. and trans. Caryl Emerson. Minneapolis: University of Minneapolis Press.

Barrett, Rusty (1994). "She is NOT white woman!": The appropriation of white women's language by African American drag queens. In Mary Bucholtz, A. C. Liang, Laurel Sutton, and Caitlin Hines (eds.), *Cultural Performances: Proceedings of the Third Berkeley Women and Language Conference.* Berkeley, CA: Berkeley Women and Language Group, 1–14.

Barrett, Rusty (1995). Supermodels of the world, unite!: Political economy and the language of performance among African American drag queens. In William L. Leap (ed.), *Beyond the Lavender Lexicon: Authenticity, Imagination and Appropriation in Lesbian and Gay Languages.* Newark: Gordon & Breach, 207–26.

Barrett, Rusty (1998). Markedness and style switching in performances by African American drag queens. In Carol Myers-Scotton (ed.), *Linguistic Choices as Social Messages.* New York: Oxford University Press, 139–61.

Bauman, Richard (1977). *Verbal Art as Performance.* Prospect Heights, IL: Waveland Press.

Beame, Thom (1983). Racism from a black perspective. In Michael J. Smith (ed.), *Black men, white men.* San Francisco: Gay Sunshine Press, 57–62.

Berendt, John (1994). *Midnight in the Garden of Good and Evil.* New York: Random House.

Berendt, John (1996). Introduction: Chablis and me. In The Lady Chablis with Theodore Bouloukos, *Hiding my Candy: The Autobiography of the Grand Empress of Savannah.* New York: Pocket Books, 12–18.

Boykin, Keith (1996). *One More River to Cross: Black and gay in America.* New York: Anchor Books.

Briggs, Charles L. (1988). *Competence in Performance: The Creativity of Tradition in Mexicano verbal art.* Philadelphia: University of Pennsylvania Press.

Bucholtz, Mary (1995). From mulatta to mestiza: Passing and the linguistic reshaping of ethnic identity. In Kira Hall and Mary Bucholtz (eds.), *Gender Articulated: Language and the Socially Constructed Self.* New York: Routledge, 351–73.

Bucholtz, Mary (1999) Purchasing power: the gender and class imaginary on the shopping channel, pp. 348–68 in Mary Bucholtz, A. C. Liang and Laurel A. Sutton (eds) *Reinventing Identities.* Oxford: Oxford University Press.

Bucholtz, Mary, and Kira Hall (1995). Introduction: Twenty years after *Language and Woman's Place.* In Kira Hall and Mary Bucholtz (eds.), *Gender Articulated: Language and the Socially Constructed Self.* New York: Routledge, 1–22.

Bullough, Vern L., and Bonnie Bullough (1993). *Cross Dressing, Sex, and Gender.* Philadelphia: University of Pennsylvania Press.

Butler, Judith (1990). *Gender Trouble: Feminism and the Subversion of Identity.* New York: Routledge.

Butler, Judith (1993). *Bodies That Matter: On the Discursive Limits of "Sex."* New York: Routledge.

Davies, Bronwyn, and Rom Harré (1990). Positioning: The discursive production of selves. *Journal for the Theory of Social Behaviour* 20(1):43–63.

Davis, Angela (1983). *Women, Race and Class.* New York: Random House.

DeMarco, Joe (1983). Gay racism. In Michael J. Smith (ed.), *Black Men, White Men.* San Francisco: Gay Sunshine Press, 109–18.

Duberman, Martin (1993). *Stonewall.* New York: Dutton.

Eckert, Penelope, and Sally McConnell-Ginet (1992). Think practically and look locally: Language and gender as community-based practice. *Annual Review of Anthropology* 21:461–90.

Feinberg, Leslie (1996). *Transgender Warriors: Making History from Joan of Arc to RuPaul.* Boston: Beacon Press.

Fleisher, Julian (1996). *The Drag Queens of New York: An Illustrated Field Guide.* New York: Riverhead Books.

Frye, Marilyn (1983). *The Politics of Reality: Essays in Feminist Theory.* Trumansburg, NY: Crossing Press.

Garber, Marjorie (1992). *Vested Interests: Cross-Dressing and Cultural Anxiety.* New York: Routledge.

Gates, Henry Louis, Jr. (1988). *The Signifying Monkey: A Theory of African-American Literary Criticism*. Oxford: Oxford University Press.

Gilbert, Sandra M. (1982). Costumes of the mind: Transvestism as metaphor in modern literature. In Elizabeth Abel (ed.), *Writing and Sexual Difference*. Chicago: University of Chicago Press, 193–220.

Glass, Lillian (1992). *He Says, She Says: Closing the Communication Gap between the Sexes*. New York: Putnam.

Hall, Kira (1995). Lip service on the fantasy lines. In Kira Hall and Mary Bucholtz (eds.), *Gender Articulated: Language and the Socially Constructed Self*. New York: Routledge, 183–216.

Harper, Phillip Brian (1993). Eloquence and epitaph: Black nationalism and the homophobic impulse in responses to the death of Max Robinson. In Michael Warner (ed.), *Fear of a Queer Planet: Queer Politics and Social Theory*. Minneapolis: University of Minnesota Press, 239–63.

Hilbert, Jeffrey (1995). The politics of drag. In Corey K. Creekmur and Alexander Doty (eds.), *Out in Culture: Gay, Lesbian and Queer Essays on Popular Culture*. Durham, NC: Duke University Press, 463–9.

hooks, bell (1989). *Talking Back: Thinking Feminist, Thinking Black*. Boston: South End Press.

Hymes, Dell (1981). *"In vain I tried to tell you": Essays in Native American Ethnopoetics*. Philadelphia: University of Pennsylvania Press.

Kroskrity, Paul V. (1993). *Language, History, and Identity: Ethnolinguistic Studies of the Arizona Tewa*. Tucson: University of Arizona Press.

Labov, William (1972). *Language in the Inner City: Studies in the Black English Vernacular*. Philadelphia: University of Pennsylvania Press.

The Lady Chablis, with Theodore Bouloukos (1996). *Hiding my Candy: The Autobiography of the Grand Empress of Savannah*. New York: Pocket Books.

Lakoff, Robin (1975). *Language and Woman's Place*. New York: Harper & Row.

Le Page, R. B., and Andrée Tabouret-Keller (1985). *Acts of Identity: Creole-Based Approaches to Language and Ethnicity*. Cambridge: Cambridge University Press.

Lurie, Allison (1981). *The Language of Clothes*. New York: Random House.

MacKenzie, Gordene Olga (1994). *Transgender Nation*. Bowling Green, OH: Bowling Green State University Popular Press.

Marcus, Eric (1992). *Making History: The Struggle for Gay and Lesbian Equal Rights 1945–1990. An Oral History*. New York: Harper and Row.

McElhinny, Bonnie S. (1995). Challenging hegemonic masculinities: Female and male police officers handling domestic violence. In Kira Hall and Mary Bucholtz (eds.), *Gender Articulated: Language and the Socially Constructed Self*. New York: Routledge, 217–43.

McLemore, Cynthia Ann (1991). The pragmatic interpretation of English intonation: Sorority speech. Ph.D. diss., University of Texas, Austin.

Mitchell-Kernan, Claudia (1972). Signifying and marking: Two Afro-American speech acts. In John J. Gumperz and Dell Hymes (eds.), *Directions in Sociolinguistics*. New York: Holt, Rinehart and Winston, 161–79.

Monteiro, Kenneth P., and Vincent Fuqua (1994). African American gay youth: One form of manhood. *High School Journal* 77(1–2):20–36.

Morgan, Marcyliena (1991). Indirectness and interpretation in African American women's discourse. *Pragmatics* 1(4):421–35.

Morgan, Marcyliena (1999) "No woman, no cry", claiming African American women's place, pp. 27–45 in Mary Bucholtz, A. C. Liang and Laurel A. Sutton (eds) *Reinventing Identities*. Oxford: Oxford University Press.

Newton, Esther (1979). *Mother Camp: Female Impersonation in America*. Chicago: University of Chicago Press.

Ochs, Elinor (1992). Indexing gender. In Alessandro Duranti and Charles Goodwin (eds.), *Rethinking Context*. Cambridge: Cambridge University Press, 335–58.

Peterson, John L. (1992). Black men and their same-sex desires and behaviors. In Gilbert Herdt (ed.), *Gay Culture in America: Essays from the Field.* Boston: Beacon Press, 87–106.

Preston, Dennis (1992). Talking black and talking white: A study in variety imitation. In Joan H. Hall, Nick Doane, and Dick Ringler (eds.), *Old English and New: Studies in Language and Linguistics in Honor of Frederic G. Cassidy.* New York: Garland, 327–54.

Raymond, Janice (1994). *The Transsexual Empire: The Making of the She-Male.* New York: Teachers College Press. (Original work published 1979).

Raymond, Janice (1996). The politics of transgenderism. In Richard Ekins and Dave King (eds.), *Blending genders: Social Aspects of Cross-Dressing and Sex-Changing.* New York: Routledge, 215–23.

RuPaul (1995). *Lettin It All Hang Out: An Autobiography.* New York: Hyperion.

Showalter, Elaine (1983). Critical cross-dressing: Male feminists and the woman of the year. *Raritan* 3(2):130–49.

Simmons, Ron (1991). Tongues untied: An interview with Marlon Riggs. In Essex Hemphill (ed.), *Brother to Brother: New Writings by Black Gay Men.* Boston: Alyson, 189–99.

Smith, Max C. (1986). By the year 2000. In Joseph Beam (ed.), *In the Life: A Black Gay Anthology.* Boston: Alyson, 224–9.

Smitherman, Geneva (1977). *Talkin and Testifyin: The Language of Black America.* Boston: Houghton Mifflin.

Stevens, Jennifer Anne (1990). *From Masculine to Feminine and All Points in Between: A Practical Guide for Transvestites, Cross-dressers, Transgenderists, Transsexuals, and Others who Choose to Develop a More Feminine Image ... and for the Curious and Concerned.* Cambridge, MA: Different Path Press.

Tinney, James S. (1986). Why a gay Black church? In Joseph Beam (ed.), *In the Life: A Black Gay Anthology.* Boston: Alyson, 70–86.

Trudgill, Peter (1983). *On Dialect: Social and Geographical Perspectives.* New York: New York University Press.

Walters, Keith (1996). Contesting representations of African American language. In Risako Ide, Rebecca Parker, and Yukako Sunaoshi (eds.), *SALSA III: Proceedings of the Third Annual Symposium about Language and Society – Austin (Texas Linguistics Forum* 36). Austin: University of Texas, Department of Linguistics, 137–51.

White, Edmund (1980). The political vocabulary of homosexuality. In Leonard Michaels and Christopher Ricks (eds.), *The State of the Language.* Berkeley: University of California Press, 235–46.

Williamson, Judith (1986). *Consuming Passions: The Dynamics of Popular Culture.* London: Marion Boyars.

Woolard, Kathryn (1995). Gendered peer groups and the bilingual repertoire in Catalonia. In Pamela Silberman and Jonathan Loftin (eds.), *SALSA II: Proceedings of the Second Annual Symposium about Language and Society – Austin (Texas Linguistics Forum* 35). Austin: University of Texas, Department of Linguistics, 200–20.

31

Language and Sexuality in Spanish and English Dating Chats

Marisol del-Teso-Craviotto

Source: Journal of Sociolinguistics 10(4) (2006), pp. 460–80. Reprinted with permission of Wiley-Blackwell.

1 Introduction

[...]

The investigation of language and sexuality is rich indeed, and with a relatively long tradition, although until recently, researchers had mostly explored the connection between language and sexual identity (e.g. Harvey and Shalom 1997; Leap 1996; Livia and Hall 1997). Researchers are calling, however, for an expansion of the object of study and the range of social situations and linguistic phenomena to be investigated (Cameron and Kulick 2003; Campbell-Kibler, Podesva, Roberts and Wong 2002), such as how people construct desire and their sexual selves in interaction (Channel 1997; Tainio 2002) or how people talk about desire (Hall 1995; Hoey 1997; Knowles 1997; Langford 1997; Radway 1991). Studies on how desire emerges in naturally occurring conversations are scarce, and thus the present study of how people flirt, express attraction, or use erotic talk in dating Internet chat rooms can advance our knowledge of the social dimension of desire in general, and the role of language in the expression and construction of desire in particular.

Although it is not my purpose to establish a direct comparison between online and offline situations, I want to underscore that the discursivity of eroticism in dating chats is not unique nor a mere consequence of this particular medium of interaction, where language is the only means to establish and develop a relationship or to express sexual desire. Adult phone lines are a clear example of the importance of language in sexuality (Hall 1995), and even in situations where physical contact is possible, such as Japanese hostess clubs (Allison 1994), people also rely on language for the shaping of desire.

[...]

2   Sexual Desire in Cyberspace

As is the case in linguistic studies of sexuality in general, cybersex has been investigated mostly through indirect methods such as personal interviews, although there are also some analyses of conversations of sexual content that take place in public rooms (Ito 1997; McRae 1997; Menon 1998; Waskul 2003). These studies seem to indicate that Internet users engage in cybersex or participate in erotic conversations for different reasons and experience them in different ways. McRae (1997: 75), for instance, argues that 'while some may well find technologically facilitated eroticism to be a disembodied, alienating and ultimately meaningless experience, others, however, have discovered that it can be as involving, intense and transformative as the best kinds of embodied erotic encounters.' Crucially, these online experiences are constituted in and through language and as the joint accomplishment of the participants in the interactions.

This is the case of the chat rooms that I have chosen for my investigation, which are a variety of Computer-Mediated Communication (CMC) based on the exchange of text messages devoid of visual and aural cues.[1] Internet chats are divided into virtual rooms, and people need to choose a screen name before they log on, which guarantees their anonymity and provides an opportunity for a creative presentation of the self. Dating chats, in particular, are conceived of as a virtual space where people can meet other people who are potentially interested in initiating a sexual, romantic, or friendship relationship, although conversations do not necessarily run along those lines. Once in the room, participants exchange typed messages in real time, although the resulting conversations are unlike face- to-face interactions in their lack of a strict turn structure because of the time lag between the posting of the message and its appearance on the screen, the existence of multiple threads of conversation, and the interruption of people logging on and off. The discursive characteristics of conversations in synchronous CMC such as chats have been widely discussed, establishing parallels and contrasts with face-to-face interactions (Blanco-Rodríguez 2002; Crystal 2001; Herring 1996; Murray 2000; Rintel and Pittam 1997; Wilkins 1991; Wyss 1999). Unfortunately, we still know little about the conversational features of online eroticism and how specifically language creates and maintains sexual or erotic relationships in this context. My research addresses this issue by examining the discursive strategies associated with sexual desire in dating chat interactions, although it does not examine cybersex *per se* (which takes place in private chat rooms), but the flirtatious and erotic conversations taking place in public rooms.

3   Methodology

3.1   Data collection

For the analysis of Internet chats in English, I selected conversations taking place in five chat rooms hosted by America Online (AOL), a US online service: 'Thirties Love', 'Lesbian 30s', 'Gay 30s', 'Catholic Singles', and 'Ethnic Latin'. This selection reflects the overall criteria used in AOL for the organization of staff-created romance rooms at the time of the gathering of the data: gender and sexual orientation, religious affiliation, and ethnic groups. During April 2002, I downloaded half-hour conversations in each of these rooms on five random days around the same time each day. For the analysis of chat interactions in Spanish, I followed the same procedure with mIRC, an interface that operates in the Internet Relay Chat network (IRC). Users have to download the mIRC software into their computer and then use an Internet connection to join one of the hundreds of rooms in mIRC. I selected four rooms from the mIRC channel #Hispanic, namely 'Lesbianas', 'Gays', 'Más_de_30' (*More_than_30*), and 'Amor' (*Love*), and recorded five half-hour conversations during May 2003. Although the channel #Hispanic can be accessed from anywhere in the world and AOL is available in several countries, users of the selected rooms appeared to be geographically located in Spain and USA, respectively.

I adopted a participant-observer role, although not as is traditionally understood in ethnolinguistics or anthropological linguistics, where the researcher is physically on the scene and known to the participants. First, I did not participate in the interactions that were actually recorded so as not to interfere with the data. Instead, I participated in the chat rooms when the conversations were not being recorded to familiarize myself with the environment, language, and dynamics of the interactions under investigation. Second, given the difficulties present in informing all participants about my goals or obtaining their consent.[2] I was not able to reveal my role as researcher or the purpose of my investigation, nor could I ask for permission to reproduce the conversations. This obviously raises some ethical concerns that I had to weigh against the nature of the data and the technical characteristics of the medium. I followed Sharf (1999) in considering the implications that my research would have in terms of privacy, confidentiality, informed consent, and appropriation of others' stories, and in the end, I decided to proceed as described. Furthermore, chat conversations are similar to television or radio interactions in that they happen in a public medium and, therefore, are accessible to anyone. Even if participants could feel that their privacy is somehow invaded, their identity is preserved at all times by the use of screen names. Therefore, I followed the normal practice in the field and downloaded the conversations without making participants aware of my presence or requesting their consent to reproduce the interactions.

3.2   Data analysis

Chat conversations are certainly unusual because they take place in written mode and they are not strictly simultaneous, but just as face-to-face conversations, they are interactive and locally managed (Blanco-Rodríguez 2002). More importantly for the present research, however, is the fact that in this medium, participants do not have the kind of information given away by visual or aural cues in offline conversations. In the analysis of the data, therefore, the researcher, just as the participants themselves, cannot rely on any contextual information except that emerging from the conversation itself. An approach like Conversation Analysis (CA), which has a long tradition of analyzing talk-in-interaction (e.g. Atkinson and Heritage 1984; Sacks, Schegloff and Jefferson 1978; Schegloff 1982, 1992, 1993, 2001) can be most useful in understanding how desire is constituted in and through talk in chat rooms. The general approach of CA to the analysis of talk-in-interaction rests upon the discourse analytic idea that social and psychological phenomena are partly constituted in and through discourse, whether written or spoken. The investigation of which actions are accomplished in talk does not rely on external information about the speakers' backgrounds or their relationships. Such an independence from external information is possible because conversation analysts examine the orientations, meanings, and interpretations that are manifestly privileged by the participants themselves as they unfold in the interaction, without relying on external evidence. Since the purpose of the investigation is to underscore the social and interactional nature of sexual desire, I follow CA procedures and examine the particular linguistic expressions of eroticism that are privileged by the participants in the chat rooms, regardless of why or for what purpose they were participating in the conversations.

What this participant-oriented approach has meant for the study of language, gender, and sexuality, however, is the almost exclusive reliance on explicit (mostly lexical) mentions of gender or sexuality (Edwards 1998; Hopper and LeBaron 1998). Such analyses are well within the CA preference for participant orientation that I have just described, but limiting the study of gender and sexuality in talk to explicit references seems excessively restricting for researchers interested in the construction of the social world, as suggested by a rich tradition of language, gender, and sexuality studies that have shown that the linguistic construction of gender and other social identities goes well beyond the use of certain lexical items (see, for instance, Bergvall, Bing and Freed 1996; Bucholtz, Liang and Sutton 1999; Campbell-Kibler et al. 2002; Eckert and McConnell-Ginet 2003). In the analysis of the dating chat rooms, therefore, I have followed a growing group of conversation analysts who argue for an integration of the knowledge that analysts have as members of society in making claims about the relevance of gender and sexuality in an interaction (Kitzinger 2002; Stokoe and Smithson 2001, 2002), and use in the analysis and discussion of the data the knowledge of chat rooms that I obtained through my participant observations, and my own knowledge of the societies that inform and sustain the specific forms of sexual desire that we find in chat rooms. Drawing from this knowledge does not constitute an act of researcher's imperialism, as Schegloff (1997) would argue, any more than would working with the battery of theoretical and methodological tools that conversation analysts bring into their research (Billig 1999a, 1999b). No analysis, not even in the hard sciences, is completely objective. What we should aim for, and what I have personally adopted for my own research, is a conscious reflexivity about one's position as a researcher, and an analysis that is firmly grounded in linguistic and social theories.

4 The Shame and Joy of Romance and Eroticism on the Net

People participate in chats and other recreational varieties of CMC for several reasons, but in most cases, there is a high level of personal satisfaction derived from the social contact with other participants. Despite occasional flaming (an Internet term for verbal aggressive behavior), the conversations in dating chats that I observed proceeded in a relaxed and overall fun atmosphere. Some of the social activities taking place online, however, are often regarded as a substitute for the 'real' social life, the one that takes place without an intervening computer. Interpersonal communication research seems to support this popular belief, suggesting that CMC is less likely to foster effective relationships than face-to-face situations would, although a growing body of literature suggests that this may not be necessarily the case (Walther, Loh and Granka 2005). The fact remains that even if people enjoy chatting or playing on the Internet, their pleasure is compromised by the problematic social reputation of CMC. This situation is not unlike that of other popular culture products such as women's magazines (Hermes 1995), romance novels (Radway 1991), or soap operas (Baym 1995), where people often feel the need to legitimize and justify their consumption and enjoyment of these products. Given the purpose of dating chat rooms, conversations are often riveted by erotic innuendoes, flirty remarks, or sexually-explicit jokes, which adds an additional social stigma to the participation in these cyberspaces, namely, the negative connotations associated with actively looking for sex, love, and romance – as opposed to the 'natural' way, which is letting destiny or Cupid do the work for you. Consequently, participants find pleasure in getting involved in the dynamics of Internet flirting, but at the same time they must show to other participants that they are not losers, people without social skills, or psychopaths. Occasional conversations, such as Example 1, show that participants are potential victims of flaming because of the conflict inherent in their practice.[3] While Ladynightstar33 participates in the relaxed and joyful spirit of dating chat rooms with her flirty compliment, JeffTheGentleman voices in a very 'ungently' manner the prejudices of those who consider Internet social relationships as the last resource for those who cannot have 'real' lovers or a 'real' life (glosses are given in italics throughout examples):

Example 1: Thirties Love

LADYNIGHTSTAR33:	I think you are very sexy
JEFFTHEGENTLEMAN:	TY LADY
	thank you, Lady
JEFFTHEGENTLEMAN:	IM TOLD THAT LIKE 50 TIMES A DAY
JEFFTHEGENTLEMAN:	GETS OLD
JEFFTHEGENTLEMAN:	ESPECIALLY FROM A BUNCH OF KEY BOARD LOVERS
JEFFTHEGENTLEMAN:	LOL
	laughing out loud
JEFFTHEGENTLEMAN:	BECAUSE IN REAL LIFE
JEFFTHEGENTLEMAN:	WELL, THEY HAVE NO REAL LIFE, LMAO
	well, they have no real life, laughing my ass off

Participants in dating chat rooms also have to find a solution to the potential risks inherent in public manifestations of sexual desire. Talking about penises, suggesting sexual attraction, or presenting an eroticized self can be socially sanctionable in most situations that involve interaction among strangers or in a public situation, whether online or offline. Moreover, when sexual desire is embedded in the construction of personal relationships, people are placed in a potentially vulnerable position, since they can be rejected, made fun of, or simply ignored.

5   The Play Frame

The need for a critical stance while maintaining involvement, and the risks of engaging in sexual conversations in a public medium are two sources of tension that influence how people experience and give meaning to the act of chatting in dating rooms, and more importantly, they partly determine how desire is constructed and understood. In AOL and mIRC dating chat rooms, this tension is partly managed interactionally by drawing on the notion of play – materialized in several linguistic strategies – to conceptualize and justify their participation in dating chat rooms and to frame the expression of desire. By defining (implicitly or explicitly) their interactions as play, participants seem to establish a safe distance between their real (critical) selves and their virtual (enjoying) selves, although this separation is never absolute. Framing interactions as a game also creates a safety net for the participants, since breaches of social norms and expectations regarding the appropriateness of sexuality in public situations can be excused because all is done in jest. At the same time, engaging in conversational games enhances the feeling of intimacy and complicity among the participants in the chat room, building solidarity and creating (the illusion of) friendship and closeness, which in turn, reduces the public dimension of chat rooms.

The notion of play is not the only concept that participants orient to in their conversations in dating chat rooms, but it is the most salient framework of interpretation for most of the interactions where desire is constructed. This interpretive framework is similar to the frames of experience that Danet, Ruedenberg-Wright and Rosenbaum-Tamari (1997) identified in their analysis of the conversations in an IRC channel. [...]

I propose a definition of frames that includes three fundamental aspects. First, a frame is an ideological construct made up of culturally shared ideas that people invoke in their interactions to legitimize and make sense of the activity they are accomplishing. This is not simply saying that participants must share and draw on a common set of ideas to enable communication. After all, in every interaction there must be a common ground for speakers to be able to understand each other, such as a common language, common conversational rules, common spatial and temporal coordinates, or common mechanisms of inference. Frames refer to more specific sets of ideas that participants use to give meaning to the particular social practice in which they are participating. For instance, let us imagine two friends who meet on the street, both with children. In the course of the conversation, they may show interest in each other's children, comment on the difficulties of being parents, or give advice on parenting. This does not mean, however, that these two friends are interpreting their encounter and conversation under the frame of parenthood. If they were asked to explain why they are having such an interaction, they would probably refer to their common history, their friendship, or the social norms that regulate which topics are appropriate for a casual chat, all of which could function as frames for the situation. Likewise, people tend to invoke the idea of play and fun to explain and make sense of their participation in the rooms; play functions, therefore, as a frame for dating chat interactions.

Second, frames are not the result of a conscious rationalization of the people involved in any given activity. Frames (or in Hermes's 1995 terminology, repertoires) are a researcher's reconstruction: they are analytical interpretations of what a particular group of people is doing to make sense of their practices. Therefore, upon claiming that participants in dating chats invoke the play frame in their interactions, I am not implying that they are making explicit statements in this regard, although this is always a possibility. People are not fully aware of the frames they invoke because frames have an emergent nature. They are not there and ready for use; rather, they emerge from discourse contexts based on what is available and what is needed. There is no guarantee, therefore, that the frames will survive over time or will be shared among wider communities.

Third, although frames are abstract concepts, they are instantiated in specific stylistic and linguistic strategies that repeatedly appear in the conversations. It is the researcher's task to identify those strategies and interpret them by paying attention to the details of the conversation and to the participants' own orientation. As in any other kind of discourse analysis, we should not imply that there is a simple, one-to-one correspondence between the linguistic strategies and the frames. A particular strategy may be related to more than one frame, and a frame may be expressed by more than one strategy. In what follows, I describe the linguistic features that are associated with the notion of play, focusing on how these features contribute to expressing sexual desire.

5.1   Laughter

In the dating chats under study, laughter is by far the most common face-saving strategy used by participants when engaging in flirty conversations. Laughter is expressed through onomatopoeia ('ja', 'he'), with emoticons (graphic representations of facial expressions, such as:-) or x-D), or with acronyms (e.g. 'lol' *laughing out loud*, or 'lmao' *laughing my ass off*). These laughs can be used in isolation (Example 2) or directed at somebody else, which also reproduces the gaze in face-to-face encounters (Example 3):

Example 2: Lesbianas
<noe_c>   antes estabas desnuda?
          you were naked before?

<noe_c>   deberias habermelo dicho antes
          you should have told me before

<noe_c>   xDD
          big laugh

Example 3: Thirties Love
Sweetjucee: IT'S ABOUT TIME THE MEN CAME IN THE ROOM

SoftNSweetLips: lol Sweet
                  laughing out loud, Sweet

The force of the idea of play as an ideological frame invoked in dating chats is evident in the particular ways that participants use laughter, illustrated in the previous examples. In Example 2, noe_c uses laughter to frame her flirty complaint as humor and thus save a potentially face-threatening situation, and in Example 3, laughter is a response to the sexual connotations of Sweetjucee's comment. Sweetjucee, however, did not mark her message as humorous (Is she complaining? Is she just stating a fact? Is she joking?). Despite the ambiguity of Sweetjucee's comment, SoftNSweetLips interprets the message as playful and responds with laughter. This response can only be understood if both participants use the notion of play to give meaning to their participation in general and this conversation in particular.

5.2   Humorous speech

Another very salient way of enhancing the feeling of playfulness is by reproducing a very casual pronunciation in the typed messages. This is especially noticeable in the case of Spanish IRC channels, where participants reproduce a pronunciation that in oral speech is associated with familiarity, and, importantly, also with being funny or silly. The following conversation from the mIRC room 'Amor' illustrates the most typical features of this humorous pronunciation, which includes graphemic representations: of colloquial phonetic processes such as the deletion of intervocalic [d] in participles ('preguntao' instead of 'preguntado'); of phonetic segments stereotypically associated with low class speech ('tos' instead of 'todos'); of phonetic features of the Andalusian Spanish dialect ('argo' instead of 'algo', or 'dises' [dises] instead of 'dices' [diθes]); and of childish pronunciation of words ('te vi a pone' instead of 'te voy a poner').[4]

Example 4: Amor

<XMORENOX>   M-a-r-a que me has preguntaoooooooooo
                M-a-r-a what did you say?

...

<M-A-R-A>   xmorenox ke si te conozco?!? xD
                xmorenox just seeing if i knew ya! lol

...

<XMORENOX>   por foto solo
                only by my pic

...

<M-A-R-A>   XMorenoX y ke foto!! pffffffffffffffff
                XMoreno X oh, btw nice pic, whoa
<XMORENOX>   o me conoces de argo y no me lo disessssssssssss
                what? u know me from somethin else youre not sayin?

...

<M-A-R-A>   XMorenoX te vi a pone en la mesita de nose jajajajajaja
                XMorenoX im gonna put your pic by my bed, hahahahaha

...

<M-A-R-A>   xmorenox no hijo no ke a gente asiii ojala conociera ms:DDDD
                xmorenox no man, i wish i know more people like you! lol

...

<XMORENOX>   lo diras por lo simpatico que zoy no???????
                you're telling me im the best, huh???????

...

<M-A-R-A>   xmorenox siii por eso siii xDDDDDDDDD
                xmorenox riiiiight, totally haha

...

<XMORENOX>   M-a-r-a a ver si me vas a decir que soy un capullo xDDDDDDD
                DDDDDDDDDDDDDDD
                M-a-r-a you think im a dick or somethin?

...

<M-A-R-A>   xmorenox no te voy a decir ke lo ERES sino que lo TIENES como tos los
                tiOs xDDDDDDD
                *xmorenox im not saying that you ARE one just that ya GOT one, like all
                guys lol*

Colloquial, low class, and childish speech styles, and Mock Andalusian[5] are often used by comedians or in comic acting roles, and in everyday situations, the features just mentioned are also used when someone wants to be funny. Because the speech styles that participants reproduce are often associated with comedy, they enhance the feeling of enjoyment and play. The feeling of parody of this humorous pronunciation is thus a useful resource for participants to manage the tension inherent in the act of chatting in dating rooms, since they can defend themselves in case sexuality or flirting is deemed inappropriate.

More important, perhaps, is the fact that the type of pronunciation reproduced in these chats is not normally used in formal situations or among strangers, and they are often a marker of familiarity and friendship among the interactants, which seems to indi-cate that Internet chatting has the same status as a conversation among friends, despite the fact that most of the participants have never met before either online or offline. Support for this conclusion is provided by the fact that those participants that have already established an online relationship are much more likely to use these features with each other than with newcomers. In 'Más_de_30', for instance, several participants make reference to previous encounters with other users in the same room. From the very beginning, these participants use a humorous pronunciation with each other, but they tend to be more formal with people they have not met before, at least initially. Therefore, just as in face-to-face situations, language signals the type of relationship among the interactants, which in this case, is one of familiarity. Although the speech styles that participants reproduce in the Spanish IRC channels do not only appear in messages with erotic innuendos or sexual comments, it is often the case that when participants in mIRC bring up any aspect of sexuality or desire, they do so using one or more of the features described above. Part of the reason is that this familiar and humorous pronunciation can create the illusion of an intimacy that is usually associated with sexual desire, especially in the case of the childish pronunciation, which can also evoke erotic images of innocence.[6] AOL participants also modify the standard spelling of words, but this strategy does not create the same humorous effect as it does in the Spanish mIRC. Although there are numerous examples of very creative ways of spelling words or phrases (e.g. 'brb' instead of 'be right back' or '18er' instead of 'later'), these orthographic variations are not obviously related to the expression of sexuality.

5.3   Appropriation

In humorous appropriations, participants take one element from a previous message and give it a different meaning than was intended, humor being the product of the contrast between the original and the new interpretation of a message. This type of humor is interactional because the sender of the original message does not usually coincide with the participant that produces the appropriation, although people can 'appropriate' their own previous contribution for purposes of humor. Appropriation can target the content or the form of a word or phrase, taking advantage of its ambiguity or generality, or giving it an interpretation that was probably not anticipated or intended in the original message, as illustrated below. Humor in Example 5 is derived from changing the verb of XMorenoX's turn, going from 'ser un capullo' (*to be a dick*) to 'tener un capullo' (*to have a dick*). In Example 6, Dustyroad57 takes the screen name of another participant ('Godzfreekyest') and modifies it to give it a sexual meaning by changing adjectives but maintaining the structure of the screen name ('Godzhorniest').

Example 5: Amor
<XMORENOX>   a ver si me vas a decir que soy un capullo xDDDDDDD
                        M-a-r-a you think im a dick or somethin?

<M-A-R-A>   no te voy a decir ke lo ERES sino que lo TIENES como tos los tios xDDD
                        xmorenox im not saying that you ARE one just that ya GOT one, like all guys
                        lol

Example 6: Ethnic Latin
GODZFREEKYEST: 23-FEMALE-JERSEY

...

DUSTYROAD 57:   <~~Godzhorniest:

Appropriation is often used in teases. Teases are mocking but playful jibes against someone. They often foreground some weakness or put another (unwilling) participant on the spot. Teases typically use the appropriation strategy: a participant makes a mocking comment about another participant's utterance, focusing on a meaning that was clearly not intended in the original utterance. In the following example, one of the participants chooses an 'unfortunate' term to indicate that she is about to log out of the room. Other participants are quick to pick up on this and tease SportsSaints as if she was actually describing a sexual feeling:

Example 7: Catholic Singles

SPORTSSAINTS:	Baby you still here? [talking to boo]
...	
SPORTSSAINTS:	Cause I'm getting off
...	
GODPOET 88:	lol
	laughing out loud
BOGEY GOLF GIRL:	WITH YOUR FINGERS OR YOUR TOY?
...	
SULTRY MAE WEST:	getting off?????
...	
BOGEY GOLF GIRL:	SCREAM OUR NAME

Humorous appropriation accomplishes two important functions. First, the playful nature of appropriation helps create a more daring attitude regarding sexual desire. Second, since appropriation is a joint accomplishment, it creates rapport and complicity among the participants, and contributes to the overall feeling of play and enjoyment. Teases, in particular, have been proposed as an index of intimacy or acquaintance, the assumption being that teasing is mostly done between friends or intimates (Drew 1987). The use of teasing in chats, where participants do not usually know each other, suggests that under certain circumstances, teasing can create intimacy or the illusion of intimacy, and foster feelings of solidarity and closeness. In other words, in chat rooms, friendship is not a pre-requisite for teasing, but teasing creates friendship and thus helps reduce the risks inherent in interacting in a public medium.

5.4   Alter personae

In many cases, participants in chats choose to interact through the *alter egos* created by the screen names. It is not Josh from Ithaca and Pam from Natchitoches that interact, but 'MrReb' and 'DreamyAngel' who engage in situations where they move around, sit next to each other, take road trips, or serve a beer. In dating chats, we can observe an ideological process similar to the transgressions and identity changes that characterize carnival and other play genres such as charades (Danet 1998). Participants use their screen names as masks and enter a space that is marked as different from everyday reality, hence acquiring a certain degree of unaccountability. Through their *alter personae*, participants can go beyond the verbal expression of sexuality and engage in erotic or flirty actions, as illustrated in Examples 8 and 9:

Example 8: Catholic Singles[7]

DARLA8881:	RACER, WHEN ARE YOU GONNA COME GET ME AND RUN AWAY WITH ME?
RACERXGUNDAM:	lol
	laughing out loud

DARLA8881:	NOTE: I KNOW RACER HS A GIRLIE, I ASK THIS EVERYDAY, IT IS JUST A JOKE *Note: I know Racer has a girlfriend, I ask this everyday, it is just a joke*
GODPOET88:	LOL Julie .... he does but I don't *Laughing out loud. Julie. .... he does, but I don't*
DARLA8881:	C'MERE POEY BABY *Come here, Godpoet88, baby*
GODPOET88:	walking over to Julie
SULTRY MAE WEST:	<<<<<<<<watchin Darla move
ECCE X:	DARLA MOVES?
DARLA8881:	LOL POEY, SWEETY YOU WOULDN'T LOOK AT ME ONCE MUCH LESS TWICE
GODPOET88:	yes I would because I have Julie

Example 9: Lesbian 30s[8]

SPECIALK1975:	LAURA, I AM GONNA COME AND WHOOP YOUR ASS
...	
WED1963:	:(*sad face*
...	
ZUUKIE:	dont worry Laura i kiss it and make it all better
...	
WED1963:	lol. ... ty. ... z *laughing out loud ... thank you...Zuukie*
...	
WED1963:	u so sweet to me
...	
WED1963:	hurts on both sides......z

The fact that *alter personae*, which enhance the feeling of playfulness and suspension of reality, are often the main actors of desire in these chat rooms (in AOL to a much larger extent than in mIRC) is not a coincidence. Crucially, the carnivalesque character of many of the interactions in these chat rooms alternates with glimpses of the real people behind the screen and their real lives. As illustrated in the last two examples, there is a constant movement back and forth between the real and the virtual worlds; both conversations started as comments about the participants in relation to their offline selves, but the conversations turned into interactions between their *alter personae*. This alternation of virtual and material realities, although an end in itself, is also one of the participants' strategies to create a distance that saves them from accusations of being social outcasts while at the same time showing a high involvement in the conversations.

6   Discussion

As we have seen, conversations very often present a tinge of eroticism: there are sexualized presentations of the self, flirtatious teasing and implied sexual meanings, or references to sexual body parts such as penises. Expressing erotic feelings, making passes at someone, or presenting a sexualized identity are socially risky, because people can lose face easily in such situations, both online and offline. The social risk is even greater when interacting with strangers or in a public medium, which is the case of dating chat rooms. I would argue that the play frame is fundamental in reducing chat participants' vulnerability when expressing sexual desire. It is no coincidence that most instances of eroticism are expressed through the linguistic strategies that we have seen: smiling emoticons are often postposed to sexually bold statements; flirtation and erotic actions are usually performed through *alter personae* in AOL chats; in mIRC, a humorous pronunciation rarely fails to accompany spicy comments; appropriation often targets implied sexual meanings. In all these instances, participants are not only creating a humorous atmosphere, but they are also engaging in games – sometimes playing with words, sometimes playing with their online *personae* – and in doing so they are expressing their sexual desire under the play frame, which allows them to keep a safe disengagement from the socially risky actions and attitudes they are displaying in the chat room. In other words, although participants in dating chats flirt with and express attraction to other participants, they do so in a playful way so that in the end they can always fall back on the 'I was just kidding' strategy. Yet the play frame is not only a face-saving strategy, it has an instrumental function. As mentioned, chat participation fulfills important social needs and it is a pleasant and satisfying activity. By engaging in linguistic games, people are able to derive their enjoyment not from physical contact with other people, but from the unrealized or unrealizable promise of it. Sexual desire is thus present in the conversations not as a physical pleasure but as an interactional pleasure under the play frame.

The type of eroticism and sexuality that surfaces in dating chat rooms seems to support the idea that CMC cannot simply be equated or contrasted with offline practices, but has to be understood in its own terms. At the same time, however, CMC is a tool for interpersonal communication just like our voice, telephone, or letters, and therefore it is embedded in and informed by the same social structures and ideologies as are other forms of human communication. From a sociolinguistic point of view, we cannot examine chat conversations as isolated or unique practices. For some users, chats are instrumental because they allow them to meet people for other types of encounter beyond the chat room, but for some others, chatting is a goal in itself. Likewise, many people go to parties, bars, and other social spaces with the purpose of meeting new people, but in other instances they also look forward to dancing, having fun, or having a drink with friends. Conversations with new acquaintances may be a simple chit-chat, but may also involve flirting, have some erotic purpose, or be motivated by the hope of finding romance. Dating Internet chat rooms are thus not unique in their purpose or in the types of interactions that take place in them.

Finally, the importance of language in dating Internet chats and other social practices such as adult phone lines, Japanese hostess clubs, or even more venerable traditions such as Courtly Love shows that 'we do not engage in sexual activity only out of the desire for a particular physiological object, but for a social object. The notion of a 'purely physical attraction' is a mystification – a dehistoricized version of what is in fact an eminently social course of learning' (Eckert 2002: 109). Eroticism, desire, and pleasure are ingrained in the construction of our social selves, and go beyond issues of sexual identity and sexual activities. As linguistic creations, they also go beyond physicality understood in strictly biological terms. What these social practices compel us to do, therefore, is to rethink our definition of sexual desire to include a wider variety of situations and phenomena.

7   Conclusion

People seem to enjoy flirting, insinuating, courting, eroticizing talk, and pushing the social limits of appropriate behavior for their own sakes, and in many cases, relationships are initiated, developed, and terminated within the public virtual space. It is very possible that participants in dating chat rooms, just as business men in Japanese hostess clubs, are drawn to the opportunity to play with the idea of eroticism without necessarily having to act upon it. We cannot label as exceptional the flirtatious and erotic talk that can be observed in dating chats, and this is why I believe that understanding the discursive processes of dating chat rooms can provide useful insights into the creation of desire that takes place in more intimate and private situations that do not lend themselves easily for observation. I am not arguing, of course, that we can simply assume that the social construction of desire is similar in dating chats to that in other environments, or that we can simply transfer what we learn about dating chat rooms to other contexts. Studies like this one, however, can help us to formulate hypotheses about the discursive nature of desire in other situations. With the knowledge of the specific linguistic strategies that can be used in creating eroticism, we are in a better position to undertake the linguistic study of desire in other settings.

The examination of Internet chats affiliated with two different countries/cultures and two different languages suggests that there are important similarities as well as differences in terms of what specific resources participants use in order to flirt with one another. This point deserves further investigation if we aim to understand to what extent the technology of the medium facilitates transnational and transcultural approaches to communication, and whether participants bring to CMC their own baggage of expectations and culturally learned patterns of interaction to construct sexual desire.

Notes

I would like to thank Margarita Suñer, Hongyin Tao, and very specially, Sally McConnell-Ginet for their help in the elaboration of my dissertation, upon which this article is based.

1　There are Internet chats that incorporate sound and image. In this study, however, I concentrate on text-based chat rooms in which the written word is the primary means of communication. For more information on the structure of chat rooms, see for instance: Blanco-Rodríguez (2002); Crystal (2001); Noblia (2000); Werry (1996).
2　In chats there is a constant variation in membership: although some participants remain in the room for long periods of time, many others log in only for a few minutes or even seconds.
3　I have not altered the spelling or order of the messages in the examples, but I have deleted some of the participants' messages and substituted dotted lines for them when they are part of parallel conversations and thus not relevant for the purposes of the discussion.
4　The translation of this conversation is not literal but tries to capture the flirty and humorous key, and the informal written conventions of the original Spanish messages. Thanks to Christine Norgard for her help with the translation.
5　I follow Hill's (1998) use of 'Mock Spanish', and define Mock Andalusian as the appropriation of presumed linguistic features of the Andalusian dialect by speakers of other Peninsular Spanish dialects for the purposes of creating humor, thus covertly derogating the language and culture of Andalusians. For other strategic uses of Andalusian see Pujolar i Cos (1997, 2000).
6　I want to thank an anonymous reviewer for this sexual reading of the childish pronunciation.
7　Julie (a pseudonym) is Darla8881's offline name.
8　Laura (a pseudonym) is Wed1963's offline name.

References

Allison, Anne. 1994. *Nightwork: Sexuality, Pleasure, and Corporate Masculinity in a Tokyo Hostess Club*. Chicago: University of Chicago Press.

Atkinson, J. Maxwell and John Heritage (eds.). 1984. *Structures of Social Action: Studies in Conversation Analysis.* Cambridge: Cambridge University Press.

Baym, Nancy K. 1995. The performance of humor in computer-mediated communication. *Journal of Computer-Mediated Communication* 2. www.ascusc.org/jcmc/vol1/issue2/baym.html Accessed October 2003.

Bergvall, Victoria, Janet Bing and Alice Freed (eds.). 1996. *Rethinking Language and Gender Research: Theory and Method.* London: Longman.

Billig, Michael. 1999a. Whose terms, whose ordinariness? Rhetoric and ideology in Conversation Analysis. *Discourse and Society* 10: 543–58.

Billig, Michael. 1999b. Conversation Analysis and the claims of naivety. *Discourse and Society* 10: 572–6.

Blanco-Rodríguez, María-José. 2002. El chat: La conversación escrita. *Estudios de Lingüística* 16: 43–87.

Bucholtz, Mary, A. C. Liang and Laurel A. Sutton. 1999. *Reinventing Identities: The Gendered Self in Discourse.* Oxford: Oxford University Press.

Cameron, Deborah and Don Kulick. 2003. *Language and Sexuality.* Cambridge: Cambridge University Press.

Campbell-Kibler, Kathryn, Robert J. Podesva, Sarah J. Roberts and Andrew Wong. 2002. *Language and Sexuality: Contesting Meaning in Theory and Practice.* Stanford, CA: CSLI Publications.

Channel, Joanna. 1997. 'I just called to say I love you': Love and desire on the telephone. In Keith Harvey and Celia Shalom (eds.) *Language and Desire: Encoding Sex, Romance and Intimacy.* New York: Routledge. 143–69.

Crystal. David. 2001. *Language and the Internet.* Cambridge: Cambridge University Press.

Danet, Brenda. 1998. Text as mask: Gender, play, and performance on the Internet. In Steve G. Jones (ed.) *Cybersociety 2.0: Revisiting Computer-Mediated Communication and Community.* Thousand Oaks, CA: Sage. 129–58.

Drew, Paul. 1987. Po-faced receipts of teases. *Linguistics* 25: 219–53.

Eckert, Penelope. 2002. Demystifying sexuality and desire. In Kathryn Campbell-Kibler, Robert J. Podesva, Sarah J. Roberts and Andrew Wong (eds.) *Language and Sexuality: Contesting Meaning in Theory and Practice.* Stanford, California: CSLI Publications. 99–110.

Eckert, Penelope and Sally McConnell-Ginet. 2003. *Language and Gender.* Cambridge: Cambridge University Press.

Edwards, Derek. 1998. The relevant thing about her: Social identity categories in use. In Charles Antaki and Sue Widdicombe (eds.) *Identities in Talk.* London: Sage. 15–33.

Hall, Kira. 1995. Lip service on the fantasy lines. In Kira Hall and Mary Bucholtz (eds.) *Gender Articulated: Language and the Socially Constructed Self.* New York: Routledge. 183–216.

Harvey, Keith and Celia Shalom (eds.). 1997. *Language and Desire: Encoding Sex, Romance and Intimacy.* New York: Routledge.

Hermes, Joke. 1995. *Reading Women's Magazines.* Cambridge: Polity Press.

Herring, Susan (ed.). 1996. *Computer-Mediated Communication: Linguistic, Social and Cross-Cultural Perspectives.* Philadelphia, PA: John Benjamins.

Hill, Jane. 1998. Language, race, and white public space. *American Anthropologist* 100: 680–689.

Hoey, Michael. 1997. The organisation of narratives of desire: A study of first-person erotic fantasies. In Keith Harvey and Celia Shalom (eds.) *Language and Desire: Encoding Sex, Romance and Intimacy.* New York: Routledge. 85–105.

Hopper, Robert and Curtis LeBaron. 1998. How gender creeps into talk. *Research on Language and Social Interaction* 31: 59–74.

Ito, Mizuko. 1997. Virtually embodied: The reality of fantasy in a Multi-User Dungeon. In David Porter (ed.) *Internet Culture.* New York: Routledge. 87–109.

Kitzinger, Celia. 2002. Doing feminist conversation analysis. In Paul McIlvenny (ed.) *Talking Gender and Sexuality.* Amsterdam and Philadelphia, PA: John Benjamins. 49–78.

Knowles, Murray. 1997. 'You would if you loved me': Language and desire in the teen novel. In Keith Harvey and Celia Shalom (eds.) *Language and Desire: Encoding Sex, Romance and Intimacy*. New York: Routledge. 123–40.

Langford. Wendy. 1997. 'Bunnikins, I love you snugly in your warren': Voices from subterranean cultures of love. In Keith Harvey and Celia Shalom (eds.) *Language and Desire: Encoding Sex, Romance and Intimacy*. New York: Routledge. 170–85.

Leap, William L. 1996. *Word's Out: Gay Men's English*. Minneapolis, MN: University of Minnesota Press.

Livia, Anna and Kira Hall. 1997. *Queerly Phrased: Language, Gender and Sexuality*. Oxford: Oxford University Press.

McRae, Shannon. 1997. Flesh made word: Sex, text and the virtual body. In David Porter (ed.) *Internet Culture*. New York: Routledge. 73–86.

Menon, Goutham M. 1998. Gender encounters in a virtual community: Identity formation and acceptance. *Computers in Human Services* 15: 55–69.

Murray, Denise E. 2000. Protean communication: The language of computer-mediated communication. *TESOL Quarterly* 34: 397–421.

Noblia, María Valentina. 2000. Conversación y comunidad: Las Chats en la comunidad virtual. *Discurso y Sociedad* 2: 77–99.

Pujolar i Cos. Joan. 1997. Masculinities in a multilingual setting. In Ulrike Hanna Meinhof and Sally Johnson (eds.) *Language and Masculinity*. Cambridge, MA: Blackwell. 86–106.

Pujolar i Cos, Joan. 2000. *Gender, Heteroglossia and Power: A Sociolinguistic Study of Youth Culture*. Berlin: Walter De Gruyter.

Radway, Janice. 1991. *Reading the Romance: Women, Patriarchy and Popular Literature*. Chapel Hill, NC: University of North Carolina Press.

Rintel. E. Sean and Jeffery Pittam. 1997. Strangers in a strange land: Interaction management on Internet Relay Chat. *Human Communication Research* 23:507–34.

Sacks, Harvey, Emanuel A. Schegloff and Gail Jefferson. 1978. A simplest systematics for the organization of turn-taking for conversation. In Jim Schenkein (ed.) *Studies in the Organization of Conversational Interaction*. New York: Academic Press. 7–55.

Schegloff, Emanuel A. 1982. Discourse as an interactional achievement: Some uses of 'uh huh' and other things that come between sentences. In Deborah Tannen (ed.) *Analysing Discourse: Text and Talk*. Washington, DC: Georgetown University Press. 71–93.

Schegloff, Emanuel A. 1992. In another context. In Charles Goodwin and Alessandro Duranti (eds.) *Rethinking Context: Language as an Interactive Phenomenon*. Cambridge: Cambridge University Press. 191–227.

Schegloff, Emanuel A. 1993. Reflections on quantification in the study of conversation. *Research on Language and Social Interaction* 26: 99–128.

Schegloff, Emanuel A. 1997. Whose text, whose context? *Discourse and Society* 8: 165–87.

Schegloff, Emanuel A. 2001. Getting serious: Joke → serious 'no'. *Journal of Pragmatics* 33: 1947–55.

Sharf. Barbara. 1999. Beyond netiquette: The ethics of doing naturalistic discourse research on the Internet. In Steve G. Jones (ed.) *Doing Internet Research: Critical Issues and Methods for Examining the Net*. Thousand Oaks, CA: Sage. 243–56.

Stokoe, Elizabeth and Janet Smithson. 2001. Making gender relevant: Conversation Analysis and gender categories in interaction. *Discourse and Society* 12: 217–44.

Stokoe, Elizabeth and Janet Smithson. 2002. Gender and sexuality in talk-in-interaction: Considering conversation analytic perspectives. In Paul McIlvenny (ed.) *Talking Gender and Sexuality*. Amsterdam and Philadelphia, PA: John Benjamins. 79–110.

Tainio, Lisa. 2002. Negotiating gender identities and sexual agency in elderly couples' talk. In Paul McIlvenny (ed.) *Talking Gender and Sexuality*. Amsterdam and Philadelphia, PA: John Benjamins. 207–36.

Walther, Joseph B., Tracy Loh and Laura Granka. 2005. Let me count the ways: The interchange of verbal and nonverbal cues in computer-mediated and face-to-face affinity. *Journal of Language and Social Psychology* 24: 36–65.

Waskul, Dennis D. 2003. *Self-Games and Body-Play: Personhood in Online Chat and Cybersex.* New York: Peter Lang.

Werry, Christopher C. 1996. Linguistic and interactional features of Internet Relay Chat. In Susan Herring (ed.) *Computer-Mediated Communication: Linguistic, Social and Cross-Cultural Perspectives.* Philadelphia, PA: John Benjamins. 47–63.

Wilkins, Harriete. 1991. Computer talk: Long-distance conversations by computer. *Written Communication* 8: 56–78.

Wyss, Eva Lia. 1999. Iconicity in the digital world: An opportunity to create a personal image? In Max Nänny and Olga Fischer (eds.) *Form, Miming, Meaning. Iconicity in Language and Literature.* Amsterdam and Philadelphia, PA: John Benjamins. 285–306.

Part VII

Theoretical Debates (1): Gender or Power?

Each of the next three sections takes as its focus a key theoretical debate in the language and gender field. The first looks at the debate over whether it is power rather than gender which determines how people speak. The second examines two competing theoretical frameworks, known as the difference approach and the dominance approach. The third looks at the debate over whether or not analysts need to provide evidence to justify any claim that gender is relevant in a particular stretch of talk. The first two of these debates began in the 1970s and 1980s; the third has come to prominence more recently.

The present section will focus on the debate which questions whether the linguistic features said to be typical of women's speech are actually associated with lack of power. The paper which first raised this question – William O'Barr and Bowman Atkins' " 'Women's Language' or 'Powerless Language'?" – is now dated in several ways, but is included because of its historical importance in the debate. O'Barr and Atkins studied language variation in American courtrooms and became interested in questions of gender through noticing that legal manuals give special advice on the behavior of female witnesses. Using the linguistic features highlighted by Robin Lakoff (1975), they analyzed the speech of a range of witnesses, both male and female, to see if their language use varied along gender lines. While they found some female witnesses who used language in a way which accorded with Lakoff's categories, they found others who did not: these were typically expert witnesses, women of high social status, who spoke confidently and assertively in court. Male witnesses varied in the same way, with less statusful individuals using language with more "female" features. These findings led O'Barr and Atkins to claim that what Lakoff described as "women's language" would be better termed "powerless language," since these features are associated with speakers of low status, irrespective of gender. The fact that the female witnesses in their sample were more likely than men to use powerless language they explain in terms of social structure: American society allocates women to relatively powerless social positions.

There are several problems with O'Barr and Atkins' account. The first is its uncritical use of Lakoff's set of "women's language" features, features which Lakoff arrived at through introspection and personal observation, not through empirical research. The second is its assumption that any linguistic form, such as a hedge or a tag question, can

Language and Gender: A Reader, Second Edition. Edited by Jennifer Coates and Pia Pichler.
© 2011 Blackwell Publishing Ltd except for editorial material and organization. © 2011 Jennifer Coates and Pia Pichler. Published 2011 by Blackwell Publishing Ltd.

be matched, one-to-one, with a specific function. This means that their analysis assumes that a hedge such as *sort of*, or *you know*, for example, must express tentativeness. This view has been challenged (see Cameron et al. 1989), and many linguists have written about the multi-functional nature of such linguistic forms (see, for example, Holmes 1984, 1995; Coates 1987, 1996).

More fundamentally, O'Barr and Atkins make the assumption that the value placed on the set of linguistic forms they call WL (Women's Language) is independent of culture; in other words, they seem to believe that hedges, for example, are *intrinsically* weak or tentative. Feminist linguists in English-speaking countries have suggested that the low value placed on forms like hedges might have less to do with hedges and more to do with their supposed association with female speakers. In other words, because female speakers have low status, linguistic forms said to be typical of women will acquire low status by association. As Janet Holmes (1986: 18) puts it: "one (female) person's feeble hedging may well be perceived as another (male) person's perspicacious qualification."

Strong support for this position is given by the next paper in this section, Patricia Wetzel's "Are 'Powerless' Communication Strategies the Japanese Norm?". Wetzel investigates the notion of "powerless" language. She shows that the conversational patterns associated with women and powerlessness in the West are associated with male speakers and with power in Japan. This rather undermines the idea that such conversational patterns are intrinsically weak or powerless. Wetzel's discussion of this issue puts power center-stage: she examines culture-specific features of power, and shows how it is only through an understanding of the power-structures of a society that we can come to an understanding of the meaning of any given conversational strategy. It is salutary to learn that the array of conversational strategies viewed in the West as strong, assertive, powerful, and macho are considered immature and childish by Japanese speakers. This paper is a forceful reminder that linguistic forms themselves mean nothing: it is the cultural value placed on these forms that matters.

In the third paper in this section – "When the Doctor is a 'Lady'" – Candace West sets out to disentangle the independent variables of status and gender. Her paper is a report of an exploratory study of doctor–patient talk. The doctor–patient relationship is essentially asymmetrical: doctors have institutional power in the context of the doctor's surgery; patients have little or no power. West carried out a detailed analysis of all the interruptions which occurred in these doctor–patient encounters, focusing on interruptions because they are a linguistic strategy which both demonstrates and accomplishes dominance (see West and Zimmerman's paper in Part III). As anticipated, West found that doctors interrupted patients disproportionately, except where the doctor was female, when patients interrupted as much as or more than the doctors. West explains this apparent anomaly by arguing that gender outweighs social status in determining social (including linguistic) behavior. In other words, while male doctors use interruptions as devices for exercising control over interaction, women doctors are interrupted by their patients, which undermines their authority. These results are supported by the work of Woods (1989), who found that, in the work setting, gender was more important than status in predicting linguistic behavior, with female bosses regularly interrupted by male subordinates. On the other hand, a more recent study of doctor–patient interaction in an outpatient clinic in Vienna, Austria (Menz and Al-Roubaie 2008), showed that status does outweigh gender with respect to interruptions, as both male and female doctors interrupted their patients more than vice versa. However, gender outweighed status with respect to supportive conversational behavior, which was displayed by women doctors and patients alike much more than by their male counterparts.

This is a complex debate. It throws up many questions. What is the relationship between gender, power, and status? Should we see gender and power as being in an either/or relationship (as O'Barr and Atkins assume), or as being in a both/and relationship (as West assumes)? Is it more accurate to argue that gender and power are intertwined, so that when a man interrupts a woman (for example) he is not just "doing gender" but also "doing power"? These three papers present a range of answers, not all compatible, and all products of their time. The debate continues, and in the twenty-first century more sophisticated ideas about gender and also about power, inspired in particular by the work of Foucault, are stimulating new questions and new answers.

References

Cameron, Deborah, McAlinden, Fiona, and O'Leary, Kathy (1989) "Lakoff in context: the social and linguistic functions of tag questions," pp. 74–93 in Jennifer Coates and Deborah Cameron (eds) *Women in their Speech Communities*. London: Longman.

Coates, Jennifer (1987) "Epistemic modality and spoken discourse," *Transactions of the Philological Society*, 110–31.

Coates, Jennifer (1996) *Women Talk: Conversation Between Women Friends*. Oxford: Blackwell.

Holmes, Janet (1984) "Hedging your bets and sitting on the fence: some evidence for hedges as support structures," *Te Reo* 27, 47–62.

Holmes, Janet (1986) "Functions of *you know* in women's and men's speech," *Language in Society* 15(1), 1–21.

Holmes, Janet (1995) *Women, Men and Politeness*. London: Longman.

Lakoff, Robin (1975) *Language and Woman's Place*. New York: Harper & Row.

Menz, Florian and Ali Al-Roubaie (2008) "Interruptions, status and gender in medical interviews: the harder you brake, the longer it takes," *Discourse & Society* 19(5), 645–66.

Woods, Nicola (1989) "Talking shop: sex and status as determinants of floor apportionment in a work setting," pp. 141–57 in Jennifer Coates and Deborah Cameron (eds) *Women in their Speech Communities*. London: Longman.

Recommended Further Reading

Cameron, Deborah, McAlinden, Fiona, and O'Leary Kathy (1989) "Lakoff in context: the social and linguistic functions of tag questions," pp. 74–93 in Jennifer Coates and Deborah Cameron (eds) *Women in their Speech Communities*. London: Longman.

Coates, Jennifer (1996) *Women Talk: Conversation Between Women Friends*. Oxford: Blackwell. See especially chapters 7 and 8.

Fairclough, Norman (1989) *Language and Power*. London: Longman.

Fairclough, Norman (1992) *Discourse and Social Change*. Cambridge: Polity Press.

Simpson, Paul and Mayr, Andrea (2009) *Language and Power: A Resource Book for Students*. London: Routledge.

Thornborrow, Joanna (2002) *Power Talk*. London: Longman.

Thimm, Caja, Koch, Sabine C., and Schey, Sabine (2003) "Communicating gendered professional identity: competence, cooperation and conflict in the workplace." In Janet Holmes and Miriam Meyerhoff (eds). *The Handbook of Language and Gender*. Oxford: Blackwell.

32

"Women's Language"
or "Powerless Language"?

William M. O'Barr and Bowman K. Atkins

Source: Sally McConnell-Ginet et al. (eds), *Women and Language in Literature and Society*. New York: Praeger (1980), pp. 93–110. Reprinted with permission of ABC Clio.

Introduction

The understanding of language and sex in American culture has progressed far beyond Robin Lakoff's influential and provocative essays on "women's language" written only a few years ago (Lakoff 1975). The rapid development of knowledge in what had been so significantly an ignored and overlooked area owes much to both the development of sociolinguistic interest in general and to the woman's movement in particular. But as a recent review of anthropological studies about women pointed out, this interest has grown so quickly and studies proliferated so fast that there is frequently little or no cross-referencing of mutually supportive studies and equally little attempt to reconcile conflicting interpretations of women's roles (Quinn 1977). A similar critique of the literature on language and sex would no doubt reveal many of the same problems. But in one sense, these are not problems – they are marks of a rapidly developing field of inquiry, of vitality, and of saliency of the topic.

Our interest in language and sex was sharpened by Lakoff's essays. Indeed, her work was for us – as it was for many others – a jumping off point. But unlike some other studies, ours was not primarily an attempt to understand language and sex differences. Rather, the major goal of our recent research has been the study of language variation in a specific institutional context – the American trial courtroom – and sex-related differences were one of the kinds of variation which current sociolinguistic issues led us to consider. Our interest was further kindled by the discovery that trial practice manuals (how-to-do-it books by successful trial lawyers and law professors) often had special sections on how female witnesses behave differently from males and thus special kinds of treatment they require.

In this paper, we describe our study of how women (and men) talk in court. The research we report here is part of a 30-month study of language variation in trial courtrooms which has included both ethnographic and experimental components. It is the thesis of this study that so-called "women's language" is in large part a language of powerlessness, a condition that can apply to men as well as women. That a complex of such features should have been called "women's language" in the first place reflects the generally powerless position of many women in American society, a point recognized but not developed extensively by

Language and Gender: A Reader, Second Edition. Edited by Jennifer Coates and Pia Pichler.
© 2011 Blackwell Publishing Ltd except for editorial material and organization. © 2011 Jennifer Coates and Pia Pichler. Published 2011 by Blackwell Publishing Ltd.

Lakoff (1975: 7–8). Careful examination in one institutional setting of the features which were identified as constituting "women's language" has shown clearly that such features are simply not patterned along sex lines. Moreover, the features do not, in a strict sense, constitute a *style* or *register* since there is not perfect co-variation.

This paper proceeds as follows: first, it examines the phenomenon of "women's language" in the institutional context of a court of law; second, it shows that the features of "women's language" are not restricted to women and therefore suggests renaming the concept "powerless" language due to its close association with persons having low social power and often relatively little previous experience in the courtroom setting; [...] and finally, it calls for a refinement of our studies to distinguish powerless language features from others which may in fact be found primarily in women's speech.

How to Handle Women in Court – Some Advice from Lawyers

One of the means which we used in our study of courtroom language to identify specific language variables for detailed study was information provided to us in interviews with practicing lawyers. More useful, however, were *trial practice manuals* – books written by experienced lawyers which attempt to discuss systematically successful methods and tactics for conducting trials. Typically, little effort is devoted to teaching and developing trial practice skills in the course of a legal education. Rather it is expected that they will be acquired through personal experimentation, through watching and modeling one's behavior after successful senior lawyers, and through reading the advice contained in such manuals. Those who write trial practice manuals are experienced members of the legal profession who are reporting on both their own experiences and the generally accepted folklore within the profession. In all these situations, the basis for claims about what works or what does not tends to be the general success of those who give advice or serve as models – judged primarily by whether they win their cases most of the time.

One kind of advice which struck us in reading through several of these manuals was that pertaining to the special treatment which should be accorded women. The manuals which discuss special treatment for women tend to offer similar advice regarding female witnesses. Readers are instructed to behave generally the same toward women as men, but to note that, in certain matters or situations, women require some special considerations. Some of this advice includes the following:

1. *Be especially courteous to women.* ("Even when jurors share the cross-examiner's reaction that the female witness on the stand is dishonest or otherwise undeserving individually, at least some of the jurors are likely to think it improper for the attorney to decline to extend the courtesies customarily extended to women.") (Keeton 1973: 149.)

2. *Avoid making women cry.* ("Jurors, along with others, may be inclined to forgive and forget transgressions under the influence of sympathy provoked by the genuine tears of a female witness." "A crying woman does your case no good.") (Keeton 1973: 149; Bailey and Rothblatt 1971: 190.)

3. *Women behave differently from men and this can sometimes be used to advantage.* ("Women are contrary witnesses. They hate to say yes. ... A woman's desire to avoid the obvious answer will lead her right into your real objective – contradicting the testimony of previous prosecution witnesses. Women, like children, are prone to exaggeration; they

generally have poor memories as to previous fabrications and exaggerations. They also are stubborn. You will have difficulty trying to induce them to qualify their testimony. Rather, it might be easier to induce them to exaggerate and cause their testimony to appear incredible. An intelligent woman will very often be evasive. She will avoid making a direct answer to a damaging question. Keep after her until you get a direct answer – but always be the gentleman.") (Bailey and Rothblatt 1971: 190–1.)

These comments about women's behavior in court and their likely consequences in the trial process further raised our interest in studying the speech behavior of women in court. Having been told by Lakoff that women do speak differently from men, we interpreted these trial practice authors as saying that at least some of these differences can be consequential in the trial process. Thus, one of the kinds of variation which we sought to examine when we began to observe and tape record courtroom speech was patterns unique to either women or men. We did not know what we would find, so we started out by using Lakoff's discussion of "women's language" as a guide.

Briefly, what Lakoff had proposed was that women's speech varies from men's in several significant ways. Although she provides no firm listing of the major features of what she terms "women's language" (hereafter referred to in this paper as WL), we noted the following features, said to occur in high frequency among women, and used these as a baseline for our investigation of sex-related speech patterns in court.

1   *Hedges.* ("It's sort of hot in here."; "I'd kind of like to go."; "I guess ..."; "It seems like ..."; and so on.)
2   *(Super) polite forms.* ("I'd really appreciate it if ..."; "Would you please open the door, if you don't mind?"; and so on.)
3   *Tag questions.* ("John is here, isn't he?" instead of "Is John here?"; and so on.)
4   *Speaking in italics.* (Intonational emphasis equivalent to underlining words in written language; emphatic *so* or *very* and so on.)
5   *Empty adjectives.* (*Divine; charming; cute; sweet; adorable; lovely,* and so on.)
6   *Hypercorrect grammar and pronunciation.* (Bookish grammar; more formal enunciation.)
7   *Lack of a sense of humor.* (Women said to be poor joke tellers and to frequently "miss the point" in jokes told by men.)
8   *Direct quotations.* (Use of direct quotations instead of paraphrases.)
9   *Special lexicon.* (In domains like colors where words like *magenta, chartreuse,* and so on are typically used only by women.)
10 *Question intonation in declarative contexts.* (For example, in response to the question, "When will dinner be ready?", an answer like "Around 6 o'clock?", as though seeking approval and asking whether that time will be okay.)

What We Found

During the summer of 1974, we recorded over 150 hours of trials in a North Carolina superior criminal court. Although almost all of the lawyers we observed were males, the sex distribution of witnesses was more nearly equal. On looking for the speech patterns described by Lakoff, we quickly discovered some women who spoke in the described manner. The only major discrepancies between Lakoff's description and our findings were in features which the specific context of the courtroom rendered inappropriate, for example, *tag questions* (because witnesses typically answer rather than ask questions) and *joking* (because there is little humor in a courtroom, we did not have occasion to observe the specifically female patterns of humor to which she referred).

In addition to our early finding that some women approximate the model described by Lakoff, we also were quick to note that there was considerable variation in the degree to which women exhibited these characteristics. Since our observations were limited to about ten weeks of trials during which we were able to observe a variety of cases in terms of offense (ranging from traffic cases, drug possession, robbery, manslaughter, to rape) and length (from a few hours to almost five days), we believe that our observations cover a reasonably good cross-section of the kinds of trials, and hence witnesses, handled by this type of court. Yet, ten weeks is not enough to produce a very large number of witnesses. Even a single witness may spend several hours testifying. In addition, the court spends much time selecting jurors, hearing summation remarks, giving jury instructions, and handling administrative matters. Thus, when looking at patterns of how different women talk in court, we are in a better position to deal with the range of variation we observed than to attempt any precise frequency counts of persons falling into various categories. Thus, we will concentrate our efforts here on describing the range and complement this with some non-statistical impressions regarding frequency.

Our observations show a continuum of use of the features described by Lakoff.[1] We were initially at a loss to explain why some women should speak more or less as Lakoff had described and why others should use only a few of these features. We will deal with our interpretation of these findings later, but first let us examine some points along the continuum from high to low.

A. Mrs. W,[2] a witness in a case involving the death of her neighbor in an automobile accident, is an extreme example of a person speaking WL in her testimony. She used nearly every feature described by Lakoff and certainly all those which are appropriate in the courtroom context. Her speech contains a high frequency of *intensifiers* ("*very* close friends," "*quite* ill," and so on often with intonation emphasis); *hedges* (frequent use of "you know," "sort of like," "maybe just a little bit," "let's see," and so on); *empty adjectives* ("this *very* kind policeman"); and other similar features. The first example below is typical of her speech and shows the types of intensifiers and hedges she commonly uses.[3] (To understand what her speech *might* be like without these features, example (2) is a rewritten version of her answers with the WL features eliminated.)

(1) L: State whether or not, Mrs. W., you were acquainted with or knew the late Mrs. E. D.

   W: Quite well.
   L: What was the nature of your acquaintance with her?
   W: Well, we were, uh, very close friends. Uh, she was even sort of like a mother to me.

(2) L: State whether or not, Mrs. W., you were acquainted with or knew the late Mrs. E. D.
   W: Yes, I did.
   L: What was the nature of your acquaintance with her?
   W: We were close friends. She was like a mother to me.

Table 1   Frequency distribution of Women's Language features[a] in the speech of six witnesses in a trial courtroom

	Women			Men		
	A	*B*	*C*	*D*	*E*	*F*
Intensifiers[b]	16	0	0	21	2	1
Hedges[c]	19	2	3	2	5	0
Hesitation Forms[d]	52	20	13	26	27	11
W asks L questions[e]	2	0	0	0	0	0
Gestures[f]	2	0	0	0	0	0
Polite Forms[g]	9	0	2	2	0	1
Sir[h]	2	0	6	32	13	11
Quotes[i]	1	5	0	0	0	0
Total (all powerless forms)	103	27	24	85	47	24
# of Answers in Interview	90	32	136	61	73	52
Ratio (# powerless forms for each answer)	1.14	0.84	0.18	1.39	0.64	0.46

[a] The particular features chosen for inclusion in this table were selected because of their saliency and frequency of occurrence. Not included here are features of WL which either do not occur in court or ones which we had difficulty operationalizing and coding. *Based on direct examinations only.*

[b] Forms which increase or emphasize the force of assertion such as *very, definitely, very definitely, surely, such a*, and so on.

[c] Forms which reduce the force of assertion allowing for exceptions or avoiding rigid commitments such as *sort of, a little, kind of*, and so on.

[d] Pause fillers such as *uh, um, ah*, and "meaningless" particles such as *oh, well, let's see, now, so, you see*, and so on.

[e] Use of question intonation in response to lawyer's questions, including rising intonation in normally declarative contexts (for example, "thirty?, thirty-five?") and questions asked by witness of lawyer like. "Which way do you go ...?".

[f] Spoken indications of direction such as *over there*, and so on.

[g] Include *please, thank you*, and so on. Use of *sir* counted separately due to its high frequency.

[h] Assumed to be an indication of more polite speech.

[i] Not typically allowed in court under restrictions on hearsay which restrict the situations under which a witness may tell what someone else said.

Source: Original data.

Table 1 summarizes the frequency of several features attributed to WL by Lakoff. Calculated as a ratio of WL forms for each answer, this witness's speech contains 1.14 – among the highest incidences we observed.

B.   The speech of Mrs. N, a witness in a case involving her father's arrest, shows fewer WL features. Her ratio of features for each answer drops to .84. Her testimony contains instances of both WL and a more assertive speech style. Frequently, her speech is punctuated with responses like: "He, see, he thought it was more-or-less me rather than the police officer." Yet it also contains many more straightforward and assertive passages than are found in A's speech. In example (3), for instance, Mrs. N is anything but passive. She turns questions back on the lawyer and even interrupts him. Example (4) illustrates the ambivalence of this speaker's style better. Note how she moves quickly to qualify – in WL– an otherwise assertive response.

(3) L: All right. I ask you if your husband hasn't beaten him up in the last week?
    W: Yes, and do you know why?
    L: Well, I ...
    W: Another gun episode.
    L: Another gun episode?
    W: Yessiree.

(4) L: You've had a controversy going with him for a long time, haven't you?
    W: Ask why – I mean not because I'm just his daughter.

C. The speech of Dr. H, a pathologist who testifies as an expert witness, exhibits fewer features of WL than either of the other two women. Her speech contains the lowest incidence of WL features among the female witnesses whose speech we analyzed. Dr. H's ratio of WL features is .18 for each answer. Her responses tend to be straightforward, with little hesitancy, few hedges, a noticeable lack of intensifiers, and so on. (See table 1.) Typical of her speech is example (5) in which she explains some of her findings in a pathological examination.

(5) L: And had the heart not been functioning, in other words, had the heart been stopped, there would have been no blood to have come from that region?
    W: It may leak down depending on the position of the body after death. But the presence of blood in the alveoli indicates that some active respiratory action had to take place.

What all of this shows is the fact that some women speak in the way Lakoff described, employing many features of WL, while others are far away on the continuum of possible and appropriate styles for the courtroom. Before discussing the reasons which may lie behind this variation in the language used by women in court, we first examine an equally interesting finding which emerged from our investigation of male speech in court.

We also found men who exhibit WL characteristics in their courtroom testimony. To illustrate this, we examine the speech of three male witnesses which varies along a continuum of high to low incidence of WL features.

D. Mr. W exhibits many but not all of Lakoff's WL features.[4] Some of those which he does employ, like intensifiers, for example, occur in especially high frequency – among the highest observed among all speakers, whether male or female. His ratio of WL features for each answer is 1.39, actually higher than individual A. Example (6), while an extreme instance of Mr. W's use of WL features, does illustrate the degree to which features attributed to women are in fact present in high frequency in the speech of some men.

(6) L: And you saw, you observed what?
    W: Well, after I heard – I can't really, I can't definitely state whether the brakes or the lights came first, but I rotated my head slightly to the right, and looked directly behind Mr. Z., and I saw reflections of lights, and uh, very, very, very instantaneously after that, I heard a very, very loud explosion – from my standpoint of view it would have been an implosion because everything was forced outward, like this, like a grenade thrown into a room. And, uh, it was, it was terrifically loud.

E. Mr. N, more toward the low frequency end of the continuum of male speakers, shows some WL features. His ratio of features for each answer is .64, comparable to individual B. Example (7) shows an instance of passages from the testimony of this speaker in which there are few WL features. Example (8), by comparison, shows the same hedging in a way characteristic of WL. His speech falls between the highest and lowest incidences of WL features we observed among males.

(7) L: After you looked back and saw the back of the ambulance, what did you do?
     W: After I realized that my patient and my attendant were thrown from the vehicle, uh, which I assumed, I radioed in for help to the dispatcher, tell her that we had been in an accident and, uh, my patient and attendant were thrown from the vehicle and I didn't know the extent of their injury at the time, to hurry up and send help.

(8) L: Did you form any conclusion about what her problem was at the time you were there?
     W: I felt that she had, uh, might have had a sort of heart attack.
     F: Officer G, among the males lowest in WL features, virtually lacks all features tabulated in table 1 except for hesitancy and using *sir*. His ratio of WL forms for each answer is .46. Example (9) shows how this speaker handles the lack of certainty in a more authoritative manner than by beginning his answer with "I guess …". His no-nonsense, straightforward manner is illustrated well by example (10), in which a technical answer is given in a style comparable to that of individual C.

(9) L: Approximately how many times have you testified in court?
     W: It would only have to be a guess, but it's three or four, five, six hundred times. Probably more.

(10) L: You say that you found blood of group O?
     W: The blood in the vial, in the layman's term, is positive, Rh positive. Technically referred to as a capital r, sub o, little r.

Taken together these findings suggest that the so-called "women's language" is neither characteristic of all women nor limited only to women. A similar continuum of WL features (high to low) is found among speakers of both sexes. These findings suggest that the sex of a speaker is insufficient to explain incidence of WL features, and that we must look elsewhere for an explanation of this variation.

Once we had realized that WL features were distributed in such a manner, we began to examine the data for other factors which might be associated with a high or low incidence of the features in question. First, we noted that we were able to find *more* women toward the high end of the continuum. Next, we noted that all the women who were aberrant (that is, who used relatively few WL features) had something in common – an unusually high social status. Like Dr. H, they were typically well-educated, professional women of middle-class background. A corresponding pattern was noted among the aberrant men (that is, those high in WL features). Like Mr. W, they tended to be men who held either subordinate, lower-status jobs or were unemployed. Housewives were high in WL features while middle-class males were low in these features. In addition to social status in the society at large, another factor associated with low incidence of WL is previous courtroom experience. Both individuals C and F testify frequently in court as expert witnesses, that is, as witnesses who testify on the basis of their professional expertise. However, it should be noted that not all persons who speak with few WL features have had extensive courtroom experience. The point we wish to emphasize is that a powerful position may derive from either social standing in the larger society and/or status accorded by the court. We carefully observed these patterns and found them to hold generally.[5] For some individuals whom we had observed in the courtroom, we analyzed their speech in detail in order to tabulate the frequency of the WL features as shown in table 1. A little more about the background of the persons we have described will illustrate the sort of pattern we observed.

A is a married woman, about 55 years old, who is a housewife.

B is married, but younger, about 35 years old. From her testimony, there is no information that she works outside her home.

C is a pathologist in a local hospital. She is 35–40 years old. There is no indication from content of her responses or from the way she was addressed (always *Dr.*) of her marital status. She has testified in court as a pathologist on many occasions.

D is an ambulance attendant, rather inexperienced in his job, at which he has worked for less than 6 months. Age around 30. Marital status unknown.

E is D's supervisor. He drives the ambulance, supervises emergency treatment and gives instructions to D. He has worked at his job longer than D and has had more experience. Age about 30–35; marital status unknown.

F is an experienced member of the local police force. He has testified in court frequently. Age 35–40; marital status unknown.

"Women's Language" or "Powerless Language"?

In the previous section, we presented data which indicate that the variation in WL features may be related more to social powerlessness than to sex. We have presented both observational data and some statistics to show that this style is not simply or even primarily a sex-related pattern. We did, however, find it related to sex in that more women tend to be high in WL features while more men tend to be low in these same features. The speech patterns of three men and three women were examined. For each sex, the individuals varied from social statuses with relatively low power to more power (for women: housewife to doctor; for men: subordinate job to one with a high degree of independence of action). Experience may also be an important factor, for those whom we observed speaking with few WL features seemed more comfortable in the courtroom and with the content of their testimony. Associated with increasing shifts in social power and experience were corresponding decreases in frequency of WL features. These six cases were selected for detailed analysis because they were representative of the sorts of women and men who served as witnesses in the trials we observed in 1974. Based on this evidence, we would suggest that the phenomenon described by Lakoff would be better termed *powerless language*, a term which is more descriptive of the particular features involved, of the social status of those who speak in this manner, and one which does not link it unnecessarily to the sex of a speaker.

Further, we would suggest that the tendency for more women to speak powerless language and for men to speak less of it is due, at least in part, to the greater tendency of women to occupy relatively powerless social positions. What we have observed is a reflection in their speech behavior of their social status. Similarly, for men, a greater tendency to use the more powerful variant (which we will term *powerful language*) may be linked to the fact that men much more often tend to occupy relatively powerful positions in society.

[…]

Conclusion

In this study, we have attempted to argue that our data from studying male–female language patterns in trial courtrooms suggest that Lakoff's concept of "woman's language" is in need of modification. Our findings show that, in one particular context at least, not all women exhibit a high frequency of WL features and that some men do. We have argued that instead of being primarily sex-linked, a high incidence of some or all of these features appears to be more closely related to social position in the larger society and/or the specific context of the courtroom. Hence, we have suggested a re-naming of the phenomenon as "powerless language." What has previously been referred to as "women's language" is perhaps better thought of as a composite of features of powerless language (which can but need not be a characteristic of the speech of either women or men) and of some other features which may be more restricted to women's domains.

Thus, Lakoff's discussion of "women's language" confounds at least two different patterns of variation. Although our title suggests a dichotomy between "women's language" and "powerless language," these two patterns undoubtedly interact. It could well be that to speak like the powerless is not only typical of women because of the all-too-frequent powerless social position of many American women, but is also part of the cultural meaning of speaking "like a woman." Gender meanings draw on other social meanings; analyses that focus on sex in isolation from the social positions of women and men can thus tell us little about the meaning of "women's language" in society and culture.

[…]

Notes

The research reported here was supported by a National Science Foundation Law and Social Science Program Grant (No. GS-42742), William M. O'Barr, principal investigator. The authors wish to thank especially these other members of the research team for their advice and assistance: John Conley, Marilyn Endriss, Bonnie Erickson, Bruce Johnson, Debbie Mercer, Michael Porter, Lawrence Rosen, William Schmidheiser, and Laurens Walker. In addition, the cooperation of the Durham County, North Carolina, Superior Court is gratefully acknowledged.

1 Actually each feature should be treated as a separate continuum since there is not perfect co-variation. For convenience, we discuss the variation as a single continuum of possibilities. However, it should be kept in mind that a high frequency of occurrence of one particular feature may not necessarily be associated with a high frequency of another.
2 Names have been changed and indicated by a letter only in order to preserve the anonymity of witnesses. However, the forms of address used in the court are retained.
3 These examples are taken from both the direct and cross examinations of the witnesses, although table 1 uses data only from direct examinations. Examples were chosen to point out clearly the differences in style. However, it must be noted that the cross examination is potentially a more powerless situation for the witness.
4 This speaker did not use some of the intonational features that we had noted among women having high frequencies of WL features in their speech.
5 We do not wish to make more of this pattern than our data are able to support, but we suggest that our grounds for these claims are at least as good as Lakoff's. Lakoff's basis for her description of features constituting WL are her own speech, speech of her friends and acquaintances, and patterns of use in the mass media.

References

Bailey, F. Lee and Rothblatt, Henry B. (1971) *Successful Techniques for Criminal Trials.* Rochester, NY: Lawyers Cooperative Publishing Co.

Keeton, Robert E. (1973) *Trial Tactics and Methods.* Boston: Little, Brown.

Lakoff, Robin (1975) *Language and Woman's Place.* New York: Harper & Row.

Quinn, Naomi (1977) 'Anthropological studies of women's status'. *Annual Review of Anthropology,* 6, 181–225.

33

Are "Powerless" Communication Strategies the Japanese Norm?

Patricia J. Wetzel

Source: Language in Society 17(4) (1988), pp. 555–64. Reprinted with permission of Cambridge University Press.

Introduction

This article examines strikingly parallel claims concerning Japanese communication strategies and female communication strategies in the West. Miscommunication between Japan and the West is found to resemble miscommunication between the sexes in the West, yet the similarities are superficial. Any investigation into (mis)communication across cultures must take into account the cultural fabric within which interaction takes place. The notion of power is taken to be central to these issues, and a closer examination of how the notion of power in the West contrasts with the notion of power in Japan is shown to be one key to understanding miscommunication between Japan and the West.

[…]

Female Communication – Japanese Communication

Differences between Japan and the United States are the subject of a great deal of discussion – perhaps nowhere as much as the US business community, which finds itself at once challenged and baffled by Japanese behavior. Consider the following generalization from Christopher's popular 1983 book, *The Japanese mind:*

> In their conversations … Japanese religiously shun explicit, carefully reasoned statements in favor of indirect and ambiguous ones basically designed not to communicate ideas but to feel out the other person's mood and attitudes. As the Japanese see it, plain speaking has one overwhelming drawback: it tends to commit the speaker to a hard-and -fast position, and thus can easily provoke direct confrontation – which all Japanese dread. (Christopher 1983: 43)

Though by no means scholarly in its approach to language, Christopher's statement nonetheless reflects a strong awareness of how different Japanese communication patterns are from those of the West. Or are they? A breakdown of those features of communication

Language and Gender: A Reader, Second Edition. Edited by Jennifer Coates and Pia Pichler.
© 2011 Blackwell Publishing Ltd except for editorial material and organization. © 2011 Jennifer Coates and Pia Pichler. Published 2011 by Blackwell Publishing Ltd.

which surface again and again in research on Japan show a remarkable similarity to features that have been said to mark female interaction patterns in the West. The following is a direct comparison of some of the more striking parallels between observed female interaction patterns in the West and Japanese interaction patterns:[1]

Women show a greater tendency to make use of positive minimal responses, especially "mm hmm" and are more likely to insert these throughout the interchange not at the end. (Maltz and Borker 1982: 197 [reprinted in Part VIII of this volume], citing Hirschman [1973] and Fishman [1978]	If properly empathetic, Alter assures and reassures Ego of his receptivity, congeniality, or agreement by frequently nodding and exclaiming "I'm listening," "That is so," or "Yes." ... The listener constantly breaks his silence to let the speaker know that he is listening with interest and agreement. (Lebra 1976: 39)
Women are more likely than men to make utterances that demand or encourage responses from their fellow speakers. (Maltz and Borker 1982: 197)	Japanese conversation is marked by the frequency with which Ego interjects his speech with the particle *ne* ("isn't it"), which sounds as if he is soliciting Alter's agreement. (Lebra 1976: 39)
Men make more direct declarations of fact or opinion than do women ... they are more likely to challenge or dispute their partners' utterances. (Maltz and Borker 1982: 198, citing Fishman [1978] and Hirschman [1973])	[T]here is an extremely strong attitude of consideration toward others and concern about what they are thinking. The Japanese seem to be speaking so as not to collide with each other. (Mizutani 1981: 78)
[Features of women's speech] have been coded under the general category of "positive reactions" including solidarity, tension release, and agreeing. (Maltz and Borker 1982: 197, citing Strodbeck and Mann 1956)	While debate is accepted to a certain degree ... if outsiders will be present, the Japanese think about ways to turn them into insiders rather than ways to carry on the debate in words and thereby achieve certain results. (Mizutani 1981: 71–2)
[W]omen are more likely to adopt a strategy of silent protest after they have been interrupted. (Maltz and Borker 1982: 197–8, citing Zimmerman and West [1975] and West and Zimmerman [1977, reprinted in Part III of this volume])	Once conflict is generated, the victim A may express his frustration or anger to B, the source ... by not communicating it ... in a message of silence. (Lebra 1984: 43)
The general orientation among women is interactional, relational, participatory, and collaborative. (Treichler and Kramarae 1983: 120)	[E]mpathy (*omoiyari*) ranks high among the virtues considered indispensable for one to be really human, morally mature, and deserving of respect. *Omoiyari* refers to the ability and willingness to feel what others are feeling. (Lebra 1976: 38)
Girls frame their accusations as reports about offenses heard from an intermediary (Goodwin 1980a: 172). Rather than stating the offense directly ... [the] accusation is phrased in terms of a report by some intermediate party. (Goodwin 1980b: 682)	The request or protest is made in the name of another, which is less offensive to a Japanese listener (Lebra 1984: 46). Ego meets Alter face-to-face but conveys his message as being that of someone else. Ego thus pretends to be a delegate or messenger for a third party. (Lebra 1976: 123).

[W]omen attempt to link their utterance to the one preceding it by building on the previous utterance ... [a signal] of women's desire to create continuity in conversation, and Hirschman 1973 describes elaboration as a key dynamic of women's talk. (Maltz and Borker 1982: 210)

In conversation the speaker does not complete a sentence but leaves it open-ended in such a way that the listener will take it over before the former clearly expresses his will or opinion, thereby showing a concern for maintaining consensus. (Lebra 1976: 38–9).

Japanese–Western Miscommunication

Maltz and Borker predict miscommunication between men and women based on the fact that their culturally determined rules for interaction are different. Based on the preceding, we might extend this and predict miscommunication of a similar nature between Japanese and males in the West.

Consider the following advice, written by a male for a primarily male audience – Western business concerns considering business ventures in Japan:

> [T]he purpose of the business luncheon in Japan is not to discuss problems or work out solutions. Rather it is to enhance a sense of intimacy between business affiliates and to serve as a lubricant for present or future negotiations. If you are being invited to such a lunch, this may not mean that there are any business matters to be discussed, but perhaps that your prospective partner or client would simply like to check out your personality. (*Business Japanese II*: 138)

The same textbook on business strategies in Japan provides the following characterization of negotiation in Japan:

> It has been observed that [executives in the West] arrive at the negotiation table with an itemized list of all the goals they intend to achieve, and then expect to proceed at a brisk pace right down this list so as not to waste everyone's precious time (*Business Japanese*: 246). [S]uccessful presentations in Japan are not always direct or logical, nor do they revolve primarily around a product's merits. Instead, a Japanese sales presentation is often rambling, ambiguous, and full of "unrelated" information about the product's (or company's) ongoing contributions to society and mankind – what we in the West sometimes jokingly refer to as "hearts and flowers". (*Business Japanese II*: 28)

I suggest that the feminine imagery here ("hearts and flowers") is not accidental.

A recent flyer for a seminar on doing business with the Japanese poses a series of questions which, presumably, perenially baffle the Western business*man*.

> "Why can't we get down to business?" "Why can't we give each other a simple 'yes' or 'no'?" "Why does it take so long to work things out?" "Who's responsible for conflicts?" ... This seminar will provide an understanding of the American and Japanese business*man*'s [emphasis mine] way of thinking and will present skills necessary to communicate effectively with each other for maximum business success. ("Maximizing your business effectiveness in Japan/America" offered by the Japan–America Society of Oregon, 1986)

All of this sounds remarkably similar to traditional male evaluations of female behavior, and the parallels with Maltz and Borker's predictions about male–female miscommunication are also striking.

It is tempting to conclude that Japanese tend to use language akin to women's language in the West. However, this would be a gross oversimplification of the facts and would ignore the cultural framework within which linguistic behavior takes place. Rather, the parallels between Western women's communication styles and Japanese communication styles is taken here to indicate that analysis of both is somehow lacking and that the terms in which we describe this behavior should be reexamined.

Is Japanese–Female Communication Powerless?

First of all, research indicates that in the West, at least, differences in communication style often correlate less with gender than with factors such as role and status. O'Barr and Atkins (1980 [reprinted in Part VII of this volume]) found in their courtroom testimony data, for example, that women who tend to exhibit few or no features of *women's language* (as defined by Lakoff [1975]) had something in common: They were typically well-educated, professional, middle-class women. Correspondingly, men who tended to use features of women's language were typically men who held subordinate, lower status jobs or were unemployed (103–4). O'Barr and Atkins conclude that "the tendency for women to speak powerless language and for men to speak less of it is due, at least in part, to the greater tendency of women to occupy relatively powerless social positions" (104). Hence, they suggest a renaming of the concept of women's language as *powerless language*. They also allow that the two patterns – women's language and powerless language – interact and that it is part of the cultural meaning of speaking "like a woman" to speak powerlessly.[2]

Can we conclude, then, that the Japanese communicate in a "powerless" mode? Or, turning the perspective around, should we instead ask what these powerless features convey within a Japanese communicative context?

In their discussions of those qualities which make a child *ningen-rashii*, or "human-like" according to the Japanese, White and Levine (1986) observe that within Japan, first of all, to be *ningen-rashii* means to be able to maintain harmony in human relationships (56). And high among qualities that Japanese value in child rearing is "*yutaka*, meaning 'empathetic', 'receptive', or 'open hearted'" (58). "Sensitivity and anticipation of the needs of others," they go on to say, "sound passive and *feminine* [emphasis mine] to Western ears, but appearances are deceptive, *yutaka* has a very positive, active connotation and suggests a mature vigor" (58).

Given what it means to be a mature adult and *ningen-rashii* in Japan, it stands to reason that "nonconfrontational modes [of communication] must be exhausted" before resorting to other strategies (Lebra 1984: 42). The Japanese value those patterns of communication that indicate sensitivity to the other: demonstrations or signals of empathy, solicitation of agreement, concern about what others are thinking, silent protest as a strategy for signaling disagreement or displeasure, and use of intermediaries – strategies that we in the West associate with female, and thereby powerless, interaction.

Contrast this with the strategies that we in the West associate with powerful communication style: assertion of dominance, interrupting while others have the floor, challenging or disputing others' utterances, ignoring comments of others, making direct declarations of fact or opinion. All contrast with what it means to be a mature adult in a Japanese framework, and as such are much more likely to be viewed as immature or childish behavior.

What, then, are the communicative strategies by which individuals assert power in Japan? The relationship between communication style, or any behavior, and perceptions of power is undeniably complex. In the case where we wish to compare linguistic strategies in Japan and the West, however, examination of a notion as basic as *power* is indispensable.

Power: Japan Versus the West

One striking feature of claims regarding powerful versus powerless language is the way in which the notion of power itself is taken for granted. *Power* is a complex term and the subject of a great deal of debate as regards its nature and forms (see, e.g., Galbraith 1983; Janeway 1981; Korda 1975; and McClelland 1975). Within the wide range of research on language and the sexes, only Henley (1977) provides a working definition of power: "Power is thus based on the control of resources, and their defense" (19). She distinguishes power from other related terms such as *dominance* (like power, but with a connotation of more blatancy), *authority* (power that is somehow legitimized, such as through law or tradition), and *status* (social position) (19–20).

Galbraith (1983: 2) introduces his discussion of power by defining it as follows: "Power is: the possibility of imposing one's will upon other persons." Webster's *Third international unabridged dictionary* contains the following sub-entry (one of many) for power: "2. The possession of sway or controlling influence over others; authority; command; government; influence; ascendancy, whether personal, social, or political; also, occasionally, permission or liberty to act."

The striking feature of all these English descriptions of power is that they define power as a substantive phenomenon, as something possessed by the individual.[3] It is safe to say that, in the West, the individual is generally viewed as the locus of power (Hengeveld 1984: 10).

A search for an appropriate equivalent for English *power* in Japanese yields two possibilities: *kenryoku* and *tikara*.[4] *Kenryoku* may be defined generally as "power, authority, or influence" while *tikara* is defined as "strength, force, power, ability, or capacity" (*Shogakukan progressive Japanese–English dictionary*, 1986). Yet neither of these provides a way of describing powerful and powerless language in Japanese. The phrase *tikara ga aru/nai hanasikata* "powerful/less speech style" is misleading in that it describes moving or affective speech but not powerful/less speech style in the sense sought here. The phrase *kenryoku ga aru/nai hanasikata* "powerful/less speech style", rather than being misleading, conveys nothing in Japanese. (Hengeveld [1984: 1] briefly relates her own experience wrestling with this problem of talking about powerful and powerless speech in Japanese.) The reasons for this translation problem, in large part, have to do with the nature of power in Japan.

Hengeveld (1984) observes that power in Japan is less an attribute of the individual than of role and position. Japanese analyses of power (Maruyama 1964; Matsushita 1978; Matsuzawa 1978; Nakane 1970) reflect such a relational view of power and place emphasis on role interaction within the power structure or hierarchy and far less on the individual. Individuals may make use of the power inherent in the role or position that they occupy, but as Hengeveld observes, "*kenryoku* isn't 'held over someone' as 'power' is in English. Rather, it simply exists in a particular individual within a given sphere, and the severing of power from the [concomitant] network of obligations will result in an instant loss of *kenryoku*" (85–6). In short, to speak of an individual as possessing a powerful speech style is to view the individual as the locus of power, and this is not how Japanese perceive the phenomenon of power.

Conclusion

Parallels between descriptions of female interaction in the West and Japanese interaction are not coincidental. Much of Japanese behavior viewed from a Western perspective is reminiscent of what we consider to be feminine (and therefore powerless) interaction.

What this investigation suggests is that the cultural underpinnings of a unified set of linguistic behaviors in the West (such as those that connote power or powerlessness) may be radically different from what underlies similar behavior in Japan. In both our practical dealings with the Japanese and in our theoretical analysis of Japanese and Western linguistic behavior, we would do well to realize this.

Similarly, the search for powerful and powerless speech styles in Japanese that parallel this distinction in the West will prove misleading or meaningless if our assumptions about the nature of power do not allow for cultural variation. Our descriptions of Japanese linguistic behavior should take into account the differences that distinguish Japanese culture from our own, as should our descriptions of cross-ethnic (mis)communication.

Notes

I would like to thank Elizabeth Hengeveld for her painstaking readings and lengthy discussions of earlier versions of this paper, and Mari Noda for her comments on the final analysis. Their help is evident throughout.

1 These observations reflect a variety of perspectives on female and Japanese interaction patterns, including anthropological and sociological research. There are, in fact, more data supporting the claims made regarding female communication strategies than there are supporting the claims made regarding Japanese communication strategies. Only recently has data-oriented sociolinguistic research on Japanese begun to appear in the literature (e:g., Shibamoto 1985). Nonetheless, the data that have appeared tend to support the observations cited above.

2 What is problematic about this analysis is the fact that it continues to implicitly promote "the assumption that white, heterosexual, male speech constitutes the norm for American speakers of English" (Hayes 1979: 28). It is this issue that Kramarae (1980) and others have begun to address by recognizing that, "By and large men have controlled the norms of use; and this control, in turn, has shaped the language system available for use by both sexes and has influenced the judgements made about the speech of women and men" (58). We might also ask whether men and women in the West, particularly in the United States, evaluate power differently. Gilligan (1982) addresses this issue in her analysis of women's moral development.

3 One exception to this is Janeway (1981), who looks very carefully at the relational nature of power. Is it coincidental that Janeway is female and tends to write from and affirm the female perspective?

4 The Chinese character for *tikara* is the same as the one used for *ryoku* in *kenryoku*.

References

Business Japanese, vols. I and II. (1985). Tokyo: Nissan Motor Company.

Christopher, R. C. (1983). *The Japanese Mind: The Goliath Explained.* New York: Linden Press/ Simon & Schuster.

Fishman, P. M. (1978). Interaction: The work women do. *Social Problems* 25(4): 397–406.

Galbraith, J. K. (1983). *The anatomy of power.* Boston: Houghton Mifflin.

Gilligan, C. (1982). *In a Different Voice: Psychological Theory and Women's Development.* Cambridge, MA: Harvard University Press.

Goodwin, M. (1980a). Directive–response speech sequences in girls' and boys' task activities. In S. McConnell-Ginet et al. (1980), 157–73.

Goodwin, M. (1980b). He-said-she-said: Formal cultural procedures for the construction of a gossip dispute activity. *American Ethnologist* 7(4): 674–95.

Hayes, P. (1979). Lesbians, gay men, and their "languages." In J. W. Cheesbro (ed.), *Gayspeak: Gay Male and Lesbian Communication*. New York: Pilgrim, 28–42.

Hengeveld, E. C. (1984). The lexicographic representation of power vocabulary in Japanese. Unpublished M.A. thesis, Cornell University, Ithaca, NY.

Henley, N. M. (1975). Power, sex, and nonverbal communication. In B. Thorne and N. Henley (1975), 184–203.

Henley, N. M. (1977). *Body politics*. Englewood Cliffs, NJ: Prentice-Hall.

Hirschman, L. (1973). Female–male differences in conversational interaction. Paper presented at Linguistic Society of America, San Diego.

Janeway, E. (1981). *Powers of the Weak*. New York: Morrow Quill.

Korda, M. (1975). *Power: How To Get It, How To Use It*. New York: Random House.

Koschman, J. V. (ed.) (1978). *Authority and the Individual in Japan*. Tokyo: Tokyo University Press.

Kramarae, C. (1980). Proprietors of language. In S. McConnell-Ginet et al. (1980), 58–68.

Kraus, E. S., Rohlen, T. P., and Steinhoff, P. G. (eds.) (1984). *Conflict in Japan*. Honolulu: University of Hawaii Press.

Lakoff, R. (1975). *Language and Woman's Place*. New York: Harper & Row.

Lebra, T. S. (1976). *Japanese Patterns of Behavior*. Honolulu: University of Hawaii Press.

Lebra, T. S. (1984). Nonconfrontational strategies for management of interpersonal conflicts. In E. S. Kraus et al. (1984), 41–60.

Maltz, D. N., and Borker, R. A. (1982). A cultural approach to male–female miscommunication. In J. J. Gumperz (ed.), *Language and Social Identity*. Cambridge: Cambridge University Press, 196–216.

Maruyama, M. (1964). Some problems of political power [translation of *Sihai to hukuzyuu*, 1953, D. Sisson, trans]. In I. Morris (ed.), *Thought and Behavior in Modern Japanese Politics*. London: Oxford University Press, 268–89.

Matsushita, K. (1978). Citizen participation in historical perspective. In J. V. Koschman (1978), 171–88.

Matsuzawa, H. (1978). "Theory" and "organization" in the Japanese communist party. In J. V. Koschman (1978), 108–27.

McClelland, D. C. (1975). *Power: The Inner Experience*. New York: Irvington.

McConnell-Ginet, S., Borker, R., and Furman, N. (eds.) (1980). *Women and Language in Literature and Society*. New York: Praeger.

Mizutani, O. (1981). *Japanese: The Spoken Language in Japanese Life*. Tokyo: The Japan Times.

Nakane, C. (1970). *Japanese Society*. Berkeley: University of California Press.

O'Barr, W. M., and Atkins, B. K. (1980). "Women's language" or "powerless language"? In S. McConnell-Ginet et al. (1980), 93–110.

Shibamoto, J. (1985). *Japanese Women's Language*. Orlando, Fla: Academic.

Stevenson, H., Azuma, H., and Hakuta, K. (eds.) (1986). *Child Development in Japan*. New York: W. H. Freeman.

Strodbeck, F. L., and Mann, R. D. (1956). Sex role differentiation in jury deliberations. *Sociometry* 19: 3–11.

Thorne, B., and Henley, N. (eds.) (1975). *Language and Sex: Difference and Dominance*. Rowley, MA: Newbury House.

Treichler, P. A., and Kramarae, C. (1983). Women's talk in the ivory tower. *Communication Quarterly* 31(2): 118–32.

West, C., and Zimmerman, D. H. (1977). Women's place in everyday talk: Reflections on parent–child interaction. *Social Problems* 24(5): 521–9.

White, M. I., and Levine, R. A. (1986). What is an *ii ko* (good child)? In H. Stevenson et al. (1986), 55–62.

Zimmerman, D. H., and West, C. (1975). Sex roles, interruptions, and silences in conversations. In B. Thorne and N. Henley (1975), 105–29.

34

When the Doctor is a "Lady": Power, Status and Gender in Physician–Patient Encounters

Candace West

Source: *Symbolic Interaction* 7 (1984), pp. 87–106. Reprinted with permission of the University of California Press.

Introduction

[...] Spoken interaction is widely recognized as a fundamental means of regulating social activities and organizing social relationships (e.g., Goffman, 1981; Hymes, 1974; Labov and Fanshel, 1977; Scherer and Giles, 1979.) For example, an extensive body of research indicates that men interrupt women much more often than the reverse, across a variety of situations (Argyle et al., 1968; Eakins and Eakins, 1976; McMillan et al., 1977; Natale et al., 1979; Octigan and Niederman, 1979; Willis and Williams, 1976.) A succession of studies by West and Zimmerman (Zimmerman and West, 1975; West and Zimmerman, 1977 [reprinted in Part III of this volume]; West, 1979, 1982; West and Zimmerman, 1983) leads them to conclude that men's interruptions of women in cross-sex conversations constitute an exercise of power and dominance over their conversational partners.

To be sure, power is an important facet of many other social relationships, such as those between whites and Blacks, bosses and employees, and – of immediate interest – doctors and patients. Moreover, a great deal of our existing knowledge of sex differences in behavior confounds gender with status. Given a world in which men make more money, earn greater prestige, and exert more control over public affairs, it is hardly surprising to find women are less "dominant."[1] Yet the lesser dominance (or lesser power) of women in society cannot be attributed to their gender without considering their lesser opportunities in the marketplaces where commodities are distributed. Where women earn less, are accorded less prestige, and exert less control over affairs, we might reasonably expect to discover them in subordinate positions to men. What happens, though, when the conventional stratification of the sexes is reversed, e.g., when a doctor is a "lady"?[2]

Insofar as the physician–patient relationship is essentially asymmetrical by our cultural standards, it is here that we would expect to find highlighted the micropolitical dynamics of social interaction, through, among other things, a greater proportion of interruptions initiated by superordinate parties to talk. This paper reports results of an exploratory study of interruptions in encounters between physicians and patients during actual "visits to the doctor." My findings offer some empirical support for an asymmetrical view of the physician–patient relationship; male physicians interrupt patients far more often than the reverse, and they appear to use interruptions as a means of exerting control over patients. However, encounters between patients and female physicians display markedly different patterns: there, patients interrupt as much or more than physicians, and their interruptions seem to subvert the physicians' authority. Consideration of these results leads me to address such issues as the respective roles of power, status and gender in face-to-face interaction.

Methods

Data collection

Data for this analysis consist of 21 dyadic encounters between doctors and patients recorded in a family practice center in the southern United States. The doctors involved were residents in family practice, a specialty requiring three years of additional training beyond medical school.[3] Residents are typically in their late twenties to early thirties when completing their training at the Center. Seventeen of the encounters involve white male physicians, and four involve white females. (These four female physicians were among the first cohort – i.e., group of more than two women – ever to enter the program at the Center.)

Patients in these exchanges range in age from 16 to 82 years. They come from a variety of backgrounds, including those of professional, domestic, construction worker and unemployed carpenter. Of the 21 encounters, five involve Black female patients, six, white females, four, Black males, and six, white males.

All of these encounters were recorded during actual "visits to the doctor." Thus, they are not standardized by duration of interaction, purpose of visit, or length of relationship between physician and patient. The family practice center at which they were recorded has employed video taping for many years now, as part of the medical education of residents. With patients' signed consent, they are recorded with their doctors via ceiling microphones and unobtrusive cameras located in the corners of examining rooms. Hence, recordings were not made for purposes of this study but they were later transcribed for these purposes.[4]

[…]

Coding interruptions

West and Zimmerman's studies of interruptions in cross-sex interaction (e.g., 1977, 1983) base their definition of "interruption" on Sacks, Schegloff and Jefferson's (1974) model of turn-taking in talk. There, it is argued that speech exchange systems in general are arranged to ensure that (1) one party speaks at a time and (2) speaker change recurs. These features thus organize a variety of forms of speech exchange including casual conversation, interviewing, formal debate and high ceremony.

Sacks et al. (1974) suggest that a turn consists of the right and obligation to speak which is allocated to a particular speaker. Turns are built out of what they call "unit-types," consisting of possibly complete words, phrases, clauses or sentences, depending on their context. Unit-types are described as "projective" devices in that they allow enough information prior to their completion to allow a hearer to anticipate an upcoming transition place. The end of a possibly complete unit-type is the proper place for turn transition between speakers.[5]

West and Zimmerman (1977) employ these ideas to distinguish between two categories of simultaneous speech: overlaps (briefly, errors in transition timing) and interruptions (violations of speaker turns.) Overlaps are defined as stretches of simultaneity initiated by a "next" speaker just as a current speaker arrives at a possible turn-transition point (West and Zimmerman, 1977: 523). For example, these may occur where a current speaker stretches or drawls the final syllable of an utterance, or adds a tag-question to an otherwise possibly complete statement:

(DYAD 19: 305–307)[6]
PATIENT: I li:ve better and so I- they don' bo:ther
             me too mu:ch. ⌈y'know?⌉
PHYSICIAN: ⌊O::kay. ⌋

Here (as indicated by the brackets), the physician begins an "Okay" just at what would ordinarily be the proper end of the patient's utterance ("They don't bother me too much"). But the patient's addition of a tag-question ("Y'know?") results in their collision. Such an instance of simultaneous speech would be regarded as a possible error in transition timing (cf. West and Zimmerman, 1977) rather than as an indication that the physician is not listening. Certainly, one must listen very carefully in order to anticipate the upcoming completion of a current speaker's utterance and begin speaking precisely on cue with no intervening silence.[7]

Interruptions, in contrast, are defined as deeper incursions into the internal structure of a current speaker's utterance (West and Zimmerman, 1977: 523). Operationally, they are found more than a syllable away from a proper place for turn transition. Since the rules for turn-taking assign a current speaker the rights to a turnspace until a possible turn-transition point is reached, interruptions are seen as violations of current speakers' rights to be engaged in speaking. Just below, we see an example of their potential disruptiveness:

(Dyad 1: 945–954)
((Here, doctor and patient debate the effectiveness of sleeping pills over
extended intervals. The doctor argues that the patient will be better off
without such medication: the patient argues that her anxieties over
a forthcoming trip will interfere with her effectiveness on the job for which
the trip is to be taken.))
PHYSICIAN: ... prob'ly settle dow:n gradjully, a little
             bit, once yuh get used to it. =
PATIENT: = The- press:: ⌈ure's gonna-   ⌉
PHYSICIAN: ⌊Well if it doe::sn',⌋
             Seco*bar*:bital's not gonna help.
                          (.2)
PATIENT: We:ll,
                          (.2)
PHYSICIAN: It's gonna make things worse.

Here, the physician's intrusion ("Well, if it doesn't, Secobarbital's not gonna help") occurs at a point at which the patient is nowhere near completion of her utterance – and the patient drops out, leaving her utterance hanging incomplete. As noted in the preface to this excerpt, the physician and patient had been arguing about whether or not he ought to prescribe sleeping pills for her. One might imagine that the physician's impatience with the argument might have induced his cutting off the patient's protests, especially since the patient was asking for renewals of sixteen other medications (including Valium and Serax) prior to making her trip. The point here is that the way in which the physician imposes his opinion over the patient's is through interruption of her turn at talk – technically, violation of her right to speak.

Later, I will address the content of such incursions in some detail. But next, I turn to general distributions of interruptions between physicians and patients in my collection.

Findings

First, I located all instances of simultaneous speech in the 532 pages of transcribed encounters. Using the criteria specified above, instances of interruption (i.e., deep incursions more than a syllable away from possible turn-transition places) were separated from other types of simultaneity. Then I examined the initiations of interruptions by physician and patient in each dyad in the collection.[8]

Inspecting table 1, we see that a total of 188 instances of interruption occurred. Of these, physicians initiated 67% (126) and patients initiated 33% (62). Thus, in the aggregate, doctors interrupted patients far more often than the reverse. Moreover, in the two encounters that contained more interruptions by patients than physicians (those to which the footnotes are appended), the patient is hard of hearing in one case, and mentally retarded in the other. With the exception of these encounters, doctors interrupted patients more in every dyad in this collection.

However, this collection is comprised only of encounters between patients and male physicians. When we turn to the distributions of interruptions between patients and *female* physicians, we can see that the asymmetries depicted in table 1 are exactly reversed (see table 2). Whereas male physicians (as a group) initiated 67% of all interruptions relative to their patients' 33%, female physicians (as a group) initiated only 32% of interruptions relative to their patients' 68%. Moreover, patients in encounters with female physicians interrupted as much or more than their physicians in each dyad in this collection.

While the collection of encounters involving women physicians only contains four dyads, it is at least worth noting that the two encounters that display nearly symmetrical relations between the parties involved (the first two listed in table 2) are same-sex interactions between female doctors and female patients. These symmetries are all the more noteworthy when one considers the differences in race and age between them (the patients in both dyads are Black and the physicians are white; the patients are both much older than their physicians). Zimmerman and West's (1975) earlier research on same-sex interactions between white females conversing in public places also indicates that casual conversations between females tend to display symmetrical distributions of interruptions.

Obviously, the variety of race, age and gender combinations in a sample of this size precludes extensive extrapolation regarding the composite effects of these factors. There is, for example, only one white male patient engaged in interaction with a white female physician; and, there is only one sixty-seven year old patient engaged in talk with a physician of half her years. Still, the consistency of patterns of interruption displayed in tables 1 and 2 offer evidence of an asymmetrical relationship between doctors and patients in this collection – *except* when the doctor is a "lady."

Table 1 Interruptions in encounters between patients and male physicians

	Physician Interruptions	Patient Interruptions	
Black male patient, 26 years	100% (7)	—	(0)
Black female patient, 20 years	100% (1)	—	(0)
White male patient, 16 years	100% (1)	—	(0)
White female patient, 17 years	100% (1)	—	(0)
Black female patient, 16 years	91% (10)	9	(1)
White female patient, 58 years	80% (4)	20	(1)
Black female patient, 31 years	77% (20)	23	(6)
White female patient, 36 years	73% (11)	27	(4)
White female patient, 53 years	71% (29)	29	(12)
White female patient, 32 years	67% (10)	33	(5)
Black male patient, 36 years	67% (4)	33	(2)
White male patient, 16 years	67% (2)	33	(1)
White male patient, 31 years	60% (3)	40	(2)
White male patient, 36 years	58% (7)	42	(5)
Black male patient, 17 years	56% (5)	44	(4)
White female patient, 82 years[*]	37% (7)	63	(12)
White male patient, 56 years[**]	36% (4)	64	(7)
TOTAL	67% (126)	33% (62)	

[*] This patient is hard of hearing.
[**] This patient is mentally retarded.

Table 2 Interruptions in encounters between patients and female physicians

	Physician Interruptions	Patient Interruptions	
Black female patient, 52 years	50% (7)	50	(7)
Black female patient, 67 years	40% (6)	60	(9)
Black male patient, 58 years	28% (5)	72	(13)
White male patient, 38 years	8% (1)	92	(11)
TOTAL	32% (19)	68% (40)	

It is important to remember that this collection of encounters does not represent a random sample of physicians, patients, or physician–patient exchanges. The data analyzed here were initially collected for purposes of resident training rather than for purposes of my research. Thus, my lack of control over many factors (e.g., length of exchange or past acquaintanceship between doctor and patient) resulted in a non-standardized corpus of materials, involving exchanges of various durations and including doctors and patients with different bases for relationships. Some encounters transpired between parties with well-established relationships of three years' standing, while others constituted the occasions on which physicians and patients met for the first time. Some encounters involved physical examinations, while others were devoted exclusively to verbal interactions. The collection of encounters does not constitute a probability sample of physicians, patients, or medical exchanges, and simple projections from these findings to physicians, patients, or medical encounters generally cannot be justified with the usual logic of statistical inference. The stability of any empirical finding cannot, in any event, be established by a single piece of research. My purpose in presenting these quantitative trends is twofold. First, their consistency offers a rough indication that relations between patients and female physicians constitute a site that merits "drilling for oil" (i.e., through collection of a larger, systematic sample of such interactions). Second, these quantitative data provide a general framework for the detailed qualitative analysis of interruptions that follows.

Interruptions, Dominance and Control

West and Zimmerman's (1977) comparisons of conversations between men and women and interactions between parents and children lead them to suggest that males' use of interruptions may display dominance and control to females (and to any witnesses), just as parents' interruptions communicate aspects of parental control to children and others present. If patients can be likened to children (as proposed by Parsons and Fox, 1952), then we might regard the violations of their speaking rights by male physicians as displays of the physicians' interactional control.

For example, the key to the therapeutic practice of medicine is, for Parsons (1951, 1975), the essential *asymmetry* of the physician–patient relationship. Because, at least within Western cultures, it is the physician who is charged with the legal responsibility for restoring the patient to normality:

> ... The practitioner must have control over the interaction with the patient, ensuring that the patient will comply with the prescribed regimen. If patient compliance is not ensured, then the ability of the practitioner to return the patient to a normal functioning state is undermined. (Wolinsky, 1980: 163, explicating Parsons)

In this view, patients' situational dependency on physicians, physicians' professional prestige and their authority over patients all ensure physicians the necessary leverage for controlling interpersonal encounters. But, if physicians' control is to be exerted in actual exchanges with patients, one would expect some ready vehicle might be available in *any* medical encounter for demonstrating the physician's dominance.

Although medical sociologists place heavy emphasis on social roles as determinants of behaviors (cf. Wilson, 1970: 13–14), the actual behaviors of persons in social roles remain to be enacted in particular situations. Whatever the scripts that may exist for the physician–patient encounter, they must always be negotiated on the basis of the situational exigencies of social life. Fortunately, as Zimmerman (1978: 12) notes, social life is rife with opportunities for enacting them:

> It would surely be odd if a society were designed so that its institutions were partly constructed of role-relationships but lacked any systematic mechanism for articulating societal roles within the features of various interactional settings. [And] stranger still if this articulation were itself not socially organized. Strangest of all would be a state of affairs in which the instantiation of a role in an actual situation had no bearing on the understanding of roles in general, or the sense of "objectivity" and transcendence of the role.

Zimmerman's observations invite us to look more closely at the ways in which the social identities of "doctor" and "patient" are played out in the actual organization of interaction between the two.

Hence, rather than regarding the physician's authority as superimposed *onto* encounters with patients in "well-rehearsed", script-like fashion (cf. Parsons, 1951, 1975; Wilson, 1970), we can examine the dynamics of actual medical exchanges to see how dominance and control are constituted by participants in these social situations. A telling example is offered in the fragment used earlier to display the potential effects of interruption itself. There, a disagreement between a (male) physician and (female) patient was ultimately resolved by the doctor's interruption of the patient's opinion (regarding sleeping pills) with his own contrary view ("They won't help"). In that excerpt, we saw interruption used to advance the physician's (expert) perspective while simultaneously cutting off the patient's (lay) point of view.

Another aspect of the relationship between interruptions and interactional control was first brought to my attention by a friend – in this case, a male physician. Prior to writing up the results of this study, I discussed with him the tendency of male physicians to interrupt patients in these encounters. My friend did not find this trend a surprising one, and explained. "That's because so many patients are still answering your last question when you're trying to ask them the *next* one!" His "explanation" was of interest for two reasons. First, it fails as an explanation on the grounds that answers follow questions, rather than the other way around. Hence, a speaker interrupting an answer with a "next question" is disavowing the obligation to listen to the answer to a prior question. But second, my doctor-friend's explanation was of analytical interest, since I had already begun to notice that a great many physician-initiated interruptions in these data were composed of doctors' questions to their patients.

Consider the following fragment, which shows the staccato pace at which physicians' "next" questions can follow their "last" ones:

```
(Dyad 20: 053–074)
PATIENT:     It us:ually be (1.0) ((she reaches
             down to touch her calf with her left
             hand)) in: he:ah. You: know, it
             jus' ⌈be a li:l            ⌉
PHYSICIAN:        ⌊Can y' pull up⌋ yer cuff there
             for me? (.6) Duh yuh have the pain right no::w?
             (.2)
PATIENT:     Um-um. No, it ⌈ha:ppens                   ⌉
PHYSICIAN:                 ⌊It's not happening right now::?⌋
PATIENT:     =ss- some- only one: time when ah w⌈as heah.  ⌉
PHYSICIAN:                                      ⌊Can y  ⌋uh take
             yer shoe: off for me please?
             (.8) ((Patient removes her shoe))
PATIENT:     ⌈But I-  ⌉
PHYSICIAN:   ⌊WHU::T'RE YUH DO::ING, when yuh no:tice the pai:n
             (.4) ((Physician bends over to touch the patient's legs))
PATIENT:     We:ll, I thi:nk that- Well, so:metime I jus' be si:ttin'
             theah, (1.0) An' yih: know: ih ji:st- (1.2) ((she
             shrugs, holding up both palms)) Then I fee:l a liddul
             pai:n in theah, (.2) Yih know, ji:st- gra:dually (.4)
PATIENT:     It gradually c⌈ome on.     ⌉
PHYSICIAN:                 ⌊Take thi:s⌋ shoe: off?
```

We can note here that each of the physician's intrusions into his patient's turn at talk is patently reasonable and warranted by the external constraints of medical examination and treatment. To ask where a patient is feeling pain, how often, when or under what conditions is all justified by, even required for, precise diagnosis of a problem (cf. Cicourel, 1975; 1978). However, when these inquiries cut off what the patient is in the process of saying, particularly when what she is saying is presumably the necessary response to a "prior" needed question, then the physician is not only violating the patient's rights to speak, but he is also systematically cutting off potentially valuable information *on which he must himself rely* to achieve a diagnosis.[9]

Just below, a similar pattern is evident:

(Dyad 2: 085–099)
((Here, the doctor is inquiring about a recent injury
to the patient's back caused by an auto accident.))

PATIENT: When I'm sitting *up*right. Y'know =
PHYSICIAN: = More so than it
           was even before?
PATIENT: Yay::es =
PHYSICIAN: = Swelling 'r anything like that thet chew've no:ticed?
           (.)
PATIENT: Nuh:o, not the ⌈t I've nodi-
PHYSICIAN: ⌊TEN::DER duh the tou⌋ ch? Press:ing any?
PATIENT: No::, jus' when it's- si::tting.
PHYSICIAN: Okay: =
PATIENT: = Er lying on it.
PHYSICIAN: Even ly:ing, Stan:ding up? Walking aroun:d? ((sing-song))
PATIENT: No: ⌈jis-
PHYSICIAN: ⌊Not so mu:ch.⌋ Jis'- ly:ing on it. Si:tting on it.
           Jis' then.

In this excerpt [...] on two occasions, the physician's "next" utterance cuts off the patient's completion of her answer to his "last" one. The staccato pacing and intrusions into the patient's turnspaces demonstrate that – in essence and in fact – a simple "yes" or "no" is all this doctor will listen to. Such practices also serve to demonstrate who is in control in the exchange.

In the case of both excerpts, it appears that the use of interruptions by male doctors is a *display* of dominance or control to the patient, just as males' and parents' interruptions (West and Zimmerman, 1977) are employed to communicate control in cross-sex and parent–child interactions. But also in these exchanges (as in West and Zimmerman's study), it appears that the use of interruptions is *in fact* a control device, as the incursions (especially when repeated) disorganize the local construction of conversational topics. Insofar as the over-arching conversational topic is, in the medical exchange, the state of the patient's health, interruptions in these encounters may have further serious consequences than in casual conversation.

When the doctor is a "lady"

The above analysis notwithstanding, the fact remains that results for four of the 21 exchanges in this collection defy the general pattern. Interactions between female doctors and female patients display distributions that approximate symmetry. Moreover, encounters between female physicians and male patients show the male patient (not the female physician) interrupting most (92% of interruptions in one exchange and 72% in another.) It must be reiterated that there are very few dyads involving female physicians in the collection of materials here analyzed. Thus, attention to these encounters might best be viewed as a variant of case study rather than a survey of such interactions in general. However, since these proportions parallel – rather than contradict – the actual distributions of females in medicine (where women, notes Lorber, are "invisible professionals and ubiquitous patients," 1975), they warrant at least preliminary inspection here.

[...]

In our society, Hughes (1945: 353–4) observes, the auxiliary characteristics that have emerged around the status "physician" are "white," "Protestant" and "male." Hence, when persons assuming the powerful status of physician are not properly equipped with whiteness, Protestantism or maleness, there tends to be what Hughes terms a "status contradiction" – or even, a "status dilemma" – both for the individuals themselves and for those with whom they associate.

The "lady doctor" is a case in point, the adjective "lady" (or "woman" or "female") serving to underscore the presumed maleness of the status "physician." Hughes notes that particular statuses (e.g., "Black") operate as "master status-determining traits", i.e., powerful characteristics that outshine any others with which they may be clustered. So, for persons (e.g., women) whose master status conflicts with other very potent statuses (e.g., physician), a dilemma is likely to ensue over whether to treat them as members of the social category "women" *or* as members of the profession "physician."

In the context of these considerations, we are well-advised to remember that the appropriate behaviors of persons occupying social roles remain to be acted out in everyday life. Hughes' (1945) description might lead us to an overly-deterministic perspective that depicts "choices" between two conflicting status-determining characteristics (e.g., "woman" and "physician"), as if the resolution of status dilemmas were an individual matter. However, the issue is more complex than can be described by the "choice" or "nonchoice" of individuals who are caught in status dilemmas, since they must interact with others in their social worlds. For example, the Black man who would "pass" as a white one must rely on others' willingness to read various physical characteristics as constitutive of his "whiteness." Similarly, the woman who would become a physician must rely on others' willingness to honor her displays of professionalism over those of her gender.

While the evidence is far from conclusive, there is reason to believe that Hughes' (1945) analysis is pertinent to my results. Recall, for example, that the four female physicians involved in these encounters were among the first cohort of women ever to enter the residency program at the Family Practice Center. In this sense, they constituted what Hughes terms "a group of some new and peculiar type." Moreover, at the time they began their training at the Center, there was only one woman doctor among the medical faculty members. Hence, there was only one faculty member who might assist these "new and peculiar" entrants into what was formerly an all-male preserve. Even the medical faculty in charge of resident training remarked on the "exceptional" status of the first cohort of women. For example, those who assisted me in my data collection took great pains to include "our new women residents" in the final collection of exchanges.[10] Through such descriptions they helped make gender a salient characteristic of women residents (e.g., not once did I hear a male doctor described as a "man resident").

More telling still were the words of patients themselves. For example, one patient bade her new woman physician farewell, commenting that she had "enjoyed meeting" her since she had never had "a female doctor" before. Another patient, asked by his woman physician if he was having any problems passing urine, responded "You know, the *doctor* asked me that." In this instance, it was difficult to tell who "the doctor" *was*: "the doctor" was *not*, evidently, the female physician who was treating him.

Finally, consider the excerpt below, in which a female physician attempts to provide her professional opinion on a patient's problem:

(Dyad 4: 213–231)
((To this point, the patient has complained about his
weight, and the doctor and patient have been discussing
possible ways for reducing. One suggestion offered by
the physician was to slow down while eating: but the
patient has *just countered* that suggestion with a complaint
– he does not like cold food.))

PATIENT:　　… An' they take twe:nny 'r thirdy minutes

.

.

.

Tuh eat.
PHYSICIAN:　Wull what chew 　⌈could DO:
PATIENT:　　　　　　　 ⌊An' then by the⌋ time they
get through: their foo:d is col::d an' uh-
'ey li:kes it y'know
PHYSICIAN:　⌈engh-hengh-hengh-hengh-hengh⌉ .hh=
PATIENT:　 ⌊An' th' they enjoy that　　　 ⌋ 　 = but I- I
'on't *like* cole foo:d.
(.2)
PHYSICIAN:　One thing yuh could *d*⌈*o::*
PATIENT:　　　　　　　　 ⌊Spesh'ly⌋ food thet's
not suhpoze: be col'=
PHYSICIAN:　　　　　　　　 = O:kay .h = is tuh ea:t. say.
the *meat* firs'. Yuh know:, but if yuh have a
*sal:*ad tuh eat, t' sa:ve that till *after* yuh eat
the meat. (.) Cuz the sal:ad's suhpose tuh be
col:d.

Here, the physician's attempts to advance her solution are interrupted repeatedly by the patient's ongoing elaboration of his (already evident) problem.

In the same encounter, the patient earlier questioned his physician about a medication he is taking for his high blood pressure. He said that he had heard a radio report indicating that this medicine "might" cause cancer, and then another report, indicating that people should continue with use of the drug. Following this, the doctor checked the patient's blood pressure and explained that she had looked into this problem. There was, she said, no alternative medication available, and there was, in her view, no better present alternative than to continue it. At this juncture, the patient shifted to a slightly different complaint:

(Dyad 4: 430–454)
PATIENT:　　… If there wuz any way possible duh git me some
diffrun' type a pill thet li:ke yuh take twi:ce a
da::y instead of three:. .hh an' have th' same
effek with this (allernate) 'n u:h- *wah*dur pi:ll.

PHYSICIAN: OhKa:y, that's egzakly what we: were try:ing
 tuh do:: .hh=
PATIENT: =Ah kno:w, but tho:se-
 I- (.) heard ⌈what ⌉ th' man sai:d.
PHYSICIAN: ⌊We:ll.⌋
 Ay:::e- checked *in*:ta tha:t. oka::y? an:::d-
 (1.0) No:t No:t- *exten*sively. I didn' search
 all the lidda'chure =
PATIENT: = ((clears throat))
 (.4)
PHYSICIAN: .h Bu::t uh:m (.6) ((sniff)) Ah feel *comf*trable
 us:in' thuh dru::g? An' would take it muhself:::
 °If I needed tuh. ((Looking directly at the patient))
 (6.0)
PHYSICIAN: So it ⌈'s u:p- .hh It's u:p tuh you:: ⌉ :: =
PATIENT: ⌊But if all they sa:y- if there's *any*-⌋ =Ah
 know::w, it's u:h-uh ⌈bud it's u:h- ⌉ Ah'm try:in'
PHYSICIAN: ⌊It's up tuh you:⌋
PATIENT: to: uh- .h ((clears throat)) i:s there: *any other*
 ty::*pe* that chew could u:h fi:gger ...

To spare readers, I have omitted the next several lines, in which the doctor again asserts that there is nothing else the patient can take and in which the patient again asserts his desire to get around taking this medication. Below, however, is the resolution of their argument:

(Dyad 4: 471–479)
PHYSICIAN: *If I* brought cha some *ar*duhcul(s) saying thet this
 wuz Ok*ay:::*, would juh bih*lie:::ve* me? .h
PATIENT: Ye:ah, su:re, defin ⌈at'ly. ⌉
PHYSICIAN: ⌊OKa:y.⌋
 (.)
PHYSICIAN: O ⌈kay:, ⌉o::kay =
PATIENT: ⌊But u:h-⌋ = ((clears throat)) .h
 Whether I would cha:nge to it 'r no:t, it would
 be a diff- y'know, a nuther thi::ng.

Note: the patient might "believe" this woman physician if she brought him some articles supporting her opinions, but whether or not he would follow her advice "would be a nuther thi::ng."

My concern here is *not* with the possible carcinogenic effects of the drug (though important) – nor with the alternatives to it. Rather, I am interested in the way in which this woman physician is "heard" by her (male) patient. As noted earlier, Parsons (1951, 1975) asserts that the therapeutic practice of medicine is predicated on institutionalized asymmetry between physician and patient. In his view, physicians are in a position of situational authority vis-à-vis their patients, since only physicians are possessed of the technical qualifications (and institutional certification) to provide medical care.

Yet these excerpts show that neither technical qualifications (conferred by the training and medical degree) nor personal assurances ("I would take this myself," "I checked into it") are sufficient for the woman physician to have her authority (*as a physician*) respected by the patient. Elsewhere, Hughes (1958) suggests that clients of professionals do not simply grant them authority and autonomy as *faits accompli*. Given a recent history of increasing challenges to medical authority in the United States (cf. Reeder, 1972; Ruzek,

1979; Mendelsohn, 1981), it is entirely possible that patients in general are taking increased initiative in their own health care and questioning physicians more frequently. But, nowhere else in these data did I find a patient who questioned the opinion of a male physician as forcefully or as repeatedly as the case noted here.

Conclusions

These are preliminary findings, based on suggestive but far from definitive results. These data originated in a small and essentially haphazard collection of exchanges between patients and Family Physicians. Thus, generalizations based on them to medical encounters at large cannot be substantiated through quantitative extrapolation. I report them here to call attention to their potential significance for the study of gender, power and interaction.

Encounters between patients and male physicians lend support to conventional descriptions (cf. Parsons, 1951; Parsons and Fox, 1952; Parsons, 1975) of asymmetry in the physician–patient relationship. Face-to-face with one another, male doctors interrupted their patients far more often than the reverse, and they appeared to use interruptions as devices for exercising control over interaction. However, where female physicians were involved, the asymmetrical relationship was exactly reversed: patients interrupted their female doctors as much or more than these doctors interrupted them. Hence, my findings for female physicians conflict with the general pattern.

At this point, any discussion of the implications of this gender-associated difference must be speculative. But, in engaging in such discussion, I hope to eliminate possible misinterpretations of its significance. I am not claiming that female physicians are "better listeners" than their colleagues (although they may be). These preliminary analyses have focused on the distribution of interruptions *between* physicians and patients. While the female physicians in this collection were interrupted disproportionately, it makes as much sense to attribute this finding to their patients' gender-associated "disrespect" as it does to attribute it to the physicians' own communication skills. Neither inference is warranted at this point. What *is* warranted, for the findings reported here, is the suggestion that gender can have primacy over status where women physicians are concerned. These data indicate that gender can amount to a "master" status (Hughes, 1945), even where other power relations are involved.

Notes

A revised version of this paper was presented at the American Sociological Association Annual Meeting. New York, August 1980.

I wish to thank Sarah F. Berk, Richard M. Frankel, Erving Goffman, Wendy Martyna, Ann Stromberg, and Gilly West for their helpful comments on the earlier versions of this paper. The financial assistance provided by the Southern Regional Educational Board, the Committee on Faculty Research at the University of California, Santa Cruz, and the Organized Research Unit in Institutional Analysis and Social Policy at Santa Cruz (Robert R. Alford, Director) is gratefully acknowledged. Finally, I offer thanks and appreciation to the Department of Family Medicine, Medical University of South Carolina, Charleston.

1   My use of the term *dominant* is not meant in the conventional psychological sense (i.e., as a personality attribute). Rather, I use it sociologically to describe control of and supremacy over one group by another.

2 I use quotation marks around *lady* to illustrate its ironic connotations in this context. For example, Lakoff (1975: 21) contends that this term operates as a euphemism for *woman*:

> Just as we do not call whites "Caucasian-Americans," there is no felt need to refer to men commonly as "gentlemen." And just as there is a need for such terms as "Afro-Americans," there is similarly felt a need for "lady." One might even say that when a derogatory epithet exists, a parallel euphemism is deemed necessary.

To the extent that *lady* does indeed operate as a euphemism (i.e., rendering the very fact of femaleness less distasteful and more respectable than *woman*), it is especially peculiar to see it coupled with prestigious occupations (e.g., "lady lawyer," "lady doctor" or "lady engineer").

3 Two physicians included in the collection were not residents. One was an alumnus of the training program who continued to see patients at the Center after completing his residency four years earlier; the other was a faculty member who also saw patients there. With regard to the analysis which follows, I found no differences evidenced between these doctors' exchanges with patients and those of resident physicians.

4 In the transcriptions, anything which might identify participants has been altered. Transcription Conventions are given on p. x.

5 The criteria for determining a possibly complete utterance, and hence an interrupted turn at talk, are only partially syntactic. For example, the status of a word as a unit-type is also a sequential and thus, social-organizational issue, as where one party says "Yes" in response to another's question (West and Zimmerman, 1977: 522, fn. 1). However, both syntactic and sequential criteria are fundamentally linked to the above-mentioned characteristic of speech exchange systems, i.e., one party speaks at a time. That this characteristic of talk is seen to describe speech exchange in general, rather than conversation in particular, is of central concern to this paper. For, while Sacks et al.'s (1974) model of turn-taking is intended to account for observed features of actual conversation, it may be that the talk which goes on in medical encounters is not entirely conversational in nature (cf. Frankel, in press).

6 Superscripts to these excerpts denote dyads and line numbers of transcripts in this corpus of materials.

7 To be sure, there are instances of simultaneous speech that appear to ratify – rather than disrupt – the talk of a current speaker, even when they intrude deeply into the current speaker's turnspace (West, 1979: 83). For example, Jefferson (1973) identifies two of these as (1) the emphatic "YEAH" interjected to display recognition of that which is in-the-course-of-being-said, and (2) the display of independent knowledge achieved by saying the same thing at the same time that a current speaker produces it. Following West (1979), I exempted such instances of simultaneous speech from the category, interruptions.

8 I am grateful to Linda Guiffre, who coded these instances of simultaneous speech independently. The categorization of instances involved a detailed coding scheme (West, 1979) designed to distinguish violations of speakers' rights (interruptions) from other types of simultaneity (e.g., errors in transition timing, displays of active listening, simultaneous starts, and continuations of prior incomplete turns). Despite its complexity, the coding scheme yielded substantial inter-coder reliability: in this case 87% between the two coders. Disagreements (typically, over instances of overlap rather than interruption) were resolved by discussion of the individual utterances in question.

9 An anecdote may help to illustrate this point. A friend of mine has suffered all of her life from a chronic but rare lung disorder. Prior to the discovery of sulfa drugs, people died from this disorder: now, it is manageable with routine monitoring and treatment. My friend has traveled around the world and visited numerous physicians for treatment of her condition. Since her disorder is a rare one, she often discovers that she knows more about her problem than the doctors she goes to for treatment. And yet, she observes that most physicians insist on going through a standard battery of questions before they begin to treat her complaints seriously. Thus, suggestions that she tries to raise concerning new ways of coping with her disorder are often aborted by physicians' insistence on a litany of complaints and disorders described in medical textbooks.

10   In passing, it is worth noting Hogan's (1978) contention that the use of personal pronouns in this context ("our new women residents") implies proprietorship rather than collegial relations (e.g., "our girls at the main desk," "my gal at the office," etc.).

References

Argyle, Michael, Mansur Lalljee, and Mark Cook (1968) "The effects of visibility on interaction in a dyad." *Human Relations* 21: 3–17.

Braslow, Judith B. and Marilyn Heins (1981) "Women in medical education: a decade of change." *New England Journal of Medicine* 304: 1129–35.

Cicourel, Aaron V. (1975) "Discourse and text: cognitive and linguistic processes in studies of social structure." *Versus: Quaderni di Studi Semotici* 12: 33–84.

Cicourel, Aaron V. (1978) "Language and society: cognitive, cultural and linguistic aspects of language use." *Sozialwissenschaftliche Annalen.* Band 2. Seite B25–B58. Vienna: Physica-Verlag.

Eakins, Barbara Westbrook and R. Gene Eakins (1976) *Sex Differences in Human Communication.* Boston: Houghton Mifflin.

Frankel, Richard M. (in press) "Talking in interviews: a dispreference for patient-initiated questions in physician–patient encounters." In G. Psathas (ed.), *Interactional Competence.* New York: Irvington.

Goffman, Erving (1981) *Forms of Talk.* Philadelphia: University of Pennsylvania Press.

Hogan, Patricia (1978) "A woman is not a girl and other lessons in corporate speech." pp. 168–72 in Bette Ann Stead (ed.), *Women in Management.* Englewood Cliffs, NJ: Prentice-Hall.

Hughes, Everett C. (1945) "Dilemmas and contradictions of status." *American Journal of Sociology* 50: 353–354.

Hughes, Everett C. (1958) *Men and Their Work.* New York: The Free Press.

Hymes, Dell (1974) *Foundations in Sociolinguistics: An Ethnographic Approach.* Philadelphia: University of Pennsylvania Press.

Jefferson, Gail (1973) "A case of precision timing in ordinary conversation: overlapped tag-positioned address terms in closing sequences." *Semiotica* 9: 47–96.

Labov, William and David Fanshel (1977) *Therapeutic Discourse: Psychotherapy as Conversation.* New York: Academic Press.

Lakoff, Robin (1975) *Language and Woman's Place.* New York: Harper Colophon.

Lorber, Judith (1975) "Women and medical sociology: invisible professionals and ubiquitous patients", pp. 75–105 in M. Millman and R. M. Kanter (eds), *Another Voice: Feminist Perspectives on Social Life and Social Science.* Garden City, NY: Anchor Press/Doubleday.

Mattera, Marianne Dekker (1980) "Female doctors: why they're on an economic treadmill." *Medical Economics* (February 18): 98–110.

McMillan, Leslie R., A. Kay Clifton, Diane McGrath, and Wanda S. Gale (1977) "Women's language: uncertainty or interpersonal sensitivity and emotionality?" *Sex Roles* 3: 545–59.

Mendelsohn, Robert S. (1981) *Male Practice: How Doctors Manipulate Women.* Chicago: Contemporary Books.

Natale, Michael, Elliot Entin, and Joseph Jaffee (1979) "Vocal interruptions in dyadic communication as a function of speech and social anxiety." *Journal of Personality and Social Psychology* 37: 865–78.

Octigan, Mary and Sharon Niederman (1979) "Male dominance in conversation." *Frontiers* 4: 50–4.

Parsons, Talcott (1951) *The Social System.* New York: The Free Press.

Parsons, Talcott (1975) "The sick role and the role of the physician reconsidered." *Millbank Memorial Fund Quarterly* 53: 257–77.

Parsons, Talcott and Renee C. Fox (1952) "Illness, therapy and the modern urban American family." *Journal of Social Issues* 8: 31–44.

Reeder, Leo G. (1972) "The patient-client as a consumer: some observations on the changing professional-client relationship." *Journal of Health and Social Behavior* 13: 406–12.

Ruzek, Sheryl Burt (1979) *The Women's Health Movement.* New York: Praeger.

Sacks, Harvey, Emanuel A. Schegloff, and Gail Jefferson (1974) "A simplest systematics for the organization of turn-taking for conversation." *Language* 50: 696–735.

Scherer, Klaus R. and Howard Giles (eds.) (1979) *Social Markers in Speech.* Cambridge: Cambridge University Press.

West, Candace (1979) "Against our will: male interruptions of females in cross-sex conversation." *Annals of the New York Academy of Sciences* 327: 81–97.

West, Candace (1982) "Why can't a woman be more like a man? An interactional note on organizational game-playing for managerial women." *Sociology of Work and Occupations* 9: 5–29.

West, Candace and Don H. Zimmerman (1977) "Women's place in everyday talk: reflections on parent–child interaction." *Social Problems* 24: 521–9.

West, Candace and Don H. Zimmerman (1983) "Small insults: a study of interruptions in cross-sex conversations between unacquainted persons." pp. 86–111 in Barrie Thorne, Cheris Kramarae and Nancy Henley (eds.), *Language, Gender and Society.* Rowley, MA: Newbury House.

Willis, Frank N. and Sharon J. Williams (1976) "Simultaneous talking in conversation and sex of speakers." *Perceptual and Motor Skills* 43: 1067–70.

Wilson, Robert N. (1970) *The Sociology of Health: An Introduction.* New York: Random House.

Wolinsky, Frederic D. (1980) *The Sociology of Health: Principles, Professions and Issues.* Boston: Little, Brown.

Zimmerman, Don H. (1978) "Ethnomethodology." *The American Sociologist* 13: 6–14.

Zimmerman, Don H. and Candace West (1975) "Sex roles, interruptions, and silences in conversation." pp. 105–129 in Barrie Thorne and Nancy Henley (eds.), *Language and Sex: Difference and Dominance.* Rowley, MA: Newbury House.

Part VIII

Theoretical Debates (2): Difference or Dominance?

In this section we focus on a debate involving two of the main approaches used in language and gender research: the dominance approach and the difference approach. This debate precedes the rise of social constructionism, the approach now adopted by most language and gender researchers, but shows that in the 1980s dissatisfaction with the two approaches was beginning to be articulated. You will have already read several papers relevant to this debate: most of the papers in Part III (on gender, power, and dominance) adopt a dominance perspective, while Davies in Part II and Coates in Part IV are good examples of papers orienting to a difference perspective. To put it very simply, research which takes a dominance perspective interprets the differences between women's and men's linguistic usage as reflexes of the dominant-subordinate relationship holding between women and men. Research which takes a difference perspective, by contrast, sees the differences between women's linguistic usage and men's linguistic usage as arising from the different subcultures in which women and men are socialized (this approach is sometimes called the subcultural or two-cultures approach).

Early work on language and gender took a dominance approach. The reaction against this, and the subsequent flourishing of the difference approach, arose *not* because researchers denied the existence of dominance and oppression in male–female relationships, but because researchers, particularly feminist researchers, became unhappy at the negative portrayal of women in work using the dominance approach. Women's language was often described as weak, unassertive, or tentative, and women were presented as losers, as victims.

Researchers who began using the difference model in the 1980s argued that the dominance model had become a *deficit* model, that is, a way of interpreting the linguistic facts which represented men's language as the norm and women's language as deviant. The advantage of the difference model was that it allowed researchers to show the strengths of linguistic strategies characteristic of women and to celebrate women's ways of talking. For those carrying out research involving mixed talk, the dominance approach provides a useful explanatory framework, but for researchers investigating same-sex talk it seems less appropriate, since dominance and oppression are not obviously helpful categories for analyzing all-female talk. (It is only relatively recently that researchers have turned their attention to the informal talk of all-male groups, frequently adopting a constructionist rather than the difference approach – see the papers in Part IV.)

The first paper in this section is the one which, it can be argued, initiated this debate: Daniel Maltz and Ruth Borker's "A Cultural Approach to Male–Female Miscommunication." This paper explicitly claims to present a new (anthropological) framework for discussing gender differences in language. Until 1982, when the paper was published, most researchers had assumed a dominance model, so there is no one paper which sets out the dominance approach (though the papers produced in the 1970s and early 1980s by West and Zimmerman on interruptions could be seen as archetypal – see their "Women's Place in Everyday Talk" in Part III above). Maltz and Borker's paper is not based on new data, but rather presents a synthesis of work on gender and language in a variety of fields. Their argument rests on the claim that the "difficulties" found in cross-sex communication – like the "difficulties" found in cross-ethnic communication – are the result of cultural difference and should be seen as miscommunication. They argue that boys and girls are socialized largely in same-sex peer groups between the ages of 5 and 15, and that they learn to use language in very different ways. This means that, when male and female speakers interact as adults, they are working with a different set of assumptions about the way interaction works. In the concluding section of their paper Maltz and Borker make some sensible suggestions about future research in the language and gender field, and summarize the contribution they think a difference approach could offer to language and gender research.

At the time it was published, many sociolinguists found Maltz and Borker's paper refreshing: it certainly gave impetus to those linguists wanting to carry out research into women's talk outside a framework of dominance and oppression. So, for research into talk in single-sex groups, the difference approach had a lot to offer. But, like all frameworks, the difference approach has its limitations. Probably the main problem with the approach is its assumption that all interactional difficulties can be called "miscommunication."

However, this idea – the notion that miscommunication is at the heart of male–female problems – had, and still has, immense popular appeal. This became evident when Deborah Tannen's book *You Just Don't Understand* (1990) became a best-seller and made gender differences in language a topic for discussion all over the English-speaking world. The second paper in this section is "Asymmetries: Women and Men Talking at Cross-Purposes," the second chapter of Tannen's book, in which she presents her main argument about women and men and miscommunication. This is the one selection in this Reader which comes from a popular book rather than an academic source. But it is vital for an understanding of the difference–dominance debate to read some of Tannen's work. What Tannen did in this book was to take Maltz and Borker's argument to its logical extreme: women and men belong to different subcultures; interactional problems between women and men are cross-cultural miscommunication; if we all take the trouble to understand each other a bit better, these problems can be overcome.

You Just Don't Understand received some of the most critical reviews ever seen in the sociolinguistic world (see, for example, Troemel-Ploetz 1991; Cameron 1992; Freed 1992). Theoretical debates do not generally generate such emotional heat, but in this case sociolinguists, particularly feminist linguists, felt very strongly that Tannen's account of gender differences in language misrepresented research findings in the area, as well as over-simplifying the explanatory framework.

The third paper in this section, Senta Troemel-Ploetz's "Selling the Apolitical," is the fiercest of these reviews. Troemel-Ploetz articulates the widely held feeling that Tannen has taken the difference approach too far: dominance and power have disappeared from the analysis. Troemel-Ploetz claims that Tannen fails to make clear that women's and men's different ways of talking are *not* different-but-equal, arguing, rather, that men's ways of talking have high status in society while women's talk is denigrated. Moreover, Tannen's book fed into the genre of self-help books aimed at women which, it can be argued, perpetuate the view that, where things aren't working, then it is women who need to adapt (see Cameron 1995 and Crawford 1995 for a fuller exposition of this point).

The after-effects of Tannen's book were significant: the difference approach became stigmatized and researchers were forced to recognize the limitations of a theoretical framework which treated women and men as if they came from different planets. As Freed (1992) ripostes in the title of her review, "We understand perfectly." The dominance approach also went into decline, since it was apparent that, on its own, it was inadequate for dealing with same-sex talk (though more recently it has reappeared in a revised form in sociolinguistic work on talk in the public sphere – see Part V). The feminist principles which were behind both these approaches (the dominance approach emphasizing patriarchal power structures; the difference approach celebrating women's voices) were muted for a time, but have been reasserted in recent work (see Part X on recent developments, especially the paper by Holmes). The most significant outcome of the debate was the adoption of a new theoretical framework – social constructionism – and a new understanding that language does not reflect society but is actively involved in the construction and maintenance of social categories such as gender.

References

Cameron, Deborah (1992) "Review of Tannen *You Just Don't Understand*," *Feminism and Psychology* 2, 465–8.

Cameron, Deborah (1995) *Verbal Hygiene*. London: Routledge.

Crawford, Mary (1995) *Talking Difference: On Gender and Language*. London: Sage.

Freed, Alice (1992) "We understand perfectly: a critique of Tannen's view of miscommunication," pp. 144–52 in Kira Hall et al. (eds) *Locating Power: Proceedings of the Second Berkeley Women and Language Conference*. BWLG group, University of California.

Tannen, Deborah (1990) *You Just Don't Understand*. New York: Ballantine Books.

Troemel-Ploetz, Senta (1991) "Selling the apolitical," *Discourse & Society* 2(4), 489–502.

Recommended Further Reading

Cameron, Deborah (1995) *Verbal Hygiene*. London: Routledge. See especially chapter 5.

Cameron, Deborah (1998) "'Is there any ketchup, Vera?': gender, power and pragmatics," *Discourse & Society* 9(4), 437–55.

Cameron, Deborah (2009) "Theoretical issues for the study of gender and spoken interaction," pp. 1–17 in Pia Pichler and Eva Eppler (eds) *Gender and Spoken Interaction*. London: Palgrave Macmillan.

Coates, Jennifer (1989) "Introduction – language and sex in connected speech," pp. 63–73 in Jennifer Coates and Deborah Cameron (eds) *Women in their Speech Communities*. London: Longman.

Crawford, Mary (1995) *Talking Difference: On Gender and Language*. London: Sage.

Holmes, Janet (2007) "Social constructionism, postmodernism and feminist sociolinguistics," *Gender and Language* 1(1), 51–66; reproduced in Part X of this Reader.

A Cultural Approach to Male–Female Miscommunication

Daniel N. Maltz and Ruth A. Borker

Source: John Gumperz (ed.), *Language and Identity*. Cambridge: Cambridge University Press (1982), pp. 195–216. Reprinted with permission of Cambridge University Press.

Introduction

This chapter presents what we believe to be a useful new framework for examining differences in the speaking patterns of American men and women. It is based not on new data, but on a reexamination of a wide variety of material already available in the scholarly literature. Our starting problem is the nature of the different roles of male and female speakers in informal cross-sex conversations in American English. Our attempts to think about this problem have taken us to preliminary examination of a wide variety of fields often on or beyond the margins of our present competencies: children's speech, children's play, styles and patterns of friendship, conversational turn-taking, discourse analysis, and interethnic communication. The research which most influenced the development of our present model includes John Gumperz's work on problems in interethnic communication (1982) and Marjorie Goodwin's study of the linguistic aspects of play among black children in Philadelphia (1978, 1980a, 1980b).

Our major argument is that the general approach recently developed for the study of difficulties in cross-ethnic communication can be applied to cross-sex communication as well. We prefer to think of the difficulties in both cross-sex and cross-ethnic communication as two examples of the same larger phenomenon: cultural difference and miscommunication.

The Problem of Cross-Sex Conversation

Study after study has shown that when men and women attempt to interact as equals in friendly cross-sex conversations they do not play the same role in interaction, even when there is no apparent element of flirting. We hope to explore some of these differences, examine the explanations that have been offered, and provide an alternative explanation for them.

Language and Gender: A Reader, Second Edition. Edited by Jennifer Coates and Pia Pichler.
© 2011 Blackwell Publishing Ltd except for editorial material and organization. © 2011 Jennifer Coates and Pia Pichler. Published 2011 by Blackwell Publishing Ltd.

The primary data on cross-sex conversations come from two general sources: social psychology studies from the 1950s such as Soskin and John's (1963) research on two young married couples and Strodbeck and Mann's (1956) research on jury deliberations, and more recent sociolinguistic studies from the University of California at Santa Barbara and the University of Pennsylvania by Candace West (Zimmerman and West 1975; West and Zimmerman 1977 [reprinted in Part III of this volume]; West 1979), Pamela Fishman (1978), and Lynette Hirschman (1973).

Women's Features

Several striking differences in male and female contributions to cross-sex conversation have been noticed in these studies.

First, women display a greater tendency to ask questions. Fishman (1978: 400) comments that "at times I felt that all women did was ask questions," and Hirschman (1973: 10) notes that "several of the female–male conversations fell into a question–answer pattern with the females asking the males questions."

Fishman (1978: 408) sees this question-asking tendency as an example of a second, more general characteristic of women's speech, doing more of the routine "shitwork" involved in maintaining routine social interaction, doing more to facilitate the flow of conversation (Hirschman 1973: 3). Women are more likely than men to make utterances that demand or encourage responses from their fellow speakers and are therefore, in Fishman's works, "more actively engaged in insuring interaction than the men" (1978: 404). In the earlier social psychology studies, these features have been coded under the general category of "positive reactions" including solidarity, tension release, and agreeing (Strodbeck and Mann 1956).

Third, women show a greater tendency to make use of positive minimal responses, especially "mm hmm" (Hirschman 1973: 8), and are more likely to insert "such comments throughout streams of talk rather than [simply] at the end" (Fishman 1978: 402).

Fourth, women are more likely to adopt a strategy of "silent protest" after they have been interrupted or have received a delayed minimal response (Zimmerman and West 1975; West and Zimmerman 1977: 524).

Fifth, women show a greater tendency to use the pronouns "you" and "we," which explicitly acknowledge the existence of the other speaker (Hirschman 1973: 6).

Men's Features

Contrasting contributions to cross-sex conversations have been observed and described for men.

First, men are more likely to interrupt the speech of their conversational partners, that is, to interrupt the speech of women (Zimmerman and West 1975; West and Zimmerman 1977; West 1979).

Second, they are more likely to challenge or dispute their partners' utterances (Hirschman 1973: 11).

Third, they are more likely to ignore the comments of the other speaker, that is, to offer no response or acknowledgment at all (Hirschman 1973: 11), to respond slowly in what has been described as a "delayed minimal response" (Zimmerman and West 1975: 118), or to respond unenthusiastically (Fishman 1978).

Fourth, men use more mechanisms for controlling the topic of conversation, including both topic development and the introduction of new topics, than do women (Zimmerman and West 1975).

Finally, men make more direct declarations of fact or opinion than do women (Fishman 1978: 402), including suggestions, opinions, and "statements of orientation" as Strodbeck and Mann (1956) describe them, or "statements of focus and directives" as they are described by Soskin and John (1963).

Explanations Offered

Most explanations for these features have focused on differences in the social power or in the personalities of men and women. One variant of the social power argument, presented by West (Zimmerman and West 1975; West and Zimmerman 1977), is that men's dominance in conversation parallels their dominance in society. Men enjoy power in society and also in conversation. The two levels are seen as part of a single social-political system. West sees interruptions and topic control as male displays of power – a power based in the larger social order but reinforced and expressed in face-to-face interaction with women. A second variant of this argument, stated by Fishman (1978), is that while the differential power of men and women is crucial, the specific mechanism through which it enters conversation is sex-role definition. Sex roles serve to obscure the issue of power for participants, but the fact is, Fishman argues, that norms of appropriate behavior for women and men serve to give power and interactional control to men while keeping it from women. To be socially acceptable as women, women cannot exert control and must actually support men in their control. In this casting of the social power argument, men are not necessarily seen to be consciously flaunting power, but simply reaping the rewards given them by the social system. In both variants, the link between macro and micro levels of social life is seen as direct and unproblematic, and the focus of explanation is the general social order.

Sex roles have also been central in psychological explanations. The primary advocate of the psychological position has been Robin Lakoff (1975). Basically, Lakoff asserts that, having been taught to speak and act like "ladies," women become as unassertive and insecure as they have been made to sound. The impossible task of trying to be both women and adults, which Lakoff sees as culturally incompatible, saps women of confidence and strength. As a result, they come to produce the speech they do, not just because it is how women are supposed to speak, but because it fits with the personalities they develop as a consequence of sex-role requirements.

The problem with these explanations is that they do not provide a means of explaining why these specific features appear as opposed to any number of others, nor do they allow us to differentiate between various types of male–female interaction. They do not really tell us why and how these specific interactional phenomena are linked to the general fact that men dominate within our social system.

An Alternative Explanation: Sociolinguistic Subcultures

Our approach to cross-sex communication patterns is somewhat different from those that have been previously proposed. We place the stress not on psychological differences or power differentials, although these may make some contribution, but rather on a notion of cultural differences between men and women in their conceptions of friendly conversation, their rules for engaging in it, and, probably most important, their rules for interpreting it. We argue that American men and women come from different sociolinguistic subcultures, having learned to do different things with words in a conversation, so that when they attempt to carry on conversations with one another, even if both parties are attempting to treat one another as equals, cultural miscommunication results.

The idea of distinct male and female subcultures is not a new one for anthropology. It has been persuasively argued again and again for those parts of the world such as the Middle East and southern Europe in which men and women spend most of their lives spatially and interactionally segregated. The strongest case for socio-linguistic subcultures has been made by Susan Harding from her research in rural Spain (1975).

The major premise on which Harding builds her argument is that speech is a means for dealing with social and psychological situations. When men and women have different experiences and operate in different social contexts, they tend to develop different genres of speech and different skills for doing things with words. In the Spanish village in which she worked, the sexual division of labor was strong, with men involved in agricultural tasks and public politics while women were involved in a series of networks of personal relations with their children, their husbands, and their female neighbors. While men developed their verbal skills in economic negotiations and public political argument, women became more verbally adept at a quite different mode of interactional manipulation with words: gossip, social analysis, subtle information gathering through a carefully developed technique of verbal prying, and a kind of second-guessing the thoughts of others (commonly known as "women's intuition") through a skillful monitoring of the speech of others. The different social needs of men and women, she argues, have led them to sexually differentiated communicative cultures, with each sex learning a different set of skills for manipulating words effectively.

The question that Harding does not ask, however, is, if men and women possess different subcultural rules for speaking, what happens if and when they try to interact with each other? It is here that we turn to the research on interethnic miscommunication.

Interethnic Communication

Recent research (Gumperz 1977, 1978a, 1978b, 1979; Gumperz and Tannen 1978) has shown that systematic problems develop in communication when speakers of different speech cultures interact and that these problems are the result of differences in systems of conversational inference and the cues for signalling speech acts and speaker's intent. Conversation is a negotiated activity. It progresses in large part because of shared assumptions about what is going on.

Examining interactions between English-English and Indian-English speakers in Britain (Gumperz 1977, 1978a, 1979; Gumperz et al. 1977), Gumperz found that differences in cues resulted in systematic miscommunication over whether a question was being asked, whether an argument was being made, whether a person was being rude or polite, whether a speaker was relinquishing the floor or interrupting, whether and what a speaker was emphasizing, whether interactants were angry, concerned, or indifferent. Rather than being seen as problems in communication, the frustrating encounters that resulted were usually chalked up as personality clashes or interpreted in the light of racial stereotypes which tended to exacerbate already bad relations.

To take a simple case, Gumperz (1977) reports that Indian women working at a cafeteria, when offering food, used a falling intonation, e.g. "gravy," which to them indicated a question, something like "do you want gravy?" Both Indian and English workers saw a question as an appropriate polite form, but to English-English speakers a falling intonation signalled not a question, which for them is signalled by a rising intonation such as "gravy," but a declarative statement, which was both inappropriate and extremely rude.

A major advantage of Gumperz's framework is that it does not assume that problems are the result of bad faith, but rather sees them as the result of individuals wrongly interpreting cues according to their own rules.

The Interpretation of Minimal Responses

How might Gumperz's approach to the study of conflicting rules for interpreting conversation be applied to the communication between men and women? A simple example will illustrate our basic approach: the case of positive minimal responses. Minimal responses such as nods and comments like "yes" and "mm hmm" are common features of conversational interaction. Our claim, based on our attempts to understand personal experience, is that these minimal responses have significantly different meanings for men and women, leading to occasionally serious miscommunication.

We hypothesize that for women a minimal response of this type means simply something like "I'm listening to you; please continue," and that for men it has a somewhat stronger meaning such as "I agree with you" or at least "I follow your argument so far." The fact that women use these responses more often than men is in part simply that women are listening more often than men are agreeing.

But our hypothesis explains more than simple differential frequency of usage. Different rules can lead to repeated misunderstandings. Imagine a male speaker who is receiving repeated nods or "mm hmm"s from the woman he is speaking to. She is merely indicating that she is listening, but he thinks she is agreeing with everything he says. Now imagine a female speaker who is receiving only occasional nods and "mm hmm"s from the man she is speaking to. He is indicating that he doesn't always agree; she thinks he isn't always listening.

What is appealing about this short example is that it seems to explain two of the most common complaints in male–female interaction: (1) men who think that women are always agreeing with them and then conclude that it's impossible to tell what a woman really thinks, and (2) women who get upset with men who never seem to be listening. What we think we have here are two separate rules for conversational maintenance which come into conflict and cause massive miscommunication.

Sources of Different Cultures

A probable objection that many people will have to our discussion so far is that American men and women interact with one another far too often to possess different subcultures. What we need to explain is how it is that men and women can come to possess different cultural assumptions about friendly conversation.

Our explanation is really quite simple. It is based on the idea that by the time we have become adults we possess a wide variety of rules for interacting in different situations. Different sets of these rules were learned at different times and in different contexts.

We have rules for dealing with people in dominant or subordinate social positions, rules which we first learned as young children interacting with our parents and teachers. We have rules for flirting and other sexual encounters which we probably started learning at or near adolescence. We have rules for dealing with service personnel and bureaucrats, rules we began learning when we first ventured into the public domain. Finally, we have rules for friendly interaction, for carrying on friendly conversation. What is striking about these last rules is that they were learned not from adults but from peers, and that they were learned during precisely that time period, approximately age 5 to 15, when boys and girls interact socially primarily with members of their own sex.

The idea that girls and boys in contemporary America learn different ways of speaking by the age of five or earlier has been postulated by Robin Lakoff (1975), demonstrated by Andrea Meditch (1975), and more fully explored by Adelaide Haas (1979). Haas's research on school-age children shows the early appearance of important male–female differences in patterns of language use, including a male tendency toward direct requests and information giving and a female tendency toward compliance (1979: 107).

But the process of acquiring gender-specific speech and behavior patterns by school-age children is more complex than the simple copying of adult "genderlects" by preschoolers. Psychologists Brooks-Gunn and Matthews (1979) have labelled this process the "consolidation of sex roles"; we call it learning of gender-specific "cultures."

Among school-age children, patterns of friendly social interaction are learned not so much from adults as from members of one's peer group, and a major feature of most middle-childhood peer groups is homogeneity; "they are either all-boy or all-girl" (Brooks-Gunn and Matthews 1979). Members of each sex are learning self-consciously to differentiate their behavior from that of the other sex and to exaggerate these differences. The process can be profitably compared to accent divergence in which members of two groups that wish to become clearly distinguished from one another socially acquire increasingly divergent ways of speaking.[1]

Because they learn these gender-specific cultures from their age-mates, children tend to develop stereotypes and extreme versions of adult behavior patterns. For a boy learning to behave in a masculine way, for example, Ruth Hartley (1959, quoted in Brooks-Gunn and Matthews 1979: 203) argues that:

> both the information and the practice he gets are distorted. Since his peers have no better sources of information than he has, all they can do is pool the impressions and anxieties they derived from their early training. Thus, the picture they draw is over-simplified and overemphasized. It is a picture drawn in black and white, with little or no modulation and it is incomplete, including a few of the many elements that go to make up the role of the mature male.

What we hope to argue is that boys and girls learn to use language in different ways because of the very different social contexts in which they learn how to carry on friendly conversation. Almost anyone who remembers being a child, has worked with school-age children, or has had an opportunity to observe school-age children can vouch for the fact that groups of girls and groups of boys interact and play in different ways. Systematic observations of children's play have tended to confirm these well-known differences in the ways girls and boys learn to interact with their friends.

In a major study of sex differences in the play of school-age children, for example, sociologist Janet Lever (1976) observed the following six differences between the play of boys and that of girls: (1) girls more often play indoors; (2) boys tend to play in larger groups; (3) boys' groups tend to include a wider age range of participants; (4) girls play in predominantly male games more often than vice versa; (5) boys more often play competitive games, and (6) girls' games tend to last a shorter period of time than boys' games.

It is by examining these differences in the social organization of play and the accompanying differences in the patterns of social interaction they entail, we argue, that we can learn about the sources of male–female differences in patterns of language use. And it is these same patterns, learned in childhood and carried over into adulthood as the bases for patterns of single-sex friendship relations, we contend, that are potential sources of miscommunication in cross-sex interaction.

The World of Girls

Our own experience and studies such as Goodwin's (1980b) of black children and Lever's (1976, 1978) of white children suggest a complex of features of girls' play and the speech within it. Girls play in small groups, most often in pairs (Lever 1976; Eder and Hallinan 1978; Brooks-Gunn and Matthews 1979), and their play groups tend to be remarkably homogeneous in terms of age. Their play is often in private or semi-private settings that require participants be invited in. Play is cooperative and activities are usually organized in noncompetitive ways (Lever 1976; Goodwin 1980b). Differentiation between girls is not made in terms of power, but relative closeness. Friendship is seen by girls as involving intimacy, equality, mutual commitment, and loyalty. The idea of "best friend" is central for girls. Relationships between girls are to some extent in opposition to one another, and new relationships are often formed at the expense of old ones. As Brooks-Gunn and Matthews (1979: 280) observe, "friendships tend to be exclusive, with a few girls being exceptionally close to one another. Because of this breakups tend to be highly emotional," and Goodwin (1980a: 172) notes that "the non-hierarchical framework of the girls provides a fertile ground for rather intricate processes of alliance formation between equals against some other party."

There is a basic contradiction in the structure of girls' social relationships. Friends are supposed to be equal and everyone is supposed to get along, but in fact they don't always. Conflict must be resolved, but a girl cannot assert social power or superiority as an individual to resolve it. Lever (1976), studying fifth-graders, found that girls simply could not deal with quarrels and that when conflict arose they made no attempt to settle it; the group just broke up. What girls learn to do with speech is cope with the contradiction created by an ideology of equality and cooperation and a social reality that includes difference and conflict. As they grow up they learn increasingly subtle ways of balancing the conflicting pressures created by a female social world and a female friendship ideology.

Basically girls learn to do three things with words: (1) to create and maintain relationships of closeness and equality, (2) to criticize others in acceptable ways, and (3) to interpret accurately the speech of other girls.

To a large extent friendships among girls are formed through talk. Girls need to learn to give support, to recognize the speech rights of others, to let others speak, and to acknowledge what they say in order to establish and maintain relationships of equality and closeness. In activities they need to learn to create cooperation through speech. Goodwin (1980a) found that inclusive forms such as "let's," "we gonna," "we could," and "we gotta" predominated in task-oriented activities. Furthermore, she found that most girls in the group she studied made suggestions and that the other girls usually agreed to them. But girls also learn to exchange information and confidences to create and maintain relationships of closeness. The exchange of personal thoughts not only expresses closeness but mutual commitment as well. Brooks-Gunn and Matthews (1979: 280) note of adolescent girls:

> much time is spent talking, reflecting, and sharing intimate thought. Loyalty is of central concern to the 12- to 14-year old girl, presumably because, if innermost secrets are shared, the friend may have 'dangerous knowledge' at her disposal.

Friendships are not only formed through particular types of talk, but are ended through talk as well. As Lever (1976: 4) says of "best friends," "sharing secrets binds the union together, and 'telling' the secrets to outsiders is symbolic of the 'break-up'."

Secondly, girls learn to criticize and argue with other girls without seeming overly aggressive, without being perceived as either "bossy" or "mean," terms girls use to evaluate one another's speech and actions. Bossiness, ordering others around, is not legitimate because it denies equality. Goodwin (1980a) points out that girls talked very negatively about the use of commands to equals, seeing it as appropriate only in role play or in unequal relationships such as those with younger siblings. Girls learn to direct things without seeming bossy, or they learn not to direct. While disputes are common, girls learn to phrase their arguments in terms of group needs and situational requirements rather than personal power or desire (Goodwin 1980a). Meanness is used by girls to describe nonlegitimate acts of exclusion, turning on someone, or withholding friendship. Excluding is a frequent occurrence (Eder and Hallinan 1978), but girls learn over time to discourage or even drive away other girls in ways that don't seem to be just personal whim. Cutting someone is justified in terms of the target's failure to meet group norms and a girl often rejects another using speech that is seemingly supportive on the surface. Conflict and criticism are risky in the world of girls because they can both rebound against the critic and can threaten social relationships. Girls learn to hide the source of criticism; they present it as coming from someone else or make it indirectly through a third party (Goodwin 1980a, 1980b).

Finally, girls must learn to decipher the degree of closeness being offered by other girls, to recognize what is being withheld, and to recognize criticism. Girls who don't actually read these cues run the risk of public censure or ridicule (Goodwin 1980b). Since the currency of closeness is the exchange of secrets which can be used against a girl, she must learn to read the intent and loyalty of others and to do so continuously, given the system of shifting alliances and indirect expressions of conflict. Girls must become increasingly sophisticated in reading the motives of others, in determining when closeness is real, when conventional, and when false, and to respond appropriately. They must learn who to confide in, what to confide, and who not to approach. Given the indirect expression of conflict, girls must learn to read relationships and situations sensitively. Learning to get things right is a fundamental skill for social success, if not just social survival.

The World of Boys

Boys play in larger, more hierarchically organized groups than do girls. Relative status in this ever-fluctuating hierarchy is the main thing that boys learn to manipulate in their interactions with their peers. Nondominant boys are rarely excluded from play but are made to feel the inferiority of their status positions in no uncertain terms. And since hierarchies fluctuate over time and over situation, every boy gets his chance to be victimized and must learn to take it. The social world of boys is one of posturing and counterposturing. In this world, speech is used in three major ways: (1) to assert one's position of dominance, (2) to attract and maintain an audience, and (3) to assert oneself when other speakers have the floor.

The use of speech for the expression of dominance is the most straightforward and probably the best-documented sociolinguistic pattern in boys' peer groups. Even ethological studies of human dominance patterns have made extensive use of various speech behaviors as indices of dominance. Richard Savin-Williams (1976), for example, in his study of dominance patterns among boys in a summer camp uses the following speech interactions as measures of dominance: (1) giving of verbal commands or orders, such as "Get up," "Give it to me," or "You go over there"; (2) name calling and other forms of verbal ridicule, such as "You're a dolt"; (3) verbal threats or boasts of authority, such as "If you don't shut up, I'm gonna come over and bust your teeth in"; (4) refusals to obey orders; and (5) winning a verbal argument as in the sequence: "I was here first"/"Tough," or in more elaborate forms of verbal duelling such as the "dozens."[2]

The same patterns of verbally asserting one's dominance and challenging the dominance claims of others form the central element in Goodwin's (1980a) observations of boys' play in Philadelphia. What is easy to forget in thinking about this use of words as weapons, however, is that the most successful boy in such interaction is not the one who is most aggressive and uses the most power-wielding forms of speech, but the boy who uses these forms most successfully. The simple use of assertiveness and aggression in boys' play is the sign not of a leader but of a bully. The skillful speaker in a boys' group is considerably more likeable and better liked by his peers than is a simple bully. Social success among boys is based on knowing both how and when to use words to express power as well as knowing when not to use them. A successful leader will use speech to put challengers in their place and to remind followers periodically of their nondominant position, but will not brow-beat unnecessarily and will therefore gain the respect rather than the fear of less dominant boys.

A second sociolinguistic aspect of friendly interaction between boys is using words to gain and maintain an audience. Storytelling, joke telling, and other narrative performance events are common features of the social interaction of boys. But actual transcripts of such storytelling events collected by Harvey Sacks (Sacks 1974; Jefferson 1978) and Goodwin (1980a), as opposed to stories told directly to interviewers, reveal a suggestive feature of storytelling activities among boys: audience behavior is not overtly supportive. The storyteller is frequently faced with mockery, challenges and side comments on his story. A major sociolinguistic skill which a boy must apparently learn in interacting with his peers is to ride out this series of challenges, maintain his audience, and successfully get to the end of his story. In Sacks's account (1974) of some teenage boys involved in the telling of a dirty joke, for example, the narrator is challenged for his taste in jokes (an implication that he doesn't know a dirty joke from a non-dirty one) and for the potential ambiguity of his opening line "Three brothers married three sisters," not, as Sacks seems to imply, because audience members are really confused, but just to hassle the speaker. Through catches,[3] put-downs, the building of suspense, or other interest-grabbing devices, the speaker learns to control his audience. He also learns to continue when he gets no encouragement whatever, pausing slightly at various points for possible audience response but going on if there is nothing but silence.

A final sociolinguistic skill which boys must learn from interacting with other boys is how to act as audience members in the types of storytelling situations just discussed. As audience member as well as storyteller, a boy must learn to assert himself and his opinions. Boys seem to respond to the storytelling of other boys not so much with questions on deeper implications or with minimal-response encouragement as with side comments and challenges. These are not meant primarily to interrupt, to change topic, or to change the direction of the narrative itself, but to assert the identity of the individual audience member.

Women's Speech

The structures and strategies in women's conversation show a marked continuity with the talk of girls. The key logic suggested by Kalčik's (1975) study of women's rap groups, Hirschman's (1973) study of students and Abrahams's (1975) work on black women is that women's conversation is interactional. In friendly talk, women are negotiating and expressing a relationship, one that should be in the form of support and closeness, but which may also involve criticism and distance. Women orient themselves to the person they are talking to and expect such orientation in return. As interaction, conversation requires participation from those involved and back-and-forth movement between participants. Getting the floor is not seen as particularly problematic; that should come about automatically. What is problematic is getting people engaged and keeping them engaged – maintaining the conversation and the interaction.

This conception of conversation leads to a number of characteristic speech strategies and gives a particular dynamic to women's talk. First, women tend to use personal and inclusive pronouns, such as "you" and "we" (Hirschman 1973). Second, women give off and look for signs of engagement such as nods and minimal response (Kalčik 1975; Hirschman 1973). Third, women give more extended signs of interest and attention, such as interjecting comments or questions during a speaker's discourse. These sometimes take the form of interruptions. In fact, both Hirschman (1973) and Kalčik (1975) found that interruptions were extremely common, despite women's concern with politeness and decorum (Kalčik 1975). Kalčik (1975) comments that women often asked permission to speak but were concerned that each speaker be allowed to finish and that all present got a chance to speak. These interruptions were clearly not seen as attempts to grab the floor but as calls for elaboration and development, and were taken as signs of support and interest. Fourth, women at the beginning of their utterances explicitly acknowledge and respond to what has been said by others. Fifth, women attempt to link their utterance to the one preceding it by building on the previous utterance or talking about something parallel or related to it. Kalčik (1975) talks about strategies of tying together, filling in, and serializing as signs of women's desire to create continuity in conversation, and Hirschman (1973) describes elaboration as a key dynamic of women's talk.

While the idiom of much of women's friendly talk is that of support, the elements of criticism, competition, and conflict do occur in it. But as with girls, these tend to take forms that fit the friendship idiom. Abrahams (1975) points out that while "talking smart" is clearly one way women talk to women as well as to men, between women it tends to take a more playful form, to be more indirect and metaphoric in its phrasing and less prolonged than similar talk between men. Smartness, as he points out, puts distance in a relationship (Abrahams 1975). The target of criticism, whether present or not, is made out to be the one violating group norms and values (Abrahams 1975). Overt competitiveness is also disguised. As Kalčik (1975) points out, some stories that build on preceding ones are attempts to cap the original speaker, but they tend to have a form similar to supportive ones. It is the intent more than the form that differs. Intent is a central element in the concept of "bitchiness," one of women's terms for evaluating their talk, and it relates to this contradiction between form and intent, whether putting negative messages in overtly positive forms or acting supportive face to face while not being so elsewhere.

These strategies and the interactional orientation of women's talk give their conversation a particular dynamic. While there is often an unfinished quality to particular utterances (Kalčik 1975), there is a progressive development to the overall conversation. The conversation grows out of the interaction of its participants, rather than being directed by a single individual or series of individuals. In her very stimulating discussion, Kalčik (1975) argues that this is true as well for many of the narratives women tell in conversation. She shows how narrative "kernels" serve as conversational resources for individual women and the group as a whole. How and if a "kernel story" is developed by the narrator and/or audience on a particular occasion is a function of the conversational context from which it emerges (Kalčik 1975: 8), and it takes very different forms at different tellings. Not only is the dynamic of women's conversation one of elaboration and continuity, but the idiom of support can give it a distinctive tone as well. Hannerz (1969: 96), for example, contrasts the "tone of relaxed sweetness, sometimes bordering on the saccharine," that characterizes approving talk between women, to the heated argument found among men. Kalčik (1975: 6) even goes so far as to suggest that there is an "underlying esthetic or organizing principle" of "harmony" being expressed in women's friendly talk.

Men's Speech

The speaking patterns of men, and of women for that matter, vary greatly from one North American subculture to another. As Gerry Philipsen (1975: 13) summarizes it, "talk is not everywhere valued equally; nor is it anywhere valued equally in all social contexts." There are striking cultural variations between subcultures in whether men consider certain modes of speech appropriate for dealing with women, children, authority figures, or strangers; there are differences in performance rules for story-telling and joke telling; there are differences in the context of men's speech; and there are differences in the rules for distinguishing aggressive joking from true aggression.

But more surprising than these differences are the apparent similarities across subcultures in the patterns of friendly interaction between men and the resemblances between these patterns and those observed for boys. Research reports on the speaking patterns of men among urban blacks (Abrahams 1976; Hannerz 1969), rural Newfoundlanders (Faris 1966; Bauman 1972), and urban blue-collar whites (Philipsen 1975; LeMasters 1975) point again and again to the same three features: storytelling, arguing and verbal posturing.

Narratives such as jokes and stories are highly valued, especially when they are well performed for an audience. In Newfoundland, for example, Faris (1966: 242) comments that "the reason 'news' is rarely passed between two men meeting in the road – it is simply not to one's advantage to relay information to such a small audience." Loud and aggressive argument is a second common feature of male–male speech. Such arguments, which may include shouting, wagering, name-calling, and verbal threats (Faris 1966: 245), are often, as Hannerz (1969: 86) describes them, "debates over minor questions of little direct import to anyone," enjoyed for their own sake and not taken as signs of real conflict. Practical jokes, challenges, put-downs, insults, and other forms of verbal aggression are a third feature of men's speech, accepted as normal among friends.

LeMasters (1975: 140), for example, describes life in a working-class tavern in the Midwest as follows:

> It seems clear that status at the Oasis is related to the ability to "dish it out" in the rapid-fire exchange called "joshing": you have to have a quick retort, and preferably one that puts you "one up" on your opponent. People who can't compete in the game lose status.

Thus challenges rather than statements of support are a typical way for men to respond to the speech of other men.

What Is Happening in Cross-Sex Conversation

What we are suggesting is that women and men have different cultural rules for friendly conversation and that these rules come into conflict when women and men attempt to talk to each other as friends and equals in casual conversation. We can think of at least five areas, in addition to that of minimal responses already discussed, in which men and women probably possess different conversational rules, so that miscommunication is likely to occur in cross-sex interaction.

(1)   There are two interpretations of the meaning of questions. Women seem to see questions as a part of conversational maintenance, while men seem to view them primarily as requests for information.

(2)   There are two conventions for beginning an utterance and linking it to the preceding utterance. Women's rules seem to call for an explicit acknowledgment of what has been said and making a connection to it. Men seem to have no such rule and in fact some male strategies call for ignoring the preceding comments.

(3)   There are different interpretations of displays of verbal aggressiveness. Women seem to interpret overt aggressiveness as personally directed, negative, and disruptive. Men seem to view it as one conventional organizing structure for conversational flow.

(4)   There are two understandings of topic flow and topic shift. The literature on storytelling in particular seems to indicate that men operate with a system in which topic is fairly narrowly defined and adhered to until finished and in which shifts between topics are abrupt, while women have a system in which topic is developed progressively and shifts gradually. These two systems imply very different rules for and interpretations of side comments, with major potential for miscommunication.

(5)   There appear to be two different attitudes towards problem sharing and advice giving. Women tend to discuss problems with one another, sharing experiences and offering reassurances. Men, in contrast, tend to hear women, and other men, who present them with problems as making explicit requests for solutions. They respond by giving advice, by acting as experts, lecturing to their audiences.[4]

Conclusions

Our purpose in this paper has been to present a framework for thinking about and tying together a number of strands in the analysis of differences between male and female conversational styles. We hope to prove the intellectual value of this framework by demonstrating its ability to do two things: to serve as a model both of and for sociolinguistic research.

As a model *of* past research findings, the power of our approach lies in its ability to suggest new explanations of previous findings on cross-sex communication while linking these findings to a wide range of other fields, including the study of language acquisition, of play, of friendship, of storytelling, of cross-cultural miscommunication, and of discourse analysis. Differences in the social interaction patterns of boys and girls appear to be widely known but rarely utilized in examinations of sociolinguistic acquisition or in explanations of observed gender differences in patterns of adult speech. Our proposed framework should serve to link together these and other known facts in new ways.

As a model *for* future research, we hope our framework will be even more promising. It suggests to us a number of potential research problems which remain to be investigated. Sociolinguistic studies of school-age children, especially studies of the use of speech in informal peer interaction, appear to be much rarer than studies of young children, although such studies may be of greater relevance for the understanding of adult patterns, particularly those related to gender. Our framework also suggests the need for many more studies of single-sex conversations among adults, trying to make more explicit some of the differences in conversational rules suggested by present research. Finally, the argument we have been making suggests a number of specific problems that appear to be highly promising lines for future research:

(1) A study of the sociolinguistic socialization of "tomboys" to see how they combine male and female patterns of speech and interaction;

(2) An examination of the conversational patterns of lesbians and gay men to see how these relate to the sex-related patterns of the dominant culture;

(3) An examination of the conversational patterns of the elderly to see to what extent speech differences persist after power differences have become insignificant;

(4) A study of children's cultural concepts for talking about speech and the ways these shape the acquisition of speech styles (for example, how does the concept of "bossiness" define a form of behavior which little girls must learn to recognize, then censure, and finally avoid?);

(5) An examination of "assertiveness training" programs for women to see whether they are really teaching women the speaking skills that politically skillful men learn in boyhood or are merely teaching women how to act like bossy little girls or bullying little boys and not feel guilty about it.

We conclude this paper by reemphasizing three of the major ways in which we feel that an anthropological perspective on culture and social organization can prove useful for further research on differences between men's and women's speech.

First, an anthropological approach to culture and cultural rules forces us to reexamine the way we interpret what is going on in conversations. The rules for interpreting conversation are, after all, culturally determined. There may be more than one way of understanding what is happening in a particular conversation and we must be careful about the rules we use for interpreting cross-sex conversations, in which the two participants may not fully share their rules of conversational inference.

Second, a concern with the relation between cultural rules and their social contexts leads us to think seriously about differences in different kinds of talk, ways of categorizing interactional situations, and ways in which conversational patterns may function as strategies for dealing with specific aspects of one's social world. Different types of interaction lead to different ways of speaking. The rules for friendly conversation between equals are different from those for service encounters, for flirting, for teaching, or for polite formal interaction. And even within the apparently uniform domain of friendly interaction, we argue that there are systematic differences between men and women in the way friendship is defined and thus in the conversational strategies that result.

Third and finally, our analysis suggests a different way of thinking about the connection between the gender-related behavior of children and that of adults. Most discussions of sex-role socialization have been based on the premise that gender differences are greatest for adults and that these adult differences are learned gradually throughout childhood. Our analysis, on the other hand, would suggest that at least some aspects of behavior are most strongly gender-differentiated during childhood and that adult patterns of friendly interaction, for example, involve learning to overcome at least partially some of the gender-specific cultural patterns typical of childhood.

Notes

1 The analogy between the sociolinguistic processes of dialect divergence and genderlect divergence was pointed out to us by Ron Macaulay.
2 In the strict sense the term "dozens" refers to a culturally specific form of stylized argument through the exchange of insults that has been extensively documented by a variety of students of American black culture and is most frequently practiced by boys in their teens and pre-teens. Recently folklorist Simon Bronner (1978) has made a convincing case for the existence of a highly similar but independently derived form of insult exchange known as "ranking," "mocks," or "cutting" among white American adolescents. What we find striking and worthy of note is the tendency for both black and white versions of the dozens to be practiced primarily by boys.
3 "Catches" are a form of verbal play in which the main speaker ends up tricking a member of his or her audience into a vulnerable or ridiculous position. In an article on the folklore of black children in South Philadelphia, Roger Abrahams (1963) distinguishes between catches which are purely verbal and tricks in which the second player is forced into a position of being not only verbally but also physically abused as in the following example of a catch which is also a trick:

> A: Adam and Eve and Pinch-Me-Tight
>   Went up the hill to spend the night.
>   Adam and Eve came down the hill.
>   Who was left?
> B: Pinch-Me-Tight
> [A pinches B]

What is significant about both catches and tricks is that they allow for the expression of playful aggression and that they produce a temporary hierarchical relation between a winner and loser, but invite the loser to attempt to get revenge by responding with a counter-trick.
4 We thank Kitty Julien for first pointing out to us the tendency of male friends to give advice to women who are not necessarily seeking it, and Niyi Akinnaso for pointing out that the sex difference among Yoruba speakers in Nigeria in the way people respond verbally to the problems of others is similar to that among English speakers in the US.

References

Abrahams, R. (1963) "The 'Catch' in negro Philadelphia". *Keystone Folklore Quarterly*, 8(3), 107–11.
Abrahams, R. (1975) "Negotiating respect: patterns of presentation among black women", in C. Farrar (ed.) *Women in Folklore*. Austin: University of Texas Press.

Abrahams, R. (1976) *Talking Black*. Rowley, MA: Newbury House.

Bauman, R. (1972) "The La Have Island General Store: sociability and verbal art in a Nova Scotia community". *Journal of American Folklore*, 85, 330–43.

Bronner, S. (1978) "A re-examining of white dozens". *Western Folklore*, 37(2), 118–28.

Brooks-Gunn, J. and Matthews, W. (1979) *He and She: How Children Develop Their Sex-Role Identity*. Englewood Cliffs, NJ: Prentice-Hall.

Eder, D. and Hallinan, M. (1978) "Sex differences in children's friendships", *American Sociological Review*, 43, 237–50.

Faris, J. (1966) "The dynamics of verbal exchange: a Newfoundland example", *Anthropologica (Ottawa)*, 8(2), 235–48.

Fishman, P. (1978) "Interaction: the work women do", *Social Problems*, 25(4), 397–406.

Goodwin, M. (1978) Conversational Practices in a Peer Group of Urban Black Children. Doctoral dissertation, University of Pennsylvania, Philadelphia.

Goodwin, M. (1980a) "Directive–response speech sequences in girls' and boys' task activities", in S. McConnell-Ginet, R. Borker and N. Furman (eds) *Women and Language in Literature and Society*. New York: Praeger.

Goodwin, M. (1980b) "He-said-she-said: formal cultural procedures for the construction of a gossip dispute activity", *American Ethnologist*, 7(4), 674–95.

Gumperz, J. (1977) "Sociocultural knowledge in conversational inference", in M. Saville-Troike (ed.) *Linguistics and Anthropology (Georgetown University Round Table on Languages and Linguistics)*. Washington, DC: Georgetown University Press.

Gumperz, J. (1978a) "The conversational analysis of interethnic communication", in E. Lamar Ross (ed.) *Interethnic Communication*. Athens, GA: University of Georgia Press.

Gumperz, J. (1978b) "Dialect and conversational inference in urban communication", *Language in Society*, 7(3), 393–409.

Gumperz, J. (1979) "The sociolinguistic basis of speech act theory", in J. Boyd and S. Ferrara (eds) *Speech Act Ten Years After*. Milan: Versus.

Gumperz, J. (1982) *Discourse Strategies*. Cambridge: Cambridge University Press.

Gumperz, J., Agrawal, A. and Aulakh, G. (1977) *Prosody, Paralinguistics and Contextualisation in Indian English*. MS, Language Behavior Research Laboratory, University of California, Berkeley.

Gumperz, J. and Tannen, D. (1978) "Individual and social differences in language use", in W. Wang and C. Fillmore (eds) *Individual Differences in Language Ability and Language Behavior*. New York: Academic Press.

Hass, A. (1979) "The acquisition of genderlect", in J. Orasanu, M. Slater and L. Adler (eds) "Language, Sex and Gender: Does La Différence Make a Difference?" *Annals of the New York Academy of Sciences*, 327, 101–13.

Hannerz, U. (1969) *Soulside*. New York: Columbia University Press.

Harding, S. (1975) "Women and words in a Spanish village", in R. Reiter (ed.) *Toward an Anthropology of Women*. New York: Monthly Review Press.

Hirschman, L. (1973) Female–Male Differences in Conversational Interaction. Paper presented at Linguistic Society of America, San Diego.

Jefferson, G. (1978) "Sequential aspects of storytelling in conversation", in J. Schenker (ed.) *Studies in the Organisation of Conversational Interaction*. New York: Academic Press.

Kalčik, S. (1975) "'… Like Anne's gynaecologist or the time I was almost raped': personal narratives in women's rap groups", in C. Farrar (ed.) *Women in Folklore*. Austin: University of Texas Press.

Lakoff, R. (1975) *Language and Woman's Place*. New York: Harper & Row.

LeMasters, E. (1975) *Blue Collar Aristocrats: Life-Styles at a Working-Class Tavern*. Madison: University of Wisconsin Press.

Lever, J. (1976) "Sex differences in the games children play", *Social Problems*, 23, 478–83.

Lever, J. (1978) "Sex differences in the complexity of children's play and games", *American Sociological Review*, 43, 471–83.

Meditch, A. (1975) "The development of sex-specific speech patterns in young children", *Anthropological Linguistics*, 17, 421–33.

Philipsen, G. (1975) "Speaking 'like a man' in Teamsterville: cultural patterns of role enactment in an urban neighbourhood", *Quarterly Journal of Speech*, 61, 13–22.

Sacks, H. (1974) "An analysis of the course of a joke's telling in conversation", in R. Bauman and J. Sherzer (eds) *Explorations in the Ethnography of Speaking*. Cambridge: Cambridge University Press.

Savin-Williams, R. (1976) "The ethnological study of dominance formation and maintenance in a group of human adolescents", *Child Development*, 47, 972–9.

Soskin, W. and John, V. (1963) "The study of spontaneous talk", in R. Barker (ed.) *The Stream of Behavior*. New York: Appleton-Century-Crofts.

Strodbeck, F. and Mann, R. (1956) "Sex role differentiation in jury deliberations", *Sociometry*, 19, 3–11.

West, C. (1979) "Against our will: male interruptions of females in cross-sex conversation", in J. Orasanu, M. Slater and L. Adler (eds) "Language, Sex and Gender: Does La Différence Make a Difference?" *Annals of the New York Academy of Sciences*, 327, 81–100.

West, C. and Zimmerman, D. (1977) "Women's place in everyday talk: reflections on parent–child interaction", *Social Problems*, 24(5), 521–9.

Zimmerman, D. and West, C. (1975) "Sex roles, interruptions, and silences in conversation", in B. Thorne and N. Henley (eds) *Language and Sex: Difference and Dominance*. Rowley, MA: Newbury House.

36

Asymmetries: Women and Men Talking at Cross-Purposes

Deborah Tannen

Source: Deborah Tannen, *You Just Don't Understand: Women and Men in Conversation*. William Morrow and Co. (1990), chapter 2 (pp. 49–95). Reprinted with permission of HarperCollins Publishers USA, and Little, Brown Book Group UK.

Eve had a lump removed from her breast. Shortly after the operation, talking to her sister, she said that she found it upsetting to have been cut into, and that looking at the stitches was distressing because they left a seam that had changed the contour of her breast. Her sister said, "I know. When I had my operation I felt the same way." Eve made the same observation to her friend Karen, who said, "I know. It's like your body has been violated." But when she told her husband, Mark, how she felt, he said, "You can have plastic surgery to cover up the scar and restore the shape of your breast."

Eve had been comforted by her sister and her friend, but she was not comforted by Mark's comment. Quite the contrary, it upset her more. Not only didn't she hear what she wanted, that he understood her feelings, but, far worse, she felt he was asking her to undergo more surgery just when she was telling him how much this operation had upset her. "I'm not having any more surgery!" she protested. "I'm sorry you don't like the way it looks." Mark was hurt and puzzled. "I don't care," he protested. "It doesn't bother me at all." She asked, "Then why are you telling me to have plastic surgery?" He answered, "Because you were saying *you* were upset about the way it looked."

Eve felt like a heel: Mark had been wonderfully supportive and concerned throughout her surgery. How could she snap at him because of what he said – "just words" – when what he had done was unassailable? And yet she had perceived in his words metamessages that cut to the core of their relationship. It was self-evident to him that his comment was a reaction to her complaint, but she heard it as an independent complaint of his. He thought he was reassuring her that she needn't feel bad about her scar because there was something she could *do* about it. She heard his suggestion that she do something about the scar as evidence that *he* was bothered by it. Furthermore, whereas she wanted reassurance that it was normal to feel bad in her situation, his telling her that the problem could easily be fixed implied she had no right to feel bad about it.

Eve wanted the gift of understanding, but Mark gave her the gift of advice. He was taking the role of problem solver, whereas she simply wanted confirmation for her feelings.

A similar misunderstanding arose between a husband and wife following a car accident in which she had been seriously injured. Because she hated being in the hospital, the wife asked to come home early. But once home, she suffered pain from having to move around more. Her husband said, "Why didn't you stay in the hospital where you would have been more comfortable?" This hurt her because it seemed to imply that he did not want her home. She didn't think of his suggestion that she should have stayed in the hospital as a response to her complaints about the pain she was suffering; she thought of it as an independent expression of his preference not to have her at home.

"They're My Troubles – Not Yours"

If women are often frustrated because men do not respond to their troubles by offering matching troubles, men are often frustrated because women do. Some men not only take no comfort in such a response, they take offense. For example, a woman told me that when her companion talks about a personal concern – for example, his feelings about growing older – she responds, "I know how you feel; I feel the same way." To her surprise and chagrin, he gets annoyed; he feels she is trying to take something away from him by denying the uniqueness of his experience.

A similar miscommunication was responsible for the following interchange, which began as a conversation and ended as an argument:

HE: I'm really tired. I didn't sleep well last night.
SHE: I didn't sleep well either. I never do.
HE: Why are you trying to belittle me?
SHE: I'm not! I'm just trying to show that I understand!

This woman was not only hurt by her husband's reaction; she was mystified by it. How could he think she was belittling him? By "belittle me," he meant "belittle my experience." He was filtering her attempts to establish connection through his concern with preserving independence and avoiding being put down.

"I'll Fix It for You"

Women and men are both often frustrated by the other's way of responding to their expression of troubles. And they are further hurt by the other's frustration. If women resent men's tendency to offer solutions to problems, men complain about women's refusal to take action to solve the problems they complain about. Since many men see themselves as problem solvers, a complaint or a trouble is a challenge to their ability to think of a solution, just as a woman presenting a broken bicycle or stalling car poses a challenge to their ingenuity in fixing it. But whereas many women appreciate help in fixing mechanical equipment, few are inclined to appreciate help in "fixing" emotional troubles.

The idea that men are problem solvers was reinforced by the contrasting responses of a husband and wife to the same question on a radio talk show.[1] The couple, Barbara and William Christopher, were discussing their life with an autistic child. The host asked if there weren't times when they felt sorry for themselves and wondered, "Why me?" Both said no, but they said it in different ways. The wife deflected attention from herself: She said that the real sufferer was her child. The husband said, "Life is problem solving. This is just one more problem to solve."

This explains why men are frustrated when their sincere attempts to help a woman solve her problems are met not with gratitude but with disapproval. One man reported being ready to tear his hair out over a girlfriend who continually told him about problems she was having at work but refused to take any of the advice he offered. Another man defended himself against his girlfriend's objection that he changed the subject as soon as she recounted something that was bothering her: "What's the point of talking about it any more?" he said. "You can't do anything about it." Yet another man commented that women seem to wallow in their problems, wanting to talk about them forever, whereas he and other men want to get them out and be done with them, either by finding a solution or by laughing them off.

Trying to solve a problem or fix a trouble focuses on the message level of talk. But for most women who habitually report problems at work or in friendships, the message is not the main point of complaining. It's the metamessage that counts: Telling about a problem is a bid for an expression of understanding ("I know how you feel") or a similar complaint ("I felt the same way when something similar happened to me"). In other words, troubles talk[2] is intended to reinforce rapport by sending the meta-message "We're the same; you're not alone." Women are frustrated when they not only don't get this reinforcement but, quite the opposite, feel distanced by the advice, which seems to send the metamessage "We're not the same. You have the problems; I have the solutions."

Furthermore, mutual understanding is symmetrical, and this symmetry contributes to a sense of community. But giving advice is asymmetrical. It frames the advice giver as more knowledgeable, more reasonable, more in control – in a word, one-up. And this contributes to the distancing effect.

The assumption that giving advice can be oneupmanship underlies an observation that appeared in a book review. In commenting on Alice Adams's *After You've Gone,* reviewer Ron Carlson explained that the title story is a letter from a woman to a man who has left her for a younger woman. According to Carlson, the woman informs her former lover about her life "and then steps up and clobbers him with sage advice. Here is clearly a superior woman. ..."[3] Although we do not know the intention of the woman who wrote the story, we see clearly that the man who reviewed it regards giving advice as a form of attack and sees one who gives advice as taking a superior position.

Parallel Tracks

These differences seem to go far back in our growing up. A sixteen-year-old girl told me she tends to hang around with boys rather than girls. To test my ideas, I asked her whether boys and girls both talk about problems. Yes, she assured me, they both do. Do they do it the same way? I asked. Oh, no, she said. The girls go on and on. The boys raise the issue, one of them comes up with a solution, and then they close the discussion.

Women's and men's frustrations with each other's ways of dealing with troubles talk amount to applying interpretations based on one system to talk that is produced according to a different system. Boys and men do not respond to each other the way women respond to each other in troubles talk. The roots of the very different way that men respond to talk about troubles became clear to me when I compared the transcript of a pair of tenth-grade boys talking to each other to the transcripts of girls' conversations from videotapes of best friends talking, recorded as part of a research project by psychologist Bruce Dorval.[4]

Examining the videotaped conversations, I found that the boys and girls, who expressed deep concerns to each other, did it in different ways – ways that explain the differences that come up in daily conversations between women and men. The pairs of girls at both the sixth grade and tenth grade talked at length about one girl's problems. The other girl pressed her to elaborate, said, "I know," and gave supporting evidence. The following brief excerpts from the transcripts show the dramatic difference between the girls and boys.

The tenth-grade girls are talking about Nancy's problems with her boyfriend and her mother. It emerges that Nancy and Sally were both part of a group excursion to another state. Nancy suddenly left the group and returned home early at her mother's insistence. Nancy was upset about having to leave early. Sally reinforces Nancy's feelings by letting her know that her sudden departure was also upsetting to her friends:[5]

NANCY: God, it was *bad*. I couldn't believe she made me go home.

SALLY: I thought it was kind of weird though, I mean, one minute we were going out and the next minute Nancy's going, "Excuse me, gotta be going." [Both laugh] I didn't know what was going *on*, and Judy comes up to me and she whispers (the whole place knows), "Do you know that Nancy's going home?" And I go, "What?" [Both laugh] "Nancy's going home." I go, *"Why?"* She goes, "Her mom's making her." I go [makes a face], "Ah." She comes back and goes, "Nancy's left." Well, I said, "WELL, that was a fine thing TO DO, she didn't even come and say goodbye." And she starts boiling all over me. I go [mimicking yelling], *"All right!!"* She was upset, Judy. I was like "God" –

Sally's way of responding to her friend's troubles is to confirm Nancy's feelings of distress that her mother made her leave the trip early, by letting her know that her leaving upset her friends. In contrast, examining the transcript of a conversation between boys of the same age shows how differently they respond to each other's expressions of troubles.

The tenth-grade boys also express deep feelings. Theirs too is troubles talk, but it is troubles talk with a difference. They don't concentrate on the troubles of one, pursuing, exploring, and elaborating. Instead, each one talks about his own troubles and dismisses the other's as insignificant.

In the first excerpt from these boys' conversation, Richard says he feels bad because his friend Mary has no date for an upcoming dance, and Todd dismisses his concern:

RICHARD: God, I'm going to feel so bad for her if she stays home.

TODD: She's not going to stay home, it's ridiculous. Why doesn't she just ask somebody?

Yet Todd himself is upset because he has no date for the same dance. He explains that he doesn't want to ask Anita, and Richard, in turn, scoffs at his distress:

TODD: I felt so bad when she came over and started talking to me last night.

RICHARD: Why?

TODD: I don't know. I felt uncomfortable, I guess.

RICHARD: **I'll never understand that.** [Laugh]

Far from trying to show that he understands, Richard states flatly that he doesn't, as shown in boldface type.

Richard then tells Todd that he is afraid he has a drinking problem. Todd responds by changing the subject to something that is bothering him, his feelings of alienation:

RICHARD: When I took Anne home last night she told me off.
TODD: Really?

...

RICHARD: You see when she found out what happened last Thursday night between Sam and me?
TODD: Mhm.
RICHARD: She knew about that. And she just said – and then she started talking about drinking. You know? ... And then she said, you know, "You, how you hurt everybody when you do it. You're always cranky." And she just said, "I don't like it. You hurt Sam. You hurt Todd. You hurt Mary. You hurt Lois."

...

I mean, when she told me, you know I guess I was kind of stunned. [Pause] I didn't really drink that much.
TODD: **Are you still talking to Mary, a lot, I mean?**
RICHARD: Am I still talking to Mary?
TODD: Yeah, 'cause that's why – that's why I was mad Friday.
RICHARD: Why?
TODD: Because.
RICHARD: 'Cause why?
TODD: 'Cause I didn't know why you all just wa- I mean I just went back upstairs for things, then y'all never came back. I was going, "Fine. I don't care." I said, "He's going to start this again."

As the lines printed in boldface show, when Richard says that he is upset because Anne told him he behaved badly when he was drunk, Todd responds by bringing up his own concern: He feels left out, and he was hurt when Richard disappeared from a party with his friend Mary.

Throughout the conversation, Todd expresses distress over feeling alienated and left out. Richard responds by trying to argue Todd out of the way he feels. When Todd says he felt out of place at a party the night before, Richard argues:

RICHARD: **How could you feel out of place? You knew Lois, and you knew Sam.**
TODD: I don't know. I just felt really out of place and then last night again at the party, I mean, Sam was just running around, he knew everyone from the sorority. There was about five.
RICHARD: **Oh, no, he didn't.**
TODD: He knew a lot of people. He was – I don't know.
RICHARD: **Just Lois. He didn't know everybody.**

...

TODD: I just felt really out of place that day, all over the place. I used to feel, I mean –
RICHARD: Why?
TODD: I don't know. I don't even feel right in school anymore.
RICHARD: I don't know, last night, I mean –
TODD: I think I know what Ron Cameron and them feels like now. [Laugh]
RICHARD: [Laugh] **No, I don't think you feel as bad as Ron Cameron feels.**
TODD: I'm kidding.

RICHARD: Mm-mm. **Why should you? You know more people –**
   TODD: I can't talk to anyone anymore.
RICHARD: **You know more people than me.**

By telling Todd that his feelings are unjustified and incomprehensible, Richard is not implying that he doesn't care. He clearly means to comfort his friend, to make him feel better. He's implying, "You shouldn't feel bad because your problems aren't so bad."

Matching Troubles

The very different way that women respond to the telling of troubles is dramatized in a short story, "New Haven," by Alice Mattison.[6] Eleanor tells Patsy that she has fallen in love with a married man. Patsy responds by first displaying understanding and then offering a matching revelation about a similar experience:

> "Well," says Patsy. "I know how you feel."
> "You do?"
> "In a way, I do. Well, I should tell you. I've been sleeping with a married man for two years."

Patsy then tells Eleanor about her affair and how she feels about it. After they discuss Patsy's affair, however, Patsy says:

> "But you were telling me about this man and I cut you off. I'm sorry. See? I'm getting self-centered."
> "It's OK." But she is pleased again.[7]

The conversation then returns to Eleanor's incipient affair. Thus Patsy responds first by confirming Eleanor's feelings and matching her experience, reinforcing their similarity, and then by encouraging Eleanor to tell more. Within the frame of Patsy's similar predicament, the potential asymmetry inherent in revealing personal problems is avoided, and the friendship is brought into balance.

What made Eleanor's conversation with Patsy so pleasing to Eleanor was that they shared a sense of how to talk about troubles, and this reinforced their friendship. Though Eleanor raised the matter of her affair, she did not elaborate on it until Patsy pressed her to do so. In another story by the same author, "The Knitting," a woman named Beth is staying with her sister in order to visit her sister's daughter Stephanie in a psychiatric hospital. While there, Beth receives a disturbing telephone call from her boyfriend, Alec. Having been thus reminded of her troubles, she wants to talk about them, but she refrains, because her sister doesn't ask. She feels required, instead, to focus on her sister's problem, the reason for her visit:

> She'd like to talk about her muted half-quarrels with Alec of the last weeks, but her sister does not ask about the phone call. Then Beth thinks they should talk about Stephanie.[8]

The women in these stories are balancing a delicate system by which troubles talk is used to confirm their feelings and create a sense of community.

When women confront men's ways of talking to them, they judge them by the standards of women's conversational styles. Women show concern by following up someone else's statement of trouble by questioning her about it. When men change the subject, women think they are showing a lack of sympathy – a failure of intimacy. But the failure to ask probing questions could just as well be a way of respecting the other's need for independence. When Eleanor tells Patsy that she is in love with Peter, Patsy asks, "Are you sleeping with him?" This exploration of Eleanor's topic could well strike many men – and some women – as intrusive, though Eleanor takes it as a show of interest that nourishes their friendship.

Women tend to show understanding of another woman's feelings. When men try to reassure women by telling them that their situation is not so bleak, the women hear their feelings being belittled or discounted. Again, they encounter a failure of intimacy just when they were bidding to reinforce it. Trying to trigger a symmetrical communication, they end up in an asymmetrical one.

A Different Symmetry

The conversation between Richard and Todd shows that although the boys' responses are asymmetrical if looked at separately – each dismisses the other's concerns – they are symmetrical when looked at together: Todd responds to Richard's concern about his drinking in exactly the same way that Richard responds to Todd's feeling of alienation, by denying it is a problem:

> RICHARD: Hey, man, I just don't feel – I mean, after what Anne said last night, I just don't feel like doing that.
> TODD: **I don't think it was that way. You yourself knew it was no big problem.**
> RICHARD: Oh, Anne – Sam told Anne that I fell down the levee.
> TODD: **It's a lie.**
> RICHARD: I didn't fall. I slipped, slid. I caught myself.
> TODD: **Don't worry about it.**
> RICHARD: But I do, kind of. I feel funny in front of Sam. I don't want to do it in front of you.
> TODD: **It doesn't matter 'cause sometimes you're funny when you're off your butt.**

Todd denies that Richard was so drunk he was staggering ("It's a lie") and then says that even if he was out of control, it wasn't bad; it was funny.

In interpreting this conversation between tenth-grade boys, I initially saw their mutual reassurances and dismissals, and their mutual revelations of troubles, in terms of connection and sameness. But another perspective is possible.[9] Their conversation may be touching precisely because it was based on asymmetries of status – or, more precisely, a deflecting of such asymmetries. When Todd tells his troubles, he puts himself in a potentially one-down position and invites Richard to take a one-up position by disclaiming troubles and asymmetrically offering advice or sympathy. By offering troubles of his own, Richard declines to take the superior position and restores their symmetrical footing, sending the metamessage "We're just a couple of guys trying to make it in a world that's tough on both of us, and both of us are about equally competent to deal with it."

From this perspective, responding as a woman might – for example by saying, "I can see how you feel; you must feel awful; so would I if it happened to me" – would have a totally different meaning for boys, since they would be inclined to interpret it through the lens of status. Such a response would send a metamessage like "Yes, I know, you incompetent jerk, I know how awful you must feel. If I were as incompetent as you, I'd feel the same way. But, lucky for you, I'm not, and I can help you out here, because I'm far too talented to be upset by a problem like that." In other words, refraining from expressing sympathy is generous, insofar as sympathy potentially condescends.

Women are often unhappy with the reactions they get from men when they try to start troubles talk, and men are often unhappy because they are accused of responding in the wrong way when they are trying to be helpful. But Richard and Todd seem satisfied with each other's ways of reacting to their troubles. And their ways make sense. When men and women talk to each other, the problem is that each expects a different kind of response. The men's approach seeks to assuage feelings indirectly by attacking their cause. Since women expect to have their feelings supported, the men's approach makes them feel that they themselves are being attacked.

"Don't Ask"

Talking about troubles is just one of many conversational tasks that women and men view differently, and that consequently cause trouble in talk between them. Another is asking for information. And this difference too is traceable to the asymmetries of status and connection.

A man and a woman were standing beside the information booth at the Washington Folk Life Festival, a sprawling complex of booths and displays. "You ask," the man was saying to the woman. "I don't ask."

Sitting in the front seat of the car beside Harold, Sybil is fuming. They have been driving around for half an hour looking for a street he is sure is close by. Sybil is angry not because Harold does not know the way, but because he insists on trying to find it himself rather than stopping and asking someone. Her anger stems from viewing his behavior through the lens of her own: If she were driving, she would have asked directions as soon as she realized she didn't know which way to go, and they'd now be comfortably ensconced in their friends' living room instead of driving in circles, as the hour gets later and later. Since asking directions does not make Sybil uncomfortable, refusing to ask makes no sense to her. But in Harold's world, driving around until he finds his way is the reasonable thing to do, since asking for help makes him uncomfortable. He's avoiding that discomfort and trying to maintain his sense of himself as a self-sufficient person.

Why do many men resist asking for directions and other kinds of information? And, it is just as reasonable to ask, why is it that many women don't? By the paradox of independence and intimacy, there are two simultaneous and different metamessages implied in asking for and giving information. Many men tend to focus on one, many women on the other.

When you offer information, the information itself is the message. But the fact that you have the information, and the person you are speaking to doesn't, also sends a metamessage of superiority. If relations are inherently hierarchical, then the one who has more information is framed as higher up on the ladder, by virtue of being more knowledgeable and competent. From this perspective, finding one's own way is an essential part of the independence that men perceive to be a prerequisite for self-respect. If self-respect is bought at the cost of a few extra minutes of travel time, it is well worth the price.

Because they are implicit, metamessages are hard to talk about. When Sybil begs to know why Harold won't just ask someone for directions, he answers in terms of the message, the information: He says there's no point in asking, because anyone he asks may not know and may give him wrong directions. This is theoretically reasonable. There are many countries, such as, for example, Mexico, where it is standard procedure for people to make up directions rather than refuse to give requested information. But this explanation frustrates Sybil, because it doesn't make sense to her. Although she realizes that someone might give faulty directions, she believes this is relatively unlikely, and surely it cannot happen every time. Even if it did happen, they would be in no worse shape than they are in now anyway.

Part of the reason for their different approaches is that Sybil believes that a person who doesn't know the answer will say so, because it is easy to say, "I don't know." But Harold believes that saying "I don't know" is humiliating, so people might well take a wild guess. Because of their different assumptions, and the invisibility of framing, Harold and Sybil can never get to the bottom of this difference; they can only get more frustrated with each other. Keeping talk on the message level is common, because it is the level we are most clearly aware of. But it is unlikely to resolve confusion since our true motivations lie elsewhere.

To the extent that giving information, directions, or help is of use to another, it reinforces bonds between people. But to the extent that it is asymmetrical, it creates hierarchy: Insofar as giving information frames one as the expert, superior in knowledge, and the other as uninformed, inferior in knowledge, it is a move in the negotiation of status.

It is easy to see that there are many situations where those who give information are higher in status. For example, parents explain things to children and answer their questions, just as teachers give information to students. An awareness of this dynamic underlies one requirement for proper behavior at Japanese dinner entertainment, according to anthropologist Harumi Befu. In order to help the highest-status member of the party to dominate the conversation, others at the dinner are expected to ask him questions that they know he can answer with authority.

Because of this potential for asymmetry, some men resist receiving information from others, especially women, and some women are cautious about stating information that they know, especially to men. For example, a man with whom I discussed these dynamics later told me that my perspective clarified a comment made by his wife. They had gotten into their car and were about to go to a destination that she knew well but he did not know at all. Consciously resisting an impulse to just drive off and find his own way, he began by asking his wife if she had any advice about the best way to get there. She told him the way, then added, "But I don't know. That's how I would go, but there might be a better way." Her comment was a move to redress the imbalance of power created by her knowing something he didn't know. She was also saving face in advance, in case he decided not to take her advice. Furthermore, she was reframing her directions as "just a suggestion" rather than "giving instructions."

"I'll Fix It If It Kills Me"

The asymmetry implied in having and giving information is also found in having and demonstrating the skill to fix things – an orientation that we saw in men's approaches to troubles talk. To further explore the framing involved in fixing things, I will present a small encounter of my own.

Unable to remove the tiny lid that covers the battery compartment for the light meter on my camera, I took the camera to a photography store and asked for help. The camera salesman tried to unscrew the lid, first with a dime and then with a special instrument. When this failed, he declared the lid hopelessly stuck. He explained the reason (it was screwed in with the threads out of alignment) and then explained in detail how I could take pictures without a light meter by matching the light conditions to shutter settings in accordance with the chart included in rolls of film. Even though I knew there wasn't a chance in the world I would adopt his system, I listened politely, feigning interest, and assiduously wrote down his examples, based on an ASA of 100, since he got confused trying to give examples based on an ASA of 64. He further explained that this method was actually superior to using a light meter. In this way, he minimized the significance of not being able to help by freeing the battery lid; he framed himself as possessing useful knowledge and having solved my problem even though he couldn't fix my camera. This man wanted to help me – which I sincerely appreciated – but he also wanted to demonstrate that he had the information and skill required to help, even though he didn't.

There is a kind of social contract operating here. Many women not only feel comfortable seeking help, but feel honor-bound to seek it, accept it, and display gratitude in exchange. For their part, many men feel honor-bound to fulfill the request for help whether or not it is convenient for them to do so. A man told me about a time when a neighbor asked him if he could fix her car, which was intermittently stalling out. He spent more time than he could spare looking at her car, and concluded that he did not have the equipment needed to do the repair. He felt bad about not having succeeded in solving her problem. As if sensing this, she told him the next day, and the next, that her car was much better now, even though he knew he had done nothing to improve its performance. There is a balance between seeking help and showing appreciation. Women and men seem equally bound by the requirements of this arrangement: She was bound to show appreciation even though he hadn't helped, and he was bound to invest time and effort that he really couldn't spare, in trying to help.

Another example of the social contract of asking for help and showing appreciation occurred on a street corner in New York City. A woman emerged from the subway at Twenty-third Street and Park Avenue South, and was temporarily confused about which direction to walk in to reach Madison Avenue. She knew that Madison was west of Park, so with a little effort she could have figured out which way to go. But without planning or thinking, she asked the first person to appear before her. He replied that Madison did not come down that far south. Now, she knew this to be false. Furthermore, by this time she had oriented herself. But instead of saying, "Yes, it does," or "Never mind, I don't need your help," she found a way to play out the scene as one in which he helped her. She asked, "Which way is west?" and, on being told, replied, "Thank you. I'll just walk west."

From the point of view of getting directions, this encounter was absurd from start to finish. The woman didn't really need help, and the man wasn't in a position to give it. But getting directions really wasn't the main point. She had used the commonplace ritual of asking directions of a stranger not only – and not mostly – to find her way on emerging from the subway, but to reinforce her connection to the mass of people in the big city by making fleeting contact with one of them. Asking for help was simply an automatic way for her to do this.

"I'll Help You If It Kills You"

Martha bought a computer and needed to learn to use it. After studying the manual and making some progress, she still had many questions, so she went to the store where she had bought it and asked for help. The man assigned to help her made her feel like the stupidest person in the world. He used technical language in explaining things, and each time she had to ask what a word meant she felt more incompetent, an impression reinforced by the tone of voice he used in his answer, a tone that sent the meta-message "This is obvious; everyone knows this." He explained things so quickly, she couldn't possibly remember them. When she went home, she discovered she couldn't recall what he had demonstrated, even in cases where she had followed his explanation at the time.

Still confused, and dreading the interaction, Martha returned to the store a week later, determined to stay until she got the information she needed. But this time a woman was assigned to help her. And the experience of getting help was utterly transformed. The woman avoided using technical terms for the most part, and if she did use one, she asked whether Martha knew what it meant and explained simply and clearly if she didn't. When the woman answered questions, her tone never implied that everyone should know this. And when showing how to do something, she had Martha do it, rather than demonstrating while Martha watched. The different style of this "teacher" made Martha feel like a different "student": a competent rather than stupid one, not humiliated by her ignorance.

Surely not all men give information in a way that confuses and humiliates their students. There are many gifted teachers who also happen to be men. And not all women give information in a way that makes it easy for students to understand. But many women report experiences similar to Martha's, especially in dealing with computers, automobiles, and other mechanical equipment; they claim that they feel more comfortable having women explain things to them. The different meanings that giving help entails may explain why. If women are focusing on connections, they will be motivated to minimize the difference in expertise and to be as comprehensible as possible. Since their goal is to maintain the appearance of similarity and equal status, sharing knowledge helps even the score. Their tone of voice sends metamessages of support rather than disdain, although "support" itself can be experienced as condescension.

If a man focuses on the negotiation of status and feels someone must have the upper hand, he may feel more comfortable when he has it. His attunement to the fact that having more information, knowledge, or skill puts him in a one-up position comes through in his way of talking. And if sometimes men seem intentionally to explain in a way that makes what they are explaining difficult to understand, it may be because their pleasant feeling of knowing more is reinforced when the student *does not* understand. The comfortable margin of superiority diminishes with every bit of knowledge the student gains. Or it may simply be that they are more concerned with displaying their superior knowledge and skill than with making sure that the knowledge is shared.

A colleague familiar with my ideas remarked that he'd seen evidence of this difference at an academic conference. A woman delivering a paper kept stopping and asking the audience, "Are you with me so far?" My colleague surmised that her main concern seemed to be that the audience understand what she was saying. When he gave his paper, his main concern was that he not be put down by members of the audience – and as far as he could tell, a similar preoccupation was motivating the other men presenting papers as well. From this point of view, if covering one's tracks to avoid attack entails obscuring one's point, it is a price worth paying.

This is not to say that women have no desire to feel knowledgeable or powerful. Indeed, the act of asking others whether they are able to follow your argument can be seen to frame you as superior. But it seems that having information, expertise, or skill at manipulating objects is not the primary measure of power for most women. Rather, they feel their power enhanced if they can be of help. Even more, if they are focusing on connection rather than independence and self-reliance, they feel stronger when the community is strong.

"Trust Me"

A woman told me that she was incredulous when her husband dredged up an offense from years before. She had been unable to get their VCR to record movies aired on HBO. Her husband had looked at the VCR and declared it incapable of performing this function. Rather than accepting his judgment, she asked their neighbor, Harry, to take a look at it, since he had once fixed her VCR in the past. Harry's conclusion was the same as that of her husband, who was, however, incensed that his wife had not trusted his expertise. When he brought it up years later, the wife exclaimed in disbelief, "You still remember that? Harry is dead!" The incident, though insignificant to the wife, cut to the core of the husband's self-respect, because it called into question his knowledge and skill at managing the mechanical world.

Trust in a man's skill is also at issue between Felicia and Stan, another couple. Stan is angered when Felicia gasps in fear while he is driving. "I've never had an acident!" he protests. "Why can't you trust my driving?" Felicia cannot get him to see her point of view – that she does not distrust *his* driving in particular but is frightened of driving in general. Most of all, she cannot understand why the small matter of involuntarily sucking in her breath should spark such a strong reaction.

"Be Nice"

Having expertise and skill can reinforce both women's and men's sense of themselves. But the stance of expert is more fundamental to our notion of masculinity than to our concept of femininity. Women, according to convention, are more inclined to be givers of praise than givers of information. That women are expected to praise is reflected in a poster that was displayed in every United States post office branch inviting customers to send criticism, suggestions, questions, and compliments. Three of these four linguistic acts were represented by sketches of men; only compliments were represented by a sketch of a woman with a big smile on her face, a gesture of approval on her fingers, and a halo around her head. The halo is especially interesting. It shows that the act of complimenting frames the speaker as "nice."

Giving praise, like giving information, is also inherently asymmetrical. It too frames the speaker as one-up, in a position to judge someone else's performance. Women can also be framed as one-up by their classic helping activities as mothers, social workers, nurses, counselors, and psychologists. But in many of these roles – especially mothers and nurses – they may also be seen as doing others' bidding.

Overlapping Motivations

When acting as helpers, women and men typically perform different kinds of tasks. But even the same task can be approached with eyes on different goals, and this difference is likely to result in misjudgments of others' intentions. The end of my camera story underlines this. At a family gathering, I brought the camera to my brother-in-law, who has a reputation in the family for mechanical ability. He took it to his workshop and returned an hour and a half later, having fixed it. Delighted and grateful, I commented to his daughter, "I knew he would enjoy the challenge." "Especially," she pointed out, "when it involves helping someone." I felt then that I had mistaken his displayed concern with the mechanics of the recalcitrant battery cover as reflecting his ultimate concern. But fixing the camera was a way of showing concern for me, of helping me with his effort. If women directly offer help, my brother-in-law was indirectly offering help, through the mediation of my camera.

A colleague who heard my analysis of this experience thought I had missed an aspect of my broken-camera episode. He pointed out that many men get a sense of pleasure from fixing things because it reinforces their feeling of being in control, self-sufficient, and able to dominate the world of objects. (This is the essence of Evelyn Fox Keller's thesis that the conception of science as dominating and controlling nature is essentially masculine in spirit.) He told me of an incident in which a toy plastic merry-go-round, ordered for his little boy, arrived in pieces, having come apart during shipping. His wife gave the toy to her uncle, renowned in the family as a fixer and helper. Her uncle worked for several hours and repaired the toy – even though it was probably not worth more than a few dollars. The uncle brought this up again the next time he saw them, and said he would have stayed up all night rather than admit he couldn't put it together. My colleague was convinced that the motivation to gain dominion over the plastic object had been stronger than the motivation to help his sister and nephew, though both had been present.

Furthermore, this man pointed out that he, and many other men, take special pleasure in showing their strength over the world of objects for the benefit of attractive women, because the thanks and admiration they receive is an added source of pleasure and satisfaction. His interpretation of my revised analysis was that my niece and I, both women, would be inclined to see the helping aspect of an act as the "real" or main motive, whereas he still was inclined to see the pleasure of demonstrating skill, succeeding where the camera expert had failed, and whacking the recalcitrant battery lid into line as the main ones.

The element of negotiating status that characterizes many men's desire to show they are knowledgeable and skillful does not negate the connection implied in helping. These elements coexist and feed each other. But women's and men's tendencies to place different relative weights on status versus connection result in asymmetrical roles. Attuned to the metamessage of connection, many women are comfortable both receiving help and giving it, though surely there are many women who are comfortable only in the role of giver of help and support. Many men, sensitive to the dynamic of status, the need to help women, and the need to be self-reliant, are comfortable in the role of giving information and help but not in receiving it.

The View from a Different Mountain

In a story by Alice Mattison, "The Colorful Alphabet," a man named Joseph invites another man, Gordon, to visit his family in the country, because Gordon's wife has just left him. During the visit, they all climb a mountain. On the way down, they stop to rest, and Gordon realizes that he left his beloved old knapsack on the mountaintop. Joseph volunteers to climb back up to get it, because Gordon is not used to climbing and his feet are sore. Joseph's wife goes with him, but she is too tired to climb all the way to the top, and he leaves her on the path to complete the mission himself. When he finds her again, he is empty-handed: The bag wasn't there. He says then that he knew it wouldn't be, because he had seen a man carrying the bag pass them when they all stopped to rest. He explains why he didn't just say that he had seen someone go by with the bag: "I couldn't tell him I'd seen it and hadn't been smart enough to get it back for him." Instead, he says, "I had to *do* something."

Exhausted and frustrated, the wife is not so much angry as incredulous. She can't understand how he could have preferred reclimbing the mountain (and making her reclimb it too) to admitting that he had seen someone carrying Gordon's bag. "I would never have done that," she says, but she speaks "more in wonder than anger." She explains, "I'd have just blurted it out. I'd have been upset about making the mistake – but not about people *knowing*. That part's not a big deal to me." Her husband says, "Oh, is it ever a big deal to me."

This story supports the view of men's style that I have been proposing. Joseph wanted to help Gordon, and he did not want to let it be known that he had done something he thought stupid. His impulse to do something to solve the problem was stronger than his impulse not to climb a mountain twice. But what struck me most strongly about the story was the wife's reflections on the experience. She thinks:

> It was one of the occasional moments when I'm certain I haven't imagined him: I would never have done what he'd done, wouldn't have dreamt it or invented it – Joseph was, simply, *not me*.[10]

This excerpt reflects what may be the subtlest yet deepest source of frustration and puzzlement arising from the different ways that women and men approach the world. We feel we know how the world is, and we look to others to reinforce that conviction. When we see others acting as if the world were an entirely different place from the one we inhabit, we are shaken.

We look to our closest relationships as a source of confirmation and reassurance. When those closest to us respond to events differently than we do, when they seem to see the same scene as part of a different play, when they say things that we could not imagine saying in the same circumstances, the ground on which we stand seems to tremble and our footing is suddenly unsure. Being able to understand why this happens – *why* and *how* our partners and friends, though like us in many ways, are *not* us, and different in other ways – is a crucial step toward feeling that our feet are planted on firm ground.

Notes

1 The Christophers were discussing their book *Mixed Blessings* on *The Diane Rehm Show,* WAMU, Washington, DC, June 6, 1989.
2 I have borrowed the term *troubles talk* from Gail Jefferson. See, for example, her article "On the Sequential Organization of Troubles-Talk in Ordinary Conversation." *Social Problems* 35(4), 1988.
3 The quotation is from "Clobbering Her Ex," a review of Alice Adams's *After You've Gone* in *The New York Times Book Review,* October 8, 1989, p. 27.
4 Bruce Dorval videotaped friends talking at a range of ages. He describes the tapes and how he collected them in a book he edited, *Conversational Coherence and Its Development* (Ablex, 1990). That book includes chapters in which scholars from different disciplines analyze selected videotapes. My analysis of gender differences in the videotapes is included in that collection and is also the basis for this chapter.

5   Excerpts are from transcripts originally prepared by Bruce Dorval and his assistants. I have checked and occasionally refined the transcripts, and made a few changes in punctuation to enhance readability for the nonspecialist reader.
6   "New Haven," like all the other stories by Alice Mattison that I quote, is in *Great Wits* (New York: William Morrow, 1988). This quotation is from p. 63.
7   Mattison, "New Haven," p. 64.
8   Mattison, "The Knitting," p. 36.
9   The alternative interpretation of the boys' dismissal of each other's concerns was pointed out to me by Ralph Fasold.
10 Mattison, "The Colorful Alphabet," p. 125.

37

Selling the Apolitical

Senta Troemel-Ploetz

Source: *Discourse & Society* 2(4) (1991), pp. 489–502. Reprinted with permission of SAGE.

Review of Deborah Tannen's You Just Don't Understand (New York: Ballantine Books, 1990).

Reading Tannen's *You Just Don't Understand* – the lamentation of the title alone places it squarely into the profuse relationship literature à la Ann Landers, along with books of the caliber of Norwood's *Women Who Love Too Much* and selling as well – one might believe feminism had never happened in this country.

This is a book for the present period of restoration, undoing the upsetting politics of the last three decades, adjusting and accommodating to those in power, namely men, providing appeasement for the male chauvinist backlash so that it does not hurt the wrong women, and appealing to readers who have lived through these decades untouched and untroubled by the analyses of social and economic injustice all around them. That such a deeply reactionary book should appeal to so many readers informs us, disconcerting as it may be, that what is non-threatening to the status quo sells better than critical analysis.

This is a dishonest book precisely because of its non-engaged and apolitical stance. It veils and conceals the political analysis to which women have given their energy during the last 30 years, and the changes they have brought about with the help of fair men. It waters down our insights; it equalizes where differences have to be acknowledged; it hardly ever talks about inequity – and never with real concern; it again and again stops short of drawing any political inferences that would suggest that significant changes are needed in the communication and relationships between women and men.

The author shields her readers also from linguistic knowledge. Thus if one did not know, one would never find out that there is an enormous body of feminist literature presenting a critical analysis of the differences in power and access to power between women and men, on all levels, public and private, and in all areas – work, pay, family, sexuality, the professions, the institutions, e.g. medicine, the court system, even academia (where Tannen is located), and even conversational analysis (which is her field).

The main thesis of Tannen's book is that women's and men's conversation *is* (not even *is patterned like*) cross-cultural communication (pp. 18, 42, 47). This is entirely unsupported and unproven. What Tannen claims, that 'if adults learn their ways of speaking as children growing up in separate social worlds of peers, then conversation between women and men is cross-cultural communication' (p. 47), simply does not follow. Even if it were true that girls and boys grow up in different linguistic worlds, it would not follow. Girls and boys, women and men (always remaining within the white middle class) live together in shared linguistic worlds, be it in the family, in schoolrooms, in the streets, in colleges, in jobs; they are probably spending more time in mixed-sex contexts than in single-sex contexts, and, above all, they are not victims of constant misunderstandings. On the contrary, they understand each other quite well. They know who is allowed to use dominant speech acts, like commands, orders, explanations, contradiction, doubts, advice, criticism, evaluations, definitions, punishment, attacks, challenges, accusations, reproaches; and who has to apologize, defend, ask for favors, beg, request permission, justify herself, agree, support, adjust, accommodate, and accept someone else's definition of the situation.

By using these speech acts to a large extent asymmetrically, a conversational reality is being constructed in which men claim more authority and autonomy for themselves, and women become more dependent and non-autonomous. We are acting out our social roles and producing, via our speech acts, a conversational world in which our social reality is reflected and corroborated: men have power, women submit.

Consequently, we find two conversational cultures or two different styles that are not equal. Men, the speakers of the dominant style, have more rights and privileges. They exhibit their privileges and produce them in every conversational situation. Men are used to dominating women; they do it especially in conversations: they set the tone as soon as they enter a conversation, they declare themselves expert for almost any topic, they expect and get attention and support from their female conversational partners, they expect and get space to present their topics and, above all, themselves – their conversational success is being produced by the participants in that conversation. Women are trained to please; they have to please also in conversations, i.e. they will let men dominate and they will do everything not to threaten men: not set the tone, not insist on their own topics or opinions, package opposing views pleasantly, not refuse support, not take more space than men, i.e. let men win conversationally and renounce their own conversational success and satisfaction in the process.

Men also exhibit and produce their conversational rights: the right to dominate, the right to self-presentation or self-aggrandizement at the expense of others, the right to have the floor and to finish one's turn, the right to keep women from talking (by disturbance or interruption), the right to get attention and consideration from women, the right to conversational success. Women, on the other hand, have conversational obligations: they must not disturb men in their dominating and imposing behavior; they must support their topics, wait with their own topics, give men attention, take them seriously at all times, and, above all, listen and help them to their conversational success. By assuming, attributing and reconstructing men's rights and privileges and women's obligations in every conversation, status differences between women and men are being confirmed and produced in most mixed-sex interactions – the social hierarchy remains intact.

Reading through what a German critic called Professor Tannen's 'chatter', one searches in vain for concepts like dominance, control, power, politics of gender, sexism, discrimination, and finds two of them mentioned after 200 pages but not explored, borrowed probably from another author. Concepts like feminism or patriarchy never occur, being evidently far too radical for the author. Tannen is selling political naïveté, but neither is sociology quite so naïve nor linguistics quite as apolitical as Tannen would have us believe. In both fields women have, long before Tannen started publishing on mixed-sex communication,

given political analyses of their data and introduced new concepts from a feminist perspective that suggested a revision of the existing male models, e.g. Labov's model of the male
storyteller as the protagonist; Labov's model of the language of youth which was neither
the language of youth nor of black youth but the language of male black youth; Sacks' and
Schegloff's turn-taking model, etc.

Significantly, the feminist literature in her own field is not even mentioned by Tannen
or, where mentioned en passant, as in the case of Aries, Edelsky, Goodwin, Spender, it is
reduced in such a way that its spark is neutralized and its critical impetus watered down
so as not to offend anyone or lead him to think. But we do not hear about Lee Jenkins
(1981, 1982) who first worked on story-telling in a women's group concentrating on
women's competence and their high degree of cooperation, in the process doing away
with the stereotypes of women's style found in linguistics as elsewhere. We do not hear
about new work done on women's discourse, work on women's friendships, women's
professional style, emphasizing the competence of women whose style lends itself very
well to all kinds of verbal endeavors, from psychotherapy to teaching to management,
and whose success is appreciated independently in these fields. Conspicuous by its
absence too is the work of the psychologists of the Stone Center at Wellesley, although
Tannen is tampering in relationships.

All these works, apparently, would be far too feminist to be considered by Tannen,
since they attack the principle of male superiority and male dominance. Even staying
within sociolinguistics, however, there is no mention of the important work by Sue
Fisher and Alexandra Todd (Fisher, 1984, 1986; Fisher and Todd, 1983, 1986; Todd,
1984, 1989) who analyzed medical discourse as an unequal power contest where male
doctors use their power at the expense of women and their organs. We do not hear about
the analysis by Candace West (1984), looking at female doctors and male and female
patients respectively, and corroborating the asymmetries as we know them in mixed-sex
conversations, even where the doctor is a woman and the patient male. We do not hear
about West's interesting result, the construction of symmetry – with respect to interruptions – between the woman doctor and her female patients, giving the first indication
that women use power differently than men. We do not hear about Pamela Fishman's
work on couples in private conversations which shows male dominance and points out
that, when dominance is threatened, the man has recourse to verbal and physical violence. Of course, we do not hear about sexual antagonism (Whitehead, 1976), sexual
harassment or verbal insults – Tannen stays with polite conversation.

But even discussing certain topics, e.g. gossip, the powerful analyses of Reiter (1975)
and Harding (1975) are missing; in talking about body language, there is no reference
to the important *Body Politics* by Henley; the discussion of jokes (pp. 90, 140) is done
without using the extensive literature on the politics of humor which shows at whose
expense the jokes are made, and who does the work to construct the success of the
jokers.

Tannen chooses to ignore all this work because it takes a political stand, because it is
looking at interactions between women and men in terms of mechanisms of control and
exertion of power, in terms of unequal rights. It is informed by a sense of justice and its
authors, each in her own field, are committed to social change. Only an author who is
not in touch with the women in her field could write a book in 1990 on conversations
between women and men without understanding that women cannot simply adopt the
male style and be powerful, too; and also that men will not voluntarily give up their style
and be powerless like women. Of course, Tannen never considers such a radical option as
men giving up their style to adopt a more humane one; she suggests 'mutual adjustment'.

Reading some of the women in her field, understanding the criticism of her work as it is offered in Henley/Kramarae (1991) might have helped her to avoid the superficial dilettantism of her analysis.

Unfortunately, Tannen is also not in touch with other professional women, e.g. women in law, in politics, in journalism, who are fighting for their credibility and their status. The work of these women depends entirely on language as their instrument. Acting in their professions is nothing but speaking. They are trained like the men; they speak with authority – still their experience in their professions is very different from that of men. Tannen has no explanation for this and apparently is unfamiliar with the concept of status dilemma – I return to this point later.

And as to linguistics, readers who do not know will not learn, in this book written by a linguist, that speaking has been analyzed since Austin (1962) as a social act in a social context. Utterances are acts that reflect as well as construct differences in status and power among speakers, and as such they can hurt and degrade another, they can decrease respect for and credibility of another, they can ignore, diminish, ridicule, i.e. discriminate against others. They can do this quite without conscious intention by their speakers. But, of course, as social beings situated in a certain cultural context, we have the obligation to inform ourselves about which acts are seen as discriminatory, i.e. as sexist or racist or both, by our hearers and we have to guarantee that our speech acts are such that they are not offensive if we do not want to offend. If we do not want to exclude someone, we have to guarantee that our advertisement or invitation is such that they feel included. If we want to comfort someone, we have to speak in such a way that the hearer can accept it as comfort. If we fail to follow the conventions of our language to address or comfort someone then our speech acts do not succeed, they 'misfire', as Austin said. We are responsible for how we speak. We cannot arbitrarily produce speech acts and claim idiosyncratic intentions for them – there is a limit to how an utterance can be both understood and misunderstood.

This has to be kept in mind when reading Tannen where again and again what is meant by one speaker and what is understood by another is described as having merely the most tenuous connection. Tannen's linguistically innocent stance gives us no clue that speakers, when talking, are active in a social exchange that can legitimate and produce the domination of men and the subordination of women, and that their interaction just as well could undo social inequality by not reproducing utterances and acts that discriminate, by producing fairer language and more symmetric conversations.

Here may be the reason why Tannen's book is without passion, even 'linguistic' passion as we find it in Labov or Chomsky or Lakoff (Robin Lakoff, of course). Its author does not envisage change anywhere, she does not allow herself linguistic passion or political passion. She is writing in the service of the male research perspective, not making any value judgements, especially none that would threaten the existing hierarchies, i.e. the status quo. However, in selling the status quo, her by-intention apolitical book becomes a highly political act. As such, it is not even in the tradition of American linguistics which all in all has had a deep political and social concern embodied foremost in Chomsky, but also in Labov, who in the 1960s salvaged Black English from primitive status by showing it as a creative endeavor with complex linguistic practices that white standard speakers could not dream to match. Even the anthropologist-linguists of old were more political than Tannen and more concerned with equality. They defended Native American languages (called Indian languages, then) as just as good and just as rich to express the relevant concerns of Native American life as was Standard English with respect to the concerns of its speakers. But none of these linguists would have dismissed the power differences between the speakers of Native American languages or Black English and standard speakers.

Turning away now from academia and her colleagues, to the women and men who are the subjects of Tannen's *You Just Don't Understand*, it is difficult to believe that they could feel their communication adequately described. The plaintive reproach of the title is obviously a woman's utterance, resigned to not being understood instead of insisting on being understood. This is indicative of what is to come. As a critic wrote: 'Tannen's wailing lament about male conversational behaviour is bound to frustrate frustrated women even more' (*Spiegel* 18, 1991: 223). Women are being told that men who are unempathic, who do not care about women's feelings or their wishes, who are selfish and self-centered, speak a different language, called a language of report, and are interested in a different goal, namely the solution of problems. This will not comfort the women who think that men should also be able to communicate on an emotional level and who want to educate men to their emotional culture. Are they to give up the idea of a loving heterosexual relationship based on mutual sharing?

Take for instance the woman who had a breast operation and felt she had been cut into and that the seam of the stitches 'had changed the contour of her breast' (p. 49). Her husband replies with only one sentence to his wife's distress: 'You can have plastic surgery to cover up the scar and restore the shape of your breast' (p. 49). Then the following dialogue evolves (p. 50):

WOMAN: I'm not having any more surgery! I'm sorry you don't like the way it looks.
MAN: I don't care. It doesn't bother me at all.
WOMAN: Then why are you telling me to have plastic surgery?
MAN: Because you were saying *you* were upset about the way it looked.

Note that in this dialogue the man has the last word and the woman afterwards 'felt like a heel'. We hear a lot about her feelings – e.g. she felt guilty about snapping at him – but we hear nothing about his feelings, only that he was reacting to her complaint by reassuring her that there is something she could do about it. Tannen concludes: 'Eve wanted the gift of understanding, but Mark gave her the gift of advice. He was taking the role of problem-solver, whereas she simply wanted confirmation of her feelings' (p. 50). Tannen's analysis ends here.

It is interesting to see who gets their needs fulfilled. The man solved a problem and presented his solution – he did what he needed to do. The woman did not get what she needed in her situation. There is not the slightest suggestion that especially in a difficult situation of that kind the man should perhaps for once not react to his wife with the usual unempathic, unconcerned, cold, problem-solving response. Is this woman to accept that even when she most needs compassion and empathy (a word that does not occur in Tannen's book), she is not going to get it? And should she believe Tannen's explanation that her husband did not *understand* what she wanted?

Many women know that men just do not *want* to be interested in what they need and it often shows most dramatically in situations where a woman is sick or pregnant or becomes disabled or gets old. It is not that men do not understand what women want and, if they only knew, they would generously give it. Neither women nor men are as dumb as Tannen wants us to believe: 'Many men honestly do not know what women want, and women honestly do not know why men find what they want so hard to comprehend and deliver' (p. 81). Many men, however, must appreciate Tannen's analysis – they do not have to find out what women want and, above all, they do not have to change.

My thesis is that men understand quite well what women want but they give only when it suits them. In many situations they refuse to give and *women cannot make them give*.

To claim, as Tannen does, that women want comfort and do not want advice or solution of problems, and that men can give only the latter but not the former, is simply ridiculous. Women also want advice and solutions to problems and men also want empathy. What is wrong is that most of the time men are getting both from women, and women often (as in the case of Tannen's Eve) get neither.

Conversations between women and men are not as superficial as suggested by this book, and they do not fail because of miscommunication. Dialogues also do not stop where they do in this book; often women and men do go on to inquire what went wrong. They both know that they are not just expressing their caring, loving, selfless thoughts in two different ways, but that they are doing essentially different things: women care for, and support, men; empathize with them, comfort them, and especially work for men in conversations and relationships, at home and at work; men take women's energy and work, and use it for themselves (what Tannen calls their love of independence and autonomy), and return when and what and if they feel like returning. The majority of relationships between women and men in our society are fundamentally asymmetrical to the advantage of men. If they were not, we would not need a women's liberation movement, women's commissions, houses for battered women, legislation for equal opportunity, antidiscrimination laws, family therapy, couple therapy, divorce. We would not even need Tannen's book.

To pursue the subjects of Tannen's book a bit further – just like Eve, other women in her examples have to submit to male domination: The woman who came out of the hospital early and 'had to move around more' (p. 50) (obviously because her husband was not doing for her what strange nurses did for her in the hospital), was told by her husband: 'Why didn't you stay in the hospital where you would have been more comfortable?' (p. 50). A perfectly reasonable answer 'to her complaint about the pain she was suffering' from the person closest to her? Tannen herself surely would have taken such a response in her stride, understanding her husband's suggestion just as it was intended. Or the woman who, when she braked, extended her right arm to protect the man beside her from falling forward (p. 35), an automatic gesture which infuriated this man, who thought she should keep both hands on the wheel. This woman ends up 'training herself to resist this impulse with Maurice to avoid a fight, but *she felt sadly constrained* by what she saw as his irrational reaction' (p. 50, my emphasis). Or the woman who had asked her husband 'Would you like to stop for a drink?', and he said 'no', whereupon they did not stop (p. 15). Now, apart from the fact that even a very dense man can infer the indirect meaning of a request from this question, it is again interesting to see who did what he wanted to do, and who accommodated to his wishes and did not do what she wanted to do.

Although women are submitting, annoyed, hurt and losing out in one example after the other, and men are getting their needs fulfilled, Tannen ends up rescuing the men. She explains them to us so we can perceive them as they should be perceived: in their puzzlement, confusion, frustration, while they all get their way.

However, at one point Tannen's explanation stops: men don't talk to their heterosexual partners, Tannen claims, but she does not tell us why. She fails to explain why men who talk all day long, whose business is talk, including talk of a high degree of indirectness, in politics, law, advertising, sales, journalism, on school boards, in academia, cannot say two sentences to their wives at home. Take the man who cannot answer his wife's question 'What's new with X?' and says 'Nothing' (p. 80). Do you think if his boss asked him the same question about the same X, he would say 'nothing'? And if he did indeed, and his boss reacted in anger, would he not know why? As a native speaker he knows that his answer means not only there is nothing new about X but also that it has an indirect message of 'I don't care to talk with you now', and is a refusal to enter into further conversation. But how is it that a man, when talking to his female boss, knows more about indirect meaning and indirect speech acts than when he talks with his wife? Because he can afford to. He *has to* supply information to his boss, but at home *his wife has to* work at drawing information out of him and he gives it only when he is good and ready.

So let us now look at the men in Tannen's book. So far, we have learned that although they are emotionally retarded and impoverished, morose and taciturn – Tannen calls it 'hampered by their style' (p. 146) – they always have the best of intentions. To be sure, they are being sold for stupid as far as their proficiency in their native language is concerned, but that does not matter since they can maintain their privileges. Take the man who is moving out of the house and wants to tell his 12-year-old son (pp. 146–7). He ends up talking about wars and politics instead of the new situation and his feelings, not to mention his son's feelings and fears. Tannen considers him handicapped by his style. Did he get his need to lecture fulfilled, did the boy get his needs fulfilled? Should we accept that men are total emotional illiterates even when it comes to their children? Should we accept that they do not have to be knowledgeable about emotions, not even their own? That it is just their style which makes them know more about wars than about their relationships with the most important people in their lives? And so they can lecture forth about wars and weapons, and Japan and Russia, but not say one empathic comforting word to their children or their wives when they are in distress.

Is it a matter of style that men in this country spend three minutes a day talking to their small children?

Has anyone found out how much time they spend talking to their wives?

Should we really believe what Tannen tells us about men not talking at home, namely 'many men are deeply frustrated by feeling they have disappointed their partners, without understanding how they failed or how else they could have behaved' (p. 82).

If men were that frustrated, they would change, and talk to their wives. If women could make them talk, they would, but women accommodate because that is all they can do. Those who do not accommodate get to feel the consequences. Women even accommodate where it is not necessary because of their family, job, or economic situation, i.e. they allow themselves to be dominated even when they could walk out of a doctor's office or tell a man to shut up, without negative consequences.

A beautiful case in point is the author (Tannen) herself who, after giving a talk in a bookstore for an audience of mainly women, found that 'the discussion was being conducted by men in the audience. At one point', to follow her insightful description, 'a man sitting in the middle was talking at such great length that several women in the front rows began shifting in their seats and rolling their eyes at me. Ironically, what he was going on about was how frustrated he feels when he has to listen to women going on and on about topics he finds boring and unimportant' (p. 76). Again, the story ends here. There is no comment on the fact that a man dominated all the women in the audience, including the speaker; no comment on her letting the man 'conduct the discussion' at the expense of the women present. These poor women learned the lesson over that they already know: who talks and who listens, who feels disappointed and frustrated, and who feels satisfied. Only this time they learned it from the expert, by her shining example.

If you leave out power, you do not understand any talk, be it the discussion after your speech, the conversation at your own dinner-table, in a doctor's office, in the back yards of West Philadelphia, in an Italian village, on a street in Turkey, in a courtroom or in a day-care center, in a women's group or at a UN conference. It is like saying Black English and Oxford English are just two different varieties of English, each valid on its own; it just so happens that the speakers of one variety find themselves in high-paying positions with a lot of prestige and power of decision-making, and the others are found more in low-paying jobs, or on the streets and in prisons. They don't always understand each other, but they both have the best intentions; if they could only learn a bit from each other and understand their differences as a matter of style, all would be well.

I prefer an analysis that has more descriptive and explanatory adequacy – and also more passion, an analysis like that of Henley/Kramarae (1991: 20) that takes into consideration that 'Hierarchies determine whose version of the communication situation will prevail; whose speech style will be seen as normal; who will be required to learn the communication style, and interpret the meaning, of the other; whose language style will be seen as deviant, irrational, and inferior; and who will be required to imitate the other's style in order to fit into the society' (p. 20); or that views US culture as 'requiring (and teaching through popular magazines) females, not males, to learn to read the silence, lack of emotional expression, or brutality of the other sex as not only other than, but more benign than, it appears' (p. 23). Tannen's book is such a product of US culture, quite comparable to popular magazines and teaching just that.

In my own research (Troemel-Ploetz, 1981, 1982) I have shown that the gender hierarchy is stronger than the hierarchy created by social status. Thus even when women have a high social status, i.e. when they have experience and expertise, age and high professional position, younger or less-qualified men often succeed in constructing a higher conversational status for themselves.

Tannen supplies us with several examples where her expertise is questioned by men who contradict, doubt or challenge her, but she seems to have no problem with these male attempts to construct a higher status for themselves. She takes such challenges as an invitation to show her expertise (p. 145), and presumably submits, just like she let herself and her women audience be dominated by a few men. Professional women, women in politics, the women doctors of West (1984), the judges and attorneys in reports on *Women in the Courts* (1984 to present), usually arrive at different interpretations in similar situations. They know that they are questioned more because they are women, and they are challenged in ways men would not be. They would laugh at Tannen's naïve suggestion that a man's challenge is 'a sign of respect and equal treatment' (pp. 128–9), or that they are 'misinterpreting challenges as personal attacks on their credibility' (p. 129). But significantly, professional women, working women, intellectual women hardly occur in Tannen's book. The women she describes do not even read the paper (pp. 80–2). The women she describes do not talk about politics or professional matters, but about 'who was at the bus stop, who called, what they said, how they made them feel' (p. 80). Her women are the adjusting, begging, nagging, wailing women, who regularly eat the chicken back (p. 184), and keep complying, but who are, in spite of all their efforts, just not understood.

But take a woman judge who can insist on being understood in the courtroom. She still must construct her professional competence against male attempts to deconstruct it. Kathryn Stechert describes in *Sweet Success* (1986: 185) the efforts of a female justice of the peace to demonstrate power so she can use it. The judge does this by 'maintaining a sense of awe' in the courtroom, by a stern facial expression, by raising her voice at times, by being very cold. The judge says: 'I think of it as acting and it does have an effect on people'. Stechert concludes: 'with other accoutrements of power, the black robe, the gavel, and court room bench, that place her higher than the lawyers and litigants who come before her, she retains the power that goes with her position' (p. 185).

Or take a woman attorney, who depends on making herself understood and is competent to do so. In one of the reports of *Women in the Courts*, an attorney stated that when she came up to the bar in a child custody suit, the male judge asked her: 'Are you the child?' I wonder if Tannen would analyze this insult as the male judge's 'different habitual style' or as his 'creating an imbalance'. Telling the woman attorney that 'the real problem is conversational style', 'women and men have different ways of talking', 'men are handicapped by their style', or 'hurtful and unjustified misinterpretations can be avoided by understanding the conversational styles of the other gender' (p. 95) would not be very helpful in this situation.

Fortunately, some American lawyers believe more in the power of words than the linguist Deborah Tannen does. They would throw out immediately Tannen's wishy-washy explication: 'The culprit then is not an individual man or even men's styles alone, but the difference between women's and men's styles. If that is the case, then both can make adjustments' (p. 95). They would point out to Tannen that men do not voluntarily make adjustments and women should not have to. Feminist lawyers actually did something about the 'different ways of talking' men use in the courtroom and they *made* men change *their* way of talking. They found that it was quite systematic talk used by men, to and about women, to violate women's credibility and professionalism. They defined such talk as sexist, and have shown that sexist bias against women is damaging to women on all levels in the court system, as accused and as witnesses, as jurors and court personnel, as lawyers and secretaries and judges; it does not make for justice.

Whereas Tannen tries to explain away male insensitivity, many sensitive men have been taking a stand during the last ten years, looking critically at themselves and their colleagues. They have supported feminist lawyers, instituted task forces in one US state after the other to identify discriminatory verbal behavior in the courts; they have worked for change. Ironically, Tannen's understanding of the social and political function of language falls below what sensitive and reasonable men in high positions know, without being linguists. To quote one of them, Robert N. Wilentz, Chief Justice of New Jersey:

> There's no room for gender bias in our system ... there's no room for the funny joke and the not-so-funny joke, there's no room for conscious, inadvertent, sophisticated, clumsy, or any other kind of gender bias, and certainly no room for gender bias that affects substantive rights.
> There's no room because it hurts and it insults. It hurts female lawyers psychologically and economically, litigants psychologically and economically, and witnesses, jurors, law clerks and judges who are women. It will not be tolerated in any form whatsoever. (The First Year Report of the New Jersey Supreme Court Task Force on *Women in the Courts*, June 1984)

I do not think this man will change his politics to a watered-down stance about men's different style of communication. I hope other self-critical and fair men will also refuse Tannen's thesis, recognizing it for what it aims at: the cementation of patriarchy.

Knowledge gained about discourse in the courtroom or in medical practice can easily be extended to private conversations, for what is going on in this arena is, after all, not that different. The repertoire of speech acts is quite the same; the construction of dominance and superiority is quite similar. The difference is that private talk among lovers or wife and husband *could* be symmetrical. Hierarchy in private relationships is not as formalized as in the court system. Private talk has a chance courtroom interaction, unless there is an enlightened judge, does not have. (How could the attorney who was called a child demand and construct symmetry?)

This is why Tannen's book is so depressing. In one example after the other she is trying to make the man's responses understandable, to explain his ignorance, his disinterest, selfishness or rudeness. She is telling women who have gained insight into the power politics of talk that men and women do not understand each other (without her explanation). She completely misses the point that conversations are constructed, that people don't 'fall into differences of their interactional habits' (p. 125) or 'find themselves arrayed in an asymmetrical alignment' (p. 125), but that we produce equality or inequality, symmetry or asymmetry in every conversation, only it is usually the more powerful who have the choice to give up some of their privileges and rights, and the less powerful who cannot just demand equality or symmetry and get it.

To tell professional women, who have worked for two decades in rape crisis centers, with domestic violence, in universities and state women's commissions with sexual harassment, defining it on a scale from verbal utterance to date rape or acquaintance rape, to tell women lawyers and doctors who have worked with sexual abuse of girls and baby girls at home by fathers and male relatives, that 'the real problem is conversational style' (p. 79) or 'misunderstandings arise because the styles are different' (p. 47), or 'that men have a different way of showing they care' (p. 298), is more than absurd. These women know that underlying the conversational politics and the body politics is the power politics of female–male relationships where men have social control of women and, if need be, recourse to violence. There are many other manifestations of the power relationship between the sexes, e.g. an analysis of women's and men's economics shows men earn 90 percent of the world income, own 99 percent of the world property, while doing only one-third of the world's work (UN Report of 1980 – with the growing poverty of women also in the USA, these figures have probably changed for the worse in the last decade).

I hope Tannen's readers will see through her 'explanations', will not be kept at the naïve level of ignorance the author assigns them to. The chances are good, because many of the women readers are giving the book to their husbands to read (p. 85). A follow-up study showing that all husbands now put down their paper at breakfast and talk, talk, talk empathically will (against all of Tannen's predictions) not be forthcoming.

I hope Tannen's readers will not stay in their place. I hope they will see through the patterns of domination in their exchanges with men. I hope they will see that *their* understanding the masculine style does not help them (p. 123) and that nothing changes if men just *understand* female style without valuing it as more humane and changing their style to become more empathic and caring. I hope they test Tannen's claim of the good intentions in males and insist on symmetry – if they are listening supportively to a man's problem, they should get the same, if they are freely giving information, they should get it just as freely, if they are open, their partner should also open up. I hope they know that the 'hope for the future' (p. 48) does not lie in *their* changing their style, but in men being less dominant, and learning from women.

This book trivializes our experience of injustice and of conversational dominance; it disguises power differences; it conceals who has to adjust; it veils differences again and again and equalizes with a leveling mania any distinction in how we experience women and men.

References

Allen, Sheila and Barker, Diana Leonard, eds (1976) *Dependence and Exploration in Work and Marriage*. London: Longman.

Austin, John L. (1962) *How to Do Things with Words*. Oxford: Clarendon.

Coupland, Nikolas, Giles, Howard and Wiemann, John M., eds (1991) '*MisCommunication' and Problematic Talk*. Newbury Park, CA: Sage.

528 Theoretical Debates (2): Difference or Dominance?

Fisher, Sue (1984) 'Was Ärzte sagen – was Patientinnen sagen: Die Mikropolitik des Entscheidungsprozesses im medizinischen Gespräch', in Senta Troemel-Ploetz (1984).

Fisher, Sue (1986) *In the Patient's Best Interest.* New Brunswick, NJ: Rutgers University Press.

Fisher, Sue and Todd, Alexandra, eds (1983) *The Social Organization of Doctor–Patient Communication.* Washington, DC: The Center for Applied Linguistics.

Fisher, Sue and Todd, Alexandra, eds (1986) *Discourse and Institutional Authority: Medicine, Education, Law.* Norwood, NJ: Ablex Publishing Corporation.

Harding, Susan (1975) 'Women and Words in a Spanish Village', in Rayna R. Reiter (1975).

Henley, Nancy M. and Kramarae, Cheris (1991) 'Gender, Power and Miscommunication!', in Nikolas Coupland et al. (1991).

Jenkins, Lee (1981) 'The Development and Structure of Stories in a Women's Rap Group', Paper presented at Speech Communication Association, Anaheim, CA.

Jenkins, Lee (1982) 'Stories Women Tell: An Ethnographic Study of Personal Experience Narratives in a Women's Rap Group', Paper given at the 10th World Congress of Sociology, Mexico City, Mexico.

Reiter, Rayna R., ed. (1975) *Toward an Anthropology of Women.* New York: Monthly Review Press.

Todd, Alexandra (1984) '"Die Patientin hat nichts zu sagen": Kommunikation zwischen Frauenärzten und Patientinnen', in Senta Troemel-Ploetz (1984).

Todd, Alexandra (1989) *Intimate Adversaries: Cultural Conflict between Doctors and Women Patients.* Philadelphia: University of Pennsylvania Press.

Troemel-Ploetz, Senta (1981) '"Sind Sie angemessen zu Wort gekommen?": Zur Konstruktion von Status in Gesprächen', Paper presented at the 3rd Annual Conference of the German Society for Linguistics, University of Regensburg, March 1981. Published in Senta Troemel-Ploetz (1982).

Troemel-Ploetz, Senta (1982) *Frauensprache: Sprache der Veränderung.* Frankfurt: Fischer Taschenbuch Verlag.

Troemel-Ploetz, Senta (1982) 'The Construction of Conversational Differences in the Language of Women and Men', Paper presented at the 10th World Congress of Sociology, Mexico City, August 1982. Published in Senta Troemel-Ploetz (1984).

Troemel-Ploetz, Senta, ed. (1984) *Gewalt durch Sprache: Die Vergewaltigung von Frauen in Gesprächen.* Frankfurt: Fischer Taschenbuch Verlag.

West, Candace (1984) *Routine Complications: Troubles with Talk between Doctors and Patients.* Bloomington: Indiana University Press.

Whitehead, Ann (1976) 'Sexual Antagonism in Herefordshire', in Sheila Allen and Diana Leonard Barker (1976).

Women in the Courts:

The First Year Report of the New Jersey Supreme Court Task Force on *Women in the Courts,* June 1984.

The Second Report of the New Jersey Supreme Court Task Force on *Women in the Courts,* June 1986.

Report of the New York Task Force on *Women in the Courts,* March 1986. Published in *Fordham Urban Law Journal* XV (1), 1986–8: 11–198.

See also:

Lynn Hecht Schafran (1987) 'Documenting Gender Bias in the Courts: The Task Force Approach', *Judicature* 70 (5), February–March: 280–90.

Gail Diane Cox (1990) 'Reports Track Discrimination: Fourteen Volumes Chronicle How Women Are Treated in Court', *The National Law Journal* no. 12, 26 November.

Part IX

Theoretical Debates (3): When is Gender Relevant?

This section focuses on a lively ongoing debate in language and gender studies. It asks the question: how do we know that gender is relevant to a particular stretch of talk? Ideas about gender have developed a great deal in the last 10 years or so, with the notion of gender as a static social variable that can be straightforwardly correlated with particular linguistic features being superseded by an understanding of gender as socially constructed. This constructionist idea of gender has been adopted by most scholars in the field, but discourse and conversation analysts disagree on the question of gender relevance.

Researchers from a strict Conversation Analysis (CA) background argue that you can only say that a particular linguistic form or a particular utterance is constructing gender *if* the speaker explicitly or at least demonstrably orients to gender in what they say. Many sociolinguists and discourse analysts, on the other hand, argue that gender is often inferred on the basis of pre-existing background assumptions that speakers and analysts draw on. This point about the indirect relationship between language and (gendered) meaning was made in 1992 in a seminal paper by Elinor Ochs. Ochs argues that there are only very few features which index gender directly in the English language (for example "he" and "she"). Instead, Ochs argues that gender (and other social meaning) is usually only "indexed indirectly." For example, certain linguistic features can index assertiveness, but, on a secondary/indirect level, they have also come to index masculinity. Critical discourse analysts such as Norman Fairclough (2001, 2003) argue that speakers' interactional and social practices and identities are frequently shaped by social structures and belief systems (such as dominant ideologies) which are not always visible and therefore may not be "oriented to" by the speakers in their talk.

The three papers which have been chosen for this section take up the debate in various ways. The first is a seminal paper by Emanuel Schegloff, "Whose Text, Whose Context?", which provides a clear exposition of the CA perspective. The paper arose as a contribution to a conference where participants responded to the question: Are all ways of "doing" discourse analysis equally legitimate? Schegloff argues that discourse analysis too often relies on the analyst's perspective in interpreting the linguistic data, whereas he himself urges us to consider the participants' perspective. The danger is, according to Schegloff, that analysts'

Language and Gender: A Reader, Second Edition. Edited by Jennifer Coates and Pia Pichler.
© 2011 Blackwell Publishing Ltd except for editorial material and organization. © 2011 Jennifer Coates and Pia Pichler. Published 2011 by Blackwell Publishing Ltd.

categories are imposed on the data, when in fact there is no evidence, or "warrant," to justify this. He calls this "a kind of theoretical imperialism." Two extracts are analyzed in the paper, and Schegloff's careful micro-analysis of talk-in-interaction illustrates the way Conversation Analysis is done: only what participants in interaction orient to in their talk is considered relevant to the interpretation of the text. So in Schegloff's first extract, "Stolen," a telephone conversation between estranged parents, gender is not mentioned in the talk and is therefore not to be considered of relevance to participants. But in the second extract, where a participant says "Ladies last" after he has helped himself to butter before passing it to one of the women present at the dinner table, Schegloff argues that gender is made relevant to the talk by the explicit use of the term "ladies."

Ann Weatherall's short paper, "Gender Relevance in Talk-In-Interaction and Discourse," is a direct response to Schegloff's. She argues that, in his analysis of the extract "Stolen," he provides background information about the participants which helps to make the analysis coherent. He describes participants in terms of age (Joey is a teenager) and marital status (Marsha and Tony are Joey's parents but live apart), among other things. Weatherall queries whether this is any different from drawing attention to the gender of the participants. Gender, she argues, is "a pervasive social category," one that is omnipresent in our lives. Recognizing that this is the case does not make researchers theoretical imperialists. She also claims that impartiality is impossible in any research: as researchers, we all bring our own baggage to our analysis of texts. What is important is that we reflect on what we do. A conscious reflexivity, in Weatherall's words, makes for "more objective" analysis.

The final paper in this debate is Joan Swann's "Yes, But Is It Gender?". Arguing that there has been a shift in language and gender research, from seeing both language and gender in relatively fixed terms to seeing them as relatively fluid, Swann focuses on the issue of "warrants." What evidence should an analyst draw on to justify claiming that gender is relevant to a particular piece of talk-in-interaction? She provides a list of possible warrants used by researchers, ranging from general patterns derived from large corpora, through "participants' orientations" as evident in the text, to analysts' intuitions, to the simple fact that speakers are female or male or drag queens or whatever. She pays particular attention to Schegloff's critique of what he calls "a priori" assumptions about the relevance of gender based on analysts' concerns and categories rather than on participant orientations. Swann's critique of Schegloff's argument echoes Weatherall's, and sums up many of the questions that have been raised in reaction to his paper, including: Do participants need explicitly (or even knowingly) to put gender on record for gender to be seen as important in an interaction? and Don't all analysts, including Conversation Analysts, impose their own concerns on data? Stokoe and Smithson (2001), for example, argue that background knowledge is a valid interpretational resource for analysts. Swann concludes her review by encouraging language and gender scholars to be open to a wide range of warrants and research methods, employing comparisons and/or quantification of larger corpora in addition to local and contextualized studies of language and gender.

This is a debate which continues to preoccupy discourse analysts of all kinds. Those working in a strict CA framework continue to pay scrupulous attention to participants' orientations and to avoid assuming that gender is relevant in any particular stretch of conversation. Other analysts take the view that gender is not just any social variable and that gender ideologies structure every aspect of our lives. The value of this debate is that it has made all researchers more conscious of the way we provide evidence or warrants for our interpretation of texts. Greater reflexivity in the analysis of spoken interaction can only improve the quality of linguistic research.

References

Fairclough, Norman (2001) *Language and Power* (2nd edn). London: Longman.

Fairclough, Norman (2003) *Analysing Discourse. Textual Analysis for Social Research*. London: Routledge.

Ochs, Elinor (1992) "Indexing gender," pp. 335–58 in Alessandro Duranti and Charles Goodwin (eds) *Rethinking Context: Language as an Interactive Phenomenon*. Cambridge: Cambridge University Press.

Stokoe, Elizabeth and Smithson, Janet (2001) "Making gender relevant: conversation analysis and gender categories in interaction," *Discourse & Society* 12(2), 217–44.

Recommended Further Reading

Bucholtz, Mary (2003) "Theories of discourse as theories of gender: discourse analysis in language and gender studies," pp. 43–68 in Janet Holmes and Miriam Meyerhoff (eds) *The Handbook of Language and Gender*. Oxford: Blackwell.

Bucholtz, Mary and Hall, Kira (2005). "Identity and interaction: a sociocultural linguistic approach," *Discourse Studies* 7(3), 585–614.

Cameron, Deborah (2005) "Relativity and its discontents: language, gender, and pragmatics," *Intercultural Pragmatics* 2–3, 321–34.

Harrington, Kate, Saunston, Helen, Litosolliti, Lia, and Sunderland, Jane (eds) (2008) *Gender and Language: Theoretical and Methodological Approaches*. Basingstoke: Palgrave Macmillan.

Kitzinger, Celia (2007) "Is 'woman' always relevantly gendered?" *Gender and Language* 1(1), 39–50.

McElhinny, Bonnie (2003) "Theorising gender in sociolinguistics and linguistic anthropology," pp. 21–42 in Janet Holmes and Miriam Meyerhoff (eds) *The Handbook of Language and Gender*. Oxford: Blackwell.

Stokoe, Elizabeth (2005) "Analysing gender and language," *Journal of Sociolinguistics* 9(1), 118–33.

38

Whose Text? Whose Context?

Emanuel A. Schegloff

Source: *Discourse & Society* 8(2) (1997), pp. 165–87. Reprinted with permission of SAGE.

Introduction

The title of this paper is 'Whose Text? Whose Context?' Perhaps I would do well to begin by saying what I mean to thematize by the use of that title.

It is surely by now a commonplace observation that persons who can be characterized by one set of category terms – such as male or female – can be characterized by many sets of category terms – terms of age, ethnicity, nationality, religion, residence locale, occupation, culinary disposition (vegetarian), pet preference, etc. One consequence of that is that it does not suffice to ground the use of one of these category terms to refer to people by saying that they *are*, after all, such a one (Sacks, 1972; Schegloff, 1991a). It is not enough to justify referring to someone as a 'woman' just because she is, in fact, a woman – because she is, by the same token, a Californian, Jewish, a mediator, a former weaver, my wife, and many others.

Similarly, the ways of formulating the context within which something occurred are multiple. The observations which I just made were in the context of introductory remarks to a talk, in the context of a panel on politics and aesthetics, in a potentially polemical context, in the context of American Association of Applied Linguistics (AAAL) meetings, of a professional convention, in the American midwest, in the Intercontinental hotel, in a setting specially attuned to multicultural concerns, in the absence of my wife, etc. These are also all true, and one cannot fully or distinctively ground the use of any one of them by virtue of its truth.

Finally, if one had to characterize what I am doing at the moment, one might say that I am presenting a paper, introducing my remarks, reading a text, arguing a point of view, responding to our chairs' invitation, gesticulating occasionally and suppressing gesticulation mostly, managing recurrent eye contact with members of the audience, and many others. And a similar stricture can be introduced here: none of these characterizations can get an adequate warrant by saying that it was employed because it is *true* – even though it *is* true. They are *all* true.

At a time when there appears to be deep skepticism about the possibility of establishing *anything* as true, we have here an embarrassment of truths. And of course this is why we have such a skepticism: because each truth, or at least many of them, is said to be appropriate to, the product of, but relative to, the perspective brought to the matter at hand. And in the apparent multiplicity, and continuing multiplication, of perspectives, truth seems to disappear in a hall of perspectival mirrors.

It is one thing to register that there are many ways to characterize a person, a stretch of conduct, or a setting or context in which the person enacts that conduct. It is quite another to claim that they are all equally warranted, equally legitimate, entitled to identical uptake and weight. But how should one discriminate? On what grounds should some characterization of any of these aspects of a sociocultural event be preferred to another?

One solution has been that of explanatory adequacy. In the social sciences, this point of view has a history which warrants calling it 'positivistic', though this is just one usage of that much abused term. On this view, that way of characterizing social actors, the context in which they act, and the things they say and do – that way is best which most reliably yields 'findings' – repeatable, reliable, objective, significant (for some, statistically significant) observations about the world. Some would add to this that the characterizations should not only yield such worthy observations, but that they also be elements of a theory or theoretical apparatus which lends those observations more general import.

Another solution – one which I will be defending – takes a different tack. For the events of human conduct, we are dealing with sentient beings who themselves orient to their context under some formulation or formulations; who grasp their own conduct and that of others under the jurisdictions of some relevancies and not others; who orient to some of the identities they separately and collectively embody and, at any given moment, not others. And because it is the orientations, meanings, interpretations, understandings, etc. of the *participants* in some sociocultural event on which the course of that event is predicated – and especially if it is constructed interactionally over time, it is *those* characterizations which are privileged in the *constitution of socio-interactional reality*, and therefore have a prima facie claim to being privileged in efforts to *understand* it.

Now, as peculiar (and even outrageous) as it might seem to some, critical and political stances toward discourse often appear – in this way of thinking about the matter – to be 'positivistic'. But let us leave off the scientistic resonance of that term, for to some these days it is very nearly an insult, and I do not mean to insult anyone. Instead let me put it differently. The former of the two stances I have described allows students, investigators, or external observers to deploy the terms which preoccupy *them* in describing, explaining, critiqueing, etc. the events and texts to which they turn their attention. There is no guaranteed place for the endogenous orientations of the participants in those events; there is no principled method for establishing those orientations; there is no commitment to be constrained by those orientations. However well-intentioned and well-disposed toward the participants – indeed, often enough the whole rationale of the critical stance is the championing of what are taken to be authentic, indigenous perspectives – there is a kind of theoretical imperialism involved here, a kind of hegemony of the intellectuals, of the literati, of the academics, of the critics whose theoretical apparatus gets to stipulate the terms by reference to which the world is to be understood – when there has already *been* a set of terms by reference to which the world was understood – by those endogenously involved in its very coming to pass. (The issue is not unlike those who speak of Columbus having 'discovered' America, as if there were not already indigenous people living there.)

What I mean by 'Whose text? Whose context?', then, refers to this. Whose characterization of the conduct, and the context of the conduct, is to shape, to determine, to control our treatment of discourse? The very use of the term 'text' in my title was meant as a provocation, for it imposes on everything in the world the terminology of that praxis at which intellectuals, and literary intellectuals in particular, excel. I know that there is a technical usage involved here – a 'text' meaning only a field of significations, etc. Still, this is to insist, to impose, upon a world which may have very different concerns a preoccupation with its conduct as a field of significations.

Note that I said '… a world which *may have* very different concerns …' And this brings me to a final point in this prefatory theme-setting. The term 'discourse' itself is in some respects like 'text' – demarcating a universe more for the concerns of those who will address it academically than for those whose efforts produced its objects. What gets addressed under the rubric 'discourse' is so varied that the default expectation should be the *non*-generalizability of what is said about some type of discursive object of attention to others. And this applies to what I have said so far as well. The considerations I have tried to establish early in this paper are the product of trying to come to terms with the events of *talk-in-interaction*. I think they have a kind of prima facie validity beyond that, but this is surely defeasible. On the other hand, the reach of talk-in-interaction may be more extensive than is at first realized, and even if limited to this sub-domain, these introductory comments may have a bearing worth weighing heavily. Those who are preoccupied with very different kinds of discourse may nonetheless want to reflect on the relevance of the themes treated here to their materials.

In any case, the Colloquium's titular question – Are politics and aesthetics compatible? – requires a small modification of the question from my point of view, for 'aesthetics' isn't quite the word for the alternative to 'politics' for talk-in-interaction. I take the upshot of what is meant to be the 'design features' of the object under study, which make it – and make it recognizable as – what it is: a poem, a haiku, an aphorism, an interview, a conversation. In the arts and humanities we commonly subsume these design features under the rubric 'aesthetics'. Outside the arts/humanities domain they will be something else, but very likely still something formal. So perhaps the question can be rephrased as 'Are politics and formal analysis compatible?'.

With that modification, the answer I want to put forward to the question is, 'who knows'. But before we *can* know the answer, we need first to understand the object – the conversational episode – in its endogenous constitution, what it was for the parties involved in it, in its course, as embodied and displayed in the very details of its realization. Only then can we even begin to explore what forms a critical approach to it might take, and what political issue if any it allows us to address. […]

By the time I finish, I want to have spoken to, or provided grounds for, three points. First, why I think that talk-in-interaction has an internally grounded reality of its own that we can aspire to get at analytically. Second, how the mandate to first understand the target 'text' in its own terms applies to talk-in-interaction. And third, the need to rethink the issue of what a context can be – what can serve as *the context*, and *whose* context – whose *orientation* to context – is the consequential and warrantable one for our analysis. And so to the data.

The Data, with Preliminary 'Critical' Gloss

In their proposal for this Colloquium, Claire Kramsch and Ruth Wodak noted that the several approaches invited to come together here 'each tends to choose texts that best illustrate its proponents' views'. […] And so, in selecting a 'text' to serve as the focus for my contribution, I have tried to select one that might be seen as involving at least some of the issues which most engage those who bring critical and political concerns to this Colloquium.

Let me initially characterize the data by reference to those concerns, thereby *introducing* their relevance, which I otherwise would wish to *contest*. The episode involves interruption and overlap, which are commonly taken to embody issues of conflict and differential power; its protagonists are male and female participants in a strained relationship, and the occasion is one in which moral evaluation and censure are at issue.

Marsha and Tony are the parents – now separated or divorced – of the teenaged Joey, who lives with his father in northern California, but has just spent a period of vacation from school with his mother in southern California. This was the day he was scheduled to drive back up north, and the exchange on which I will focus comes from the quite brief telephone conversation which Tony makes to Marsha. Here is what precedes the target excerpt, followed by the excerpt itself at lines 35–54 (for transcription conventions, see p. x):

(1) Stolen, 1:01–2:17

```
                    ((ring))
 1   MARSHA:   Hello:?
 2   TONY:     Hi: Marsha?
 3   MARSHA:   Ye:ah.
 4   TONY:     How are you.
 5   MARSHA:   Fi::ne.
 6             (0.2)
 7   MARSHA:   Did Joey get home yet?
 8   TONY:     Well I wz wondering when 'e left.
 9             (0.2)
10   MARSHA:   .hhh Uh:(d) did Oh: .h Yer not in on what pen'. (hh)(d)
11   TONY:     No(h)o=
12   MARSHA:   =He's flying.
13             (0.2)
14   MARSHA:   En Ilene is going to meet im:.Becuz the to:p wz ripped
15             off'v iz car which is tih say someb'ddy helped th'mselfs.
16   TONY:     Stolen.
17             (0.4)
18   MARSHA:   Stolen.=Right out in front of my house.
19   TONY:     Oh: f'r crying out loud,=en eez not g'nna eez not
20             g'nna bring it ba:ck?
21   MARSHA:   ·hh No so it's parked in the g'rage cz it wz so damn
22             co:ld. An' ez a matter fact snowing on the Ridge Route.
23             (0.3)
24   MARSHA:   ·hhh So I took him to the airport he couln' buy a ticket.
25             (·)
26   MARSHA:   ·hhhh Bee- he c'd only get on standby.
27             (0.3)
28   TONY:     Uh hu:[h,
29   MARSHA:        [En I left him there et abou:t noo:n.
30             (0.3)
31   TONY:     Ah ha:h.
32             (0.2)
33   MARSHA:   Ayund uh,h
34             (0.2)
35   TONY:     W't's 'e g'nna do go down en pick it up later? er
36             somethin like (    ) [well that's aw]:ful
37   MARSHA:                        [H i s friend  ]
```

38	MARSHA:	Yeh h[is friend Stee-]
39	TONY:	[That really makes] me ma:d,
40		(0.2)
41	MARSHA:	·hhh Oh it's disgusti[ng ez a matter a'f]a:ct.
42	TONY:	[P o o r J o e y,]
43	MARSHA:	I- I, I told my ki:ds. who do this: down et the Drug
44		Coalition ah want th'to:p back.h ·hhhhhhhhh ((1.0))
45		SEND OUT the WO:RD.hhh hnh
46		(0.2)
47	TONY:	Yeah.
48	MARSHA:	·hhh Bu:t u-hu:ghh his friend Steve en Brian er driving
49		up. Right after:: (0.2) school is out. En then hi'll
50		drive do:wn here with the:m.
51	TONY:	Oh I see.
52	MARSHA:	So: in the long run, ·hhh it (·) probly's gonna save a
53		liddle time 'n: energy.
54	TONY:	Okay.
55	MARSHA:	But Ile:ne probably (0.8) is either at the airport er
56		waiting tuh hear fr'm in eess
57		((conversation continues))

Tony has called to find out when Joey left, presumably so as to know when to expect him. It turns out that there is trouble: Joey's car has been vandalized, and this has happened, as they say, on Marsha's watch (as she puts it at line 18, 'Right out in front of *my house*'). What is worse, nobody has bothered to inform Tony. In the segment of this conversation before us, two issues appear to be of concern: Joey and his itinerary, and the car and *its* itinerary. When Tony raises the latter issue (at lines 19–20: 'an eez not g'nna […] bring it back?'), Marsha gives it short shrift – providing the minimal answer (line 21: 'No') and rushing ahead into a continuation of the telling she has been engaged in (the 'so' marks the remainder of the turn, which could have stood as an account for the 'no', as disjunctive with it, and conjunctive with her earlier talk). When that telling is brought to an analyzable conclusion (lines 29–33), Tony returns to the issue which he had raised before – the fate of the car (line 35). This is the segment on which we focus.

As it might be formulated both vernacularly and for the purposes of critically oriented analysis, we have here an interaction across gender lines, in which the asymmetries of status and power along gender lines in this society are played out in the interactional arena of interruption and overlapping talk, and this exchange needs to be understood in those terms. In this interactional contest, it may be noted, Marsha is twice 'beaten down' in a metaphoric sense but nonetheless a real one, being twice induced to terminate the talk which she is in the process of producing (at line 37, 'His friend'; and again at line 38, 'his friend Stee-'), thereby indexing the power processes at work here. On the other hand, in the third interruption in this little episode (at lines 41–2), although Marsha does not this time yield to Tony's interruptive talk, neither does Tony yield to Marsha's. He starts while Marsha is talking, and brings his exclamation of commiseration to completion in spite of Marsha's ongoing, continuing talk. One could almost imagine that we capture in this vignette some of the elements which may account for these people no longer living together.

Now I find this way of casting and grasping this exchange problematic on many counts, as perhaps many of you do. There is, of course, much analysis along these lines out there, in terms both more and less sophisticated, in both the professional and the popular literature. Some of the issues raised by such analysis are raised in even its highly sophisticated versions (even if I have not produced one here). The reservation I wish to feature here is that such analyses make no room for the overtly displayed concerns of the participants themselves, the terms in which they relate to one another, the relevancies to which they show themselves to be oriented. Such analyses insist instead on characterizations of the parties, the relevancies, and the context, to which the *analyst* is oriented. I wish, then, to provide a moderately detailed (though quite compressed) analytic rendering of this exchange, the goal of which is to establish a version – even if only a partial version – of what was going on in it *for the participants, in its course*. And I wish finally to reconsider the bearing which this analytic account of the episode has – or should have – on the critically oriented take on it with which I began.

Let me say at the outset that one conclusion which I will want to draw from this exercise is that even where critical analysis is wanted, is justifiable, and can have its basic preconditions met, what it should properly be brought to bear on is an internally analyzed rendering of the event, the episode, the exchange, the 'text', if you wish to insist on literary diction. Whatever the differences between the analysis of literary discourse and quotidien talk-in-interaction, in this respect they are alike. You need to have technical analysis *first*, in order to constitute the very object to which critical or sociopolitical analysis might sensibly and fruitfully be applied. And then one may find it no longer in point.

And so I turn to a partial account of the object itself.

Talk-in-Interaction: The Sequence as a Course of Action

We begin with Tony's return to the issue of the car at line 35.

> TONY: W't's 'e g'nna <u>do</u> go down en pick it <u>up</u> lat<u>er</u>? er
> somethin like (   )

The design of the first unit of this turn is: WH-Question + candidate response + hedge via class extrapolation.

The Wh-Question – 'What's he gonna do' – is thoroughly indexical; it does not specify what course of action is being asked about. Until specified by the candidate response, it could be, 'What's he gonna do, take the first flight on Southwest, or take any airline he can get?'. That indeterminacy insulates it partially from premature response, but it is in any case designed and delivered in a fashion that marks it as a frame for a subsequent part. (It may be worth considering – though not now – what is getting done by framing it this way, rather than just asking, 'Is he gonna go down and pick it up later?' or even just 'Is he gonna pick it up later?'. What would each of these do or not do, as compared to the actually used form and construction?)

The subsequent turn-component offers a candidate answer to 'what's he gonna do', and that is 'go down and pick it up later'. The fact is Tony *does* put into the candidate response not only 'pick it up later' but also 'go down'. This may appear nit-picking, but there are several kinds of evidence that the nit turns out to be picked – by *Marsha*.

First, and least central for how the sequence develops but nonetheless probative, is the reappearance of the word 'down' in Marsha's subsequent response ('down at the <u>Drug</u> Coalition ...' at line 43), a usage which echoes an element of vernacular poetics already included in Tony's turn, with its masked contrast pair, 'go DOWN and pick it UP', where the directionality is at best metaphoric in each.

Second, and most telling, is that Marsha's reply, when she gets to articulate it, addresses itself virtually exclusively to the 'going down'. She remarks that Joey will be 'driving

DOWN with friends' (lines 49–50) and therefore will 'save a little time and energy' (lines 52–3), not to mention the money for another plane fare. There is no mention of his 'picking it up' or anything else after his driving back 'down' with his friends. I take this as some vindication of pitching the analysis at this level of detail; if the parties are hearing that way and responding that way – that is, with an orientation to this level of turn design – we are virtually mandated to analyze it that way.

I pass lightly over the third component of the turn unit noting only that it hedges commitment to the particular candidate response Tony has put forward, and that on completion of this component, the turn as a whole comes to possible completion. And Marsha apparently hears it that way, for just after this, she starts a next turn (lines 35–7).

> TONY: W't's 'e g'nna <u>do</u> go down en pick it <u>up</u> lat<u>er</u>? er
>   somethin like (   ) [well that's <u>aw</u>]:ful
> MARSHA: [H i s <u>f</u>riend]

On possible completion of Tony's turn and question, Marsha starts an answer. That it is an 'answer' which she has begun is not obvious on delivery, at least not in the same ways in which it is obvious that a 'why' question is being answered when a next turn begins with 'Becuz ...'. The claim that it is an *answer* which she is beginning can be warranted in post hoc fashion by noting that she tries twice to get this out (at lines 37 and 38) before succeeding on her third try (at line 48). Marsha builds these to be recognizable as three tries at the same utterance by starting each time with the same words. It is, of course, possible to say the same thing in different words; 'using the same words' is a canonical practice for displaying or claiming that a current saying is the same as a prior saying or partial saying was *trying* to be (Schegloff, 1996). Seeing that what the third try comes to is an answer to Tony's question, we can see that that is what Marsha was *starting* to do at lines 37 and 38, hence my earlier claim that at Tony's possible completion, Marsha starts an answer. But of course Tony does not have this resource for making this determination. The whole of the answer hasn't happened yet, and the utterance's start is not designed to display 'answerness'.

Although Tony's turn *had* come to possible completion, it turns out not to have been complete. (That is why we talk about *possible* completion as the strategic element of a turn for turn-taking purposes.) After the possible completion of his turn, Tony produces a wholly new turn unit, and one engaged in a quite different action than the one which he has just brought to possible completion.

It should be noted that Tony does not do this, as far as we can tell, *by virtue* of Marsha's talk, for example, by virtue of its start not being engaged in 'doing answering'. For Tony launches this new unit virtually simultaneously with the start of Marsha's turn. So he's not 'interrupting' in the conventional vernacular sense.

Tony's additional unit stands in a different relationship to what had preceded than did the first. They are two different orders of response to what has happened: an 'emotional' one on his own and his son's behalf, and a pragmatic one on the car's behalf. As we saw, the two cohabited an earlier turn (at lines 19–20) in the opposite order, and here they are again. Their relatively disjunctive character is marked by the start of the second unit with 'well' – a so-called 'discourse marker' whose usual home is turn-initial position; but here it is, displaced well into a turn.

To call what Tony adds here 'an emotional response' is clearly a vernacular gloss. As a matter of action- and turn-construction, it is in the first instance an assessment of what has happened. As a matter of sequence organization, such an assessment makes relevant next an agreement or disagreement with the assessment. And so it is not just that Marsha's answering of Tony's question about the car is interfered with by his simultaneous talk. That simultaneous talk by Tony mandates *its own response next*, leaving Marsha with two things to do – answer the earlier question, and respond to the assessment. What does Marsha do?

TONY:	W't's 'e g'nna <u>do</u> go down en pick it <u>up</u> la<u>ter</u>? er
	somethin like ( ) [well that's <u>aw</u>]:ful
MARSHA:	[H i s <u>friend</u>]
MARSHA:	Yeh h[is <u>friend Stee-</u>]
TONY:	[That really makes] me ma:d,

What Marsha does is momentarily quit. Just for the one syllable 'ful' in 'awful' she drops out of the overlap, leaving off production of her turn-so-far. On possible completion of Tony's assessment, she offers an agreement token as a response to it ('yeh'), and then tries again to produce the answer she was providing to Tony's question, using again the words she had used before, but getting a little bit further (one syllable further – 'His friend Stee-'). In doing so, she is adopting the canonical practice for responding to a turn which has made *two* responses relevant like a turn with two questions (Sacks, 1987 [1973]): deal with them in reverse order, responding to the second one first, and the first after that (if it is still relevant and possible). Here, Marsha has stopped the response to the first of Tony's moves when she hears that there is a second, she responds to the second, and then returns to respond to the first. The only problem is the character of the response which she has provided to Tony's assessment.

Pomerantz (1984) has shown that in offering second assessments, and in designing agreements with a first assessment, it is often not enough to offer another assessment term of the same class or valence. Effective agreements ordinarily require some *upgrading* relative to the assessment with which they are agreeing. Same-valence assessments which are not upgraded, or simple agreement tokens, can constitute 'weak agreements', and can be taken as tantamount to virtual *dis*agreement or non-agreement. Commonly, the producers of the first assessment respond to such weak agreements with upgrades.

Marsha's response here to Tony's 'awful' is 'yeh'. And this is far from an optimal agreement. It is virtually pro forma, a token response to dispose of something which needed responding to, but hardly a vigorous alignment with the stance which Tony has taken up. It is, then, in various respects, a less than adequate response to his second move. And when Marsha restarts her answer to Tony's question, she finds herself in collision again, this time with Tony's reaction to her problematic response to his assessment.

Tony's reaction embodies an upgrade not only relative to Marsha's pallid 'yeh', but relative to his own prior assessment. He has upped the ante. This is carried, first, in the personalization of the assessment; it is no longer the event which is being described, but Tony's reaction to it – its effect on Tony. And second in the intensified strength of the assessment term itself, '*really* makes me mad'. An 'intensifier' is after all precisely an instrument for upgrading. Here then is the response to weak agreement I described a moment ago – upgrading in response, seeking to draw the previously weak stance into a more vigorous alignment with the initial assessment.

Note, by the way, that Tony's intervention here has the effect of getting the sequential follow-through to the second action in his prior turn brought to satisfactory resolution before the first part is addressed. In this respect he is aligned with what Marsha is doing. And the competing talk in which he does his assessment upgrade prompts Marsha again to drop out of the overlap, to abandon her incipient answer to the question about the car, and to deal again with the issue of the assessment of what has happened to Joey's car, and aligning with that assessment (lines 35–50).

```
TONY:      W't's 'e g'nna do go down en pick it up later? er
           something like (   ) [well that's aw]:ful
MARSHA:                         [H i s friend ]
MARSHA:    Yeh h[is friend Stee-   ]
TONY:           [That really makes] me ma:d,
           (0.2)
MARSHA:    hhh Oh it's disgusti[ng ez a matter a'f ]a:ct.
TONY:                          [P o o r J o e y,]
MARSHA:    I- I, I told my ki:ds. who do this: down et the Drug Coalition
           ah want th'to:p back.h ·hhhhhhhhh ((1.0)) SEND OUT the
           WO:RD.hhh hnh
           (0.2)
TONY:      Yeah.
MARSHA:    ·hhh Bu:t u-hu:ghh his friend Steve en Brian er driving up.
           Right after:: (0.2) school is out. En then hi'll drive do:wn here
           with the:m.
```

Marsha's reaction to Tony's reaction is to provide a proper agreement, here by offering an assessment which is an upgrade on each aspect of what Tony has done. With respect to the assessment of what has happened, i.e. of the mischief itself, she upgrades 'awful' to 'disgusting'. As this is coming to possible completion, Tony chimes in with an expression of sympathy for their son, a position on which they can come together. But Marsha seems already committed to something else.

Although the transcript reads, and the tape sounds, as if Marsha is saying 'Oh it's disgusting as a matter of fact', there are substantial grounds for parsing this differently, namely, 'Oh it's disgusting. As a matter of fact I told my kids …'. But we haven't the time to work through the grounds for this assertion.

What then is this about? 'As a matter of fact' often marks the claim that what is to be told, or has been told, is so, and is said, independent of local interactional grounds for saying it. It is used as a form of 'coincidence marker'. Here, Marsha's 'disgusting' is vulnerable to suspicion that it has been coerced by Tony's interruptive upgrade of his prior assessment in reaction to Marsha's tepid agreement; that Marsha is just going along, is saying what is necessary. Marsha can then be undertaking to offer evidence that this is not so, that she is articulating a view she had held independent of Tony's coaxing, and she offers in evidence an independent event which embodies it. In doing so, she adds to her assessment of the event (as 'disgusting') a depiction of its effect on her, her counterpart to Tony's 'really makes me mad'. Marsha's telling completely overrides 'Poor Joey'.

The alignment on assessments having been achieved, Marsha once again tries to produce her answer to Tony's earlier question, and now is able to bring it to conclusion. There is, of course, more to be said about this, but we will have to do without.[1]

Suffice it to say that an account that would treat this brief exchange as but another exemplar of gendered discourse, whatever was further to be made of that, would have missed what it was demonstrably about *in the first instance – for the parties*. Can compelling critical discourse analysis sacrifice that?

But what could be meant by 'what it was demonstrably about *in the first instance – for the parties*'? Literarily speaking, what is meant resonates with the now commonplace assertion that meaning is use (Wittgenstein, 1953), or with the claim that the import of an utterance is its way of speaking (Garfinkel, 1967: 29). The import of 'a way of speaking' – a practice of speaking – is what it can be used to do, the possible actions it can accomplish … at least in part; a way of speaking, a practice, may have other import as well (for example, furnished by the distinctive biographical associations it may have come to have), but it – the practice – has at least this import.

But what could 'a practice of speaking' be 'used to do'? Specifying this is one task of analysis – of what I have been calling 'formal' analysis. It involves: (a) specifying the 'it', that is, that there is a practice underlying a bit of conduct, and what that practice is. In the preceding analysis, for example, that rebeginning a turn with the same words consti-tutes a practice of talking, deployed in characterizable contexts, for example, overlapping talk (first described as a methodical practice in Schegloff, 1987 [1973]); (b) showing what that practice seems designed and deployed to do (Schegloff, 1987 [1973], and, more generally, on the practice of using the same words to show one is saying the same thing that one was saying or trying to say earlier, Schegloff, 1996); and (c) showing that the products of that practice are understood by interactional co-participants to be pos-sibly doing that action, that is, that this understanding is not merely the imposition of an external academic or professional analyst, but is the understanding of the co-participant, as revealed in ensuing talk which is built on just that understanding (Schegloff, 1987 [1973]; Sacks et al., 1974).

When the account of the exchange between Marcia and Tony claims to represent 'the import for the parties', it draws on work which shows that the practices deployed there are members' practices of talk-in-interaction, used on behalf of certain projects and linked to certain outcomes. In addition to the work cited in the previous paragraph, there is the work of Pomerantz (1984) cited earlier and that of Goodwin and Goodwin (1992). That responses to assessments are examined by co-participants for their align-ment with the preceding assessment, that 'merely' same valence assessments or 'weak agreements' are not taken to be agreements but are treated as non-alignments with the first assessment, that the speaker of the first assessment may display such an understand-ing and act on it by re-doing the assessment with an upgraded assessment term, etc., these are all grounded in demonstrable conduct of parties to interaction, and thereby are shown to be indigenous practices of interaction (Pomerantz, 1984; and the abbrevi-ated account in Schegloff, 1996). The analysis of Tony re-entering the talk with 'That really makes me mad' as responsive to the weakness of Marcia's 'yeh' as a response to his prior assessment 'well that's awful' is, then, not a casual characterization, nor one war-ranted by claimed commonsense plausibility or by the cogency of some theoretical apparatus. Each of these 'contributions' has the prima facie appearance-in-context of the exercise of a members' practice of talking, fitted to a sequential and interactional context of deployment, and thereby made available for co-participant understanding along such lines, an understanding which the immediately ensuing talk seems to show was in fact accorded it. Although defeasible, this is a strong analytically focussed and empirically grounded case for the claim that these understandings are 'the understand-ings of the participants', unlike assertions of the sort most likely to enter into critically accented analyses, which either do not make this claim, or do not make it explicitly, or do not offer empirical grounding for it. Again then: Can compelling critical discourse analysis sacrifice that?

An Impossible Hurdle?[2]

There is nothing in the preceding discussion which necessarily either undercuts or underwrites critical discourse analysis. The upshot is only that critical discourse analysis be applied to a world refracted through the prism of disciplined and molecular observation,

observation at the level of the lived reality of the events which compose it, and not to the world as refracted through the prism of 'casual' vernacular observation, constrained neither by the discipline of interactional participation nor by that of systematic empirical inquiry.

Though it prompts impatience in those who aspire to more global claims and assertions, over and over again close examination of brief exchanges which may initially appear to casual inspection to be utterly unremarkable, or even transparently characterizable in vernacular or commonsense terms, turn out to yield rather more complex, and differently complexioned, understandings. More sweeping accounts appear then to depend on *not* examining single moments or episodes closely, and this may help understand the common impatience, and often intolerance, of close analysis ... this, and the fact that such analysis often yields results uncomfortably at variance with commonsense understanding or ideological predilections. All the more reason, then, to have critical concerns be brought to bear only after an initial formal analysis has brought to the fore the import of the events for the participants.

Of course, understanding along such lines, for example along gender lines, can also, in principle, be shown in any particular case to be 'the understanding of the participants', but this needs to be *shown*. It *can* be shown. Before concluding this essay, a brief examination of another data segment may serve to demonstrate that no impossible hurdles have been erected here; that even after a stretch of interaction can be shown to implicate on the participants' part orientations to activity-relevant identities, aspects of central interest to critical discourse analysis may still be shown to be oriented to by the participants, even when these are ostensibly irrelevant to the activity at hand.

In the following exchange, Michael and Nancy are having dinner with Shane and Vivian. The occasion is being videotaped by Vivian for a course in which she has enrolled; the exchange occurs shortly after the start of the tape.

(2) Chicken Dinner 1: 18–29

```
 1   SHANE:      [·hehh huh ·hhhh Most wishful thinkin
 2        →      hey hand me some a 'dat fuckin budder will you?
 3               (0.8)
 4  ?SHANE:      °°Oh::yeah°°
 5               (1.1)
 6   NANCY:→     C'n I have some t[oo
 7   MICHAEL:                     [mm-hm[hm:
 8   NANCY:                            [hm-hm-^h[m    [^he-ha-]ha ·hehh ]
 9   VIVIAN:→                                  [Ye[h [I wa]nt ]sometoo.]
10   SHANE:                                       [N[o:. ]  [( )-
11   SHANE:      No.
12               (0.2)
```

Shane's talk at line 1 is implicated in the closing of the preceding topic talk, and the 'hey' marks a disjunction and the start of a new sequence. Shane's body behavior has preceded his talk in this regard; his gaze shifts toward the butter – which is by Michael's place at the table – at the second syllable of 'wishful', he begins to point to the butter at the second syllable of 'thinkin', and he brings his arm pointing at the butter to full extension at the 'some' on line 2. Without spelling out in full the detail of the practice by which it is accomplished, it can be noted that Shane here (line 2) produces a request, that it is addressed to Michael, that Michael understands it to be a request and one which is addressed to him, and shows all this by beginning a compliant response. Indeed, he does this before the object of the request has been lexically formulated – he begins to reach for the butter just as Shane's point to it reaches maximum extension, at the word 'some'. For the activity enacted in this sequence-so-far, Shane and Michael are relevantly requester and requestee (or request recipient), respectively.

In the immediately following moments they become in effect deliverer and recipient respectively, as Michael and Shane consumate the request–grant sequence which Shane had initiated. This involves a choreography of movement which, were it not so common, one would be inclined to term extraordinary, in which Shane's hand shifts from a pointing to a receiving deployment in close coordination with Michael's reaching for the butter, grasping it and extending it toward Shane – a collaborative enterprise whose detailed explication is out of place in the present context.[3] Suffice it to say that its shape and reciprocity embody an orientation by Shane and Michael to their complementary capacities as deliverer and recipient, respectively.

While the request is still being articulated by Shane, Nancy and Vivian eye the butter, track its movement to Shane and his cutting a slab for himself, and produce the two requests at lines 6 and 9, respectively. These are requests to Shane, requests which potentially compete with each other and with his taking butter for himself. His response is the ironic or mock rejection of Nancy's request at line 10 and of Vivian's at line 11. Here, then, *they* are the requesters and *he* is the request recipient, and the request rejector. But then, after a moment's delay, he adds what can be taken as an account for the rejection. Here is the entire exchange:

(2) Chicken Dinner 1:18–19

```
 6  NANCY:→   C'n I have some t[oo
 7  MICHAEL:                  [mm-hm[hm:
 8  NANCY:                          [hm-hm-^h[m    [^he-ha-]ha hehh ]
 9  VIVIAN:→                                [Ye[h [I wa]nt ]sometoo.]
10  SHANE:                                    [N[o:. ]    [( )-
11  SHANE:        No.
12               (0.2)
13  SHANE:→   Ladies la:st.
```

At line 13, Shane's utterance displays an orientation on his part to categorical identities of the parties ostensibly unimplicated in the just-current activity and not otherwise evidently warrantable in context. Gender is relevant here after all, and 'counter-intuitively'. How so?

No extended account is possible here, but some suggestions may be in order to sketch one direction such an account might take, one which treats this next utterance as grounded in the activities just preceding, and seeks to understand the relevance of introducing gender as prompted by what has preceded.

The two requests by Nancy and Vivian while Shane is just helping himself to the butter can be seen to confront Shane with competing proprieties of action, ones embodied in various adages concerning orders of service: on the one hand 'first come, first served', on the other hand 'ladies first'. 'First come, first served' yields as the proper next action that Shane continue to help himself to the butter. 'Ladies first' yields as the proper next action that Shane defer continuing to serve himself and pass the butter (though to whom turns out to be problematic in his eventual actual passing behavior). 'Ladies last' is a reformulation of the rule which he is *not* observing, a reformulation which would be in accord with the course of action he adopts, and is offered as (an ironic) account of it.[4]

This is hardly a form of account which is likely to appeal to critical discourse analysts, but it does show that categories of analysis which are often central to such approaches can turn out to be relevant to discourse, and to be oriented to by the parties, even when not ostensibly relevant to the activities otherwise ongoing. Although in this case this orientation is made overt by the explicit mention of a category term, this is by no means necessary to establish the relevant orientation by the participants which earlier sections of this essay have argued for. Various accounts have been offered of conduct by which orientation to gender (to cite only one common pre-occupation of critical discourse analysis) can be manifested without being explicitly named or mentioned (for example, Garfinkel, 1967: 116–85; Ochs, 1992; West and Zimmerman, 1987; see also Sacks, 1992, I: 590–96, II: 360–6; Schegloff, 1992b: liii–liv; 1992c: xxx–xxxi). One line of analysis which could enrich both 'formal' and critical discourse analysis would be the elaboration of those forms of conduct by which persons 'do' gender, class or ethnicities of various sorts, and by which they may be shown to display and invoke participants' orientations to those features of the interactional context.

I understand that critical discourse analysts have a different project, and are addressed to different issues, and not to the local co-construction of interaction. If, however, they mean the issues of power, domination, and the like to connect up with discursive material, it should be a serious rendering of that material. And for conversation, and talk-in-interaction more generally, that means that it should at least be compatible with what was demonstrably relevant for the parties – not necessarily their sequentially directed preoccupations, but, whatever it was, demonstrably relevant to them as embodied in their conduct. Otherwise the critical analysis will not 'bind' to the data, and risks ending up merely ideological.

Conclusion

In his essay, 'Explaining the Obvious' (1994: 124), the remarkable music analyst and pianist Charles Rosen – known for his treatment of western music in broad socio-historical context – comments on an analysis he has just offered of some music of Schubert:

> This may appear at first sight to be an issue of purely formal and technical description. Nevertheless, it is only by getting the formal aspect right that we can see how Schubert's music conveys a different view of experience, and reflects his age in its attempt to go beyond the rendering of what might be conceived as the underlying static conditions of appearance – the structure beneath the skin, so to speak – and to represent instead the very movement of phenomena. In Europe, after the intoxication of the French Revolution …

What Rosen finds, then, is that 'getting the formal aspect right' is necessary for getting into a position even to *see* in Schubert's music the larger cultural and political themes one may wish to argue it embodies. And he concludes his essay with a theme purportedly distinctive to music, but perhaps even more relevant to discourse (p. 126):

> It is natural to look outside or beyond the music, to find the ways in which it can temporarily and provisionally assume different kinds of significance. Nevertheless, music will not acknowledge a context greater than itself – social, cultural or biographical – to which it is conveniently subservient. To paraphrase Goethe's grandiose warning to the scientist: do not look behind the notes, they themselves are the doctrine.

In our times, the relativization and perspectivalization of cultural analysis threaten the virtual disintegration of stable meaning and import into indeterminacy, and nowhere more than in discourse analysis. By analogy to physical entropy, there is here a kind of interpretive en-tropism. Discourse is too often made subservient to contexts not of its participants' making, but of its analysts' insistence. Relevance flies in all directions; the text's center cannot hold in the face of the diverse theoretical prisms through which it is refracted.

But ordinary talk-in-interaction, it seems to me, offers us leverage. The interaction embodies and displays moment-to-moment the products of its own, endogenous mechanisms of interpretation and analysis, both of the utterances and actions which compose it and of the oriented-to context. These are the understandings *of the participants*. And their robustness and inescapable relevance is ensured by having subsequent moments in the trajectory of the interaction grounded in those very understandings, and built on them. More than music, more than literature, more than the visual arts, then, whose understanders and interpreters may have (many now think) no Archimedean leverage, either with respect to the objet d'art or with respect to other interpreters, talk-in-interaction *does* provide such an Archimedean point. But it is not *external*, as in the classical imagery. It is *internal* to the object of analysis itself. It is the product of the organization of practices of conversation itself, whose consequence is that contributions display their speakers' understanding of what has preceded.[5]

That is a big part of what we study in 'formal' analysis; that is how we try to ground *our* analysis. It has the virtue, if well done, of capturing – at least partly – the demonstrable indigenous import of the events and of their context *for their participants*. And if that is not what *critical* discourse analysis is to address itself to – discursive events *in their import for their participants*, then I'm not sure what it is about and what is to be hoped for from it. If it *is* what critical discourse analysis is to address itself to, then critical analysis and formal analysis are not competitors or alternatives. One presupposes the other; serious critical discourse analysis presupposes serious formal analysis, and is addressed to its product. Whether politics and aesthetics are compatible turns, in this view, on whether this arrangement can be made to work by those whose central impulse is critical.

Notes

This paper was prepared for the invited colloquium, 'Understanding Discourse: Are Politics and Aesthetics Compatible?' organized by Claire Kramsch and Ruth Wodak for the American Association of Applied Linguistics Annual Conference, 23–26 March, 1996, Chicago, Illinois. For transcription conventions, see p. x.

1   One intervention from the floor noted that what has been offered here was 'just one interpretation', and asked, 'aren't there others?' and 'which is right?'. There are undoubtedly others, though cogent ones are not quite as easy to produce as the comment intimates. Even more demanding is the challenge of providing other 'interpretations' for which evidence can be provided that the parties are oriented to that grasp or version of what is transpiring, and/or which are grounded in independent analyses of talk-in-interaction which explicate the practices which yield such interpretable stretches of talk and which show the methodicity with which such practices are linked to such outcomes (e.g. such types of responses to assessments to be linked to agreement or disagreement). The preceding discussion – in its effort to address these undertakings – aims to convert interpretation into warranted analysis. Whether or not there are 'other analyses' awaits the submission of efforts along those lines; determinations of 'which is right' awaits juxtaposition of the proposals and a determination whether comparative assessment is relevant and/or possible.

2   I am indebted to Gene Lerner for suggesting the usefulness of adding a discussion that speaks to the actual feasibility of introducing themes of interest to critical discourse

analysis after formal analysis had already been employed to characterize what is going on in a spate of interaction.

3 My account of this exchange – both the detail given and the detail withheld – has profited from early work on 'object transfers' done by Blaine Roberts at the University of California, Irvine in the early 1970s.

4 That Shane deals with matters of etiquette, and shows his orientation to them, by reversing them, can be seen elsewhere in this exchange as well, for example, in his including in his request a term of impoliteness (indeed, obscenity) where a term of politeness ('please') might have been relevant.

5 The text of Goethe's paraphrased in the earlier-cited excerpt from Rosen reads, 'Do not look behind the phenomena, they themselves are the doctrine'.

References

Garfinkel, H. (1967) *Studies in Ethnomethodology.* Englewood Cliffs, NJ: Prentice-Hall.

Goodwin, C. and Goodwin, M.H. (1992) 'Assessments and the Construction of Context', in A. Duranti and C. Goodwin (eds) *Rethinking Context: Language as an Interactive Phenomenon,* pp. 151–89. Cambridge: Cambridge University Press.

Ochs, E. (1992) 'Indexing Gender', in A. Duranti and C. Goodwin (eds) *Rethinking Context: Language as an Interactive Phenomenon,* pp. 335–58. Cambridge: Cambridge University Press.

Pomerantz, A. (1984) 'Agreeing and Disagreeing with Assessments: Some Features of Preferred/ Dispreferred Turn Shapes', in J. M. Atkinson and J. Heritage (eds) *Structures of Social Action: Studies in Conversation Analysis,* pp. 57–101. Cambridge: Cambridge University Press.

Rosen, C. (1994) *The Frontiers of Meaning: Three Informal Lectures on Music.* New York: Hill and Wang.

Sacks, H. (1972) 'An Initial Investigation of the Usability of Conversational Materials for Doing Sociology', in D. N. Sudnow (ed.) *Studies in Social Interaction,* pp. 31–74. New York: Free Press.

Sacks, H. (1987 [1973]) 'On the Preferences for Agreement and Contiguity in Sequences in Conversation', in G. Button and J. R. E. Lee (eds) *Talk and Social Organisation,* pp. 54–69. Clevedon: Multilingual Matters.

Sacks, H. (1992) *Lectures on Conversation,* 2 vols, ed. Gail Jefferson, with Introductions by Emanuel A. Schegloff. Oxford: Blackwell.

Sacks, H., Schegloff, E. A. and Jefferson, G. (1974) 'A simplest systematics for the organisation of tum-taking for conversation', *Language* 50: 696–735.

Schegloff, E. A. (1987 [1973]) 'Recycled Turn Beginnings: A Precise Repair Mechanism in Conversation's Turn-taking Organisation', in G. Button and J. R. E. Lee (eds) *Talk and Social Organisation,* pp. 70–85. Clevedon: Multilingual Matters.

Schegloff, E. A. (1991a) 'Reflections on Talk and Social Structure', in D. Boden and D.H. Zimmerman (eds) *Talk and Social Structure,* pp. 44–70. Cambridge: Polity Press.

Schegloff, E. A. (1992b) 'Introduction', in G. Jefferson (ed.) *Harvey Sacks: Lectures on Conversation,* Vol. 1, pp. ix–lxii. Oxford: Blackwell.

Schegloff, E. A. (1992c) 'Introduction', in G. Jefferson (ed.) *Harvey Sacks: Lectures on Conversation,* Vol. 2, pp. ix–lii. Oxford: Blackwell.

Schegloff, E. A. (1996) 'Confirming Allusions', *American Journal of Sociology* 104(1): 161–216.

West, C. and Zimmerman, D. H. (1987) 'Doing Gender', *Gender & Society* 1(2): 125–51.

Wittgenstein, L. (1953) *Philosophical Investigations,* trans. by G. E. M. Anscombe. New York: Macmillan.

39

Gender Relevance in
Talk-in-Interaction and Discourse

Ann Weatherall

Source: Discourse & Society 11(2) (2000), pp. 286–8. Reprinted with permission of SAGE.

The topic of gender and language is not new but as recent volumes of *Discourse & Society* attest, it is one that continues to attract considerable scholarly attention. The centrality of language to social relationships and power has made it an important domain for interrogating the creation and recreation of the gendered status quo. Of particular importance to feminists has been understanding how language is implicated in the reproduction of male dominance, female subordination and hetero-normativity with a view to developing strategies for subverting those processes.

Of fundamental significance for feminist work on gender and language is an issue discussed by Schegloff (1997 reprinted in Part IX of this volume, 1998) and Wetherell (1998). That is, to what extent is it justifiable or even desirable to invoke gender as an analytic category when it is not transparently relevant to participants engaging in an interaction? Representing a conversation analytic position, Schegloff (1997) suggested that it is a self-indulgent act of intellectual hegemony for scholars to impose categories that preoccupy them onto data. A more principled approach, according to Schegloff, is conversation analysis where researchers restrict themselves to those categorizations of the data that the participants overtly privilege as being relevant and consequential to the interaction. Following Schegloff, the use of gender as an analytic category would only be appropriate when it was an observably salient feature of the participants' talk and conduct. For example, when actors call attention to the use of a masculine pronoun because the sex of the subject is unknown, then gender is explicitly relevant to the context of the interaction.

Restricting the analytic frame of reference to include gender only when it is explicitly displayed as concerning the parties involved is supported by Schegloff on two counts. On the one hand it provides a solution to the problem of when to privilege gender over other possible dimensions of social identity (e.g. age, ethnicity) that may be relevant to the interactional context. On the other hand, it avoids the kind of imperialism that feminist researchers may practise when they impose their theoretical preoccupations with gender on the target text. Schegloff acknowledges that such restraints may limit scholars' ability to engage in social criticism. Nevertheless, constraining the analysis to what is demonstrably relevant to the participants functions to maintain empirical rigour in

Language and Gender: A Reader, Second Edition. Edited by Jennifer Coates and Pia Pichler.
© 2011 Blackwell Publishing Ltd except for editorial material and organization. © 2011 Jennifer Coates and Pia Pichler. Published 2011 by Blackwell Publishing Ltd.

discourse analytic work and, Schegloff argues, is necessary for establishing a foundation upon which a critical analysis must rest.

To illustrate his argument, Schegloff (1997) presented an analysis of a telephone conversation labelled 'Stolen' between Marsha and Tony concerning Joey. He suggests that formulating the patterns of interruption and overlap displayed in the conversation along gender lines, as a critically orientated analyst may do, would be problematic because there is no explicit evidence that gender is directly relevant to the participants during their conversation. An analysis of the conversational extract is then presented that claims to restrict itself to an account of what the exchange was about for the parties involved. However, Schegloff does provide considerable background information about the parties involved (i.e. Marsha and Tony are Joey's parents; Joey is a teenager; Marsha and Tony live apart; Joey lives with Tony), that is not explicit from the interaction but gives the analysis coherence. Thus Schegloff seems to commit the very kind of act that he describes as self-indulgent.

A point upon which both Wetherell (1998) and Schegloff (1997) agree is that conversation is a (or maybe 'the') prime site for examining the intersubjective construction of meaning and social order. Indeed, analyses of talk-in-interaction have produced important insights into the structures of conversation that constitute shared resources for co-ordinating understanding and social action. Hopper and LeBaron (1998) provide one example of what a conversation analytic approach can bring to the study of gender and language. They found, for example, that linguistic markers of gender provide a structural resource for increasing the ease with which gender can be occasioned, and its relevance extended, in social interaction.

In contrast to Schegloff (1997), Wetherell (1998) argues that for a more complete rather than just a technical analysis of texts, it is necessary to consider the 'discursive articulation' or the 'argumentative texture of social life' that constitutes the fabric upon which everyday sense-making practices depend. Thus Schegloff's analysis of 'Stolen' may be enhanced by identifying, what might be called, the discursive articulation of parental concern. That identification may evoke further questions about the conversation, such as why Tony seeks a confirmation of Marsha's identity but fails to explicitly identify himself or, why Tony extends the opening sequence of the conversation so that it is Marsha who ultimately poses the question about their son's whereabouts. The issue at stake is whether it is actually more indulgent to ignore the common-sense categories necessary for understanding the text, than it is to invoke them.

Here I wish to reiterate a point made by feminist philosophers of science for a long time – the impossibility of impartiality in any analytic approach. Values and biases enter into the most rigorous of empirical approaches by, for example, the types of questions asked and the kinds of interpretations made. Thus what becomes desirable, or 'more objective' for any analysis is a conscious reflexivity about the position one brings to a piece of research and a consideration of what is hidden by taking that perspective. As Hopper and LeBaron's (1998) work illustrates, there is nothing wrong with limiting the scope of an analysis of conversation to that which the actors observably orientate to. However, to claim such an analysis is inherently more objective and less self-indulgent than some other approach must be treated with suspicion.

Gender is a pervasive social category. The identification of a person as belonging to one of two gender groups is a fundamental guide to how they are perceived, how their behaviour is interpreted and how they are responded to in every interaction and throughout the course of their life. Linguistic indexes of gender may occur at every level of language. So, even if gender is not explicitly privileged by participants as relevant to the conversation, it is an omnipresent feature of all interactions. Compelling evidence that gender constitutes part of the 'argumentative texture' for meaning-making was Cameron's (1998) analysis of a vignette, 'Is there any ketchup Vera?'. The utterance, produced by Vera's husband, was used to illustrate how gender subtly influences communication and social interaction in a pragmatic sense. In this example, Vera understands that her husband is not inquiring as to the presence of ketchup in the house, but is requesting that she fetch it for him. The relevance of gender here is not marked by 'gender noticing' but through a consideration of the pragmatics of the exchange (i.e. a similar request from a daughter may have received a different response).

A recognition of gender's omnirelevance does not necessarily constitute an act of theoretical imperialism, nor does a conversation analytic approach curb a critical perspective. An example of the latter was Kitzinger and Frith's (1999) use of conversation analytic work on the normative structure of refusals, to question the effectiveness of the 'no means no' slogan for date rape prevention. It seems then that conversation analysis is no more or less able to step outside the argumentative texture of social life, than any other approach. Thus the kind of critical discursive social psychology that is advocated by Wetherell (1998) which synthesizes a range of analytical approaches seems to advance the most promising approach for understanding and subverting dominant discourses of gender and sexuality.

Note

I would like to thank Margaret Wetherell for encouraging me to contribute to this discussion. I would also like to thank Nicola Gavey for her prompt and insightful feedback on an earlier draft.

References

Cameron, D. (1998) ' "Is There any Ketchup, Vera?": Gender, Power and Pragmatics', *Discourse & Society* 9(4): 437–55.

Hopper, R. and LeBaron, C. (1998) 'How Gender Creeps into Talk', *Research on Language and Social Interaction* 31: 59–74.

Kitzinger, C. and Frith, H. (1999) 'Just Say No? The Use of Conversation Analysis in Developing a Feminist Perspective on Sexual Refusal', *Discourse & Society* 10(3): 293–316.

Schegloff, E. (1997) 'Whose Text? Whose Context?', *Discourse & Society* 8(2): 165–88.

Schegloff, E. (1998) 'Reply to Wetherell', *Discourse & Society* 9(3): 413–16.

Wetherell, M. (1998) 'Positioning and Interpretative Repertoires: Conversation Analysis and Post-structuralism in Dialogue', *Discourse & Society* 9(3): 387–412.

40

Yes, But Is It Gender?

Joan Swann

Source: This is a revised version of chapter 2 of L. Litosseliti and Jane Sunderland (eds), *Gender Identity and Discourse Analysis*. Amsterdam: John Benjamins (2002). With kind permission of John Benjamins Publishing Company, Amsterdam/Philadelphia.

Introduction

> *Rethinking Language and Gender Research* is the first book focussing on language and gender to explicitly challenge the dichotomy of female and male use of language. It represents a turning point in language and gender studies, addressing the political and social consequences of popular beliefs about women's language and men's language and proposing new ways of looking at language and gender. (Blurb for Bergvall, Bing and Freed, 1996)

Rethinking language and gender research has been very much in the air over the past few years. Bergvall, Bing and Freed (1996) is one of a number of books (I do not think it is actually the first) that sets out to challenge earlier research practices and the theories (implicit or explicit) that informed them. There is a danger of caricaturing earlier traditions in order to establish the novelty of what we do now – by no means all earlier work on language and gender proposed a strict dichotomy between female and male language users. The general picture that emerged from reviews of such work was always one of general tendencies that admitted of some variability: female speakers tended to use language in one way, male speakers in another.[1] Nevertheless, there has been a general shift that might best be characterised as running from relative fixity to relative fluidity in terms of how 'language' and 'gender' are conceived and how the two are seen to interrelate.

I shall refer to the current, relatively fluid, position as broadly postmodernist, in the sense that it is part of a more general intellectual trend towards the questioning, if not the subversion of any notion of discrete categories of identity that has been associated with postmodernist thinkers.[2] I am using this term for want of a better one, and do not mean to imply by this that all contemporary language and gender researchers explicitly acknowledge a common theoretical base in postmodernism, or even that they all acknowledge an explicit theoretical base. Academic ideas and traditions are notoriously leaky, and the ideas I discuss here seem to me to be widespread and not just to apply to fully paid-up postmodernists.

Recent preoccupations in language and gender research have to do with diversity (differences amongst women and amongst men), context (seeing language/meaning as context dependent, and gender as a contextualised social practice) and uncertainty/ambiguity

Language and Gender: A Reader, Second Edition. Edited by Jennifer Coates and Pia Pichler.
© 2011 Blackwell Publishing Ltd except for editorial material and organization. © 2011 Jennifer Coates and Pia Pichler. Published 2011 by Blackwell Publishing Ltd.

(in terms of the meanings of what speakers say and do). The respects in which this is a shift from a more fixed view of language and gender can be exemplified by considering research on classroom language. Such reseach, carried out since the late 1970s, suggests that there are differences in girls' and boys' interactional styles. These lead to boys dominating the interactional space. Girls provide more interactional support, but this in effect leads to them 'giving away power' in mixed-sex contexts (for a review see Swann, 1992). There are clear practical implications arising from such research: the 1980s saw the development of a number of equal opportunities and anti-sexist initiatives designed to redress the inequalities that had been documented, and Holmes, writing in 1994 about the situation in English language teaching classrooms discusses the continuing need to 'improv[e] the lot of female language learners').

Such generalised patterns of difference and disadvantage are, however, challenged by more fluid models of language and gender: these would point to the need for contextualised interpretations of language use, which may throw up ambiguities and analytical uncertainties; to differences between girls and between boys (not all girls are 'supportive'); and to the resultant fragmentation of formerly fixed social categories such as 'girl' or 'boy'. The practical implications of such a shift are by no means clear.

In working with such models I have found myself getting 'stuck' on a number of issues, and I want to work through some of these in the remainder of this paper. My interests here are quite practical. I am interested in the empirical analysis of language: in how an analyst approaches an utterance or text, how they interpret this, and what 'warrants' (to borrow a term from conversation analysis) they draw on (implicitly or explicitly) to support their interpretation. In particular, I want to consider whether the models of language and gender I have outlined above allow an analyst to make any general statements about gendered language use; and whether it matters if they don't.

The points I am making can be related to recent commentaries on 'critical' approaches to language analysis. Emanuel Schegloff (1997), for instance, in 'Whose Text? Whose Context?' [reprinted in Part IX of this volume] argues against what he terms the 'theoretical imperialism' of critical researchers who analyse texts from their own ideological perspective rather than seeking to understand speakers'/participants' orientations. And Michael Stubbs (1997) criticizes the reliance of much critical discourse analysis (CDA) on small amounts of data that may (even if unwittingly) have been selected to support the analyst's viewpoint. While both Schegloff and Stubbs are concerned with how analysts may produce a valid interpretation of data, their approach to this question and the solutions they propose are somewhat different. I shall return to their work below.

The discussion in the remainder of this paper will apply, at some level, to all aspects of written and spoken language, but I shall focus primarily on the study of spoken interaction, which is the area I am most familiar with as a researcher.

Problematizing 'Language'

The analysis of 'gendered language' has traditionally been bedevilled by what is sometimes known as the 'form/function' problem. For instance, findings that male speakers interrupt female speakers more than *vice versa* were based on studies of linguistic forms: interruptions were usually identified as speech that began before a previous speaking turn was complete, or almost complete (precise definitions varied from one study to another). What was important, however, was not the identification of differences in the use of certain linguistic forms, but the functions that could be 'read off' from these. Seeing certain types of overlapping speech as interruptions suggested that these were hostile incursions into another speaker's turn (e.g. Zimmerman and West, 1975; West and Zimmerman, 1983). The problem here was that it was possible to attribute differing functions to the same, or very similar linguistic forms. Thus large amounts of overlapping speech were seen as supportive in informal talk between women (Coates, 1996).

Janet Holmes' research on a corpus of New Zealand data differed from earlier formal studies by taking an explicitly functional approach. Holmes recognised that the same linguistic form could have different functions, and looked at how these functions were distributed between female and male speakers. Her discussion of tag questions (Holmes, 1984) provides a useful illustration of this approach. Tag questions (of the form 'It's hot in here, *isn't it?*) have been controversial in language and gender research. While Robin Lakoff (1975) speculated that women used these forms more than men, findings from subsequent empirical investigations have been inconsistent (e.g. Baumann, 1979; Dubois and Crouch, 1975; Preisler, 1986). Holmes identified distinct functions of tag questions in her data, and showed that women and men used these differently: for instance, women used more tags that could be interpreted as facilitative or supportive. While this is, in many respects, an improvement on earlier formal studies, the functional approach itself is not without problems. Deborah Cameron et al. (1989) tried to replicate Holmes' functional classification of tag questions in an analysis of British conversational data. Their findings were sometimes inconsistent with those of Holmes but, more importantly, they found it was not always possible to assign tag questions unambiguously to one category or another. Tag questions were often ambiguous and they could have more than one function simultaneously. (For a more complete account of Holmes' functional analysis, see Holmes, 1995.)

These findings are in line with the more recent approaches to language I mentioned above, which see meanings, or functions, as relatively unstable, potentially ambiguous and heavily context-dependent. One of the clearest statements of this position comes from Deborah Cameron's discussion of *Feminism and Linguistic Theory*. Cameron explicitly rejects the 'fixed code' model of language that she claims underpins much of traditional linguistics as well as certain feminist accounts of language. She proposes, as an alternative, 'integrational linguistics' (Harris, 1981), a model in which language is regarded as a communicative phenomenon, rooted in context and used creatively by speakers:

> language is *radically* contextual. It is not just a matter of context affecting the system, the system has no existence outside a context. Thus language cannot be abstracted from time and space, or from the extralinguistic dimensions of the situation in which it is embedded. Just as modern biologists regard even simple organisms' behaviour as produced by incredibly complex interactions of genetic and environmental phenomena, so even the simplest linguistic exchange involves a constellation of factors – linguistic, contextual, social and so on – which is always more than the sum of its parts. And this also implies, of course, that meaning is radically indeterminate and variable. (Cameron, 1992:192; italics as in original)

This suggests, to Cameron, that some women's feelings of 'alienation' from language derive, not from the language system itself but from their exclusion from certain linguistic practices that have traditionally been dominated by men.[3]

While Cameron is concerned with language and (feminist) politics, her statement, in emphasising the indeterminacy of language meaning, also has implications for the language or discourse analyst. If one accepts such a fluid conception of language and meaning, for instance, what implications does this have for the authority with which analysts interpret texts? How do analysts establish the meaning of an utterance? Is one interpretation as good as any other? The reliance on context is also problematical: for the analyst, what should count as *relevant* context, and what sort of warrants do analysts need to make inferences about this? Such problems relate not just to how one handles language, but also to gender, which I turn to below.

Problematizing 'Gender'

Like language, gender as a social category has come to be seen as highly fluid, or less well defined than it once appeared. In line with gender theory more generally, researchers interested in language and gender have focussed increasingly on plurality and diversity amongst female and male language users, and on gender as performative – something that is 'done' in context, rather than a fixed attribute.[4] The whole notion of gender, and identity in general, is challenged when this is seen, rather like language itself, as fluid, contingent and context dependent. This is mainly an alternative theoretical conception of gender, though there are also suggestions that identities are loosening, so that in many contexts people now have a wider range of identity options.[5]

'Traditional' research on gender and spoken language has been challenged on several counts. Shan Wareing (1996), for instance, took issue with the methodology adopted in some earlier studies, arguing that rather large generalisations about female and male language use had been made on the basis of inadequate evidence. If one accepts this critique, an implication might be that such studies could be improved upon: research using (say) larger samples, or a wider range of contexts, could produce more reliable evidence of the relationship between gender and language. Recent conceptions of gender/identity, however, go several steps further: they would seem to call into question any generalized claims about language and gender.

Such ideas are prevalent amongst contemporary studies (see, e.g., the the papers in Bergvall, Bing and Freed, 1996; Bucholtz, Liang and Sutton, 1999; Hall and Bucholtz, 1995; Johnson and Meinhof, 1997; and Wodak, 1997). As an illustration, Bergvall, Bing and Freed (1996) *Rethinking Language and Gender Research*, which I cited above, has an explicit emphasis on challenging 'traditional' binary distinctions between female and male language users, and a focus on the diversity of women's and men's experiences. Hall and Bucholtz (1995) *Gender Articulated* focusses on women. As in Bergvall et al. there is an emphasis on diversity amongst women and on the fluid nature of social identity: the collection takes Robin Lakoff's early work as a canonical text for its starting point, but claims to be moving from 'Woman's Place' to 'Women's Places'. Johnson and Meinhof (1997) *Language and Masculinity* has, overall, a fluid conception of masculinity; in a similar vein to the other volumes, it focusses on the variable nature of masculine identities.

Sally Johnson, one of the editors of *Language and Masculinity*, gives a clear statement of this position:

> Work within pro-feminist approaches to masculinity has explored men in terms of 'multiple subjectivities', and this has led writers to abandon the idea of 'masculinity' in the singular, in preference for the pluralized 'masculinities'. The concept of 'male power' is then dislodged by the notion of 'hegemonic' or 'hierarchical' masculinities, perhaps best characterized as those forms of masculinity able to marginalize and dominate not only women, but also other men, on the grounds of, say, class, race and/or sexuality (Connell, 1987).
>
> According to this view of masculinities, where gender identities and power relations are seen as highly contextualised practices, it becomes rather more difficult to make clear and

generalizable statements about how men are or what they do. (Johnson, 1997: 19–20; note, the Connell referred to is Bob Connell's work on gender and power; see also Connell (1995) on masculinities)

Johnson's emphases here on the *pluralisation* of gender and on gender as a *contextualised practice* have major implications for the language analyst. 'Pluralization', on its own, is the lesser challenge. Relating gender to social attributes such as class, race and sexuality suggests a focus on interactions between different aspects of identity: rather than looking at the language of 'men', we can look at 'working class white heterosexual men' ... or whatever. But this on its own leaves the boundaries between different social identities fairly stable and untroubled. Seeing gender as a contextualised practice is a more important theoretical shift. If gender identity is something that is done, in context, this begs the question of how an analyst is able to interpret any utterance in terms of masculinity (or working class, white, heterosexual masculinity). How does the analyst assess whether a speaker is doing gender, or another aspect of identity? How does this relate to any one of a number of other things speakers and listeners may be doing in an interaction? (There are similar problems in assessing whether a speaker is carrying out certain activities associated with gender – e.g. doing power.) The situation is compounded in that, with this more fragmented model of identity, there is no need to stick to 'established' categories such as gender, class, race, sexuality: a whole set of identity features (being a manager, someone's mother, a sensible person) is potentially relevant; furthermore, a speaker may be stacking a number of complementary identities, or trying to balance sets of competing identities. The analyst, then, faces a major task in deciding what aspects of identity are relevant – or, slightly paraphrasing Nicholson (1990), in determining what aspects of 'difference' make a difference.

Interpreting 'Gendered Language'

I want to examine below some of the challenges produced by this shift in conceptions of language and gender for the language analyst. As a starting point, it seems useful to consider the warrants actually used by researchers, both historically and at present, to draw inferences about language and gender. Across a whole range of empirical studies, it is possible to identify a series of warrants for gender; that is, a series of decision procedures adopted by analysts that justify interpreting data (an utterance, or a linguistic construction, or a set of linguistic features) as, in some way, gendered. I have set out below those that occur to me, and I shall work through each of these in turn.

Warrants for gender in language and gender research

- quantitative and/or general patterns (derived from correlational studies of language use, large (computerised) corpora or other systematic comparison between the language of different social groups)
- indirect reliance on quantitative/general patterns
- 'participants' orientations' as evident in the text
- speakers'/participants' solicited interpretations
- analysts' theoretical positions
- analysts' intuitions
- speakers/participants are female, male (or whatever)

Quantitative and/or general patterns

By this I mean work that attempts a systematic comparison between some aspects of language used by female and male (or different types of female/male) speakers. The comparison need not involve quantification but frequently does so.

A great deal of work that identifies generalised differences between female and male speech has been carried out within what Deborah Cameron and Jennifer Coates (1989) termed the 'quantitative paradigm': this refers to traditional 'variationist' studies of (usually) pronunciation or grammatical features that chart the distribution of these features across social groups and across contexts. Variationist studies are able to identify systematic differences between social groups in terms of their language use. Earlier studies have usually taken social class as their primary social division, and have compared the speech of women and men from 'the same' social class. One of their most important (and certainly most discussed) findings is that women tend to use more standard or 'prestige' features of language, and men more nonstandard or vernacular features (see, e.g., Labov, 1966; Macaulay, 1978; Newbrook, 1982; Trudgill, 1974; Wolfram, 1969).[6] More recent variationist studies have qualified some of these highly general findings, relating language use not just to gender *per se*, but to women's and men's lifestyles, the social networks they form part of, and the activities they engage in, as well as to more complex interactions between gender and other aspects of speakers' identities (e.g. Eckert, 1998; Holmes, 1996; Horvath, 1985; Milroy, 1980, 1992; Thomas, 1989).

While quantification has frequently been associated with variationist studies, many studies of interactional or conversational features (such as interruptions) have adopted quantitative methods to allow comparison between women's and men's language use. An example from the classroom is Jane Sunderland's (1996) study looking at the distribution of different kinds of speaking turn between girls and boys. Vivian de Klerk (1997) has also drawn a quantitative comparison between girls' and boys' reported use of expletives. Other studies of interaction have established general differences between female and male speakers without employing quantitative methods – e.g. Jennifer Coates' claim, made on the basis of systematic study of audio recordings and transcripts, that 'while women talking with women friends tend to adopt a collaborative floor, men talking with male friends stick to a one-at-a-time floor' (1997: 108).

Computerised corpora allow the quantitative analysis of huge volumes of data so that analysts can see patterns in the distributions and associations of certain words and phrases; in the language used in different types of text; and in the language used by different types of speaker/writer. The use of electronic spoken language corpora to investigate language and gender is still relatively undeveloped. One or two studies, however, while not focussing primarily on gender, have findings of relevance to language and gender researchers – e.g. Rayson, Leech, and Hodges' (1997) study of social (including gender) differentiation in the use of English vocabulary; and McEnery, Baker and Hardie's (1999 and 2009) studies of the use of swearing and abuse in British English. Michael Stubbs (1996) provides good illustrations of the possibilities of corpus-based methods for 'socially-oriented' linguistic research, although the examples that are most relevant to gender focus on written texts. An analysis of two short texts – the final messages of Baden-Powell to guides and scouts – revealed that, alongside conventionally 'sexist' language, words such as *happy* and *happiness* had different collocations, or associations, in each text: for instance, guides were frequently exhorted to make others happy, whereas scouts were more frequently told to be happy themselves. Stubbs was also able to compare the collocations of *happy* and *happiness* in these two texts with those in a much larger computerised corpus of spoken and written English.[7]

The value of all the work I have discussed in this section is precisely that, if decision procedures are followed correctly, it allows systematic and potentially large-scale comparison between the language used by different groups of speakers. Such work should also, in principle, be *replicable* (similar studies carried out in similar contexts should obtain similar results).[8] There are, however, acknowledged problems in the interpretation of generalised/quantitative patterns. I referred above to the fact that female or male speakers' use of certain linguistic features may be associated with some other factor (e.g. employment) rather than, directly, with gender. Eckert and McConnell-Ginet (1998) point to the need to take into account a variety of data in the search for general patterns, to consider 'exceptions' (e.g. in variationist research, cases in which women's language is not more standard than men's), and to relate observations of language behaviour to the practices of particular communities. On its own, the establishment of general patterns in the distribution of linguistic features is a limited and potentially reductive exercise which tells us nothing about how language is used by women and men in specific contexts, nor about what speakers are doing as they talk.

Indirect reliance on quantitative and/or general patterns

By 'indirect reliance' I mean the fact that some small-scale and/or contextualised studies are explicitly reliant on general patterns derived from individual larger studies, or from the general 'body of work' on language and gender. Small-scale/contextualised studies may go on to qualify or question general patterns while still deriving their raison d'être, in part, from the prior existence of these patterns. An example of this comes from my own earlier work on classroom talk. In one study, a colleague and I questioned traditional patterns of 'male dominance' in the classroom, pointing out (for instance) that 'dominance', where it existed, was accomplished interactionally by all participants; and that this accomplishment drew on context-specific interactional resources (Swann and Graddol, 1988; Swann, 1989). However, beginning to approach the data in terms of dominance (ie seeing this as an issue worth developing further and perhaps qualifying) depended on the existence of a substantial body of evidence of male dominance in the classroom and elsewhere.

'Participants' orientations' as evident in the text

A useful statement of this position comes from the conversation analyst Emanuel Schegloff, whose criticism of 'theoretical imperialism' I referred to above. Schegloff (1997; reprinted in Part IX of this volume) is concerned to demonstrate that a text (he focusses on spoken interaction) may be understood 'in its own terms' and that its meaning may be revealed by close formal analysis. He argues that any aspects of context that are seen to be relevant to an interaction (including the social characteristics of participants/speakers) should derive from the orientations of the participants/speakers themselves, and not from those of the analyst. Schegloff is actually talking about something more limited than the expression 'participants' orientations' may suggest. He is referring to just those features that are made visible (or audible) in an interaction.[9] Schegloff's position contrasts with that of quantitative researchers, but also with that of any critical researchers who seek to interpret a text in terms of gender unless there is some explicit warrant for this in the text itself.

Schegloff's examples are, in fact, concerned with gender. In one of these, he quotes an extract from a conversation between four people: Michael and Nancy, Shane and Vivian, who are having dinner together:

```
 1   SHANE:                    [ůhɛhh huh ůhhhh Most wịshful thịnkin
 2            →     hey hand mɛ some a 'dat fuckin budder will you?
 3                  (0.8)
 4   ?SHANE:       °° Oh::yeah °°
 5                  (1.1)
 6   NANCY: →      C'n I have some t[oo
 7   MICHAEL:                    [mm-hm[hm:
 8   NANCY:                            [hm-hm-^h[m     [^he-ha-]ha ůhɛhh]
 9   VIVIAN: →                                 [Ye[h [I̲ wa]nt] some to̲o]
10   SHANE:                                       [N[o̲:.  ]  [( )-
11   SHANE:        No.
12                  (0.2)
13   SHANE:→       L̲adies l̲a:st.
```
(Schegloff, 1997: 181–2; see p.x for transcription conventions)

Schegloff points out that Shane's initial request for the butter (line 2) is directed towards Michael. Michael passes the butter to Shane, and this process is tracked by Nancy and Vivian. Nancy's, and then Vivian's requests for the butter (lines 6 and 9) are directed towards Shane. Shane's ironic rejection of their requests is justified by the comment 'ladies last' in line 13. Schegloff argues that this may be interpreted in terms of gender because there is evidence that the participants themselves are orienting towards gender – Shane's explicit reference to 'ladies'. Schegloff concedes that gender may be relevant without being explicitly named in this way but argues that such an interpretation would still depend upon participants' (demonstrable) orientation towards gender.

Schegloff raises interesting questions about how an analyst can determine the salience of 'contextual' features such as gender, but his solution itself raises further questions. For participants in an interaction, for instance, what is left unsaid may be as important as what is actually uttered, but Schegloff's framework would rule out anything not visibly (or audibly) attended to in the interaction.

The focus in this case on a single utterance is also problematic. Shane's interjection of 'ladies last' suggests that gender is a potentially salient category for Shane – it is something that may be invoked, or foregrounded. Because Shane utters the phrase in this context, this means he also assumes his co-conversationalists will recognise gender as (potentially) salient. However, the interactional scope of 'ladies last' remains unclear: does this mean that gender is a continuing interactional theme, attended to by Shane (and other participants)? Or does Shane's remark represent a sudden shift – an attempt to recast the interaction in terms of gender? The analytical limits imposed by Schegloff make it difficult to address such issues.

A further problem resides in the priority Schegloff accords to participants' (or, in this case, one participant's) apparent orientation to gender. This raises the question of who has the power to attribute meaning in a text. Do participants need explicitly (or even knowingly) to put gender on record for gender to be seen as important in an interaction? Shane seems here to be commenting on (and so offering an interpretation of) his own actions – but is his interpretation any more valid than that of another participant, or an overhearer – or, of course, an analyst?

Schegloff's paper has provoked considerable debate in *Discourse in Society*, the journal in which it was published. Commentators such as Margaret Wetherell (1998) and Michael Billig (1999a) have pointed out that analysts necessarily impose their own concerns on data (e.g. in selecting extracts for analysis and bringing particular analytic concepts to bear on these). Billig argues further that, rather than being ideologically neutral, conversation analysis conveys a 'non-critical' view of the social world: its 'foundational rhetoric' (incuding the way speakers are referred to and conversations described) represents a world characterised by equality and participation (this point is disputed by Schegloff – for the full debate see Schegloff, 1999a and 1999b and Billig, 1999b). Wetherell suggests that, in combination with certain post-structuralist traditions, conversation analysis may contribute to a more complete analysis that takes into account the broader 'interpretative resources' speakers have at their disposal – including 'the conversational or discursive history which makes this particular conversation possible' (1998: 403). Wetherell's own concern is with the role of discourse analysis within social psychology: her illustrative data come not from naturally-occurring conversation but from talk elicited in a group interview focussing on aspects of masculinities. In this case, she illustrates how young male speakers negotiate multiple and conflicting identities for one member of the group, and how these are related to the 'interpretative repertoires' available to the speakers (see also Schegloff's rejoinder to Wetherell – Schegloff, 1998). In a later paper in the *Discourse and Society* debate, Elizabeth Stokoe and Janet Smithson (2001) discuss the role played by analysts' 'background' or 'common sense' knowledge in interpreting conversational data. They argue that such knowledge is an important, and valid, interpretational resource that allows analysts to comment on the wider social significance of the highly localised 'working out' of gender – although this necessarily involves analysts in going beyond speakers' own demonstrable orientation to gender.[10]

Speakers'/participants' solicited interpretations

A strict adherence to Schegloff's framework would rule out actually consulting participants on their interpretations of their own and others' utterances. This approach has, however, been used within interactional sociolinguistics, most notably by John Gumperz and his associates. (See, e.g., Gumperz (1982) for discussion and illustration of the value of soliciting both participants' and others' interpretations of utterances – in this case in relation to research on codeswitching and intercultural communication.) Within language and gender research, Jane Sunderland's study of discourse in modern language lessons provides an illustration. Sunderland was interested in what she termed a 'telling case' – a single instance when gender became overt in an interaction (in this respect it is similar to Schegloff's 'ladies last' example). In one of the lessons studied by Sunderland, a teacher had asked for volunteers to perform a German dialogue. It was the boys' turn to perform, but no male volunteers were forthcoming. Three girls then called out, in succession, 'We're boys', thereby gaining an opportunity to perform. Sunderland points out that the episode was treated as quite unremarkable by all those involved. A friend to whom she mentioned the incident suggested that the girls' calling out was purely instrumental, and that if the teacher had said she wanted two dogs to perform the dialogue, the girls would have claimed to be dogs. Consultations with the girls, some of the boys and the teacher, however, suggested more interesting interpretations – for instance, there were some disagreements between participants about the meaning of the utterance; there was, however, an agreement that it was possible for girls to call out 'we're boys', but that a reversal of this – for boys to call out 'we're girls' – would be unacceptable. On the basis of her consultations, Sunderland claims that the utterance is highly gendered, and also a 'potentially *gendering* use of language' (1995: 163).

Clearly it would be a mistake to think that, in commenting on an interaction they have taken part in, participants are providing direct access to their original understandings or responses. Reflecting on an interaction is quite a different activity from taking part in this as a speaker/listener. Participants will also be tailoring their comments to a particular audience (the researcher) and a perceived purpose. It is clear from social psychological research that the beliefs and attitudes expressed by individuals are variable and context dependent, and sometimes appear contradictory (e.g. Potter and Wetherell, 1987). Participants may also (as in Sunderland's research) disagree about the meaning of an utterance – and patterns of disagreement may themselves be interesting. Participant consultations, then, cannot be expected to lead to a definitive interpretation of an utterance. They do, however, provide a broader interpretational base than can come from an analyst working alone, and so may provide a stronger warrant for making claims about gender.[11]

Analysts' theoretical positions

Analysts' interpretations are always informed by some sort of theory or position on language and how it works, and/or on gender and how it works. However, there are differences in the extent to which particular theorists, or theoretical positions, are explicitly drawn on to validate certain judgements, or interpretations of data. Early variationist work has been criticised for being relatively weak on social theory, for instance. By contrast, work carried out in more critical traditions often makes an explicit appeal to one or more social theories.

Mary Bucholtz (1996) draws on the framework of Black feminist theory – in particular the work of Patricia Hill Collins (1990) – in her analysis of the language use of contributors to a US radio panel discussion of race relations. Bucholtz intends to illustrate how a close textual analysis can serve as a vehicle for the exploration of social theory; and how Black feminist theory may shed light on African American women's everyday linguistic practices. The relevance of Collins, for Bucholtz, is that she 'locates potential commonalities in the experiences of African American women that in turn may give rise to a particular collection of shared perspectives towards those experiences'; such perspectives are 'produced and tested through a Black feminist epistemology, or theory of knowledge, that functions as an alternative to dominant ways of thinking' (pp. 268–9). There are four elements to this Black feminist epistemology:

1 the dialogic evaluation of knowledge claims, in which truth is arrived at through discussion with others;
2 an ethic of personal accountability, which holds all individuals responsible for moral behaviour;
3 an ethic of caring, often manifested as affective involvement in interaction;
4 concrete experience as a criterion of knowledge, which is prized at least as highly as the authority of the scholar or expert.

(Bucholtz, 1996: 269)

Bucholtz concedes that there is a danger of essentialism in this claim, but suggests that 'overstated accounts' of unity may be necessary to create a space in which diversity may be explored (p. 270).

Bucholtz's own empirical study focusses on a radio panel discussion of civil unrest following the acquittal of four policemen charged with beating up an African American man. She argues that two Black women on the panel subverted certain panel discussion norms (e.g. by asking questions that challenged the moderator's role in the discussion) and that this practice both illustrated and could be explained by Collins' theory. Challenging the moderator, for instance, could be seen as emphasizing the dialogic evaluation of knowledge claims and the personal accountability of knowledge producers.

The value of this and similar studies resides in their attempt to link specific linguistic practices with broader social theories. A particular theoretical perspective may also provide useful analytical insights. At issue, however, is the level and type of evidence required to substantiate (or challenge) a theory. Small-scale studies of highly contextualised practices are at best suggestive in this respect. Stubbs' concern about critical discourse analysis, which I mentioned above, also seems particularly relevant here: there is inevitably a danger of researchers, however unwittingly, tailoring their interpretations to support certain theories.

Analysts' intuitions

Intuitions have played an important role in linguistic research, particularly in research concerned with aspects of linguistic structure (such as syntax, semantics). In order to test the grammaticality of a particular form, researchers may draw on their own intuitions as members of a speech community, or they may consult the intuitions of other speakers. One of the earliest language and gender researchers, Robin Lakoff, explicitly appealed to her intuitions as a member of a (North American) speech community in arguing for the existence of a set of linguistic features that were associated primarily with women. At the time Lakoff made this claim there was still relatively little in the way of empirical research on women's (or men's) language. Her work proved useful as a stimulus for further studies (although, as I mentioned above, her intuitions have not been consistently supported by such studies).

Researchers today would be unlikely to make explicit use of intuition to support an empirically based claim about women's/men's language use. Intuition is, however, necessarily used (though not always acknowledged) in attributing meanings to particular texts or utterances. Attributing functions, or meanings to tag questions, or overlapping speech, or particular phrases ('ladies last') depends, in part, on analysts' intuitions. This practice is based on at least a tacit assumption that analysts will hold these in common with others – that the interpretation is a plausible one, and not idiosyncratic. My use of the term 'intuition' here has something in common with Stokoe and Smithson's (2001) reference to analysts' 'background knowledge' in relation to the interpretation of conversational data.[12]

Speakers/participants are male or female

The weakest warrant that one could have for interpreting a piece of language data – say, an interaction – in terms of gender, and one that few language and gender analysts would explicitly appeal to, is that the speakers or participants involved simply happen to be female, or male (or working class, male … etc). However, in the case of certain forms of research – particularly research focussing uniquely on female or male speakers – it is not always clear what other plausible warrants are available. I mentioned earlier Jennifer Coates' comparison between the conversational styles of female and male speakers. Coates is rather better known for her work on informal talk between women friends, involving detailed studies of narratives, of turn-taking and conversation management, and of the use of certain conversational devices such as hedges and questions (see Coates, 1996 for an overview). The research tells us a great deal about the structure and functions of informal conversation, and has enabled Coates to challenge some established ideas about aspects of conversation management. There has been an issue, however, about the extent to which this is *women's* talk. At one level, it clearly is, since the participants in Coates' research are all women. She does point out that they are a particular group of women, with certain social characteristics (e.g. British, middle-class). But without some form of comparison with male speakers it is difficult to be sure that the conversational styles Coates identifies are distinctive to women. (Coates' subsequent comparison with male speakers does in fact provide some evidence of differences in conversational style, see Coates, 1997, 2003.)

Scott Kiesling (1997), in a study of men's talk in a US fraternity, was concerned with differences in the strategies employed by the men to 'do power' in interactions. Kiesling illustrates, from an election meeting, how speakers construct powerful identities (appealing to factors such as specialist knowledge, seniority or status) to support their judgements about the suitability of different candidates. Kiesling focusses on power as something that is frequently associated with masculinity, but is able to demonstrate how each man adopts a unique discursive strategy in order to create and demonstrate power. In common with other recent work the study emphasizes differences between forms of masculinity, and how these are constituted in relation to one another and not simply in opposition to femininity/ies. These insights are valuable in their own right, but the study raises issues about the identification of the men's behaviour as masculine *at all*. In the absence of some form of comparison with women's behaviour, or some other independent warrant, it seems that this is *men's* talk largely because those doing the talking are men.[13]

Discussion and Conclusions

The shift in conceptions of language and gender that I referred to earlier in this paper would support a focus on highly contextualised research intended to document the localised 'working out' of gender, or an aspect of gender. It is worth conceding, first of all, that this does not always follow in practice. For instance, Vivian de Klerk's (1997) study of girls' and boys' use of expletives is a quantitative piece of work that draws statistical comparisons between the reported swearing behaviour of female and male students in different types of school in South Africa. The study appeared in Johnson and Meinhof's *Language and Masculinity*, but its approach seems barely consistent with Johnson's differentiated and contextualised model of gender/masculinity: individual contributors, then, do not always practise what their editors preach. On the whole, however, there does seem to have been a shift towards more localised studies (I shall use this term as a shorthand) consistent with a more general shift in models of language and gender. With regard to the warrants discussed above, far less reliance is placed on quantifiable and/or general patterns and the warrants drawn on are less powerful in terms of allowing researchers to make any generalised statements about language and gender. In the case of highly localised studies it becomes hard to say anything that goes beyond this interaction, these speakers, this context.

Localised studies are framed by the earlier research that established patterns of gender difference: they may constitute a reaction against the sometimes overstated claims of earlier work, but they are also dependent upon this. They are of interest partly because they are able to qualify, or complexify, or introduce counter examples. Part of the interest of Kiesling's paper, for instance, is that it is read against a backdrop of beliefs about male power. Kiesling focusses on the local 'working out' of power relations between men. However, there is only so much mileage to be got out of a focus purely on localised research. Researchers, or at least the research field, need also to go beyond this, and attempt some refurbishment of the backdrop.

Despite the current emphasis on context and performativity, I do not think language and gender researchers actually do dispense with gender as an *a priori* explanatory category – it would be impossible to do so. Claims about gender (or masculinity/femininity, or an aspect of masculinity/femininity) as a contextualised practice necessarily depend upon prior assumptions about the relevance of gender (masculinity/femininity). The danger is that researchers may make such assumptions without an appropriate warrant to support them.

We need, I think, some sort of pragmatic eclecticism: a wider range of warrants and associated research methods drawn on as and when to target specific questions and issues; and a more explicit acknowledgement of the possibilities and limitations of all methodological choices. This would include direct, even quantifiable comparisons across groups and contexts so that we can more clearly establish commonalities and differences between these. Quantitative approaches may also complement an analysis of more contextualised examples – e.g. employing large corpora to check the representativeness of data, or throw up general patterns, alongside a more contextualised analysis to show how these patterns are worked out in practice, draw attention to complexities, get into cracks that aren't visible in the larger analysis, explore counter-examples … etc.

Janet Holmes (1996) discusses the value of such a combination of methods in variationist research. Quantitative studies, she argues, make important contributions to the search for general (even universal) sociolinguistic processes. They also provide a background for more detailed qualitative research. Holmes illustrates this latter point with reference to a survey of language use in New Zealand. The survey drew on quantitative methods to establish general patterns of variation in the language use of different social groups (e.g. female and male speakers, Maori and Pakeha speakers). Further complementary research could then look at individual speakers' language choices in specific interactions. As an example, Holmes provides an analysis of a joking interaction between two young Maori men. Several features – e.g. use of syllable-timed speech – were drawn on to emphasize the young men's adherence to Maori culture (in this case the young men were joking about tricking a female relative who worked outside the Maori community). Holmes comments that the earlier quantitative analysis had demonstrated an association between syllable-timed speech and young Maori speakers – and that this enabled a more confident interpretation to be made of the use of this feature in this particular context.

A further example of a combination of quantitative and qualitative approaches comes from a study by Rupert Wegerif and Neil Mercer of children's use of collaborative or 'exploratory' talk in the classroom. The study was not concerned with gender issues, but may nevertheless be of interest because of its attempt to combine (computerized) corpus-based methods with the qualitative exploration of transcripts of children's talk. Wegerif and Mercer (1997) were interested in the quality of children's talk before and after an intervention in which they were taught the use of certain features of exploratory talk.[14] Transcript evidence suggested that, after the intervention, the children's talk changed – for instance they spent more time discussing problems and considering alternative solutions before eventually agreeing on their answer. Wegerif and Mercer point out, however, that the evidence they were able to present in support of this claim might not be seen as convincing because it consisted only of one or two brief extracts from transcripts. Using a computerised concordancing program enabled them both to extend their initial analysis and to present complementary evidence. The value of a concordancing program for Wegerif and Mercer, as for other researchers, is that it allowed them to move between different levels and types of analysis – listing certain expressions (in this case words associated with verbal reasoning, such as *cos* or *because*, *if*, *so*) in smaller or larger amounts of linguistic context; homing in on certain examples for more detailed (more contextualised) analysis; abstracting and quantifying certain usages of words over a whole transcript or series of transcripts. Wegerif and Mercer restricted their use of concordancing to their own small corpus of classroom data, but in principle patterns from small-scale studies may be compared with those in much larger corpora.[15]

I suggested above that de Klerk's (1997) approach to the study of reported swearing practices seemed inconsistent with Johnson's highly contextualised model of language and gender, proposed in the same edited volume. It may be argued more generally that generalised/quantitative and localised/qualitative approaches are necessarily underpinned by fundamentally incompatible models of language/gender, which would rule out their combination in the way I have suggested.[16]

I think, however, that researchers need to be more flexible and 'open' in their approach to models of language and gender. Language and gender are multi-facetted, their interrelationship is highly complex and it operates on different levels. On this last point, for instance, while language and gender are clearly contextualised practices, neither is context bound: both language and gender necessarily transcend specific contexts – to make a rather obvious point, if they did not, communication, along with any form of identity construction, would be impossible. Language and gender may, then, legitimately be viewed from different perspectives: a pragmatic combination of methods and approaches, along with an acknowledgement of their possibilities and limitations, might allow us to focus on different aspects of the relationship between language and gender, or have a wider range of things to say about this.

Notes

1 For reviews of relevant studies see for instance Coates (1993) and Graddol and Swann (1989).

2 For interesting material on postmodernism and its relationship to feminist issues see the studies in Nicholson (1990).

3 See also Cameron's (2005) discussion of the 'postmodern turn' in language and gender research.

4 On gender and performativity see Butler (1990).

5 I have discussed briefly gender and identity hopping in relation to computer-mediated communication in Mesthrie et al. (2000); see also McAdams (1996) and Turkle (1995).

6 Feminist linguists have criticised the methodology employed in traditional variationist studies, focussing on aspects of data collection (e.g. the use of 'sociolinguistic interviews'); the basis on which women and men are assigned to social class groups; and the interpretation of gender differences in terms of (for instance) women's greater conservatism or status-consciousness – see Cameron (1992); Coates and Cameron (1989); Coates (1993); Graddol and Swann (1989).

7 See also papers in Harrington et al (2008) for discussion of the potential of corpus linguistic approaches in language and gender research.

8   The value of replicability as a warrant was emphasised by Michael Stubbs at a recent BAAL/
    CUP-funded seminar on analysing talk (18/19 October, 1999: Open University).

9   Martyn Hammersley (personal communication) comments on Schegloff's position: 'The
    oddity is that it is nothing to do with taking account of participants' perspectives but rather
    of focussing entirely on what interactants formulate themselves as doing in the course of
    doing it. In other words, the model is of the person as interactant, and is an abstraction. In
    a way, the conversation analyst could be said to be reading his/her peculiar orientation into
    the behaviour of the participants; though this is not simply invention.'

10 For a further illustration of a strong Schegloffian position in relation to language and gender
    see Speer (2005).

11 Pichler (2008) provides an interesting illustration of how evidence from spontaneous interac-
    tion and ethnographic interviews may be combined.

12 From a rather different tradition, researchers adopting an ethnographic or anthropological
    approach to language and gender seek to gain access to insider meanings and interpretations.
    Were I to be writing this chapter today I would probably put ethnographic evidence or
    insights as a separate category. While some of the warrants identified here (including speak-
    ers'/participants' solicited interpretations and analysts' intuitions) are evident in ethnograph-
    ically-oriented analyses of spoken interaction, such analyses are also supported by close and
    prolonged participative observation and an attempt to ground interpretations in participants'
    perspectives on events. As an example see Maybin (2006, chs. 3 and 5).

13 Coates has pointed out (personal communication) that her initial group of women friends was
    formed *as* a women's group and that they went on to be called (affectionately but ironically)
    'The Ladies' Group' or just 'Ladies'. This would therefore support an interpretation of the
    talk as 'gendered'. My own view is that a group explicitly identified as a 'women's group' may
    have certain (interpersonal, political, ideological etc) preoccupations associated with the rea-
    sons for their formation. This may affect the nature of their interaction. However I think that,
    on its own, such an identification would still be a weak warrant for interpreting any ensuing
    talk as necessarily gendered. It would be an empirical question whether the talk of the group
    under study satisfied other warrants – for instance, whether gender was frequently oriented to
    by participants (in the Schegloffian sense discussed earlier); whether participants adopted
    styles associated with female speakers in other (comparative) studies; whether participants
    themselves interpreted their talk as in some way gendered.

14 Exploratory talk is defined by Wegerif and Mercer as 'talk in which reasons are given for asser-
    tions and reasoned challenges made and accepted within a cooperative framework oriented
    towards agreement' (1997: 277).

15 Stubbs (1996), whom I referred to earlier in connection with corpus-based research, provides
    further examples of making comparisons across different sets of data.

16 The problems and possibilities of combining quantitative and qualitative approaches have been
    the subject of ongoing debate in several academic areas. For an overview of this debate within
    classroom-based research see, for instance, Edwards and Westgate (1994).

References

Bauman, M. (1979) 'Two features of "women's speech"?', in Dubois, B. L. and Crouch, I. (eds)
    The Sociology of the Languages of American Women. Papers in Southwest English IV. San
    Antonio: Trinity University.

Bergvall, V. L., Bing, J. M. and Freed, A. F. (1996) *Rethinking Language and Gender Research:
    Theory and Practice*. London and New York: Longman.

Billig, M. (1999a) 'Whose terms? Whose ordinariness? Rhetoric and ideology in conversation
    analysis.' *Discourse and Society*, 10(4): 543–58.

Billig, M. (1999b) 'Conversation analysis and the claims of naivety.' *Discourse and Society*, 10(4):
    572–6.

Bucholtz, M. (1996) 'Black feminist theory and African American women's linguistic practice', in Bergvall, V. L., Bing, J. M. and Freed, A. F. *Rethinking Language and Gender Research: Theory and Practice*. London and New York: Longman.

Bucholtz, M., Liang, A. C., and Sutton, L. (eds) (1999) *Reinventing Identities: The Gendered Self in Discourse*. New York: Oxford University Press.

Butler, J. (1990) *Gender Trouble: Feminism and the Subversion of Identity*. New York: Routledge.

Cameron, D. (1992) *Feminism and Linguistic Theory* (2nd edn). Basingstoke: Macmillan.

Cameron, D. (2005) 'Language, gender and sexuality: current issues and new directions.' *Applied Linguistics*, 26(4): 482–502.

Cameron, D. and Coates, J. (1989) 'Some problems in the sociolinguistic explanation of sex differences', in Coates, J. and Cameron, D. (eds) (1989) *Women in their Speech Communities*. London, Longman.

Cameron, D., McAlinden, F. and O'Leary, K. (1989) 'Lakoff in context: the social and linguistic functions of tag questions', in Coates, J. and Cameron, D. (eds) *Women in their Speech Communities*. London and New York: Longman.

Coates, J. (1993) *Women, Men and Language* (2nd edn). London: Longman.

Coates, J. (1996) *Women Talk*. Oxford: Blackwell.

Coates, J. (1997) 'One-at-a-time: the organization of men's talk', in Johnson, S. and Meinhof, U. (eds) *Language and Masculinity*. Oxford: Blackwell.

Coates, J. (2003) *Mentalk: Stories in the Making of Masculinities*. Oxford: Blackwell.

Coates, J. and Cameron, D. (eds) (1989) *Women in their Speech Communities*. London: Longman.

Collins, P. H. (1990) *Black Feminist Thought*. Boston: Unwin Hyman.

Connell, R. W. (1987) *Gender and Power: Society, the Person and Sexual Politics*. Cambridge: Polity Press.

Connell, R. W. (1995) *Masculinities*. Cambridge: Polity Press.

de Klerk, V. (1997) 'The role of expletives in the construction of masculinity', in Johnson, S. and Meinhof, U. (eds) *Language and Masculinity*, Oxford: Blackwell.

Dubois, B. L. and Crouch, I. (1975) 'The question of tag questions in women's speech: they don't really use more of them, do they?'. *Language in Society*, 4: 289–94.

Eckert, P. (1998) 'Gender and sociolinguistic variation', in Coates, J. (ed.) *Language and Gender: A Reader*. Oxford: Blackwell.

Eckert, P. and McConnell-Ginet, S. (1998) 'New generalizations and explanations in language and gender research'. *Language in Society*, 28: 185–201.

Edwards, A. and Westgate, D. (1994) *Investigating Classroom Talk*. London: Falmer Press.

Gumperz, J. J. (1982) *Discourse Strategies*. Cambridge: Cambridge University Press.

Graddol, D. and Swann, J. (1989) *Gender Voices*. Oxford: Blackwell.

Hall, K. and Bucholtz, M. (1995) *Gender Articulated: Language and the Socially Constructed Self*. New York and London: Routledge

Harrington, K., Litosseliti, L., Saunston, H. and Sunderland, J. (eds) (2008) *Language and Gender Research Methodologies*. Basingstoke: Palgrave Macmillan.

Harris, R. (1981) *The Language Myth*. Duckworth.

Holmes, J. (1984) 'Hedging your bets and sitting on the fence: some evidence for hedges as support structures', *Te Reo* 27: 47–62.

Holmes, J. (1994) Improving the lot of female language learners, in J. Sunderland (ed.) *Exploring Gender: Questions and Implications for English Language Education*. London: Prentice-Hall.

Holmes, J. (1995) *Women, Men and Politeness*. Harlow, Essex: Longman.

Holmes, J. (1996) 'Women's role in language change: a place for quantification', in N. Warner, J. Ahlers, L. Bilmes, M. Oliver, S. Wertheim and M. Chen (eds.) *Gender and Belief Systems: Proceedings of the Fourth Berkeley Women and Language Conference*, April 19–21 1996. Berkeley, CA: Berkeley Women and Language Group.

Horvath, B. M. (1985) *Variation in Australian English: The Sociolects of Sydney*. Cambridge: Cambridge University Press.

Johnson, S. (1997) 'Theorizing language and masculinity', in Johnson, S. and Meinhof, U. (eds) *Language and Masculinity*, Oxford: Blackwell.

Johnson, S. and Meinhof, U. (eds) (1997) *Language and Masculinity*, Oxford: Blackwell.

Kiesling, S. F. (1997) 'Power and the language of men', in Johnson, S. and Meinhof, U. (eds) *Language and Masculinity*, Oxford: Blackwell.

Labov, W. (1966) *The Social Stratification of English in New York City*. Washington, DC: Center for Applied Linguistics.

Lakoff, R. (1975) *Language and Woman's Place*. New York: Harper & Row.

Macaulay, R. K. S. (1978) 'Variation and consistency in Glaswegian English', in Trudgill, P. (ed.) *Sociolinguistic Patterns in British English*. London: Edward Arnold.

McAdams, M. (1996) Gender Without Bodies, *CMC Magazine*, March 1, 1996.

McEnery, T., Baker, P. and Hardie, A. (1999) 'Assessing claims with corpus data – the case of swearing', in Kirk, J. (ed.) *Corpora Galore*. Amsterdam: Rodopi.

McEnery, T., Baker, P. and Hardie, A. (2009) 'Swearing and abuse in modern English', in Lewandowska-Tomaszczyk, B. and Melia, P. J. (eds) *Practical Applications of Language Corpora*. Hamburg: Peter Lang.

Maybin, J. (2006) Children's Voices: talk, knowledge and identity. Basingstoke: Palgrave Macmillan.

Mesthrie, R., Swann, J., Deumert, A. and Leap, W.L. (2000; 2nd edn 2009) *Introducing Sociolinguistics*. Edinburgh: Edinburgh University Press.

Milroy, L. (1980) *Language and Social Networks*. Oxford: Basil Blackwell.

Milroy, L. (1992) 'New perspectives in the analysis of sex differentiation in language', in Bolton, K. and Kwok, H. (eds) *Sociolinguistics Today: International Perspectives*. London and New York: Routledge.

Newbrook, M. (1982) *Sociolinguistic Reflexes of Dialect Interference in West Wirral*. Unpublished PhD thesis, University of Reading.

Nicholson, L. J. (1990) Introduction to Nicholson, L. J. (ed.) *Feminism/Postmodernism*. New York and London: Routledge.

Pichler, P. (2008) 'Gender, ethnicity and religion in spontaneous talk and ethnographic-style interviews: balancing perspectives of researcher and researched', in Harrington et al. (eds) (2008).

Potter, J. and Wetherell, M. (1987) *Discourse and Social Psychology*. London: Sage.

Preisler, B. (1986) *Linguistic Sex Roles in Conversation: Social Variation in the Expression of Tentativeness in English*. Berlin: Mouton de Gruyter.

Rayson, P., Leech, G. and Hodges, M. (1997) 'Social differentiation in the use of English vocabulary: some analyses of the conversational component of the British National Corpus', *International Journal of Corpus Linguistics*, 2(1): 133–52.

Schegloff, E. A. (1997) 'Whose text? Whose context?'. *Discourse and Society*, 8(2): 165–87.

Schegloff, E. A. (1998) 'Reply to Wetherell'. *Discourse and Society*, 9(3): 413–16.

Schegloff, E. A. (1999a) '"Schegloff's texts" as "Billig's data": a critical reply'. *Discourse and Society*, 10(4): 558–72.

Schegloff, E. A. (1999b) 'Naivete vs sophistication or discipline vs self-indulgence: a rejoinder to Billig.' *Discourse and Society*, 10(4): 577–82.

Speer, S. A. (2005) *Gender Talk: Feminism, Discourse and Conversation Analysis*. London and New York: Routledge.

Stokoe, E. H. and Smithson, J. (2001) 'Making gender relevant: conversation analysis and gender categories in interaction.' *Discourse and Society*, 12(2): 217–44.

Stubbs, M. (1996) *Text and Corpus Analysis: Computer-Assisted Studies of Language and Culture*. Oxford: Blackwell.

Stubbs, M. (1997) 'Whorf's children: critical comments on Critical Discourse Analysis (CDA)', in Ryan, A. and Wray, A. (eds) *Evolving Models of Language: Papers from the Annual Meeting of the British Association for Applied Linguistics, 1996*. Clevedon: British Association for Applied Linguistics in association with Multilingual Matters.

Sunderland, J. (1995) ' "We're boys, miss!": finding gendered identities and looking for gendering of identities in the foreign language classroom', in Mills, S. (ed.) *Language and Gender: Interdisciplinary Perspectives*. Harlow, Essex: Longman.

Sunderland, J. (1996) *Gendered Discourse in the Foreign Language Classroom: Teacher–Student and Student–Teacher Talk and the Social Construction of Children's Femininities and Masculinities*. Unpublished PhD thesis: University of Lancaster.

Swann, J. (1992) *Girls, Boys and Language*. Oxford: Blackwell.

Swann, J. (1989) 'Talk control: an illustration from the classroom of problems in analysing male dominance of conversation', in Coates, J. and Cameron, D. (eds) (1989) *Women in their Speech Communities*, London: Longman.

Swann, J. and Graddol, D. (1988) 'Gender inequalities in classroom talk', *English in Education*, 22(1): 48–65.

Thomas, B. (1989) 'Differences of sex and sects: linguistic variation and social networks in a Welsh mining village', in Coates, J. and Cameron, D. (eds) *Women in their Speech Communities*. London and New York: Longman.

Trudgill, P. (1974) *The Social Differentiation of English in Norwich*. Cambridge: Cambridge University Press.

Turkle, S. (1995) *Life on the Screen: Identity in the Age of the Internet*. New York: Simon & Schuster.

Wareing, S. (1996) 'What do we know about language and gender?' Paper presented at *Sociolinguistics Symposium 11*, Cardiff, 5–7 September 1996.

Wegerif, R. and Mercer, N. (1997) 'Using computer-based text analysis to integrate quantitative and qualitative methods in the investigation of collaborative learning', *Language and Education*, 11(4): 271–86.

West, C. and Zimmerman, D. H. (1983) 'Small insults: a study of interuptions in cross-sex conversations between unacquainted persons', in Thorne, B., Kramarae, C. and Henley, N. (eds) *Langue, Gender and Society*. Rowley, MA: Newbury House.

Wetherell, M. (1998) 'Positioning and interpretive repertoires: conversation analysis and poststructuralism in dialogue', *Discourse and Society* 9(3): 387–412.

Wodak, R. (ed.) (1997) *Gender and Discourse*. London: Sage Publications.

Wolfram, W. (1969) *A Sociolinguistic Description of Detroit Negro Speech*. Washington, DC: Center for Applied Linguistics.

Zimmerman, D. H. and West, C. (1975) 'Sex roles, interruptions and silences in conversation' in Thorne, B. and Henley, N. (eds) *Language and Sex: Difference and Dominance*. Rowley, MA: Newbury House.

Part X

New Directions in Language and Gender Research

This final section consists of three papers, all of which focus on theory and methodology in language and gender research and which signpost the way language and gender research is moving in the twenty-first century. The last 20 years have been tumultuous, with researchers disagreeing on the goals of language and gender research and on the theoretical frameworks and methodologies best suited to achieving these goals. (We have looked at some of these disagreements in the three sections devoted to theoretical debates – Parts VII, VIII, and IX.) During these last 20 years, ideas about language and gender have changed considerably. What used to be called "language" is now seen instead as a heterogeneous collection of competing discourses. Gender is no longer viewed as monolithic or static but as multiple and fluid. Researchers have moved on to observing the discursive production of a wide range of femininities and masculinities, and have broadened the range of communities investigated, both geographically and also in terms of gay, lesbian, bisexual, and transgender speakers (see the papers in Part VI). In this final section it is not possible to survey the whole range of new ideas and new frameworks. Instead, we have selected three papers which deal with key concepts in the developing field of language and gender. They deal, respectively, with the concept of Communities of Practice and the importance of "looking locally"; with the significance of ideologies – in particular, language and gender ideologies – in structuring both language and society; and, lastly, with the importance of reasserting feminist goals and putting women back at the center of language and gender research.

One of the key developments in sociolinguistic research has been the adoption of the concept of "the Community of Practice" (or CoP). This was introduced to sociolinguistics by Penelope Eckert and Sally McConnell-Ginet, drawing on the work of Etienne Wenger (1998). They argue that language and gender research needs to be grounded in "detailed investigations of the social and linguistic practice of specific communities of practice" (Eckert and McConnell-Ginet 1995: 469). This concept has largely replaced the older, somewhat nebulous concept of "the speech community." The first paper in this section is, accordingly, Penelope Eckert and Sally McConnell-Ginet's "Communities of Practice: Where Language, Gender and Power All Live," the paper (together with

Eckert and McConnell-Ginet 1992) which brought this new concept to the attention of sociolinguists. In this paper they urge researchers to avoid generalizing, to avoid abstractions, and to "think practically and look locally." They argue that the community of practice is a concept which asserts the dynamism of living communities: who we are is not constructed in a vacuum, but in the many communities of practice each of us belongs to. Gender, one aspect of who we are, is not a given, but is constantly created and re-created in social interaction with others in these communities of practice. Moreover, gender is complex: there are many different ways of being a woman or a man. (Papers in the Reader which draw on and develop this concept are those by Bucholtz (Part IV), Pichler (Part IV), Shaw (Part V), Ostermann (Part V) and Holmes and Schnurr (Part V).)

More recently, language and gender researchers have developed an awareness of the role played by ideology in structuring society. Even though we now talk in terms of the fluidity and plurality of gender, we need to acknowledge the power of the social ideology of gender as dichotomous. Most people in most cultures align themselves with this ideology. The second paper in this section is Deborah Cameron's "Gender and Language Ideologies." Ideologies of gender and language have varied over the last 200 years, but one thing that is constant is "the insistence that in any identifiable social group, women and men are *different*" (italics in original). In this paper, Cameron argues that we need to understand the way ideologies work if we are to understand the way ideological representations of language and gender "inform everyday linguistic and social practices among real women and men." She looks at how language and gender ideologies vary through time and in different cultures. She argues that the role of ideologies is to make the (unequal) relationship between women and men in any society appear natural, rather than unjust. She also charts what she calls "the fall and rise of women's language," arguing that women's language skills are no longer seen as deficient, but as superior to men's. (However, this new ideology of women as great communicators has not resulted in better pay or higher-status jobs for women, who are simply seen as doing what they are "naturally" good at.) "Communication" is now the buzzword – Cameron describes it as "the language ideology of late modernity." "Communication" has become so important because we live in a society where social networks are much weaker than in the past, and where the individual has to invent her/himself through a process of self-reflexivity (something Anthony Giddens (1991) refers to as the "reflexive project"). Interestingly, Cameron shows how, while working-class males are disadvantaged by these new ideologies, powerful men combine the new "feminine" communicative skills (emotional expressiveness, good listening, rapport) with traditionally masculine ones (authority, enterprise, and leadership). Good examples of such men in the recent past are Bill Clinton, former president of the USA, and Tony Blair, late prime minister of the UK. Cameron points out that, while men who combine the masculine and the feminine like this are widely admired, women in senior positions are not rewarded for developing masculine characteristics: "Nobody ever said approvingly of Margaret Thatcher that she was 'in touch with her masculine side'." Finally, Cameron urges language and gender researchers to be more reflexive about the ideologies which have shaped their thinking. (The significance of ideology in the construction of gender norms is explored in the papers by Yang in Part III, by Bucholtz in Part IV, and by Ostermann and by Ehrlich in Part V).

The final paper, Janet Holmes' "Social Constructionism, Postmodernism and Feminist Sociolinguistics," reviews the current state of the language and gender field and considers the role of feminism in language and gender research. Many of the papers included in the Reader are implicitly feminist, but no paper discusses this question explicitly. We think it important to end the Reader with a paper which reasserts the significance of feminism to language and gender research. Holmes' paper first appeared in 2007 in the very first issue of the new journal *Gender and Language*. The establishment of this new journal was a landmark in language and gender studies, marking the language and gender field as a distinct and evolving area of research. Holmes' paper is both an overview of the tensions and conflicts of the previous 20-odd years in language and gender research and also a challenge to researchers to put women back at the center of that research. Calling for the sensitive use of "strategic essentialism," Holmes argues that anti-essentialism went too far and was ultimately unproductive; the insistence on a multiplicity of femininities and of the multiple intersections between gender and other social variables such as class, ethnicity, and sexuality made it impossible to see "women" as a social group who are systematically oppressed. Holmes argues that the category of "women" as a group (and some level of generalization about this category) is still "strategically indispensable" if the aim of the scholar is to explore the "gender order," that is, the "ways in which women are the victims of repressive ideologies and discriminatory behaviour," particularly in the workplace and other institutional contexts. This leads her to conclude that women need to be "put back at the centre of language and gender research."

References

Eckert, Penelope and McConnell-Ginet, Sally (1992) "Think practically and look locally: language and gender as community based practice," *Annual Review of Anthropology* 21, 461–90.

Eckert, Penelope and McConnell-Ginet, Sally (1995) "Constructing meaning, constructing selves: snapshots of language, gender and class from Belten High," pp. 469–507 in Kira Hall and Mary Bucholtz (eds) *Gender Articulated: Language and the Socially Constructed Self*. London: Routledge.

Giddens, Anthony (1991) *Modernity and Self-Identity: Self and Society in the Late Modern Age*. Cambridge: Polity.

Wenger, Etienne (1998) *Communities of Practice*. Cambridge: Cambridge University Press.

Recommended Further Reading

Bergvall, Victoria, Byng, Janet, and Freed, Alice (eds) (1997) *Rethinking Language and Gender Research: Theory and Practice*. London: Longman.

Bucholtz, Mary, Laing, Anita, and Sutton, Laurel (eds) (1999) *Reinventing Identities: The Gendered Self in Discourse*. New York: Oxford University Press.

DeFrancisco, Victoria Pruin and Palczewski, Catherine Helen (2007). *Communicating Gender Diversity: A Critical Approach*. Thousand Oaks, CA: Sage.

Eckert, Penelope and McConnell-Ginet, Sally (2003) *Language and Gender*. Cambridge: Cambridge University Press.

Eckert, Penelope and McConnell-Ginet, Sally (2007) "Putting communities of practice in their place," *Gender and Language* 1(1), 27–37.

Hall, Kira and Bucholtz, Mary (eds) (1995) *Gender Articulated. Language and the Socially Constructed Self*. London: Routledge.

Harrington, Kate, Litosolliti, Lia, Saunston, Helen, and Sunderland, Jane (eds) (2008) *Gender and Language Research Methodologies*. London: Palgrave.

Holmes, Janet and Meyerhoff, Miriam (eds) (2003) *The Handbook of Language and Gender*. Oxford: Blackwell.

Litosolliti, Lia and Sunderland, Jane (eds) (2002) *Gender Identity and Discourse Analysis.* Amsterdam: John Benjamins.

McElhinny, Bonny (2003) "Theorising gender in sociolinguistics and linguistic anthropology," pp. 21–42 in Janet Holmes and Miriam Meyerhoff (eds) *The Handbook of Language and Gender.* Oxford: Blackwell.

Pichler, Pia and Eppler, Eva (eds) (2009) *Gender and Spoken Interaction.* London: Palgrave.

41

Communities of Practice: Where Language, Gender, and Power All Live

Penelope Eckert and Sally McConnell–Ginet

Source: Kira Hall et al. (eds), *Locating Power. Proceedings of the 2nd Berkeley Women and Language Conference*. Berkeley: BWLG (1992), pp. 89–99.

Introduction: Too Much Abstraction Spoils the Broth

Studies of language and gender in the past twenty years have looked at many different dimensions of language use and have offered a rich variety of hypotheses about the inter-action between gender and language and especially about the connection of power to that interaction. On the one hand, language has been seen as supporting male domi-nance; on the other, it has been seen as a resource for women resisting oppression or pursuing their own projects and interests. We have all learned a lot by thinking about such proposals, most of which have been supported by interesting and often illuminating observations. But their explanatory force has been weakened by the absence of a coher-ent theoretical framework within which to refine and further explore them as part of an ongoing research community.

The problem is not an absence of generalizations. Our diagnosis is that gender and language studies suffer from the same problem as that confronting sociolinguistics and psycholinguistics more generally: too much abstraction. Abstracting gender and lan-guage from the social practices that produce their particular forms in given communities often obscures and sometimes distorts the ways they connect and how those connections are implicated in power relations, in social conflict, in the production and reproduction of values and plans. Too much abstraction is often symptomatic of too little theorizing: abstraction should not substitute for theorizing but be informed by and responsive to it. Theoretical insight into how language and gender interact requires a close look at social practices in which they are jointly produced. What we want to do in this paper is to sketch the main outlines of a theoretical perspective on language, gender, and power that can help us continue to make progress toward a productive community of language–gender scholars who hold themselves accountable both to one another's work and to relevant developments in linguistics, social theory, and gender studies.

Why is abstraction so tempting and yet so dangerous? It is tempting because at some level and in some form it is irresistible, an inevitable part of theoretical inquiry. People and their activities, including their use of language, are never viewed in completely concrete or

Language and Gender: A Reader, Second Edition. Edited by Jennifer Coates and Pia Pichler.
© 2011 Blackwell Publishing Ltd except for editorial material and organization. © 2011 Jennifer Coates and Pia Pichler. Published 2011 by Blackwell Publishing Ltd.

particularistic terms. With no access to abstract constructs like linguistic systems and social categories and relations like class and race and gender, we could not hope to engage in any kind of illuminating investigation into how and why language and gender interact. The danger, however, is that the real force and import of their interaction is erased when we abstract each uncritically from the social practices in which they are jointly produced and in which they intermingle with other symbolic and social phenomena. In particular, if we view language and gender as self-contained and independent phenomena, we miss the social and cognitive significance of interactions between them. Abstraction that severs the concrete links between language and gender in the social practices of communities kills the power that resides in and derives from those links.

The notions of "women" and "men," for example, are typically just taken for granted in sociolinguistics. Suppose we were to take all the characterizations of gender that have been advanced to explain putatively gender-differentiated linguistic behavior. Women's language has been said to reflect their (our) conservatism, prestige consciousness, upward mobility, insecurity, deference, nurturance, emotional expressivity, connectedness, sensitivity to others, solidarity. And men's language is heard as evincing their toughness, lack of affect, competitiveness, independence, competence, hierarchy, control. Linguists are not, of course, inventing such accounts of gender identities and gender relations out of whole cloth. Not only commonplace stereotypes but also social-scientific studies offer support for the kinds of characterizations linguists offer in explanation of language use. But the social-science literature must be approached critically: the observations on which such claims about women and men are based have been made at different times and in different circumstances with different populations from those whose linguistic behavior they are being used to explain.

The problem is too much or at least too-crude abstraction. Gender is abstracted whole from other aspects of social identity, the linguistic system is abstracted from linguistic practice, language is abstracted from social action, interactions and events are abstracted from community and personal history, difference and dominance are each abstracted from wider social practice, and both linguistic and social behavior are abstracted from the communities in which they occur. When we recombine all these abstractions, we really do not know what we have. Certainly we don't seem to find real women and men as sums of the characteristics attributed to them.

What we propose is not to ignore such abstract characterizations of gender identities and relations but to take responsibility for connecting each such abstraction to a wide spectrum of social and linguistic practice in order to examine the specificities of its concrete realization in actual communities. This can happen only if we collectively develop a community of analytic practice that holds itself responsible for language and gender writ large.

This means that we are responsible to linguistic theory and research beyond the areas of our particular specializations. Furthermore, we cannot excuse our inattention to social theory and gender studies on the grounds that we are "just linguists," not if we hope to make responsible claims about language and gender interactions. And perhaps the most important implication is that we cannot abandon social and political responsibility for how our work is understood and used, especially given what we know about sexism and racism and elitism and heterosexism in so many of the communities where our research might be disseminated.

Our major aim is to encourage a view of the interaction of gender and language that roots each in the everyday social practices of particular local communities and sees them as jointly constructed in those practices: our slogan, "Think practically and look locally." To think practically and look locally is to abandon several assumptions common in gender and language studies: that gender works independently of other aspects of social identity and relations, that it "means" the same across communities, and that the linguistic manifestations of that meaning are also the same across communities. Such assumptions can be maintained only when the language–gender partnership is prematurely dissolved by abstraction of one or both partners.

Language, Power, and Gender Viewed Locally

Becoming language users and becoming gendered members of local communities both involve participating with other members in a variety of practices that often constitute linguistic, gender, and other social identities and relations at one and the same time. Many such activities have been described in the papers in Hall et al., 1992: instigating or taking the plaintiff or defendant role in a he-said-she-said dispute (Goodwin, 1992), providing sexy talk on the 900 lines (Hall, 1992), participating in "Father Knows Best" dinnertime dramas (Ochs & Taylor, 1992), taking a police report from a bleeding woman (McElhinny, 1992, reprinted in this volume, p. 309), joining in a debate about rape and race and responsibility on the walls of a bathroom stall (Moon-womon, 1992), smiling at the boss's "Sleazy bitch" (Case, 1992), silencing a planned anecdote during a conference paper when you note its (male) protagonist in the audience (Lakoff, 1992), criticizing or defending a colleague's bestseller (Freed, 1992).

In the course of engaging with others in such activity, people collaboratively construct a sense of themselves and of others as certain kinds of persons, as members of various communities with various forms of membership, authority, and privilege in those communities. In all of these, language interacts with other symbolic systems – dress, body adornment, ways of moving, gaze, touch, handwriting style, locales for hanging out, and so on. And the selves constructed are not simply (or even primarily) gendered selves: they are unemployed, Asian American, lesbian, college–educated, post-menopausal selves in a variety of relations to other people. Language is never encountered without other symbol systems, and gender is always joined with real people's complex forms of participation in the communities to which they belong (or have belonged or expect to join).

Individuals may experience the language–gender interface differently in the different communities in which they participate at a given time or at different stages of their lives. Using *Mrs. Jones* may be important for avoiding the condescension of *Mary* when a professionally employed woman addresses the woman who cleans her house; for that professional woman, receiving address as *Mrs. Smith* (particularly from her colleagues) may seem to emphasize her subordination to a husband and to deny her individual identity as Joan Doe, who (as she sees it) simply happens to be married to John Smith. On the other hand, acquiring a new name of *Mrs. John Smith* upon marriage may have functioned thirty years ago for the young Joan Doe as a mark of her achieving fully adult status as a married woman (a possibility denied her lesbian sister who rejects marriage). And the woman who with a tolerant smile receives *Mary* from the six-year-old daughter of her employer may insist in her local residential community on *Mrs. Jones* from her own daughter's friends.

Exploring any aspect of the language–gender interface requires that we address the complexities of its construction within and across different communities: what *Mrs. Jones* means, what social work is done by the use of that title, can be understood only by considering its place in the practices of local communities (and in the connections among

those communities). Analysts not only jump too readily from local observations to global claims; they/we also too often ignore the multiple uses of particular linguistic
resources in the practices of a given community. We can see the confusion that results by
trying to put together some of the general claims about the social and psychological
underpinnings of language use common in the variation literature with claims about
gender such as those common in interaction studies.

A methodological cornerstone of variation studies is the notion that all speakers step
up the use of vernacular variants when they are at their most emotional. It is also generally accepted that vernacular variants function to establish solidarity. If women are more
emotional than men or more interested in promoting solidarity, as so many interaction-
ists have claimed, the variationists might be expected to predict that vernacular variants
typify women's rather than men's language. But the general claim in variation studies has
been that men's language exemplifies the vernacular whereas women's aspires toward
standard or prestige variants. The explanation offered is not men's emotionality or greater
interest in social connections but women's supposed prestige-consciousness and upward
mobility (often accompanied by claims of women's greater conservatism). Even in situations in which some vernacular variant is more frequent in women's than men's speech,
analysts do not consider how their explanations relate to their own claims about the social
meanings of vernaculars. There are many other tensions and potential contradictions
when we try to put together all the different things said about language, gender, and
power. The standard or prestige variants are associated with the speech of those who have
economic and political power, the social elite; at the same time, standard speech is associated with women and "prissiness," and the vernacular is heard as tough and "macho."
Once we take seriously the connections among gender characterizations and the various
aspects of language that we study and try to develop a coherent picture, it quickly becomes
apparent that the generalizations to be found cannot be integrated with one another as
they now stand. This suggests serious difficulties in adopting as our primary goal the
search for generalizations about "women" and "men" as groups with some kind of global sociolinguistic unity that transcends social practices in local communities.

Statements like "Women emphasize connection in their talk whereas men seek status"
may have some statistical support within a particular community. Statistics being what
they are, there is, of course, no guarantee that the actual women and men whose behavior supports one such generalization will overlap very much with those supporting
another – say, that women prefer standard and men vernacular variants in everyday talk
with their peers – and this is true even if our statistics come from a single community.
The more serious problem, however, is that such generalizations are seldom understood
as simple reports of statistics.

Most American women are under five feet nine inches tall and most American men are
over five feet six inches tall, but it would sound odd indeed to report these statistical facts
by saying, "Women are under five feet nine inches tall" and "Men are over five feet six
inches tall" without some explicit indicator of generalization like *most*. Although unmodified claims about "women" and "men" do allow for exceptions, such claims, which we
have certainly made ourselves, often seem to imply that individuals who don't satisfy the
generalization are indeed exceptional "as women" or "as men," deviants from some normative model (perhaps deviants to admire but nonetheless outsiders in some sense). This
is especially true when women and men are being characterized as "different" from one
another on some particular dimension. But if gender resides in difference, what is the
status of the tremendous variability we see in actual behavior within sex categories? Too
often dismissed as "noise" in a basically dichotomous gender system, differences among

men and among women are, in our view, themselves important aspects of gender. Tomboys and goody-goodies, homemakers and career women, body-builders and fashion models, secretaries and executives, basketball coaches and French teachers, professors and students, grandmothers and mothers and daughters – these are all categories of girls and women whose mutual differences are part of their construction of themselves and each other as gendered beings. When femaleness and maleness are differentiated from one another in terms of such attributes as power, ambition, physical coordination, rebelliousness, caring, or docility, the role of these attributes in creating and texturing important differences among very female identities and very male identities becomes invisible.

The point here is not that statistical generalizations about the females and the males in a particular community are automatically suspect. But to stop with such generalizations or to see finding such "differences" as the major goal of investigations of gender and language is problematic. Correlations simply point us toward areas where further investigation might shed light on the linguistic and other practices that enter into gender dynamics in a community. An emphasis on difference as constitutive of gender draws attention away from a more serious investigation of the relations among language, gender, and other components of social identity; it ignores the ways difference (or beliefs therein) function in constructing dominance relations. Gender can be thought of as a sex-based way of experiencing other social attributes like class, ethnicity, or age (and also less obviously social qualities like ambition, athleticism, and musicality). To examine gender independently as if it were just "added on" to such other aspects of identity is to miss its significance and force. Certainly, to interpret broad sex patterns in language use without considering other aspects of social identity and relations is to paint with one eye closed. Speakers are not assembled out of separate independent modules: part European American, part female, part middle-aged, part feminist, part intellectual. Abstracting gender away from other aspects of social identity also leads to premature generalization even about normative conceptions of femaleness and maleness. While most research that focuses on sex difference is not theoretically committed to a universalizing conception of women or of men, such research has tended to take gender identity as given at least in broad strokes at a relatively global level.

Too much abstraction and too-ready generalization are encouraged by a limited view of theorizing as aimed at accounts of gender difference that apply globally to women and men. In the interests of abstraction and global generalization, William Labov has argued that ethnographic studies of language and society must answer to the results of survey studies – that generalized correlations reflect a kind of objective picture that must serve as the measure of any locally grounded studies. Others cite the objectivity of controlled experimental studies. We argue instead that ethnographic studies must answer to each other, and that survey and experimental studies in turn must answer to them (see Eckert, 1990). Surveys typically examine categories so abstracted from social practice that they cannot be assumed to have independent status as sociolinguistically meaningful units, and they rely heavily on interviews, a special kind of social activity. Experimental studies also abstract in ways that can make it hard to assess their relevance to the understanding of naturally occurring social practice, including cognition. To frame abstractions so that they help explain the interaction of language and social practice, we need a focus of study and analysis that allows us to examine them each on something like an equal footing. This requires a unit of social analysis that has explanatory power for the construction of both language and gender. It is mutual engagement of human agents in a wide range of activities that creates, sustains, challenges, and sometimes changes society and its institutions, including both gender and language, and the sites of such mutual engagement are communities. How the community is defined, therefore, is of prime importance in any study of language and gender, even those that do not use ethnographic methods (e.g., survey or experimental studies).

Language, Gender, and Communities of Practice

Sociolinguists have located linguistic systems, norms, and social identities within a loosely defined construct, the *speech community*. Although in theory sociolinguists embrace John Gumperz's (1982) definition of a speech community as a group of speakers who share rules and norms for the use of language, in practice community studies have defined their populations on the basis of location and/or population. Differences and relations among the speakers who people sociolinguists' speech communities have been defined in terms of abstracted characteristics: sex, age, socio-economic class, ethnicity. And differences in ways of speaking have been interpreted on the basis of speculative hypotheses about the relation between these characteristics and social practice. Sociolinguistic analysis, then, attempts to reconstruct the practice from which these characteristics, and the linguistic behavior in question, have been abstracted. While participation in community practice sometimes figures more directly into classification of speakers, sociolinguists still seldom recognize explicitly the crucial role of practice in delineating speech communities and more generally in mediating the relation between language, society, and consciousness.

To explore in some detail just how social practice and individual "place" in the community connect to one another, sociolinguists need some conception of a community that articulates place with practice. For this reason, we adopt Jean Lave and Etienne Wenger's notion of the *community of practice*.[1] The community of practice takes us away from the community defined by a location or by a population. Instead, it focuses on a community defined by social engagement – after all, it is this engagement that language serves, not the place and not the people as a collection of individuals.

A community of practice is an aggregate of people who come together around mutual engagement in some common endeavor. Ways of doing things, ways of talking, beliefs, values, power relations – in short, practices – emerge in the course of their joint activity around that endeavor. A community of practice is different as a social construct from the traditional notion of community, primarily because it is defined simultaneously by its membership and by the practice in which that membership engages. Indeed, it is the practices of the community and members' differentiated participation in them that structures the community socially.

A community of practice might be people working together in a factory, regulars in a bar, a neighborhood play group, a nuclear family, police partners and their ethnographer, the Supreme Court. Communities of practice may be large or small, intensive or diffuse; they are born and they die, they may persist through many changes of membership, and they may be closely articulated with other communities. Individuals participate in multiple communities of practice, and individual identity is based in the multiplicity of this participation. Rather than seeing the individual as some disconnected entity floating around in social space, or as a location in a network, or as a member of a particular group or set of groups, or as a bundle of social characteristics, we need to focus on communities of practice. Such a focus allows us to see the individual as an actor articulating a range of forms of participation in multiple communities of practice.

Gender is produced (and often reproduced) in differential membership in communities of practice. People's access and exposure to, need for, and interest in different communities of practice are related to such things as their class, age, and ethnicity, as well as their sex. Working-class people are more likely on the whole than middle-class people to be members of unions, bowling teams, close-knit neighborhoods. Upper-middle-class people, on the other hand, are more likely than working-class people to be members of tennis clubs, orchestras, professional organizations. Men are more likely than women to be members of football teams, armies, and boards of directors. Women, on the other hand, are more likely to be members of secretarial pools, aerobics classes, and consciousness-raising groups.

And associated with differences in age, class, and ethnicity are differences in the extent to which the sexes belong to different communities of practice. Different people, for a variety of reasons, will articulate their multiple memberships differently. A female executive living in a male-dominated household will have difficulty articulating her membership in her domestic and professional communities of practice, unlike a traditional male executive "head of household." A lesbian lawyer "closeted" within the legal community may also belong to a women's community whose membership defines itself in opposition to the larger heterosexual world. And the woman who scrubs toilets in the household "managed" by the female executive for her husband and also in the home of the lesbian lawyer and her artist lover may be a respected lay leader in her local church, facing a different set of tensions than either of her employers does in negotiating multiple memberships.

Gender is also produced and reproduced in differential forms of participation in particular communities of practice. Women tend to be subordinate to men in the workplace, women in the military do not engage in combat, and in the academy, most theoretical disciplines are overwhelmingly male with women concentrated in descriptive and applied work that "supports" theorizing. Women and men may also have very different forms of participation available to them in single-sex communities of practice. For example, if all-women groups do in fact tend to be more egalitarian than all-men groups, as some current literature claims (e.g., Aries, 1976), then women's and men's forms of participation will be quite different. Such relations within same-sex groups will, of course, be related in turn to the place of such groups in the larger society.

The relations among communities of practice when they come together in overarching communities of practice also produce gender arrangements. Only recently, for example, have female competitive sports begun to receive significant recognition, and male sports continue to bring far greater visibility, power, and authority both to the teams and to the individual participants in those teams. The (male) final four is the focus of attention in the NCAA basketball world every spring, with the women's final four receiving only perfunctory mention. Many a school has its Bulldogs and Lady Bulldogs, its Rangers and Rangerettes. This articulation with power and stature outside the team in turn translates into different possibilities for relations within. The relation between male varsity sports teams and female cheerleading squads illustrates a more general pattern of men's organizations and women's auxiliaries. Umbrella communities of this kind do not offer neutral membership status. And when several families get together for a meal prepared by the women who then team up to do the serving and clearing away while the men watch football, gender differentiation (including differentiation in language use) is being reproduced on an institutional level.

The community of practice is where the rubber meets the road – it is where observable action and interaction do the work of producing, reproducing, and resisting the organization of power in society and in societal discourses of gender, age, race, etc. Speakers develop linguistic patterns as they engage in activity in the various communities in which they participate. Sociolinguists have tended to see this process as one of acquisition of something relatively "fixed" – the linguistic resources, the community, and the individual's relation to the two are all viewed as fixed. The symbolic value of a linguistic form is taken as given, and the speaker simply learns it and uses it, either mechanically or strategically. But in actual practice, social meaning, social identity, community membership, forms of participation, the full range of community practices, and the symbolic value of linguistic form are being constantly and mutually constructed.

And so although the identity of both the individual and the individual community of practice is experienced as persistent, in fact they both change constantly. We continue to adopt new ways of talking and discard some old ways, to adopt new ways of being women and men, gays and lesbians and heterosexuals, even changing our ways of being feminists or being lovers or being mothers or being sisters. In becoming police officers or psychiatrists or physicists or professors of linguistics, we may change our ways of being women and perhaps of being wives or lovers or mothers. In so doing, however, we are not negating our earlier gendered sociolinguistic identities; we are transforming them, changing and expanding forms of femininity, masculinity, and gender relations. And there are many more unnamed ways of thinking, being, relating, and doing that we adopt and adapt as we participate in different ways in the various communities of practice to which we belong.

What sociolinguists call the *linguistic repertoire* is a set of resources for the articulation of multiple memberships and forms of participation. And an individual's ways of speaking in a particular community of practice are not simply a function of membership or participation in that community. A way of speaking in a community does not simply constitute a turning on of a community-specific linguistic switch, or the symbolic laying of claim to membership in that community, but a complex articulation of the individual's forms of participation in that community with participation in other communities that are salient at the time. In turn, the linguistic practices of any given community of practice will be continually changing as a result of the many saliencies that come into play through its multiple members.

The overwhelming tendency in language and gender research on power has been to emphasize either speakers and their social relations (e.g., women's disadvantage in ordinary conversations with men) or the meanings and norms encoded in the linguistic systems and practices historically available to them (e.g., such sexist patterns as conflating generic human with masculine in forms like *he* or *man*). But linguistic forms have no power except as given in people's mouths and ears; to talk about meaning without talking about the people who mean and the community practices through which they give meaning to their words is at best limited.

Conclusion: A Scholarly Community of Practice

Susan Gal (1992) has called for the integration of the wide range of endeavors that come under the rubric of language and gender. […] Mary Talbot (1992) shows us how a teen magazine attempts to create an imaginary community around the consumption of lipstick. It provides many of the requirements of a community of practice – knowledge, membership, history, practices – inviting the readers to become engaged in lipstick technology and to form their own real communities of practice around the consumption of lipstick. Many people studying gender dynamics in everyday conversation may not immediately see the relation between their work and studies of the discourses of gender as revealed in teen magazines. But just as gender is not given and static, it is also not constructed afresh in each interaction or each community of practice. Those of us who are examining the minutiae of linguistic form need to build detailed understanding of the construction of gender in the communities of practice that we study. But part of the characterization of a community of practice is its relation to other communities of practice and to the wider discourses of society. Thus while we do our close examination, we need to work within a consciously constructed broader perspective that extends our own necessarily limited view of the communities we study.

Significant advances in the study of language and gender from now on are going to have to involve integration on a level that has not been reached so far. The integration can come only through the intensive collaboration of people in a variety of fields, developing shared ways of asking questions and of exploring and evaluating possible answers. Language and gender studies, in fact, require an inter-disciplinary community of scholarly practice. Isolated individuals who try to straddle two fields can often offer insights, but real progress depends on getting people from a variety of fields to collaborate closely in building a common and broad-based understanding. We will cease to be a friendly but scattered bunch of linguists, anthropologists, literary critics, etc., when we become mutually engaged in the integration of our emerging insights into the nexus between language, gender, and social practice.

Sometimes our mutual engagement will lead us to controversy. And some researchers have been concerned about the development of controversy over the cultural-difference model. It is true that argument that is not grounded in shared practice can reduce to unpleasant and *ad feminam* argument. But rich intellectual controversy both requires and enhances mutual engagement. Without sustained intellectual exchange that includes informed and detailed debate, we will remain an aggregate of individuals with vaguely related interests in language and gender. With continued engagement like that begun in works such as Hall et al. (1992) we may become a productive scholarly community.

Note

Many of the ideas expressed in this paper have appeared also in Penelope Eckert and Sally McConnell-Ginet (1992).

1 See Etienne Wenger (1990, 1998); and Jean Lave and Etienne Wenger (1991).

References

Aries, Elizabeth (1976). Interaction patterns and themes of male, female, and mixed groups. *Small Group Behaviour* 7: 7–18.

Case, Susan (1992). Organizational inequity in a steel plant: A language model. In Hall et al. (eds) (1992).

Eckert, Penelope (1990). The whole woman: Sex and gender differences in variation. *Language Variation and Change* 1: 245–67.

Eckert, Penelope, and Sally McConnell-Ginet (1992). Think practically and look locally: Language and gender as community-based practice. *Annual Review of Anthropology* 21: 461–90.

Freed, Alice F. (1992). We understand perfectly: A critique of Tannen's view of cross-sex communication. In Hall et al. (eds) (1992).

Gal, Susan (1992). Language, gender, and power: An anthropological view. In Hall et al. (eds) (1992).

Goodwin, Marjorie Harness (1992). Orchestrating participation in events: Powerful talk among African American girls. In Hall et al. (eds) (1992).

Gumperz, John J. (1982). *Discourse strategies.* Cambridge: Cambridge University Press.

Hall, Kira (1992). Women's language for sale on the fantasy lines. In Hall et al. (eds) (1992).

Hall, Kira, Mary Bucholtz and Birch Moonwomon (eds) (1992) *Locating Power. Proceedings of the 2nd Berkeley Women and Language Conference.* Berkeley, CA: Berkeley Women & Language Group.

Lakoff, Robin Tolmach (1992). The silencing of women. In Hall et al. (eds) (1992).

Lave, Jean, & Etienne Wenger (1991). *Situated learning: Legitimate Peripheral Participation.* Cambridge: Cambridge University Press.

McElhinny, Bonnie S. (1992). "I don't smile much anymore": Affect, gender, and the discourse of Pittsburgh police officers. In Hall et al. (eds) (1992).

Moonwomon, Birch (1992). Rape, race, and responsibility: A graffiti text political discourse. In Hall et al. (eds) (1992).

Ochs, Elinor, and Carolyn Taylor (1992). Mothers' role in the everyday reconstruction of "Father knows best." In Hall et al. (eds) (1992).

Talbot, Mary (1992). A synthetic sisterhood: False friends in a teenage magazine. In Hall et al. (eds) (1992).

Wenger, Etienne (1990). *Toward a Theory of Cultural Transparency.* Palo Alto: Institute for Research on Learning.

Wenger, Etienne (1998). *Communities of Practice: Learning, Meaning and Identity.* Cambridge: Cambridge University Press.

42

Gender and Language Ideologies

Deborah Cameron

Source: Janet Holmes and Miriam Meyerhoff (eds), *The Handbook of Language and Gender*. Oxford: Blackwell (2003), pp. 447–67. Reprinted with permission of Wiley-Blackwell.

1 Introduction

Language ideologies have emerged in recent years as a distinct focus for research and debate among sociolinguists and linguistic anthropologists (see e.g. Schieffelin, Woolard, and Kroskrity 1998). The term "language ideologies" is generally used in this literature to refer to sets of *representations* through which language is imbued with cultural meaning for a certain community. In these representations of language, certain themes recur: examples include where and how language originated, why languages differ from one another and what that means, how children learn to speak, and how language should properly be used. Accounts of these matters may be more or less widely diffused. Some myths of linguistic origin, for example, are localized to a single small community; others, such as the biblical account in the Book of Genesis of Adam naming God's creatures, have been much more widely disseminated. A more recent example of a "diffused" ideology of language is the representation of ancestral vernacular languages as privileged carriers of the identity or spirit of a people. Originating in the thought of German-speaking philosophers and historically associated with the political ideology of nationalism, this language ideology has spread and persisted: it remains salient in the post-colonial and post-Cold War debates of the present day.

It is worth commenting briefly on the definition of language ideologies in terms of *representations* of language rather than, say, *beliefs* or *attitudes* relating to it. The term "ideology" is often used in ordinary discourse to denote beliefs or belief systems (e.g. "communism," "feminism," "racism"), and it is especially likely to be used in connection with belief systems which the speaker takes to be misguided and/or partisan. Explicitly or implicitly, "ideology" is opposed to "truth" (or sometimes more specifically to "science," as a mode of thinking which makes particularly strong claims to truth). One reason why academic commentators prefer not to equate "language ideology" with "beliefs about language" is precisely to avoid this common-sense identification of ideology with false or objectionable beliefs. The linguist's axiom "all languages are equal" will probably be regarded by readers of this book as both scientifically "true" and socially "progressive" – which is to say, neither false nor objectionable – but it is nevertheless also

Language and Gender: A Reader, Second Edition. Edited by Jennifer Coates and Pia Pichler.
© 2011 Blackwell Publishing Ltd except for editorial material and organization. © 2011 Jennifer Coates and Pia Pichler. Published 2011 by Blackwell Publishing Ltd.

"ideological." It is part of a "liberal" ideology which has deeply influenced the social and human sciences since the mid-twentieth century. This example also shows why "language ideologies" cannot be equated simply with folklinguistic stereotypes (see Talbot 2003).

In addition, such terms as "attitude" and "belief" denote, or are commonly assumed to denote, *mental* constructs which essentially "belong" to individuals. Ideologies, by contrast, are *social* constructs: they are ways of understanding the world that emerge from interaction with particular (public) representations of it. The study of language ideologies, then, involves examining the texts and practices in which languages are represented – not only spoken and written but also spoken and written *about*. It is from these representations that language users learn how linguistic phenomena are conventionally understood in their culture. That need not imply, however, that they internalize a particular understanding as a set of fixed beliefs: representation is also a means for *contesting* current understandings of language and creating new alternatives.

Challenging established ideologies of language has been among the aims of many social and political movements, including feminism. Nineteenth- and twentieth-century feminist writings on language took up the subject of what I have been calling "language ideologies" long before that term was used in its present scholarly sense. It was a salient issue for feminists because of the salience of gender itself in many (pre- and non-feminist) representations of language. Ideas about how women and men use language, and how they ought ideally to use it, have been a recurring theme in discourse about language produced by many societies in many historical periods. Women in particular have also been prime targets for the kind of ideological discourse I have elsewhere labelled "verbal hygiene" (Cameron 1995), which sets out actively to intervene in language use with the aim of making it conform to some idealized representation.

These observations suggest a number of questions which need to be considered in an essay about gender and language ideologies. How has the relationship between language and gender been represented in different times and places, and what purposes have been served by representing it in particular ways? Has political (feminist) intervention succeeded in changing the repertoire of representations? How and to what extent do ideological representations of the language/gender relationship inform everyday linguistic and social practice among real women and men?

Before I examine these questions in more detail, though, it is relevant to consider the more general question of what ideological work is done by representations of language. In an earlier discussion (Cameron 1995), I argued that many such representations belong to a "double discourse" in which language is simultaneously both itself and a symbolic substitute for something else. Pronouncements on the "proper" uses of language at one level express the desire to control and impose order on *language*, but at another level they express desires for order and control in other spheres. Putting language to rights becomes a surrogate for putting the world to rights. One familiar example of this is the persistent equation of grammatical "correctness" with law-abiding behavior, and of failure to follow prescriptive grammatical rules with lawlessness or amorality.

Recent writers on language ideologies have also called attention to their symbolic dimension, the sense in which they are always concerned with more than just the linguistic issues they purport to be about. Kathryn Woolard (1998: 4) quotes Raymond Williams: "a representation of language is always a representation of human beings in the world," while Susan Gal (1995: 171) reminds us that ideas about what is desirable in language are always "systematically related to other areas of cultural discourse such as the nature of persons, of power, and of a desirable moral order." These insights are highly relevant to any analysis of representations which focus on the relation of language to gender. In many cases it is not difficult to argue that the underlying subject of these representations is gender itself: one purpose of making statements about men's or women's language is to instruct the hearer or reader in what counts as gender-appropriate behavior. To take a now notorious example, Otto Jespersen's assertion that "... women exercise a great and universal influence on linguistic development through their instinctive shrinking from coarse and vulgar expressions and their preference for refined and (in certain spheres) veiled and indirect expressions" (1922: 246) is readily understood as an expression of what were at the time mainstream societal views on proper femininity.

Yet the idea of the "double discourse" suggests that language does not only stand in for other things when it is represented, it also remains "itself." It might be observed, for instance, that Jespersen's assertion about women's linguistic refinement is not only a representation of gender, it is also part of a discourse on the supposed nature of language. If you read the whole chapter in which Jespersen expounds on the subject of "The Woman," it becomes clear that he is adopting a view of languages as ideally balanced between "masculine" and "feminine" elements. The natural inclinations of men are needed to give a language "variety and vigour," while those of women are needed to keep it within the bounds of propriety that civilized society requires. As well as telling us something about historical understandings of gender, this tells us something about historical understandings of language.

2   Representing Language and Gender: Uniformity and Diversity

Jespersen's chapter "The Woman" provides us with a prototypical example, from early twentieth-century Europe, of what is probably the most general, most culturally widespread, and most historically persistent of all language ideologies pertaining to gender: that there are clear-cut, stable differences in the way language is used by women and by men. In many versions of this ideology the differences are seen as natural, and in most they are seen as desirable. Beyond that, however, representations of gendered linguistic behavior are extremely variable historically and culturally. From the most accessible popular texts on the subject (e.g. Lakoff 1975; Spender 1980; Tannen 1990) it would be easy to get the impression that women have always and everywhere been measured against a similar linguistic ideal, constituted by such qualities as reticence, modesty, deference, politeness, empathy, supportiveness, and cooperation. On inspection, however, the picture is more complicated.

Joel Sherzer (1987) has suggested one useful overarching generalization: that in any community the normal linguistic behavior of women and men will be represented in ways congruent with the community's more general representation of the essential natures of the two groups. If women are said to be "naturally" modest, for example, their speech will be represented as expressing that modesty – community members may explain that "women don't like to speak in public," for instance. In observed reality, there may be little evidence for this generalization, or the evidence may be contradictory. Or it may be that women do indeed behave "modestly," precisely because the representation of women as modest has the force of a norm, which is enforced in various ways (e.g. denying women the opportunity to practice speaking in public, or sanctioning individual women who are insufficiently reticent). Women themselves may actively try to conform to prevailing ideals of feminine behavior, though the effort and calculation this often demands makes clear that the behavior in question is not simply "natural."

As Sherzer also points out, while the assumption that women's language proceeds from women's nature is culturally very widespread, there is considerable cross-cultural variation in precisely what "women's nature," and therefore women's language, is taken to consist of. Jespersen thought women more "refined" than men, and claimed that this was reflected in women's instinctive avoidance of coarse, vulgar, and abusive language. In the Papua New Guinea village of Gapun, however, a distinctive genre of speech called a *kros* in Tok Pisin, which is a tirade of obscene verbal abuse delivered in monologue, is represented by villagers as a primarily female genre (Kulick 1993). Women in this community are not regarded as more reticent, delicate, or verbally co-operative than men. Among the Malagasy of Madagascar, a highly valued traditional style of speech known as *kabary*, which is characterized by a high degree of indirectness, is associated with men, on the grounds that women are by nature direct speakers (Keenan 1974). Among Western anglophones, by contrast, the opposite belief prevails: men are supposed to be more direct speakers than women.

It is also the case that cultural representations of gendered speech may change over time. The ideal most frequently criticized by feminists – that of the modest, deferential, and publicly silent woman – is sometimes presented as if it had prevailed throughout recorded history, but in some times and places, the ideal woman speaker was represented very differently. In a discussion of the "conduct books" which instructed readers in proper behavior from the medieval period onward, Ann Rosalind Jones (1987) observes that texts of this genre addressed to upper-class women in the royal courts of Renaissance Europe were very far from exhorting women to be silent and deferential. On the contrary, the court lady was expected to hold her own in verbal duels and witty exchanges which took place in public and in mixed company. The "silent woman" ideal with which we are now more familiar emerged, Jones argues, with the rise to prominence of the European bourgeoisie. Especially where they espoused puritan religious beliefs, the bourgeois class had different notions of the proper relationship between women and men. Conduct literature written for a bourgeois readership emphasized the subordination of wives to husbands, and the confinement of women to the domestic sphere. The specifically linguistic corollary of this can be seen in the following extract from a 1614 conduct book entitled *A Godly Forme of Household Gouernmente* (quoted in Armstrong and Tennenhouse 1987: 8). The respective linguistic duties of men and women in a household are graphically laid out in two columns:

Husband	*Wife*
Deal with many men	Talk with few
Be "entertaining"	Be solitary and withdrawn
Be skillfull in talk	Boast of silence

Jones also points out that bourgeois conduct literature was often intended as an implicit or explicit critique of the "decadent" aristocracy. The license of aristocratic women to speak freely in public was represented in bourgeois texts as a sign of the immorality of the upper classes. Discourse on the ideal of the silent woman, then, was not just part of an ideology of gender, but also played a part in an ideological conflict between social classes. In this particular conflict, the bourgeoisie were the eventual victors. Over time, Jones observes, gender norms which were once specifically bourgeois would be adopted by the upper class as well, becoming an ideal to which women in general were exhorted to aspire. In later eras, the withdrawn and reticent middle-class woman would be favorably contrasted not with the articulate but immoral aristocrat, but with the vulgar and undisciplined working-class woman. Even today, in British English at least, a loose and vulgar female tongue is still sometimes figured in the person of the "fishwife," though few people have ever encountered a real member of that traditional occupational category.

The examples just given remind us that there is *intra-* as well as inter-cultural variation in the representation of language and gender. From outside a culture this variation may not be salient or even visible, but inside, the representation of differences *between* women, or between men, does ideological work. The "fishwife," for example, represents a supposedly general (not just gendered) characteristic of low-status speakers – their lack of refinement compared to higher-status speakers. The effect of the interaction of class and gender representations is to define low-status women as "unfeminine." Or, we could consider the commonplace representation (which is not confined to a single culture[1]) of Asian speakers – of both sexes – as more reticent and polite than Western speakers. The interaction between ethnic and gendered representations in this case leads to the stereotypical perception of Asian women as "superfeminine." Though this stereotype can be exploited for its positive value (in parts of the sex industry, for instance, and by the Asian airlines who use the subservience of their female cabin crew as a selling point), it can also prompt more negative evaluations of Asian women as *excessively* feminine. The work done by representations like these is to establish a norm of desirable feminine behavior which is identified with a particular *kind* of femininity – in the cases I have used as examples here, the norm is White, Western, and middle-class. Of course, the norm is not necessarily an accurate description of the way White middle-class women in a given community really behave: rather, it is a representation incorporating the characteristics ideologically ascribed to them as female members of a favored social group. But the way "other" women are represented foregrounds the idea that they are *different* from the norm – just as women-in-general are typically represented as different from the "human" norm, that is, from men.

Ideologies of language and gender, then, are specific to their time and place: they vary across cultures and historical periods, and they are inflected by representations of other social characteristics such as class and ethnicity. What is constant is the insistence that in any identifiable social group, women and men are *different*. Gender differences are frequently represented as complementarities, that is, whatever men's language is, women's language is not. But as the examples in the above discussion illustrate, there may be great variation in the actual substance of claims about how men and women speakers differ from or complement one another.

Whatever their substance, though, these representations of gender and language are part of a society's apparatus for maintaining gender distinctions in general – they help to naturalize the notion of the sexes as "opposite," with differing aptitudes and social responsibilities (see Talbot 2003). In many cases they also help to naturalize gender *hierarchies*. Jespersen may praise the "refinement" he attributes to women speakers, but this quality is readily invoked to exclude women from certain spheres of activity on the grounds they are too refined to cope with the linguistic demands of, say, military service. Among the Malagasy and in Gapun, the qualities attributed to men's speech are also ones the society accords particular respect to. In these communities too, we find women being excluded or marginalized from certain important public forums, in part because it is supposed they cannot master the appropriate public language.

Here it may be as well to remind ourselves that ideological representations do not, in and of themselves, accomplish the exclusion, marginalization, or subordination of women. Their particular role in those processes is to make the relationship of women and men in a given society appear natural and legitimate rather than merely arbitrary and unjust. Conversely, attacks on particular representations (such as feminist criticisms of the idea that women are "naturally" silent/modest/delicate) do not in and of themselves produce changes in the position of a subordinate group. Rather, they help to undermine the legitimacy of the present order, the sense that the way things are is desirable, natural, and immutable. If enough people can be induced to doubt that the status quo is natural or legitimate, a climate is created in which demands for change are much harder for their opponents to resist.

Feminist demands for change have often included demands that restrictions on women's linguistic behavior be removed, and those demands have often been supported by criticism of the ideological representations which justified the restrictions. The 1848 Seneca Falls Convention, a landmark event in nineteenth-century American feminism, demanded for instance that women be accepted as speakers at mixed public gatherings such as political meetings, attacking the argument that public speaking was incompatible with respectable femininity. Christian religious women have challenged the idea that women cannot be effective preachers (an argument often deployed by opponents of women's ordination to the priesthood). These challenges have been successful: while for a variety of reasons it remains true that discourse in many public forums is dominated by men, the argument that women should not be permitted to speak publicly because it is indecent, or because they are incompetent to do so, have been fairly decisively discredited. When these arguments are heard today, they are widely perceived as eccentric and reactionary; and when instances from the past are cited (such as the solemn debate within the BBC during the 1970s on whether a woman television newsreader would so inflame male viewers' passions as to render them incapable of concentrating on current events) they are received with incredulity. In the matter of women's public speech, at least, mainstream ideologies of language and gender have changed dramatically in recent decades.

In the very last decade of the twentieth century, another shift in representations of language and gender began to become apparent. In the following sections I will examine this shift, exploring what it might tell us about changing concepts of both gender and language.

3   Shifting Ideological Landscapes: The Fall and Rise of "Women's Language"

Much of the feminist criticism produced on the subject of language ideologies since the mid-1970s has addressed itself in particular to the idea, implied if not stated in most mainstream representations of "women's language," that women are linguistically *inferior* to men. The tradition of commentary that 1970s feminists inherited portrayed women's language by and large as a deviation from the (implicitly masculine) norm, and this deviance tended to be evaluated in negative terms. Despite Jespersen's overt championing of male/female complementarity, it is difficult not to read his account of male/female differences as sexist – not merely stereotypical but biased in favor of men's alleged vigor, creativity, and more complex sentence structure. Early feminist commentators, most notably Robin Lakoff (1975), also made use of what would now be labeled a "deficit model," according to which women's characteristic way of speaking was, indeed, a factor making women unsuitable candidates for positions of public authority and responsibility. Feminists, however, differed from prefeminists like Jespersen in pointing out that women were not "naturally" weak and deferential speakers: rather they were socialized into "feminine" ways of behaving, in a sexist society which systematically strove to keep women in their (subordinate) place. Nevertheless, the solution proposed by many feminists was for women to adopt alternative and "better" ways of speaking. This was the idea behind, for example, "assertiveness training" for women (Cameron 1995; Crawford 1995; Gervasio and Crawford 1989). The late twentieth-century equivalents of conduct literature (self-help books, radio and TV talkshows, and articles in women's magazines, for example) often advised women in a more piecemeal manner on how to be taken more seriously by deliberately eschewing such "women's language" features as high pitch, "swoopy" intonation, expansive body language, allowing oneself to be interrupted, phrasing commands in the form of questions, adding question tags to statements, and producing declaratives with rising intonation. As I have argued elsewhere (Cameron 1995), a good deal of this advice implicitly boils down to "talk [more] like a man" – or more exactly, perhaps, since we are dealing here with representations rather than empirical realities, "try to approximate the popular linguistic stereotype of a man."

This kind of guidance still circulates, but the climate in which it now exists is no longer one in which it is generally assumed that women are "deficient" as language users. On the contrary, more and more mainstream discourse on language and gender stresses the opposite proposition – that women are actually *superior* to men. The problem of the unassertive or insecure woman speaker may not have disappeared entirely, but it is increasingly being eclipsed by anxiety about a quite different phenomenon, namely the problem of the inarticulate, linguistically unskilled man. In the new deficit model, it is men who are represented as deficient, and women whose ways of speaking are frequently recommended as a model for them to emulate. To illustrate this point, I will reproduce a number of texts in which the proposition "women are superior language users" is explicitly or implicitly asserted.

Example (1) comes from an advertisement, part of an extended multimedia advertising campaign run by British Telecom (the UK's largest provider of telephone services) in the late 1990s. The idea that men should emulate women's styles of speaking was central to this campaign, a primary goal of which (according to a spokesperson for the advertising agency) was to encourage men to make more extended telephone calls, after market research had found significant differences in men's and women's attitudes to talking on the phone. Here I reproduce part of the text of a print advertisement, which provides a particularly striking example of the strategy BT's advertisers adopted (in fact it is the first part of a text whose second part is quoted by Talbot 2003; see also Talbot 2000). It should be acknowledged, by the way, that this strategy includes some degree of irony: it is not clear that the claims made about gender difference (e.g. "men make phone calls standing up") are meant to be taken at face value. However, even if these claims are made entirely in jest (which is not clear either), the joke depends on readers' familiarity with the more "serious" discourse they allude to. Serious or not, then, this text affirms certain generalizations about language and gender as "common knowledge."

(1): *British Telecom advertisement*
      (*Radio Times* magazine, December 1994)
      Men and women communicate differently. Have you noticed? Women like to sit down to make phone calls. They know that getting in touch is much more important than what you actually say. Men adopt another position. They stand up. Their body language says this message will be short, sharp and to the point. "Meet you down the

pub, all right?" That's a man's call. Women can't understand why men are so abrupt. Why can't they share the simple joys of talking as other men have? "Conversation is one of the greatest pleasures of life. But it wants leisure." W. Somerset Maugham. Or, as another writer said, "The conversation of women is like the straw around china. Without it, everything would be broken."

Example (2) comes from an interview conducted by two sociologists with the manager of a call center in the northeast of England. Call centers are workplaces where employees sell products and/or provide customer services by telephone: they are a rapidly growing sector of the "new" hi-tech service economy. In this extract from the interview transcript, the manager is explaining why the call center operators he recruits are predominantly women, even though his center is in an area of high unemployment where any job attracts numerous applicants of both sexes.

(2):   *Interview with a call center manager*
       (Tyler and Taylor 1997: 10)
       … We are looking for people who can chat to people, interact, build rapport. What we find is that women can do this more, they're definitely more natural when they do it anyway. It doesn't sound as forced, perhaps they're used to doing it all the time anyway … women are naturally good at that sort of thing. I think they have a higher tolerance level than men … I suppose we do, yes, if we're honest about it, select women sometimes because they are women rather than because of anything they've particularly shown at the interview.

Example (3) comes from an advice booklet with the subtitle *How To Get More Out of Life Through Better Conversations* (BT 1997). Like example (1), this was produced on behalf of British Telecom, but for a different purpose. It was part of a community service project undertaken by BT under the heading "TalkWorks," which involved producing and distributing learning materials on the theme of "better communication." This particular text was written by an external consultant, with the assistance of a qualified psychologist and counsellor. It was available at no charge to any UK household requesting it (i.e. not just customers of BT), and more than two million copies were distributed in the 18 months following its appearance.

(3):   *Advice booklet*
       (British Telecom 1997: 17–18)
       Just as we can only get to know about another person's "real self" through their words, we can only become familiar with our own real self by communicating openly and fully with other people. Conversation, it turns out, is the best way we have of exploring the full range and diversity of our own thoughts, memories and emotions … talking candidly about ourselves not only helps other people get to know us, it also helps us to get to know ourselves and be more genuine. … Some people actively struggle to avoid becoming known by other people. We now know that this struggle can lead to a form of stress which is capable of producing a whole set of physical and emotional problems … As a rule, women are more comfortable with talking about their real selves than men. Women also live longer than men. This may not be a coincidence.

Example (4) comes from a document entitled *Boys and English*, produced by a British government agency, the Office for Standards in Education, in 1993. The function of

Ofsted is to assess and monitor the standards achieved by schools in England and Wales; it also issues guidance to schools on improving standards. This text is addressing a subject that has featured prominently in discussions of education in Britain since the late 1990s, namely the academic "under-achievement" of boys relative to girls. It summarizes recent research findings and offers guidance on how boys could be helped to do better in English, a subject where the gender gap in achievement is particularly striking.

> (4):   *Ofsted Report on Boys and English*
>   (1993: 16, emphasis in original)
>   [Boys] were more likely [than girls] to interrupt one another, to argue openly and to
>   voice opinions strongly. They were also less likely to listen carefully to and build upon
>   one another's contributions ... *It is particularly important for boys to develop a clearer
>   understanding of the importance of sympathetic listening as a central feature of success-
>   ful group and class discussion.*

These texts show how pervasive a particular representation of language and gender has become in recent years, at least in the UK where all four examples were produced. The texts are drawn from different genres, including both "popular" ones like advertising and advice literature, and "expert" ones like the Ofsted report. They represent language and gender differences in a range of contexts: personal relationships (examples (1) and (3)), work (example (2)) and education (example (4)). But what they say about language and gender is essentially similar: each one represents the verbal behavior of men as in some way problematic, and contrasts it unfavorably with the behavior of women in the same situation. In all four texts the "problem" is defined explicitly or implicitly as a lack of skill in using language for the purpose of creating and maintaining rapport with other people. Males in these texts do not spend sufficient time interacting with friends and relatives, do not share their feelings and problems openly, cannot chat to customers in a "natural" manner, and are unable to listen "sympathetically" in group discussions designed to promote learning. These deficiencies are represented as having serious consequences for men, including educational underachievement (example (4)), unemployment (example (2)), personal unhappiness and even premature death (example (3)).

The consistent focus on men's communicational shortcomings in these texts (and many others which I do not have space to reproduce) marks a real shift in public discourse on men, women, and language. For most of the 1970s and 1980s, representations of language and gender – both popular and expert – focused either on women's alleged shortcomings as language users (e.g. their lack of skill in public speaking and performance genres such as comedy or political debate) or else, where discussion was informed by feminist ideas, on the relationship between women's speech styles and their subordinate position in society. Even those feminists who valued women's language positively were apt to represent it as an obstacle to women's advancement because of the widespread prejudice it inspired. Today, by contrast, women are regularly represented as model language users: their verbal skills are seen, moreover, as central to what is portrayed as the fulfillment of that old prophecy, "the future is female." Compared to their male peers, today's women and girls are said to be doing better in education, gaining employment more easily, living happier as well as longer lives – and it is suggested that they owe this good fortune at least partly to their linguistic accomplishments.

What accounts for this shift, and how should it be interpreted? A number of possibilities suggest themselves. One might be that the new representations reflect real gains made by feminism since the 1970s. The value of women's ways of doing things has been recognized, and women are finally getting the (material and symbolic) rewards they deserved all along. Another possibility is that on the contrary, all this discourse about women's superiority is intended to distract attention from factual evidence suggesting that in material reality, women are still "the second sex." It is evident, for instance, that women's superior educational qualifications have not translated into higher-status and better-paid jobs: one Australian study found that boys leaving school with low levels of literacy were soon out-earning not only girls with similar qualifications, but also girls who had left school with high or very high levels of literacy (Gilbert 1998). There is still a significant gender gap in earnings, and women remain more likely than men to end their lives in poverty.

In the following section, however, I will argue that the shift toward a language ideology of female superiority and male deficit is neither a simple case of successful feminist intervention in a tradition of sexist representations, nor straightforwardly part of a "backlash" discourse in which feminism has "gone too far," leaving men as the new victims of sexist oppression. I would agree that these are both elements in the new discourse of female verbal superiority. But that discourse, in my view, is more fundamentally a product of changing ideals concerning language itself – what it is for, and what constitutes skill in using it. In contemporary Western societies, recent social changes have given new value to linguistic genres and styles that were and are symbolically associated with femininity. It is this development, more than any radical change in gender relations as such, that underlies the new discourse of female verbal superiority.

4   "Communication": The Language Ideology of Late Modernity?

In the foregoing section I have referred to the "female verbal superiority" discourse as instantiating a *change* in the way gendered language is represented. Yet readers might well ask themselves how much has really changed. The idea that women are better than men at sharing their feelings or listening sympathetically to others is hardly novel: on the contrary, it is a hoary old stereotype. Complaints about men's taciturnity, insensitivity, and lack of emotional openness are not new either. And the idea that women are more inclined to use talk as a means for maintaining close relationships, and are more skilled at doing so than men, was emphasized in a number of spectacularly successful self-help and advice texts published in the early 1990s, notably Deborah Tannen's *You Just Don't Understand* (1990) and John Gray's *Men are from Mars, Women are from Venus* (1992). However, neither Tannen nor Gray overtly argued for the superiority of women. Rather, both took the line that the sexes are "different but equal" and need to understand and accept one another's differences in order to avoid misunderstandings. Nevertheless, their texts seem to have been read by many people as implicitly suggesting that women are superior and that men would do well to emulate them. Subsequent works of advice literature (example (3), for instance) have drawn that conclusion more explicitly. What has changed, then, is not the dominant stereotypes of men's and women's linguistic behavior, but the value judgments made on that behavior. And the obvious question is, why?

To put briefly what I have argued at greater length elsewhere (Cameron 2000), the conditions obtaining in late modern societies have given rise to a new linguistic ideal: the skilled interpersonal communicator who excels in such verbal activities as cooperative problem-solving, rapport-building, emotional self-reflexivity and self-disclosure, "active" listening, and the expression of empathy. If we ask what it is about contemporary life that brings this ideal to the fore, two important considerations immediately suggest themselves. One is the changing nature of work in the global economy, especially in post-industrial societies where most work is no longer about manufacturing objects, but rather involves selling services. Service sector workers are required to engage intensively in interaction with other people. And this interaction is not purely instrumental in nature, but foregrounds the interpersonal functions of language. A good server does not just provide efficient service, s/he creates rapport with customers, making them feel that they are individually valued and cared for, and that their needs are more important than the server's own. It is a role that has elements of both nurturance and low status or powerlessness – qualities which also figure in many familiar representations of "women's language." Hence the assertion by the call center manager quoted in example (2) above that women are more "naturally" suited than men to customer service work.

The other relevant consideration is the changing nature of *personal* life in late modern societies, some key features of which are described by the sociologist Anthony Giddens (1991). Late modern subjects, Giddens asserts, live in a more complex, mobile, rapidly changing, and individualistically oriented society than their ancestors did, and their sense of identity depends on being able to order the various fragments of their life-experience into a coherent, ongoing autobiographical narrative. This requires a high degree of self-reflexivity, the ability and willingness to reflect on one's experience. As Giddens puts it, the self in late modern society becomes a "reflexive project," something subjects must think about and work on rather than simply taking for granted. Another thing late modern subjects have to work at is the creation of intimate relationships with others. The individualism and mobility of contemporary societies weaken social networks, making it more difficult to become close to others while at the same time raising our expectations of the few people to whom we *are* close (modern marriages, for instance, are no longer economic and social alliances between extended families, but are ideally supposed to be unions between "soul mates" who will meet one another's needs for friendship as well as sex, romance, and domesticity). Under these conditions, intimacy has to be created and sustained through mutual self-disclosure, the open and honest sharing of experiences and feelings. The reflexively constructed self cannot remain a private creation, then, but must be *communicated* continuously to significant others. In that context it becomes easier to understand why such skills as emotional expressiveness and empathetic listening are so idealized in many present-day representations of language.

In a study of what the term "communication" meant to mainstream Americans, Katriel and Phillipson (1981) found that their informants differentiated it from mere "talk" or "chat." "Communication" for them meant honest, serious, problem-solving talk within significant relationships, where it functioned as a means for overcoming the otherwise invincible isolation of the individual. They also represented "communication" as a kind of "work," worthwhile but also difficult and requiring continuous effort. As Katriel and Phillipson note (1981: 304), from the perspective on the world which their informants adopted, communication is "both vitally important and highly problematic. If people are unique, the kind of mutual disclosure and acknowledgement entailed in communication provide a necessary bridge from self to others. But if people are unique, they also lack the mutuality necessary for achieving interpersonal meaning and co-ordination." This problem can only be overcome by working hard to develop the skills "communication" demands.

It is because "communication" has come to be conceived in this way, as a means to greater self-knowledge and more satisfying intimate relationships (or in the service economy, more convincingly *simulated* intimate relationships), that contemporary advice literature on speech is so different from the advice literature of the past.[2] Victorian authorities, or the denizens of eighteenth-century salons who wrote treatises on the art of conversation, would scarcely recognize British Telecom's late twentieth-century account of what constitutes "better conversation." Nor would the authors of early modern conduct books like the one quoted earlier in this chapter. The advice writers of the past emphasized qualities such as wit, taste, propriety, politeness, and modesty. Invariably, for example, they dwelt on the vulgarity of talking about oneself and recommended that "delicate" topics be avoided in polite company. Today's authorities are equally insistent that talking about oneself (self-disclosure or "sharing") is a crucial skill for communicators to master, and that personal problems of every kind can and should be addressed by talking about them. In the past, advice writers about conversation were usually literary and cultural luminaries, or else high-ranking members of polite society who took it upon themselves to share their knowledge of that milieu with others who aspired to join. By contrast, today's authorities are psychologists and therapists – their expertise is in the area of human behavior and relationships, and many of the linguistic strategies they recommend (e.g. "being assertive," "sharing your feelings," "listening without judging") originated as rules specifically for various kinds of therapeutic discourse.

In the last few paragraphs I have been discussing what I take to be a pervasive and powerful ideology of language in late modern societies, the ideology of "communication" as a set of skills which are needed to sustain both personal identity and interpersonal relationships. One effect of the rise of this "communication" ideology has been to alter prevailing definitions of linguistic "skill," so that the interpersonal skills of, for instance, self-disclosure and empathetic listening are foregrounded while traditionally admired skills of a more forensic or rhetorical kind – such as the ability to engage in formal debate or public oratory – recede into the background.[3] The shift could also be analyzed as a foregrounding of "private" linguistic genres relative to "public" ones, illustrating a phenomenon discussed by a number of analysts of language and social change (notably Fairclough 1992), namely the growing "informalization" or "conversationalization" of Western public discourse. Service encounters, for instance, increasingly simulate personal conversations between acquainted parties; addresses by politicians and even monarchs, influenced strongly by the demands of the television medium for which most of them are now primarily designed, are less "oratorical" and more "personal" (Montgomery 1999); institutional written documents such as job specifications and health education materials adopt a more informal and direct mode of address than they did in the past.

What does all this have to do with *gender*, and more specifically with the recent tendency to represent women as linguistically superior to men? My answer would be that the representation of women as model language users is a logical consequence of defining "skill" in communication as primarily skill in using language to maintain good interpersonal relationships, and of emphasizing traditionally "private" speech genres (e.g. conversations about personal feelings and problems) rather than "public" ones. The management of feelings and of personal relationships are culturally coded as female domains, and have been throughout the modern era in the West. Nancy Armstrong and Leonard Tennenhouse, discussing early modern conduct books, point out that this literature helped to establish a division of the social world into "public and private, economic and domestic, labor and leisure, according to a principle of gender that placed the household and sexual relations under *female* authority" (Armstrong and Tennenhouse 1987: 12, my emphasis).

In late modern societies, however, the public/private boundary is increasingly blurred. Ways of speaking traditionally associated with the private sphere (e.g. emotionally expressive ones) are now equally favored in public contexts and economic transactions (e.g. service encounters), while the conduct of domestic, sexual, and other intimate relations is no longer just a matter for private contemplation, but a major preoccupation of the popular media. By the gendered logic that has prevailed in the West for several centuries, these changes are bound to be perceived as *feminizing* the values and the language of public discourse, and consequently as advantaging women while simultaneously marginalizing men.

What kind of ideological work is done by the representations of language and gender I have been examining in this discussion? To begin with, they do the usual work of affirming the existence of fundamental differences between women and men. The differences are represented variously as biologically based (e.g. Skuse et al. 1997, a widely publicized study suggesting that there is a gene on the X chromosome controlling certain social and verbal skills), as "facts of life" which are "natural" in some unspecified way (cf. the comments of the call center manager in example (2) above), as socially constructed but too "deep" to be amenable to change (this is Deborah Tannen's (1990) position), or as constructed and alterable with effort (probably the commonest position, exemplified by examples (1), (3), and (4) above). In all cases, however, one effect of the representations is to reproduce the proposition that gender difference or complementarity is part of the normal order of things.

In discussions of globalization and the new economy, representations of female verbal superiority and male deficit do particular ideological work. As example (2) demonstrates, common-sense ideas about women as "naturally" skilled communicators help to naturalize the way women are channeled into low-paid and low-status service occupations – as if the issue were all about women's aptitude for the work and not at all about their greater willingness (born of historical necessity rather than choice) to accept the low pay, insecurity, and casualization which were endemic to "women's work" in the past and are now becoming the lot of many more workers. Example (2) also shows that ideas about "natural" gender difference can license discrimination in the workplace: the call center manager admits that he sometimes hires women "because they are women rather than because of anything they've particularly shown at the interview." Here representation (what women are said to be "good at") takes precedence over reality (how the woman in front of you actually performs).

A corollary of employers selecting women for certain occupations "because they are women" is, presumably, *not* selecting men because they are men. Another kind of ideological work done by current representations of language and gender is, in fact, to scapegoat men (or more exactly, certain groups of them, especially young working-class men) for misfortunes not of their making. Economic globalization has particularly affected the life-chances of non-elite male workers in Western societies by exporting the jobs they would once have expected to do to parts of the world where labor is cheaper, thus leaving many Western working-class men chronically un- or under-employed. A good deal of discourse on boys' educational underachievement arises from anxiety about this development (for a feminist critique, see Epstein et al. 1998; Mahony 1998). Some of this discourse blames young men for being unable or unwilling to develop the communication skills that would make them employable in new conditions. It is implied, and sometimes said, that if boys and young men made more effort to improve their communication skills, they would not be unemployed, poor, socially marginalized, and disaffected – though arguably it is a naive oversimplification of the economic realities to suggest that young men by their own efforts could avoid the inevitable systemic problems associated with the transition to a post-industrial order. Men's alleged poor verbal and social skills are also sometimes invoked in a "pathologizing" way, to explain the involvement of lower-class males in disruptive classroom behavior, violence, and criminal activity. Some commentators propose remedial instruction in communication and "emotional literacy" skills as a solution (e.g. Goleman 1995; Phillips 1998). Others suggest that anti-social males may be suffering from various clinical syndromes which could be controlled by medication (see Mariani 1995). Once again, this approach obscures the impact on certain men of systemic factors, particularly economic deprivation and inequality.

I will close this discussion by pointing out, however, that the "communication ideology" with which new representations of gendered language are strongly linked does ideological work of a broader kind – it is not concerned only or even primarily with gender, but is engaged in constructing a new model of the "good *person*." It presents, for the contemplation of women and men alike, a new ideal which, symbolically speaking, has both masculine and feminine elements: the enterprising, self-aware, interpersonally skilled individual who will flourish rather than flounder in the demanding conditions of twenty-first-century life. Despite the emphasis currently given to the "feminine" qualities of the good communicator, the individuals who most closely approximate the new ideal in the real world are often men: men who combine the traditionally "masculine" qualities of authority, enterprise, and leadership with a command of the more "feminine" language of emotional expressiveness and rapport. Outstanding examples of this type include the former US president Bill Clinton and the British Prime Minister Tony Blair. That both are male only underlines the point that valuing "feminine" characteristics need not threaten the dominant position of men in a society. On the contrary, a man who has some of these characteristics – always provided he remains clearly a man – will often be particularly applauded for his "sensitivity," whereas the same qualities in a woman attract no special approbation, since after all, they are "only natural" (which is to say, they are normative) for women. At the same time, women receive less credit for adopting characteristics that are admired when displayed by men, such as competitiveness, decisiveness, and strength of will. Nobody ever said approvingly of Margaret Thatcher that she was "in touch with her masculine side."

5   Representations and Realities

The comments just made bring us back to one of the questions posed in the introduction to this chapter: what is the relationship between language ideologies, the representations of language that circulate within a culture, and the actual linguistic behavior of that culture's members? Overall there is something rather contradictory about feminist discussions of this question. On one hand feminists have been at pains to stress the gulf that exists between representations and reality. Many empirical studies have been undertaken in an effort to disprove common gender stereotypes, such as that women don't swear and men don't gossip. The claim here is that actual gendered behavior is typically remote from cultural representations of it. On the other hand, sexist representations are sometimes criticized as pernicious, precisely because it is supposed that regular exposure to them may cause people to take them as models for their own behavior. Here, there is an implicit claim that representations *do* affect behavior. Ideological statements such as "women's language lacks forcefulness" can become self-fulfilling prophecies; that is why it is important to challenge them so vigorously. In which case, it might well be asked why so many common stereotypes find little support in empirical studies of naturally occurring language use.

In my view, the way out of this contradiction is to bear in mind that human beings do not "behave," they *act*. They are not just passive imitators of whatever they see and hear around them: they must actively produce their own ways of behaving – albeit not always in a fully conscious and deliberate way and never, as Marx said in another context, "under conditions of their own choosing." Since human beings are social beings, their identities and practices are produced from social (which is to say, collective rather than purely individual) resources. And the representations that circulate in a culture are among those collective resources. They do not determine our behavior in the way the laws of physics determine the behavior of matter, but neither are they entirely irrelevant to it. Occasionally we may learn ways of acting from them directly (as when people claim they learned to kiss or to smoke from scenes in movies), but more usually we integrate them into the broader understandings of the world on which we base our own actions.

That this process is both active and selective is illustrated by reception studies carried out with readers of self-help books (e.g. Lichterman 1992; Simonds 1992). No genre could be more overtly didactic than self-help, and one might suppose that no group of readers would be more susceptible to the ideological norms embedded in representations than self-help readers. Yet both the researchers cited above found that their informants claimed not to read self-help books for the advice they offered – indeed they often could not remember, when questioned, what a recently enjoyed text had recommended readers to do. Rather, the informants said they read self-help for the pleasure of "recognizing" themselves. They said that the texts helped them to understand themselves better, and that far from being inspired by this to change themselves, they usually felt "reassured" that their own ways of acting were normal, even if they were also problematic.

What these readers described doing with self-help texts can be readily linked to what Anthony Giddens calls "the reflexive project of the self," the process whereby people ongoingly construct autobiographical narratives in an effort to understand themselves in relation to the world. It could be argued that representations are particularly powerful in shaping this kind of understanding, precisely because they are *not* accurate reproductions of the complexity of lived experience. Compared to an actual life, for example, a life *story* is simpler, more condensed, and far more orderly. It is private and personal experience ordered by public generic (in this case, narrative) conventions, and as such it provides the reader with a template s/he can use to order and reflect on his/her own experience.

If representations are resources for the work of producing identities and actions, then the interesting question about them becomes less "what does this representation say about language and gender – is it accurate or misleading, sexist or anti-sexist?" than "what do people *do* with this representation of language and gender?" – always bearing in mind, of course, that different people may do different things with it. It is by investigating what people do with representations *in* reality that we will discover the relationship *between* representations and reality.

Language and gender scholars are not excluded from the category of "people who do things with representations of language and gender." Just as those representations are resources for the production of gender in everyday life, so they are also resources for the production of theoretical understandings of gender. A simple illustration is the way empirical research on language and gender has often begun from folklinguistic stereotypes (e.g. "women talk incessantly"). Researchers may be motivated by a wish to explode the stereotype, but still the stereotype has set the agenda – and the researcher cannot avoid recirculating it, even if she presents it critically. Of course, popular representations do not always set research agendas, but there is no escaping the influence of prior "expert" representations: it is a strict rule of academic discourse that one *must* refer to (and so recirculate) the discourse of one's predecessors in the same field of inquiry. Nor is this necessarily an undesirable limitation. Even if one *could* think without reference to prior understandings of the phenomenon one is trying to think about, the resulting ideas would be difficult or impossible for others to integrate into their own understandings of the world, and therefore useless as a contribution to public discourse. (This is a particularly salient point for feminists who view their scholarship as a contribution to a movement for social *change*.)

It is impossible to "transcend" ideology, but it is not impossible for language and gender scholars to be *reflexive* about the cultural resources that have shaped their own understandings, as well as the understandings of the people whose language use they study. This, too, is an argument for the serious study of language ideologies. Cultural representations of language and gender are part of our inheritance, as social beings and also as linguists. Arguably, the better we understand them – where they "come from" and how they work – the more control we will have over what we do with them.

Notes

1 This is an "orientalist" representation, i.e. it portrays Asia from a Western standpoint, but I hesitate to call it simply "Western" because the idea of Asian speakers as more polite and reticent is often found in Asian *self*-representations too. On the appropriation and internalization of others' stereotypes by members of the group they stereotype, see Talbot.
2 On the history of advice literature about conversation, see Burke 1993; Zeldin 1998.
3 In a sample of recent "communication skills" texts and training materials I examined, most of which were produced for professional rather than personal self-improvement purposes, there was virtually no reference – in some texts, none at all – to any speech event that necessitated addressing an audience or using formal generic conventions. Even such routine responsibilities as chairing a business meeting often went unmentioned. By contrast, a sample of comparable materials from the 1930s and 1950s placed emphasis on such rhetorical performances as "making a presentation" or "proposing a toast." (See further Cameron 2000.)

References

Armstrong, Nancy and Tennenhouse, Leonard (eds) 1987: *The Ideology of Conduct: Essays on Literature and the History of Sexuality*. New York: Methuen.

BT 1997: *Talk Works: How To Get More Out of Life Through Better Conversations*. London: British Telecommunications plc.

Burke, Peter 1993: *The Art of Conversation*. Ithaca, NY: Cornell University Press.

Cameron, Deborah 1995: *Verbal Hygiene*. London and New York: Routledge.

Cameron, Deborah 2000: *Good To Talk? Living and Working in a Communication Culture*. London and Thousand Oaks, CA: Sage.

Crawford, Mary 1995: *Talking Gender*. London: Sage.

Dunbar, Robin 1996: *Grooming, Gossip and the Evolution of Language*. London: Faber & Faber.

Epstein, Debbie, Elwood, Jannette, Hey, Valerie, and Maw, Janet (eds) 1998: *Failing Boys: Issues in Gender and Achievement*. Buckingham: Open University Press.

Fairclough, Norman 1992: *Discourse and Social Change*. Cambridge: Polity.

Gal, Susan 1995: Language, gender and power: An anthropological review. In Kira Hall and Mary Bucholtz (eds) *Gender Articulated: Language and the Socially Constructed Self*. London: Routledge, pp. 169–82.

Gervasio, Amy and Crawford, Mary 1989: Social evaluations of assertiveness: A critique and speech act reformulation. *Psychology of Women Quarterly* 13: 1–25.

Giddens, Anthony 1991: *Modernity and Self-Identity: Self and Society in the Late Modern Age.* Cambridge: Polity.

Gilbert, Pam 1998: Gender and schooling in new times: The challenge of boys and literacy. *Australian Educational Researcher* 25(1): 15–36.

Goleman, Daniel 1995: *Emotional Intelligence.* New York: Bantam Books.

Gray, John 1992: *Men are from Mars, Women are from Venus.* New York: HarperCollins.

Jespersen, Otto 1922: *Language: Its Nature, Development and Origin.* London: Allen & Unwin.

Jones, Ann Rosalind 1987: Nets and bridles: Early modern conduct books and sixteenth century women's lyrics. In Nancy Armstrong and Leonard Tennenhouse (eds) *The Ideology of Conduct: Essays on Literature and the History of Sexuality.* New York: Methuen, pp. 39–72.

Katriel, Tamar and Phillipson, Gerry 1981: "What we need is communication": "Communication" as a cultural term in some American speech. *Communication Monographs* 48: 301–17.

Keenan, Elinor Ochs 1974: Norm-makers, norm-breakers: Uses of speech by men and women in a Malagasy community. In Richard Bauman and Joel Sherzer (eds) *Explorations in the Ethnography of Speaking.* Cambridge: Cambridge University Press, pp. 125–43.

Kulick, Don 1993: Speaking as a woman: Structure and gender in domestic arguments in a New Guinea village. *Cultural Anthropology* 8(4): 510–41.

Lakoff, Robin 1975: *Language and Woman's Place.* New York: Harper & Row.

Lichterman, Philip 1992: Self help reading as a thin culture. *Media, Culture & Society* 14: 421–47.

Mahony, Pat 1998: Girls will be girls and boys will be first. In Debbie Epstein, Jannette Elwood, Valerie Hey, and Janet Maw (eds) *Failing Boys: Issues in Gender and Achievement.* Buckingham: Open University Press, pp. 37–55.

Mariani, Philomena 1995: Law-and-order science. In Maurice Berger, Brian Wallis, and Simon Watson (eds) *Constructing Masculinity.* New York: Routledge, pp. 135–56.

Montgomery, Martin 1999: Speaking sincerely: Public reactions to the death of Diana. *Language and Literature* 8(1): 5–33.

Office for Standards in Education (Ofsted) 1993: *Boys and English.* London: Ofsted.

Phillips, Angela 1998: *Communication: A Key Skill for Education.* London: BT Forum.

Schieffelin, Bambi, Woolard, Kathryn, and Kroskrity, Paul (eds) 1998: *Language Ideologies: Practice and Theory.* New York and Oxford: Oxford University Press.

Sherzer, Joel 1987: A diversity of voices: Men's and women's speech in ethnographic perspective. In Susan Philips, Susan Steele, and Christine Tanz (eds) *Language, Gender and Sex in Comparative Perspective.* New York: Cambridge University Press, pp. 95–120.

Simonds, Wendy 1992: *Women and Self-Help Culture: Reading Between the Lines.* New Brunswick, NJ: Rutgers University Press.

Skuse, D. H., James, R. S., Bishop, D. V. M., et al. 1997: Evidence from Turner's syndrome of an imprinted X-linked locus affecting cognitive function. *Nature* 387(6634): 705–8.

Spender, Dale 1980: *Man Made Language.* London: Routledge and Kegan Paul.

Talbot, Mary 2000: "It's good to talk?" The undermining of feminism in a British Telecom advertisement. *Journal of Sociolinguistics* 4: 108–19.

Talbot, Mary 2003: Gender stereotypes: reproduction and challenge. In Janet Holmes and Mirain Meyerhoff (eds) *The Handbook of Language and Gender.* Oxford: Blackwell, pp. 68–86.

Tannen, Deborah 1990: *You Just Don't Understand.* New York: William Morrow.

Tyler, Melissa and Taylor, Steve 1997: "Come Fly With Us": Emotional Labour and the Commodification of Sexual Difference in the Airline Industry. Paper presented to the Annual International Labour Process Conference, Edinburgh.

Woolard, Kathryn 1998: Language ideologies as a field of inquiry. In Bambi Schieffelin, Kathryn Woolard, and Paul Kroskrity (eds) *Language Ideologies: Practice and Theory.* New York and London: Oxford University Press, pp. 3–47.

Zeldin, Theodore 1998: *Conversation: How Talk Can Change Your Life.* London: Harvill Press.

43

Social Constructionism, Postmodernism and Feminist Sociolinguistics

Janet Holmes

Source: *Gender and Language* 1(1) (2007), pp. 51–66. Reprinted with permission of Equinox Publishing Ltd.

Introduction

When the essentialist presuppositions behind questions such as 'How do women and men speak differently?' and 'Are women more polite than men?' were exposed and challenged in the early 1990s (e.g. Butler 1990; Freed 1992), the field of language and gender research was engulfed in a wave of social constructionism. Instead of 'women's language' being distinguished from 'men's talk' on the basis of identifiable linguistic features, language was rather seen as one important resource for constructing gender roles and gendered social identities. At the same time, researchers challenged the binary nature of social conceptions of gender (e.g. Bing and Bergvall 1996), and even of biological sex (e.g. Bem 1993; Nicholson 1994), pointing to the arbitrariness of such distinctions in some cases, and to the evidence from cultures that recognise more than two biological categories, as well as more than two sociocultural and linguistic categories (e.g. Hall and O'Donovan 1996). The emphasis moved to an appreciation of the continuum of experience and the fuzziness of social boundaries, including gender boundaries, and to a greater awareness of the diverse, dynamic, and context-responsive ways in which people 'do gender' (among other identities) in different situations, and even from moment to moment within a situation. Linguistic features associated with 'women talk' (Coates 1996) were noted in interactions between men in some contexts (e.g. Freed 1996; Cameron 1997), and researchers documented contexts in which women used the discourse of power and authority (e.g. Wodak 1995), or adopted the emotionally inexpressive interactional style widely associated with masculinity (e.g. McElhinny 1995).

A developing appreciation of the diverse and dynamic ways in which people construct their complex social identities led to the rejection by some feminist linguists of the ways in which gender had been operationalised in sociolinguistics and discourse analysis, together with pleas to eschew research which reinforced dichotomous thinking and emphasised gender stereotypes (e.g. Freed 1992, 2003). One logical result of a positive response to such appeals, one might think, would be the disappearance of language and gender studies (Holmes and Meyerhoff 2003:10). To be consistent, such researchers should surely move into other areas, and orient their analyses to dimensions other than gender. And, to some extent, this did in fact occur, particularly among those whose focus was discourse rather than more traditional linguistic features. Nonetheless, many researchers continue to be entranced by the interaction of gender and language in its broadest sense, with this journal as concrete evidence of our preoccupation. Some of us continue to see a role for researchers interested in analysing the interface between gender and language (where 'language' includes 'discourse'). It is interesting to speculate why.

The Gender Order

One reason for the persistence of gender and language as a vibrant area of research is surely that although gender is only one of many factors accounting for how we talk, language nonetheless plays an important part in constructing what Connell (1987) calls 'the gender order', the repressive ideology which ensures that deviation from gender norms (by women or men) entails penalties. Examining how this process is accomplished is an important task for feminist linguists. And nowhere is the gender order more apparent than in professional workplaces where lip-service is paid to equality of opportunity, while the reality is that women are grossly under-represented at senior levels in most organisations (Bass and Avolio 1997; Burke and Davidson 1994; McConnell-Ginet 2000; Olsson 1996; Still 1996). Organisational power and authority is frequently concentrated in the hands of a very few men rather than shared between women and men. Despite decades of Equal Employment Opportunity schemes and gender equity initiatives, many professional work-places are still rife with examples of systemic gender discrimination in which language plays an important role (see Holmes 2005). Stereotypes rule; and in many societies stereotypes of workplace leaders are still predominantly both male and masculine (see, for example, Gunnarsson 2001; Harris 2002; Hearn and Parkin 1989; Kendall and Tannen 1997; Maier 1997; Sinclair 1998). I return to this issue below, but first I briefly address two relevant issues which have emerged in recent discussions of language and gender research: firstly, the issue of how social constructionism is interpreted by many gender and language researchers; and, secondly, the issue of the status of the category 'women' in postmodernist language and gender research.

Sociolinguists and Social Constructionism[1]

There has been extensive debate over the last few years between Conversation Analysis (CA) researchers, discursive psychologists, and proponents of other approaches over how overtly speakers must mark their orientation to and the conversational salience of gender in order for it to be analysed as a social category being attended to in talk (e.g. Benwell and Stokoe 2006; Bucholtz 2003; Sidnell 2003; Speer 2005). I do not intend to rehearse here the details of that debate (see Part IX in this volume). Rather, I focus briefly on the wider issue of how exactly sociolinguists and non-CA discourse analysts employ a social constructionist framework, and how this differs from the way ethnomethodologists and proponents of CA use it.

   One issue, as I see it, is that, because social constructionism has at least some roots in ethnomethodological soil, some CA researchers have claimed a monopoly on judgments of what counts as a valid social constructionist approach and methodology, and they criticise those who depart from their very strict criteria.[2] Sociolinguists who adopt a social constructionist approach simply do not accept that social categories need to be observably and explicitly salient for participants in order to be considered relevant to their analyses. To the contrary, social and pragmatic meanings may be, and frequently are, inferred using contextualisation cues; and language systematically evokes contextual presuppositions (e.g. Gumperz 1999:456), including assumptions about gender norms.

Privileging context in this way, and making use of culturally specific situated inferences, language and gender researchers, and especially those engaged in discourse analysis, have embraced the perspective that gender is socially constructed through context embedded practices of various kinds. Thus, the focus of much current empirical research is 'how in everyday talk and text [people] constitute the world, themselves, and other people, as recognisably, take-for-grantedly, gendered' (Stokoe 2005:126). This approach offers a very powerful way of analysing the dynamic way that gender is constructed in context-embedded everyday talk, but it is not entirely unproblematic for those interested in examining the diverse ways in which sexist and discriminatory behaviours disadvantage women as a group. As Sidnell succinctly puts it there is 'an underlying tension here in so far as many researchers advance anti-essentialist, theoretical conceptions of gender (suggesting that gender emerges through practices of talk) but at the same time employ the very same categories in their analysis' (Sidnell 2003:347). Labelling such researchers as 'essentialist', however, is at least unhelpful, and could even be interpreted as offensive, since 'essentialist' is currently a very dirty word in language and gender studies. Nonetheless, the problem remains if the goal is to avoid circularity.

A second issue, identified by Stokoe (2005:125), is what she calls the widespread misappropriation of social constructionism by some language and gender researchers, as evidenced by their conflation of social constructionism (vs. essentialism) with social/cultural (vs. biological) understandings of gender (2005:126). This is a perceptive point. These different dimensions are clearly separable since the social category of gender (as opposed to the biological category of sex) can, in principle, be viewed through essentialist spectacles and analysed using a binary approach. In fact, however, during the 1990s, insights about the distinction between social/cultural vs. biological categories developed alongside perceptions concerning culturally gendered ways of talking; and the indexing of femininity and masculinity through interactional style became strongly identified with social constructionist approaches (Cameron and Kulick 2003; Ochs 1992). The focus was on the process of gendering, the on-going accomplishment of gender, as well as the dynamism and fluidity of the process (Eckert and McConnell-Ginet 2003). Hence, preexisting binary categories were rejected for a range of reasons, including evidence that neither behaviour nor biology provided a sound basis for dividing human beings into two neat categories.

In practice, then, the position that many language and gender researchers now espouse may not fit Sidnell's or Stokoe's characterisations of social constructionism, but it nonetheless provides a viable and valuable analytical approach. Adopting this position, ways of talking are associated with particular roles, stances (e.g. authoritative, consultative, deferential, polite), activities, or behaviours (Ochs 1992), and to the extent that these are 'culturally coded as gendered ... the ways of speaking associated with them become indices of gender' (Cameron and Kulick 2003:57). We bring this knowledge to our interactions and we use it to assess and interpret the linguistic behaviour of the participants. Gender is one particular type of social meaning, one aspect of social identity conveyed, usually indirectly, by particular linguistic features, which may, of course, concurrently convey other meanings as well (Holmes 1997). Needless to say, the significance of such features as indices of gender needs to be demonstrated by careful contextual analysis, with particular attention to participants' interpretations within a particular community of practice.

Women, Language and Postmodernism

Just as it could be considered superficially surprising that feminist linguists who reject essentialism and gender binarism continue to study the relationship between language and gender, so it may seem puzzling that postmodern feminist linguists continue to discuss systemic discrimination against women. How can 'women' be treated as a uniform social category when a postmodern approach regards a word like 'women' as an indefensible generalisation concealing untold depths of variation and diversity?

Mills (2003:240) argues, for example, against the use of 'Second Wave feminist concepts such as patriarchy, which seem to suggest that women are universally oppressed and that all men benefit from their oppression'. On the other hand, she notes that 'within Third Wave [i.e. postmodern] feminism … it does seem to be possible to argue that women are still systematically discriminated against, and that this discrimination occurs both at a structural level (institutions and the state), and at a local level (relationships and families)' (2003:240–1). So, she claims, despite the fact that 'the notion of "women" has been destabilised to a certain extent and is difficult to use except with provisos, it is still a concept which it is important to retain in order to be able to describe the systematic nature of the discrimination that many women experience' (2003:241). This apparent inconsistency can perhaps be interpreted as the 'strategic use of positivist essentialism in a scrupulously visible political interest' (Spivak 1985 cited in Landry and Maclean 1996:205), a form of 'strategic essentialism' (Boyne 1990:170), one tactic for regaining the strength which is inevitably dissipated when the focus is on difference and diversity, rather than on what is shared. As Susan Phillips (2003:260) notes:

> While a great deal was gained by the new feminist conceptualizing of women as intersections of various aspects of social identity, a great deal was lost too. The rhetorical force of the focus on the universal key problem of a very broad men's power over women, rather than the particularities of problems like domestic violence and rape, was obscured, and really has not regained center stage in feminist writing since.

Because essentialism has been 'aged in the keg' and promoted as 'common sense' (Wilchins 2002:33), naming and defining relevant social categories has the advantage of providing some degree of social intelligibility, and thus permitting potential access to social resources for oppressed groups. Consequently, for researchers who are concerned to identify ways in which women are the victims of repressive ideologies and discriminatory behaviour, some level of generalisation, albeit appropriately qualified, about women as a group is strategically indispensable.

So where does all this leave empirically based language and gender research? While gender and language researchers can usefully challenge the rigidity of binary gender categories, expose the unwarranted assumptions or ideological baggage they encapsulate, and point out displacements and ruptures which regularly occur in social interaction, it is also important to recognise that political efficacy may entail the formulation of generalisations, and the identification of salient social categories in the interests of strategic essentialism.[3] And although caution must be exercised in using categories such as 'women' and 'men', 'boys' and 'girls', with generalisations restricted to groups who share sufficient numbers of relevant non-linguistic characteristics, the gain in social intelligibility could be regarded as providing adequate justification in cases of political oppression.[4] This approach encourages a focus on ways in which gendered assumptions about appropriate behaviours may restrict women's social and professional opportunities (e.g. Eckert and McConnell-Ginet 2003; Holmes 2005; Martín Rojo 1998; McConnell-Ginet 2000), while not precluding analysis of the subtle ways in which gender interacts with other factors at different points in everyday talk. If we wish to make political progress, it makes strategic sense to acknowledge that most of the world continues to treat 'women' and 'men', 'female' and 'male' as fundamental social categories, not least in describing interpersonal communication styles (Moore Quinn 2005).[5] In the next section, I return to the issue of the role of the feminist sociolinguist, using a social constructionist approach to workplace discourse.

Gender and Language in the Workplace

The pervasive, systemic constraints which prevent many women from reaching positions of authority, status, power, or leadership in their organisations are often instantiated in subtly sexist interactional and discursive behaviours. Gender is a significant and salient variable in organisational interaction, a 'pervasive social category' (Weatherall 2000:287), even when it is not overtly referred to. Gender stereotypes and normative expectations about appropriate behaviour are particularly evident when we examine the pressures on women in workplace leadership positions, and the range of strategies they develop to manage the pervasive double-bind that potentially undermines their institutional effectiveness. The diverse responses which feminist research has documented in different communities of practice (e.g. Baxter 2003; Holmes 2006; Martín Rojo and Esteban 2003, 2005; Wodak 2003, 2005) indicate the pressure of normative expectations on women leaders. They also provide evidence that norms are being contested and restrictive stereotypes are being challenged. As Freed (2003:717) notes, there is 'persistent confirmation that long-established notions of sex-determined and gender-determined differences are being destabilized'.

It could be argued, however, that maintaining coherent links between the detailed analyses of particular interactions which have dominated language and gender research in the last fifteen years on the one hand, and the big picture ('the gender order') on the other presents something of a theoretical challenge. In our own research, following Eckert and McConnell-Ginet (1992 [see also their paper in this section]), we have found the concept of community of practice especially useful, and we have focused on particular social and ethnic groups, in particular social contexts, such as workplace meetings both large and small (e.g. Holmes and Marra 2002; Holmes and Stubbe 2003a). Moreover, we have examined particular aspects of interaction for evidence of gendering: e.g. styles of humour, meeting management styles, instantiations of power in the workplace (e.g. Holmes, Burns, Marra, Stubbe and Vine 2003; Holmes 1999, 2005). The results have provided some interesting indications of the ways in which women and men at work 'do gender' as one aspect of their workplace identity.

The analyses which have emerged from the work of the Wellington Language in the Workplace Project (LWP) team demonstrate, for instance, that women and men in positions of power in their organisations draw on diverse discursive resources (including normatively masculine and feminine discourse styles) to effectively 'do leadership' (Holmes 2006; Marra, Schnurr and Holmes 2006; Schnurr 2006). They also demonstrate that, in many organisations, leaders who are women cannot avoid addressing, in some way, the deeply embedded assumption that effective leadership entails stereotypically masculine discourse behaviours (Gal 1991; Gunnarsson 2001; Jackson and Parry 2001; Kendall and Tannen 1997; Sinclair 1998). To handle this unavoidable double-bind ('If she talks like a manager she is transgressing the boundaries of femininity: if she talks like a woman she no longer represents herself as a manager', Jones 2000:196), these women select from a range of strategies, some more normatively masculine and some more conventionally feminine in discourse style, according to features of the context, but also according to the type of workplace and workplace culture in which they are operating.

Hence, in male-dominated workplaces with normatively masculinist institutional values (Baxter 2003), some women in leadership positions largely conform to expectations and favour the more masculine end of the range of discursive practices which are considered appropriate. Other women leaders choose to work in woman-friendly communities of practice, where conventionally feminine styles of interaction are interpreted as unmarked and normal (e.g. where pre-meeting talk topics include personal and family topics without attracting comment, where humour tends to be collaborative and non-abrasive, and where it is acceptable to instantiate leadership in relatively negotiative and less authoritarian ways – see Holmes 2006; Holmes and Schnurr 2006). Still other women in leadership roles attempt, to varying degrees and in a variety of ways, to challenge the existing gendered discourse norms of their workplaces. In order to be treated with respect, such women often need to prove they can foot it discursively in meetings with male colleagues (cf. Baxter 2003), and they adopt a contestive and authoritarian style at appropriate points to match their colleagues. But some women managers also effectively switch between normatively gendered styles of discourse, or strategically integrate aspects of normatively feminine discourse styles into their workplace talk, skilfully meshing transactional and relational discourse features, for instance, even in masculinist and male-dominated workplace contexts (Holmes and Marra 2004; Holmes 2006).

This third strategy is important, since it suggests ways in which discursive behaviours and interactional norms may gradually be transformed in workplace interaction. By appropriating normatively masculine discourse strategies to 'do power', it can be argued that women in leadership positions contribute both to de-gendering the leadership role as well as the discourse strategies they use to enact that role. They co-opt these strategies as tools of leadership discourse, and challenge their exclusive association with male speakers.

Yet another strategy used by some senior women in the workplace is to 'do femininity' quite explicitly and confidently in a variety of ways in their workplace interactions, constructively creating positive 'feminine' spaces and asserting the value of more feminine discursive styles within their male-dominated and masculinist workplaces (Holmes and Schnurr 2006 [see Part V, in this volume]). These women are actively challenging the devaluation of behaviours associated with women, and contesting the widespread interpretation of 'feminine' as a negative concept (Holmes and Schnurr 2006).

Examining the behaviour of a number of women in leadership positions across a range of communities of practice makes it possible to identify the different ways in which these women respond to the repressive, predominantly masculine, discourse norms in their workplaces. The patterns become apparent only when we are willing to risk strategic generalisations, with social intelligibility as a legitimate political goal. Such generalisations are encouraging, since they suggest that some women are troubling the gendered discourse norms which characterise so many workplaces, and which constantly reinforce the glass ceilings which prevent many women from progressing to more senior positions. So while detailed descriptions of the discourse of specific women in specific communities of practice illustrate the diverse and creative ways in which women respond to the well-known double-bind, it is also strategically worthwhile to identify the bigger picture, the evidence of the gender norms which become apparent only through analysis of a large amount of accumulated data.

Conclusion

There is no doubt that the last decade of research in language and gender studies has enriched our understanding of 'the complexity and the fluidity of the concept of gender' (Freed 2003:699) as well as our appreciation of the heterogeneity within women's and men's linguistic practices. Those who oppose binary approaches have argued that by drawing attention to the relatively small areas of gender difference, as opposed to the much larger areas of overlap in women's and men's ways of speaking, we assign differences an unwarranted level of importance, and feed the media frenzy which, as Cameron (1995) and Freed (2003) note, has become more and more obsessed with identifying differences in the ways women and men speak as the areas of difference contract. While this may be true especially for middle class women and men in informal conversational contexts, it is also important to acknowledge that there are still many contexts where gendered expectations about normative ways of speaking persist, and workplaces are one such area (Holmes and Stubbe 2003b; Holmes 2006).

I have argued that a focus on women's ways of talking is warranted, at least in the study of workplace discourse. Despite gradual change, there is abundant evidence that women are still under-represented as a group at senior levels in many occupations. Language and gender research can usefully identify the many ways in which subtle and not so subtle patterns in organisational discourse contribute to this repression. Leadership discourse has been dominated by masculinist norms and conventionally masculine styles of interaction for decades. Social constructionism offers both an explanatory framework and a tool for documenting change. As Freed (2003:714) notes:

> Perhaps when a sufficiently large number of men and women deviate from the stereotyped expectations that society has had for them, change actually begins to take hold ... The real threat to the two-gender system may be that people are increasingly aware that women and men are able to recreate themselves (that is, create different selves) in part through language. People are experiencing first hand, the constructed nature of gender and grasping the degree to which gender is 'performed' and variable. Changes and variations in speech behavior thus become symbolic (or even represent concrete evidence) that things are not the way they used to be or perhaps, that things never were as they had been represented.

In conclusion, then, I am arguing along with others (e.g. Baxter 2003; Philips 2003; Sunderland 2004) that we need to put women back at the centre of language and gender research. As linguists, we can highlight discursive behaviours which penalise women in many workplace contexts, on the one hand, while documenting active discursive resistance to sexist behaviours on the other. Research which focuses on effective ways of contesting repressive norms and restrictive stereotypes offers a way out of what has been experienced by some as a depressing cul de sac, as well as providing an optimistic indication that feminist linguists have much to contribute to social transformation.

Notes

I would like to thank Sally McConnell-Ginet, Miriam Meyerhoff, Meredith Marra and Stephanie Schnurr, as well as the anonymous reviewer, for valuable comments on a draft of this paper.

1 After this paper was completed, I read Deborah Cameron's (2006) more extended and very valuable discussion of the similarities, differences, and overlaps between what she calls 'modern' and 'postmodern' approaches.
2 See, for example, Kitzinger (2000:171–2); Sidnell (2003:347–9); Stokoe (2004) and Speer (2005) for discussion of this issue.
3 The formulation of this point owes a good deal to the helpful comments of the anonymous reviewer.
4 As Judith Butler (2004:30) observes 'To be oppressed you must first become intelligible'.
5 But see Freed 2003.

References

Bass, Bernard and Bruce Avolio. 1997. Shatter the glass ceiling: Women may make better managers. In Keith Grint (ed.). *Leadership. Classical, Contemporary, and Critical Approaches*. Oxford: Oxford University Press, pp. 199–210.

Baxter, Judith. 2003. *Positioning Gender in Discourse: A Feminist Methodology*. Basingstoke: Palgrave Macmillan.

Bem, Sandra L. 1993. *The Lenses of Gender: Transforming the Debate on Sexual Inequality*. New Haven, CT: Yale University Press.

Benwell, Bethan and Elizabeth Stokoe. 2006. *Discourse and Identity*. Edinburgh: Edinburgh University Press.

Bing, Janet M. and Victoria L. Bergvall. 1996. The question of questions: Beyond binary thinking. In Victoria L. Bergvall, Janet M. Bing and Alice F. Freed (eds). *Rethinking Language and Gender Research: Theory and Practice*. New York: Longman, pp. 1–30.

Boyne, Roy. 1990. *Foucault and Derrida: The Other Side of Reason*. London: Unwin Hyman.

Bucholtz, Mary. 2003. Theories of discourse as theories of gender: Discourse analysis in language and gender studies. In Janet Holmes and Miriam Meyerhoff (eds). *The Handbook of Language and Gender*. Oxford: Blackwell, pp. 43–68.

Burke, Ronald and Marilyn Davidson. 1994. Women in management: Current research issues. In Marilyn Davidson and Ronald Burke (eds). *Women in Management. Current Research Issues*. London: Paul Chapman, pp. 1–8.

Butler, Judith. 1990. *Gender Trouble: Feminism and the Subversion of Identity*. New York: Routledge.

Butler, Judith. 2004. *Undoing Gender*. New York: Routledge.

Cameron, Deborah. 1995: *Verbal Hygiene*. London: Routledge.

Cameron, Deborah. 1997. Performing gender identity: Young men's talk and the construction of heterosexual masculinity. In Sally Johnson and Ulrike Hanna Meinhof (eds). *Language and Masculinity*. Oxford: Blackwell, pp. 47–65.

Cameron, Deborah. 2006. Language, gender, and sexuality: Current issues and new directions. *Applied Linguistics* 26(4):482–502.

Cameron, Deborah and Don Kulick. 2003. *Language and Sexuality*. Cambridge: Cambridge University Press.

Coates, Jennifer. 1996. *Women Talk*. Oxford: Blackwell.

Connell, Robert W. 1987. *Gender and Power: Society, the Person and Sexual Politics*. Stanford: Stanford University Press.

Eckert, Penelope and Sally McConnell-Ginet. 1992. Think practically and look locally: Language and gender as community-based practice. *Annual Review of Anthropology* 21:461–90.

Eckert, Penelope and Sally McConnell-Ginet. 2003. *Language and Gender*. Cambridge: Cambridge University Press.

Freed, Alice F. 1992. We understand perfectly: A critique of Tannen's view of cross-sex communication. In Kira Hall, Mary Bucholz and Birch Moonwomon (eds). *Locating Power: Proceedings of the Second Berkeley Women and Language Conference*. Berkeley, CA: Berkeley Women and Language Group, pp. 144–52.

Freed, Alice F. 1996. Women, men and type of talk: What makes the difference. *Language in Society* 25(1):1–26.

Freed, Alice F. 2003. Epilogue: Reflections on language and gender research. In Janet Holmes and Miriam Meyerhoff (eds). *The Handbook of Language and Gender*. Oxford: Blackwell, pp. 699–721.

Gal, Susan. 1991. Between speech and silence: The problematics of research on language and gender. In Micaela di Leonardo (ed.). *Gender at the Crossroads of Knowledge*. Berkeley, CA: University of California Press, pp. 180–201.

Gumperz, John J. 1999. On interactional sociolinguistic method. In Srikant Sarangi and Celia Roberts (eds). *Talk, Work and Institutional Order*. Berlin: Mouton de Gruyter, pp. 453–71.

Gunnarsson, Britt-Louise. 2001. Academic women in the male university field: Communicative practices at postgraduate seminars. In Bettina Baron and Helga Kotthoff (eds). *Gender in Interaction*. Amsterdam: John Benjamins, pp. 247–81.

Hall, Kira and Veronica O'Donovan. 1996. Shifting gender positions among Hindi-speaking Hijras. In Victoria Bergvall, Janet Bing and Alice Freed (eds). *Rethinking Language and Gender Research: Theory and Practice*. London: Longman, pp. 228–66.

Harris, Thomas E. 2002. *Applied Organizational Communication*. Second edition. Mahwah, NJ: Lawrence Erlbaum.

Hearn, Jeff and Wendy Parkin. 1989. Women, men, and leadership: A critical review of assumptions, practices, and change in the industrialized nations. In Nancy Adler and Dafna Izraeli (eds). *Women in Management Worldwide*. London: M. E. Sharpe, pp. 17–40.

Holmes, Janet. 1997. Women, language and identity. *Journal of Sociolinguistics* 2(1):195–223.

Holmes, Janet. 1999. Women at work: Analysing women's talk in New Zealand work-places. *Australian Review of Applied Linguistics (ARAL)* 22(2):1–17.

Holmes, Janet. 2005. Power and discourse at work: Is gender relevant? In Michelle Lazar (ed.). *Feminist Critical Discourse Analysis*. London: Palgrave, pp. 31–60.

Holmes, Janet. 2006. *Gendered Talk at Work*. Oxford: Blackwell.

Holmes, Janet, Louise Burns, Meredith Marra, Maria Stubbe and Bernadette Vine. 2003. Women managing discourse in the workplace. *Women in Management Review* 18(8):414–24.

Holmes, Janet and Meredith Marra. 2002. Having a laugh at work: How humour contributes to workplace culture. *Journal of Pragmatics* 34:1683–1710.

Holmes, Janet and Meredith Marra. 2004. Relational practice in the workplace: Women's talk or gendered discourse? *Language in Society* 33:377–98.

Holmes, Janet and Miriam Meyerhoff. 2003. Different voices, different views: An introduction to current research in language and gender. In Janet Holmes and Miriam Meyerhoff (eds). *The Handbook of Language and Gender*. Oxford: Blackwell, pp. 1–17.

Holmes, Janet and Stephanie Schnurr. 2006. Doing 'femininity' at work: More than just relational practice. *Journal of Sociolinguistics* 10(1):31–51.

Holmes, Janet and Maria Stubbe. 2003a. *Power and Politeness in the Workplace. A Sociolinguistic Analysis of Talk at Work*. London: Longman.

Holmes, Janet and Maria Stubbe. 2003b. 'Feminine' workplaces: Stereotypes and reality. In Janet Holmes and Miriam Meyerhoff (eds). *The Handbook of Language and Gender*. Oxford: Blackwell, pp. 573–99.

Jackson, Brad and Ken Parry. 2001. *The Hero Manager: Learning from New Zealand's Top Chief Executives*. Auckland: Penguin.

Jones, Deborah. 2000. Gender trouble in the workplace: 'Language and gender' meets 'feminist organisational communication'. In Janet Holmes (ed.). *Gendered Speech in Social Context: Perspectives from Gown and Town*. Wellington: Victoria University Press, pp. 192–210.

Kendall, Shari and Deborah Tannen. 1997. Gender and language in the workplace. In Ruth Wodak (ed.). *Gender and Discourse*. London: Sage, pp. 81–105.

Kitzinger, Celia. 2000. Doing feminist conversation analysis. *Feminism & Psychology* 10:163–93.

Landry, Donna and Gerald Maclean. 1996. *Selected Works of Gayatri Chakravorty Spivak*. New York: Routledge.

Maier, Mark. 1997. Gender equity, organizational transformation and challenger. *Journal of Business Ethics* 16(9):943–62.

Marra, Meredith, Stephanie Schnurr and Janet Holmes. 2006. Effective leadership in New Zealand workplaces: Balancing gender and role. In Judith Baxter (ed.). *Speaking Out: The Female Voice in Public Contexts*. Basingstoke: Palgrave Macmillan, pp. 240–60.

Martín Rojo, Luisa. 1998. Intertextuality and the construction of a new female identity. In M. Bengoechea and R. Sola Bull (eds). *Intertextuality*. Alcala de Henares: Universidad de Alcala de Henares, pp. 81–98.

Martín Rojo, Luisa and Conception Gomez Esteban. 2003. Discourse at work: When women take on the role of manager. In Gilbert Weiss and Ruth Wodak (eds). *Critical Discourse Analysis: Theory and Interdisciplinarity*. New York: Palgrave Macmillan, pp. 241–71.

Martín Rojo, Luisa and Conception Gomez Esteban. 2005. The gender of power: The female style in labour organizations. In Michelle Lazar (ed.). *Feminist Critical Discourse Analysis*. London: Palgrave, pp. 61–89.

McConnell-Ginet, Sally. 2000. Breaking through the 'glass ceiling': Can linguistic awareness help? In Janet Holmes (ed.). *Gendered Speech in Social Context: Perspectives from Gown and Town*. Wellington: Victoria University Press, pp. 259–82.

McElhinny, Bonnie. 1995. Challenging hegemonic masculinities: Female and male police officers handling domestic violence. In Kira Hall and Mary Bucholtz (eds). *Gender Articulated*. New York: Routledge, pp. 217–43.

Mills, Sara. 2003. *Gender and Politeness*. Cambridge: Cambridge University Press.

Moore Quinn, Eileen. 2005. Review of *The Handbook of Language and Gender*, ed. Janet Holmes and Miriam Meyerhoff. *Journal of English Linguistics* 33(3):298–302.

Nicholson, Linda. 1994. Interpreting gender. *Signs* 20(1):79–105.

Ochs, Elinor. 1992. Indexing gender. In Alessandro Duranti and Charles Goodwin (eds). *Rethinking Context: Language as an Interactive Phenomenon*. Cambridge: Cambridge University Press, pp. 335–58.

Olsson, Su. 1996. A takeover? Competencies, gender and the evolving discourses of management. In Su Olsson and Nicole Stirton (eds). *Women and Leadership: Power and Practice*. Palmerston North: Massey University, pp. 359–78.

Philips, Susan U. 2003. The power of gender ideologies in discourse. In Janet Holmes and Miriam Meyerhoff (eds). *The Handbook of Language and Gender*. Oxford: Blackwell, pp. 252–76.

Schnurr, Stephanie. 2006. Leadership, humour and gender: An analysis of workplace discourse. Unpublished PhD thesis, Victoria University of Wellington, Wellington, New Zealand.

Sidnell, Jack. 2003. Constructing and managing male exclusivity in talk-in-interaction. In Janet Holmes and Miriam Meyerhoff (eds). *The Handbook of Language and Gender*. Oxford: Blackwell, pp. 327–52.

Sinclair, Amanda. 1998. *Doing Leadership Differently. Gender, Power and Sexuality in a Changing Business Culture*. Melbourne: Melbourne University Press.

Speer, Susan. 2005. *Gender Talk: Feminism, Discourse and Conversation Analysis*. London and New York: Routledge.

Still, Leonie. 1996. Women as leaders: The cultural dilemma. Conference Proceedings. In Su Olsson and Nicole Stirton (eds). *Women and Leadership: Power and Practice*. Palmerston North: Massey University, pp. 63–76.

Stokoe, Elizabeth H. 2004. Gender and discourse, gender and categorization: Current developments in language and gender research. *Qualitative Research in Psychology* 1:107–29.

Stokoe, Elizabeth H. 2005. Analysing gender and language. *Journal of Sociolinguistics* 9(1):118–33.

Sunderland, Jane. 2004. *Gendered Discourses*. London: Palgrave Macmillan.

Weatherall, Ann. 2000. Gender relevance in talk-in-interaction and discourse. *Discourse and Society* 11:290–2.

Wilchins, Riki. 2002. A certain kind of freedom: Power and truth of bodies – four essays on gender. In Joan Nestle, Clare Howell and Riki Wichins (eds). *GenderQueer: Voices from Beyond the Sexual Binary*. Los Angeles: Alyson Books, pp. 23–66.

Wodak, Ruth. 1995. Power, discourse and styles of female leadership in school committee meetings. In David Corson (ed.). *Discourse and Power in Educational Organizations*. Cresskill, New Jersey: Hampton Press, pp. 31–54.

Wodak, Ruth. 2003. Multiple identities: The roles of female parliamentarians in the EU parliament. In Janet Holmes and Miriam Meyerhoff (eds). *The Handbook of Language and Gender*. Oxford: Blackwell, pp. 671–98.

Wodak, Ruth. 2005. Gender mainstreaming and the European Union. In Michelle Lazar (ed.). *Feminist Critical Discourse Analysis*. London: Palgrave, pp. 90–113.

Index